HABITS of the HEART

HABITS *of the* HEART

*Individualism
and Commitment
in American Life*

With a New Preface

**ROBERT N. BELLAH
RICHARD MADSEN
WILLIAM M. SULLIVAN
ANN SWIDLER
STEVEN M. TIPTON**

University of California Press
Berkeley   Los Angeles   London

University of California Press, one of the most distinguished university presses in the United States, enriches lives around the world by advancing scholarship in the humanities, social sciences, and natural sciences. Its activities are supported by the UC Press Foundation and by philanthropic contributions from individuals and institutions. For more information, visit www.ucpress.edu.

University of California Press
Berkeley and Los Angeles, California

University of California Press, Ltd.
London, England

ISBN 978-0-520-25419-0 (pbk. : alk. paper)

The Library of Congress has cataloged the earlier edition of this book as follows:

Library of Congress Cataloging-in-Publication Data

Habits of the heart : individualism and commitment in American life /
[edited by] Robert N. Bellah . . . [et al.].—Updated ed., with a
new introduction, 1st California paperback ed.
       p.   cm.
Includes bibliographical references and index.
ISBN 0-520-20568-5 (pbk. : alk. paper)
    1. National characteristics, American.   2. United States—
Civilization—1945–   3. Individualism.   4. Civics.   I. Bellah,
Robert Neely, 1927–
E169.12.H29   1996
973.9—dc20   95-51286
                                                                 CIP

29   28   27   26   25   24   23   22   21   20
10   9   8   7   6   5   4

Contents

CONCLUSION

Preface to the 2008 Edition

The great struggles of our time are characterized as the conflict between democracy and tyranny. Since those seem to be the only options, we Americans take it for granted that democracy is a good thing, indeed, politically, the best thing, and whatever opposes it is a very bad thing. But we do not spend much time thinking about what we mean by democracy. We often mean societies that have free elections, a problematic idea when the free elections are won by opponents of democracy. In *Habits of the Heart* we draw heavily from Tocqueville's *Democracy in America*, a book that went far in making *democracy* a good word.[1] It is worth remembering that in most of Western history democracy was thought to be a bad form of government, quite different from a republic, which was usually viewed as a "mixed constitution," with monarchic, aristocratic, and democratic elements, none of them predominating. The founders of the American republic were consciously opposed to democracy, and our constitution was written with the idea of a mixed constitution in mind: there would be a monarchical element (the presidency), an aristocratic element (the Senate), and a democratic element (the House of Representatives).

Democracy comes from the Greek word *demokratia*, which means rule by the people, and this meant direct rule, not representative rule, as the ancient Greeks had no idea of representative democracy. The most successful example of ancient democracy was fifth-century BC Athens, where free adult male citizens did indeed rule through their participation in the assembly that made all important political decisions, an assembly in which anyone could speak and all could vote. Unfortunately we know most about Athenian democracy from its critics, above all Plato and Aristotle. Aristotle calls democracy not "the rule of the people" but "the rule of the poor," because the majority of the citizens were, relatively at least, poor. But in the eyes of its critics, the rule of the poor was biased against those who were not poor and so was unjust. It must be said that Plato and Aristotle criticized oligarchy, the rule of the few, as biased in favor of the rich and so also unjust. And although Plato favored the rule of a philosopher king, while admitting the idea was most unrealistic, both Plato and Aristotle were bitterly opposed to tyranny, the rule of one man serving his own interest alone. Aristotle was one of the first to favor the idea of a mixed constitution, which he called a *politeia*.

What this excursus into the history of the idea of democracy tells us is not only that since fifth-century Athens the term *democracy* was not positive until very late in the day, perhaps less than two hundred years ago, but that *democracy* and *tyranny* are only two of several terms in classical political philosophy for forms of government. As early as Herodotus we find the description of three basic forms of government: the rule of one, the rule of the few, and the rule of the many. What the democracy/tyranny contrast omits is Herodotus's second form, oligarchy, or rule of the few, meaning in practice the nobles and richer elements of the political community.

In the classical view, the first two kinds of government had good and bad forms—the rule of one could be a monarchy or a tyranny, and the rule of the few could be an aristocracy or an oligarchy—but the rule of the many was pretty much always bad. Within this tradition Tocqueville worked not only with the contrast between democracy and tyranny (we might remember that he still shared traditional fears about democracy when he spoke of the possibility that there could be "democratic tyranny" as well as "democratic liberty," though holding that American institutions favored democratic liberty), but also the contrast between democracy and aristocracy, since he thought the French tradition had been largely aristocratic and, though it had its merits, as such was fundamentally opposed to liberty.[2] Although he does not use the word *oligarchy*, the classic term for the bad form of the rule of the few, he often uses the word *aristocracy* for the selfish rule of the few. Furthermore, he saw it not only as characteristic of a past rapidly fading away, though he hoped that would be the case, but also as possibly arising again even in the midst of democracy. His most famous admonition in this regard had to do with new forms of economic organization only incipient in his own day, as described in volume 2, part 2, chapter 20, ominously entitled "How an Aristocracy May Be Created by Industry."[3] In the final paragraphs of this chapter Tocqueville modulates his criticism at the same time that he emphasizes it:

> I think that, generally speaking, the manufacturing aristocracy which we see rising before our eyes is one of the hardest that have appeared on earth. But at the same time, it is one of the most restrained and least dangerous.

> In any event, the friends of democracy should keep their eyes anxiously fixed in that direction. For if ever again permanent inequality of conditions and aristocracy make their way into the world, it will have been by that door that they entered.[4]

It is the tendency to oligarchy, with its threats to republican liberty, that we believe is today on the rise, especially in the United States.

In *Habits of the Heart*, we followed Tocqueville's pioneering analysis of the social results of the new political form of democracy. Tocqueville saw a variety of unique features in American democracy, especially what he called equality of condition and, famously, individualism. While he affirmed the historical tendency toward equality as divinely inspired, he worried about the consequences of the tendency toward individualism. In volume 2, part 4, chapter 6 of *Democracy in America*, entitled "What Sort of Despotism Democratic Nations Have to Fear," Tocqueville considers some of the despotic potentialities that lie within democracy.[5] The sort of despotism democracies have to fear has been called "soft despotism": that is, a sort of despotism that comes on almost without being noticed. One condition for this to happen is the individualism that Tocqueville warned is the Achilles heel of the American experiment. As he described it, "Each one of them [the citizens], withdrawn into himself, is almost unaware of the fate of the rest. Mankind, for him, consists in his children and his personal friends. As for the rest of his fellow citizens, they are nothing." Under these circumstances those in power may become absolute almost without the citizens being aware of what is happening. He writes that an "orderly, gentle, peaceful slavery," such as he described, "could be combined, more easily than is generally supposed, with some of the external forms of freedom, and there is a possibility of its getting itself established even under the shadow of the sovereignty of the people."[6]

When Tocqueville pointed to the possibility of a new industrial and financial aristocracy (we might more accurately call it an oligarchy), he did not imagine the mechanisms it would develop to underpin its rule, a rule that would continue the form but not the substance of democracy and lead to increasing inequality as well. The enormous power of money to determine election outcomes, the fact that in the United States both major parties are beholden to the financial magnates, these could not have been clear in his day. He foresaw the soft despotism at home, but he did not foresee a foreign policy that would support hard despotism abroad wherever it serves our interests. And of course he could not foresee the ecological crisis and the growing demand for fossil fuel in the face of decreasing supply that is sparking ever more violent global conflict.

Recently John Dunn has described the strange history of the term *democracy* and has argued that only in the French Revolution did the idea of democracy, for the first time since ancient Greece, become a political possibility: "It was Robespierre above all who brought democracy back to life as a focus of political allegiance: no longer merely an elusive or blatantly implausible form of government, but a glowing and perhaps in the long run irresistible pole of attraction and source of power."[7] He points to the revolutionary leader Babeuf, an extremist even in a moment of extremes, as describing the two possibilities of democracy: it could produce an order of equality or an order of egoism, depending on whether private property was socialized or sacralized.[8] For nearly two hundred years after the French Revolution the struggle between these two options continued, ending only with the fall of European communism at the end of the 1980s. Ironically, both forms of "democracy" created regimes of great inequality: a totalitarian state in the name of equality of property, and the greatest inequality in human history in the order of egoism, better known as the free-market economy.[9]

Tocqueville saw many things, but, writing in the first half of the nineteenth century, he could not see everything. His sense that equality was on the march turns out to have been a mistake after all, though his fear that democracy could end up more as form than substance seems to be coming true before our eyes. Since *Habits of the Heart* first appeared more than twenty years ago, the United States has witnessed a great increase in inequality of life chances among its citizens, especially in the areas of health care, economic security, and educational opportunity. The growth in this kind of inequality has been much greater in the United States than in other developed countries. Even though overall economic productivity has risen considerably during this period, thanks in part to new information technologies, almost all the profits from that growth have gone to a few at the very top of the income distribution. Why, then, have Americans been unwilling or unable to halt the growth of inequality or to use our increasing wealth for the common welfare?

Here we believe Tocqueville's analysis still has much to teach us. The link between individualism and a strong suspicion of government, especially the national government—at just the time private wealth and control of government has grown enormously—is a major reason for our drift toward oligarchy. These developments make Tocqueville's warning about the reentry of "aristocracy," or, as we would prefer to call it, oligarchy, directly applicable. Indeed, since the publication of *Habits*, the growth of global inequality has continued its ominous march, and awareness of it is increasing, even to the point where Marxism in some quarters is making a comeback, as Tony Judt has recently warned.[10] No one in his right mind should welcome the return of a dogmatic ideological system that seems inevitably linked to a coercive state, but are we so much better off with a dogmatic market ideology, one that argues we hardly need a state at all? Does the latter really support democracy in any meaningful sense?

Twenty years later, the picture of American culture we drew in *Habits of the Heart* seems all too accurate. At the same time, however, we pointed out the role of traditions within American culture, especially aspects of biblical religion and civic republicanism, that have provided resources for countering extreme individualism by upholding aspirations to solidarity. We have been gratified that many groups of citizens who continue to work for the common good have found these ideas useful. Americans have, after all, at various times realized a greater degree of inclusion and civic equality, particularly in the still unfinished effort to overcome barriers of race and gender, than was present in our early history. The ideas that lie behind these efforts may serve us yet in dealing with our current problems.

Habits is a book about American individualism but also about the many efforts to offset its destructive consequences. Many citizen groups continue to work for a different kind of society and a different kind of world. In many ways *Habits* remains a handbook for such groups.

March 2007

Notes

1. John Dunn writes, "In Tocqueville's *Democracy in America,* we find for the first time the recognition that democracy is the key to the distinctiveness of modern political experience and that anyone who hopes to grasp the character of that experience must focus on and take in just what it is that democracy implies." Dunn, *Democracy: A History* (New York: Atlantic Monthly Press, 2006), p. 73.
2. See his preface to the twelfth edition, Alexis de Tocqueville, *Democracy in America,* trans. George Lawrence, ed. J. P. Mayer (Garden City, NY: Anchor Books, 1969), p. xii.
3. Tocqueville, *Democracy,* pp. 555–58.
4. Tocqueville, *Democracy,* p. 558.
5. Tocqueville, *Democracy,* pp. 690–95.
6. Tocqueville, *Democracy,* pp. 692–93.
7. Dunn, *Democracy,* p. 118.
8. The terms may actually derive from Babeuf's follower, Buonarroti. Dunn, *Democracy,* p. 124.
9. Dunn writes, "The market economy is the most powerful mechanism for dismantling equality that humans have ever fashioned." And its triumph leads Dunn to describe it, with capitals, as "The World Order of Egoism." Dunn, *Democracy,* pp. 137, 171.
10. Tony Judt, "Goodbye to All That?" *New York Review of Books,* September 21, 2006, pp. 88–92.

Preface to the 1996 Edition

THE HOUSE DIVIDED

"How ought we to live? . . . Who are we, as Americans?" Since we wrote those questions at the beginning of *Habits of the Heart*, over a decade ago, they have taken on a critical urgency. Their meaning has been contested since the beginning of the republic, but never more than at present, when we hear calls to "renew America" or to overcome "moral crisis."

We Americans have always wanted to make something of ourselves. We have aspired to be self-confident and energetic, trusting that, by dint of hard work and good character, we could achieve self-respect and integrity in an open society. Looking around at what is happening to us as a nation, however, everywhere we find uneasiness about the soundness of our society and concern about its future. More and more of us doubt whether we can trust our institutions, our elected officials, our neighbors, or even our ability to live up to our own expectations for our lives. And anxiety is always close to the surface, a haunting fear that things have somehow gone wrong. For many Americans, these fears come to a head in worries about crime, moral decline, and the deepening divides of income and opportunity. There is a gnawing uncertainty about the future of our jobs, of adequate income, and of our family life, especially our children's welfare.

Underlying many of these fears is the realization that, for most Americans, growth of the global economy no longer means opportunity but, rather, "downsizing," "re-engineered" jobs, and the pink slip of dismissal. Yet through all these wrenching threats to prosperity there has been curiously little public protest about the changing rules of the economic game. We are divided, we are told, by race, by culture, by creed, by differing views of the national identity. But we are united, as it turns out, in at least one core belief, even across lines of color, religion, region, and occupation: the belief that economic success or misfortune is the individual's responsibility, and his or hers alone.

How can we account for this overwhelming value consensus which seems to fly in the face of our usual picture of America as a contentious, deeply divided society? The fact becomes even more puzzling once we notice that this common American belief is shared by the population of no other industrial nation, either in Europe or in East Asia. Those nations too are experiencing the disorienting shocks of the new global economy. Yet the gap in income between the best-off and the worst-off is vastly greater in the United States than in any of them, and we continue to tolerate significantly higher rates of economic deprivation than they do. Why are we paying a higher cost, as a society, for economic change? Is this high cost related to the decline of trust and confidence? Could these developments share a common source in some of our unquestioned beliefs about individuals and their responsibilities? In other words, is this conundrum rooted in cultural values which are so taken for granted as to be nearly invisible to Americans?

Individualism Again

In *Habits of the Heart* we attempted to understand this cultural orientation. Following Alexis de Tocqueville, we called it individualism. Individualism, the first language in which Americans tend to think about their lives, values independence and self-reliance above all else. These qualities are expected to win the rewards of success in a competitive society, but they are also valued as virtues good in themselves. For this reason, individualism places high demands upon every person even as the open nature of American society entices with chances of big rewards.

American individualism, then, demands personal effort and stimulates great energy to achieve, yet it provides little encouragement for nurturance, taking a sink-or-swim approach to moral development as well as to economic success. It admires toughness and strength and fears softness and weakness. It adulates winners while showing contempt for losers, a contempt that can descend with crushing weight on those considered, either by others or by themselves, to be moral or social failures.

In *Habits* we explored this American individualism. We asked where it came from and sought to describe its anatomy. We found that it took both a "hard" utilitarian shape and a "soft" expressive form. One focused on the bottom line, the other on feelings, which often were viewed therapeutically. Most critically, we questioned whether individualism in either form serves us well as a society, whether it serves even the most successful among us, that educated upper middle class which has historically been most devoted to many of the values of individualism. Our answer then was a qualified no. We argued, again inspired by Tocqueville, that individualism has been sustainable over time in the United States only because it has been supported and checked by other, more generous moral understandings.

In times of economic prosperity, Americans have imagined individualism as a self-sufficient moral and political guide. In times of social adversity such as the present, they are tempted to say that it is up to individuals to look after their own interests. Yet many of us have felt, in times both of prosperity and of adversity, that there is something missing in the individualist set of values, that individualism alone does not allow persons to understand certain basic realities of their lives, especially their interdependence with others. These realities become more salient as individual effort alone proves inadequate to meet the demands of living. At such times in the past Americans have turned to other cultural traditions, particularly those we termed the biblical and civic republican understandings of life. These two traditions have served the nation well when united action to address common problems has been called for.

The biblical tradition, a second language familiar to most Americans through a variety of communities of faith, teaches concern for the intrinsic value of individuals because of their relationship to the transcendent. It asserts the obligation to respect and acknowledge the dignity of all. This tradition has played a crucial political role since the beginning of the republic, especially at moments of national crisis and renewal such as the Civil War, by insisting that the nation rests on a moral foundation. At such times currents in biblical religion have made common cause with the civic republicanism which guided the nation's founders, to insist that the American experiment is a project of common moral purpose, one which places upon citizens a responsibility for the welfare of their fellows and for the common good.

The key point of connection between these traditions, one which sets them off from radical individualism, is their appreciation for the social dimensions of the human person. These voices have contested individualism's mistaken identification of individuality with the typical virtues of adolescence, initiative and independence, along with their less savory concomitants of adulation of success and contempt for weakness. Civic republicanism and biblical religion remind us that being an individual—being one's own person—does not entail escaping our ties to others, and that real freedom lies not in rejecting our social nature but in fulfilling it in a critical and adult loyalty, as we acknowledge our common responsibility to contribute to the wider fellowship of life. It was these voices above all which we sought to amplify in the public conversation even as we feared that our national discourse was being impoverished by the monotones of a strident and ultimately destructive individualism.

Strongly though we emphasized the importance of individualism when we published *Habits*, we perhaps understated the ambiguity of its relationship to the biblical and republican traditions, which in some ways mitigate individualism but in other ways significantly contribute to it. As Ernst Troeltsch pointed out, ascetic Protestantism, the form of biblical religion most pervasive in our formative period and still widely influential, has a strongly anti-political, even anti-civic, side.[1] The state and the larger society are considered unnecessary because the saved take care of themselves. Even more problematic is the tendency in this same strand of Protestantism to exclude those who are considered morally unworthy—unworthiness often being determined by their lack of economic success (the undeserving poor)—from the social body altogether. This attitude is countered by other Protestants and particularly by the Catholic tradition, in which an emphasis on the common good precludes the exclusion of anyone from society's care and concern. As opposed to that strand in Protestantism which looks at work as a way individuals prove themselves, this other view sees work as a contribution to a common endeavor in which all do what they can but none is rejected because of inability. Still, we cannot forget that one influential strand of biblical religion in America encourages secession from public life rather than civic engagement, and is even tempted to condemn the most vulnerable as morally unworthy.

Further, one influential type of republicanism that we inherited from the eighteenth century, our version of the English Whig tradition, best known in its early form as anti-federalism, was anti-state and anti-urban, idealizing the yeoman farmer in all his independence. Jefferson's insistence on putting the nation's capital in a swamp was not accidental. Jefferson-Madison republicanism viewed with hostility not only cities but also taxation and virtually any functions for the state. A paranoid fear of the state is not something new, but can be seen from the earliest days of the republic.[2]

We also underestimated the *moral* meaning of the individualism we called utilitarian. In at least one version of utilitarian individualism the real focus is on moral self-discipline and self-help, not primarily on extrinsic rewards. Worldly rewards are simply signs of good moral character—an idea that developed gradually in the Calvinist tradition. The individualist focus on adolescent independence, which we certainly emphasized, involves enduring fears of a meddling, powerful father who might push one back to childish dependence, fears easily transferred to a paternalistic state seen as threatening to reduce free citizens to helpless subjects.³ This moral utilitarianism works out in class terms: the rich are independent adults and the poor are dependent children, and both have only themselves to thank or blame. American individualism resists more adult virtues, such as care and generativity, let alone wisdom, because the struggle for independence is all-consuming.

This complex culture of individualism was much more functional on the frontier (though it certainly had destructive consequences there as well) than it can be in the complex, interdependent society we have become today. If some readers of *Habits* saw us as nostalgic for an idealized past, we would now like to disabuse them. We still believe that the biblical and republican traditions are in many ways preferable to utilitarian and expressive individualism, but there is no form of them that we can appropriate uncritically or affirm without reservation.

The Crisis of Civic Membership

The consequences of radical individualism are more strikingly evident today than they were even a decade ago, when *Habits of the Heart* was published. In *Habits* we spoke of commitment, of community, and of citizenship as useful terms to contrast to an alienating individualism. Properly understood, these terms are still valuable for our current understanding. But today we think the phrase "civic membership" brings out something not quite captured by those other terms. While we criticized distorted forms of individualism, we never sought to neglect the central significance of the individual person or failed to sympathize with the difficulties faced by the individual self in our society. "Civic membership" points to that critical intersection of personal identity with social identity. If we face a crisis of civic identity, it is not just a social crisis, it is a personal crisis as well.

What we mean by the crisis of civic membership is that there are, at every level of American life and in every significant group, temptations and pressures to disengage from the larger society. Two consequences follow from this: social capital (a term we will define in the next section) is depleted, and personal identity is threatened as well. The confident sense of selfhood that comes from membership in a society in which we believe, where we both trust and feel trusted, and to which we feel we securely belong: this is exactly what is threatened by a crisis of civic membership. It is not simply a matter of disillusionment with politics, though that is bad enough. It involves a more radical disengagement that is even more threatening to social coherence than alienation from politics alone would be.

Because we think that the crisis of civic membership takes different forms in different social classes, a consideration of the widening disparities in our class system is necessary as a step toward clarifying the crisis. Americans often feel uncomfortable talking about class. Isn't ours basically a classless society? Far from it. In *Habits of the Heart* the consideration of class is largely implicit, since the book focuses on cultural ideals of middle-class identity that most Americans share. But in the past decade changes in our class structure have occurred that raise grave moral issues. An explicit treatment of class has now become unavoidable.

The pressures of the global market economy are impinging on all societies in the world. The chief consequence of these pressures is the growing disparity between winners and losers in the global marketplace. The result is not only income polarization, with the rich growing richer and the poor poorer, but also a shrinking middle class increasingly anxious about its future. Let us consider some of the tendencies these global pressures are creating everywhere, but with particular sharpness in the United States. First is the emergence of a deracinated elite composed of those Robert Reich calls "symbolic analysts," that is, people who know how to use the new technologies and information systems that are transforming the global economy.[4] Such people are located less securely in communities than in networks linking them, flexibly and transiently, to others like themselves who are scattered all over the world. Educated in the highly competitive atmosphere of excellent universities and graduate schools, such persons have learned to travel light with regard to family, church, locality, even nation. It is here, though not exclusively here, that we clearly see the cultural profile of individualization that we studied in *Habits of the Heart*.

Among this powerful elite the crisis of civic membership is expressed in the loss of civic consciousness, of a sense of obligation to the rest of society, which leads to a secession from society into guarded, gated residential enclaves and ultra-modern offices, research centers, and universities. Its sense of a social covenant, of the idea that we are all members of the same body, is singularly weak.

What is even more disturbing about this knowledge/power elite than its secession from society is its predatory attitude toward the rest of society, its willingness to pursue its own interests without regard to anyone else. Lester Thurow has spoken of the difference between an establishment and an oligarchy.[5] Japan, he argues, has an establishment, while much of Latin America suffers under an oligarchy. Both are privileged elites; the essential difference is that an establishment seeks its own good by working for the good of the whole society (*noblesse oblige*), whereas an oligarchy looks out for its own interests by exploiting the rest of society. Another way of putting it would be to say that an establishment has a strong sense of civic membership while an oligarchy lacks one. One of the principal differences has to do with taxation: an oligarchy taxes itself least; an establishment taxes itself most. In American history we have had establishments—most notably in the founding generation and the period after World War II—but we have also had oligarchies. It is not hard to see what we have today.

Thurow has pointed out more recently the growing disparity in incomes when an oligarchy replaces an establishment: "[N]ever before have a majority of American workers suffered real wage reductions while the per capita domestic product was advancing." The real per capita gross domestic product went up 29 percent between 1973 and 1993. That was a lower rate of increase than in the preceding twenty years, but it was still a significant increase. Yet that increase in per capita GDP was not shared equally: 80 percent of workers either lost ground or barely held their own. "Among men, the top 20 percent of the labor force has been winning all of the country's wage increases." This is not a feature of all high-tech economies. Other countries comparable to ours, such as Japan and Germany, shared their increase in GDP across the board.[6] And if we look at the top 20 percent of workers in the United States, we will see inordinate differences. It is the top 5 percent that has gained the most, and particularly the top 1 percent.

In tandem with the growth of this knowledge/power elite has been the growth of an impoverished underclass, the people from whom the elite are most eager to secede. Forty years ago people living in urban ghettos could go to sleep with their doors unlocked. They were poor and they were segregated, but relatively few of them were unemployed and relatively few of them had out-of-wedlock babies. They were not called the underclass, a term invented in 1963 by the Swedish social analyst Gunnar Myrdal to indicate those who suffered most from poverty and segregation.[7] He carefully hyphenated the term and put it in quotes. At first known only to a few policy specialists, by the late 1970s it had become both a term and a problem widely recognized by the general public and even by ghetto-dwellers themselves. (Although originally a neutral term used in social scientific analysis, it eventually became pejorative, a way to blame the poor for their poverty. We wish to be clear that we are using the term only in its analytical sense.)

As a term, underclass had the great advantage of being color-blind in a period when we have become sensitive about racial language. Yet among most Americans the term was primarily used to designate blacks, indeed only those blacks who still inhabited the depopulated ghettos which now resembled nothing so much as the bombed-out remnants of the thriving communities they had once been. It is worth remembering that five out of six poor people in America are white and that poverty breeds drugs, violence, and unstable families without regard to race.

How could all this have happened, and why did we let it happen? Part of the answer lies in the deindustrialization of our cities. Hundreds of thousands of blue-collar jobs, and many thousands of white-collar jobs too, have been moved out of our major cities in the last thirty years. Those African Americans with enough education to enter the professional or sub-professional skilled workforce have been able to leave the old ghetto, not for integrated housing—housing segregation remains unchanged in most areas over the last three decades—but for new black neighborhoods and suburbs with some of the amenities of white neighborhoods of comparable income: thus the depopulation of ghettos, many of which now house half or a third of the population they had in their prime.[8]

Those left behind were then subjected to the systematic withdrawal of institutional support, both public and private. The departing middle-class African Americans took with them many of the churches and clubs they had always initiated. Cities under increasing fiscal pressure closed schools, libraries, and clinics, and even police and fire stations, in ghetto areas. The most vulnerable left behind have to fend for themselves in a Hobbesian world where just making it through the month with enough to eat is often a major problem. Far from breeding dependency, life in the ghetto today requires the most urgent kind of self-reliance. Unlike some sectors of the elite, the underclass has suffered a crisis of civic membership not because its members have opted out but because they have been pushed out—denied civic membership—by economic and political forces for which they are simply redundant. Other societies, less blinded by cultural individualism, are more sensitive to these matters than we are. In France, for example, the unemployed have come to be called "*les exclus*" (the excluded) and as such have become a central concern of the whole society.[9]

This is not a story the elite wants to hear, and some journalists and even some social scientists have obliged them with another story, a story made plausible by our individualist ideology. The underclass is not, according to this alternative story, the result of the systematic withdrawal of economic and political support from the most deprived and segregated portion of our society. Members of the underclass have only themselves to blame: it is their resistance to all efforts to help them that has caused the problem. Or, in another widely believed elaboration on the underclass story, the underclass was actually *created* by the efforts to help its members, above all by the Great Society welfare programs, which caused self-perpetuating, indeed permanent, welfare dependency. The facts that welfare payments, including Aid to Families with Dependent Children, have systematically declined in real dollars over the last twenty years and that they have fallen by half during the 1980s alone are ignored by those who tell this story, as is the fact that over 70 percent of those on welfare stay on it for less than two years, and over 90 percent for less than eight years.

The underclass story, which involves blaming the victims rather than recognizing a catastrophic economic and political failure of American society, serves to soothe the conscience of the affluent, and it even allows them to wax indignant at the cost of welfare in a time of expanding deficits. But, more important, the underclass story serves to frighten and to warn all those who are not so affluent, who have seen the erosion of what they have or who have had to battle just to stay even. The underclass gives people something to define themselves against; it tells them what they are not; it tells them what it would be most fearful to become. And it gives them people to blame. The shrinking middle class, shorn of its postwar job security by the pressure of global competitiveness, is tempted to look down at those worse off as the source of our national problems. If success and failure are the result of individual effort, those at the top can hardly be blamed—unless, of course, they are politicians.

Robert Reich elaborated this three-class typology of our current socioeconomic life when he spoke of our three classes as an "overclass," living in the safety of elite suburbs, an "underclass quarantined in surroundings that are unspeakably bleak, and often violent," and a new "anxious class" trapped in "the frenzy of effort it takes to preserve their standing." More and more families are trying to patch together two and sometimes more paychecks to meet the widening income, health-care, and pension gaps that are spurring the "disintegration" of the middle class as it has historically been defined.[10] In the anxious class the crisis of civic membership takes the form of disillusion with politics and a sense of uncertainty about the economic future so pervasive that concern for individual survival threatens to replace social solidarity.[11]

In 1970, after twenty-five years of economic growth in which almost everyone shared, America reached the greatest degree of income equality in its recent history and enjoyed a vigorous civic culture. The challenges of the sixties were deeply unsettling but also stimulating, and a sense of civic membership continued to characterize the society as a whole. In 1995, after twenty-five years in which the profits of economic growth went entirely to the top 20 percent of the population, we have reached the high point of income inequality in our recent history, and our civic life is a shambles. We have seen what Michael Lind calls the revolution of the rich and what Herbert Gans calls the war against the poor.[12] A society in which most of the population is treading water, the bottom is sinking, and the top is rising is a society in which a crisis of civic membership is vividly evident at every level.[13]

Declining Social Capital

One way of characterizing the weakening of the practices of social life and civic engagement that we have called the crisis of civic membership is to speak of declining social capital. Robert Putnam, who has brought the term to public attention recently, defines social capital as follows: "By analogy with notions of physical capital and human capital—tools and training that enhance individual productivity—'social capital' refers to features of social organization, such as networks, norms, and trust, that facilitate coordination and cooperation for mutual benefits."[14] There are a number of possible indices of social capital; the two that Putnam has used most extensively are associational membership and public trust.

Putnam has chosen a stunning image as the title of a recent article: "Bowling Alone: America's Declining Social Capital."[15] He reports that between 1980 and 1993 the total number of bowlers in America increased by 10 percent, while league bowling decreased by 40 percent. Nor, he points out, is this a trivial example: nearly 80 million Americans went bowling at least once in 1993, nearly a third more than voted in the 1994 congressional elections and roughly the same as claim to attend church regularly. But Putnam uses bowling only as a symbol for the decline of American associational life, the vigor of which has been seen as the heart of our civic culture ever since Tocqueville visited the United States in the 1830s.

In the 1970s dramatic declines in membership began to hit organizations typically associated with women, such as the PTA and the League of Women Voters, in what has often been explained as the result of the massive entry of women into the workforce. In the 1980s falling membership struck traditionally male associations, such as the Lions, Elks, Masons, and Shriners, as well. Union membership has dropped by half since its peak in the middle 1950s. We all know of the continuing decline in the numbers of eligible voters who actually go to the polls, but Putnam reminds us that the number of Americans who answer yes when asked whether they have attended a public meeting on town or school affairs in the last year has fallen by more than a third since 1973.

Almost the only groups that are growing are the support groups, such as twelve-step groups, that Robert Wuthnow has recently studied. These groups make minimal demands on their members and are oriented primarily to the needs of individuals: indeed, Wuthnow has characterized them as involving individuals who "focus on themselves in the presence of others," what we might call being alone together.[16] Putnam argues that paper membership groups, such as the AARP (American Association of Retired Persons), which has grown to gargantuan proportions, have few or no civic consequences, because their members may have common interests but they have no meaningful interactions. Putnam also worries that the Internet, the electronic town meeting, and other much ballyhooed new technological devices are probably civically vacuous, because they do not sustain civic engagement. Talk radio, for instance, mobilizes private opinion, not public opinion, and trades on anxiety, anger, and distrust, all of which are deadly to civic culture. The one sphere that seems to be resisting the general trend is religion. Religious membership and church attendance have remained fairly constant after the decline from the religious boom of the 1950s, although membership in church-related groups has declined by about one-sixth since the 1960s.

What goes together with the decline of associational involvement is the decline of public trust. We are not surprised to hear that the proportion of Americans who reply that they trust the government in Washington only some of the time or almost never has risen steadily, from 30 percent in 1966 to 75 percent in 1992. But are we prepared to hear that the proportion of Americans who say that most people can be trusted fell by more than a third between 1960, when 58 percent chose that alternative, and 1993, when only 37 percent did?

The argument for decline in social capital is not one that we made in *Habits of the Heart*. *Habits* was essentially a cultural analysis, more about language than about behavior. We worried that the language of individualism might undermine civic commitment, but we pointed to the historically high levels of associational membership in America and the relative strength of such memberships here compared with those in other advanced industrial nations. Whether there has really been such a decline is still controversial, but we are inclined to believe that tendencies that were not yet entirely clear in the early 1980s when *Habits* was written are now discernible and disconcerting.[17]

We believe that the culture and language of individualism influence these trends but that there are also structural reasons for them, many of which stem from changes in the economy we have already mentioned. The decline in social capital is evident in different ways in different classes. For example, the decline in civic engagement in the overclass is indicated by their withdrawal into gated, guarded communities. It is also related to the constant movement of companies in the process of mergers and breakups. Rosabeth Kanter has recently suggested some of the consequences of this movement:

> For communities as well as employees this constant shuffling of company identities is confusing and its effects profound. Cities and towns rely on the private sector to augment public services and support community causes. There is a strong "headquarters bias" in this giving: companies based in a city tend to do more for it, contributing $75,000 a year on average more to the local United Way, than companies of similar size with headquarters elsewhere.[18]

Kanter points out that the departure of a corporate headquarters from a middle-sized city can tear holes in the social fabric of that city. Not only are thousands of jobs lost but so is the civic leadership of the corporate executives. Local charities lose not only money but board members.

Corporate volatility can lead to a kind of placelessness at the top of the pyramid: "Cut loose from society the rich man can play his chosen role free of guilt and responsibility," observes Michael Lewis. "He becomes that great figure of American mythology—the roaming frontiersman. These days the man who has made a fortune is likely to spend more on his means of transportation than on his home: the private jet is the possession that most distinguishes him from the rest of us. . . . The old aristocratic conceit of place has given way to a glorious placelessness."[19] The mansions of the old rich were certainly expressions of conspicuous consumption, but they also encouraged a sense of responsibility for a particular place (city, state, region) where they were located. Wendell Berry has spoken of "itinerant professional vandals,"[20] who are perhaps not too different from Reich's "symbolic analysts," attached to no place at all and thus tempted to act more like an oligarchy than an establishment.

Moving to the opposite end of the income spectrum, Lee Rainwater, in his classic book *What Money Buys*, shows that poverty—income insufficient to maintain an acceptable level of living—operates to deprive the poor not only of material capital but of social capital as well. In traditional hierarchical societies, low levels of material well-being can be associated with established statuses that confer the benefits of clientship. In our kind of society, with its fundamentally egalitarian ideology and its emphasis on individual self-reliance, status—even personal identity—

is conferred primarily by one's relationship to the economy, by one's work and the income derived from one's work. Lack of a socially acceptable income and any likelihood of attaining one has long-term consequences for the kind of person one becomes and the kind of life one is likely to live. As Rainwater puts it:

> As people grow up and live their lives, they are engaged in a constant implicit assessment of their likely chances for having the access and resources necessary to maintain a sense of valid identity. People's anticipation of their future chances, particularly as children, adolescents, and younger adults, seems to affect quite markedly the way they relate to others and the way they make use of the resources available to them. When individuals make the assessment that their future possibilities for participating in validating activities are low and particularly when that estimate is constantly confirmed by others in their world (teachers, police, parents), then the process of searching for alternative validating potentials that result in deviant behavior is set in motion. When people define their position in life as such that they have "nothing to lose," they are much less responsive to the efforts at social control exercised informally by those in their neighborhood and formally by official agencies of social regulation.[21]

By reducing social capital, chronic poverty blocks economic and political participation, and consequently weakens the capacity to develop moral character and sustain family life.

When we add to the consequences of poverty the consequences of residential segregation, the situation becomes devastating. We should remember that in spite of fair housing laws residential segregation for black Americans has remained unchanged in our larger cities for the last three decades.[22] What has changed is that the geographical areas with the highest poverty rates have lost retail trade outlets, government services, political influence, and, worst of all, employment that provides anything like an adequate living. Those deprived of social capital have come to be confined to "reservations" that are effectively outside the environing society.

Herbert Gans in his *Middle American Individualism* provides a picture of life in the middle reaches of our society that helps us understand what is happening to social capital in the anxious class.[23] Gans criticizes *Habits of the Heart* for being too censorious of middle American individualism. After all, says Gans, the residents of the lower-middle- and working-class suburbs who are more devoted to their family and friends than to civic life are only a generation or two away from the grinding poverty of manual labor suffered by their immigrant ancestors or the backbreaking labor of peasant agriculture in the old country. The social condition of those not-so-distant ancestors was one of vulnerable subordination, of being kicked around by people who told them what to do. Owning one's own home, taking vacations wherever one wants, being free to decide whom to see or what to buy once one has left the workplace—these are all freedoms that are especially cherished by those whose ancestors have never had them. The modest suburb is not the open frontier but it is, under the circumstances, a reasonable facsimile thereof.

Among the many ironies in the lives of at least a significant number of these middle Americans, however, is that labor union membership had much to do with their attainment of relative affluence and its attendant independence; yet for many of them the labor union has become one more alien institution from which they would like to be free. Middle Americans not only are suspicious of government, according to Gans, they don't like organizations of any kind. Relative to the upper middle class (the lower echelons of what we have been calling the overclass), they are not joiners, belonging to only one or two associations at the most, the commonest being a church. While continuing to identify strongly with the nation, they are increasingly suspicious of politics, which they find confusing and dismaying. Their political participation declines steadily.

As a consequence of tendencies that Gans is probably right in asking us to understand, middle Americans are today losing the social capital that allowed them to attain their valued independence in the first place. Above all this is true of the decline of the labor movement. This decline stems from legislative changes in the last twenty years that have deprived unions of much of their power and influence, and from congressional refusal since 1991 to raise the minimum wage from $4.25 an hour. But, as we see in France and other European countries, where loyalty to labor unions has survived, such attacks can be turned back. In America, union meetings, even where there are unions, are attended by 5 percent of the members at most. Lacking the social capital that union membership would provide, anxious-class Americans are vulnerable in new ways to the arbitrary domination they thought they had escaped. One may lose even one's home and one's recreational vehicle if one's job is downsized and the only alternative employment is at the minimum wage.

The decline of social capital in America becomes particularly distressing if we consider what has happened to our political participation. In *Voice and Equality* Sydney Verba and his colleagues have recently given us a comprehensive review of political participation in the United States.[24] Although the data concerning trends over time are not unambiguous, they do indicate certain tendencies. During the last thirty years the average level of education of the American public has risen steadily, but the level of political participation, which is usually associated with education, has not. This fact can be taken as an indication that, controlling for education, political participation has declined. Even more significant is the nature of the changes. Political party identification and membership have declined, while campaign contributions and writing to congresspersons have increased. Both of these growing kinds of activities normally take place in the privacy of one's home as one writes a check or a letter. Verba and his associates note that neither generates the personal satisfactions associated with more social forms of political participation.

Further, making monetary contributions correlates highly with income and is the most unequal form of participation in our society. The increasing salience of monetary contributions as a form of political participation, as well as the general tendency for political participation to correlate with income, education, and occupation, leads to the summary conclusion of *Voice and Equality*:

> Meaningful democratic participation requires that the voices of citizens in politics be clear, loud, and equal: clear so that public officials know what citizens want and need, loud so that officials have an incentive to pay attention to what they hear, and equal so that the democratic ideal of equal responsiveness to the preferences and interests of all is not violated. Our analysis of voluntary activity in American politics suggests that the public's voice is often loud, sometimes clear, but rarely equal.[25]

Although unequal levels of education, occupation, and income favor the originally advantaged in securing the resources for political participation, there is one significant exception. Verba and his associates note that:

> [o]nly religious institutions provide a counterbalance to this cumulative resource process. They play an unusual role in the American participatory system by providing opportunities for the development of civic skills to those who would otherwise be resource-poor. It is commonplace to ascribe the special character of American politics to the weakness of unions and the absence of class-based political parties that can mobilize the disadvantaged—in particular, the working class—to political activity. Another way that American society is exceptional is in how often Americans go to church—with the result that the mobilizing function often performed elsewhere by unions and labor or social democratic parties is more likely to be performed by religious institutions.[26]

To summarize the relationship of the decline of social capital to political participation we might consider how this relationship works out in the several social classes. Overall, with the exception of the activities centered in religious institutions, political participation has shifted away from those forms that require civic engagement to those that are essentially private, and above all to that of making monetary contributions. The unequal voice to which Verba and his associates point is an indication that the anxious class is seriously under-represented and the underclass scarcely represented at all. Even in the overclass, participation has shifted from more active forms of engagement to the more isolated forms of check- and letter-writing. Finally, Verba and his associates point out that the increasing importance of money in political life contributes to public cynicism: "In short, a participatory system in which money plays a more prominent role is one unlikely to leave either activists or the citizenry at large feeling better about politics."[27]

Individualism and the American Crisis

Most Americans agree that things are seriously amiss in our society—that we are not, as the poll questions often put it, "headed in the right direction"—but they differ over why this is so and what should be done about it. We have sought for answers in the structural problems that we have described under the rubrics of the crisis in civic membership and the decline of social capital. What are some of the other explanations? Perhaps the most widespread alternative explanation locates the source of our problems in a crisis of the family. The cry that what our society most needs is "family values" is not one to be dismissed lightly. Almost all the tendencies we have been describing threaten family life and are often experienced most acutely within the family. Being unemployed and thus unable to get married or not having enough income to support an existing family due to downsizing or part-timing, along with the tensions caused by these conditions, can certainly be understood as family crises. But why is the crisis expressed as a failure of family values?

It is unlikely that we will understand what is going on here unless we once again take into account the culture of individualism. If we see unemployment or reduced income because of downsizing as a purely individual problem rather than a structural problem of the economy, then we will seek to understand what is wrong with the unemployed or underemployed individual. If we also discern that such individuals are prone to have children out of wedlock, to divorce, or to fail to make child support payments, we may conclude that the cause is weakened family values. In *Habits of the Heart* we strongly affirmed the value of the family, and in both *Habits* and *The Good Society* we argued for renewed commitment to marriage and family responsibilities. But to imagine that problems arising from failures rooted in the structure of our economy and polity can primarily be traced to the failings of individuals with inadequate family values seems to us sadly mistaken. It not only increases the level of individual guilt, it also distracts attention from larger failures of collective responsibility.

The link between cultural individualism and the emphasis on family values has a further consequence. Families have traditionally been supported by the paid labor of men. Failure to support one's family may be taken as an indication of inadequate manhood. It is easy to draw the conclusion that if American men would only act like men, then family life would be improved and social problems solved. Some such way of thinking undoubtedly lies behind the movement known as Promise Keepers, as well as the Million Man March of 1995. While we share many of the values of these movements, we are skeptical that increased male responsibility will prove to be an adequate solution to our deep structural economic and political problems or even that it will do more than marginally diminish the severe strains on the American family. The notion that if men would only be men then all would be well in our society seems to us a sad cultural delusion.

Another common alternative explanation of our difficulties is to explain them as the failure of community. This is indeed valid, we believe, but only if our understanding of community is broad and deep enough. In many current usages of the term, however, community means face-to-face groups formed by the voluntary efforts of individuals. Used in this way, failure of community as the source of our problems can be interpreted to mean that if only more people would volunteer to help in soup kitchens or Habitat for Humanity or Meals on Wheels, then our social problems would be solved. As in the case of family values, *Habits of the Heart* strongly affirms face-to-face communities and the valuable contributions voluntary groups can make to society. But we do not believe that the deep structural problems that we face as a society can be effectively alleviated by an increase in devotion to community in this narrow sense. We would agree that an increase in the voluntary commitments of individuals can over the long haul increase our social capital and thus add to the resources we can bring to bear on our problems. But to get at the roots of our problems these resources must be used to overcome institutional difficulties that cannot be directly addressed by voluntary action alone.

We see another difficulty in emphasizing a small-scale and voluntaristic understanding of community as the solution to our problems. As we noted in discussing the work of Verba and his colleagues, voluntary activity tends to correlate with income, education, and occupation. "Joiners" are more apt to be found in the overclass than in the underclass or the anxious class, again with the significant exception of religious groups. This means that voluntary activities are less often designed to help the most deprived, though we don't want to overlook those that are, than to serve the interests of the affluent. This is particularly true of political voluntarism, as Verba and his associates have shown conclusively. Thus, dismantling structures of public provision for the most deprived in hopes that the voluntary sector will take over is misguided in three important respects. First, the voluntary sector has by no means the resources to take up the slack, as churches, charities, and foundations have been pointing out repeatedly in recent years. The second reason is that our more affluent citizens may feel they have fulfilled their obligation to society by giving time and money to "making a difference" through voluntary activity without taking into account that they have hardly made a dent in the real problems faced by most Americans. The third reason is that, as we noted, the voluntary sector is disproportionately run by our better-off citizens and a good many voluntary activities do more to protect the well-to-do than the needy.

There is another sense of community that also presents difficulties if we think the solution to our problems lies in reviving community, and that is the notion of community as neighborhood or locality. *Habits of the Heart* encourages strong neighborhoods and supports civic engagement in towns and cities. But residential segregation is a fact of life in contemporary America. Even leaving aside the hypersegregation of urban ghettos, segregation by class arising from differential housing costs is becoming increasingly evident in suburban America. Thus it is quite possible that in "getting involved" with one's neighborhood or even with one's suburban town one will never meet someone of a different race or class. One will not be exposed to the realities of life for people in circumstances different from one's own. One may even succumb to the natural human temptation to think that people who are different, particularly those lower in social status, are inferior. The anxious class does not want itself to be confused with the underclass. One of the least pleasant characteristics of the overclass, including its lower echelons in the educated upper middle class, is that they do not want to associate with middle Americans, with "Joe Six-Pack" and others who lack the proper cultural attributes. Even in the underclass, those who are not on welfare look down on those who are, and those who are on the dole briefly look down on those on it for a long time.[28] Under such circumstances an exclusive emphasis on neighborhood solidarity could actually contribute to larger social problems rather than solving them.

What the explanations of our social problems that stress the failure of family values or the failure of community have in common is the notion that our problems are individual or in only a narrow sense social (that is, involving family and local community), rather than economic, political, and cultural. A related feature that these common explanations of our troubles share is hostility to the role of government or the state. If we can take care of ourselves, perhaps with a little help from our friends and family, who needs the state? Indeed, the state is often viewed as an interfering father who won't recognize that his children have grown up and don't need him anymore.[29] He can't help solve our problems because it is in large measure he who created them.

In contrast, the market, in this mindset, seems benign, a mostly neutral theater for competition in which achievement is rewarded and incompetence punished. Some awareness exists, however, that markets are not neutral, that some people and organizations have enormous economic power and are capable of making decisions that adversely affect many citizens. From this point of view big business joins big government as the source of problems rather than their solution. Still, in America more than in most comparable societies, people are inclined to think that the market is fairer than the state.

Individualism and Neocapitalism

The culture of individualism, then, has made no small contribution to the rise of the ideology we called neocapitalism in chapter 10 of *Habits*. There we drew a picture of the American political situation that has turned out not to be entirely adequate. We suggested that the impasse between welfare liberalism and its counter-movement, neocapitalism, was coming to an end and that two alternatives, the administered society and economic democracy, were looming on the scene. As it turned out, this incipient pair of alternatives did not materialize, or at least they are enduring a long wait. Instead, neocapitalism has grown ever stronger ideologically and politically. Criticism of "big government" and "tax-and-spend liberalism" has mounted even as particular constituencies, which in the aggregate include most citizens, favor those forms of public provision that benefit them in particular, while opposing benefits they do not receive.

We do not believe we were wrong in seeing ten years ago the severe strains that the neocapitalist formula was creating for the nation. Today those strains are more obvious than ever. But we clearly underestimated the ideological fervor that the neocapitalist position was able to tap—

ironically for us, because so much of that fervor derives from the very source we focused on in our book: individualism. The neocapitalist vision is viable only to the degree to which it can be seen as an expression—even a moral expression—of our dominant ideological individualism, with its compulsive stress on independence, its contempt for weakness, and its adulation of success. Its intensity rises in time of economic trial, when individuals who "work hard and play by the rules" fail to find the rewards they feel they deserve.

Thus neocapitalism has been able to turn even its policy failures into ideological successes, at least up to the present. It has persuaded many Americans that the problems it has produced, such as a quadrupling of the national debt since 1980, are really the result of welfare liberalism, even though welfare liberalism has not set the American policy agenda for over twenty years. It manages to interpret problems arising from the drastic reduction of public provision for the poor as caused by the pitifully inadequate welfare system that still manages to survive despite decades of cuts. It holds that it would actually be charitable to the poor to cut them loose from their "dependence" on the state.

From the neocapitalist point of view, privatization in the service of economic competitiveness is the solution to almost all difficulties. Recent transformations in the health care "industry" are in some ways paradigmatic of neocapitalist solutions to public problems. In a situation of serious crisis with respect to health care, an active role of governmental investment and redistribution in order to cover everyone and control costs has been rejected in favor of the massive growth of for-profit health maintenance organizations. Services are provided in much the same way by the same people, except that less is provided by worse-paid physicians, disciplined to worry ever more about cutting costs and less about patient welfare. Nonprofit hospitals are bought up by chains and health plans that maximize profits for management and investors. The CEOs of these large conglomerates receive annual salaries of eight or even nine figures, while new investment that would make health care more productive, more effective, or—God forbid—more just is put on hold. As insurance companies raise premiums and employers require larger contributions from their workers, more people are pushed out of the private health care system altogether. If they are not actually closed down, overwhelmed public hospitals operate under dangerous conditions that would cost the taxpayers dearly to remedy. From the point of view of neocapitalist individualism, those who find themselves falling into the abyss of no health care at all have only themselves to blame, and the wealthy who siphon off the resources of the system are entitled to whatever they can take.

Neocapitalist ideology aims to convince us that all government social programs have been disastrous failures. Millions of beneficiaries of Medicare and Social Security find that position hard to believe, in spite of its ideological appeal. Those programs, then, are attacked not as intrinsically evil but as too expensive, as mortgaging the future of our children and grandchildren for the sake of older Americans. What is not adequately recognized is just how successful those programs actually are.

Americans over 65 are, largely because of Medicare, the healthiest people in their age category in the world. But for Social Security, 50 percent of our citizens over 65 would be below the poverty line, as they were as recently as 1940, instead of the 10 percent who are presently poor. Thus Social Security is keeping 40 percent of our older citizens from poverty. Our War on Poverty was on the whole a miserable failure not because, as the neocapitalist ideologues would have it, we did too much for the poor, but because we did hardly anything at all, leading Herbert Gans to call it a "Skirmish on Poverty."[30] The money that would have been required to provide an infrastructure of education and economic opportunity for those in chronic poverty was never spent. (In Western Europe, where such money *was* spent, the war on poverty was generally won.) The great exception in spending has been for Social Security. If we were not in a situation of popular attack on the state and public provision, the argument about "generational justice" could be taken more seriously, although most dire projections about rising entitlements leading to bankruptcy fail to take into account expected increases in productivity that will probably cover the rise. We do indeed keep most older people out of poverty while the number of children in poverty continues to rise. But reductions in Medicare and Social Security under present conditions will not be used to help needy younger Americans. They will simply go to reduce taxes for the rich.

During the first decades after World War II, high levels of social spending went hand in hand with high levels of economic growth. In the last twenty years, as the ideology of neocapitalism has taken hold, social spending has decreased dramatically. As spending on material and social infrastructure has declined, economic growth rates have slowed and economic inequality has rapidly increased, as we have seen. One would think anyone who had taken Economics 1 would know that if we do not invest in the future, the future will be bleak. But under the aegis of neocapitalist ideology the American economy has chosen high rates of short-term gain, however speculative, over investment for long-term growth. The results are clear even though the reasons for them are ideologically obscured by a neocapitalist ideology more impervious to disconfirmation than the most dogmatic Marxism.

The economic and political changes that have occurred in the United States in recent decades parallel changes in Western Europe (although not, interestingly enough, in East Asia), but they are more extreme in America than anywhere else. Structural causes are certainly at work here, some of them not well understood. We are convinced, however, that the extreme position of the United States compared to other countries in matters such as income inequality and the attack on public provision is due in important part to the culture of individualism, with its inability to understand the capacities and responsibilities of government.

Where Do We Go from Here?

We believe that neocapitalism offers a fatally flawed political agenda. It claims to be opposed to the state, yet it uses the state ruthlessly to enforce "market discipline." It creates problems that the market alone only exacerbates and that require for their solution effective government intervention and a strong independent sector. When we wrote *Habits* the term communitarianism had not yet come into vogue, nor had the concern with civil society, sparked as it was by the fall of Communism and the concern for the bases of democracy in post-Communist societies. *Habits* got pulled into the debate in ways beyond our anticipation. As we pointed out in the preface to *The Good Society*, if communitarianism means opposition to the neocapitalist agenda and to a theoretical liberalism for which autonomy is almost the only virtue, then we are communitarians. But if it means a primary emphasis on small-scale and face-to-face relations, with the nineteenth-century small town as its exemplar, we are not communitarians.[31] As we argued in *The Good Society* and reiterate here, only effective institutions—economic, political, and social—make complex modern societies livable.

Granted that small-scale communities alone cannot solve our problems, a tension still exists over where to look for solutions. In contemporary republicanism or even nationalism, as represented by Michael Lind's *The Next American Nation*, national consensus and national action are deemed essential to transcend our present difficulties. In opposition stands a sophisticated communitarianism or associationalism that argues for a primary emphasis on devolving functions onto lower-level associations (although not avoiding the responsibility of the state), as represented by Jonathan Boswell's *Community and the Economy*[32] or Paul Hirst's *Associative Democracy*.[33] We refuse, however, to see the two sides as antithetical, for we believe that only a national consensus could devolve responsibility onto associations in a way that does not weaken public provision.

We are impressed by the vigor of the civil society discussion even though it is inconclusive with respect to policy implications.[34] What makes us sympathetic to democratic communitarianism and democratic associationalism as represented by the proposals of Boswell and Hirst is that they do not imagine civil society to be hermetically sealed off from the state and the economy. Rather, they see community and associational life as interpenetrating government and the economy. They would give associations governance functions in both spheres. Hirst foresees associations as actually taking on the function of social welfare provision, as already happens to some degree in our society. Both of them wish to see democratic governance functions operating within the economy. They assume that the state and the economy are supposed to serve people rather than the other way around, as seems all too often to be the case today. Boswell's view of the economy is one we would affirm:

> If balanced, sustained economic performance is sought, it seems that to desire it primarily for its own sake is unwise, even self-defeating, not to mention ethically unsound. If we seriously want it, it appears that we should want something else far more, namely a social change extending particularly, though not exclusively, to the economic system itself. We would accept that enterprise makes full practical and ethical sense only *in* and *with* as well as *for* community. We would acknowledge that economic health and a community renaissance are inseparable, and that of the two it is a community renaissance that would come first.[35]

Toward the end of *Habits of the Heart* we used the notion of a social ecology to evoke a vision of a larger community that was formed out of a variety of smaller communities, each with its own agenda and needs but each affecting the whole and depending on the well-being of the whole. The forms of social relations are different at each level; each level should have its own rights and responsibilities, the nature of which should be constantly revised through public debate. In our book on social institutions that was a sequel to *Habits* we did not make community our central term but spoke instead of *The Good Society*. We emphasized that at every level this society must, while respecting the dignity of each of its members, seek the common good. We believe that this approach can provide a helpful framework for both communitarians and civil society theorists.

As long as neocapitalist ideology maintains its hegemony all these matters may seem to be academic. It is one of the dangers of the neocapitalist vision that it is determinist. It implies that there are no institutional choices: the market decides. Indeed, one of the conundrums of contemporary individualism is that it can combine an absolute belief in the freedom of individual choice with market determinism. But we believe this determinism is an ideological delusion: neither the global economy, nor the stock market, nor the profit margin can determine our institutional choices unless we as citizens let them. But the capacity to make institutional choices rests on cultural resources that are, along with material and social resources, seriously depleted. *Habits of the Heart* was a call to replenish those resources as the basis for moving our society in new directions. It is worth restating that argument in terms of the issues raised in this introduction.

Meaning and a Renewal of Civic Membership

While the idea of community, if limited to neighbors and friends, is an inadequate basis for meeting our current needs, we want to affirm community as a cultural theme that calls us to wider and wider circles of loyalty, ultimately embracing that universal community of all beings of which H. Richard Niebuhr spoke.[36] We should remember that when Jesus was asked, "Who is my neighbor?" he answered with the parable of the Good Samaritan (Luke 10:29–37), in which the true neighbor turns out to be a Samaritan, a member of a group despised in Israel. It is not that Jesus didn't think that a person living next door, or an inhabitant of one's own village, or a member of one's own ethnic group could be a neighbor. But when asked directly, he identified the neighbor as a stranger, an alien, a member of a hated ethnic group. Any community short of the universal community is not the beloved community.

Much of what has been happening in our society has been undermining our sense of community at every level. We are facing trends that threaten our basic sense of solidarity with others: solidarity with those near to us (loyalty to neighbors, colleagues at work, fellow townsfolk), but also solidarity with those who live far from us, those who are economically in situations very different from our own, those of other nations. Yet this solidarity—this sense of connection, shared fate, mutual responsibility, community—is more critical now than ever. It is solidarity, trust, mutual responsibility that allows human communities to deal with threats and take advantage of opportunities. How can we strengthen these endangered capacities, which are first of all cultural capacities to think in certain ways?

When we consider how to renew the cultural capacity for community and solidarity in each of the three classes into which our society is divided, it would be well to remember something we have already mentioned: that in American society religious associations have the strongest hold on their members and almost alone have the capacity to reach individuals in every class. We can formulate the need for a fundamental reorientation toward community and solidarity as a kind of conversion, a turning of consciousness and intention. In the biblical tradition conversion means a turning away from sin and a turning toward God. An idea of turning away from preoccupation with the self and toward some larger identity is characteristic of most of the great religions and philosophies of mankind. Conversion cannot come from willpower alone, but if it is to be enabled we must recover the stories and symbols in whose terms it makes sense.

If we think first of the overclass, the thirty-year critical assault on the dominance of white Euroamerican males in our society has not greatly dented that dominance in practice, but it has been used to justify a decline in civic responsibility on the part of the powerful and a selfish withdrawal into monetary aggrandizement. In an open society we can work to make room for more inclusive leadership without derogating the contributions of older elites. We need at least a portion of the overclass acting as a true establishment if we are to deal with our enormous problems. If the members of the overclass can overcome their own anxieties they may realize that they will gain far more self-respect in belonging to an establishment than to an oligarchy. They may come to see that civic engagement—a concern for the common good, a belief that we are all members of the same body—will not only contribute to the good of the larger society but will contribute to the salvation of their own souls as well. Only some larger engagement can overcome the devastating cultural and psychological narcissism of our current overclass. A return to civic membership, to commitments to community and solidarity, on the part of the overclass would be good not only for society as a whole but also for its individual members.

It would be well to point out that the majority of the people we interviewed in *Habits* belong to the lower echelons of the overclass, to what is commonly called the upper middle class, however much they (and we, who belong to the same class) would be uncomfortable with that terminology. Of course these are not the people who make the big decisions or who profit most from our current economy. They could even be called, in Pierre Bourdieu's pointed phrase, "the dominated fraction of the dominant class."[37] But, as we argued in *Habits*, they are the symbolic center of our society, their style of life is that to which most

Americans aspire, and they do indeed prosper more than 80 percent of their fellow citizens. Their resources are far greater than those of other classes: they have the cultural and social capital and the civic skills to influence the direction in which our society goes. The question is, can they recover a coherent view of the world which will allow them to use these resources for the common good rather than for their own aggrandizement?

The anxious class faces equally serious challenges, for its problems are not only cultural and psychological but sharply material. The average income for a white male has slowly drifted down from an all-time high in 1992 dollars of $34,231 in 1973 to $31,012 in 1992.[38] Even worse than that income decline, which in considerable degree is offset by increasing female participation in the workplace (though that creates its own problems), is the concomitant rise in economic uncertainty. We are becoming a society of what has been called "advanced insecurity." Downsizing, part-timing, and loss of benefits have become a way of life.

The anger and fear generated by acute economic anxiety are easily displaced onto "welfare queens" and illegal immigrants. These feelings also contribute to the decline of voting and associational membership, even union membership, as well as to the rise of divorce. While economic anxieties are real and must ultimately be dealt with structurally, the resulting decline of civic engagement in the anxious class only deepens its cynicism and despair. Renewed engagement with the larger society—for many, through churches first of all, certainly through labor unions, and then through civic organizations—is the most likely way to meet the very real problems that face society's largest group. And on top of its material problems the anxious class shares more than a little in the psychological and cultural problems of the overclass, for which a renewed sense of meaning giving coherence to ideas of solidarity and community would be the best antidote.

Meeting the problems of the underclass and attempting to reincorporate its members into the larger society is the most challenging task of all. The basic problem stems from economic developments that have simply rendered the twenty or thirty million members of the underclass superfluous (and, we should not forget, have rendered much of the anxious class merely marginally relevant). Only a fundamental change in public policy will begin to alter the situation, and in the present atmosphere such a change is hardly to be expected.

But even indispensable changes in public policy cannot alone meet the situation. Where social trust is limited and morale is blasted, one of the most urgent needs is a recovery of self-respect and a sense of agency that can come only from the participation that enables people to belong and contribute to the larger society. Participatory justice asks each individual to give all that is necessary to the common good of society. In turn it obliges society to order its institutions so that everyone can work to contribute to the commonweal in ways that respect their dignity and renew their freedom.[39] Not by transfer payments alone or the compassion of social workers will the problems of the underclass be solved.

In responding to the problems of the underclass, perhaps we need to turn to the principle of subsidiarity, which is derived from Catholic social teaching. The idea is that groups closest to a problem should deal with it, receiving support from higher-level groups where necessary but, wherever possible, not being replaced by those higher-level groups. This principle implies respect for the groups closest to the persons in need, but it does not absolutize those groups or exempt them from the moral standards that apply to groups at any level. A process of social reconstruction of the underclass would require massive public resources, but these should be brought to the situation by third-sector agencies, local so far as possible. Today subsidiarity language is, in contradiction to its basic meaning, used to justify cuts in government spending. In truth, subsidiarity is not a substitute for public provision but makes sense only when public provision is adequate.

Ultimately what the underclass needs is not so different from what the overclass or the anxious class needs. Its social capital is more depleted and its morale more thoroughly shattered, but, like everyone else, what its members most require is a clear sense of solidarity and community and of a future shared with the rest of society.

A House Divided

In conclusion it may be helpful to put our present situation into relation to two earlier moments in American history. The first is the crisis of the republic in the 1850s, during the dark years that would lead to the Civil War. David Greenstone has suggested that the American politics of the day were divided between what he calls a reform liberalism represented by Abraham Lincoln and a utilitarian liberalism represented by Stephen Douglas.[40] The Lincoln–Douglas debates, which took place during the Illinois senatorial campaign of 1858, were a defining moment in American history. The issue was whether slavery should be extended to the territories in the West. Douglas took the line of popular sovereignty: if they want slavery, let them have slavery. In other words, freedom to do what you want was, in this case, freedom to do what the white majority wanted. The basis of Douglas's position was a utilitarian liberalism that asked only for the summing of preferences, not about the moral quality of the preferences.

But Lincoln said that slavery was wrong, that it contradicted the nation's most fundamental principles and should not be extended to the territories no matter what the majority there might want. In other words, freedom is the right only to do that which is morally justified. The basis of Lincoln's position was a reform liberalism that had its roots in New England Puritanism. It drew upon biblical and republican sources and was committed not only to the notion of an objective moral order ("the laws of nature and of nature's God") but also to the notion that individuals live in a society that has a common good beyond the sum of individual goods. It was this moral politics that led Lincoln to his great "House Divided" speech in Springfield, Illinois, on June 16, 1858. "'A house divided against itself cannot stand,'"[41] Lincoln said. "I believe this government cannot endure, permanently half *slave* and half *free*."[42]

If we apply Lincoln's words to our situation we can say that the house today is divided not by slavery but by deepening class divisions. Douglas had no problem with a house divided, since he saw society as nothing more than the sum of individual choices and their consequences. Lincoln, however, judged certain conditions to be objectively wrong and held society accountable for changing them. Our situation today is historically linked to what Lincoln was talking about, for though slavery has been abolished, equality for African Americans has not been achieved. But we believe that it is not so much race discrimination that is the problem, though that continues to be serious enough, but, rather, the racialization of the class hierarchy—the Brazilianization of America, as Michael Lind calls it.[43]

Race differences are real in our society, but we should not let them obscure how much we have in common. Jennifer Hochschild in *Facing Up to the American Dream* has recently analyzed the ways in which Americans differ by race.[44] She shows that black and white Americans share most of the ideology of the American dream—by which she means not only material but moral aspirations—though they differ as to how far African Americans have realized it. Focusing exclusively on race differences obscures an important truth about our society: race differences are rooted in class differences. Class differences transcend race and divide all Americans.

We believe the degree of class difference today is wrong in the same sense that Lincoln believed slavery was wrong: it deprives millions of people of the ability to participate fully in society and to realize themselves as individuals. This is the festering secret that Americans would rather not face. Many nations have persisted while divided into a small elite that lives in luxury and a large mass in various stages of insecurity and misery, but this nation, with the ideals and hopes of the last 220 years, cannot permanently so endure.

This brings us to our second historical reference: John Winthrop's sermon "A Model of Christian Charity," delivered on board ship in 1630 just before the Massachusetts Bay colonists disembarked. In that sermon Winthrop warned that if we pursue "our pleasures and profits" we will surely perish out of this good land. Rather, what Winthrop, paraphrasing the Apostle Paul, tells us is that we must "entertain each other in brotherly affection, we must be willing to abridge ourselves of our superfluities, for the supply of others' necessities . . . we must delight in each other, make others' conditions our own, rejoice together, mourn together, labour and suffer together, always having before our eyes . . . our Community as members of the same Body."[45]

Under the conditions of today's America, we are tempted to ignore Winthrop's advice, to forget our obligations of solidarity and community, to harden our hearts and look out only for ourselves. In the Hebrew Scriptures God spoke to the children of Israel through the prophet Ezekiel, saying, "I will take out of your flesh the heart of stone and give you a heart of flesh" (Ez. 36:26). Can we pray that God do the same for us in America today?

January 1996

Notes

1. On page 810 of Volume II of *The Social Teaching of the Christian Churches* (London: Allen and Unwin, 1931 [1911]), Ernst Troeltsch writes that ascetic Protestantism "regards the State from a purely utilitarian standpoint" and denies that "the State [is] an ethical end in itself, which was self-evident to the Ancient World, and has reappeared within the modern world." This is "the natural result of the transference of all true life-values into the religious sphere, which means that even in the most favorable light the rest of the life-values are only regarded as means to an end." Although this is a "common Christian idea, . . . Calvinism goes much farther than Lutheranism or Catholicism."

2. Stanley Elkins and Eric McKitrick, *The Age of Federalism: The Early American Republic, 1788–1800* (New York: Oxford University Press, 1993), passim, but particularly chapter 4.

3. George Lakoff, *Moral Politics* (Chicago: University of Chicago Press, 1996).

4. Robert B. Reich, *The Work of Nations: Preparing Ourselves for 21st Century*

Capitalism (New York: Knopf, 1991), part 3, "The Rise of the Symbolic Analyst."

5. Lester Thurow, *Head to Head: The Coming Economic Battle Among Japan, Europe, and America* (New York: Warner, 1992), pp. 266–67.

6. Lester C. Thurow, "Companies Merge; Families Break Up," *New York Times*, September 3, 1995, p. E11.

7. Gunnar Myrdal, *Challenge to Affluence* (New York: Pantheon, 1963).

8. William Julius Wilson is the most reliable scholar on these matters. See his *The Truly Disadvantaged: The Inner City, the Underclass and Public Policy* (Chicago: University of Chicago Press, 1987); "The Political Economy and Urban Racial Tensions," *American Economist*, 39, 1 (Spring 1995); "The 'New Poverty:' Social Policy and the Growing Inequality in Industrial Democracies," forthcoming; and other forthcoming works.

9. Hans Koning, "A French Mirror," *Atlantic Monthly*, December 1995, p. 100. The attempt is to avoid stigmatizing the jobless by providing them with sufficient income so that they do not lose social membership. The greater centrality of Catholicism in France, together with a different kind of republicanism, accounts in part for this difference.

10. As reported in "Labor Chief Decries Middle-class Squeeze," *San Francisco Examiner*, September 25, 1994, p. A2.

11. John Gray has recently described the "ruling American culture of liberal individualism" that characterizes our affluent, educated elites as one "in which individual choice and self-realization are the only undisputed values," rendering "communal attachments" and "civic engagement as optional extras on a fixed menu of individual choice and market exchange." The consequences of this culture are mixed. As Gray puts it, "It has generated extraordinary technological and economic vitality against a background of vast social dislocation, urban desolation, and middle-class impoverishment." What Gray is saying in effect is that the consequences of a wrong belief in freedom, the belief that freedom is freedom to do whatever you want rather than freedom to do what is morally justified, is radically undermining our social coherence. See John Gray, "Does Democracy Have a Future?" *New York Times Book Review*, January 22, 1995, p. 25.

12. See Herbert J. Gans, *The War Against the Poor: The Underclass and Antipoverty Policy* (New York: Basic Books, 1995), which is particularly good on the stereotyping and stigmatizing of the poor. See also Michael Lind, *The Next American Nation: The New Nationalism and the Fourth American Revolution* (New York: Free Press, 1995), chapter 5, "The Revolution of the Rich."

13. The best current treatment of American inequality is Claude S. Fischer, Michael Hout, Martin Sanchez Jankowski, Samuel R. Lucas, Ann Swidler, and Kim Voss, *Inequality by Design: Cracking the Bell Curve Myth* (Princeton: Princeton University Press, 1996).

14. Robert D. Putnam, "The Prosperous Community: Social Capital and Public Life," *American Prospect*, 13 (Spring 1993): 35. Putnam has derived the notion from James S. Coleman, *Foundations of Social Theory* (Cambridge:

Harvard University Press, 1990), pp. 300–321, who in turn credits Glenn Loury with introducing the concept.

15. In *Journal of Democracy*, January, 1995, pp. 65–78.

16. Robert Wuthnow, *Sharing the Journey: Support Groups and America's New Quest for Community* (New York: Free Press, 1994), p. 3.

17. Seymour Martin Lipset, in a judicious review of Putnam's argument about the decline of Americans' involvement in voluntary organizations along with the relevant data, concludes that it is "not proven but probable." See his "Malaise and Resiliency in America," *Journal of Democracy*, July, 1995, p. 15.

18. Rosabeth Moss Kanter, "Upsize, Downsize," *New York Times*, September 27, 1995, p. A23. See also Rosabeth Moss Kanter, *World Class: Thriving Locally in the Global Economy* (New York: Simon and Schuster, 1995).

19. Michael Lewis, "Whatever Happened to the Leisure Class?" *New York Times Magazine*, November 19, 1995, p. 69.

20. In *Home Economics* (San Francisco: North Point Press, 1987), p. 50, Wendell Berry writes, "A powerful class of itinerant professional vandals is now pillaging the country and laying it waste. Their vandalism is not called by that name because of its enormous profitability (to some) and the grandeur of its scale."

21. Lee Rainwater, *What Money Buys: Inequality and the Social Meanings of Income* (New York: Basic Books, 1974), p. 31.

22. Douglas S. Massey and Nancy A. Denton, *American Apartheid: Segregation and the Making of the Underclass* (Cambridge: Harvard University Press, 1993).

23. Herbert J. Gans, *Middle American Individualism: The Future of Liberal Democracy* (New York: Free Press, 1988). It should be noted that Gans is talking about roughly the middle 40 percent of the income distribution in speaking of middle Americans, whereas we define the anxious class as roughly the middle 60 percent.

24. Sydney Verba, Kay Lehman Schlozman, and Henry E. Brady, *Voice and Equality*, (Cambridge: Harvard University Press, 1995).

25. Verba, *Voice and Equality*, back cover.

26. Verba, *Voice and Equality*, pp. 18–19.

27. Verba, *Voice and Equality*, p. 531.

28. Loic J. D. Wacquant in "Inside the 'Zone': The Social Art of the Hustler in the Dark Ghetto," Russell Sage Foundation, Working Papers, 1994, writes: "'It's people doin' *worser* than me,' often remark ghetto residents, including the most dispossessed of them, as if to comfort themselves, innovating a double superlative that speaks volumes about the finely differentiated microhierarchies elaborated at the very bottom of society."

29. Lakoff, *Moral Politics*.

30. Gans, *The War Against the Poor*, p. 178 n. 1.

31. We believe this regressive notion of communitarianism is largely the product of its critics; those who call themselves communitarians are not motivated by nostalgia or by fear of the modern world. See Amitai Etzioni, *The Spirit of Community* (New York: Touchstone, 1993).

32. Jonathan Boswell, *Community and the Economy: The Theory of Public Co-operation* (London: Routledge, 1990).

33. Paul Hirst, *Associative Democracy: New Forms of Economic and Social Governance* (Amherst: University of Massachusetts Press, 1994).

34. The emerging literature on civil society is vast. Important theoretical statements include: Ernst Gellner, *Conditions of Liberty: Civil Society and Its Rivals* (New York: Penguin, 1994); John Keane, *Democracy and Civil Society* (New York: Verso, 1988); Adam B. Seligman, *The Idea of Civil Society* (New York: Free Press, 1992); and Jean Cohen and Andrew Arato, *Civil Society and Political Theory* (Cambridge: MIT Press, 1992). For an explicitly religious perspective see the publications of the Corresponding Academy on Civil Society, sponsored by the German Protestant Academies, the Vesper Society, the Ecumenical Foundation of Southern Africa, and the World Council of Churches.

35. Boswell, *Community and the Economy*, p. 201.

36. H. Richard Niebuhr, *The Responsible Self* (New York: Harper and Row, 1978 [1963]), p. 88. It is interesting in view of our argument to learn from H. Richard Niebuhr's son, Richard R. Niebuhr, that "[i]n the early years of the 1930s, I sensed though scarcely comprehended my father's increasing apprehension at what he described as the 'class crucifixion' then taking place in our unhappy country." (From the foreword by Richard R. Niebuhr to H. Richard Niebuhr, *Theology, History and Culture: Major Unpublished Writings* [New Haven: Yale University Press, 1996], as reported in *Harvard Divinity Bulletin*, 25, 1 [1995]: 8.) Class crucifixion is the opposite of universal community.

37. Pierre Bourdieu, *Distinction: A Social Critique of the Judgment of Taste* (Cambridge: Harvard University Press, 1984 [1979]).

38. Thurow, "Companies Merge; Families Break Up," p. E11.

39. A particularly eloquent statement of this position can be found in *Economic Justice for All: Pastoral Letter on Catholic Social Teaching and the U.S. Economy* (Washington, D.C.: National Conference of Catholic Bishops, 1986). Catholics do not have a monopoly on this position, of course. It is rooted in the covenantal tradition that goes back to the Hebrew Scriptures and is also evidenced in Calvinist corporatism as expressed, for example, in the passage from John Winthrop's sermon "A Model of Christian Charity," quoted below. But the modern tradition of Catholic social teaching has affirmed it with especial vigor.

40. J. David Greenstone, *The Lincoln Persuasion: Remaking American Liberalism* (Princeton: Princeton University Press, 1993). It should be noted that Greenstone's own terminology is somewhat different. His contrast term to reform liberalism is humanist liberalism, called humanist because it has no transcendent reference. The editor defines humanist liberalism using Greenstone's own words as follows: "*Humanist liberalism* refers to a set of beliefs that place primary emphasis on 'equitably satisfying individual desires and preferences,' and on achieving 'the welfare of each human being as he or she defines it'" (p. 36 n. 1). We believe that is an accurate de-

scription of a utilitarian liberalism. Humanist seems a particularly unfortunate way of describing this position in the light of Greenstone's characterization of reform liberalism as "humanitarian."

41. "And if a house be divided against itself, that house cannot stand." Mark 3:25, King James Version.

42. Abraham Lincoln, *Speeches and Writings, 1832–1858* (New York: Library of America, 1989), p. 426.

43. "By Brazilianization I mean not the separation of cultures by race, but the separation of races by class. As in Brazil, a common American culture could be indefinitely compatible with a blurry, informal caste system in which most of those at the top of the social hierarchy are white, and most brown and black Americans are on the bottom—*forever*." Lind, *The Next American Nation*, p. 216.

44. Jennifer L. Hochschild, *Facing Up to the American Dream: Race, Class, and the Soul of the Nation* (Princeton: Princeton University Press, 1995).

45. John Winthrop, "A Model of Christian Charity," in Conrad Cherry, ed., *God's New Israel: Religious Interpretations of American Destiny* (Englewood Cliffs, N.J.: Prentice-Hall, 1971), p. 42. Spelling has been modernized.

Preface to the First Edition

How ought we to live? How do we think about how to live? Who are we, as Americans? What is our character? These are questions we have asked our fellow citizens in many parts of the country. We engaged them in conversations about their lives and about what matters most to them, talked about their families and communities, their doubts and uncertainties, and their hopes and fears with respect to the larger society. We found them eager to discuss the right way to live, what to teach our children, and what our public and private responsibilities should be, but also a little dismayed by these subjects. These are important matters to those to whom we talked, and yet concern about moral questions is often relegated to the realm of private anxiety, as if it would be awkward or embarrassing to make it public. We hope this book will help transform this inner moral debate, often shared only with intimates, into public discourse. In these pages, Americans speak with us, and, indirectly, with one another, about issues that deeply concern us all. As we will see, many doubt that we have enough in common to be able mutually to discuss our central aspirations and fears. It is one of our purposes to persuade them that we do.

The fundamental question we posed, and that was repeatedly posed to us, was how to preserve or create a morally coherent life. But the kind of life we want depends on the kind of people we are—on our character. Our inquiry can thus be located in a longstanding discussion of the relationship between character and society. In the eighth book of the *Republic*, Plato sketched a theory of the relationship between the moral character of a people and the nature of its political community, the way it organizes and governs itself. The founders of the American republic at the time of the Revolution adopted a much later version of the same theory. Since for them, as for the Americans with whom we talked, freedom was perhaps the most important value, they were particularly concerned with the qualities of character necessary for the creation of a free republic.

In the 1830s, the French social philosopher Alexis de Tocqueville offered the most comprehensive and penetrating analysis of the relationship between character and society in America that has ever been written. In his book *Democracy in America,* based on acute observation and wide conversation with Americans, Tocqueville described the mores—which he on occasion called "habits of the heart"[1]—of the American people and showed how they helped to form American character. He singled out family life, our religious traditions, and our participation in local politics as helping to create the kind of person who could sustain a connection to a wider political community and thus ultimately support the maintenance of free institutions. He also warned that some aspects of our character—what he was one of the first to call "individualism"—might eventually isolate Americans one from another and thereby undermine the conditions of freedom.

The central problem of our book concerns the American individualism that Tocqueville described with a mixture of admiration and anxiety. It seems to us that it is individualism, and not equality, as Tocqueville thought, that has marched inexorably through our history. We are concerned that this individualism may have grown cancerous—that it may be destroying those social integuments that Tocqueville saw as moderating its more destructive potentialities, that it may be threatening the survival of freedom itself. We want to know what individualism in America looks and feels like, and how the world appears in its light.

We are also interested in those cultural traditions and practices that, without destroying individuality, serve to limit and restrain the destructive side of individualism and provide alternative models for how Americans might live. We want to know how these have fared since Tocqueville's day, and how likely their renewal is.

While we focus on what people say, we are acutely aware that they often live in ways they cannot put into words. It is particularly here, in the tension between how we live and what our culture allows us to say, that we have found both some of our richest insights into the dilemmas our society faces and hope for the reappropriation of a common language in which those dilemmas can be discussed.

Taking our clue from Tocqueville, we believe that one of the keys to the survival of free institutions is the relationship between private and public life, the way in which citizens do, or do not, participate in the public sphere. We therefore decided to concentrate our research on how private and public life work in the United States: the extent to which private life either prepares people to take part in the public world or encourages them to find meaning exclusively in the private sphere, and the degree to which public life fulfills our private aspirations or discourages us so much that we withdraw from involvement in it.

With a small research team and a limited budget, we decided to concentrate our research on white, middle-class Americans. Apart from the fact that we could not cover all of the tremendous diversity of American life, there were several theoretical reasons for our decision. From Aristotle on, republican theorists have stressed the importance of the middle classes for the success of free institutions. These classes have traditionally provided the active public participation that makes free institutions work. In addition, the middle classes have been peculiarly central in American society. As we will argue in chapters 2, 5, and 6, America from the beginning has been a society in which the "middling condition of men" has been of primary importance, and for the past hundred years or so, the middle class, in the modern sense of the term, has so dominated our culture that neither a genuinely upper-class nor a genuinely working-class culture has fully appeared. Everyone in the United States thinks largely in middle-class categories, even when they are inappropriate. Concentration on the middle class thus made a great deal of sense for our purposes. Nonetheless, we did interview a number of working-class men and women, some of whom appear in this book, and more than a few of those who appear had working-class parents. Though we were able to include considerable ethnic diversity, we were not able to illustrate much of the racial diversity that is so important a part of our national life.

In order to get at the nature of private and public life, we decided to undertake four research projects, each carried out by a different member of our group, projects that would focus on a representative form of private or public orientation in the United States today. In thinking about private life, we decided to study love and marriage, one of the oldest ways in which people give form to their private lives, and therapy, a newer, but increasingly important, way in which middle-class Americans find meaning in the private sphere. In thinking about public life, we decided to study older forms of civic participation such as local politics and traditional voluntary associations as well as some of the newer forms of political activism that have grown out of the political movements of the sixties but operate "within the system."

Each of the field researchers chose particular communities, groups, or sets of individuals who vividly illustrated his or her particular focus. Where possible (more often in the public than in the private components of our study) interviews were supplemented with participant observation. The fieldwork was carried out from 1979 to 1984 and involved interviews with over 200 persons, some of whom we talked to several times and many of whom we observed as they participated in community activities or events. We do not claim that we have talked to "average" Americans or that we have a random sample. We have read a great many surveys and community studies, enough to know that those to whom we talked are not markedly aberrant. The primary focus of our research was not psychological, or even primarily sociological, but rather cultural. We wanted to know what resources Americans have for making sense of their lives, how they think about themselves and their society, and how their ideas relate to their actions. For this purpose, focussing on representative issues in representative communities seemed the best choice. We have talked with people about problems of American life in which we all share, allowing particular individuals struggling with particular challenges to uncover the possibilities and limits of our cultural traditions.

Ann Swidler, whose focus was on how the private realm of love and marriage gives shape and meaning to people's lives, interviewed men and women in several suburban neighborhoods in and around San Jose, California. The area is one of rapid growth, particularly because of the electronics industries of "Silicon Valley." Those she interviewed came from all parts of the country. Few were native Californians. They were either middle-class or from relatively prosperous blue-collar families. Most were mature adults (their ages ranged from twenty-seven to fifty-five, but they were predominantly in their thirties and forties), coping with the realities of love, marriage, and family life in modern society. Most were married, and somewhat fewer than half had been divorced. Among the latter, about half had remarried. Most of those she interviewed had children. Through some of those she interviewed, Swidler learned of Marriage Encounter, participated in a weekend sponsored by the movement, and interviewed a number of those for whom this movement was significant.

Steven Tipton explored another dimension of private life by interviewing therapists, psychologists, and psychiatrists of various stripes in a major Southern city and in the San Francisco Bay area. He took part in classes and clinical supervision with doctoral students training as clinical psychologists, and he attended case conferences of psychologists working in private practice and in a public mental health clinic. He also interviewed Protestant ministers and seminarians engaged in psychotherapeutic approaches to clinical pastoral education, in which he participated. Finally, he interviewed a range of clients seen by these practitioners to discover how the experience and outlook of psychotherapy affected their self-understanding and their view of social commitments and relationships in work, love, and public life.

Richard Madsen attempted to understand how Americans become involved in public life. To this end, he studied two communities, one a town not far from Boston, founded over 250 years ago, and the other a suburban area near San Diego that has been settled only in recent decades and is still largely unincorporated. Both communities were largely middle-class, but the Boston suburb had many blue-collar families. Madsen focussed on voluntary associations (YMCA, Rotary Club, Junior Chamber of Commerce, and others) and on local politics. He interviewed people about their sense of the communities in which they live, the reasons for their civic involvement, and the extent to which that involvement gives meaning and purpose to their lives. In the course of pursuing civic-minded voluntarism, he studied not only routine activities but several intense controversies that erupted while he was in the field.

William Sullivan attempted to get at the meaning of public life through a study of two political organizations, the Institute for the Study of Civic Values, which does community organizing in Philadelphia, and the Campaign for Economic Democracy, which has its greatest influence in Santa Monica, California. These two groups are both indebted to the political movements of the sixties for their dedication to political organizing in bringing about social change. Both have become involved in electoral politics, and their leaders have recently been elected to local or state offices. Sullivan interviewed leaders and members of these groups in an effort to understand their visions of the larger society and the changes needed in it, as well as to see how they have integrated their public activities with their private lives. Both groups are largely middle-class, but the Philadelphia group has been effective in working-class and minority neighborhoods.

Much as our book draws on the four research projects described, it is not simply a report of that research. We have learned from years of reading, reflection, and conversation with many who were not formally subjects of our research. Four of us are sociologists by training; one of us, Sullivan, received his degree in philosophy. We have all been deeply influenced by social science and social philosophy and seek to continue the traditions of social reflection that have nurtured us. A brief Appendix explains our position.

The people who let us into their homes and talked to us so freely during the course of our study are very much part of the authorship of this book. Their words appear in almost every chapter.[2] They made us think things we never thought before. But we have tried to make sense not only of what we saw and heard in our research but also of what we have experienced as lifetime members of American society. The story we tell is not just the story of those we interviewed. It is also our own.

We have not organized the book as a report on the four separate projects. Monographs by the four field workers will provide that. Almost every chapter here draws from all four projects. The first two provide an introduction and orientation to the study as a whole. Chapter 1 consists of four portraits of individuals, drawn from each of the four research projects, who represent different ways of using private or public life to find meaning in contemporary America. Chapter 2 provides a historical sketch and, in particular, a description of the four major traditions that we believe have been important in the self-interpretations of Americans. Chapters 3 through 6 deal with private life, going from ways of thinking of the self to marriage, the family, and other forms of personal relationship, including therapy. Chapter 6 sums up the American ideology of individualism and suggests some of the alternatives to it in our society. Chapters 7 through 10 deal with public life. Local politics, civic volunteerism, and the larger meanings of citizenship and religion are discussed in chapters 7 through 9. Chapter 10 considers several successive historical stages of interpretation of the national society and how these relate to the views of those with whom we talked. In a concluding chapter, we try to sum up the implications of our research for the future of American society.

In an ambitious and lengthy research project such as this one, there are inevitably many whose help was crucial and many to thank. Richard Sharpe, then of the Ford Foundation, was responsible in 1978 for the initial suggestion that led to the formulation of the project. Major funding came from the National Endowment for the Humanities, a federal agency that supports research in such fields as philosophy, history, literature, and the humanistic social sciences. Matching grants came from the Ford Foundation and the Rockefeller Foundation. We are grateful to NEH and the two foundations for their generosity and support. In addition, Ann Swidler and Robert Bellah would like to thank the John Simon Guggenheim Memorial Foundation for fellowships. Swidler used her fellowship year, 1982–83, in part for research for this book. Bellah used his fellowship year, 1983–84, in part for the final rewriting of *Habits of the Heart*.

An advisory committee, consisting of David Riesman, Renée Fox, Ralph Potter, and Robert Coles, gave us theoretical insight and methodological guidance during the early years of the project. They met with us frequently and some of them, particularly David Riesman, shared their reflections on our research in writing. Michael Maccoby, S. N. Eisenstadt, and Alasdair MacIntyre attended our research meetings on occasion and gave us their suggestions. Many other colleagues and friends have provided particular references as well as general encouragement. Our departments and universities have been most helpful. Those who read the manuscript in whole or in part were: John Maguire, Barbara Metcalf, Samuel Popkin, David Riesman, and Eli Sagan. We are grateful for their reactions and corrections, even when we did not heed them. Individual chapters have been read by students and colleagues too numerous to mention. Their questions and doubts prodded us toward greater clarity. John Chan provided a particularly enlightening review of the literature, and he and Rita Jalali gave valuable research assistance. Laola Hironaka contributed through her typing and many other forms of support.

We would like to thank Melanie Bellah (who also read the original manuscript) and Eli Sagan for reading the new introduction and giving us the benefit of their suggestions. We would also like to thank James Clark, Director of the University of California Press, for encouraging us to write an introduction for the new paperback edition.

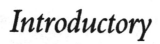

Introductory

The Pursuit of Happiness

Brian Palmer

Living well is a challenge. Brian Palmer, a successful businessman, lives in a comfortable San Jose suburb and works as a top-level manager in a large corporation. He is justifiably proud of his rapid rise in the corporation, but he is even prouder of the profound change he has made recently in his idea of success. "My value system," he says, "has changed a little bit as the result of a divorce and reexamining life values. Two years ago, confronted with the work load I have right now, I would stay in the office and work until midnight, come home, go to bed, get up at six, and go back in and work until midnight, until such time as it got done. Now I just kind of flip the bird and walk out. My family life is more important to me than that, and the work will wait, I have learned." A new marriage and a houseful of children have become the center of Brian's life. But such new values were won only after painful difficulties.

Now forty-one, his tall, lean body bursting with restless energy, Brian recalls a youth that included a fair amount of hell-raising, a lot of sex, and considerable devotion to making money. At twenty-four, he married. Shouldering the adult responsibilities of marriage and children became the guiding purpose of his life for the next few years.

Whether or not Brian felt his life was satisfying, he was deeply committed to succeeding at his career and family responsibilities. He held two full-time jobs to support his family, accepting apparently without complaint the loss of a youth in which, he himself reports, "the vast majority of my time from, say, the age of fifteen to twenty-two or twenty-three was devoted toward giving myself pleasure of one sort or another." Brian describes his reasons for working so hard after he married quite simply. "It seemed like the thing to do at the time," he says. "I couldn't stand not having enough money to get by on, and with my wife unable to contribute to the family income, it seemed like the thing to do.

I guess self-reliance is one of the characteristics I have pretty high up in my value system. It was second nature. I didn't even question the thing. I just went out and did it." Brian and his wife came to share very little in their marriage, except, as he thought, good sex, children, and devotion to his career. With his wife's support, he decided to "test" himself "in the Big League," and he made it, although at great cost to his marriage and family life. "What was my concept of what constituted a reasonable relationship? I guess I felt an obligation to care for materially, provide for, a wife and my children, in a style to which I'd like to see them become accustomed. Providing for my family materially was important. Sharing wasn't important. Sharing of my time wasn't important. I put in extremely long hours, probably averaging sixty to sixty-five hours a week. I'd work almost every Saturday. Always in the office by 7:30. Rarely out of the office before 6:30 at night. Sometimes I'd work until 10:30 or 11. That was numero uno. But I compensated for that by saying, I have this nice car, this nice house, joined the Country Club. Now you have a place you can go, sit on your butt, drink, go into the pool. I'll pay the bills and I'll do my thing at work."

For Brian's wife, the compensations apparently weren't enough. After almost fifteen years of marriage, "One day I came home. In fact, our house was for sale, and we had an offer on the house. My wife said, 'Before you accept an offer, you should probably know that once we sell this house, we will live in different houses.' That was my official notification that she was planning to divorce me."

The divorce, "one of the two or three biggest surprises of my life," led Brian to reassess his life in fundamental ways and to explore the limits of the kind of success he had been pursuing. "I live by establishing plans. I had no plan for being single, and it gave me a lot of opportunity to think, and in the course of thinking, I read for the first time in many, many years. Got back into classical music for the first time since my college years. I went out and bought my first Bach album and a stereo to play it on. Mostly the thinking process of being alone and relating to my children."

When his children chose to live with him, Brian found himself forced to shift his sense of himself and his priorities in life. "I found that being a single parent is not all that it is cracked up to be. I found it an extremely humbling experience. Whereas I go into the office in the morning and I have a personal secretary and a staff of managers and a cast of hundreds working for me, I came home and just like every Tom, Dick, and Harry in the world, I'd clean up garbage after these three big boys of mine. I'd spend two hours preparing and cleaning up after dinner, doing laundry, folding clothes, sweeping the floor, and generally doing manual labor of the lowest form. But the fact that my boys chose to live with me was a very important thing to me. It made me feel that maybe I had been doing something right in the parenting department."

Although his wife had left him, and he later found out that she had been having an affair, Brian's period of reflection led him to rethink his role in the relationship. "Being a compulsive problem solver, I analyzed the failure. I don't like failure. I'm very competitive. I like to win. So I went back and reexamined where the thing broke down and found that I had contributed at least 50 percent and, depending on the vantage point, maybe 99 percent of the ultimate demise of the institution. Mostly it was asking myself the question of why am I behaving in such and such a way. Why am I doing this at work? Why was I doing this at home? The answer was that I was operating as if a certain value was of the utmost importance to me. Perhaps it was success. Perhaps it was fear of failure, but I was extremely success-oriented, to the point where everything would be sacrificed for the job, the career, the company. I said bullshit. That ain't the way it should be."

The revolution in Brian's thinking came from a reexamination of the true sources of joy and satisfaction in his life. And it is particularly in a marriage to a woman very different from his first wife that Brian has discovered a new sense of himself and a different understanding of what he wants out of life. He has a new sense of what love can be. "To be able to receive affection freely and give affection and to give of myself and know it is a totally reciprocal type of thing. There's just almost a psychologically buoyant feeling of being able to be so much more involved and sharing. Sharing experiences of goals, sharing of feelings, working together to solve problems, etc. My viewpoint of a true love, husband-and-wife type of relationship is one that is founded on mutual respect, admiration, affection, the ability to give and receive freely." His new wife, a divorcée his own age, brings four children to their marriage, added to Brian's own three. They have five children still living at home, and a sense of energy, mutual devotion, and commitment sufficient to make their family life a joy.

In many ways, Brian's is an individual success story. He has succeeded materially, and he has also taken hold of the opportunity to reach out beyond material success to a fuller sense of what he wants from life. Yet despite the personal triumph Brian's life represents, despite the fulfillment he seems to experience, there is still something uncertain, something poignantly unresolved about his story.

The difficulty becomes most evident when Brian tries to explain why it is that his current life is, in fact, better than his earlier life built around single-minded devotion to his career. His description of his reasons for changing his life and of his current happiness seems to come down mainly to a shift in his notions of what would make him happy. His new goal—devotion to marriage and children—seems as arbitrary and unexamined as his earlier pursuit of material success. Both are justified as idiosyncratic preference rather than as representing a larger sense of the purpose of life. Brian sees himself as consistently pursuing a utilitarian calculus—devotion to his own self-interest—except that there has been an almost inexplicable change in his personal preferences. In describing the reasons for this change, he begins, "Well, I think I just reestablished my priorities." He sometimes seems to reject his past life as wrong; but at other times, he seems to say he simply got bored with it. "That exclusive pursuit of success now seems to me not a good way to live. That's not the most important thing to me. I have demonstrated to myself, to my own satisfaction, that I can achieve about what I want to achieve. So the challenge of goal realization does not contain that mystique that it held for me at one time. I just have found that I get a lot of personal reward from being involved in the lives of my children."

American cultural traditions define personality, achievement, and the purpose of human life in ways that leave the individual suspended in glorious, but terrifying, isolation. These are limitations of our culture, of the categories and ways of thinking we have inherited, not limitations of individuals such as Brian who inhabit this culture. People frequently live out a fuller sense of purpose in life than they can justify in rational terms, as we see in Brian's case and many others.

Brian's restless energy, love of challenges, and appreciation of the good life are characteristic of much that is most vital in American culture. They are all qualities particularly well-suited to the hard-driving corporate world in which he works. When Brian describes how he has chosen to live, however, he keeps referring to "values" and "priorities" not justified by any wider framework of purpose or belief. What is good is what one finds rewarding. If one's preferences change, so does the nature of the good. Even the deepest ethical virtues are justified as matters of personal preference. Indeed, the ultimate ethical rule is simply that individuals should be able to pursue whatever they find rewarding, constrained only by the requirement that they not interfere with the "value systems" of others. "I guess I feel like everybody on this planet is entitled to have a little bit of space, and things that detract from other people's space are kind of bad," Brian observes. "One of the things that I use to characterize life in California, one of the things that makes California such a pleasant place to live, is people by and large aren't bothered by other people's value systems as long as they don't infringe upon your own. By and large, the rule of thumb out here is that if you've got the money, honey, you can do your thing as long as your thing doesn't destroy someone else's property, or interrupt their sleep, or bother their privacy, then that's fine. If you want to go in your house and smoke marijuana and shoot dope and get all screwed up, that's your business, but don't bring that out on the street, don't expose my children to it, just do your thing. That works out kind of neat."

In a world of potentially conflicting self-interests, no one can really say that one value system is better than another. Given such a world, Brian sets great store by one basic principle—the importance of honesty and communication. It is through communication that people have a chance to resolve their differences, since there is no larger moral ideal in terms of which conflicts can be resolved. "Communication is critical not only to a man-and-woman relationship, it is the essence of our being on this planet in my opinion. Given open communication and the ability to think problems out, most problems can be solved." Solving conflicts becomes a matter of technical problem solving, not moral decision. Lying, which would interfere in a critical way with the ability to communicate accurately and resolve interpersonal conflicts, is thus wrong, but, even here, wrongness is largely a matter of practicality—it doesn't pay. "The bottom line of my personal value system applies to the way I conduct business. My predecessor was characterized as a notorious, habitual, and compulsive liar, and that's a difficult act to follow. That's probably one of the reasons that led to his demise—that his lies were catching up with him and he left before the walls came tumbling down."

Not lying is one of the major things Brian wants to teach his children. "Why is integrity important and lying bad? I don't know. It just is. It's just so basic. I don't want to be bothered with challenging that. It's part of me. I don't know where it came from, but it's very important." Brian says "values" are important, and he stresses the importance of teaching them to his children. But apart from the injunction not to lie, he is vague about what those values are. "I guess a lot of them are Judeo-Christian ethics of modern society, that certain things are bad." Even the things that may be "absolutely wrong," such as killing, stealing, and lying, may just be matters of personal preference—or at least injunctions against them exist detached from any social or cultural base that could give them broader meaning.

Are there some things that are just absolutely wrong? "I don't think I would pontificate and say that I'm in a position to establish values for humanity in general, although I'm sufficiently conceited to say that if the rest of the world would live by my value system it would be a better place," Brian says. The justification he offers is simply, "I'm quite comfortable with my values." Yet values, in turn, continually slip back for Brian into a matter of personal preferences, and the only ethical problem is to make the decision that accords with one's preferences. His increased commitment to family and children rather than to material success seems strangely lacking in substantive justification. "I just find that I get more personal satisfaction from choosing course B over course A. It makes me feel better about myself. To participate in this union of chaos to try and mold something, this family situation—and maybe it's because of this bringing two families together—is a challenge. Believe me, this is a challenge. Maybe that's why it fascinates me. Maybe that's why it's important to me."

Despite the combination of tenderness and admiration he expresses for his wife, the genuine devotion he seems to feel for his children, and his own resilient self-confidence, Brian's justification of his life thus rests on a fragile foundation. Morally, his life appears much more coherent than when he was dominated by careerism, but, to hear him talk, even his deepest impulses of attachment to others are without any more solid foundation than his momentary desires. He lacks a language to explain what seem to be the real commitments that define his life, and to that extent the commitments themselves are precarious.

Joe Gorman

Joe Gorman would probably call Brian Palmer's ideas about success childish. Joe lives three thousand miles from San Jose and has never met Brian. But talking about people in his own town whose lives seem totally focussed on individual success, as Brian's once was, he says they are "trying to be kids again." For Joe, being like a kid means lacking an appreciation of one's responsibilities to one's family and one's community. It means thinking primarily about what you can get out of your family and community rather than what you should give them. For Joe, success means achieving the goals set by your family and community, not using your family and community to achieve your own individual goals.

Joe Gorman is about the same age as Brian Palmer, but unlike Brian, who has moved to many different communities in his search for personal success, Joe has always lived in the small town where his father and mother have spent most of their lives: Suffolk, Massachusetts, a community of fewer than 20,000 people, about a half-hour's drive from Boston. Suffolk was founded in 1632, and about six months before one of us interviewed Joe Gorman, the town celebrated its 250th anniversary. Joe had taken charge of organizing the celebrations, although he had not originally been asked to do so. During the early phases of planning the anniversary festivities, the town manager appointed a committee of locally prominent townspeople that did not include Joe. But the problem was that practically none of its members had much experience in planning such a complicated event. To make matters worse, according to Joe, about half of them were more interested in getting their names in the paper than in doing much work. As a result, the first event in the long series of planned anniversary celebrations had been a fiasco—a large community dinner with only enough food for about half of the people who showed up. Joe Gorman knew that he had the ability to organize the celebrations successfully, and he felt a kind of duty to do whatever he could to help. So he got himself on the committee and became, in fact if not in name, its head.

Under Joe's direction, the anniversary celebration turned out to be a grand success. The festivities stretched out for nine months. There were parades, concerts, a carnival, athletic contests, dinners, dances, and ecumenical religious services, all well attended and smoothly organized. The fundamental meaning of the celebration was expressed for Joe in the slogan: "We are doing it together." As he put it, "That's so important—to work to get as many people as possible active." Another key theme was the importance of the family. The inspiration for many of the events came from the fact that that year had been proclaimed by the United Nations to be "the year of the family." For Joe, the highlight of the festivities was a softball tournament in which each team was made up of members of a different extended family. "We had eight clans—eight big families from Suffolk—in the tournament. In one of them some people came clear from Connecticut just to play softball on the side of their family. You know, for me the best time of the whole celebration was standing there back behind the bleachers after the softball games with members of the families that had played and talking with them about their families and drinking champagne. That to me was the ultimate. During the games between the clans, on many occasions, lots of people showed up besides the players to watch the game and see how people in the families were doing."

Another of the most inspiring events of the anniversary celebration was a day given over to the town's senior citizens. "We told people that this was their chance now to come together and see the people who had contributed to this town. They had an afternoon on the Common where they sold baked goods and made an awful lot of money." The whole series of anniversary celebrations was "so successful that the first thing that people said after it was over was, 'Why can't we have one every year?'" Accordingly, the town fathers decided to have an annual celebration and made Joe Gorman the head of the committee for the next year's celebration.

In Joe's vocabulary, *success* is a very important word. But throughout our conversation with him, it was consistently applied not to any status he had gained for himself or even to any accomplishment he had realized by himself. *Success* rather applied to the experience of togetherness the community had created partially through his efforts. "We had a lot of hassles [in organizing the anniversary celebration] and a lot of complaints that we had to deal with before we got it all rolling. But when it was over, the town was totally in favor of it. And even most of those people who had been opposed to various things came up to me and said that they were totally for having it again this year. So it was a great event, a great success, and it really brought the town together. If it's successful again this year, we're going to have it year after year. It was a great success. It was great for the community. But I didn't do it. The Suffolk family did it. Yes, it's the Suffolk family, and I love being a part of it."

This is not to say that Joe does not care about receiving personal rewards for his work within the community. What he considers to be one of the greatest events of his life happened to him several months after Suffolk's anniversary celebrations were finished. He was named Good Guy of the Year in Suffolk and a huge celebration was held for him by the business and civic leaders of the town. "It was a complete surprise for me. They got me to cooperate in it by telling me that they were putting on a benefit for someone else, one of my co-workers at the factory. It was really embarrassing because I was getting after some people thinking that they weren't doing enough in preparation for this celebration for this co-worker, and then I showed up and it was for me." Joe was immensely gratified at this expression of community affection. But it was important for him that it came as a surprise—that he experienced it as a reward he had not consciously worked for.

Besides enjoying the prestige the community has "spontaneously" given him, Joe also receives an income from his efforts on behalf of the community. It is, in fact, part of his profession to be a community "good guy." He is director of public relations for one of the large manufacturing companies located in Suffolk. Like most such companies, the firm that employs Joe wants to maintain good relations with the townspeople, and to do this it contributes money to community recreation programs and other charities. It is part of Joe Gorman's job to help his company decide how best to help the town. Even though much of it happens to be part of his job, however, Joe's community service work clearly remains a labor of love. He has been offered promotions to positions in his company's head office in Houston, but he has refused them. For him, his position in the community is more important than his status within his company. As he sees it, he works so hard for the town because he is a "natural citizen" of Suffolk. "I was born here. My father set up the athletic program at Suffolk High. Friendship alone with the people would keep me here. We will always stay here. It is my home."

Unlike Brian Palmer, therefore, Joe Gorman does not decide the proper goals that would constitute a successful life on the basis of current "priorities." The goals are given to him by the traditions of his family and community. Yet Joe's solution to the problem of discovering adequate goals in life is a solution that raises problems of its own.

The Suffolk Joe loves so much—the community of civic-minded, interlocking families rooted in two hundred fifty years of tradition—does not really exist. Three-fourths of Suffolk's present population have moved in within the past twenty-five years. Most of them are not deeply involved in the life of the town. If five hundred out of the town's nine thousand registered voters show up for a town meeting, that is considered a very good turnout. The work life of most Suffolk residents separates them from the town. Their jobs are in Boston or in one of the industrial parks surrounding that city. Even when they happen to work in Suffolk, they work in one of the factories located in the town's industrial parks—factories that are frequently parts of multinational conglomerates. They live in Suffolk because it happens to be conveniently located for them and the housing prices there happen to fit their budgets. Many of them readily admit that they really would prefer to live in one of the more affluent towns in the area, but stay in Suffolk because they could not afford a house in a wealthier community. Such people do not think of Suffolk as their "family," but only as a convenient suburb. They probably looked on the town's anniversary celebration as a set of quaint festivities—pleasant diversions for a weekend afternoon, not rituals expressing something important about the meaning of their lives.

To affirm the importance of Suffolk's traditions, Joe conjures up a fictitious golden age of the town that has been corrupted by modern developments. The spirit of this age can be recovered, he believes, and the task of recovering it can validate one's present life. "Behind what I'm doing is one of my hidden motives. I would like to see Suffolk get back to that type of atmosphere where fifteen people could get together, form a baseball team, go down to the park, don't need a uniform or anything like that, play some ball and just have a good time. Nowadays to do that sort of thing, people demand uniforms and leagues and regulations and so forth. They don't trust each other. But this other, older kind of spirit is what you need."

The spirit of spontaneous, trustful conviviality Joe remembers having experienced as a boy has been lost, he thinks, partly because the town's newcomers have been corrupted by the atmosphere of Boston, the big city. There is dissension in local politics because "people coming from Boston are so interested in payoffs and so convinced that the politicians are corrupt." They are also concerned only about their own private investments in the town rather than the public good. "One of their concerns is that their houses were new and they wanted them to have all the proper facilities and they wanted to make sure that their investment in them was protected." But besides the corruption that comes directly from the experience of life in the city, there is also a more subtle kind of decay, spread by the modern educational system. "It's like people are trying to be kids again. It used to be that parents would discipline their kids and tell them what to do. But now in school you have all these specialists, these psychologists, who analyze the kids and say the kids need this and need that and the parents don't give the kids discipline and become like kids themselves. Kids need discipline, but instead they get these psychic jobs done on them."

The past was almost certainly never as relaxed and innocent as Joe nostalgically remembers it, however, and even if it had been, it would be totally unrealistic to try to return to the past by isolating the town from the city and eliminating the influence of modern psychology from the school curriculum. Joe's vision of the good life, seemingly rooted so firmly in the objective traditions of his community, is in the end highly subjective. Perhaps he has to hide his hopes of returning to the good old days because even he realizes that most of his fellow townspeople would find them faintly ridiculous.

Moreover, even if Joe Gorman's vision of a good society could be realized, it is not at all clear that Joe would want to live in it. "We need more family ties, more closeness as a family group," Joe says. "I grew up in a family in a neighborhood of nine houses, and all the people in those houses were relatives, cousins. The big thing for us was Labor Day weekend. At that time, all the family would get together for a huge picnic. It was wonderful." But Joe no sooner paints this nostalgic picture of family unity than he backs away from it, affirming the need to separate himself from his family. "As kids grow up, they have to go their separate ways. So now I've become more separate from my family. I think that's needed. The way I've done it, I pick my time to get together with them. But it's important that we be by ourselves, too."

And, finally, a dangerously narrow conception of social justice can result from committing oneself to small town values. For instance, just two months after the culmination of Suffolk's 250th anniversary celebrations, the town erupted in an angry fit of local chauvinism. The town Housing Authority had been trying to provide low-cost housing for elderly citizens. To build this housing, it needed funds from the federal government. The Department of Housing and Urban Development finally offered Suffolk a grant of $5,000,000 to build such housing—but it stipulated that to qualify for the grant, the town also had to build a small number of low-cost housing units for poor families. Many townspeople feared that such units would be occupied by blacks and Cubans from Boston. In an intensely emotional town meeting, they rejected the HUD grant and voted to establish recall proceedings to remove the town officials who had applied for it. Townspeople appealed to the unity and integrity of their tradition-rooted community to justify segregationist policies.

Joe Gorman did not approve of the rejection of the HUD grant. There is a fundamental generosity to his character that makes him uneasy about the fear of minority groups that many townspeople feel. Yet his nostalgic desire to return to a mythical past provides little help in understanding how Suffolk might work out its contemporary problems and almost no framework for thinking about Suffolk in the context of the larger society.

Margaret Oldham

Margaret Oldham is a therapist, not unlike those Joe Gorman accuses of having undermined discipline in the family and the schools. Raised in a stable, solidly middle-class home, Margaret would nonetheless say that Joe's concept of the well-lived life is unrealistic and fails to take account of the realities of human nature and modern social life. People vary tremendously in their values and experiences, she would say, and all you do if you stick rigidly to your own standards is cut yourself off from others. Tolerance for others and a willingness to learn from new experience are important to Margaret, and their relative absence in the tightly knit, homogeneous community Joe longs to recreate would make it both claustrophobic and ultimately too undemanding for her. It would be too much like trying to stay forever in the comfort of the womb rather than coming out into the bright light of day. She places individual fulfillment higher than attachment to family and community.

Margaret, a composed woman in her early thirties, has a strong sense of discipline and has achieved an outstanding academic record and professional success. Indeed, she feels that one of the most important things she learned from her parents was the value of hard work—"not just work, but taking pride in your work and being responsible for your work and doing it as well as you possibly can and doing a lot of it." She also attributes much of her strong sense of responsibility to her parents, who raised her "with a lot of respect for other people and their property and their rights." But she has parted company with them in one crucial sense. "I don't think it's important to be quite that moralistic, quite that rigid," she says. "I think that I accept people the way they are more than either one of my parents has ever been able to do." Her tolerance for other people makes it easier for her to get along with a variety of people than it was for her father. Her interest in other people and her capacity to accept them is critical to what makes life interesting for Margaret, particularly in her work as a therapist in a large Southern city. "I got into psychology mostly because I was just really curious about people and what made them tick. And I was interested in why people did the things they did and why they didn't have the same ideas I did. I had a lot of friends who were intelligent people who were flunking out of school and getting into a lot of trouble and I always wondered, why? What was the motivation? What was causing them to make the kinds of decisions that they made in their lives?"

Being challenged by a variety of people different from herself is a continuing source of stimulation. As a therapist she has an "eclectic background—interactionist, Gestalt, Rogersian," she explains. It is the diversity of ideas and psychological experiences that makes life in her chosen field interesting. "If you're any kind of therapist at all, you're out there on the line all the time and you learn things from all your clients and you grow a lot yourself. Doing therapy is almost as good for me as it is for my client, so I do get a lot of that sort of reward. I think just being exposed to different people's thoughts and ideas and problems and finding out, you know, what their lives are like just sort of opens up new kinds of ideas. Every time I got a client for a while, I would totally re-think my view of the world because a client would come with all these different ideas and sort of innocently challenge things that I consider to be very basic in life and I have to go home and think about it for a while."

In Margaret's view, the most important thing in life is doing whatever you choose to do as well as you can. Summing up her sense of the meaning of life, she says: "I just sort of accept the way the world is and then don't think about it a whole lot. I tend to operate on the assumption that what I want to do and what I feel like is what I should do. What I think the universe wants from me is to take my values, whatever they might happen to be, and live up to them as much as I can. If I'm the best person I know how to be according to my lights, then something good will happen. I think in a lot of ways living that kind of life is its own reward in and of itself." Like Brian Palmer, Margaret takes "values" as given, "whatever they might happen to be."

Margaret wants to work hard at her profession, to help people, and to give and receive love in her personal relationships, including her marriage to a bright, successful engineer. But she does not think the happiness of a fulfilling life can be won without a realistic willingness to make the effort and pay the costs required. For example, you have to be willing to give to make a relationship work. What many of her clients want instead, she thinks, is an ideal relationship in which they will be loved completely without having to do anything in return. "This is the person who is going to be there to talk to, to go somewhere with them, or, you know, a person who's just going to be there and is going to understand them. Most people don't want to have to tell you how they feel. They want you to divine that. That would be perfection. Someone who would understand them so thoroughly that they would never have to say a word and just always be there for them and who would just make them feel really secure and really, oh, not alone." What people need to accept is that it is their responsibility to communicate what they need and what they feel, and to realize that they cannot expect someone else magically to make them happy. "People want to be made happy, instead of making themselves happy."

Margaret's counsel of a sober maturity fits her role. As a therapist, she cannot solve people's problems but can only help them achieve greater self-understanding so that they may deal more realistically, and perhaps more fruitfully, with life and better realize their personal preferences. She understands that human relationships require give–and–take, that you must work hard for the satisfactions you expect in life, and that you are ultimately responsible for your own life. But this clear-sighted vision of each individual's ultimate self-reliance turns out to leave very little place for interdependence and to correspond to a fairly grim view of the individual's place in the social world. Self-reliance is a virtue that implies being alone. "I do think it's important for you to take responsibility for yourself, I mean, nobody else is going to really do it. I mean people do take care of each other, people help each other, you know, when somebody's sick, and that's wonderful. In the end, you're really alone and you really have to answer to yourself, and in the end, if you don't get the job you want or, you know, meet the person you want, it's at least in part your responsibility. I mean your knight in shining armor is not going to meet you on the street and leave messages all over the world trying to find you. It's not going to happen."

Accepting personal responsibility is, then, acting like an adult, not childishly expecting other people to solve one's problems for one. But it is also simply a necessity for getting along in a world in which other people either cannot or will not help you, in which no one can make you feel "not alone," because in the end you really are alone. Margaret's image of the world sharply limits the demands she feels people can make upon one another, even in the closest, most committed relationships. Even bonds of marriage and parenthood don't overcome the isolation that is ultimately the lot of each individual: "I'm responsible for my acts and what I do." Asked whether she was responsible for others, she replied, "No." Asked whether she was responsible for her husband, she replied, "I'm not. He makes his own decisions." What about children? "I . . . I would say I have a legal responsibility for them, but in a sense I think they in turn are responsible for their acts." In relationships, as in the wider social world, "everybody likes to get their own way." So the only way to run a relationship is to strive for "fairness"—that is, "not one person making all the sacrifices or one always giving—having a relative balance between what's the giving end and getting your own way."

Since, however, there is no wider framework within which to justify common values, all one can ask from others is that they do the work of communicating their needs clearly, and one must in turn try to be clear about one's own needs and desires. If other people don't meet your needs, you have to be willing to walk out, since in the end that may well be the only way to protect your interests. The inability to make legitimate demands on others becomes an even more severe problem when one steps out of the face-to-face personal world where one may be able to negotiate differences and assure fairness through direct communication. In the world of politics, for example, the hope of cooperative effort toward common ends is necessarily disappointed: the person who thinks in terms of the common good is a "sucker" in a situation where each individual is trying to pursue his or her own interests. "Everybody wants to be on top and get their own way. It's like in a relationship. When I think about government policies, I guess I don't want them to cut off all aid to research in psychology unless they do some other things too that should be done. I mean, I don't want to be the only one who suffers. I don't want to be the only sucker. I don't want to be the fall guy for people who are not doing their part."

So while Margaret Oldham has a vision of individual fulfillment that involves deep self-knowledge, wide tolerance of differences among people, and a mature willingness to accept responsibility for one's own life, she, too, is caught in some of the contradictions her beliefs imply. She is responsible for herself, but she has no reliable way to connect her own fulfillment to that of other people, whether they be her own husband and children or the larger social and political community of which she is inevitably a part.

Wayne Bauer

Wayne Bauer would probably agree with Margaret Oldham's insistence on the need of the individual to make a psychic break with family conventions and the limitations of tradition. Wayne is a community organizer who works in California for the Campaign for Economic Democracy. He is in his middle thirties now and considers his present outlook on life to be a product of the 1960s. "During the sixties we saw a dream, we had a vision. And we had a belief that things could be much better, on many levels," he says. "I mean, it was a time of personal growth as well as political change. And what was exciting about that is that the personal change was what would be leading into a very significant political change in the country." Personal change involved a break with one's family. "A lot of us were raised either in working-class or middle-class backgrounds and believed that there were certain things that you did with your life. The status quo. You know, what your father did. How he lived his life. You go to high school, you go to college, get married, settle down, have a family, get a respectable position in society. And I think that what we had seen in the sixties was an emptiness that we saw in our families, that this was not what we wanted for ourselves, that we wanted something better."

Wayne's break with his family and quest for "something better" came in 1965, when he was seventeen. He had joined the Marine Corps. "I had come from a background of John Wayne, you know, American patriotism. This whole kind of facade of what we were all about as the American people." After boot camp he was stationed at Camp Lejeune and would come up to New York City on leave. "Nineteen sixty-five was when NYU marched and burned the draft cards and all of a sudden there was a political awareness and these people were letting their hair grow a little longer and putting earrings in their ear. And this was a real shock to me. I mean, I didn't understand this. I was in the Marine Corps." During this time, some friends of his who had gone to college in New York began to argue with him about the Vietnam War. "And after this went on, to make a long story short, for about three or four months, I realized that my best argument held no weight. And what happened was, all of a sudden, my view of who I was and my environment was shattered. It was like looking in the mirror and having the whole thing shattered on you and seeing all your values, all your beliefs, everything you thought was real just kind of crumble. And it left me without any values and it also left me in a position where I had this terrible feeling of loneliness that there was no one I could go to for help. All the people that I had trusted, I feel, essentially, they had lied to me."

Upon receiving orders to go to Vietnam, Wayne went AWOL, assumed an alias, spent eight years leading an underground life travelling around the country, eventually surrendered to the military in 1972, spent four months in a military stockade, but was spared a court-martial and, finally, released by the Marine Corps with a general discharge. He returned to his parents, found them totally uncomprehending of his understanding of life, and moved from New Jersey to Venice, California.

But Wayne's break with the conventions of family and community— the conventions that remain so important for people like Joe Gorman— did not end, as it did for Margaret Oldham, with a retreat into a preoccupation with profession and private life. If he knew her, Wayne would criticize Margaret Oldham for her lack of appreciation for issues of social justice. It was through radical politics that Wayne glued the shattered mirror of his life back together again. After he made his break with his past, "morality became a question to me. It's sort of like I wanted to put everything back together again with more durable material, one that would stand the strain." Political activism became that durable material. "Watching politics is watching civilization struggle and evolve, and it's very exciting, but it's also much more personal because it's your struggle to evolve into this picture, into this historic picture somehow." In the mid-seventies, Wayne was living in a Spanish-speaking neighborhood of Santa Monica and got involved with some of his neighbors in a dispute with their landlord. "I felt very much that they were being oppressed; they were being taken advantage of. These goddam landlords used immigration like a gun at their head and these people live in this constant state of fear. I had a very good feeling. I really liked these people, they were great people."

His tenant-organizing work led him into involvement with the Campaign for Economic Democracy. "I feel good about what I do. I feel that the work I'm involved in is directly affecting other people in beneficial ways. It's again this value question. You can spend all your time in seeing how many material goods you can get together and how much money you can make or you can spend it helping one another and working together. You know, we can adopt any type of system that we want, let's say it was socialism, communism, or what have you, but the system that we adopt isn't going to mean anything unless we can educate the people to think differently and to be different. And I see what I do as sort of an educational thing in the community, that what I do when I organize tenants is to take care of an immediate crisis that they have. But really what I do is give them a sense of power about their own lives."

When they have power over their lives, each individual will have a greater sense of efficacy, the marvellous feeling of personal growth Wayne himself has felt. "They've never made their ideas public, never shared their ideas, always felt impotent, that they couldn't affect anything. I see them coming out feeling like, well, hell! we affected something. Then the next step is to show them that there are all kinds of things that they can do in society, things they can create. And all they have to do is work as a collective to do it, to agree, to be able to agree to disagree, and then come up with some kind of consensus. Oh, it's a tremendous thing. I mean, it's very beautiful to see and very exciting to be a part of because what you're seeing is kind of an evolution of consciousness."

But what specific *kinds* of things should these newly liberated people create in society? Here Wayne becomes strangely inarticulate. They will make society "better," he says. But what does he *mean* by "better"? "I'm probably not the best person to ask," he says. Even in his area of specialty, tenants' rights, he has only vague notions of what kinds of social arrangements for providing housing tenants would work out if they had the same amount of power as their landlords. "I have a right to live in this community as long as I'm not breaking the law or damaging things— and it's a very touchy question because it deals with private property and other people's rights, investment rights—but I think you can affect that, you can control that situation, that he can make a reasonable amount of money and you can live a reasonably good life—I guess. God! I'm not being very clear."

Wayne thus has a much better idea of what he is against than of what he is for. As a result, the idea of justice that provides such a powerful focus for his life's commitments is weak in substantive content. When he speaks of justice, he talks about individual rights and legal and political systems that would give everyone a fair chance of asserting them. The language he uses provides little conception of the ways in which scarce goods should be distributed in a complex society when different individuals fairly offer competing claims to those goods.* Yet he describes his own involvement in political activism as having broadened his sense of responsibility.

---

*The interviews with Wayne Bauer on which our discussion of him in this chapter is based were carried out in 1980. Since then his ideas about distributive justice and public policy have clarified considerably. In June 1983 he was elected to the Santa Monica Rent Control Board.

Wayne has gradually reentered the Roman Catholic Church, drawn by the example of a priest who has attempted to apply the insights of the Latin American "theology of liberation" to conditions in the United States. He has also begun seriously to consider a legal career, in which he could devote himself to public service law. In spite of these moves to give more substance and direction to his political concerns, his political vocabulary at best does a partial job of explaining and developing his own sense of justice and responsibility. As we shall see, his problem is a typical one for Americans, conservative, liberal, and radical alike.

Different Voices
in a Common Tradition

Brian, Joe, Margaret, and Wayne each represent American voices familiar to us all. The arguments that we have suggested would take place among them, if they ever met, would be versions of controversies that regularly arise in public and private moral discourse in the United States. One of the reasons for these differences is that they draw from different traditions, which will be described in the next chapter. Yet beneath the sharp disagreements, there is more than a little consensus about the relationship between the individual and society, between private and public good. This is because, in spite of their differences, they all to some degree share a common moral vocabulary, which we propose to call the "first language" of American individualism in contrast to alternative "second languages," which most of us also have.

Each of the individuals that we have described in this chapter is drawn from one of the four research projects on which the book is based. We are less concerned with whether they are average than with the fact that they represent the ways in which Americans use private and public life to make sense of their lives. This is the central issue with which our book is concerned. Brian Palmer finds the chief meaning of his life in marriage and family; Margaret Oldham in therapy. Thus both of them are primarily concerned with private life. Joe Gorman gives his life coherence through his active concern for the life of his town; Wayne Bauer finds a similar coherence in his involvement in political activism. Both of them have integrated the public world deeply into their lives. Whether chiefly concerned with private or public life, all four are involved in caring for others. They are responsible and, in many ways, admirable adults. Yet when each of them uses the moral discourse they share, what we call the first language of individualism, they have difficulty articulating the richness of their commitments. In the language they use, their lives sound more isolated and arbitrary than, as we have observed them, they actually are.

Thus all four of the persons whose voices we have heard assume that there is something arbitrary about the goals of a good life. For Brian Palmer, the goal of a good life is to achieve the priorities you have set for yourself. But how do you know that your present priorities are better than those of your past, or better than those of other people? Because you intuitively appreciate that they are right for you at the present time. For Joe Gorman, the goal of a good life is intimate involvement with the community and family into which he happens to have been born. But how do you know that in this complicated world, the inherited conventions of your community and your family are better and more important, and, therefore, more worthy of your allegiance, than those of other communities and families? In the end, you simply prefer to believe that they are better, at least for you. For Margaret Oldham, the goal of a good life is liberation from precisely the kinds of conventions that Joe Gorman holds dear. But what do you aim for once you have been liberated? Simply what you yourself decide is best for you. For Wayne Bauer, the goal of a good life is participation in the political struggle to create a more just society. But where should political struggle lead us? To a society in which all individuals, not just the wealthy, will have power over their own lives. But what are they going to *do* with that power? Whatever they individually choose to do, as long as they don't hurt anybody.

The common difficulties these four very different people face in justifying the goals of a morally good life point to a characteristic problem of people in our culture. For most of us, it is easier to think about how to get what we want than to know what exactly we should want. Thus Brian, Joe, Margaret, and Wayne are each in his or her own way confused about how to define for themselves such things as the nature of success, the meaning of freedom, and the requirements of justice. Those difficulties are in an important way created by the limitations in the common tradition of moral discourse they—and we—share. The main purpose of this book is to deepen our understanding of the resources our tradition provides—and fails to provide—for enabling us to think about the kinds of moral problems we are currently facing as Americans. We also hope to make articulate the all-too-inarticulate search of those we have described in this chapter to find a moral language that will transcend their radical individualism.

Although we have based our reflections about American traditions of moral discourse on conversations with over 200 different Americans, the major themes of our book are already contained in the four stories of life quests with which we began this chapter. Those key themes are really questions: how are we Americans to think about the nature of success, the meaning of freedom, and the requirements of justice in the modern world? Our conversations with our fellow citizens have deepened our conviction that although we have to rely on our traditions to answer those questions, we will have to probe those traditions much more critically than we are used to doing if we are going to make sense of the challenges posed by the rapidly changing world in which we live.

Success

As we noted above, Americans tend to think of the ultimate goals of a good life as matters of personal choice. The means to achieve individual choice, they tend to think, depend on economic progress. This dominant American tradition of thinking about success does not, however, help very much in relating economic success to our ultimate success as persons and our ultimate success as a society.

A century and a half ago, when most Americans still lived in small towns and worked in small businesses or on family-owned farms, the requirements of economic success were perhaps more easily reconciled with understandings of success in family and civic life. In that context, running a profitable farm or business would often have required a reputation for being a good family person and a public-spirited citizen, the meanings of which would be defined in terms of the conventions of one's local community. In Joe Gorman's story, we can see a relic of the way in which the requirements of success in one's job might have encouraged one to define the success of one's life in accordance with the conventional wisdom of one's small town.

But only a small percentage of Americans now work in small businesses in small towns. Most of us work in large public or private bureaucracies. To be a success at work means to advance up the hierarchy of such corporations by helping the corporation make a good profit. But how is this kind of success related to a more fundamental kind of success in life? Even Joe Gorman now works for a large national manufacturing corporation; and he can play such an extraordinarily active part in his community because it fits in with his job as a public relations man for his corporation. If Joe's corporation should ever decide to move its Suffolk factory away from New England to a cheaper labor market, or if the company should offer Gorman an exceptionally good promotion to work at its Houston headquarters, Joe may yet face serious difficulties reconciling the requirements of economic success with his loyalties to his home town.

Someone like Brian Palmer has, of course, already encountered such difficulties. We have seen him wrestle with the question of how to integrate his ambitions to climb the corporate ladder with his desire to have a good family life. This caused him problems, not only because the pressures of work sometimes kept him from spending adequate time with his family, but, even more subtly, because the way of thinking about success that helped him move up the corporate ladder was inappropriate for adequately comprehending the goals of a good family life. And although Brian at least recognizes the problems of integrating a successful work life with a good family life, he seems blithely unconcerned with the wider political and social implications of his work.

Throughout this book, we will be wrestling, together with Brian Palmer and many others, with this question of how to think about the relationship between economic success in our centralized, bureaucratized economy and the ultimate goals of a successful private and public life.

Freedom

Freedom is perhaps the most resonant, deeply held American value. In some ways, it defines the good in both personal and political life. Yet freedom turns out to mean being left alone by others, not having other people's values, ideas, or styles of life forced upon one, being free of arbitrary authority in work, family, and political life. What it is that one might do with that freedom is much more difficult for Americans to define. And if the entire social world is made up of individuals, each endowed with the right to be free of others' demands, it becomes hard to forge bonds of attachment to, or cooperation with, other people, since such bonds would imply obligations that necessarily impinge on one's freedom. Thus Margaret Oldham, for example, sets great store on becoming an autonomous person, responsible for her own life, and she recognizes that other people, like herself, are free to have their own values and to lead their lives the way they choose. But then, by the same token, if she doesn't like what they do or the way they live, her only right is the right to walk away. In some sense, for her, freedom to be left alone is a freedom that implies being alone.

For Margaret, as for others influenced by modern psychological ideals, to be free is not simply to be left alone by others; it is also somehow to be your own person in the sense that you have defined who you are, decided for yourself what you want out of life, free as much as possible from the demands of conformity to family, friends, or community. From this point of view, to be free psychologically is to succeed in separating oneself from the values imposed by one's past or by conformity to one's social milieu, so that one can discover what one really wants. This was precisely the transformation Brian Palmer experienced. He came to feel that the success he had been seeking was a false goal that didn't meet his own needs, so he pushed it aside, feeling it an assertion of freedom to be able to step back from the demands of his company and fulfill his own vision of happiness. The difficulty, of course, is that this vision of freedom as freedom *from* the demands of others provides no vocabulary in which Brian, Margaret, or other Americans can easily address common conceptions of the ends of a good life or ways to coordinate cooperative action with others. Indeed, Brian points out that one thing he likes in California is the freedom people have to do what they want as long as they stay within the walls of their own houses and do not impinge on others. Implicit here, of course, is an image of self-sufficiency, as if Brian will, on his own in the context of his own small family, be able to imbue his children with "values" independently of what his neighbors are doing behind the walls of their own homes. The larger hope that his freedom might encompass an ability to share a vision of a good life or a good society with others, to debate that vision, and come to some sort of consensus, is precluded in part by the very definition of freedom Brian holds.

Joe Gorman and Wayne Bauer both value democratic as well as personal freedom. But even their more political and social definition of freedom—not freedom to be your own person so much as the freedom cherished in a democracy, freedom to speak out, to participate freely in a community, and to have one's rights respected, is highly individualistic. As a traditional American patriot, Joe Gorman deeply cherishes the American ideal of freedom, even though in many ways it is precisely the ideal of freedom that makes his dream of a united Suffolk family impossible to achieve. The success of Suffolk's family spirit depends, as he has discovered, on the willingness of a few people like himself to volunteer freely to sustain community life with their own efforts. Yet he recognizes that very few people in Suffolk are willing to undertake the burdens of shaping community life, and that a man like himself is therefore likely to become exhausted, repeatedly finding himself the only volunteer.

Even more, it is the freedom Joe Gorman values—freedom of each person to live where he wants, do what he wants, believe what he wants, and, certainly, do what he can to improve his material circumstances— that makes community ties so fragile. The freedom of free enterprise makes Suffolk a bedroom community to which the residents are attached mainly by housing prices, while economic opportunities tempt most of its native sons and daughters away. The ideal of freedom Joe Gorman holds most dear makes it difficult even to discuss the question of how a just economy or a good society might best be developed in modern circumstances. For Joe, freedom and community can be reconciled only in the nostalgic dream of an idealized past.

While Wayne Bauer holds what he would conceive to be social and political ideals radically different from those of Joe Gorman, he is if anything even more committed to the American ideal of freedom. He would, of course, be willing to limit the freedom of large corporations, but his guiding ideal is simply to restore what he sees as the lost freedom of everyone else. He wants to help give people back a sense that they are effective and can exercise some control over their own lives. But his passionate commitment to economic and political democracy turns out to be strangely without content. He can envision freedom from what he sees as current forms of economic exploitation, but that freedom is, for him, a virtual end in itself. The legacy of freedom is still the right of each person to feel powerful, to be free to strive after whatever he or she happens to want. Wayne's political vocabulary, despite its socialist patina, is forged from authentically American ore. He waxes passionate about how the freedom of individuals is limited by current economic and political arrangements, but he, too, has difficulty finding a way to think about what a more cooperative, just, and equal social order might look like. Like other Americans, he thinks of freedom very much as freedom *from*—from people who have economic power over you, from people who try to limit what you can do or say. This ideal of freedom has historically given Americans a respect for individuals; it has, no doubt, stimulated their initiative and creativity; it has sometimes even made them tolerant of differences in a diverse society and resistant to overt forms of political oppression. But it is an ideal of freedom that leaves Americans with a stubborn fear of acknowledging structures of power and interdependence in a technologically complex society dominated by giant corporations and an increasingly powerful state. The ideal of freedom makes Americans nostalgic for their past, but provides few resources for talking about their collective future.

Justice

Our American traditions encourage us to think of justice as a matter of equal opportunities for every individual to pursue whatever he or she understands by happiness. Equal opportunities are guaranteed by fair laws and political procedures—laws and procedures applied in the same way to everyone. But this way of thinking about justice does not in itself contain a vision of what the distribution of goods in a society would end up looking like if individuals had an equal chance to pursue their interests. Thus, there could be great disparities in the income given to people in different occupations in a just society so long as everyone had an equal chance of getting a well-paid job. But if, as is now becoming painfully apparent, there are more qualified applicants than openings for the interesting jobs, is equal opportunity enough to assure justice? What of the socially disadvantaged for whom a fair race is to no avail since they are left well short of the starting line?

Our society has tried to establish a floor below which no one will be allowed to fall, but we have not thought effectively about how to include the deprived more actively in occupational and civic life. Nor have we thought whether it is healthy for our society to give inordinate rewards to relatively few. We need to reach common understandings about distributive justice—an appropriate sharing of economic resources—which must in turn be based on conceptions of a substantively just society. Unfortunately, our available moral traditions do not give us nearly as many resources for thinking about distributive justice as about procedural justice, and even fewer for thinking about substantive justice.

Even a self-styled radical such as Wayne Bauer has a difficult time going beyond notions of procedural justice. He is outraged because in Santa Monica the political cards have been stacked against poor tenants in favor of wealthy landlords. He wants to liberate tenants from this unfair system, to give them the same opportunities as rich people to exercise their wills individually. But he becomes confused when asked what kind of society, with what kind of distribution of wealth, the tenants should try to create once they have achieved a fair chance. There is, after all, not enough land near the coast in Southern California to accommodate everyone who would want to live there. If the mechanisms of the free market are not to determine who should live in places like Santa Monica, how should that determination be made? How, in short, should scarce resources be distributed in the new social order created by liberated tenants? What would a just society really look like? To answer such questions, Wayne would have to do more than think about the fair procedures that should be created to give individuals the ability to exercise power over their own lives. He would need some sense of substantive goals, some way to think about distributive justice. But here his cultural resources fail him, as they do most of us.

We now turn to the traditions that have shaped our language and our lives for what they may tell us about our present predicament.

□

Culture and Character: The Historical Conversation 2

To an American reader, the individualism that pervades the four lives described in chapter 1 may at first glance seem not to have anything to do with cultural tradition, but simply to express the way things are. Yet when we look more closely, we see that there are subtle differences among our four characters. There are different modes even within the vocabularies of each individual. Brian Palmer, for example, was at one time in his life single-mindedly devoted to career success, sacrificing everything to attainment of that goal. Later, he came to value quite different things—classical music, books, relationships, the immediate enjoyment of life—and left behind his total devotion to career. Both these modes are individualistic, but they are rooted in different traditions and have different implications. We propose to call the former mode "utilitarian individualism" and the latter "expressive individualism." Joe Gorman and Wayne Bauer combine their individualism with somewhat different languages of civic responsibility. Margaret Oldham holds a more sharply formulated version of Brian's individualism.

These differences derive from a historical past of which none of our characters is entirely aware. In our forward-facing society, however, we are more apt to talk about the future than the past and to imagine that the differences between us derive largely from a conflict of current interests. Yet even in the debate about our future, our cultural tradition, in its several strands, is still very much present, and our conversation would probably be more to the point if we were aware of that fact.

So long as it is vital, the cultural tradition of a people—its symbols, ideals, and ways of feeling—is always an argument about the meaning of the destiny its members share.[1] Cultures are dramatic conversations about things that matter to their participants, and American culture is no exception. From its early days, some Americans have seen the purpose and goal of the nation as the effort to realize the ancient biblical hope of a just and compassionate society. Others have struggled to shape the spirit of their lives and the laws of the nation in accord with the ideals of republican citizenship and participation. Yet others have promoted dreams of manifest destiny and national glory. And always there have been the proponents, often passionate, of the notion that liberty means the spirit of enterprise and the right to amass wealth and power for oneself. The themes of success, freedom, and justice that we detected in chapter 1 are found in all three of the central strands of our culture—biblical, republican, and modern individualist—but they take on different meanings in each context. American culture remains alive so long as the conversation continues and the argument is intense.

The Biblical and Republican Strands

Most historians have recognized the importance of biblical religion in American culture from the earliest colonization to the present. Few have put greater emphasis on the religious "point of departure" of the American experiment than Alexis de Tocqueville, who went so far as to say, "I think I can see the whole destiny of America contained in the first Puritan who landed on those shores." Just as we have used several individuals to introduce aspects of contemporary American culture, we will look at several representative individuals to introduce earlier strands.

John Winthrop (1588–1649) was one of those "first Puritans" to land on our shores and has been taken as exemplary of our beginnings by commentators on American culture from Cotton Mather to Tocqueville to Perry Miller.[2] Winthrop was elected first governor of the Massachusetts Bay Colony even before the colonists left England. Just over forty years of age, he was a well-educated man of good family and earnest religious convictions, determined to start life anew in the wilderness in company with those of like religious commitment. In the sermon "A Model of Christian Charity," which he delivered on board ship in Salem harbor just before landing in 1630, he described the "city set upon a hill" that he and his fellow Puritans intended to found. His words have remained archetypal for one understanding of what life in America was to be: "We must delight in each other, make others conditions our own, rejoyce together, mourn together, labor and suffer together, always having before our eyes our community as members of the same body." The Puritans were not uninterested in material prosperity and were prone when it came, unfortu-

nately, to take it as a sign of God's approval. Yet their fundamental criterion of success was not material wealth but the creation of a community in
which a genuinely ethical and spiritual life could be lived. During his
twelve terms as governor, Winthrop, a relatively rich man for those days,
devoted his life to the welfare of the colony, frequently using his own
funds for public purposes. Near the end of his life, he had to step down
from the governorship because his neglected estate was threatened with
bankruptcy. The Puritan settlements in the seventeenth century can be
seen as the first of many efforts to create utopian communities in America.
They gave the American experiment as a whole a utopian touch that it has
never lost, in spite of all our failings.[3]

For Winthrop, success was much more explicitly tied to the creation of
a certain kind of ethical community than it is for most Americans today.
His idea of freedom differs from ours in a similar way. He decried what he
called "natural liberty," which is the freedom to do whatever one wants,
evil as well as good. True freedom—what he called "moral" freedom, "in
reference to the covenant between God and man"—is a liberty "to that
only which is good, just and honest." "This liberty," he said, "you are to
stand for with the hazard of your lives."[4] Any authority that violates this
liberty is not true authority and must be resisted. Here again, Winthrop
perceives an ethical content to the central idea of freedom that some other
strands of the American tradition have not recognized.

In like manner, Winthrop saw justice as a matter more of substance
than of procedure. Cotton Mather describes Winthrop's manner of governing as follows: "He was, indeed, a governor who had most exactly
studied that book which, pretending to teach politics, did only contain
three leaves, and but one word in each of those leaves, which word was
'Moderation.'" When it was reported to him during an especially long
and hard winter that a poor man in his neighborhood was stealing from
his woodpile, Winthrop called the man into his presence and told him
that because of the severity of the winter and his need, he had permission
to supply himself from Winthrop's woodpile for the rest of the cold season. Thus, he said to his friends, did he effectively cure the man from
stealing.[5]

The freemen of Massachusetts did not always appreciate Winthrop's
leniency, for it made it seem that there was no law but the governor's
will. He was voted out of office and quietly served in minor posts for
several years before being recalled to leadership. Petty leaders in far-
flung colonial outposts have not always taken demotion with such equa-
nimity. Winthrop accepted the procedural principles of self-government
enough to temper his own preference for magnanimous, if personal,
substantive justice.[6] If our "whole destiny" is not quite contained in Win-

throp, as Tocqueville thought, something very important about our tradition nonetheless derives from him and from his fellow Puritans.

The founding generation of the American republic produced so many individuals exemplary of the republican tradition that it is hard to choose among them. George Washington seemed to his contemporaries like some figure out of the early Roman republic. Though he would have preferred to live quietly on his country estate, Washington responded to his country's call to be commander-in-chief of the revolutionary army and, later, first president of the United States. After graduating from Harvard College, John Adams of Massachusetts, a descendant of the Puritans, devoted his talents as a young lawyer to the constitutional defense of the rights of his fellow colonists, and subsequently to the revolutionary cause. Thomas Jefferson (1743–1826), however, as author of the Declaration of Independence and leader of the popular cause, stands out as a particularly appropriate example of republican thinking.

Jefferson came from the planter class of western Virginia.[7] After graduating from William and Mary College, he early took an active part in the politics of the Virginia colony. At the age of thirty-three, he drafted the Declaration of Independence, and with the words "All men are created equal" gave enduring expression to his lifelong commitment to equality. Jefferson did not believe that human beings are equal in all respects. By equality, he meant fundamentally political equality. No man, he believed, is born with a saddle on his back for another man to ride. Therefore, however much he temporized on the practical issue of emancipation, Jefferson vigorously opposed slavery in principle.[8]

Though he held that equality is a universal principle, true at all times and places, Jefferson was a genuine adherent of the republican tradition in believing that it is only effective politically at certain times and places where relatively rare conditions allow it to be operative. Political equality can only be effective in a republic where the citizens actually participate. "The further the departure from direct and constant control by the citizens," he said, "the less has the government of the ingredient of republicanism." Indeed, the ideal of a self-governing society of relative equals in which all participate is what guided Jefferson all his life. In comparison to Europe, he thought this ideal was realizable in the United States in large part because Americans, at least white Americans, were not divided into a few very rich aristocrats and a poverty-stricken mass. Jefferson's ideal was the independent farmer who could at the same time make his living and participate in the common life. Cities and manufacturing he feared precisely because they would bring great inequalities of class and corrupt the morals of a free people.[9]

Late in life, he saw that manufactures were necessary if the nation itself was not to lose its liberty, but at the same time he more insistently than ever stressed the principle of citizen participation. He proposed to subdivide counties into "wards" of approximately 100 citizens that would be "small republics" in which every citizen could become "an acting member of the Common government, transacting in person a great portion of its rights and duties, subordinate indeed, yet important, and entirely within his own competence."[10] Such small republics would help to guarantee the health of the large one. In such a society, Jefferson's injunction "Love your neighbor as yourself, and your country more than yourself" could have an immediate meaning to the citizens. But Jefferson feared that "our rulers will become corrupt, our people careless." If people forgot themselves "in the sole faculty of making money," he said, the future of the republic was bleak and tyranny would not be far away.[11] Like Winthrop, Jefferson left office much poorer than he entered it and faced bankruptcy in his later years.

Freedom was not so tightly tied to substantive morality for Jefferson as it had been for Winthrop. Indeed, Jefferson's first freedom, freedom of religion, aimed at ensuring that people like Winthrop would not have legal power to force their views on others. In general, Jefferson favored freedom of the person from arbitrary state action and freedom of the press from any form of censorship. Yet he also believed that the best defense of freedom was an educated people actively participating in government. The notion of a formal freedom that would simply allow people to do what they pleased—for example, solely to make money—was as unpalatable to Jefferson as it had been to Winthrop. However important formal freedom was to either of them, freedom only took on its real meaning in a certain kind of society with a certain form of life. Without that, Jefferson saw freedom as quickly destroying itself and eventuating in tyranny.[12]

Listing the essential principles of government in his first inaugural address, Jefferson began with: "Equal and exact justice to all men, of whatever state or persuasion, religious or political." While he certainly believed in the procedural justice of our legal system, he could not forget that there is a higher justice that sits in judgment over human justice: "the laws of nature and of nature's God." In considering the continued existence of slavery, Jefferson wrote, "Indeed I tremble for my country when I reflect that God is just; that his justice cannot sleep forever." The profound contradiction of a people fighting for its freedom while subjecting another to slavery was not lost on Jefferson and gave rise to anxiety for our future if this contradiction were not solved.[13]

Utilitarian and Expressive Individualism

Benjamin Franklin (1706–1790) was long regarded at home and abroad as the quintessential American. Though uncomfortable with the Puritanism of his native Boston, Franklin learned much of practical use from Cotton Mather, whose life his own overlapped by twenty-two years. One of the founders of the American republic, Franklin often gave evidence of his republican convictions. And yet it is finally neither for his Christian beliefs, which he embraced rather tepidly and perhaps more for their social utility than for their ultimate truth, nor for his republicanism, which he more genuinely espoused, that he is best known. Rather he is the archetypal poor boy who made good. It is the *Autobiography* that recounts Franklin's worldly success and the maxims from *Poor Richard's Almanack* advising others how to attain the same that are most indelibly associated with him.

Born the son of a soap and candle maker, Franklin was largely self-educated, for he could not afford the college education that Adams and Jefferson took as their due. Seeking a respectable craft, he apprenticed himself to his older brother, a printer. So began the vicissitudes of a career too familiar to readers of the *Autobiography* to need summary here. Suffice it to say that by the age of forty-two Franklin was established in Philadelphia as a printer and publisher and had made a sufficient fortune to be able to retire from the active direction of his business to devote himself to his political, philanthropic, and scientific interests for the rest of his life.

The *Autobiography,* a secular version of John Bunyan's *Pilgrim's Progress,* which had much impressed Franklin in his youth, is the archetypal story of a young man who, though poor, attains success by dint of hard work and careful calculation. Both famous and revealing is Franklin's account of how he attempted to lead a virtuous life by making a "little book" in which he allotted a page to each of the virtues and marked his progress as in a ledger. The twelve virtues themselves, derived from classical and Christian tradition, undergo a subtle revision in the direction of utilitarianism. "Chastity," for instance, is given a somewhat novel meaning: "Rarely use Venery but for Health or Offspring, Never to Dulness, Weakness, or the Injury of your own or another's Peace or Reputation."[14]

Even more influential than the *Autobiography* are the aphorisms in *Poor Richard's Almanack* which have passed into the common sense of Americans about the way to attain wealth: "Early to bed and early to rise, makes a man healthy, wealthy, and wise." "God helps those that help themselves." "Lost time is never found again." "Plough deep, while Sluggards sleep, and you shall have Corn to sell and to keep, says Poor

Dick." In short, Franklin gave classic expression to what many felt in the eighteenth century—and many have felt ever since—to be the most important thing about America: the chance for the individual to get ahead on his own initiative. Franklin expressed it very clearly in his advice to Europeans considering immigration to America: "If they are poor, they begin first as Servants or Journeymen; and if they are sober, industrious, and frugal, they soon become Masters, establish themselves in Business, marry, raise Families, and become respectable Citizens."[15]

What Franklin thought about freedom and justice followed pretty plainly from his understanding of success. Defending popular government in the Pennsylvania Colony in 1756, he wrote: "The people of this Province are generally of the middling sort, and at present pretty much upon a Level. They are chiefly industrious Farmers, Artificers, or Men in Trade; they enjoy and are fond of Freedom, *and the meanest among them thinks he has a Right to Civility from the greatest.*"[16] Franklin understood, with Jefferson, that it was only a certain kind of society that was likely to give such scope to ordinary citizens, to protect their rights, and to secure their equal treatment before the law. But for many of those influenced by Franklin, the focus was so exclusively on individual self-improvement that the larger social context hardly came into view. By the end of the eighteenth century, there would be those who would argue that in a society where each vigorously pursued his own interest, the social good would automatically emerge. That would be utilitarian individualism in pure form. Though Franklin never himself believed that, his image contributed much to this new model of human life.[17] Along with biblical religion and republicanism, utilitarian individualism has been one of the strands of the American tradition since Franklin's time.

By the middle of the nineteenth century, utilitarian individualism had become so dominant in America that it set off a number of reactions. A life devoted to the calculating pursuit of one's own material interest came to seem problematic for many Americans, some of them women, some of them clergymen, and some of them poets and writers. The cramped self-control of Franklin's "virtues" seemed to leave too little room for love, human feeling, and a deeper expression of the self. The great writers of what F. O. Matthiessen has called the "American Renaissance" all reacted in one way or another against this older form of individualism.[18] In 1855 Herman Melville published *Israel Potter*, a novel that subjected Franklin himself to bitter satire. Emerson, Thoreau, and Hawthorne put aside the search for wealth in favor of a deeper cultivation of the self. But it is perhaps Walt Whitman who represents what we may call "expressive individualism" in clearest form.

Walt Whitman (1819–92), like Franklin, was the son of an artisan (in his case, a carpenter), was too poor to go to college, largely educated himself, and became a printer and journalist. But there the resemblance ends. At the age of thirty-six, Whitman brought out a slim volume of poems entitled *Leaves of Grass*, and he spent the rest of his life nurturing it through one edition after another, with little financial security. The first edition of *Leaves of Grass* begins with a poem he would later aptly call "Song of Myself," whose first line is "I celebrate myself." Franklin was not above celebrating himself, but he would not have put it so bluntly. The fourth line, however, is hardly one to which Franklin would have given assent: "I loaf and invite my soul."[19]

For Whitman, success had little to do with material acquisition. A life rich in experience, open to all kinds of people, luxuriating in the sensual as well as the intellectual, above all a life of strong feeling, was what he perceived as a successful life. Whitman identified the self with other people, with places, with nature, ultimately with the universe. The expansive and deeply feeling self becomes the very source of life, as in "Passage to India":

> Passage indeed O soul to primal thought,
> Not lands and seas alone, thy own clear freshness,
> The young maturity of brood and bloom,
> To realms of budding bibles.
>
> O soul, repressless, I with thee and thou with me,
> Thy circumnavigation of the world begin,
> Of man, the voyage of his mind's return,
> To reason's early paradise,
> Back, back to wisdom's birth, to innocent intuitions,
> Again with fair creation.[20]

Freedom to Whitman was above all the freedom to express oneself, against all constraints and conventions:

> Afoot and light-hearted I take to the open road,
> Healthy, free, the world before me,
> The long brown path before me, leading wherever I choose.[21]

The frankness of Whitman's celebration of bodily life, including sexuality, was shocking to nineteenth-century Americans and led to more than a few difficulties, though he never compromised the integrity of his expression. His homosexuality, vaguely but unmistakably expressed in the poetry, was another way in which he rejected the narrow definition of the male ego dominant in his day.

For all his unconventionality, there was a strong element of the republican tradition in Whitman, particularly evident in *Democratic Vistas* (1871) and elsewhere in his prose writings.[22] The self-sufficient farmer or artisan capable of participation in the common life was Whitman's ideal as well as Jefferson's and Franklin's. He would thus have shared their idea of justice. But for Whitman, the ultimate use of the American's independence was to cultivate and express the self and explore its vast social and cosmic identities.

Early Interpretations of American Culture

One of the first to speak of the specifically American character was J. Hector St. John de Crèvecoeur, a French settler who published his *Letters from an American Farmer* in 1782. He set the tone for many future discussions when he observed that Americans tended to act with far greater personal initiative and self-reliance than Europeans and that they tended to be unimpressed by social rank or long usage. He describes the transformation of the European immigrant into an American: "From nothing to start into being; from a servant to the rank of a master; from being the slave to some despotic prince, to become a free man, invested with lands, to which every municipal blessing is annexed! What a change indeed! It is in consequence of that change that he becomes an American."[23]

Schooled by the *philosophes* of the eighteenth-century French Enlightenment, Crèvecoeur had no difficulty appraising the typical American as a kind of "new man," an emancipated, enlightened individual confidently directing his energies toward the environment, both natural and social, aiming to wring from it a comfortable happiness. The type of personality Crèvecoeur sketched approximated the rational individual concerned about his own welfare that had been the model character of Enlightenment thought and that was at that time receiving renewed emphasis in the writings of political economists such as Adam Smith. Crèvecoeur wrote of the American that, "Here the rewards of his industry follow with equal steps the progress of his labour; his labour is founded on the basis of nature, *self-interest;* can it want a stronger allurement?"[24] The rational, self-interested individual had emerged as Economic Man and, as such, was conceived as living most naturally in the conditions of a competitive market in which trade and exchange would replace traditional ranks and loyalties as the coordinating mechanism of social life. As Crèvecoeur said, "We are all animated with the spirit of an industry which is unfettered and unrestrained, because each person works for himself."[25]

Clearly, among our four exemplary Americans, it is Benjamin Franklin, at least the Franklin of legend, who comes closest to Crèvecoeur's ideal of American character. Indeed, Franklin was taken as both an ideal American and an ideal *philosophe* by many French intellectuals of the day, a number of whom created a virtual cult of Franklin during his years in Paris. But Crèvecoeur's exclusive emphasis on this aspect of American culture and character blinded him to other facets. He saw American religion as gradually fading away into bland tolerance or indifference—as, according to Enlightenment views, it should. Crèvecoeur did not understand the strand of American tradition represented by John Winthrop, and one would not know from his writings that a great series of religious revivals was about to begin around 1800. He ignored almost as completely the specifically republican political culture that was so much a part of the revolutionary generation. He did not see what many Americans of his generation did, that a purely economic man would be as unsuited to a self-governing society as would the rank-bound subject of traditional regimes. Fortunately, another Frenchman, Alexis de Tocqueville, who visited the United States in the 1830s, gave a much more adequate view. Nonetheless, Crèvecoeur's view as to the essential nature of American character and society has long been influential, appearing in recent times in the much-quoted books of Louis Hartz and Daniel Boorstin.[26]

For Tocqueville, the optimism of the Enlightenment had been tempered by the experience of the French Revolution and its aftermath, and the prophecies of the early political economists were finding an alarmingly negative fulfillment in the industrial infernos of English mill towns. Tocqueville came to the United States as a sympathetic observer, eager to determine what lessons the first fifty years of the first truly modern nation might have to teach prudent and uncertain Europeans. He added to Crèvecoeur's earlier sketch a more penetrating and complex understanding of the new society, informed by republican convictions and a deep sensitivity to the place of religion in human life.

In *Democracy in America* (published in two parts, in 1835 and 1840), Tocqueville was concerned to understand the nature of the democratic society he saw everywhere coming into existence but most fully exemplified in the United States. In particular, he was attempting to assess whether such democratic societies would be able to maintain free political institutions or whether they might slip into some new kind of despotism. He appreciated the commercial and entrepreneurial spirit that

Crèvecoeur had emphasized but saw it as having ambiguous and problematic implications for the future of American freedom.

Tocqueville argues that while the physical circumstances of the United States have contributed to the maintenance of a democratic republic, laws have contributed more than those circumstances and mores (*moeurs*) more than the laws.[27] Indeed, he stresses throughout the book that their mores have been the key to the Americans' success in establishing and maintaining a free republic and that undermining American mores is the most certain road to undermining the free institutions of the United States. He speaks of mores somewhat loosely, defining them variously as "habits of the heart"; notions, opinions and ideas that "shape mental habits"; and "the sum of moral and intellectual dispositions of men in society."[28] Mores seem to involve not only ideas and opinions but habitual practices with respect to such things as religion, political participation, and economic life.

In short, Tocqueville, unlike Crèvecoeur, saw the great importance, in the American mores of his day, of the continuing biblical and republican traditions—the traditions of Winthrop and Jefferson. He also saw very vividly the way in which Americans operated in the tradition of Benjamin Franklin, and to describe this, he helped to give currency to a new word. "'Individualism' is a word recently coined to express a new idea," he wrote. "Our fathers only knew about egoism." Individualism is more moderate and orderly than egoism, but in the end its results are much the same: "Individualism is a calm and considered feeling which disposes each citizen to isolate himself from the mass of his fellows and withdraw into the circle of family and friends; with this little society formed to his taste, he gladly leaves the greater society to look after itself."[29] As democratic individualism grows, he wrote, "there are more and more people who, though neither rich nor powerful enough to have much hold over others, have gained or kept enough wealth and enough understanding to look after their own needs. Such folk owe no man anything and hardly expect anything from anybody. They form the habit of thinking of themselves in isolation and imagine that their whole destiny is in their hands." Finally, such people come to "forget their ancestors," but also their descendants, as well as isolating themselves from their contemporaries. "Each man is forever thrown back on himself alone, and there is danger that he may be shut up in the solitude of his own heart."[30] Tocqueville mainly observed the utilitarian individualism we have associated with Franklin. He only in a few instances discerns something of the expressive individualism that Whitman would come to represent.

Tocqueville saw the isolation to which Americans are prone as ominous for the future of our freedom. It is just such isolation that is always encouraged by despotism. And so Tocqueville is particularly interested in all those countervailing tendencies that pull people back from their isolation into social communion. Immersion in private economic pursuits undermines the person as citizen. On the other hand, involvement in public affairs is the best antidote to the pernicious effects of individualistic isolation: "Citizens who are bound to take part in public affairs must turn from the private interests and occasionally take a look at something other than themselves."[31] It is precisely in these respects that mores become important. The habits and practices of religion and democratic participation educate the citizen to a larger view than his purely private world would allow. These habits and practices rely to some extent on self-interest in their educational work, but it is only when self-interest has to some degree been transcended that they succeed.

In ways that Jefferson would have understood, Tocqueville argues that a variety of active civic organizations are the key to American democracy. Through active involvement in common concerns, the citizen can overcome the sense of relative isolation and powerlessness that results from the insecurity of life in an increasingly commercial society. Associations, along with decentralized, local administration, mediate between the individual and the centralized state, providing forums in which opinion can be publicly and intelligently shaped and the subtle habits of public initiative and responsibility learned and passed on. Associational life, in Tocqueville's thinking, is the best bulwark against the condition he feared most: the mass society of mutually antagonistic individuals, easy prey to despotism. These intermediate structures check, pressure, and restrain the tendencies of centralized government to assume more and more administrative control.

In Tocqueville's still-agrarian America, as indeed throughout the nineteenth century, the basic unit of association, and the practical foundation of both individual dignity and participation, was the local community. There a civic culture of individual initiative was nurtured through custom and personal ties inculcated by a widely shared Protestant Christianity. The mores Tocqueville emphasized were still strong. Concern for economic betterment was widespread, but it operated within the context of a still-functional covenant concern for the welfare of one's neighbor. In the towns, the competitive individualism stirred by commerce was balanced and humanized by the restraining influences of a fundamentally egalitarian ethic of community responsibility.

These autonomous small-scale communities in the mid-nineteenth century were dominated by the classic citizens of a free republic, men of middling condition who shared similar economic and social positions and whose ranks less affluent members of the population aspired to enter, often successfully. Most men were self-employed, and many who worked for another were saving capital to launch themselves on their own. Westward expansion, as Tocqueville noted, reproduced this pattern of a decentralized, egalitarian democracy across the continent. American citizenship was anchored in the ethos and institutions of the face-to-face community of the town.[32]

The Independent Citizen

It was this Tocquevillean image of the American town that Joe Gorman evoked as his own vision when we met him in chapter 1. For American republicans of the nineteenth century, the town at its best was a moral grid that channeled the energies of its enterprising citizens and their families into collective well-being. The moral life of the community, it was believed, would simultaneously increase material welfare and nourish public spirit. The life of the towns was tightly bounded, however, and if it could yoke individual initiative for the common good, it could also exclude the different and suffocate the unconforming. The strictures of town morality were in part generated by the citizens' unease at trying to create community while navigating the flood of geographical, demographic, and economic expansion. For, as Tocqueville saw, the American, that new kind of person, was a tentative character type shaped by inherited values on the one hand and the challenges of the expanding frontier on the other.

A representative character is a kind of symbol.[33] It is a way by which we can bring together in one concentrated image the way people in a given social environment organize and give meaning and direction to their lives. In fact, a representative character is more than a collection of individual traits or personalities. It is rather a public image that helps define, for a given group of people, just what kinds of personality traits it is good and legitimate to develop. A representative character provides an ideal, a point of reference and focus, that gives living expression to a vision of life, as in our society today sports figures legitimate the strivings of youth and the scientist represents objective competence.

Tocqueville's America can be viewed as an interlocking network of specific social roles: those of husband, wife, child, farmer, craftsman, clergyman, lawyer, merchant, township officer, and so on. But the distinctive quality of that society, its particular identity as a "world" different from other societies, was summed up in the spirit, the mores, that animated its members, and that spirit was symbolized in the representative character of what we can call the independent citizen, the new national type Tocqueville described.[34] In many ways, the independent citizen continued the traditions of Winthrop and Jefferson. He held strongly to biblical religion, and he knew the duties as well as the rights of citizenship. But the model of Benjamin Franklin, the self-made man, loomed ever larger in his defining traits. Abraham Lincoln was perhaps the noblest example of the mid-nineteenth-century American independent citizen. In his language, he surpassed the biblical eloquence of John Winthrop and his understanding of democratic republicanism was even more profound than that of the man he always recognized as his teacher, Thomas Jefferson. And yet it was Lincoln the railsplitter who went from log cabin to White House rather than Lincoln the public theologian or Lincoln the democratic philosopher who captured the popular imagination.

In any case, representative characters are not abstract ideals or faceless social roles, but are realized in the lives of those individuals who succeed more or less well in fusing their individual personalities with the public requirements of those roles. It is this living reenactment that gives cultural ideals their power to organize life. Representative characters thus demarcate specific societies and historical eras. The new American republic of the nineteenth century was the era of the independent citizen as surely as it was defined by the town and national expansion.

Because representative characters are the focal point at which a society encounters its problems as interpreted through a specific set of cultural understandings, they have frequently been mainstays of myth and popular feeling. Certainly, powerful American myths have been built around the self-reliant, but righteous, individual whose social base is the life of the small farmer or independent craftsman and whose spirit is the idealized ethos of the township. These myths are important sources of meaning in the lives of a number of the characters we describe in this book, and they have lately come to play a large, if somewhat disingenuous, role in national political rhetoric. Myths often tell important truths about the tensions people experience and their hopes for resolving those tensions or somehow turning them to constructive use.

Tocqueville depicted the conflicts between the democratic citizen's concern for individual advancement and security on the one hand and religion and local political participation on the other. He traced privatizing tendencies to the new spirit of individualism attendant on nascent commercial capitalism and concern for community to the republican and biblical traditions.

The focus of the new democratic culture was on male roles. But the ethic of achievement articulated by men was sustained by a moral ecology shaped by women. Among artisans and farmers, the household unit played a vital economic role, within which men's and women's positions, though unequal in power and prestige, were largely complementary. In the larger towns and cities, however, and particularly among the professional and business classes, women were more and more deprived of an economic role and were expected to specialize in the expressive and nurturing roles of mother and beautifier of the home, itself viewed more as a retreat from the everyday world than as a part of it.[35] As women reacted differently to these new pressures, the first consciousness of, and opposition to, the inequality of women came to be expressed in America. By the end of the nineteenth century, the fact that women were not "independent citizens" was experienced as a major social strain.

The relevance of Crèvecoeur and Tocqueville for orienting our understanding of the present is suggested by the echoes of their respective analyses in the characters of our study. Brian Palmer's relatively private and optimistic orientation rehearses Crèvecoeur, while Joe Gorman's anxiety and Margaret Oldham's sense of isolation seem to confirm some of Tocqueville's fears of privatism, an anticipation at least somewhat counterbalanced by the contemporary public passion of Wayne Bauer. To understand the representative characters of present-day America, we need to move beyond Tocqueville's era, but in Tocqueville's spirit, noting the evolution of new characters emerging in response to the transformation of the United States into an industrial world power.

The Entrepreneur

The citizen perceived by Tocqueville was indeed closer to being an individual "shut up in the solitude of his own heart" than earlier Americans of religious and republican stripe had been.[36] Yet he was a considerably less isolated and self-regarding figure than the entrepreneurs of the Gilded Age of the late nineteenth century or the bureaucratic managers and therapists of the twentieth.

Tocqueville voiced great misgivings about two phenomena that he thought threatened the moral balance of Jacksonian democracy. One was the slave society of the South, which not only treated blacks inhumanely but, as Tocqueville, like Jefferson, noted, degraded whites as well.[37] The second danger lay in the industrial system, which first made its appearance in the Northeast. Factories had concentrated great numbers of poor and dependent workers, often women and immigrants, into rapidly growing mill towns, and Tocqueville feared the rise of a new form of aristocracy that would make owners and managers into petty

despots and reduce workers to mechanically organized, dependent oper-
atives, a condition incompatible with full democratic citizenship.[38] Just
as the plantation system subordinated the yeoman farmer in the South,
so the spread of industrial organization both concentrated economic
control in the hands of relatively few owners and threatened to displace
the independent artisans so central to nineteenth-century democratic
life. Ironically, the traumatic Civil War that destroyed the slave civilization enormously furthered the growth of the industrial structures that
would fatally unbalance the original American pattern of decentralized,
self-governing communities.

Between the period of rapid westward expansion and industrial
growth that followed the Civil War and the entry of the United States
onto the world scene in World War I, American society passed through
the most rapid and profound transformation in its history, not excluding
our own time. Nothing less than a new national society came into being
in those years, a society within whose structure we still live, and one
markedly unlike that of most of the nineteenth century. By the end of
that century, new technologies, particularly in transport, communications, and manufacturing, pulled the many semi-autonomous local societies into a vast national market. Though fostered in many ways by the
federal government, the new expansion was largely carried out by private individuals and financial groups, who generated private wealth and
control on a previously unheard-of scale.[39]

The new economically integrated society emerging at the turn of the
century developed its own forms of social organization, political control,
and culture, including new representative characters. The new social
form, capable of extending the control of a group of investors over vast
resources, huge numbers of employees and, often, great distances, was the
business corporation. The Pennsylvania Railroad, with its tentacular
reach, its supervised, graded, and uniformed army of workers, its me-
chanical precision of operation and monopolistic ambitions, became the
model of a new institution destined eventually to affect the lives of almost
all Americans. The steel, oil, banking and finance, and insurance industries rapidly adopted the new bureaucratic form of the corporation.[40]

The old local governments and organizations lacked the capacity to
deal with problems that were increasingly national in scope. Under these
conditions, the traditional forms of social and economic life of the town
lost their dominant position, in fact, if not in symbol, and the traditional
idea of American citizenship was called into question. The new industrial order was focussed on large cities that seemed the antithesis of the
order and decency of the town. Factories, slums, immigrants, and ward
bosses seemed "foreign" and frightening. In those years, a new politics

of interest developed, with the powerful national economic interests of the corporations, banks, and their investors, and, eventually, the labor movement, competing with the old regional, ethnic, and religious interests. These developments changed the workings of the political parties in the national government. By the early decades of the twentieth century, the Progressive movement was calling for a smoother partnership between large-scale economic organizations and government at all levels to "rationalize" the tumultuous process of social and political change. If all generations of Americans have had to confront "future shock," surely the turn-of-the-century generation faced the most severe challenge.

The eclipse of the old economic and social patterns brought stormy political conflicts and complex cultural changes in its wake. One was the acceleration of a possibility always available to some in American society, the emancipation of the successful entrepreneur from the confining ties of the old town morality. The Gilded Age was the era of the spectacular "self-made" economic success: captains of industry who could ignore the clamor of public opinion and rise to truly national power and prestige by economic means alone.[41] In the predatory capitalists the age dubbed robber barons, some of the worst fears of earlier republican moralists seemed confirmed: that by releasing the untrammeled pursuit of wealth without regard to the demands of social justice, industrial capitalism was destroying the fabric of a democratic society, threatening social chaos by pitting class against class. Where, many wondered, could new limits and directions for individual initiative be found beyond the broken bounds of the local self-governing community? The inability of the old moral order effectively to encompass the new social developments set the terms of a cultural debate in which we as a nation are still engaged.[42]

The most distinctive aspect of twentieth-century American society is the division of life into a number of separate functional sectors: home and workplace, work and leisure, white collar and blue collar, public and private. This division suited the needs of the bureaucratic industrial corporations that provided the model for our preferred means of organizing society by the balancing and linking of sectors as "departments" in a functional whole, as in a great business enterprise. Particularly powerful in molding our contemporary sense of things has been the division between the various "tracks" to achievement laid out in schools, corporation, government, and the professions, on the one hand, and the balancing life-sectors of home, personal ties, and "leisure," on the other. All this is in strong contrast to the widespread nineteenth-century pattern in which, as on the often-sentimentalized family farm, these functions had only indistinct boundaries. Domesticity, love, and intimacy increasingly became "havens" against the competitive culture of work.

With the industrialization of the economy, working life became more specialized and its organization tighter. Simultaneously, industrialization made functional sectors of the economy—various industries, whole geographical regions—more interdependent than before. Yet the sectoral form of organization and the competitive pressures of the national market made this interdependence difficult to perceive. While the pressures to compete and the network of private life were immediately perceptible, the interrelationships of society as a whole were largely abstractions. The sectoral pattern of modern American society has thus often been able to contain potential conflicts by separating those who are different without impairing the economic linkages of sectors within the larger economy.[43]

Under such conditions, it is not surprising that the major problems of life appear to be essentially individual matters, a question of negotiating a reliable and harmonious balance among the various sectors of life to which an individual has access. As its points of reference contracted from an economically and occupationally diverse local community to the geographically spread, but functionally homogeneous, sector within which a person competes, success came to be defined in professional terms. The concept of one's "peers" concomitantly underwent a subtle, but important, shift of meaning. It came to signify those who share the same specific mix of activities, beginning with occupation and economic position, but increasingly implying the same attitudes, tastes, and style of life.[44]

The responses to all this that were articulated around the turn of the century have continued to shape our ways of conceiving and relating to American society. Those responses have all along been closely interwoven with new character types that, like the earlier ones, have come to seem representative approaches to the common conditions of life, giving moral meaning and direction to the lives of individuals.

The Manager

The self-sufficient entrepreneur, competitive, tough, and freed by wealth from external constraints, was one new American character. Certainly much of the moral appeal of the self-made man is his apparent freedom, not only from traditional restraints, but from the tight organization, the drudgery and banality, of so much of modern industrial life. The irony, of course, is that the entrepreneur's major historical role has been to create the modern industrial context. Celebrating the economic struggle, the self-made man of means became the legitimizing symbol for some of the aspiring middle class. Yet in practice the recurrent American dream of success has often continued to approximate the old image of the business-man as family provider and citizen. The turn-of-the-century nabobs themselves frequently sought legitimation through public philanthropy and national service, drawing on models more deferential—their critics said "feudal"—than American republican tradition countenanced. But the activist individual entrepreneur, though a continuing feature of American life and still a powerful symbol, has not represented the dominant direction of economic and social development.

The bureaucratic organization of the business corporation has been the dominant force in this century. Within the corporation, the crucial character has been the professional manager.[45] The competitive industrial order with its sectoral organization and its push toward profitability has been the indisputable reality of modern life for the manager, rather than the object of a passionate faith in "progress," as for the entrepreneur. Although the manager in effect builds upon the work of the entrepreneur and shares with him the drive to achieve and problem-solving activism that are old American traits, the social positions and outlooks of the two types differ importantly.

The essence of the manager's task is to organize the human and non-human resources available to the organization that employs him so as to improve its position in the marketplace. His role is to persuade, inspire, manipulate, cajole, and intimidate those he manages so that his organization measures up to criteria of effectiveness shaped ultimately by the market but specifically by the expectations of those in control of his organization—finally, its owners. The manager's view of things is akin to that of the technician of industrial society par excellence, the engineer, except that the manager must admit interpersonal responses and personalities, including his own, into the calculation of effectiveness.[46]

Like the entrepreneur, the manager also has another life, divided among spouse, children, friends, community, and religious and other nonoccupational involvements. Here, in contrast to the manipulative, achievement-oriented practices of the workplace, another kind of personality is actualized, often within a social pattern that shows recognizable continuity with earlier American forms of family and community. But it is an outstanding feature of industrial life that these sectors have become radically discontinuous in the kinds of traits emphasized and the moral understandings that guide individuals within them. "Public" and "private" roles often contrast sharply, as symbolized by the daily commute from green suburban settings reminiscent of rural life to the industrial, technological ambience of the workplace.

The split between public and private life correlates with a split between utilitarian individualism, appropriate in the economic and occupational spheres, and expressive individualism, appropriate in private life. For a long time such a split was incipient in American life. Early in the nineteenth century, indeed already in the eighteenth century, an appeal to calculating utility was complemented by an appeal to sentiment or emotion. Jefferson, following the eighteenth-century Scottish philosophers, believed in an innate "moral sentiment" that impelled men toward benevolence. The Puritan theologian Jonathan Edwards (1703–58) had seen religion, too, as located in the "affections." When science seemed to have dominated the explanatory schemas of the external world, morality and religion took refuge in human subjectivity, in feeling and sentiment. Morality and religion were related to aesthetics, the realm of feeling par excellence, as we saw in the case of Whitman. When morality came to be associated with the role of women and the family, and religion to be largely a matter of revivalistic emotion, the split between the utilitarian and the expressive spheres in nineteenth-century America widened. Nonetheless, theologians and moralists believed feeling had some cognitive content, some access to the external world, and Whitman certainly believed his poetry was expressing the truth not only of himself but of the world. But with the emergence of psychology as an academic field—and, even more important, as a form of popular discourse—in the late nineteenth and early twentieth centuries, the purely subjective grounding of expressive individualism became complete.

The town had provided a metaphor of a moral ecology in which the polarities of public and private, masculine and feminine, were integrated by means of generally shared codes of behavior. Preindustrial American character surely oscillated between the instrumental orientation of the "masculine" world of work achievement and the values of the "feminine" spheres of nurturing domesticity. But the cultural framework made that oscillation, including its conflicts, intelligible.

With the coming of the managerial society, the organization of work, place of residence, and social status came to be decided by criteria of economic effectiveness. Those same economic criteria further facilitated the growth of national mass marketing and, with it, expanded consumer choice. The older social and moral standards became in many ways less relevant to the lives of those Americans most directly caught up in the new system. The manager could reorganize resources for greater effectiveness in economic life. Similarly, the relatively affluent twentieth-century American could reorganize habits and styles of life experimentally to achieve a more gratifying private life. In this process, Americans learned to become more efficient in adapting to new sets of expectations and styles of consumption.

The Therapist

Like the manager, the therapist is a specialist in mobilizing resources for effective action, only here the resources are largely internal to the individual and the measure of effectiveness is the elusive criterion of personal satisfaction.[47] Also like the manager, the therapist takes the functional organization of industrial society for granted, as the unproblematical context of life. The goal of living is to achieve some combination of occupation and "lifestyle" that is economically possible and psychically tolerable, that "works." The therapist, like the manager, takes the ends as they are given; the focus is upon the effectiveness of the means.

Between them, the manager and the therapist largely define the outlines of twentieth-century American culture. The social basis of that culture is the world of bureaucratic consumer capitalism, which dominates, or has penetrated, most older, local economic forms. While the culture of manager and therapist does not speak in the language of traditional moralities, it nonetheless proffers a normative order of life, with character ideals, images of the good life, and methods of attaining it. Yet it is an understanding of life generally hostile to older ideas of moral order. Its center is the autonomous individual, presumed able to choose the roles he will play and the commitments he will make, not on the basis of higher truths but according to the criterion of life-effectiveness as the individual judges it.

The moral language and images of this culture of utilitarian and expressive individualism have influenced the lives of most of the characters in this book, and one of our chief tasks in the chapters that follow will be to delineate and understand its forms. As we shall see, the effects of this managerial and therapeutic understanding are not always benign; it does not always succeed, even by its own standards. Indeed, the very term *therapeutic* suggests a life focussed on the need for cure. But cure of what? In the final analysis, it is cure of the lack of fit between the present organization of the self and the available organization of work, intimacy, and meaning. And this cure is to take the form of enhancing and empowering the self to be able to relate successfully to others in society, achieving a kind of satisfaction without being overwhelmed by their demands. In its own understanding, the expressive aspect of our culture exists for the liberation and fulfillment of the individual. Its genius is that it enables the individual to think of commitments—from marriage and work to political and religious involvement—as enhancements of the sense of individual well-being rather than as moral imperatives.

The culture of the manager and the therapist is thus both recognizably continuous with earlier American cultural forms and yet different from them. The obvious point of similarity is the emphasis on the independence of the individual. As we have seen, self-reliance is an old American value, but only one strand of the complex cultural weft we have inherited. The expressive culture, now deeply allied with the utilitarian, reveals its difference from earlier patterns by its readiness to treat normative commitments as so many alternative strategies of self-fulfillment. What has dropped out are the old normative expectations of what makes life worth living. With the freedom to define oneself anew in a plethora of identities has also come an attenuation of those common understandings that enable us to recognize the virtues of the other.

In fact, the new culture is deeply ambiguous. It represents both the easing of constraints and dogmatic prejudices about what others should be and an idealization of the coolly manipulative style of management. In our society, with its sharply divided spheres, it provides a way for the beleaguered individual to develop techniques for coping with the often-contradictory pressures of public and private life. Yet it does so by extending the calculating managerial style into intimacy, home, and community, areas of life formerly governed by the norms of a moral ecology.

Some Recent Interpretations

Robert and Helen Lynd in *Middletown* (1929) and *Middletown in Transition* (1937) offered the most extensive sociological study hitherto undertaken of a single American community (Muncie, Indiana). The Lynds sought to show what was happening to America under the impact of industrialization and the social changes accompanying it. They took the year 1890 as a baseline with which to compare the America of the twenties and thirties that they studied firsthand. They saw the typical nineteenth-century town that Muncie had been in 1890 transformed into the rapidly changing industrial city of thirty or forty years later. In particular, they noted the split into a business class and a working class, with the former dominant and the latter in many ways excluded from full participation in community life. What becomes clear from the two Middletown books and from *Knowledge for What?* (1939), Robert Lynd's more general book about American culture, is that the Lynds brought a rich harvest of sociological detail to document what was by then an old theme among social critics—namely, the decline of the culture of the independent citizen, with its strong biblical and republican elements, in the face of the rise of the business (managerial) class and its dominant ethos of utilitarian individualism.

The Lynds viewed this change with foreboding, feeling that the future of American democracy lay in the balance.[48]

Much of the public interpreted David Riesman's widely read *The Lonely Crowd* (1950) in the same way.[49] The old independent "inner-directed" American was being replaced by new, "other-directed" corporate types, with lamentable results. Read carefully, Riesman's argument is considerably more complex, and his evaluations are rather different from the Lynds'. Riesman actually proposes four character types, not two. Tradition-directed character is what most premodern societies produce. It is represented in America largely by immigrants from peasant societies. Riesman's inner-directed type characterizes old American culture and seems to be an amalgam of our biblical, republican, and utilitarian individualistic types. Perhaps the inner-directed person is the old independent citizen, more attuned to his own internal morality than to the cues of his neighbors.[50] But Riesman is far from endorsing the inner-directed type, for the superego of the inner-directed person is itself an introject from social authority experienced in childhood. Like the other-directed person responding to the conformist pressures of the immediate social environment, the inner-directed person lacks genuine autonomy. The autonomous character is Riesman's fourth type and the only one he genuinely admires. Riesman's concept of the autonomous character is clearly related to some of the ideas of Erich Fromm and seems to be close to what we have called the expressive individualist type, especially in its relatively pure therapeutic form. Indeed, whatever its immediate reception, Riesman's book seems to herald an increasing importance of the expressive individualist style in postwar America, relative to which the other-directed, or conformist, character seems to have been a relatively transient type. That Riesman grew alarmed at some of the implications of his work, or some of the implications some readers drew from it, is documented in the prefaces he supplied in successive reprintings. But Riesman's later hesitations do not in the least detract from the value of *The Lonely Crowd* as a landmark study of the transformation of American character.

The only book that we would place together with those of the Lynds and Riesman as a major interpretive contribution to the understanding of twentieth-century American character and society is Hervé Varenne's *Americans Together* (1977).[51] Varenne's classic study of a small town in southern Wisconsin is the subtlest depiction to date of how American culture and character interacted in recent times. Varenne clearly sees the dominance of utilitarian and expressive individualism as modes of character and cultural interaction, and especially the delicate balance between them and their mutual dependence. The drive toward independence and mastery only makes sense where the individual can also find a context to express the love and happiness that are his deepest feelings and desires. Fragile communities are put together to meet the utilitarian and expressive needs of individuals, with only a peripheral survival of older biblical and republican themes. For Varenne, this balance represents a successful cultural code containing and equilibrating its inner contradictions. While our reading of modern American history makes us more doubtful about the success of this equilibrium, we remain indebted to the brilliance of his insights, which, besides those of the towering figure of his fellow Frenchman, Tocqueville, have most influenced our study.[52]

American Culture Today

Perhaps the crucial change in American life has been that we have moved from the local life of the nineteenth century—in which economic and social relationships were visible and, however imperfectly, morally interpreted as parts of a larger common life—to a society vastly more interrelated and integrated economically, technically, and functionally. Yet this is a society in which the individual can only rarely and with difficulty understand himself and his activities as interrelated in morally meaningful ways with those of other, different Americans. Instead of directing cultural and individual energies toward relating the self to its larger context, the culture of manager and therapist urges a strenuous effort to make of our particular segment of life a small world of its own.

However, the cultural hegemony of the managerial and therapeutic ethos is far from complete. It is rooted in the technological affluence of postwar society, a prosperity that has been neither equitably shared nor universally accepted. Challenges to that ethos have arisen from a variety of quarters, from those left out of that prosperity, as well as from those who, while its beneficiaries, criticize it for moral defects. Sometimes the criticism seems to be motivated by a desire to hold on to the last vestiges of the autonomous community and its ideal of the independent citizen. Sometimes it is motivated by a desire to transform the whole society, and particularly its economy, so that a more effectively functioning democracy may emerge. In either case, there is a powerful rejection of the managerial-therapeutic ethos, in which we can see not only the discontents of the present economic and social order, but also reminders of the continuing importance of the biblical and republican cultural traditions in American politics.

We see a number of surviving forms of the old ideal of the independent citizen in America today. In some cases, what we call the concerned citizen is devoted to defending the moral beliefs and practices of his or her community in the face of a permissive therapeutic culture and the decisions of administrators and managers that do not understand, and are not answerable to, local community feeling. We find what we call civic volunteers, often professionals, committed to helping their communities adjust to new challenges in a way that does not rupture tradition or destroy democratic participation. And we also find movement activists for whom the task of forming a new public, organized for discussion and action, is a major commitment. The activist works within the political order, but also hopes to influence understandings of society in the direction of significant change. None of these present-day representatives of the ideal of the independent citizen can avoid being influenced by utilitarian and expressive individualism, the pervasive world of the manager and the therapist. But they give evidence that the old cultural argument is not over, and that all strands of our tradition are still alive and still speak to our present need. Perhaps it is now clear that Brian Palmer, a manager; Margaret Oldham, a therapist; Joe Gorman, a concerned citizen; and Wayne Bauer, a movement activist, though all deeply individualist in their language, draw on a more complex tradition than any of them quite realizes.

□

Part One □ Private Life

Finding Oneself 3

Self-Reliance

In the course of our history, the self has become ever more detached from the social and cultural contexts that embody the traditions discussed in chapter 2. As mass phenomena, the nervous search for the true self and the extravagant conclusions drawn from that search are probably relatively recent in our society.[1] But the current focus on a socially unsituated self from which all judgments are supposed to flow is a development out of aspects of American selfhood that go all the way back to the beginning. *Self-reliance* is a nineteenth-century term, popularized by Ralph Waldo Emerson's famous essay of that title, but it still comes easily to the tongues of many of those to whom we talked. Self-reliance of one sort or another is common to every one of the traditions we have discussed. What, if not self-reliant, were the Puritans, many of whom, like John Winthrop, left wealth and comfort to set out in small ships on a dangerous "errand into the wilderness"? They felt called by God, but they had to rely on themselves. Thomas Jefferson chose in his draft of the Declaration of Independence to strike a note of self-reliance when he said that emigration and settlement here "were effected at the expense of our own blood and treasure, unassisted by the wealth or the strength of Great Britain,"[2] conveniently forgetting how recently the British had defended the colonists against the French and Indians, but expressing a genuinely American attitude.

The note of self-reliance had a clearly collective context in the biblical and republican traditions. It was as a people that we had acted independently and self-reliantly. With utilitarian and expressive individualism, however, the collective note became muted. The focus of the self-made printer or the poet who sang of himself was more exclusively on the individual. Emerson in his 1841 essay "Self-Reliance" even declared the individual and society to be in opposition. "Society," he said, "is everywhere in conspiracy against the manhood of every one of its members." Emerson was speaking to the world of the independent citizen and insisting that the conformity exacted by small-town America was too coercive. His friend Thoreau would push this teaching to an extreme in his classic experiment at Walden Pond. But in his essay, Emerson also expressed a more prosaic sense of self-reliance, one that has been the common coin of moral life for millions of Americans ever since. Emerson says we only deserve the property we work for. Conversely, our primary economic obligation is only to ourselves. "Then again, do not tell me, as a good man did to-day, of my obligation to put all poor men in good situations. Are they *my* poor?" he wrote.[3]

We found self-reliance common as a general orientation in many of those to whom we spoke. Therapist Margaret Oldham typically expressed it as "taking responsibility for oneself." But economic self-reliance is often seen as the bedrock on which the more general character trait rests. Asked why he worked so hard to support his wife and child after he first got married, corporate executive Brian Palmer said, as we noted in chapter 1, "I guess self-reliance is one of the characteristics I have pretty high up in my value system." As a young husband and father, Brian felt "confronted with the stark realities of being self-supporting or dropping out of the human race."

Some critics have seen the "work ethic" in decline in the United States and a "narcissistic" concern with the self emerging in its place. In our conversations, we have found that an emphasis on hard work and self-support can go hand in hand with an isolating preoccupation with the self, as Tocqueville feared would be the case. Indeed, work continues to be critically important in the self-identity of Americans, closely linked to the demand for self-reliance. The problem is not so much the presence or absence of a "work ethic" as the meaning of work and the ways it links, or fails to link, individuals to one another.

Leaving Home

In this chapter, we seek to understand how the Americans to whom we talked understand themselves—what sense of self they have. We also want to describe their sense of a course of life, insofar as they have one. Does life indeed have a purpose or end, and, if so, what are the stages along the way?

In a culture that emphasizes the autonomy and self-reliance of the individual, the primary problems of childhood are what some psychoanalysts call separation and individuation—indeed, childhood is chiefly preparation for the all-important event of leaving home. Though the issues of separation, individuation, and leaving home come to a head in late adolescence, they are recurrent themes in the lives of Americans, and few if any of us ever leave them entirely behind.

Separation and individuation are issues that must be faced by all human beings, but leaving home in its American sense is not. In many peasant societies, the problem is staying home—living with one's parents until their death and worshipping parents and ancestors all one's life. In traditional Japan, the expression "leaving home" was reserved for those entering monastic life, who abandoned all ties of ordinary existence. For us, leaving home is the normal expectation, and childhood is in many ways a preparation for it.

While it sometimes appears to be a pitched battle only the heroic or rebellious wage against the parental order, more often the drive to get out in the world on your own is part of the self-conception Americans teach their children. A young therapist remembers growing up in the South as a doctor's son: "One of the messages I got as a child was to be very respectful, to have a great deal of respect for others," he says. "Another message as a child was that you were independent, you took care of yourself. The phrase that comes to mind is 'Where is your backbone?' When things are bad, you take care of yourself, you don't ask things of other people. So in one way you were real connected to other people in terms of politeness, caring, or respect. And in other ways you were very independent and would seek to be very independent."

Self-reliant and independent notions of the self show up prominently in precisely those families whose offspring report the greatest felt continuity between their parents and themselves. One of them recalls that "in my Baby Book, my mother described me as being impulsive, inquisitive, stubborn, cheerful, curious, independent, and self-sufficient. I guess I haven't changed much." They describe their coming of age in terms of breaking away from dependency on parents and relying on themselves, though in many cases, they continue to have close relations with their parents.

This development is not new in America. Sometime after the middle of the eighteenth century, according to Daniel Calhoun, child-training practices began to change from an emphasis on peace and order in the family to the development of "independent self-sufficient individuals."[4] Interestingly enough, this had something to do with the popularization of John Locke's views on child-rearing, as contained in his *Some Thoughts Concerning Education*, just when his political views were becoming popular in the colonies. Politically, Locke was a stalwart opponent of patriarchy, arguing that kingship cannot be derived from father-hood and that government is a creation of equal adults, on whose consent it necessarily depends. In his observations on child-rearing, Locke does not call for the father to abdicate his authority. Rather, he insists that the father exercise authority firmly early in the child's life with a view to the child's developing the self-discipline that will allow independence later on. By adolescence, parents are to abandon coercive authority and treat their children as self-governing friends. In this way, Locke argues, children will be able to take care of themselves in the world and good relations between parents and children can continue into the child's adulthood. For all the changes in views of child-rearing we have undergone in the past two centuries, that underlying pattern has continued.[5]

For some of the individuals we met in chapter 1, the process of leaving home was quite smooth; for others there was considerable conflict. As Hervé Varenne has pointed out, conflict does not mean that the cultural pattern of leaving home is in doubt.[6] A degree of conflict over this issue is to some extent to be expected. However painful the process of leaving home, for parents and for children, the really frightening thing for both would be the prospect of the child never leaving home.

Of the four, Joe Gorman is the least dramatic example. In one sense, he did not leave home at all. That is what his commitment to his New England town entails. Yet in significant ways even he had to leave home. He did not follow his father's career of high school coaching but chose to go to work for a local company. He did not even choose to continue to live in the family enclave, feeling that some geographical separation, even if only in another part of the same town, was essential. Still, neighborhood and extended family continue to provide the center of this white clapboard scene. Even though their unity loosens as a new generation comes of age to start families of its own, such people remain linked by webs of friendship, work, and local economic and civic participation that span generations of the town's "natural citizens." Joe represents what may in the past have been an easier and commoner pattern to follow. One leaves home in the sense of becoming economically independent and starting a family of one's own, but one's separate life is still fundamentally similar to that of one's parents, and congenial relations with parents continue.

Margaret Oldham avoided the rebelliousness of many she saw around her and has basically fulfilled her parents' expectations of her, but for her, leaving home has involved much more extensive differences from her parents' way of life than in the case of Joe Gorman. It is worth considering her case and those of some of her colleagues because they are illustrative of how far the upwardly mobile individual moves, geographically, culturally, and psychologically, even when fulfilling, rather than disappointing, parental expectations.

Margaret Oldham had strict parents who "knew what was right and what I should be doing." But they loved her well, and she in turn heeded the lessons they both preached and practiced about "being polite and considerate of people, respecting your parents, working and keeping things clean and neat—that was a big item—and just sort of being good and not getting into any trouble." Growing up as the younger of two children in a medium-sized city in upstate New York, Margaret went through a "lot of go-arounds" about keeping her room clean and doing her part at home. She excelled in school, and enjoyed herself on dates without getting too involved, she smiles, in "any of those nasty things young people are prone to want to do."

Margaret's country-bred mother "had a good, strong religious upbringing in the whole puritan kind of tradition," and even now she "really doesn't know how to relax except by doing something that's her job or doing things for other people." Her father "feels uncomfortable in churches, but he has a real sort of basic set of ideas" and a background much like his wife's. An extremely diligent, careful, and self-demanding worker, he took a high school diploma and his technical experience in the military into the skilled craft work of manufacturing optical equipment in a long-established business, where he has gradually taken on more and more supervisory responsibility. Asked what she learned in her family about what was important in life, Margaret answers without hesitation, "Work."

Her own hard work as a talented, serious student led Margaret to one of the state's elite public universities. There she found friends who were every bit as bright and capable as she was, typically hailing from college-educated families in the big cities and the suburbs of major metropolitan areas. Many of these friends turned out to be less single-minded about their studies and in more conflict about their lives as they came of age in the early seventies on a campus swept by politics, drugs, and cultural effervescence. While others were dropping out of school and into trouble, Margaret experimented cautiously in all of this. "I had a couple of friends that were quite self-destructive and one who is no longer with us," she says. Trying to understand what was going on among them and why they responded so differently strengthened Margaret's interest in psychology and helped her decide to pursue it in graduate school. Instead of rebelling herself, Margaret made the need to understand the rebellion of her peers a motive in her choice of career.

Margaret was a dutiful child who grew up close to her parents and emulated them. Yet the very virtues of hard work and self-discipline she absorbed from them have led her away from their social circle into a more educated, urbane, and open-ended society. In the middle-class suburbs and cities where most of Margaret Oldham's student and therapist friends were raised, they talk of socialization rather than of tradition. Instead of authority or its breakdown, they recall their professional parents "sending them messages" to conform or achieve in line with more or less "adaptive values" in order to win their parents' love.

"Being smart, that's what the value was, being good at things, being right," remembers one of Margaret's classmates, the New York–bred daughter of a college professor and a social worker. "Ideas and books and travel—ideas more than anything—were important. I also got a lot of messages about being good and nice and doing what pleases people. My parents spent a lot of time sort of evaluating things, and so I got a real sense that things just had to be certain ways. Food had to be certain ways, and wine. Everything had to be right or else it was less pleasing." Asked why a person ought to be good by this account, the therapist replies, "Well, because people won't love you. I don't think I ever asked why, but that was the implicit message. That if you weren't smart and nice and sort of did things properly, you wouldn't be loved." How did that fit with her idea of succeeding or not succeeding? "I think it made me very ambivalent," she answers. "On the one hand, I wanted to be good and right and smart and all that. On the other hand, I think I wanted to test people to see if they would still love me if I wasn't those things."

In the eyes of these successful children of professionals without strong religious beliefs, parental love is narrowed to a reward for doing well. Moral standards give way to the aesthetic tastes and technical skills of the achievement-oriented upper middle class. "Being good" becomes a matter of being good *at things;* being right, a matter of having the right answers. Here the child is not a new edition of the parents' selves—the child Joe Gorman idealizes—but an ambivalent seeker after success and love, ready to venture far from parental patterns in search of those ends. These children need to feel that parents and the pressures they exert are not part of the real self.

Before he embarked on his search for the self he would like to be, Brian Palmer experienced much more conflict with his parents, especially his father, than Joe and Margaret did with theirs. The eldest of three children, Brian grew up in Cleveland, on the very edge of a school district populated by the affluent upper middle class. "My family did not have much money," he remembers. "I lived in a house that probably had a thousand square feet of living area. I went over and spent the night with a friend of mine in high school whose *foyer* had a thousand square feet of living area. Big, beautiful pillared mansion up on top of the hill. I ran with those kids." To keep up with them, Brian started working hard as a teenager doing yard jobs, caddying, helping out in a shipping department, and then selling men's clothing. "I was exposed to the good life at a very young age, and I decided I wanted a piece of it," he explains. Playing $5 and $10 poker, he "had won and lost $1,000 at the poker table before I was sixteen years old, but it was my money."

While he played with his friends in "rather princely fashion," Brian's family was straining to make ends meet at home. A college graduate in architecture swept up in World War II, his father was afterward unable to find a job in his chosen field and instead went into selling real estate. It gave him ulcers, little money, and less satisfaction. As soon as the children were all in school, Brian's mother went to work as a secretary to help pay the bills. Frustrated at work and often irritable at home, Brian's father early on came into conflict with his son. He "used to beat on me a whole bunch when I disobeyed the rules. Punctuality was one of his big things, and I used to be a dilly-dallier." An adolescent standoff between the two became "a parting of the ways" when Brian went off to the state university and "he gave me absolutely no help whatsoever. I earned my way or borrowed it." Caught in the middle, as always, Brian's mother "would occasionally send me a check for $10 when I was down to my last bowl of popcorn and my last jar of peanut butter, even though I may have had twenty-four cans of beer in the refrigerator." Away at college and on his pleasurable way to "parlaying an outstanding academic record into academic probation," Brian was out on his own at last. But as the striving son failed by a father who had faltered in the world, he had effectively left home years before. Probably Brian owes more than a little of his "self-reliance" to his father's early training, but the life he has led, even more than in the case of Margaret Oldham, has taken him into realms his parents would scarcely have imagined.

Finally, in the case of Wayne Bauer, we see an example of full-scale cultural rebellion, the rejection of the "John Wayne" image of American life he had learned at home and the adoption of the life of a radical political organizer in its stead. Still, he differs only in degree from the others described above. This, too, is a way of leaving home in America. Wayne describes his youth as a transition from the middle-class American "status quo" into a world exploded by the social conflicts, movements, and alternative lifestyles of the 1960s. Traditionally, he observes, what you were to do with your life was "what your father did. How he lived his life." We have already seen, however, that for most contemporary Americans leaving home is seldom as simple as that. And, indeed, Wayne's own early life hardly conforms to the seamless image of suburban America with which he represents his past. His parents were divorced when he was a small child, and "I never knew my father." His mother remarried, and his stepfather's frequent job transfers meant that Wayne was "always the new kid in school." In a large New Jersey high school, he made close friends with "poor people, working-class people, Catholics. And I was Protestant. My family was very WASPy. I would spend a lot of time with these friends, and my family would always tell me, 'Look, it's just as easy to make friends with people who could do something for you.' I sensed that something was wrong early in life, that the yacht club that my family belonged to and this whole social attitude really was kind of phony." Together with several of his "raunchy" friends, Wayne enlisted in the Marine Corps. But he spent his leaves in New York City with his brother's college classmates. Crawling the Village and arguing with them about Vietnam, he became convinced that the war and the military were wrong, and he deserted.

His family split by divorce, uprooted as a child by his stepfather's nationwide career moves, his youth straddling the conflicting attitudes and behavior of different social classes and crossing a cultural "generation gap," Wayne came of age along some of the dividing lines of the complex social reality that belies the suburban and small town image invoked to stand for America.

For many of those who talked to us, the family seemed to reinforce the importance of self-reliance as the cardinal virtue of individuals. The idea we have of ourselves as individuals on our own, who earn everything we get, accept no handouts or gifts, and free ourselves from our families of origin turns out, ironically enough, to be one of the things that holds us together. Like other core elements of our culture, the ideal of a self-reliant individual leaving home is nurtured within our families, passed from parent to child through ties that bind us together in solitude as well as love.[7]

Leaving Church

The self-reliant American is required not only to leave home but to "leave church" as well. This may not literally happen. One may continue to belong to the church of one's parents. But the expectation is that at some point in adolescence or early youth, one will decide on one's own that that is the church to belong to. One cannot defend one's views by saying that they are simply the views of one's parents. On the contrary, they must be particularly and peculiarly one's own. Traditionally, Protestant piety demanded that a young person experience a unique conversion experience of his or her own, even while specifying more or less clearly the content of that experience. More recently we have come to expect even greater autonomy.

Again, though such ideas may be more widespread today, they are hardly new in America. In "Self-Reliance," Emerson is even more concerned with intellectual and religious independence than he is with economic independence. He writes, "The highest merit we ascribe to Moses, Plato and Milton is that they set at naught books and traditions, and spoke not what men but what they thought. A man should learn to detect and watch that gleam of light which flashes across his mind from within, more than the lustre of the firmament of bards and sages." Emerson assumes that his fellows accept his own confidence in the individual soul: "Trust thyself: every heart vibrates to that iron string."[8]

Today religion represents a frame of reference for the self as conspicuous in its absence as in its presence. To be sure, more than nine out of ten Americans "believe in God," surveys report, and four out of ten attend church regularly.[9] Joe Gorman, for one, still takes his family faithfully to Mass every Sunday, lingering afterward to greet his fellow-parishioners and chat with the pastor. But relatively few middle-class urbanites described themselves to us as "children of God," created in his image and likeness, bound by his commandments, and inspired by his love. Liberalized versions of biblical morality tend to subordinate themes of divine authority and human duty to the intrinsic goodness of human nature, since "God does not make junk," as a liberal pastor puts it. They also underscore the power of human choice and the possibility of self-acceptance, since "you are a child of the Universe," in the widely quoted formula one ecology activist, Cassie Cromwell, who is also a Unitarian, cited as part of her credo:

> BE GENTLE WITH YOURSELF. You are a child of the Universe
> no less than the trees and the stars. You have a right to be here.
> And whether or not it is clear to you, no doubt the universe is
> unfolding as it should. Therefore be at peace with God,
> whatever you conceive Him to be. And whatever your labors
> and aspirations, in the noisy confusion of life, keep peace in
> your soul. With all its sham, drudgery and broken dreams, it is
> still a beautiful world.

Here the self as metaphoric child echoes ecology, aestheticism, and nature mysticism, not biblical revelation. Like Margaret calling her self-fulfillment "what the universe wants from me," this formula confirms our individual rights instead of calling for our obedience to God's authority. The unfolding of the universe justifies no rational principles of conduct based on natural law, as it does for a traditional Catholic such as Joe Gorman. Instead, it reassures us of our freedom to choose our own God, our own labors, and our own ultimate ends, whatever they may be.

Following on the heels of liberalized religion's relaxed sense of duty, authority, and virtue, comes the rejection of institutional religion itself on the grounds that it is morally "hypocritical." Brian Palmer, who has now worked out his own "value system," explains why he left the Protestant church in which he was raised: "I found it absurd that someone could still profess for an hour and a half on Sunday to believe a certain set of values and then see living proof of how they lived a lie," he says. "I heard what they were saying and I listened to it. It seemed reasonable to me, and everyone else was shaking their head and saying, 'Yes' and 'Amen,' and all that. Then they walked out the door, turned around, and acted 180 degrees different. It was hypocrisy." Reasonable in themselves, the teachings of Christian morality are falsified because Christians do not actually live them out. Brian goes on to praise his wife, Maryellen, because she is that rarest of "anachronisms," a "practicing Christian." His admiration focuses on her tolerance, extended even to an abusive ex-boss. "She says that's his thing—he'll be punished by God." Brian compares this with his own attitude: "I said if I worked there I'd punch the guy out. I couldn't stand that. Seeing that kind of abuse. I want to be in control of things, and I figure God put me on earth to take care of myself and not do his work for him. I'll leave the big problems for him to solve. Little ones I'll solve for him."

As opposed to Brian's picture of Christians who fail to practice what they preach, Margaret's parents "never really preached" Christianity and churchgoing. They emphasized doing good and helping others. Her mother in particular "just sort of did it herself, sort of expecting me to come along and be part of it." Margaret's mother regularly took her to church, although her father accompanied them only at Christmas and Easter. Not until her second year in college did Margaret get out of the habit of going to church, but long before that she "had a problem with religion" related to Brian's. "I just didn't think it was fair," she objects, "that just because a person happens to be born in and grow up in China, they would never go to heaven because they never knew anything about God. Just because I was lucky enough to be born into the appropriate religion, why does that entitle me to be anybody better than a billion

Chinese who love Confucius?" Majoring in psychology in college and mulling over the sort of cultural absolutism that led Jefferson to deism, Margaret came to conclusions that suggest a diluted version of Jefferson's natural reason. For her now, God is "sort of a name that's been assigned to that particular kind of function for me, to make the most of my life." She compares this function to "the physical authority of the universe. I mean there are certain laws that *are* laws."

Throughout our history, churches have tended to follow and reinforce the dividing lines of class, status, and ethnicity. Even today, the lines of class-bound religious affiliation remain visible. As a rebellious adolescent intent on enraging his WASP Presbyterian parents, Wayne Bauer began going to an Italian Catholic church with some of his rough working-class friends from high school. For a long time after he went AWOL from the Marines, Wayne found meaning outside the church, in radical politics and an interest in art; but more recently, as we have seen, he has begun to attend a Catholic church again.

The American understanding of the autonomy of the self places the burden of one's own deepest self-definitions on one's own individual choice. For some Americans, even 150 years after Emerson wrote "Self-Reliance," tradition and a tradition-bearing community still exist. But the notion that one discovers one's deepest beliefs in, and through, tradition and community is not very congenial to Americans. Most of us imagine an autonomous self existing independently, entirely outside any tradition and community, and then perhaps choosing one.

It is harder for us to see ourselves choosing our families in the same way. We are just born into them. But even here, the work of therapy is often aimed at so distancing us from our parents that we may choose, or seem to choose, freely, which aspects of them we will resemble and which not. Leaving home in a sense involves a kind of second birth in which we give birth to ourselves. And if that is the case with respect to families, it is even more so with our ultimate defining beliefs. The irony is that here, too, just where we think we are most free, we are most coerced by the dominant beliefs of our own culture. For it is a powerful cultural fiction that we not only can, but must, make up our deepest beliefs in the isolation of our private selves.

Work

The demand to "make something of yourself" through work is one that Americans coming of age hear as often from themselves as from others.

It encompasses several different notions of work and of how it bears on who we are. In the sense of a "job," work is a way of making money and making a living. It supports a self defined by economic success, security, and all that money can buy. In the sense of a "career," work traces one's progress through life by achievement and advancement in an occupation. It yields a self defined by a broader sort of success, which takes in social standing and prestige, and by a sense of expanding power and competency that renders work itself a source of self-esteem. In the strongest sense of a "calling," work constitutes a practical ideal of activity and character that makes a person's work morally inseparable from his or her life. It subsumes the self into a community of disciplined practice and sound judgment whose activity has meaning and value in itself, not just in the output or profit that results from it.[10] But the calling not only links a person to his or her fellow workers. A calling links a person to the larger community, a whole in which the calling of each is a contribution to the good of all. The Episcopal Book of Common Prayer says in the collect for Labor Day, "So guide us in the work we do, that we may do it not for the self alone, but for the common good." The calling is a crucial link between the individual and the public world. Work in the sense of the calling can never be merely private.

Though the idea of a calling is closely tied to the biblical and republican strands in our tradition, it has become harder and harder to understand as our society has become more complex and utilitarian and expressive individualism more dominant. In the mid-nineteenth-century small town, it was obvious that the work of each contributed to the good of all, that work is a moral relationship between people, not just a source of material or psychic rewards. But with the coming of large-scale industrial society, it became more difficult to see work as a contribution to the whole and easier to view it as a segmental, self-interested activity. But though the idea of calling has become attenuated and the largely private "job" and "career" have taken its place, something of the notion of calling lingers on, not necessarily opposed to, but in addition to, job and career. In a few economically marginal but symbolically significant instances, we can still see what a calling is. The ballet dancer, devoted to an ill-paid art, whose habits and practices, beautiful in themselves, are handed down in a community based on a still-living tradition, so that the lives of the public may be enriched, is an example. In any case, however we define work, it is very close to our sense of self. What we "do" often translates to what we "are."

Each of our moral traditions carries a sense of the self at work distinguished by its peculiar idea of job, career, and calling in relation to one another. The stories of Winthrop, Jefferson, Franklin, and Whitman cannot be transposed neatly to the present, but their self-understandings and our own draw on many of the same cultural categories in facing the demand to make something of ourselves. To heed it, middle-class Americans today leave home to go to school and then to work. For some, as for Margaret Oldham, what they learn in school leads smoothly into what they do in professional work. "Sometimes it feels like I've been a student all my life," she says of her dissertation research, "and when I finally finish, I'd still like to keep a hand in research and teaching besides seeing clients." But for most of those we talked to, as for Brian, school proved less a part of what they made of themselves at work. A self-described "under-achiever" in school, Brian majored in English at a midwestern state university, but devoted much of his time to parties, playing cards, and falling in love "at the drop of a skirt." English literature and the writing of romantic poetry were, however, among the things that brought him together with his first wife. After several years at a routine white-collar job to support his wife and a child, Brian returned to school for a semester of accounting courses, then entered the management training program of a major corporation. "I went in the Resources Management Program, which is made up mostly of graduates from engineering schools, mostly the top 10 percent of the class, and I finished number one in my class through that. Then I went into the Budget Office, which is made up of the top 1 percent of that group, and I finished in the top 1 percent of that group, so I figured, O.K. I can fit in that league, and I have proven that, so now let me go out and set about making a name for myself. In 1972 I was what they call on our rank structure rank four and in 1978 I was rank fourteen. My salary had increased three times over." Literary self-expression gave way to competitive self-advancement up the rungs of training "classes" set in a corporate ladder. Mastery of a discipline, for Brian, mattered less than finishing first in the class, since learning itself was chiefly a means of making it to the top of an organization structured by chains of supervisory control and salary scales.

Compare this picture of college and corporate training with Joe Gorman's memories of his hometown high school, where "the spirit was 'Everything we do, we should do together.'" Then "the big thing was to be a member of the varsity," part of a team representing the school as a whole, rather than an individual star, seeking to stand out on his own. The latter, Joe complains, is exactly "what's happening to the country" today, from selfish Little Leaguers pushed by their parents to money-hungry major leaguers holding out on their contracts. "Instead of teaching the kid the sport, nowadays it's what he can get out of it."

Joe joined his present employers as an assembly-line worker. There the personnel director found him—son of the local high school coach, popular athlete, and class officer now enrolled in night school classes— and promptly offered him a full-time job in the firm's front office. Here he has remained, steadily working his way up to become head public relations officer for the local plant and then turning down promotions that would take him away from Suffolk.

By contrast, the high road to corporate success has led Brian back and forth across the country, "picking up, selling the house, moving off to a strange city and strange state" every few years, making new friends and then leaving them behind again. Even now, he is conscious of the next step onward and upward: "I can probably make one more move locally. Beyond that I'd probably have to relocate geographically. Then I'd have to make a decision. Do I want the next level of challenges back East, or do I want to continue to enjoy the sunshine and lifestyle of California?"

Whatever his answer turns out to be, the forks in Brian's successful career continue to dramatize the split between public and private life— between the challenges a public self takes on and the pleasures a private self enjoys. Yet work means more to Brian than the goods it buys and the status it secures. Most of all, it defines him in terms of his "performance" in comparison with others. "I don't like failure," he asserts. "I'm very competitive. I like to win." Finishing first among his corporate peers and leapfrogging from one promotion to another have brought Brian to the work he does today. He describes it as follows: "I am called a business manager. I have profit-and-loss responsibilities for a business that will do about fifty million dollars in sales this year. I have about sixty people that report to my staff, and prior to that I was finance manager for the department I'm in now." His responsibilities as a business manager extend from sales strategies to the bottom line of profits and loss, and no further. He defines his work by his corporate position, quantified in terms of gross revenue, profit margin, staff size, and span of control.

Still rising toward the peak of a career that has defined his identity by its progress, Brian looks back on his twenties and thirties, devoted to advancing his career at the expense of tending his marriage and family life, and concedes, "I got totally swept up in my own progress, in promotions and financial successes." Yet even now, Brian's definition of success revolves around an open-ended career on the upswing, empty of a calling's sense of social responsibility. "I want to keep progressing to the point where I remain challenged," he testifies. "Where I come as close as I can to performing at the absolute limits of my capability. That's success." That is also the voice of a utilitarian self seeking its separate identity in the exercise of its own growing powers, ever freer of restraint by others and ever farther out in front of them.

Midlife, especially for middle-class American men such as Brian, often marks the "end of the dream" of a utilitarian self established by "becoming one's own man" and then "settling down" to progress in a career.[11] The grade grows steeper at the peak of a professional field, the ledges narrower at the top of a corporate pyramid. It becomes more difficult, or virtually impossible, to become "Number One"—sole owner-operator, chief executive officer, senior partner, or Nobel laureate. As these dreams die, the possibility fades of a self that can use work and its rewards to provide the matrix of its own transcendent identity. When the trajectory of a career flattens out, and it becomes clear that one will not, after all, make it to the top, then making it loses its meaning—as opposed to continuing in a calling and practicing law, carpentry, or scholarship as best one can, even if one cannot be the best. For many in middle age, the world of work then dims, and by extension so does the public world at large. For the fortunate among the career-weary, the private world of family and friends grows brighter, and a more expressive self comes to the fore.[12]

The alternative idea of work as a calling is conspicuously absent from Brian's pattern of success. Brian sees the value of work in terms of what it yields to a self that is separate from the actual activity work demands of him in return. In this imagery of exchange, the self stands apart from what it does, and its commitments remain calculated and contingent on the benefits they deliver. In a calling, by contrast, one gives oneself to learning and practicing activities that in turn define the self and enter into the shape of its character. Committing one's self to becoming a "good" carpenter, craftsman, doctor, scientist, or artist anchors the self within a community practicing carpentry, medicine, or art. It connects the self to those who teach, exemplify, and judge these skills. It ties us to still others whom they serve.[13]

Is the presence of a calling more evident in someone dedicated to an elite profession? Margaret Oldham, who finished at the top of her class all through college and won the chance to train as a clinical psychologist over hundreds of others, sees the personal meaning of her work from a different angle than does Brian. As we saw in chapter 1, Margaret chose psychology because of a desire to understand other people and why they were different from her. Here a self seeking to understand how we think and behave enters into a profession whose practical demands seem to strengthen personal identity. Yet academic research has turned out to be both enormously complex and artificially formalized, so that "usually by the time you get a really interesting question combed down into a research project, it's lost a lot of this complexity and stuff that made it interesting in the first place." Even when meaning is not lost in methodology, Margaret is "plagued by the idea that nothing I'm doing research-wise is ever going to have any relevance to anybody's life." The hope of becoming a person able to help others change their lives for the better guided Margaret toward a career as a therapist. But efforts to do so have all to often proved inconclusive, and sometimes simply hopeless, especially if their recipient was not "a YAVIS—young, anxious, verbal, intelligent, and sensitive." And, she adds, even "if you've done a really good job, they don't think you've helped them at all, and they think they've done it all themselves— and in a sense they have."

By most sociological measures, Margaret's work is much more rewarding in terms of prestige and meaning than the work her parents do. Yet she asks much more *from* work and *for* herself than they do, she says, and that may be one reason she finds less "fulfillment" in work than they do. "Work is really what they do with their lives," she observes. "Working is what makes them feel worthwhile." She agrees with them that "people should work for what they get," and that "once you get into doing it, it kind of becomes an end in itself as well as a means to get your money or whatever it is that you want." But she does not fully share her parents' conviction that work is simply good and "what we're supposed to do." Nor does she always feel, as they seem to, that "work is a pleasure in itself." "I'm not as convinced of the all-importance of working as they are," she concludes. "It's important for me to do nothing sometimes, to relax," and so the big shift in her life is "doing more things for myself, taking more time for myself than I think that either one of my parents take for themselves. So to that extent I have succumbed to the 'me decade,'" she jokes, secure in the knowledge that compared to her peers the extent is minimal.

Compared to representative figures of our biblical and republican past, however, Margaret is less than fully committed to her calling. She has not given up her dreams of clarifying the mind and making the world a better place, but she now wonders at times if psychology is "really the most fulfilling place for me to be." She looks back wistfully to the tangible creativity, discipline, and sense of completion she found in the pottery and craftwork she did as a student. Doing therapy does give her a sense of fulfillment: "Just the opportunity to get close to people in the way that you do in therapy is real nice and you grow a lot. You get better and better at sharing your emotions and giving to other people." But asked how therapy contributes to the larger social world or community, Margaret shakes her head and smiles ruefully, "The only community I ever think I'm adding to is the one of people who have been in therapy and talk like psychologists, you know, and that's not particularly positive."

For employed Americans, work offers not only the basis of a decent material life but a great deal of self-esteem. Unemployment is peculiarly painful for those to whom what one does is what one is. Yet even for quite successful Americans, such as Brian Palmer and Margaret Oldham, work as job or career does not seem to be enough. To identify wholly with work in that sense is suffocating, even if the higher rewards are not limited by narrowing opportunities in the upper echelons. The absence of a sense of calling means an absence of a sense of moral meaning. When they do not find it in their work, people like Brian and Margaret seek for such meaning, as we might expect, in some form of expressive individualism, to be pursued with the like-minded and loved ones. But the ties one forms in the search for meaning through expressive individualism are not those of the moral community of the calling. They are rather the ties of what we might call the lifestyle enclave.

The Lifestyle Enclave

At some point in midlife, many Americans turn toward sharing with others in intimacy instead of striving to outrace them. Thus, nearing forty, Brian discovered in the wake of an abrupt divorce that "I didn't like being alone. I like to be with someone." During an interregnum of single-parenting and evenings spent alone with music and books, he realized that "self-reliance is very important to me, but I am not an island, and I'm not satisfied as a human being as a single entity." A second marriage of "sharing, openness, and communication" with a "creative, challenging, totally self-reliant" woman ensued, as if according to the script of a well-resolved "midlife crisis." According to Gail Sheehy's enormously popular book *Passages,* midlife is the time to move "out of roles and into the self" in order to discover "an enlarged capacity to love ourselves and embrace others."[14]

Once epitomized by youthful romance, the expressive self is now supposed to revive in midlife and ripen in retirement. And, it seems, for increasing numbers of Americans, the sooner the process begins, the better. By the end of 1981, 57.1 percent of all male retirees had gone on Social Security pensions before they were sixty-five, and 60 percent of all retirements were voluntary.

The very possibility of retirement on a mass scale is a recent one, sponsored by the social insurance systems of the modern welfare state and built on the broad back of a national industrial economy. A keen observer of life in a flourishing "retirement community" reports how few of the men there seemed to regret leaving their jobs. They took pride in their career success as executives, civil servants, school teachers, and small businessmen. Yet they retired as soon as they could afford to because they were "sick of working," hated "the pressure," had "paid their dues," wanted "to get out of the rat race"—and, finally, because they "never thought their work was socially necessary." Their work "seemed only a means of achieving a satisfactory private life—a 'life style,' as some put it," concludes Frances FitzGerald. They "had had jobs, but they had no work in the sense of lifelong interests," or a calling. Yet what leisurely pursuits do these freedom- and privacy-loving individuals most enjoy? Golf and bridge, games for sociable problem solvers who love rules as much as competition, who want "security within a fixed social order" as neatly laid out and tended as the harmonious landscape of a golf course.[15]

The term "lifestyle," which Frances FitzGerald heard in Sun City Center, Florida, turned up frequently in our interviews. It is worth pondering its meaning. FitzGerald is certainly right in seeing it as an expression of private life. It is linked most closely to leisure and consumption and is usually unrelated to the world of work. It brings together those who are socially, economically, or culturally similar, and one of its chief aims is the enjoyment of being with those who "share one's lifestyle."

Though the term "community" is widely and loosely used by Americans, and often in connection with lifestyle, we would like to reserve it for a more specific meaning. Whereas a community attempts to be an inclusive whole, celebrating the interdependence of public and private life and of the different callings of all, lifestyle is fundamentally segmental and celebrates the narcissism of similarity. It usually explicitly involves a contrast with others who "do not share one's lifestyle." For this reason, we speak not of lifestyle communities, though they are often called such in contemporary usage, but of lifestyle enclaves. Such enclaves are segmental in two senses. They involve only a segment of each individual, for they concern only private life, especially leisure and consumption. And they are segmental socially in that they include only those with a common lifestyle. The different, those with other lifestyles, are not necessarily despised. They may be willingly tolerated. But they are irrelevant or even invisible in terms of one's own lifestyle enclave.

The lifestyle enclave is in important respects an outgrowth of the sectoral organization of American life described in chapter 2 as resulting from the emergence of industrialization and the national market. For a long time, private life and its leisure and consumption patterns were expressions of social status, in turn linked to social class, as in more traditional societies. But as social status and social class came to depend more and more on a national occupational system and less and less on local communities, a degree of freedom became possible in private life that would not have been conceivable in the small town or even for older urban elites. By the 1920s, a concern for lifestyle expressiveness was clearly evident in the more affluent sectors of American society, though public opinion remained ambivalent.

The massive immigration of ethnically and linguistically unfamiliar groups that accompanied the industrialization of the United States in the late nineteenth and early twentieth centuries exposed Americans to cultural diversity, and so also might seem to lie behind the current phenomenon of lifestyle enclaves. While the presence of immigrant groups did accustom Americans to the presence of the culturally different, and eventually to toleration of those who remained morally irrelevant to them, ethnic groups themselves were communities or quasi-communities rather than enclaves in our sense. They attempted to reproduce the entire institutional complex of a functioning society in rural and even, as far as possible, in urban settings.

The contemporary lifestyle enclave is based on a degree of individual choice that largely frees it from traditional ethnic and religious boundaries. Among those to whom we talked, largely middle-class and similar in occupation, we found a variety of lifestyle enclaves. The newer kind of lifestyle enclave was perhaps first visible soon after World War II in what was called the "youth culture." Patterns of recreation, dress, and taste in matters such as music or food characterized young people more or less independently of ethnic or class background. These emerging youth patterns were interpreted as reactions to the "strain" of prolonged education and delayed participation in the adult world. Whether the emergence of lifestyle enclaves in midlife and among the retired can be interpreted as a reaction to the "strain" the adult occupational system places on older people is an open question. Certainly we have some evidence that that is the case. We might consider the lifestyle enclave an appropriate form of collective support in an otherwise radically individualizing society. Or, to put it somewhat differently, since the purpose of individuation has always been linked to the ability to find others who reflect and affirm one's selfhood, perhaps the lifestyle enclave is the necessary social form of private life in a society such as ours.

Although lifestyle enclaves may be most obvious in large cities, where groups of people have little in common except the way they spend their leisure time, many aspects of American life today can be viewed as incipient lifestyle enclaves. Romantic love is a quintessential form of expressive individualism. When it becomes not only the basis for the choice of a life partner but the condition for the continuation of a marriage, it tends to make of marriage itself a lifestyle enclave. Brian Palmer's second marriage has something of that flavor. Many once genuine communities, though still referred to as communities, may be well on their way to becoming lifestyle enclaves. Joe Gorman's Suffolk, for example, has long ceased to be a community in the sense that the traditional American small town was a community. For its inhabitants, most of them recent, it is largely a residential enclave chosen as a place in which to pursue appropriate private lifestyles. In this it is no different from thousands of other American suburbs.

Wayne Bauer's Santa Monica is far from a typical suburb. His own sense of himself and of his work is very much related to an ideal of community. He sees his life as that of a full-time activist contributing to the community by organizing its members in efforts to create a more equal and just society. According to Wayne, a self defined by success on the job or in a career obscures the "truly meaningful values that will never desert" a person and "will lead to a stronger, saner world." His passion for "politics as a way of life" has crystallized the rebuilding of a once-shattered life, rescued at least a little of "what we used to dream about in the sixties," and laid the foundation for what he perceives as his lifelong calling. It does not denigrate Wayne's aspirations to point out that Santa Monica is a very special kind of place with a very high concentration of people like Wayne. Even more to the point is that Campaign for Economic Democracy activists share a lifestyle, even down to similar tastes in music, wine, and food. Thus even those who would most like to think of our society in organic communitarian forms cannot avoid the lifestyle enclave as the effective social expression of our personal lives.

To take a contrasting example, we talked to many conservative Evangelicals who have their own version of what an interdependent organic community ought to be, but who end up just as unmistakably members of lifestyle enclaves as do Wayne and his CED activist friends. This is not the whole story about either activists or Evangelicals. To the extent that their serious commitments carry them beyond private life into public endeavors, they do indeed transcend the lifestyle enclave and represent genuine community. But the tendency of contemporary American life is to pull all of us into lifestyle enclaves of one sort or another.

We should not exaggerate this tendency, however. Probably most groups in America today embody an element of community as well as an element of lifestyle enclave. The distinction is more analytic than concrete. When we hear such phrases as "the gay community" or "the Japanese-American community," we need to know a great deal before we can decide the degree to which they are genuine communities and the degree to which they are lifestyle enclaves.

When the existence of a "youth culture" was first discovered, one of its functions was thought to be providing identity symbols for adolescents engaged in the process of separation from their families but not yet prepared to go to work as adults. Those symbols would define them, however marginally, as distinct from others, and thus as having an identity of their own. In a period when work is seldom a calling and few of us find a sense of who we are in public participation as citizens, the lifestyle enclave, fragile and shallow though it often is, fulfills that function for us all.

Grounding the Self

We have looked at various ways Americans today separate out their ideas of the self from family, religion, and work, and how they seek lifestyle enclaves to find the self-expression missing from the rest of their lives. We have also seen how their forebears left their homes, churches, and careers in order to begin again. Breaking with the past is part of our past. Leaving tradition behind runs all the way through our tradition. But how is such a separate self to be shaped and grounded? Do we have answers today that correspond to those provided by Winthrop's God, Jefferson's nature, Franklin's progress, and Whitman's poetic feeling? Almost everyone who talked with us spoke of "values" in reply. Some of them, like Joe Gorman, make no bones about what those values "really" are and should be for everyone. Those who don't know better need to be told, like children, "Shut up and listen!" Those who do know need to pitch in to stem the chaos and "cooperate with each other for the good of the community." Others, like Wayne Bauer, return repeatedly to "this value question" to emphasize that we should be "helping one another and working together" instead of seeking our own success. Margaret Oldham is more conscious of the fragile basis of her "values." "It really sort of comes down to the authority I say I give my values . . . all those sorts of goals I've set up for myself, that kind of motivate me and tell me which way to go, what to avoid."

If the self is defined by its ability to choose its own values, on what grounds are those choices themselves based? For Margaret and many others, there is simply no objectifiable criterion for choosing one value or course of action over another. One's own idiosyncratic preferences are their own justification, because they define the true self. Brian Palmer explains his drastic shift from obsession with work to devotion to family by saying that he just got more personal satisfaction from course *B* than from course *A*. The right act is simply the one that yields the agent the most exciting challenge or the most good feeling about himself.

Now if selves are defined by their preferences, but those preferences are arbitrary, then each self constitutes its own moral universe, and there is finally no way to reconcile conflicting claims about what is good in itself. All we can do is refer to chains of consequences and ask if our actions prove useful or consistent in light of our own "value-systems." All we can appeal to in relationships with others is their self-interest, likewise enlightened, or their intuitive sympathies. In therapy, for example, Margaret would "try to get them to come to the realization that they're probably causing the other person a whole lot of pain and then ask, 'Do you think you ought to do anything about that?'" If confronted with a person whose values "I really couldn't tolerate," Margaret concludes, "I wouldn't see them in therapy." Where sympathy or already-congruent values are not enough to resolve moral disagreements between ourselves and others, we have no recourse except to withdraw from them.

In the absence of any objectifiable criteria of right and wrong, good or evil, the self and its feelings become our only moral guide. What kind of world is inhabited by this self, perpetually in progress, yet without any fixed moral end? There each individual is entitled to his or her own "bit of space" and is utterly free within its boundaries. In theory, at least, this civil and psychic right is extended to everyone, regardless of their race, ethnicity, or value system, insofar as their exercise of this right does not infringe on the right of others to do likewise.

But while everyone may be entitled to his or her own private space, only those who have enough money can, in fact, afford to purchase the private property required to do their own thing. As a consequence, economic inequalities necessarily delimit our individual "rights" to self-fulfillment—or unjustly violate those rights, as Wayne Bauer argues in his political struggle to control the free-market explosion of rents in affluent Santa Monica. The tolerance for various values and "lifestyles" so notable in Brian Palmer's suburban Silicon Valley is helped along by real estate prices (averaging well over $100,000 per house in the early 1980s) that exclude all but the upper middle class from buying homes there. Their livelihood does not hinge on their communal loyalties or local respectability, but on their technical skills, certified by university degrees and measured by the profit-accounting of corporations such as Brian's. Brian's separate self, in short, is socially located on private property that is marked off from the public sphere but depends entirely on the institutional structure of the society at large for its apparent freedoms.

Ted Oster, a lawyer without institutionalized religious or political commitments, who also lives in Silicon Valley, brings the world of the separate self into more extreme relief. He argues that "rigid" moral standards interfere with one's freedom and enjoyment of life, since "life is a big pinball game and you have to be able to move and adjust yourself to situations if you're going to enjoy it. You got to be able to realize that most things are not absolute. Very little is, other than life and death." If the self is to be free, it must also be fluid, moving easily from one social situation and role to another without trying to fit life into any one set of values and norms, even one's own. In fact, one's values are not really a single "system," since they vary from one social situation and relationship to the next. Life conceived as a "pinball game" has its rules, but they are all instrumental, meaningful not in themselves but only as a means to the player's enjoyment. Bending the rules makes sense if it enhances the player's satisfaction. Accordingly, with a good friend "who is dishonest with some people in a pretty fundamental way," says Ted Oster, "to enjoy him I make certain compromises in the way I look at things in order to get into him and to be able to enjoy him." "I don't think I change basically who I am. I change what I am doing, perhaps the things I say. That's another aspect of not being totally honest all the time. I won't be totally honest with somebody so that I can enjoy them a little bit more. I put some of my feelings aside. I try to adjust to their way of looking at things without changing myself."

A self free of absolute values or "rigid" moral obligations can alter its behavior to adapt to others and to various social roles. It can play all of them as a game, keeping particular social identities at arm's length, yet never changing its own "basic" identity, because that identity depends only on discovering and pursuing its own personal wants and inner impulses.

If the individual self must be its own source of moral guidance, then each individual must always know what he wants and desires or intuit what he feels. He must act so as to produce the greatest satisfaction of his wants or to express the fullest range of his impulses. The objectified moral goodness of Winthrop obeying God's will or Jefferson following nature's laws turns into the subjective goodness of getting what you want and enjoying it. Utility replaces duty; self-expression unseats authority. "Being good" becomes "feeling good." "I've always loved that thing that Mark Twain said about something moral is something you feel good after," Ted Oster remarks, "and something immoral is something you feel bad after. Which implies that you got to try everything at least once. I guess I'm pretty result-oriented, and whatever produces a good result must be right, and whatever produces a bad result must be wrong." Acts, then, are not right or wrong in themselves, but only because of the results they produce, the good feelings they engender or express.

Given this individualistic moral framework, the self becomes a crucial site for the comparative examination and probing of feelings that result from utilitarian acts and inspire expressive ones. It is to enhance the efficiency and range of such examination that Oster suggests the need to "try everything at least once." The self must be maintained as the intuitive center of the wants and impulses that define right action, and as the unimpeachable evaluator of the good or bad feelings by which the utility of our acts can be calculated and the depth of their self-expression intuited. At first glance, this picture of the self seems commonsensically obvious and problem-free. A humanistic therapist comments, "It's not so hard for people to figure out what they want. It's just they're afraid that going and getting it is going to deprive them of other things they also want. And they're not sure how to juggle everything at once. But I think people seem to by and large have an amazingly good sense somewhere in there of what makes them feel good." Individuals can easily figure out what they want, since they intuitively know, "somewhere in there," what makes them feel good. The moral problems of a predominantly utilitarian self are simply strategic or technical problems: satisfying one want may obstruct our efforts to do likewise with another, requiring us to do some juggling.

But another difficulty arises to dim the possibility of individualistic self-knowledge. How can we be sure our own feelings and wants are uncompromised by those of others and truly independent of their values? "The evaluations of others are those internalized ideas of being good, as opposed to feeling good. And they often clash," explains the therapist. "Even though I couldn't tell you what feeling good is, and some people don't ever experience it much, I think again people know when they feel good, but they may be confused about and distracted by all those other things. It's like being in love. It's so highly subjective and experienced so differently that I can't tell you what it is. But I can tell you when I feel it." Feeling good oneself now stands in opposition to "being good," seen not as some objective state of virtue, but as conformity to the evaluations of others—doing what satisfies *them* or what defers to convention. For all its unmistakable presence and intensity on occasion, the experience of feeling good, like being in love, is so highly subjective that its distinguishing characteristics remain ineffable. The touchstone of individualistic self-knowledge turns out to be shaky in the end, and its guide to action proves elusive.

Separated from family, religion, and calling as sources of authority, duty, and moral example, the self first seeks to work out its own form of action by autonomously pursuing happiness and satisfying its wants. But what are the wants of the self? By what measure or faculty does it identify its happiness? In the face of these questions, the predominant ethos of American individualism seems more than ever determined to press ahead with the task of letting go of all criteria other than radical private validation. Speaking of midlife, Gail Sheehy says:

> Let go. Let it happen to you. Let it happen to your partner. Let the feelings. Let the changes.
>
> You can't take everything with you when you leave on the midlife journey. You are moving away. Away from institutional claims and other people's agenda. Away from external valuations and accreditations, in search of an inner validation. You are moving out of roles and into the self. If I could give everyone a gift for the send-off on this journey, it would be a tent. A tent for tentativeness. The gift of portable roots.
>
> To reach the clearing beyond, we must stay with the weightless journey through uncertainty. Whatever counterfeit safety we hold from overinvestments in people and institutions must be given up. The inner custodian must be unseated from the controls. No foreign power can direct our journey from now on. It is for each of us to find a course that is valid by our own reckoning.[16]

But to what or whom do our ethical and moral standards commit us if they are "quite independent of other people's standards and agenda"? The two traditions of individualism offer us only the cost-benefit analysis of external success and the intuition of feeling inwardly more or less free, comfortable, and authentic on which to ground our self-approval. Ideas of the self's inner expansion reveal nothing of the shape moral character should take, the limits it should respect, and the community it should serve. Ideas of potentiality (for what?) tell us nothing of which tasks and purposes are worth pursuing and are blind, for example, to the differences between a job, career, and calling. Why should we do one thing rather than another, especially when we don't happen to feel like it or don't find it profitable?

It should be clear by now that "values," a term we heard constantly from almost everyone to whom we talked, are in themselves no answer. "Values" turn out to be the incomprehensible, rationally indefensible thing that the individual chooses when he or she has thrown off the last vestige of external influence and reached pure, contentless freedom. The ideal self in its absolute freedom is completely "unencumbered," to borrow a term from Michael Sandel.[17] The improvisational self chooses values to express itself; but it is not constituted by them as from a pre-existing source. This notion of an unencumbered self is derived not only from psychotherapy, but much more fundamentally from modern philosophy, from Descartes, Locke, and Hume, who affect us more than we imagine. Locke was one of the first to discuss identity in the modern sense of the term when he said, "The identity of the same man consists, viz., in nothing but a participation of the same continued life, by constantly fleeting particles of matter, in succession vitally united to the same organized body."[18]

There are a number of problems with this notion of the self that have bedevilled modern thought for a long time, and the people we talked to were at least partly conscious of them. For one thing, what guarantees the autonomy of so radically empty a self against invasion from outside? Radical empiricism starts with the autonomy of the self. But, as Locke argued, what can the self be but a succession of experiences imprinted on a "blank slate"? Psychological notions of socialization and conditioning come to the same thing. Thus Margaret, who proclaims the autonomy and final aloneness of the self, nonetheless believes that "values are shaped by the way you're brought up," the "background and experiences that you've had when you were young." The extreme of this point of view, sometimes expressed in the work of Erving Goffman, is that there is no self at all.[19] What seems to be a self is merely a series of social masks that change with each successive situation. An absolutely autonomous self and a self determined completely by the social situation do not, then, turn out to be opposites. Many of those to whom we talked can switch from one vocabulary to the other, hardly noticing the difference.

The language of "values" as commonly used is self-contradictory precisely because it is not a language of value, or moral choice. It presumes the existence of an absolutely empty unencumbered and improvisational self. It obscures personal reality, social reality, and particularly the moral reality that links person and society. We have therefore tried to use the term *value* sparingly in this book, except when quoting from our interviews.

In fact, many of those to whom we talked, including therapists, share our uneasiness about "values" and other current ways of thinking about the self. Even while affirming a self standing alone, apart from society and prior to it, some argue that there are "basic needs," perhaps rooted in biology, that everyone shares. Asked what is *worth* seeking in life, one therapist cites "ten basic things that people want and need: health, clothing, housing, food, sex, love and intimacy, work and mastery, playfulness, spiritual meaning, and security." Armed with this list, she can start to make natural law-like judgments of individual wants: "healthy" versus "neurotic" needs, "lower" versus "higher" developmental tasks. Yet such reasoning remains rooted in a nonsocial, noncultural conception of reality that provides remarkably little guidance beyond private life and intimate relations.

Another way out of the dead end of radical individualism, a way inherited from Wordsworth, Emerson, and other romantics, and presently found among some humanistic and transpersonal psychologists, is to assume that at the core of every person is a fundamental spiritual harmony that links him or her not only to every other person but to the cosmos as a whole. Here, too, external authority, cultural tradition, and social institutions are all eschewed. The self in all its pristine purity is affirmed. But somehow that self, once discovered, turns out to be at one with the universe. Romantic and psychologistic pantheism is, indeed, linked to one strand of our religious heritage, as we shall see later. But such romantic individualism is remarkably thin when it comes to any but the vaguest prescriptions about how to live in an actual society.

We want to make it clear that we are not saying that the people to whom we talked have empty selves. Most of them are serious, engaged, deeply involved in the world. But insofar as they are limited to a language of radical individual autonomy, as many of them are, they cannot think about themselves or others except as arbitrary centers of volition. They cannot express the fullness of being that is actually theirs.

The Meaning of the Life Course

Finding oneself means, among other things, finding the story or narrative in terms of which one's life makes sense. The life course and its major stages have become the subject of considerable social scientific research, and books on the life cycle have become best sellers. Periodizations of childhood intrigued Americans at least as long ago as the 1930s. Adolescence as a peculiarly significant stage of life, with its "identity crises," received widespread attention in the late 1950s and the 1960s. More recently, we have heard much of midlife crises and of the aging process. Given the ideal of a radically unencumbered and improvisational self that we have been describing in this chapter, it is perhaps not surprising that Americans should grasp at some scheme of life stages or crises to give coherence to the otherwise utterly arbitrary life patterns they seem to be asked to create.

If it is to provide any richness of meaning, the idea of a life course must be set in a larger generational, historical, and, probably, religious context. Yet much popular writing about the life course (Gail Sheehy's *Passages*, for example), as well as much of the thinking of ordinary Americans, considers the life course without reference to any social or historical context, as something that occurs to isolated individuals. In this situation, every life crisis, not just that of adolescence, is a crisis of separation and individuation, but what the ever freer and more autonomous self is free *for* only grows more obscure. Thinking about the life course in this way may exacerbate rather than resolve the problem of the meaning of the individual life.

In most societies in world history, the meaning of one's life has derived to a large degree from one's relationship to the lives of one's parents and one's children. For highly individuated Americans, there is something anomalous about the relation between parents and children, for the biologically normal dependence of children on adults is perceived as morally abnormal. We have already seen how children must leave home, find their own way religiously and ideologically, support themselves, and find their own peer group. This process leads to a considerable amnesia about what one owes to one's parents. The owner of a car-dealership whom we talked to in Massachusetts, for example, speaks of himself as a self-made man who has always done everything for himself, conveniently forgetting that his father established the business and he himself inherited it. The tendency to forget what we have received from our parents seems, moreover, to generalize to a forgetting of what we have received from the past altogether. (We have noted Jefferson's amnesia about what the colonists owed to the British.) Conversely, many Americans are uneasy about taking responsibility for children. When asked if she was responsible for her children, Margaret Oldham said hesitatingly, "I . . . I would say I have a legal responsibility for them, but in a sense I think they in turn are responsible for their acts." Frances FitzGerald found that most of the retirees in Sun City Center had quite remote relations with their children and above all dreaded any dependency on them. Tocqueville said that Americans would come to forget their ancestors and their descendants, and for many that would seem to be the case. Such inability to think positively about family continuity makes the current widespread nostalgia for "the family" all the more poignant.

Clearly, the meaning of one's life for most Americans is to become one's own person, almost to give birth to oneself. Much of this process, as we have seen, is negative. It involves breaking free from family, community, and inherited ideas. Our culture does not give us much guidance as to how to fill the contours of this autonomous, self-responsible self, but it does point to two important areas. One of these is work, the realm, par excellence, of utilitarian individualism. Traditionally men, and today women as well, are supposed to show that in the occupational world they can stand on their own two feet and be self-supporting. The other area is the lifestyle enclave, the realm, par excellence, of expressive individualism. We are supposed to be able to find a group of sympathetic people, or at least one such person, with whom we can spend our leisure time in an atmosphere of acceptance, happiness, and love.

There is no question that many Americans find this combination of work and private lifestyle satisfying. For people who have worked hard all their lives, life in a "retirement community" composed of highly similar people doing highly similar things may be gratifying. As a woman who had lived fourteen years in Sun City Center, Florida, told Frances FitzGerald, "It's the long vacation we wished we'd always had."[20]

On the other hand, a life composed mainly of work that lacks much intrinsic meaning and leisure devoted to golf and bridge does have limitations. It is hard to find in it the kind of story or narrative, as of a pilgrimage or quest, that many cultures have used to link private and public; present, past, and future; and the life of the individual to the life of society and the meaning of the cosmos.

We should not forget that the small town and the doctrinaire church, which did offer more coherent narratives, were often narrow and oppressive. Our present radical individualism is in part a justified reaction against communities and practices that were irrationally constricting. A return to the mores of fifty or a hundred years ago, even if it were possible, would not solve, but only exacerbate, our problems. Yet in our desperate effort to free ourselves from the constrictions of the past, we have jettisoned too much, forgotten a history that we cannot abandon.

Of course, not everyone in America or everyone to whom we talked believes in an unencumbered self arbitrarily choosing its "values," "entirely independent" of everyone else. We talked to Christians and Jews for whom the self makes sense in relation to a God who challenges, promises, and reassures. We even talked to some for whom the word *soul* has not been entirely displaced by the word *self.* We talked to those for whom the self apart from history and community makes no sense at all. To them, a self worth having only comes into existence through participation with others in the effort to create a just and loving society. But we found such people often on the defensive, struggling for the biblical and republican language that could express their aspirations, often expressing themselves in the very therapeutic rhetoric that they consciously reject. It is a rhetoric that educated middle-class Americans, and, through the medium of television and other mass communications, increasingly all Americans, cannot avoid. And yet even those most trapped in the language of the isolated self ("In the end you're really alone") are troubled by the nihilism they sense there and eager to find a way of overcoming the emptiness of purely arbitrary "values."

We believe that much of the thinking about the self of educated Americans, thinking that has become almost hegemonic in our universities and much of the middle class, is based on inadequate social science, impoverished philosophy, and vacuous theology. There are truths we do not see when we adopt the language of radical individualism. We find ourselves not independently of other people and institutions but through them. We never get to the bottom of our selves on our own. We discover who we are face to face and side by side with others in work, love, and learning. All of our activity goes on in relationships, groups, associations, and communities ordered by institutional structures and interpreted by cultural patterns of meaning. Our individualism is itself one such pattern. And the positive side of our individualism, our sense of the dignity, worth, and moral autonomy of the individual, is dependent in a thousand ways on a social, cultural, and institutional context that keeps us afloat even when we cannot very well describe it. There is much in our life that we do not control, that we are not even "responsible" for, that we receive as grace or face as tragedy, things Americans habitually prefer not to think about. Finally, we are not simply ends in ourselves, either as individuals or as a society. We are parts of a larger whole that we can neither forget nor imagine in our own image without paying a high price. If we are not to have a self that hangs in the void, slowly twisting in the wind, these are issues we cannot ignore.

In this chapter, we have focussed on the quintessential American task of "finding oneself." In the course of our discussion, we have seen that however much Americans extol the autonomy and self-reliance of the individual, they do not imagine that a good life can be lived alone. Those we interviewed would almost all agree that connectedness to others in work, love, and community is essential to happiness, self-esteem, and moral worth. In succeeding chapters, we will gradually widen the circle, looking first at how we relate to very significant others, the world of love and marriage.

□

Love and Marriage   4

"Finding oneself" is not something one does alone. The quest for personal growth and self-fulfillment is supposed to lead one into relationships with others, and most important among them are love and marriage. But the more love and marriage are seen as sources of rich psychic satisfactions, it would seem, the less firmly they are anchored in an objective pattern of roles and social institutions. Where spontaneous interpersonal intimacy is the ideal, as is increasingly the case, formal role expectations and obligations may be viewed negatively, as likely to inhibit such intimacy.[1] If love and marriage are seen primarily in terms of psychological gratification, they may fail to fulfill their older social function of providing people with stable, committed relationships that tie them into the larger society. As we will see in this chapter, tensions between these partially conflicting conceptions of love and marriage are endemic in our society today.

Woman's Sphere

Tocqueville strongly argued the positive social functions of love and marriage. He saw the family, along with religion and democratic political participation, as one of the three spheres that would help to moderate our individualism. The family was central to his concern with "habits of the heart," for it is there that mores are first inculcated. At times he waxes extravagant on the importance of this sphere to the success of American democracy:

> For my part, I have no hesitation in saying that although the American woman never leaves her domestic sphere and is in some respects very de-

pendent within it, nowhere does she enjoy a higher station. . . . if anyone asks me what I think the chief cause of the extraordinary prosperity and growing power of this nation, I should answer that it is due to the superiority of their women.[2]

Tocqueville sees the role of religion in America as in part dependent on its influence on women. Religion, he says, "does direct mores, and by regulating domestic life it helps to regulate the state." The rigor of American mores derives from religion, but not directly through its influence on men. In America,

> religion is often powerless to restrain men in the midst of innumerable temptations which fortune offers. It cannot moderate their eagerness to enrich themselves, which everything contributes to arouse, but it reigns supreme in the souls of the women, and it is women who shape mores. Certainly of all countries in the world America is the one in which the marriage tie is most respected and where the highest and truest conception of conjugal happiness has been conceived.[3]

Much has changed since Tocqueville's day, and we will be concerning ourselves with the changes in this chapter. Yet the conception of marriage and the family that was being worked out in the late eighteenth and early nineteenth centuries and reached a clear formulation by the 1830s, one that Tocqueville accurately grasped, is in many ways still the dominant American ideal, however subject to criticism and alternative experimentation.[4] This modern American family pattern has been called "patriarchal," but the term is inaccurate and unhelpful here. It is better applied to an earlier phase of family life, one that lasted in America from the settlement to the late eighteenth century (and in rural contexts until much later), in which the family was an economically cooperative whole, where husband, wife, and children worked side by side on the farm or in the shop for the common good of the family. The husband-father in this earlier pattern was indeed a patriarch, responsible for the peace and order of his "family government," deciding on his children's occupations and marriage choices, and controlling the property of his wife, even her wages, if she had any. The new family that was coming into being in the early nineteenth century was not egalitarian to be sure, but it was much more voluntaristic. The power of the father over the children was greatly curtailed, and children by and large made their own choices of occupation and marriage partner. Women were no longer simply subordinate. To a certain degree, they were "separate but equal" in their own sphere—"woman's sphere." This new form of family was closely related to the new commercial and incipiently industrial economy, in which men's occupations took them outside the family into the world of business, the sphere of men. The shift involved a loss of economic functions for affluent women in that they were now confined to the home economy rather than contributing directly to the family business, but it involved a rise in status. With increasing affluence, women were now literate, educated (though mainly in "female academies"), and able to participate in the voluntary associational life of society (though largely within church-affiliated associations).[5] Much of the literature directed to women in the 1830s, frequently written by clergymen, reflected the same attitudes expressed by Tocqueville in exalting "woman's sphere" as one of peace and concord, love and devotion, in contrast to the selfishness and immorality characteristic of "the world." This was the period in which the ideology of the family as a "haven in a heartless world" first came into prominence. It is still a common idea among those to whom we recently talked.

The two "spheres" that were clearly separating in the early nineteenth century are still very much in the minds of contemporary Americans, and the contrast between them is one of the most important ways in which we organize our world. The family, according to David Schneider and Raymond Smith, is a realm of "diffuse, enduring solidarity," as opposed to the anxiety, competitiveness, and achievement-orientation of the occupational realm.[6] The family is a place where one is unconditionally accepted, something almost unknown in the worlds of business and politics. Americans, aware that the family these days is often not as reliable as they might hope, nonetheless define it in terms of this contrast. The family is a place of love and happiness where you can count on the other family members. The family and all familylike relationships receive a strong positive valence relative to the public world.

Given the enormous American emphasis on independence and self-reliance that we described in the previous chapter, the survival of the family, with its strong emphasis on interdependence and acceptance, is striking. In many ways, the family represents a historically older form of life. As opposed to the new time-discipline of the world of business and industry, work in the family has continued to be task-oriented, changing in character in terms of time of day and season, responsive to individual needs and their variation, and intermixing labor and social intercourse.[7] As Nancy Cott puts it, speaking of the early nineteenth century, but in terms that still to some degree apply:

> Despite the changes in its social context adult women's work, for the most part, kept the traditional mode and location which both sexes had earlier

shared. Men who had to accept time–discipline and specialized occupations may have begun to observe differences between their own work and that of their wives. Perhaps they focused on the remaining "premodern" aspects of women's household work: it was reassuringly comprehensible, because it responded to immediate needs; it represented not strictly "work" but "life," a way of being.[8]

Morally, too, Cott points out, the family represented an older pattern: "Women's household service alone remained from the tradition of reciprocal service by family members."[9] Thus, while men's work was turning into a career or a job, women's work had the old meaning of a calling, an occupation defined essentially in terms of its contribution to the common good. It was this aspect of unselfishness and concern for others that American clergymen and our French philosopher picked up about the role of women. Contrasting it to the self-aggrandizing individualism of the men, they linked this female familial morality to Christianity and republican virtue. They saw the future of a free society dependent on the nurturing of family mores, passed on to children by mothers and exerted by wives to restrain husbands. That the cost of the moral superiority of women in modern commercial society was their own freedom and participation in the public sphere was already evident in the early nineteenth century. Tocqueville marveled that the independent, self-reliant American girl, so much more able to hold her own in public than her European counterpart, should choose to enter the lifetime commitment of marriage, which would confine her to a limited, if noble, sphere.[10] Probably women did not make the choice as easily as Tocqueville thought—"marriage trauma" was not infrequent and, if severe enough, could lead to women remaining unmarried for life.[11] Yet women did accept much of the ideology of family life and "woman's sphere." Early feminists insisted that public life take on more familial qualities at the same time that they demanded greater public participation and equal rights for women.

At the crux of family life is the relationship between a man and a woman who become husband and wife, father and mother. The love that unites the marriage partners grows into the love between parents and children. It is the characteristic virtue of love that made the family appear as the locus of a morality higher than that of the world. Indeed, the "unselfish love" of a wife and mother for her husband and children was seen as the most visible example of morality itself.

The love between a man and a woman is capable of another set of extended meanings, which has given the family an additional significance in our developing culture. Love implies not only the morality of the family as against the immorality of the business world; love implies feeling as against calculation. As the primary inhabitants of the familial sphere, women were invested with all those characteristics we noted as part of the expressive, rather than the utilitarian, orientation. The nineteenth-century way of characterizing the difference was to identify women with the heart, men with the head. Women acted out of feeling, men out of reason.[12] Nor was the contrast wholly disparaging of women, since the romantic movement exalted feeling above reason as the wellspring of genuine humanity. Women were said to have sensibility, imagination, and gaiety, whereas men were characterized by solidity, judgment, and perseverance.

However strong the contrast between these stereotypes of the sex roles, and the contrast seems to have been greater in the mid-nineteenth century than before or after, men, in one crucial respect, had to participate in what was otherwise "woman's sphere." Love was clearly a matter of the heart, not the head, and love was the essential basis of marriage for both men and women. Even in the seventeenth century, when marriages were largely arranged by parents, the couple was supposed to grow to love one another during the period of espousal and love between husband and wife was, according to Puritan theology, "a duty imposed by God on all married couples."[13] By the nineteenth century, romantic love was the culturally recognized basis for the choice of a marriage partner and in the ideal marriage was to continue for a lifetime. Perhaps it would be too much to speak of expressive *individualism* in connection with nineteenth-century marriage, even though the full set of contrast terms by which we recognize the expressive alternative to utilitarianism was used. But in the twentieth century, marriage has to some extent become separated from the encompassing context of family in that it does not necessarily imply having children in significant sectors of the middle class. Thus marriage becomes a context for expressive individualism, or a "lifestyle enclave" as we argued in the previous chapter.

To summarize the changes in the American family since the early nineteenth century, the network of kinship has narrowed and the sphere of individual decision has grown. This is truer, even today, among the middle class than among the upper and lower reaches of our population. The nuclear family is not "isolated," as some over-zealous interpreters of that metaphor have implied, but contact with relatives outside the nuclear family depends not only on geographical proximity—not to be taken for granted in our mobile society—but also on personal preference. Even relations between parents and children are matters of individual negotiation once the children have left home.

The sphere of individual decision within the family is growing. For one thing, it is no longer considered disgraceful to remain unmarried. Social pressure to marry is not absent, but it is probably weaker than ever before in American history. Most people still want to marry, but they don't feel they have to. Further, no one has to have children. Having children is a conscious decision, as is the number of children one will have. While most couples want more than one child, large families are, with a few exceptions, a thing of the past. Finally, one can leave a marriage one doesn't like. Divorce as a solution to an unhappy marriage, even a marriage with young children, is far more acceptable today than ever before.[14]

What does all this mean in terms of Tocqueville's claim that marriage and the family are defenses against individualism? The contrast between the family, where love is supposed to rule, and the world, where money rules, is, if anything, sharper today than in Tocqueville's time. And yet individualism is inside the family as well as outside it. Free choice in the family, which was already greater in Tocqueville's day than it had been before, is now characteristic of the decisions of all members of the family except the youngest children. The ideology of "woman's sphere" survives but has suffered severe criticism, particularly when it has been used to restrain women from participation in the occupational world or deny them equal rights in the marital relationship. Men and women both want to preserve "family values," but the justice of a fuller equality between the sexes is also widely recognized. How do all these changes affect the people we interviewed? How do they think about love and marriage in their own lives?

Love and the Self

Americans believe in love as the basis for enduring relationships. A 1970 survey found that 96 percent of all Americans held to the ideal of two people sharing a life and a home together. When the same question was asked in 1980, the same percentage agreed. Yet when a national sample was asked in 1978 whether "most couples getting married today expect to remain married for the rest of their lives," 60 percent said no.[15] Love and commitment, it appears, are desirable, but not easy. For, in addition to believing in love, we Americans believe in the self. Indeed, as we saw in the previous chapter, there are few criteria for action outside the self. The love that must hold us together is rooted in the vicissitudes of our subjectivity. No wonder we don't believe marriage is easy today.

Yet when things go well, love seems so natural it hardly requires explanation. A love relationship is good because it works, because it "feels right," because it is where one feels most at home. Marge and Fred Rowan have been married for twelve years and have two children. They were high school sweethearts. When asked to say how they decided to marry, Fred says "there wasn't a lot of discussion." Marge was always "the kind of girl I wanted to marry" and "somewhere along the line" he just assumed "that's where our relationship was headed." There may be reasons, both practical and romantic, for marrying the person one does, but they are almost afterthoughts. What matters is the growing sense that the relationship is natural, right. One does not so much choose as simply accept what already is. Marge, Fred's wife, describes having the sense, before she married, that Fred was the "right person." "It was, like he said, very unspoken, but absolutely that's exactly how we felt. Fred was always 'my guy.' He was just 'mine.'" They were "right on ever since high school," and even when she tried to date someone else in college, "I felt stupid about it because I knew I was in love with Fred. I didn't want to be with anybody else."

Searching for a definition of "real love" becomes pointless if one "feels good" enough about one's relationship. After all, what one is looking for is the "right place" for oneself. As Fred says, "It just felt right, and it was like being caught in the flow. That's just the way it was. It wasn't a matter of deciding, so there could be no uncertainty." A relationship of the kind Fred and Marge describe seems so natural, so spontaneous that it carries a powerful sense of inevitability. For them, their relationship embodies a deep sense of their own identity, and thus a sense that the self has found its right place in the world. Love embodies one's real self. In such a spontaneous, natural relationship, the self can be both grounded and free.

Not every couple finds the easy certainty of love that Fred and Marge convey. But most couples want a similar combination of spontaneity and solidity, freedom and intimacy. Many speak of sharing—thoughts, feelings, tasks, values, or life goals—as the greatest virtue in a relationship. Nan Pfautz, a divorced secretary in her mid-forties, describes how, after being alone for many years, she fell deeply in love. "I think it was the sharing, the real sharing of feelings. I don't think I've ever done that with another man." Nan knew that she loved Bill because "I let all my barriers down. I really was able to be myself with him—very, very comfortable. I could be as gross as I wanted or I could be as funny as I wanted, as silly as I wanted. I didn't worry about, or have to worry—or didn't anyway—about what his reaction was going to be. I was just me. I was free to be me." The natural sharing of one's real self is, then, the essence of love.

But the very sharing that promises to be the fulfillment of love can also threaten the self. The danger is that one will, in sharing too completely with another, "lose oneself." Nan struggled with this problem during her marriage, and afterward still found difficulty achieving the right balance between sharing and being separate. "Before my relationship with Bill, seven, eight years ago now, I seemed to want to hang on to people too much. It was almost as though I devoured them. I wanted them totally to be mine, and I wanted to be totally theirs, with no individuality. Melding . . . I lost all of myself that way and had nothing of *me* left."

How is it that one can "lose" oneself in love, and what are the consequences of that loss? Nan says she lost herself when she lost her "own goals." At first, her marriage was "very good. It was very give and take in those days. It really was. We went skiing the first time together, and I didn't like skiing. From then on, he went skiing on his own, and I did something I wanted to do." Thus not losing yourself has something to do with having a sense of your own interests. What can be lost are a set of independent preferences and the will to pursue them. With the birth of her son, Nan became absorbed in the mother role, and stopped asserting herself. She became "someone to walk on. Very dull and uninteresting, not enthused about anything. Oh, I was terrible. I wouldn't have wanted to be around me at all." The ironic consequence of passively adapting to others' needs is that one becomes less valuable, less interesting, less desirable. Nan's story is particularly interesting because her behavior conformed fairly well to the earlier ideology of "woman's sphere," where unselfish devotion was the ideal of wifely behavior. But giving up one's self, a subtle shift in emphasis from "unselfishness," may, in the contemporary middle class, as in Nan's case, lead to losing precisely the self that was loved—and perhaps losing one's husband.

A younger woman, Melinda Da Silva, married only a few years, has a similar way of describing her difficulties in the first years of her marriage. She acted out the role of the good wife, trying continually to please her husband. "The only way I knew to be was how my mother was a wife. You love your husband and this was the belief that I had, you do all these things for him. This is the way you show him that you love him—to be a good wife, and the fear that if you don't do all these things, you're not a good wife, and maybe you don't love your husband." Trying so hard to be a good wife, Melinda failed to put her *self* into the relationship. In trying so hard to "show Thomas that I loved him," she "was putting aside anything that I thought in trying to figure out what he thought. Everything was just all put aside." What Melinda had "put aside" was her willingness to express her own opinions and act on her own judgment, even about how best to please her husband.

Melinda sought help from a marriage counselor, and came to feel that the problem with her marriage was less her husband than the loss of her self. "That's all I thought about, was what he wanted, thinking that he would love me more if I did what he wanted. I began to realize when Thomas and I went in for counseling I wouldn't voice my opinion, and I was doing things just for him and ignoring things for myself. The very things I was doing to get his approval were causing him to view me less favorably." Thus losing a sense of who one is and what one wants can make one less attractive and less interesting. To be a person worth loving, one must assert one's individuality. Melinda could "give a lot to our marriage" only when she "felt better" about herself. Having an independent self is a necessary precondition to joining fully in a relationship.

Love, then, creates a dilemma for Americans. In some ways, love is the quintessential expression of individuality and freedom. At the same time, it offers intimacy, mutuality, and sharing. In the ideal love relationship, these two aspects of love are perfectly joined—love is both absolutely free and completely shared. Such moments of perfect harmony among free individuals are rare, however. The sharing and commitment in a love relationship can seem, for some, to swallow up the individual, making her (more often than him) lose sight of her own interests, opinions, and desires. Paradoxically, since love is supposed to be a spontaneous choice by free individuals, someone who has "lost" herself cannot really love, or cannot contribute to a real love relationship. Losing a sense of one's self may also lead to being exploited, or even abandoned, by the person one loves.

Freedom and Obligation

Americans are, then, torn between love as an expression of spontaneous inner freedom, a deeply personal, but necessarily somewhat arbitrary, choice, and the image of love as a firmly planted, permanent commitment, embodying obligations that transcend the immediate feelings or wishes of the partners in a love relationship. To trace out the inner logic of these conceptions, let us first contrast two modes of understanding love, each of which emphasizes one side of the dilemma. One approach is a traditional view of love and marriage as founded on obligation, a view we found most strongly held among certain evangelical Christians. The other is what we have called the therapeutic attitude, found among therapists and their clients, but also, at least in the middle-class mainstream, much more widely diffused.

Like the therapeutically inclined, the evangelical Christian worries about how to reconcile the spontaneous, emotional side of love with the obligations love entails. For the Christian, however, the tension is clearly resolved in favor of obligation. Describing how he counsels young singles who come to him with difficulties about relationships, Larry Beckett, a youthful evangelical minister, says: "I think most people are selfish, and when they're looking at relationships romantically, they're primarily looking at it for themselves only. And the Scriptures are diametrically opposed to that. They would say, and I would teach, that there is a love that we can have for other people that is generally selfless. We have to learn it. It's actually a matter of the will. I have to decide to go out and love people by action and by will for their own good, not because I enjoy it all the time, but because God commands it. Jesus said, 'Love your enemies.' That's one of His famous sayings. When He said that, He wasn't commanding my emotions or affections, because He can't. But He can command my will and my decision process and my actions, if I allow Him to." Love thus becomes a matter of will and action rather than of feelings. While one cannot coerce one's feelings, one can learn to obey God's commands and to love others in a selfless way. This obedience is not, however, necessarily in conflict with personal freedom. Through training and shaping the will, the Christian can come to want to do what he must do. People can "see their lives as a process of changing," in which they become "less selfish" as they accept "Christ as the standard" and "His ethic as their ethic. And they do that out of a desire to, not out of any compulsion. Their love for God becomes then the motivational source for loving other people," Larry continues. In Christian love, free choice and duty can be combined, but it is obligation that comes first. Then love of God can make one want to do what one is obligated to do.

Just as love is not simply a matter of feeling for Christians, it is also not expressed primarily in internal, emotional form, but in action. "The Scriptures say over and over, if you love in just lip service and not in action, then you're a hypocrite." For the Christian, love means putting another's interests ahead of one's own. The most important examples of love come when conflicts of interest are the most intense.

For the evangelical Christian, a crucial aspect of permanent commitment to marriage involves the relationship of feeling and will. Emotion alone is too unstable a base on which to build a permanent relationship, so Christians must subordinate or tame their feelings so that they follow the mind's guidance. Les Newman, a young businessman married only a few years, is an active member of an evangelical church, and already the father of two children. Describing his marriage, he says, "Before I thought it was all heart, all chemistry. Now I know that chemistry may be a good start, but the only thing that makes it real love that will endure, and the kind of love that is taken into marriages, is that mental decision that you're going to force that chemical reaction to keep going with each other. I think real love is something where there is that chemistry, but there is also that mental decision that there's going to be a conscious effort for two people to do what's best, instead of what's best for one individual." Emotions can be sustained, or even created, by conscious choice. Reliance on that "mental decision," in turn, guarantees a permanence or stability in relationships that would not be possible relying on feelings alone.

Howard Crossland, a scientist from a rural background and an active member of Larry Beckett's evangelical Christian church, poses the problem of reconciling feeling and obligation. Emotional and moral self-control is at the heart of Howard's theory of love. Although he feels that he and his wife, married more than a dozen years, have a good marriage, he says that without his Christian faith, he "probably would have been divorced by now." Only in the Christian faith is it "logical" to say "till death do us part." Otherwise, "if the relationship is giving you trouble, perhaps it is easier to simply dissolve the thing legally, and go your way, than it is to maybe spend five years trying to work out a problem to make a lasting relationship." The difficulty is that in any relationship there will be crises, and Christian faith allows you to "weather the storm until the calm comes back. If you can logically think through and kind of push the emotions to the back, I guess the love is always there. Sometimes it's blotted out."

Although warm, comfortable feelings of love will normally come back if one waits through difficult periods, these emotional reactions do not themselves constitute love. Love is, rather, a willingness to sacrifice oneself for others. "I have a sign hanging in my bedroom: 'Love is when another's needs are greater than your own.' I think maybe that has something to do with it. I bought it for my wife when I went on a trip one time. I felt it was appropriate." With his wife, Howard tries, where possible, to "think of ways to express my love." By this he means to do things he knows she wants, even when they are not his own preferences. These are such small matters as going out occasionally without the children, "even with a limited budget and this inflationary world." "Love" is "saying you come first, even ahead of me, where possible."

In the evangelical Christian view, then, love involves placing duty and obligation above the ebb and flow of feeling, and, in the end, finding freedom in willing sacrifice of one's own interests to others. Additional support for permanence and commitment in this view of marriage comes from an acceptance of social roles. Les Newman, the young businessman quoted earlier, stresses that marriage is a permanent bond, but one based on the fulfillment of social roles. His only expectations of marriage are that "you had that bond with another individual and you spent your lives together." But spending a lifetime together also means that one can count on one's partner. "I guess the big thing is that it's a permanent relationship between two people where they support each other all the way through life, working as a team." Les and his wife have "roles within the marriage." He is "the breadwinner and the father figure" and "the spiritual leader in the family." Susan, his wife, has "the role of the homemaker and taking care of that type of thing." Rather than being artificial, socially imposed constraints that interfere with real intimacy, roles, in this view, naturally hold people together and define their relationship. In language that would be anathema to the therapeutically inclined, the young Christian insists, "It means very much to me that a married couple is in one sense one individual, and whatever affects one, for good or bad, affects both of you. By being two of you, it just makes it that much easier to deal with the world and what's going on, and to carry out the things that you're supposed to do."

Finally, these Christians stress that, at least in modern society, there is no basis for permanent commitment in marriage apart from Christian faith itself. Larry Beckett, the evangelical minister, puts the case most strongly: the only thing that is unchangeable and can be "the foundation" of life is "the spiritual life," because "God doesn't change. Jesus Christ doesn't change." The other values on which people try to build marriage are fragile: "Whether it's career, or family, or romanticism as the center, I believe that those things are innately limited, and they are degenerative. Some time they are going to change, or get boring, or die down. If God is the center and He is unchanging, He's eternal, He is in fact our source and our maker, then by definition of who He is, He is not going to change. So what that does, it gives stability to a family. That is, the family can say, O.K., we're bored with our family life right now, but that in and of itself is not enough reason to say that I don't love you anymore. That's not enough reason to throw in the towel." Faith can tide people over when their ordinary human involvements and their changeable feelings are not enough to sustain a relationship. Les Newman, the young businessman, also insists that a marriage grounded in Christian faith is more meaningful and satisfying than one without it. "There are a lot of people who obviously have very happy marriages and get along quite well. I'd say the biggest difference would be what purpose is there, in the sense, obviously they married each other because they loved each other, but having said that, why do you get married? Why do you live the way you do? A lot of couples that I know aren't Christians are here to have a good time together and enjoy each other's company. But I guess Susan and I, our number one priority is as a pair, as a couple, to work together in the way that we think God wants us to do, and it gives direction to our lives and our relationship that I don't think other people have."

Christian love is, in the view of its practitioners, built of solider stuff than personal happiness or enjoyment. It is, first, a commitment, a form of obedience to God's word. In addition, love rests less on feeling than on decision and action. Real love may even, at times, require emotional self-denial, pushing feelings to the back in order to live up to one's commitments. Most critical in love are a firm decision about where one's obligations lie and a willingness to fulfill those obligations in action, independent of the ups and downs of one's feelings. Of course, these Christians seek some of the same qualities of sharing, communication, and intimacy in marriage that define love for most Americans. But they are determined that these are goods to be sought within a framework of binding commitments, not the reasons for adhering to a commitment. Only by having an obligation to something higher than one's own preferences or one's own fulfillment, they insist, can one achieve a permanent love relationship.

These evangelical Christians seem to be devoted to an older idea of marriage than many others to whom we talked. They are not immune to pressures for the equality of women, but they still accept a version of the traditional distinction between the sphere of men and the sphere of women. They even defend "roles" in marriage that the therapeutically inclined reject. They believe in intimacy and shared feeling in marriage, but they also believe feeling is not enough. Will and intention are also necessary. From their religious point of view, they are aware of the dangers to the family of utilitarian and expressive individualism and are concerned to resist them. Whether the limitations of their grasp on their own tradition hinder the effectiveness of their resistance, we will consider in chapter 9. But Tocqueville's linkage of religion, family, and mores seems still to some degree to apply to them.

Communicating

Most Americans long for committed, lasting love, but few are willing to accept indissoluble marriage on biblical authority alone. Rather than making a permanent choice, after which feelings of love may come and go, Americans tend to assume that feelings define love, and that permanent commitment can come only from having the proper clarity, honesty, and openness about one's feelings. At the opposite pole from evangelical Christianity, there is something we might call the therapeutic attitude, based on self-knowledge and self-realization. It emerges most fully in the ideology of many practitioners and clients of psychotherapy, but resonates much more broadly in the American middle class.

This therapeutic attitude, as we saw in chapter 3, begins with the self, rather than with a set of external obligations. The individual must find and assert his or her true self because this self is the only source of genuine relationships to other people. External obligations, whether they come from religion, parents, or social conventions, can only interfere with the capacity for love and relatedness. Only by knowing and ultimately accepting one's self can one enter into valid relationships with other people.

Asked why she went into therapy, a woman summed up the themes that recur again and again in accounts by therapists and their clients: "I was not able to form close relationships to people, I didn't like myself, I didn't love myself, I didn't love other people." In the therapeutic ideology, such incapacities are in turn related to a failure fully to accept, fully to love, one's self.

As the therapist Margaret Oldham puts it, many of the professionally trained, upper-middle-class young adults who come to her, depressed and lonely, are seeking "that big relationship in the sky—the perfect person." They want "that one person who is going to stop making them feel alone." But this search for a perfect relationship cannot succeed because it comes from a self that is not full and self-sustaining. The desire for relatedness is really a reflection of incompleteness, of one's own dependent needs.

Before one can love others, one must learn to love one's self. A therapist can teach self love by offering unconditional acceptance. As a Rogersian therapist observes, "There's nobody once you leave your parents who can just say you are O.K. with us no matter what you do." He continues, "I'm willing to be a motherer—to at least with certain parts of a personality, parts of them that they present to me, validate them." Another, more behavioristic therapist concurs, saying he works by "giving them just lots of positive reinforcement in their selves; continually pointing out things that are good about them, feeding them with it over and over again." Thus the initial ingredient in the development of a healthy, autonomous self may be love from the ideal, understanding surrogate parent-lover-friend—the therapist. Unlike that of lovers and friends, however, the purpose of the therapist's love is not to create a lasting relationship of mutual commitment, but to free people of their dependence so that ultimately they can love themselves.

Becoming a more autonomous person means learning self-acceptance. While another's love or approval may help, to be a firmly autonomous individual, one must ultimately become independent of others. To be able to enjoy the full benefits of a love relationship, one must stop needing another's love to feel complete. A California therapist in his forties says, "I think people have to feel somewhat whole, and that includes liking yourself—maybe hating yourself, parts of yourself— but accepting who you are, and feeling that you can make it in this world without a partner. If what a relationship means is that you can be dependent on someone, you can say I need you at times, but I think that unless you feel you also can do without that person, then you cannot say I need you. If you have been saying that I need you as a substitute because you do not think you can make it on your own, you are in trouble."

Therapy can help individuals become autonomous by affirming over and over again that they are worthy of acceptance as they are. But the ultimate purpose of the therapist's acceptance, the "unconditional positive regard" of post-Freudian therapy, is to teach the therapeutic client to be independent of anyone else's standards. Another therapist comments, "Ultimately I think people want to know that they're O.K., and they're looking for somebody to tell them that, but I think what's really needed is to be able to have themselves say that I, Richard, am O.K. personally. What people really need is a self-validation, and once people can admit that they're O.K., even though I have shortcomings, everybody has shortcomings, but once they can admit that, all right I've got these, but I'm really O.K., somehow, they get miraculously better." Thus the therapeutic ideal posits an individual who is able to be the source of his own standards, to love himself before he asks for love from others, and to rely on his own judgment without deferring to others. Needing others in order to feel "O.K." about oneself is a fundamental malady that therapy seeks to cure.

Discovering one's feelings allows one to get close to others. A behaviorist therapist describes how he teaches clients gradually to be more spontaneous by giving them positive feedback, telling them "there's a big difference in you now than last time. You seem more at ease; you tell me how you feel; you laugh; you smile." When they relax, he "provides praise for them and teaches them that it's O.K. to share your feelings." This ability to share feelings can then be carried over from therapy to other relationships. He continues: "That's how you get close to somebody, because you relax, you're spontaneous, you act like yourself and you open up to somebody and share those intimacies with somebody that in turn responds similarly." Thus sharing of feelings between similar, authentic, expressive selves—selves who to feel complete do not need others and do not rely on others to define their own standards or desires—becomes the basis for the therapeutic ideal of love.

Therapy not only teaches people to avoid problems in love relationships by overcoming excessive dependence or unrealistic demands on those they love. It also changes the ideal of love itself. When Melinda Da Silva feared she was "losing herself" in the early years of her marriage, she went to a marriage counselor, who taught her to assert what she wanted rather than always deferring to her husband's wishes. She came to feel that only by becoming more independent could she really love, or be loved by, her husband. For Melinda, the ideal of love changed from self-sacrifice to self-assertion. "The better I feel about myself, I feel I have a whole lot that I can contribute to Thomas, so I can value him more as opposed to idolize him. It's easier to love someone you're on a par with. You can be 'in love' with someone you idolize, but you can't 'love' someone you idolize." Thus she cannot really love unless she is enough of an independent person to make her own contribution to the relationship, rather than doing only what "I thought he wanted." Loving someone implies an active, free involvement that is incompatible with the helpless thralldom of being "in love."

This egalitarian love between therapeutically self-actualized persons is also incompatible with self-sacrifice. It must be based on the autonomous needs of two separate individuals—needs that may come into conflict. Melinda says, "Being in love one day can mean, like, being selfish. I mean, doing something just for yourself, which I never thought you can and still love." When asked to give an example, she replies, "I guess like just thinking about myself and sitting and telling Thomas. Not considering what his day was like when he comes home. Just when he comes in, saying I have to talk to him and sit him down and talk to him, which I never would have done before. There are times when I don't even think about his day, but I can still love him." In the therapeutic view, a kind of selfishness is essential to love.

Therapy also redefines the ideal love relationship. Indeed, therapy becomes in some ways the model for a good relationship, so that what truly loving spouses or partners do for each other is much akin to what therapists do for their clients. Melinda, now herself in training to be a counselor, expresses part of this therapeutic ideal of marriage. A "good relationship" requires, "first for both people to be able to be strong and weak together at different times. Our relationship, our marriage, changed as I became stronger. That allowed Thomas to be able to come home and say, 'My job was horrible today,' or 'I was really upset,' or 'I was in a situation where I got anxious again.' That allowed Thomas to be weaker, and for me to be stronger, so it felt a little more balanced." Both partners in a relationship become therapists in a reciprocal exchange, each willing to listen, to understand, to accept the other's weaknesses, and in turn ready to share their own anxieties and fears.

In its pure form, the therapeutic attitude denies all forms of obligation and commitment in relationships, replacing them only with the ideal of full, open, honest communication among self-actualized individuals. Like the classic obligation of client to therapist, the only requirement for the therapeutically liberated lover is to share his feelings fully with his partner. A divorced woman, now a social services administrator, feels uncomfortable with the word *love:* "I got married believing that I was in love, and that I was going to do everything for this person, and I did a lot. I gave up a lot, supported him financially through school, and I began to realize that I was not getting anything in return." The obligations and self-sacrifice promised by the word *love* turned out to be a false promise of security and a dangerous illusion, inducing her to give up protecting her own interests. Now she values relationships that are balanced, in which if she gives a lot, she gets a lot back. Asked what would be the worst thing in a relationship, she says: "If I felt communication was no longer possible, the relationship would be over. If I felt I could not really say what I felt. If I was not caring about how he felt about things, then it would be over. Lack of communication, I think it would be the end." In a world of independent individuals who have no necessary obligations to one another, and whose needs may or may not mesh, the central virtue of love—indeed the virtue that sometimes replaces the ideal of love—is communication.

For therapeutically liberated individuals, obligation of any kind becomes problematic in relationships. A counselor who runs a therapy group for divorced women tries to help them feel more independent. She wants them to enjoy doing things for themselves and one another and to develop confidence in their ability to live alone. Relationships are better when the partners "do not depend just on themselves or each other." When pressed to consider obligation in relationships, she answers, "I guess, if there is anyone who needs to owe anybody anything, it is honesty in letting each other know how they feel about each other, and that if feelings change, to be open and receptive, to accept those changes, knowing that people in relationship are not cement."

The therapeutic attitude liberates individuals by helping them get in touch with their own wants and interests, freed from the artificial constraints of social roles, the guilt-inducing demands of parents and other authorities, and the false promises of illusory ideals such as love. Equally important, the therapeutic attitude redefines the real self. Money, work, and social status are not central to the authentic self, which instead consists of the experience and expression of feelings. For such expressive selves, love means the full exchange of feelings between authentic selves, not enduring commitment resting on binding obligation.

Ideological Confusions

Although we have drawn a sharp contrast between the therapeutic attitude, grounded in a conception of authentic self-knowledge, and an ethic that rests on absolute and objective moral obligations, found in one form among some evangelical Christians, most Americans are, in fact, caught between ideals of obligation and freedom.

The language and some of the assumptions of the therapeutic attitude have penetrated quite deeply, at least into middle-class mainstream culture. Even Les Newman, the young Christian businessman who spoke so fervently about the need to ground marriage in larger religious truth, answers a question about what makes a relationship good by saying, "I'd say a big part of it is just being able to understand, sympathize, and empathize with each other's problems. Just to be able to talk to each other and share each other's problems, sort of counsel each other a little bit. Just helping each other deal with the world." Here the ideal of mutual help and support blends with a more therapeutic image of empathy and psychological understanding as the major goods spouses can offer each other.

Even as the therapeutic attitude spreads, however, it meets, and sometimes blends with, the countervailing aspiration of many Americans to justify enduring relationships and the obligations that would sustain such relationships. For Melinda Da Silva, for example, her enthusiastic embrace of the therapeutic ideal of love is embedded in a larger sense that a marriage should last. The richer, more equal communication she and her husband worked to develop in marriage counseling was a way of sticking with her marriage rather than running away at the first sign of difficulties. "When I married him, I said that he was the person, not that I have to spend forever and ever with, but at least I'm going to make some kind of social commitment, and say I'm going to try to work things out with this person, have a family with him, and be a family with him. If we hadn't been married, I don't know that I would have gone through counseling, marriage counseling, or couple counseling." Here reasons for commitment that go beyond the terms of the therapeutic ethic are provided by the traditional social form of marriage, her sense of being a "family" with her husband, and a pride in sticking by commitments she has made. Therapy taught Melinda to "be selfish" as a way of loving, but it also gave her a way of working through the first hard times in her marriage. Yet she still has difficulty justifying her willingness to work for an enduring marriage. She gives credit to a childhood in which "family was an important value," but she hesitates to say that that value is objectively important, that it could apply to everyone. When asked whether people should stay married to the same person their whole lives she says, "Not everyone . . . I don't know how you could stop people wanting to change. I think that a lot of things that happen in divorce are that these changes occur. You're not 'in love' anymore, and being 'in love' seems so important to everyone. When they get to a point where they're not 'in love,' they don't know what else there is, so the easiest thing is to leave that and find another 'in love.'" The search for one "in love" after another strikes Melinda as unrealistic or immature. but her choice to look for more in marriage comes down fundamentally to a matter of personal preference, based on her own idiosyncratic background. The therapeutic attitude provides her with a way of deepening the bond in her own marriage, even while validating a view of the world in which people change, relationships easily end, and the self is ultimately alone.

Despite its rejection of relationships based on socially grounded obligations, the therapeutic attitude can enrich the language through which people understand their connections to others. Those influenced by the therapeutic attitude often express extreme ambivalence about ideals of obligations and self-sacrifice, particularly when they consider their own parents' marriages. They long for the unquestioning commitment their parents seemed to have, yet they are repelled by what they take to be the lack of communication, the repression of difficulties, and, indeed, the resigned fatalism such commitment seems to imply. These respondents both envy their parents and vow never to be like them.

What sometimes replaces the social obligations of marriage is a sense that relationships can be based not only on individuals maximizing their own interests and being true to their authentic feelings, but on a shared history in which two people are bound together in part by what they have been through together. Describing her sense of how her parents "love each other very much, in their sense of the word," even though they are not "in love," Melinda Da Silva says, "I never understood until the past year, after Thomas and I had gone through counseling and everything. We shared experiences together. It's different than being in love. It's real different—because we have shared things together, time and experiences, all that." For Melinda and others like her, the therapeutic attitude, with its rich description of the selves who love and the authentic feelings such selves can share, can give texture to a sense of shared history, even if it is a history of private struggles over feelings, disconnected from any larger community of memory or meaning.

The therapeutic attitude reinforces the traditional individualism of American culture, including the concept of utilitarian individuals maximizing their own interests, but stresses the concept of expressive individuals maximizing their experience of inner psychic goods. Melinda was able to blend the commitments arising from her upbringing in a large, loving traditional family with the therapeutic stress on self-assertion and communication to become a fuller participant in her own marriage. But even Ted Oster, the success-oriented young lawyer we met briefly in chapter 3, uses aspects of the expressive individualist culture to go beyond his primarily utilitarian view of the world. It was Ted Oster who referred to life as "a big pinball game" in which in order to "enjoy it" you have to "move and adjust yourself to situations," and "to realize that most things are not absolute." He has left his family's conventional Protestantism behind, and he claims few loyalties to any ideal or standard of conduct beyond his own happiness, but this psychologically oriented pragmatist, married more than ten years, feels that he is married to the "special person" who is right for him. He acknowledges that, rationally speaking, "you see a lot of people successfully married," and "that many coincidences couldn't happen all the time." But the romantic in him insists that even if there is "more than one special person" or "quite a few people with whom you could be equally happy in a different way, you've got to find somebody from that group."

Like Melinda Da Silva, Ted Oster feels that communication and the sharing of feelings are at the heart of a good marriage. And relationships require work. "You can't have something as good as a love relationship without putting a lot of effort into it. It's a wonderful thing, but it's not going to keep going by itself just because it's wonderful. That person is not forever just because you found that special person." Unlike Melinda, however, Ted Oster does not cite his family upbringing or the public commitment of marriage in describing why he wants a lasting relationship. In his utilitarian individualist vocabulary, the fundamental reason is that he has found the best possible partner, the one who will bring him the most happiness. He is unsure whether he has any obligation to his marriage or stays married only because he continues to prefer his wife to the available alternatives. Even when asked explicitly about obligation, he rapidly returns to what works: "I think there is an element, a small element of obligation. But I think mostly it's just, you know, this person is really good. It's worked so well up to now, and it continues to do that because you expect it to, and it does, by and large." It would be "wrong" to break up his marriage only in the sense, first, that he would feel "a sense of failure at making the relationship work, because I know you have to work at it," and, second, because it would be wrong for their children "not to be able to grow up in a family." Yet despite his utilitarian language, Ted Oster deeply values an enduring marriage. When pushed, he is finally able to say why in terms that go beyond both the romantic idea that his wife Debby is "special" and pragmatic concerns about the unpleasantness of divorce. Here he relies heavily on the idea of a shared history. When he is asked why one should not go from one relationship to another if one is tired of one's spouse or finds someone else more exciting, he begins, once again, with a statement of his preferences, but moves rapidly to a discussion of the virtues of sharing: "It [shifting relationships] is just not something that interests me. I have seen us get from a good relationship in terms of sharing with each other and so on to one that's much, much deeper. I mean, we still have our hard times and good times, but it's a deeper, deeper relationship." This "deeper" sharing in turn suggests the value of a shared life, a sense of historical continuity, a community of memory. Ted continues, "You can't develop a deeper relationship over a brief period of time, and also I think it is probably harder to develop with somebody new at this stage in your life. Your having grown through the twenties with someone is good. Having first children and doing all those things, you could never do it again with somebody else." He concludes by moving from the notion that life is more enjoyable when shared with one person to the idea that only a shared history makes life meaningful. "I get satisfaction in growth with Debby in proceeding through all these stages of life together. That's what makes it all really fun. It makes life meaningful and gives me the opportunity to share with somebody, have an anchor, if you will, and understand where I am. That, for me, is a real relationship."

Here the ideal of sharing, derived in part from therapy that produces a "deeper relationship," goes at least part way toward filling the gap in Ted Oster's predominantly utilitarian moral language. At times, he seems to claim only that a lasting marriage is good for him because it is what he personally finds most satisfying, but he also develops a distinctive life-course argument, finally involving a larger sense of the purpose and direction of life, to explain why the value of a lifelong marriage transcends even the virtues of the "special person" he has married. Thus Ted Oster resourcefully finds ways to describe why for him a lasting relationship is, in fact, a good way to live, good not only in the pragmatic sense that it pleases him, but good in the sense that it is virtuous, given the nature of human beings and of a fulfilling life. Yet all these arguments continually threaten to collapse into the claim that for him, because of his own background or the peculiarities of his own psyche, this way of life is simply more enjoyable. His therapeutic ethic provides a partial way of describing why his bond to his wife transcends immediate self-interest. But he has difficulty, without a widely shared language of obligation and commitment, justifying his sense that a lasting relationship is more than a matter of personal preference.

We may now return briefly to Marge and Fred Rowan, the high school sweethearts, now married many years, whom we met early in this chapter. They illustrate both the strengths and the confusions that result from the blending of a therapeutic world view with an ethic of commitment or obligation.

Marge and Fred see themselves as a traditional couple for whom marriage and family are the center of life, in Marge's words "home-body as opposed to jet-setter" types, whose love relationship is "just a way of living, just what we are." Unlike many participants in the therapeutic culture, they do not insist on putting self first, and indeed relish a kind of old-fashioned absorption in home and family. Marge says, "I think our relationship has always been the base of just about everything I do. Sometimes I almost feel guilty if I'm out on my own too much." But the Rowans did go through active induction into the therapeutic culture through Marge's and then Fred's participation in *est* (Erhard Seminars Training). Marge, in particular, had to "find out that one little thing— that I'm O.K.," in order to assert herself more fully in her marriage and in the wider world. She echoes Melinda Da Silva's conviction that affirming herself made her a fuller participant in her own marriage. Both Marge and Fred stress the depth of communication their experience of the *est* program brought to their marriage. Fred describes the new sense of security he felt after he and Marge had worked through major problems in their marriage: "It felt safer to be here. I felt more secure in the relationship. I felt like there was more support here for me as a person."

The Rowans, like the Da Silvas and the Osters, have found a way to integrate a therapeutic understanding of self and relationship (the conviction that one must know that he or she is "O.K." before one can fully enter a relationship with another) with quite traditional views of love and marriage. For the Rowans, self-discovery went hand in hand with renewed commitment to their relationship. Therapeutic language affirmed the "rightness" they had felt about each other since high school. Yet even for this stable, committed couple, therapeutic language with its stress on openness, self-development, and change, undermines a larger language of commitment. Fred stresses the excitement that their involvement in the human potential movement brought to their marriage. "I want our relationship to keep changing. I don't want it to stay exactly the way it is. Even at moments when I am just overcome with how great our relationship is, I don't even want it to stay that way. I want it to be different. I don't want it to be stagnant or boring." Marge and Fred expect their "relationship to go on forever." But they now reject any language in which permanence could be grounded in something larger than the satisfactions provided by the relationship itself. Discussing the possibility that the changes he finds so exciting might be dangerous to their relationship, Fred says, "Intellectually I think I can justify that they might be dangerous, but I feel pretty secure about our relationship, and if one of those changes happens to be something that ends our relationship, then that's probably the way the relationship was headed anyhow. If that happens it's because our relationship didn't have what it takes or took." Marge continues his thought: "Or not that it didn't have what it takes or took, but it's just what the relationship led to."

For the Rowans, as for many others, adoption of the therapeutic language leads to a paradox. They turned to the human potential movement as a way of revitalizing their marriage and working through problems. They became more committed to the marriage by doing what Americans have classically done—each, as an individual, making a fuller, freer choice of the other based on a truer, more authentic sense of self. Both Fred and Marge had to find out that they were "O.K." as individuals precisely so that they could make a genuine commitment to their relationship—because, for them, as for most Americans, the only real social bonds are those based on the free choices of authentic selves.

For the classic utilitarian individualist, the only valid contract is one based on negotiation between individuals acting in their own self-interest. For the expressive individualist, a relationship is created by full sharing of authentic feelings. But both in hard bargaining over a contract and in the spontaneous sharing of therapeutically sophisticated lovers, the principle is in basic ways the same. No binding obligations and no wider social understanding justify a relationship. It exists only as the expression of the choices of the free selves who make it up. And should it no longer meet their needs, it must end.

Love and Individualism

How Americans think about love is central to the ways we define the meaning of our own lives in relation to the wider society. For most of us, the bond to spouse and children is our most fundamental social tie. The habits and modes of thought that govern intimate relationships are thus one of the central places where we may come to understand the cultural legacy with which we face the challenges of contemporary social life. Yet in spite of its great importance, love is also, increasingly, a source of insecurity, confusion, and uncertainty.[16] The problems we have in thinking about love are an embodiment of the difficulty we have thinking about social attachment in general.

A deeply ingrained individualism lies behind much contemporary understanding of love. The idea that people must take responsibility for deciding what they want and finding relationships that will meet their needs is widespread. In this sometimes somber utilitarianism, individuals may want lasting relationships, but such relationships are possible only so long as they meet the needs of the two people involved. All individuals can do is be clear about their own needs and avoid neurotic demands for such unrealizable goods as a lover who will give and ask nothing in return.

Such a utilitarian attitude seems plausible for those in the throes of divorce or for single people trying to negotiate a world of short-term relationships. It is one solution to the difficulties of self-preservation in a world where broader expectations may lead to disappointment or make one vulnerable to exploitation. Then love becomes no more than an exchange, with no binding rules except the obligation of full and open communication. A relationship should give each partner what he or she needs while it lasts, and if the relationship ends, at least both partners will have received a reasonable return on their investment.

While utilitarian individualism plays a part in the therapeutic attitude, the full significance of the therapeutic view of the world lies in its expressive individualism, an expanded view of the nature and possibilities of the self. Love then becomes the mutual exploration of infinitely rich, complex, and exciting selves. Many of our respondents stress that their own relationships are much better than their parents' marriages were. They insist on greater intimacy, sharing of feelings, and willingness to "work through" problems than their parents found possible.

It is true that the evangelical Christians we interviewed and others who maintain continuity with a religious tradition—liberal Protestant, Catholic, and Jewish traditions as well—find relationships deepened by being part of a wider set of purposes and meanings the partners share. Les Newman and Howard Crossland say that their marriages are strong because they share commitment to the religious beliefs of their respective churches with their wives.

Accepting religious authority as a way of resolving the uncertainties and dilemmas of personal life was relatively unusual among those to whom we talked, as was the extreme version of the therapeutic attitude that puts self-realization ahead of attachment to others. But in the middle-class members of America's mainstream, we found therapeutic language very prevalent, even among those who also retain attachment to other modes of thinking about and experiencing the world. Therapeutic understandings fit many aspects of traditional American individualism, particularly the assumption that social bonds can be firm only if they rest on the free, self-interested choices of individuals. Thus even Americans who do not share the quest for self-actualization find the idea of loving in spite of, not because of, social constraints very appealing.

On the whole, even the most secure, happily married of our respondents had difficulty when they sought a language in which to articulate their reasons for commitments that went beyond the self. These confusions were particularly clear when they discussed problems of sacrifice and obligation. While they wanted to maintain enduring relationships, they resisted the notion that such relationships might involve obligations that went beyond the wishes of the partners. Instead, they insisted on the "obligation" to communicate one's wishes and feelings honestly and to attempt to deal with problems in the relationship. They had few ideas of the substantive obligations partners in a relationship might develop. Ted Oster began to hint at some of these when he discussed how having lived your life with someone, having a shared history, bound you to her in ways that went beyond the feelings of the moment. He seemed to reach for the idea that the interests, and indeed the selves of the partners, are no longer fully separable in a long-lasting relationship, but his utilitarian individualist language kept pulling him back. In the end, he oscillated between the idea that it might in some larger sense be wrong to leave his marriage and the simple idea that he and Debby would stay together because they were well suited to each other.

Similarly, while the evangelical Christians welcomed the idea of sacrifice as an expression of Christian love, many others were uncomfortable with the idea. It was not that they were unwilling to make compromises or sacrifices for their spouses, but they were troubled by the ideal of self-denial the term "sacrifice" implied. If you really wanted to do something for the person you loved, they said, it would not be a sacrifice. Since the only measure of the good is what is good for the self, something that is really a burden to the self cannot be part of love. Rather, if one is in touch with one's true feelings, one will do something for one's beloved only if one really wants to, and then, by definition, it cannot be a sacrifice. Without a wider set of cultural traditions, then, it was hard for people to find a way to say why genuine attachment to others might require the risk of hurt, loss, or sacrifice. They clung to an optimistic view in which love might require hard work, but could never create real costs to the self. They tended instead to believe that therapeutic work on the self could turn what some might regard as sacrifices into freely chosen benefits. What proved most elusive to our respondents, and what remains most poignantly difficult in the wider American culture, are ways of understanding the world that could overcome the sharp distinction between self and other.

Marriage and Mores

We have seen that marriage and the family continue to be important for Americans—in some ways, more important than ever. We have seen that the satisfactions of marriage and family life have been increasing, though as institutions they are more fragile and difficult to maintain than ever. We would argue that the family is not so much "fading," as some have said, as changing.

Marriage and the family, while still desirable, are now in several ways optional. The authors of *The Inner American* report as the most dramatic of their findings the change between 1957 and 1976 in "increased tolerance of people who reject marriage as a way of life." Whereas the majority of Americans believed it was "sick," "neurotic," or "immoral" to remain unmarried thirty years ago, by the late seventies only a third disapproved and 15 percent thought it was preferable, while a majority felt it was up to the individual.[17] That getting married, having children, and staying married are now matters of choice, rather than things taken for granted, creates a new atmosphere for marriage and a new meaning for family life. In this more tolerant atmosphere, alternate forms of committed relationship long denied any legitimacy, such as those between persons of the same sex, are becoming widely accepted. To the extent that this new atmosphere creates more sensitive, more open, more intense, more loving relationships, as it seems to have done, it is an achievement of which Americans can justly be proud.[18] To the extent that the new atmosphere renders those same relationships fragile and vulnerable, it threatens to undermine those very achievements.

All of this means that marriage and the family may be found wanting when it comes to providing "diffuse, enduring solidarity" and "unconditional acceptance." From Tocqueville's point of view, the family today is probably less able to tie individuals securely into a sustaining social order than it was in his day, though our family in many ways simply displays a further stage of the tendency he observed for "natural feeling" to increase as deference and formality declined.[19]

It is also more difficult today for the wife and mother to be the moral exemplar that Tocqueville so admired in American women. All studies agree that women are less satisfied with family life than men.[20] Women have entered the work force in increasing numbers, so that now the majority of married women and mothers work. This they do partly to express their feelings of self-worth and desire for public involvement, partly because today many families would not survive without two incomes, and partly because they are not at all sure their marriages will last. The day of the husband as permanent meal-ticket is over, a fact most women recognize, however they feel about "women's liberation." Yet women's work is largely low-status work and the differential between men's pay and women's pay is large, though women are increasingly breaking into formerly male occupations. On top of demeaning work and low pay, working wives and mothers come home to families where the men still expect them to do the preponderance of housework and child care. There have been considerable changes in expectation in this area but not much change in actual behavior. When women are more disgruntled with marriage than men, there is good reason. If women do more than their share of caring for others, it may not be because they enjoy it, but because custom and power within the family make them have to. We should not rule out the possibility that women have developed sex-specific moral sensitivities that have much to contribute to society. Carol Gilligan and Sara Ruddick, among others, argue as much.[21] But women today have begun to question whether altruism should be their exclusive domain.

One resolution would be to see that the obligations traditionally associated with "woman's sphere" are human obligations that men and women should share. There is anxiety, not without foundation, among some of the opponents of feminism, that the equality of women could result in complete loss of the human qualities long associated with "woman's sphere." The present ideology of American individualism has difficulty, as we have seen, justifying why men and women should be giving to one another at all. Traditionally, women have thought more in terms of relationships than in terms of isolated individuals. Now we are all supposed to be conscious primarily of our assertive selves. To reappropriate a language in which we could all, men and women, see that dependence and independence are deeply related, and that we can be independent persons without denying that we need one another, is a task that has only begun.

What would probably perplex and disturb Tocqueville most today is the fact that the family is no longer an integral part of a larger moral ecology tying the individual to community, church, and nation. The family is the core of the private sphere, whose aim is not to link individuals to the public world but to avoid it as far as possible. In our commercial culture, consumerism, with its temptations, and television, with its examples, augment that tendency. Americans are seldom as selfish as the therapeutic culture urges them to be. But often the limit of their serious altruism is the family circle. Thus the tendency of our individualism to dispose "each citizen to isolate himself from the mass of his fellows and withdraw into the circle of family and friends," that so worried Tocqueville, indeed seems to be coming true. "Taking care of one's own" is an admirable motive. But when it combines with suspicion of, and withdrawal from, the public world, it is one of the conditions of the despotism Tocqueville feared.

□

Reaching Out   5

In moving from love and marriage to the way Americans relate to one another in face-to-face situations generally, we find many of the same problems encountered in the preceding chapter. When Americans have difficulty operating within traditional forms of interpersonal relationship, as with marriage, they turn more and more to therapy. This chapter deals with the significance of therapy as a general outlook on life that has spread over the past few decades from a relatively small, educated elite to the middle-class mainstream of American life.[1] We are interested in therapy as a cultural phenomenon rather than as a clinical technique—as a way of thinking rather than as a way of curing psychic disorder.

Today we are likely to see not only our marriages but also our families, work, community, and society in therapeutic terms. Life's joys and deeper meanings, and its difficulties too, are less often attributed to material conditions and interpreted in traditional moral terms than they were even a generation ago. Now the "interpersonal" seems to be the key to much of life. To understand the rise of the therapeutic as a major mode of thinking about the self and society is one of the purposes of this book. But we will understand the therapeutic mode better if we start with a review of some of the more traditional ways of relating to other people and of the conditions that gave rise to therapy in the first place.

Traditional Relationships

Kinship is an important mode of relationship in all societies and certainly in our own. In simple societies, however, kinship predominates over all other ways of relating. In more complex societies that remain traditional, kinship may provide a rich vocabulary of relationship that can be extended fictively to people who are not related. In such societies, it would not be rude for a young person to address an unrelated older person as "uncle," or "aunt," "grandfather," or "grandmother." Even in a brief encounter, such kinship terminology establishes a pattern of expected interaction. In our society, especially in the broad middle class, extended kinship is not a central mode of interaction. Yet even with us, some fictive kinship terminology continues to be important, as when Joe Gorman refers to Suffolk as a "family."

The virtue of kinship relations, and under some circumstances their liability, is that they are independent of the individual's will and can to a considerable extent be taken for granted. They provide both a support and a constraint to individuals. In our individualistic society, we are ambivalent about kinship. We tend to value family highly as one of the few contexts within which one can count on others nearly unconditionally. (As Robert Frost said, "Home is the place where, when you have to go there, / They have to take you in.")[2] Yet we are wary of the restraints on our individual decision making that kinship involvements imply. Thus we tend to choose those we especially cultivate even among blood relations. Undoubtedly, kinship and the fictive language of kinship were more important in colonial America than they are today in providing a basic pattern for our relationships, but ours never was a predominantly kinship-oriented society. In particular, lineage, in the sense of inherited status, was never decisive here. Efforts to import an English pattern of nobility always failed on American soil. Concomitantly, Americans were never, in the European sense, peasants, but rather farmers—that is, independent small-holders. Being a tenant was always viewed as a temporary condition, not the basis of a hereditary dependency.

Beyond kinship, religious commitment could provide another basis of social solidarity. In "A Model of Christian Charity," John Winthrop pointed out how membership in the body of Christ could provide a model of community that would knit individuals together in mutual support in the new world. Kinship provided important imagery for the conception of the religious community. The people were "children" of "God the Father" and "brothers and sisters in Christ." Yet Christian community was based on a universal obligation of love and concern for others that could be generalized beyond, and even take precedence over, actual kinship obligations. As we will see in chapter 9, religion continues to provide an important matrix of social relationship in America as well as symbolic resources for thinking about the society as a whole and its place in the world. Yet religion is undoubtedly less central in providing the basic pattern for our relating than it was earlier in our history.

The civic tradition also has provided important resources for thinking about human relationships in the United States. The very status of citizen provides a concept of rights and duties, of mutual respect and obligation, that in a variety of contexts has been decisive for how Americans relate to one another. As we will see in chapters 7 and 8, Americans still spend a good deal of effort in "getting involved" in civic associations and citizen groups. They value the associations and friendships that flow from these activities, but they do not understand the moral meaning that was once given to such relationships very well today.

The conception of friendship put forward by Aristotle, elaborated by Cicero, and understood for centuries in the context of the Christian conception of personhood,[3] was well known to Americans in colonial and early republican times. Since contemporary ideas of friendship are heavily influenced by the therapeutic attitude, it is worth remembering that the traditional idea of friendship had three essential components. Friends must enjoy one another's company, they must be useful to one another, and they must share a common commitment to the good. Today we tend to define friendship most in terms of the first component: friends are those we take pleasure in being with. To us the issue of usefulness seems slightly out of place in a relationship that should above all be free and spontaneous, though we are quite aware of the importance of being "friendly" to those who are potentially useful to us. What we least understand is the third component, shared commitment to the good, which seems to us quite extraneous to the idea of friendship. In a culture dominated by expressive and utilitarian individualism, it is easy for us to understand the components of pleasure and usefulness, but we have difficulty seeing the point of considering friendship in terms of common moral commitments. For Aristotle and his successors, it was precisely the moral component of friendship that made it the indispensable basis of a good society. For it is one of the main duties of friends to help one another to be better persons: one must hold up a standard for one's friend and be able to count on a true friend to do likewise. Traditionally, the opposite of a friend is a flatterer, who tells one what one wants to hear and fails to tell one the truth. This profound notion of friendship in which one loves one's friend but, first of all, the good in one's friend, includes the notion of conjugal friendship as well. The "unconditional acceptance" that was supposed to go with true love and friendship did not mean the abandonment of moral standards, even in the most intimate relationship. One has a duty to forgive, and indeed forgiveness, especially in a Christian context, is the very mark of true love and friendship. But to forgive is not to excuse. Forgiveness and the struggle better to exemplify the good go hand in hand.

Traditionally, it was the virtues indelibly associated with friendship that were central to the "habits of the heart." It is also part of the traditional view that friendship and its virtues are not merely private: they are public, even political, for a civic order, a "city," is above all a network of friends. Without civic friendship, a city will degenerate into a struggle of contending interest groups unmediated by any public solidarity.

The classical idea of friendship made sense more readily in the small face-to-face communities that characterized early American society than it does to us. In such small communities, it was obvious that people not only helped one another and enjoyed one another's company but also participated mutually in enterprises that furthered the common good. For them the idea of friendship in the classical sense was intelligible, even though its realization was never easy.

Friendships were by no means confined to local communities in early American society. Particularly where a common cause united them, people of quite different backgrounds could become friends. The revolutionary struggle against Britain and the founding of the new nation brought together men from all the colonies and produced some remarkable friendships, in spite of tensions, hostilities, and rivalries. Perhaps the classic example is the friendship of John Adams and Thomas Jefferson, chronicled in the extraordinary series of letters that passed between them during their lifetimes. Frequent in the 1780s, the letters tapered off in the 1790s when the two took opposite sides in the republic's emerging party struggle. They ceased altogether after the bitter election of 1800, when Jefferson defeated Adams's bid for a second term. But as a result of a reconciliation arranged by friends, the letters resumed in 1812 and continued with increasing richness almost up to the day on which they both died, July 4, 1826, the fiftieth anniversary of the new nation. Their reconciliation after a period of bitter estrangement illustrates their capacity to put their common concern for the public good ahead of their partisan disagreements. Jefferson expressed the basis of their friendship in a letter he wrote Adams in 1820, when they were both old men: "We have, willingly, done injury to no man; and have done for our country the good which has fallen in our way, so far as commensurate with the faculties given us. . . . In the mean time be our last as cordial as were our first affections."[4]

American Nervousness

By the 1830s, Tocqueville noticed certain features of American life that endangered traditional relationships, whether of kinship, religion, or civic friendship. He wrote: "Democracy does not create strong attachments between man and man, but it does put their ordinary relations on an easier footing." Tocqueville's argument was that in older societies, one knew where one stood relative to others because of the existence of a network of established statuses and roles, each of which implied an appropriate form of attachment. In the mobile and egalitarian society of the United States, people could meet more easily and their intercourse was more open, but the ties between them were more likely to be casual and transient. A further reason for the casualness and transience had to do with what Tocqueville calls the American's "restlessness in the midst of prosperity." "In America," he says, "I have seen the freest and best educated of men in circumstances the happiest to be found in the world; yet it seemed to me that a cloud habitually hung on their brow, and they seemed serious and almost sad even in their pleasures," because they "never stop thinking of the good things they have not got." This restlessness and sadness in pursuit of the good life is intensified, says Tocqueville, by "the competition of all," which in the United States replaces the aristocratic privilege of some. So the efforts and enjoyments of Americans are livelier than in traditional societies, but the disappointments of their hopes and desires are keener, and their "minds are more anxious and on edge." How could such restless, competitive, and anxious people sustain enduring relationships, when "they clutch everything and hold nothing fast"?[5.]

What Tocqueville noticed among the more educated urban Americans of his day came to widespread public attention in the final decades of the nineteenth century. George M. Beard's *American Nervousness* (1881) popularized the term "neurasthenia," a generalized malaise that seemed to be affecting large numbers of "civilized, refined, and educated" Americans at that time. While Beard and others blamed the new national disease on such heterogeneous phenomena as railway travel and the telegraph, overwork and more specialized occupations, rapid turnover of ideas, and so forth, they tended to sum up its causes under the phrase "modern civilization." Nervous exhaustion is "developed, fostered, and perpetuated with the progress of civilization, with the advance of culture and refinement, and . . . it is oftener met with in cities than in the country, is more marked and more frequent at the desk, the pulpit, and in the counting room than in the shop or on the farm."[6] Thus Beard was as much taking pride in this modern affliction that affected only the "most evolutionarily advanced" as he was deploring its causes.

Whatever its medical basis, the crippling effects of "neurasthenia" were amply documented in the biographies of prominent Americans in the period from 1880 to 1920. One thinks of Henry Adams, Charles Ives, William James, Jane Addams, Eugene Debs, and Woodrow Wilson among scores of others. In the social background of this first massive awakening of the concern of Americans for their mental health, we can make out a key change in the nature of interpersonal relationships. Beard himself points to "the liberty allowed, and the stimulus given, to Americans to rise out of the position in which they were born, whatever that may be, and to aspire to the highest possibilities of fortune and glory" as a force in producing American nervousness, along with the fact that "in all classes there is a constant friction and unrest—a painful striving to see who shall be highest."[7]

Indeed, the period preoccupied with "American nervousness" was also the period in which a national market was depriving the small towns and regional cities of their effective independence and throwing increasing numbers of Americans into a national occupational world based on education, mobility, and the ability to compete. This was the world in which individualism was coming more and more into its own, with ever weaker restraints from the older biblical and republican traditions. What this great social transformation meant for individuals was that they faced challenges and uncertainties for which they were not prepared. Less than ever could they count on relating to others simply on the traditional grounds of kinship, local community, or inherited status. In the new, mobile middle-class world, one autonomous individual had to deal with other autonomous individuals in situations where one's self-esteem and prospects depended on one's ability to impress and negotiate. Social interactions under these conditions were often intense, but also limited and transient. "Friendliness" became almost compulsory as a means of assuaging the difficulties of these interactions, while friendship in the classical sense became more and more difficult. People could be, and indeed had to be, useful to one another. They could also enjoy one another's company. But the concept of a common good that the relationship served became ever harder to specify in a world where individuals mainly sought their own private good or the good of the organizations that employed them. Women, too, became subject to "modern nervousness" as they entered the occupational world, however tentatively, and as they worried anxiously about the competitive success of their husbands and children.

The new world of intense, but limited, relationships that required a great deal of effort to establish and maintain and the decline of more traditional supportive relationships that could simply be taken for granted put an enormous strain on the individual and were among the main causes of the nervousness that so frequently afflicted middle-class Americans before and after the turn of the century. It is in this context that we should interpret the emergence of the therapeutic culture and therapeutic relationships that became ever more important in the twentieth century. Such therapy was probably more a support for those placed under unprecedented psychic demands than a cure for new mental ills.

Another way to view the transition we are describing is to see it as involving the emergence of the modern middle class. It is worth pondering the fact that the term "middle class" only emerged in the last decades of the nineteenth century, bearing a new cultural and social meaning. In the eighteenth century, the common expressions were "middling condition," "middling interest," and "middling rank." This middling condition was essentially the mean between wealth and poverty, a condition of equilibrium. Americans of the eighteenth century were aware that the predominance of those of middling condition here and the lack of a real aristocracy and impoverished masses were facts of great consequence for our society. They reasoned much as Aristotle would have: namely that those of middling condition would be most apt as independent citizens to support republican institutions and to oppose both monarchy and despotism.

But the nineteenth-century idea of a "middle class" was no longer one of moderation, equilibrium, and a mean between the extremes of wealth and poverty. The middle class was perceived as composed of people on the rise who were "calculating" and "ambitious." It and the society it more and more defined were seen as rising indefinitely to new levels of affluence and progress. From the point of view of this new middle class, upper and lower classes fixed in some kind of equilibrium were illegitimate and, at best, temporary. The middle-class concept of an all-encompassing process of escalation that will eventually include everyone gives us our central, and largely unchallenged, image of American society.[8]

What the new idea of a middle class meant for individuals was summed up in another new term that only gained currency in the middle and later nineteenth century: *career*, in the sense of "a course of professional life or employment, that offers advancement or honor." *Profession* is an old word, but it took on new meanings when it was disconnected from the idea of a "calling" and came to express the new conception of a career. In the context of a calling, to enter a profession meant to take up a definite function in a community and to operate within the civic and civil order of that community. The profession as career was no longer oriented to any face-to-face community but to impersonal standards of excellence, operating in the context of a national occupational system. Rather than embedding one in a community, following a profession came to mean, quite literally, "to move *up* and away." The goal was no longer the fulfillment of a commonly understood form of life but the attainment of "success," and success depended for its very persuasive power on its indefiniteness, its open-endedness, the fact that whatever "success" one had obtained, one could always obtain more.[9]

As nineteenth-century Americans came increasingly to see, life on the escalator was anything but easy. Just when he could count on fewer and fewer people for "unconditional acceptance," the individual had to be self-disciplined, competitive, ambitious, able to respond to rapidly changing situations and demands, able to leave home to go to school and follow the opportunities of professional advancement. It was under these conditions that a concern for mental health became a central American preoccupation and a wide variety of therapeutic nostrums appeared.

If Americans were discovering that they were, in George Beard's words, "the most nervous people in all history," they were not yet ready to give up older forms of moral exhortation as an answer, though the exhortations took an increasingly scientific and psychological tone. William James believed that habit and will power, properly cultivated, could take care of most of our problems. In the muscular mood of his day, James wrote, "There is no more contemptible type of human character than that of the nervous sentimentalist and dreamer, who spends his life in a weltering sea of sensibility and emotion, but who never does a concrete manly deed." Specifically, he urged his readers to "be systematically ascetic or heroic in little unnecessary points, do every day or two something for no other reason than that you would rather not do it." Ascetic will power, he thought, could turn the nervous system into a tool of moral character through habitual action. But by the 1890s, James had come to realize that the frontal assault of will alone might not be effective and advocated "The Gospel of Relaxation." In 1902, in *The Varieties of Religious Experience*, he described a wider subconscious self, whose powerful source he termed "the More." Self-surrender seemed the necessary prerequisite to self-mastery. James was only a sophisticated example of the widespread combination of popular psychology and vaguely spiritual religiosity that Americans from Mary Baker Eddy to Norman Vincent Peale have offered as the key to happiness and health.[10]

But whether the treatment offered was increased will power, a rest cure, or reliance on the Power of the Infinite, it was offered to the anxious middle-class individual for whom the ties of kinship, religious fellowship, and civic friendship were no longer, or no longer sufficiently, adequate to provide psychic support. The support that traditional relationships no longer adequately supplied to the overburdened individual now came in the form of new institutions. By the time Freud visited the United States in 1909, some ninety medical articles on "psychotherapy" had been published here, and the term had been designated a separate topic in the official medical index. Psychotherapy in twentieth-century America comes in a great variety of forms, some derived from medicine, some from religion, and some from popular psychology. But what most of the forms consist in, whatever theory may be involved, is a relationship between a patient (or client) and a professional therapist. Indeed, this relationship is itself the chief instrument of the therapy. The authors of *Mental Health in America* describe the peculiar features of this therapeutic relationship:

> The present day hero searches for the self by reliving experience in a contractual relationship which is, by definition, removed from "real life" and artificial in the sense that the feelings and emotions it contains are not indigenous to it but belong to other primary relationships in the real world. . . . Psychoanalysis (and psychiatry) is the only form of psychic healing that attempts to cure people by detaching them from society and relationships. All other forms—shamanism, faith healing, prayer—bring the community into the healing process, indeed use the interdependence of patient and others as the central mechanism in the healing process. Modern psychiatry isolates the troubled individual from the currents of emotional interdependence and deals with the trouble by distancing from it and manipulating it through intellectual / verbal discussion, interpretation, and analysis.[11]

While we have no accurate statistics on the number of people using psychotherapy in twentieth-century America, there is reason to believe that there has been a steady increase, particularly since World War II, with three times as many Americans seeing "mental health professionals" now as did twenty years ago. Young, urban, well-educated people from professional backgrounds are the most likely to have actually sought professional therapeutic help, but by 1976 all sectors of society turned more frequently to professional care.[12]

Therapy as a Model Relationship

Therapy is a special kind of relationship. We need to understand its particular characteristics before we can begin to see how it more and more becomes a model for all relationships. Thinking about what makes therapy different from love or friendship, therapist Elizabeth Shulin argues that it is a unique combination of closeness and distance. "The focus is really on one person, and there isn't a relationship outside of this circumscribed one. And yet it's a relationship with a very narrow and a very, very deep nature. And so there can be a kind of frankness that isn't possible with a more sort of vested interest. And yet the distance is exactly what makes it possible to reveal so . . . so much. So it's a funny combination of business and closeness. It provides a really special place for someone to view and examine themselves in a safe and free context, free of other people's stuff, as can be obtained." For all its genuine emotional content, closeness, and honesty of communication, the therapeutic relationship is peculiarly distanced, circumscribed, and asymmetrical. Most of the time, one person talks and the other listens. The client almost always talks about himself and the therapist almost never does. The client pays a fee for professional services rendered, making it an economic exchange: the client's money for the therapist's time. The relationship is tightly regulated by "businesslike" procedural rules that fix its fees, delimit its fifty-minute hours, and schedule its meetings, while precluding sexual behavior or such conventions of friendship as shared meals. Just such a "narrow" focus is taken to allow therapy its "depth" of insight. The therapist's authority seems to derive from psychological knowledge and clinical skill, not from moral values. The therapist is there not to judge but to help clients become able to make their own judgments. The therapist is, nonetheless, even in not judging, a model for the client.

As a personal conversation focussed on one person and a professional service rendered for a fee, psychotherapy is at once intimate and instrumental. "I pay for the service," emphasizes a middle-aged social worker. "It's not a mutual sharing, and it never will be. I'm in there to get something for myself, not for the therapist. He's there to give me support in getting it and to do a good job. He may disclose personal experience, but it's only because he thinks that will facilitate my growth." This asymmetry encourages people to see the therapeutic relationship as a means to their own ends, not an end of which they are a part or an enduring set of practices that unifies their ends. This same social worker reports that she "fell deeply in love" with her therapist, but she reflects: "It wasn't love—well, the experience felt the way it felt—but what it was, of course, was transference." The therapeutic relationship underscores the intersubjective nature of reality. It alerts the participants to discrepant definitions of the situation stemming from different personal histories. It cautions them against projecting their feelings on others and overgeneralizing their own views of what is going on between them.

Compared to the practices members of a traditional family, church, or town share over a lifetime, the therapeutic relationship leaves us with relatively little to *do* together except communicate, and much less time in which to do it. In this, the therapeutic relationship resembles many other relationships in our complex, functionally differentiated society, particularly in professional and managerial life. We often have to relate to others briefly, specifically, and sometimes intensely and it is here that we indeed need to become "better communicators"—factually accurate, emotionally attuned, and intersubjectively subtle—if we are effectively to coordinate our actions with those of others. Diverse, rapidly changing, and often demanding interaction with others requires of us an articulate energy for which the therapeutic relationship provides a kind of training.

Therapy and Work

The relevance of therapy is enhanced by the fit of the therapeutic attitude of self-realization and empathic communication to the increasingly interpersonal nature of the work we do.[13] As the managerial and service sectors of the economy gradually take in a wider and wider slice of the U.S. labor force, more of us do work for which therapy serves as a model rather than a contrast.

Not only is therapy work, much of our work is a form of therapy. Preston, a human potential therapist, describes how he prepares for work: "Ninety percent of communication is body, tone, facial expression. It's who you are and how you sit there and react to someone. So when I prepare to do group therapy, my co-therapist and I go to dinner before every group. We have an hour-and-a-half dinner. When we sit down, we don't talk about our clients. Only in the last few minutes do we plan and go into strategy for the session. We talk about each other. We complain, we give each other therapy, we comb each other's feelings. We fall back in love. We need to, because we don't see each other except then. We are in love by the time we go into that group. That is the basic work we need to do, because then when we enter that room, we are a unit." The same sort of interpersonal communication runs the gamut from work to love and back again. Co-workers "give each other therapy" to cement teamwork. Individuals who meet only on the job make use of intimacy as a method to become more effective as a working "unit." Their sensitive and caring conversation is not a break from the job. It's part of the job. Conversely, therapy's fee-for-services exchange and its strict procedural regulation (in which being a few minutes early or late, missing appointments, or forgetting payments all acquire personal significance) tie it into the bureaucratic and economic structure of the larger society. Therapy's stress on personal autonomy presupposes institutional conformity. The modern self's expressive freedom goes hand in hand with the modern world's instrumental control.

The therapeutic attitude shapes itself to follow the contours of both entrepreneurial and corporate work. It encourages adaptation to such work, whether enthusiastic or skeptical. At the entrepreneurial and enthusiastic ends of the spectrum, its effects are much like those lauded by a hard-driving thirty-five-year-old insurance broker reporting on what a year's therapy has meant to him in the wake of his divorce: "It's made me more disciplined. I can handle my feelings better when I'm feeling depressed, anxious, whatever. That's helped me handle my relationships better, too. It's been good for me from a personal standpoint and it's good for business." Asked how, he explains: "I share more of myself now. The more I share and get out and meet people, the better I do. If I'm sharing with people, they know I can take care of their business and look after their interests. If they know who I am, they're gonna care for me for who I am. There's not gonna be any secrets about me." Therapy enables us to "handle" our feelings more effectively and thereby manage others' responses to us more successfully in business and social life. More sensitive self-expression allows more effective self-assertion. "Being sensitive makes you stronger, not weaker," agrees the broker. Yet simultaneously the therapeutic attitude reaffirms an expressive axiom, that such acceptance and success follow on the genuine goodness of the self so revealed. I succeed because others know and care for me "for who I am," not simply because I am more poised.

In larger bureaucratic settings, therapy at its most ambitious seeks to humanize the corporation and, in so doing, to make it more productive. Echoing the human-relations approach to industrial management, therapists attest to the powerful effects of engaging fellow-workers in sensitive and caring communication.[14] One explains how a client, a data-processing manager for the phone company, transforms their "general prescription that you tell people what to do and make sure they do it and just generally act like a horse's ass" into therapeutic terms: "She approaches everybody in a very perceptive manner. There's four or five different people in her group and each one is absolutely different from the other one. And she's approached each one absolutely differently and she's getting that particular group going from the least productive to the most productive in that organization." Recognizing the uniqueness of each individual appears here as an expressive end in itself *and* as a method of putting people to more efficient use as human resources.

More subtly, therapeutic habits of monitoring one's own and others' responses enter bureaucratic work even when self-expression is subordinated to the organization's "bottom line" goals. The county supervisor of a state welfare agency, for example, explains how she relies on therapeutic insights to keep her office "problem-focused and problem-solving": "I've learned to listen to myself and listen to other people, step into their shoes and see it from their perspective. I've also learned not to over-identify, since that gets in my way as a manager." By way of example, she thinks of "a conflict situation, where someone is trying to make you angry." As a sensitive yet efficient manager, "you have to know it's there and behave as though it's not. Don't raise your voice, don't put them down. Don't lose control. Own your own projections, and make them take responsibility for theirs. Don't get hooked into their stuff." Communication and sympathy cannot fully humanize the world of bureaucratic work, but they can make it more comfortable and cooperative. They can smooth conflict between people and help them through the regulated channels they must negotiate to get the job done while looking out for themselves. "It *is* a jungle out there, and you *do* have to look out for number one," concedes the welfare supervisor, "but you can do it without hurting people and creating more jungle."

When the faith that personal authenticity and occupational success fit neatly together begins to falter, therapy assumes another, less optimistic stance toward the world of work. A humanistic psychologist who often works with pressured middle managers, sales directors, and lawyers skeptically assesses such work as a "game" demanding self-concealment if one is to make a living. She advises them to "play the game when you have to, but know it's a game. Don't buy into it. Choose where and when to play it." She sees herself helping her clients make decisions about their lives in terms of the "tradeoffs" between the "money, power and glamor payoffs" of necessary, but personally unfulfilling, work and the genuine joys of marriage, leisure, and home life.

The fit between the therapeutic outlook and the autonomous, yet routine, pattern of bureaucratic life eases the impersonality of corporate settings but does not eliminate the tension between conceptions of people as ends in themselves and as means to organizational ends. So the same welfare supervisor who defended her own therapeutic style of management can also criticize her driving, yet psychologically skilled, boss for much the same sort of approach: "She'll bring in homemade cookies and flowers for your desk [and] at the same time she'll do anything necessary to get the organizational results she wants and advance her career." The welfare supervisor recalls a client's suicide in which all her boss cared about was "whether we were covered legally." Then she sums up her discontent as a therapeutic individual working in a bureaucratic world: "What's so frustrating to me is this confusion between what's personal and what isn't, not being able to sort it out. There's this sense of seduction and feeling scared you're going to be used." Therapeutic techniques and practices lend themselves to working relationships at odds with therapy's own formal ideals but in line with the bureaucratic institutions in which its clients live. "In the system I work in," says the welfare supervisor, "our motto could be, 'If you don't have to report it, it didn't happen.' Appearances and regulations are all that count!" she exclaims. "There's no meaning except what's legal. That devalues the human reality of what is, the human relatedness between people." A sense of conflict between organizational goals and bureaucratic defensiveness may be unusually acute among professional helpers employed in a state agency. But many of us share the cultural conviction that the meaning of our lives lies apart from the rules and regulations that surround us. Ubiquitous, yet purely procedural and institutionally variable, they compel our conformity without capturing our spirit in some larger vision of the good. Social integration by such means remains a tactical effort apart from self-integration.

In response, we may search for friendship at work, free of manipulation. We may play our work roles tongue in cheek, making tradeoffs there for the sake of authenticity at home or leisure. But such juggling of roles and relationships can leave us with the feeling that who we really are lies beyond them all. Preston encourages clients with this familiar feeling to "balance your meal of activities and pace yourself to get more done," while invoking the image of a healthy person as an ever-growing plant: "The image is that a healthy person is a plant, and that you never stop growing. Most of us don't need tomato stakes. We're basically good, and so with enough sunshine and water, we'll grow beautifully. You can grow in any direction and that adds to the variety of the world. That goes counter to the whole puritanical side of America, that there's one way of life and we're gonna fit you into it. Therapy is like the democratic side. If you become a unique person and grow in a different direction, that helps you, everybody, and society, too." Such an ideal self feeds on its role-bound activities to grow beyond them. The belief that personal growth goes on endlessly and in any direction points up the ultimately aimless nature of the organic metaphor in such post-Freudian therapeutic hands. What is not questioned is the institutional context.

One's "growth" is a purely private matter. It may involve maneuvering within the structure of bureaucratic rules and roles, changing jobs, maybe even changing spouses if necessary. But what is missing is any collective context in which one might act as a participant to change the institutional structures that frustrate and limit. Therapy's "democratic side" lacks any public forum. Its freedom is closer to the free choice of a market economy than to the shared argument and action of free citizens in a republic.

The therapeutic self, as we saw in chapter 3, is defined by its own wants and satisfactions, coordinated by cost-benefit calculation. Its social virtues are largely limited to empathic communication, truth-telling, and equitable negotiation. Preston's reference to American democracy reminds us how closely these therapeutic interpersonal virtues resemble the longstanding social virtues of modern liberalism, in which an individualistic and egalitarian society emphasizes each person's rights and liberties, held in balance by contractual negotiation and reciprocal exchange. The democratic analogy reminds us, too, that our individuality depends on the "different directions" of choice a differentiated society allows us in matters of work, schooling, worship, residence, and lifestyle. It also depends on the uniform compliance the society imposes on us through those regulations—from traffic laws and licenses to office hours and procedures—that coordinate the complexity of our institutions.

Therapy helps us translate our experience of this society into personal meanings, and then back into social action. In its quest to reunify the self, the therapeutic attitude distances us from particular social roles, relationships, and practices; and from their attendant measures of authority, duty, and virtue. Yet therapy itself is a tightly regulated and carefully balanced relationship. It etches the social contract into our intimacy. It echoes in our hearts the "go along to get along" idea of procedurally regulated cooperation with others for the sake of utilities with which to purchase our private pleasures.[15]

The problem posed by therapy is not that intimacy is tyrannically taking over too much of public life.[16] It is that too much of the purely contractual structure of the economic and bureaucratic world is becoming an ideological model for personal life.[17] The model rings true to our experience, which has been gained as interpersonal feelings do more and more of the face-to-face work in a managerial and personal-services economy. The prevalence of contractual intimacy and procedural cooperation, carried over from boardroom to bedroom and back again, is what threatens to obscure the ideals of both personal virtue and public good. When it moves beyond the private self, the therapeutic attitude sees the value of the welfare state. But beyond the limits of enlightened self-interest, the social contract, and a minimal obligation not to injure, it can say little about the nature and purpose of personal or public life.

Therapeutic Contractualism

In describing therapy as a process of self-clarification that interprets commitment in terms of personal choice and interpersonal agreement, its practitioners stress the primary importance of "knowing how you're feeling." As we saw in chapter 3, the larger enterprise of self-identification that enables individuals to fulfill themselves and to relate effectively to others depends on this first step. In these terms, Ellen Schneider, a forty-five-year-old neo–Freudian therapist, explains that "the way I use therapy or the way a person operates in a healthy sense are one and the same process. You have to know honestly how you're feeling about the situation. You have to know what your values are and how these feelings certainly relate to them, whether that's the way you want to feel or not. But then you have to look at what your priority is in view of those values and feelings. And be able to generate a lot of possible alternatives. A lot of people have blinders. They think, 'I'll either kill myself or get the promotion.' They don't see a few alternatives in between. And then you have to be able to, if you can, choose the best, the most constructive alternative for yourself at that point, and be able to follow through." A healthy person moves from discovering feelings to defining values, from setting priorities among values to generating alternative strategies to realize a priority, from selecting one such strategy to following through on it: these steps provide a checklist for strategic action aimed at self-fulfillment. This is how a "healthy" person lives, and so by implication how we ought to live. It sounds not altogether different from a textbook description of decision making in a school of management.

By taking each person's values as given or self-defined, the therapist seems to make no moral judgments. "Life's made up of ebb and flow," observes Ellen Schneider. "It's not a concrete 'these are the rules of the game and this is how you play it' thing. The fun of looking at life is that everything is variable, and that makes you tolerate being able to do therapy." In chapter 3, we saw how those with so relativist a stance may yet assume a "balanced" or "centered" self, attuned to "authentic" as opposed to "neurotic" needs, to assure its plausibility. Its most obvious implication, however, is a view of interpersonal relationships centered on contractual exchange, enacted in communication and negotiation, and grounded in each person's ultimate responsibility to himself or herself alone.

This therapeutic view not only refuses to take a moral stand, it actively distrusts "morality" and sees therapeutic contractualism as a more adequate framework for viewing human action. A Gestalt therapist sketched the transition from "morality" to its therapeutic successor. Morality begins with "picking up values from parents, authority-figures, or important 'significant others' from religion and school, from laws or mores or whatever." It continues by "incorporating those values into how I should be, operating out of that, finding out what the result is that goes with those kinds of expectations." Then a turning point may emerge: "If and when the expectations don't pan out, then they begin saying 'What happened? Why didn't this pan out? Why didn't I get orange blossoms and rosebuds because I was good?'" Therapy advances this line of questioning, and it helps clients reformulate their outlooks in different terms: "At that point they begin to develop values on the basis of wishes and wants, what they're willing to give to get it and what they're not willing to give to get it. Establishing a perception of the world that has more to do with how things work rather than how they ought to work, and doing some basic experimenting." The question "Is this right or wrong?" becomes "Is this going to work for me now?" Individuals must answer it in light of their own wants. The workings of the world are best seen in terms of the costs it exacts and the satisfactions it yields. Each of us faces cost-benefit "tradeoffs" in satisfying some wants at the expense of others.

This model of exchange highlights "differences in values," for these are the elements least susceptible to rationalization and most in need of sympathetic intuition. Sharpened by therapy, these intuitions of others' "values" can then be fed into interpersonal calculations that put behavior on the bottom line: "You can become sensitive to what the impact of what you do is going to be on the other person and start predicting if I do this, he's going to do that," Ellen Schneider explains. "And then you have to judge the relative merits. Is it worth getting him angry to maybe get something important done in this relationship, or is it not worth it? And that way people can start putting in perspective that it doesn't make sense to get mad about who takes out the garbage. It does make sense to get mad about, you know, getting the kids to a doctor." In theory, each person is supposed to decide what it is "important" to do in relation to the other and "judge the relative merits" of acts in relation to the other's reactions. Each must do so in the light of self-set values and accept that "you can only be responsible for your own actions." These are the tasks that make the moral life of a therapeutic individual so ascetic. In fact, the formal demands of the therapeutic contract for such acute insight, sympathy, and calculation between people, and such strict self-accounting, are usually mitigated by their actually shared recognition of common "human needs" to be met, injuries to be avoided, and duties to be done, such as those involved in getting a sick child to the doctor.

By its own logic, a purely contractual ethic leaves every commitment unstable. Parties to a contract remain free to choose, and thus free to remake or break every commitment, if only they are willing to pay the price for doing so.[18] "Commitments take work, and we're tired of working," sighs Alec, a young therapist. "And we come home from work, the last thing I want to do, you know, is for people to sit down and say, 'Well, let's sit and work on our relationship. Let's talk about it.' Yes, but I worked eight and a half hours today, you know. Let's just sit down and watch the boob tube." His protest ends in a confession: "It's like you periodically ask yourself, like, 'Is this worth my effort? Is this worth that?'" Faced with ongoing demands to work on their relationships as well as their jobs, separate and equal selves are led to question the contractual terms of their commitments to one another: Are they getting what they want? Are they getting as much as they are giving? As much as they could get elsewhere? If not, they are tempted to withdraw and look elsewhere for fulfillment. Therapeutic experts may counsel them that lasting commitments are necessary for self-fulfillment. But within this "giving-getting" model, individuals must test such claims against their own experience, case by case, and judge them in the light of their own "values." Because each person's feelings and values are subjective, the difficulties in figuring out the bottom line and interacting appropriately with others are daunting enough to make "long-term relationships" almost as unstable in their actual prospects as they are formidable in their therapeutic demands. Perhaps a contract model, appropriate in the context of professional and managerial work, cannot carry the weight of sustained and enduring commitments.

Therapy and Politics

The common definition of politics as "the art of the possible" sees it as a way of seeking compromise for the sake of coexistence between a welter of competing individuals, groups, and communities. We might expect therapists to recognize some kinship between their own understanding of human interaction, including the "therapeutic contractualism" we have just described, and such politics, and so voice confidence in it. But often this is not the case. Instead, they express frustration, disappointment, and disillusionment with politics. Indeed, for many of them, suspicion of politics amounts to a sense of the moral impossibility of politics. It will be instructive to inquire how the therapeutic attitude that is so congenial to aspects of our economic and professional life has such difficulty with our political life.

One reason for the therapists' doubts about politics has to do with the problem of moral relativity, which is difficult enough in one-to-one relationships but becomes simply unmanageable where large numbers of people are involved. Alec, whom we have just heard emphasizing the work that interpersonal commitments require, explains why commitments to citizenship pose even more discouraging demands: "If the public can't believe or agree on what is rewarding and what isn't rewarding, then it's going to be pretty difficult to believe or unilaterally decide any one thing. Abortion, you know? It's like one side thinks, 'Well, it's important that we be in control of our bodies.' The other side thinks it's terrible that we can take life when they cannot protect themselves. What people see as right, rewardingly right, is different and so all of this is essentially—it's like the goal of politics is somehow to bring some kind of debate to a close. To finish, and you can't finish. And so it's like politics is just essentially a dead end." Objecting that politics does not seek such final closure, but instead aims to make fair and practical decisions in the course of an ongoing debate misses the deeper thrust of the therapist's complaint. For the validity of such a debate would imply the presence of something approaching an underlying moral consensus on such things as the nature of the self and on what it would mean to give individuals their due, rather than merely tallying preferences. But the therapist does not believe such a moral consensus exists. Even between two people, such a consensus is attained only by the carefully cultivated empathy of face-to-face conversation. Among many it is not to be expected.

Given this belief, therapists rarely see any political persuasiveness in moral argument, which is often dismissed as "intellectualizing" and therefore evasive, or, worse, an attempt at coercion. Yet they commonly find their own trained empathy and interpersonal sensitivity ineffectual in the political sphere. Ellen Schneider, long involved in county mental health and child abuse programs, struggles to explain why politics is so "frustrating" and why she finds herself "having no impact" on it: "The complexity of it is what astounds me," she marvels. "It's just overwhelming how many aspects of the situation there are, but there's no one solution. I usually see the points that the opposite side holds. Not on certain things, like on abortion—I just feel strongly about that. But I can see enough of why other people feel the need to, like the welfare thing. I guess there are people who, you know, cheat. I don't feel that way, but you know you can appreciate that people don't want to waste their tax dollars. And from their viewpoint they don't see the people that I see, and so, of course, they're going to feel that way." She shakes her head in exasperation. "So it is hard to, it's like the blind men examining the elephant, and it's like, 'Will somebody *please* get me the overall picture so we can all work with the same information!'" When asked if there is any process whereby such an overall picture might indeed emerge, Ellen replies, "No, at times I'm convinced there isn't any way for that to happen. I see that because we do a lot of work with grants, and I'm active in child abuse areas. That's probably the most political area, and it's amazing how much time is spent trying to find out what somebody else is doing, the state, the region, the nation. . . . It's just crazy!" The complexity of such issues as abortion, welfare, and child abuse is only increased by emphasis on the relativity of individual feelings, values, and priorities with respect to them. Given the objective complexity of the issues and the chaos of conflicting subjective reactions to them, therapy's empathic face-to-face communication can make little headway. It cannot span the gap between the one-on-one situation and the great social scale and bureaucratic density of public life. Even though it might ideally be possible for the highly educated and sensitive to sit down and talk through the issues, the managers and professionals who could are already "reaching burnout" because of overwork, professional commitments, and family obligations. Ellen does not see her own decision to minimize her political involvement as a choice of self-interest over the public good but rather as a necessity for psychic survival.

The practical difficulties of objective and subjective complexity, aggravated by lack of time and empathic ability to reach agreement, lead to an even deeper deadlock in the therapist's view of politics: politics is both profoundly inauthentic and inescapable. Elizabeth explains some of the experiences that led her to this conclusion. The daughter of a chemistry professor and a social worker, she thinks back on her gradual disenchantment with politics as an undergraduate in a large liberal university rife with student movements. "It got too rigid," she says in summary. Activists took up unequivocal, moralistic positions on such complicated matters as welfare economics and military defense, which she came to feel were far from clear. Radical organizations imposed inflexible rules on individual feelings—they even had "rules about what to do when people cried at meetings." These were symptoms of a greater difficulty, the inability of politics, whether conducted by radicals or the president, to respect life's fluidity. "I don't think there are answers in life," Elizabeth concludes. "I think there are only really good dialogues." Asked what a dialogue in public life might be like, she replies that it would be one where "there's just no one right." Yet in Elizabeth's view that is not the way politics works and probably not the way politics can work: "I mean I think political action *needs* to happen by people who are convinced that there's one right. I don't think it works any other way. And in fact it doesn't work very well if the people within it are always dialoguing. I mean you've just got to go out and change the world based on what you believe. I just can't do that."

The irony of this discussion and its pathos is that politics is at once criticized as morally bankrupt and accepted as practically inevitable. Only if politics were a true public dialogue would it deserve our participation. Yet in reality it requires not such dialogue but absolutists and self-interested infighters, what Elizabeth calls "fanatics," in order to function. For Elizabeth and many of the therapeutically minded, lacking the notion of a common language of moral discourse in terms of which public debate can reach at least occasional consensus, there are only the authentic, but ineffectual, voices of countless individuals on the one hand and the inauthentic, but necessary, assertion of one right way on the other.

Not all the therapeutically inclined have so negative a view of politics. Some of them believe that bringing "communication" into politics might have beneficial results. For others politics may seem a field for self-development or self-expression. As a New Mexico activist, expressing his political motivation, said to Robert Coles, "I am in the struggle because it means a lot to me. It's where I'm at."[19] But when disillusion sets in, as it did for Elizabeth, such enthusiasm may quickly turn to withdrawal.

It would seem that the "giving-getting" model so prominent in contemporary American culture, which, as we have seen, has difficulty sustaining enduring commitments between two individuals, has even more trouble coming up with any substitute for civic friendship that might sustain enduring political commitments. Indeed, the ideal therapeutic world is one in which impersonal bureaucratic rules guarantee free access to market choices and the opportunity for empathic communication in open and intense interpersonal relations. It is a world without politics and almost, it would seem, without community. But the therapeutic vision cannot ignore community, a positive idea linked to the central therapeutic concept of communication itself. Nevertheless, the nature of therapeutic relationships may define a community that is bound to remain more an aspiration than a reality.

The Therapeutic Quest for Community

The therapeutic conception of community grows out of an old strand of American culture that sees social life as an arrangement for the fulfillment of the needs of individuals. In a "community of interest," self-interested individuals join together to maximize individual good. Dale Carnegie's advice on "how to win friends and influence people" is an earlier twentieth-century example of this utilitarian conception of community. Taking the salesman as a working model of social life, and economic success as its goal, Carnegie unabashedly urged his students to "say to yourself, over and over, my popularity, my success, and my income depend to no small extent on my skill in dealing with people." For Carnegie, friendship was an occupational tool for entrepreneurs, an instrument of the will in an inherently competitive society.[20]

Speaking to managers and professionals who succeed by subtler skills, therapists today propose a different sort of friendship. It offers self-fulfillment and a sense of self-worth to basically benign people in a well-coordinated, yet often lonely, social world. "People feel less depressed if they can maintain friendships and be with people," observes Ellen Schneider. Friendship "is positively related to good emotional adjustment. The more socially isolated he is, the more emotional problems a person is likely to have." In both the earlier and the more recent versions, friendship is commended on the grounds of utility, but now psychic benefits have replaced economic ones. The good things of life, those objects that make up "the good life," are still important, but they now take second place to the subjective states of well-being that make up a sense of self-worth.

Much the same shift shows up in therapeutic pictures of the larger community. There the associational model of elaborated interests and reciprocal exchange works outward from intimate relationships through a circle of friends, seen as "personal support networks." Individuals link up to exchange "support" in order to "meet their needs and validate themselves." A therapist welcomes community involvements in his clients since, he says, they are "really useful to them and supportive of them." Asked for examples, he replies, "I do a lot of work with addicts, and AA is an absolutely irreplaceable support group. School is essential to a lot of young people that are working their way up in life. All these things where there's a community of interest. These are extremely valuable." Therapeutic, educational, and social service organizations for individuals come most readily to mind in such thinking about community, in which it appears as an avenue of opportunity, a marketplace for exchange, or a meeting place for individuals on their own.

Some therapists point out that the very mobility, privacy, and urban living we value rob us of opportunities to get "to know each other at a reasonably intimate level in casual, unforced circumstances." Consequently, they advise clients looking for friends, a lover, or a spouse to use community groups as hunting grounds for such significant others. "Get on a team, get on a political organization, join a church," says one to single and divorced young adults. "Go back to school, even if you don't want to learn anything." "You need to get to know people," counsel these therapists, since "well-connected" persons live longer, healthier lives. On the grounds of interpersonally enlightened self-interest, therefore, such therapists advocate "love and closeness" over the "noncaring, self-actualizing pursuits" encouraged by therapies whose individualism relies on naive ideas of self-sufficiency. By contrast, these more "community-oriented" therapists call for "caring networks, an interconnected system of family, friends, intimates, and community that is needed to restore and sustain those now-absent feelings of belonging."

While the emphasis on connectedness and community would seem to be an advance over "noncaring self-actualization," one must still ask whether the relentless emphasis on self-interest does not raise doubts as to whether there has really been a shift. Are friends that one makes in order to improve one's health really friends enough to improve one's health? The popular language of therapy is so radically individualistic that it has difficulty imagining an alternative even when the inadequacy of "self-sufficiency" is recognized. Only occasionally do we find therapists who recognize, and then often only fitfully, that "community" is not a collection of self-seeking individuals, not a temporary remedy, like Parents Without Partners, that can be abandoned as soon as a partner has been found, but a context within which personal identity is formed, a place where fluent self-awareness follows the currents of communal conversation and contributes to them. Reflecting on her socially isolated clients as "human blanks," a therapist affirms that "everybody needs to belong to a group" because "everybody needs to have an identity." The group does not simply give one an identity, but neither, as in the associational model, does it simply sum up the individuals who join it. This alternative sense of identity in which the person is never wholly separate from others is clearest in the family. It is a context in which identity is formed in part through identifying with and incorporating aspects of other members. When therapists see the family, and particularly the parent-child relationship, not only as the context in which external standards are imposed on the child, but as one in which a person is formed and a character takes shape, then there are resources for a deeper understanding of what it means to be part of a group in general.

Faced with the fragility of commitments in current middle-class life, some therapists begin to reflect on how deep attachments might be understood and sustained. "All you see is marriages breaking up," sighs a therapist about her suburban practice, while much of what she hears from her unmarried clients is "If I just found somebody and was married, I wouldn't ever have to be alone again." While both the lament and the wish may be translated into the "giving-getting" model of therapeutic contractualism, some therapists see that only an understanding of personality as socially and historically situated might begin to remedy the situation. Therapy, which often acts to take apart one's life history so as to "liberate" one from it, can, on the other hand, help us recover the narrative unity of our lives woven through family ties into the social tapestry of communities situated in a given time, place, and culture. Having worked to differentiate the self from its family of origin, therapy can also serve to reincorporate it into this wider context. Insofar as therapy reveals our identity to be inseparable from our history, and our personal history to be essentially social, it returns the separate self to communities of practical meaning. "I certainly look at things in terms of early childhood experiences and marital kinds of stuff," says Ruth Levy, an analytically schooled family therapist. "I also like to view a person's history as the sum of *all* the forces that went on. Not doing it solely from the analytic mommy-daddy-child routine, but really stretching it out in terms of history." The therapeutic composition of such personal history can exercise memory and imagination in narrative form to unify the individual's life story with the community's ideals of a good life.

Yet even when these insights are present, it is often difficult, working with the resources of popular therapeutic language, to give a full account of social and historical context. A therapist deeply concerned about the integrity of our lives and what threatens it, often has only an impoverished language in which to think about such issues. Asked about work that compromises a person's character, such as corporate bribery, one such therapist answers in utilitarian style that we have to "ask ourselves what it costs us." Then she adds that such costs are "cumulative." "You don't just do it once and then it's done; do it again, it's done," she argues, "'cause you carry your history and remember those things, and at twelve it may be one thing and at twenty it's another, and at thirty-five it's another thing altogether." She stresses the point: "Looking back over thirty-five years, you see a lot more. I've given a little away each time and I have to stop and say wait a minute, is this going to work for me now? How diminished am I going to be at eighty when I come back to look at myself and say, do I have self-esteem?" Straining its logic to follow the trajectory of moral character over a lifetime, the language of costs and benefits can give us only a thin, quantitative facsimile of it. Miscalculated tradeoffs add up to "diminish" the sum total of ourselves, as if the unity of our character and the duration of our history were merely a matter of additive units. Judgments of character as "self-esteem" and of action as what "works for me now" only dimly depict the meaning of work well done, a family well raised, and a life well lived, as if all such judgments were merely a matter of subjective feeling.

Ruth Levy, whom we heard above speaking of people in terms of their history, understands that more than cost accounting is involved. She believes a central therapeutic goal is "reconnecting people with families" and, given the conventional family's fragility, it follows that "it doesn't always have to be blood relations." Yet she sees that isolated families on their own will not be enough. People can "generate families on their own" and nurture them only by drawing on the larger community and its many subcultural worlds more self-consciously than in the past. Thinking of her own renewed commitment to the local synagogue, Ruth notes that "two people aren't enough" to care for children or even for each other. "You need to put into the pot. You need to be there if something needs to be done. To make courtesy calls and sympathy calls and to deliver food. But the other part is that you are also a beneficiary and when you are stuck and need to have someone for your kid to play with or when disasters strike, you have support. On the joyous occasions, a bris [circumcision] or a wedding, you have people to share those with as well. The event itself is wonderful. It's magnified when you have other people who are as happy as you and you can share in other people's happy occasions." In this passage, we hear the familiar language of exchange and support, but we also hear something else—that meaning is "magnified" when it is shared with others.

Ruth explains why she and her husband decided to keep kosher for the first time since leaving their parents: "I keep kosher because of structure, because at some point I remember thinking, twelve years ago or so, you know the universe is chaotic, there is so much going on, so much turbulence, and the only thing that imparts meaning isn't some external source—God, or the Communist Party or whomever—that's not where it comes from." We cannot know who we are without some practical ritual and moral "structure" that orders our freedom and binds our choices into something like habits of the heart. Yet we also hear the familiar therapeutic hostility to external authorities who would impose meaning on our lives, and with that the whole ambiguity of the therapeutic attitude. For if there is no grounding in reality for our action, communal ties and religious commitments can be recommended only for the benefits they yield to the individual, for the social, emotional, and cultural functions they perform—providing help with daycare, enhanced feelings of joy, psychic structure in a turbulent universe. However subtly stated, such ideas return us to the contractual contingencies of a society predicated on individual interests and feelings.

Perhaps that is as far as the therapeutic conception of community can go and why, for the therapeutically inclined, community is something hoped for, something yearned for, something sadly missing most of the time, and, when found, as in the case of Ruth Levy, something that therapeutic language cannot really make sense of. In chapter 4, we saw long marriages generating commitment transcending the therapeutic limitations of the marriage partners' language; similarly, with Ruth Levy, we see a recognition that moves beyond her presuppositions: "The woman who took care of my daughter when she was little was a Greek Jew. She was very young, nine, ten, eleven, when the war broke out, and was lying at the crematorium door when the American troops came through. So that she has a number tattooed on her arm. And it was always like being hit in the stomach with a brick when she would take my baby and sit and circle her with her arm, and there was the number." So encircled by love and suffering shared, we are no longer in the "giving-getting" mode. We know ourselves as social selves, parents and children, members of a people, inheritors of a history and a culture that we must nurture through memory and hope.

The Persistence of Traditional Forms

We have spent much of this chapter discussing therapeutic modes of relating. This is because most of the people that we talked to over the past several years, particularly the more affluent and better educated, used a language influenced by therapy to articulate their thoughts about interpersonal relationships. This is not surprising in our predominantly middle-class society, where pressures for achievement and mobility have placed individuals under great strain, with few social supports that can simply be taken for granted.

We have seen that therapy has developed an acute concern for the monitoring and managing of inner feelings and emphasizes their expression in open communication. Therapy thus continues the tradition of expressive individualism that we considered earlier in this book. But we have seen, too, how therapeutic language is preoccupied with strategic considerations of costs and benefits, and has thus also incorporated much of what we have called utilitarian individualism. Indeed, in contemporary therapeutic language, the managerial and the therapeutic modes seem to be coalescing as our professional and economic life involves more and more subtle forms of interpersonal relating. We have, in fact, seen that therapeutic understandings of interaction work best in bureaucratic and market situations where individuals are under pressure and need to coordinate their activities with precision.

The benefits of the increasing importance of therapy in our lives are tangible. Americans today, especially, but not exclusively, middle-class Americans, are more "in touch with their feelings," better able to express them, and more able to seek what they want in relationships. The increase in psychological sophistication has apparently brought an increase in feelings of personal well-being.[21]

But there is a cost. Anxiety and uncertainty about more important and enduring relationships are increasing rather than decreasing. Therapists have grown increasingly concerned about the lack of "community" in modern life, and, as we have seen in our discussion of the therapeutic quest for community, have often suggested that people need to "reconnect" to families, join a church, or become involved in political activity. These admonitions suggest that therapy cannot really replace older forms of relationship, but must somehow seek to reinvigorate them. Yet, as we have seen, the very language of therapeutic relationship seems to undercut the possibility of other than self-interested relationships.

The contradictions we have described make us wonder if psychological sophistication has not been bought at the price of moral impoverishment. The ideal therapeutic relationship seems to be one in which everything is completely conscious and all parties know how they feel and what they want. Any intrusion of "oughts" or "shoulds" into the relationship is rejected as an intrusion of external and coercive authoritarianism. The only morality that is acceptable is the purely contractual agreement of the parties: whatever they agree to is right. But just as the notion of an absolutely free self led to an absolutely empty conception of the self, complete psychological contractualism leads to the notion of an absolutely empty relationship. And this empty relationship cannot possibly sustain the richness and continuity that the therapeutically inclined themselves most want, just as they want not empty but rich and coherent selves.

We are not suggesting that the trouble with the therapeutic conception of life is that it is self-indulgent and encourages narcissism. In a way, we are suggesting almost the opposite: that the relentless insistence on consciousness and the endless scanning of one's own and others' feelings while making moment-by-moment calculations of the shifting cost /benefit balances is so ascetic in its demands as to be unendurable. It is the moral content of relationships that allows marriages, families, and communities to persist with some certainty that there are agreed-upon standards of right and wrong that one can count on and that are not subject to incessant renegotiation. It is that third element of the classical idea of friendship, common commitment to the good, that allows traditional relationships to persist coherently even when the "giving-getting" balances shift, as they inevitably do.

In one sense, the therapeutic critique of traditional relationships and their moral basis is legitimate. Where standards of right and wrong are asserted with dogmatic certainty and are not open to discussion, and, even worse, where these standards merely express the interests of the stronger party in a relationship, while clothing those interests in moralistic language, then the criticism is indeed justified. Unfortunately, in all existing societies, traditional social practices and the moral standards that govern them are subject to just these distortions. But the therapeutically inclined are wrong to think that morality itself is the culprit, that moral standards are inherently authoritarian and in the service of domination. The therapeutically inclined fear any statement of right or wrong that is not prefaced by a subjective disclaimer such as "I think" or "it feels to me" because they believe moral judgments are based on purely subjective feelings and cannot meaningfully be discussed. While negotiation between individuals seeking to maximize their own positive feelings is intelligible to them, reason-giving moral argument is feared as inevitably leading to either conflict or coercion.

Traditional moral discourse, while subject in particular cases to the distortions the therapeutically inclined fear, is not the monolith of external authority and coercion that they imagine. Whether philosophical or theological, traditional ethical reflection is based on the understanding that principles and exemplars must be interpreted to be applied, and that good people may differ on particular cases. Nonetheless, there is some confidence that a rough consensus is possible so that there can be common understandings of moral obligations. Not everything is up in the air all the time, although there is nothing that is in principle closed to discussion. It is true that in periods of rapid social change, when moral standards seem to be crumbling and relativism seems to be pervasive, some people are tempted to assert a simple and unquestionable morality and, in some circumstances, to force it on their neighbors. But such people deeply misunderstand tradition even when they seek to embrace it. They defend not tradition but traditionalism, and, as Jaroslav Pelikan has said, whereas tradition is the living faith of the dead, traditionalism is the dead faith of the living.[22] A living tradition is never a program for automatic moral judgments. It is always in a continuous process of reinterpretation and reappropriation. Such a process assumes, however, that tradition has enough authority for the search for its present meaning to be publicly pursued as a common project.

It is just that assumption that the therapeutically inclined defenders of expressive and utilitarian individualism challenge. In asserting a radical pluralism and the uniqueness of each individual, they conclude that there is no moral common ground and therefore no public relevance of morality outside the sphere of minimal procedural rules and obligations not to injure. In so doing, they do not realize the degree to which their own individualism has become the common cultural coin. There is no moment when the therapeutically inclined sound more similar than when they are asserting their uniqueness.[23] In thinking they have freed themselves from tradition in the pursuit of rationality and personal authenticity, they do not understand the degree to which their views are themselves traditional. Even being anti-traditional is part of the individualist tradition. Nor do they realize that their minimalist insistence on justice, fairness, and respect for individuals is rooted in a much richer defense of the same things in the religious and civic philosophical traditions. Indeed, by not seeing the extent to which their own beliefs are part of a pervasive common culture, they run the risk of doing just what they attack in the older moral traditions—that is, accepting as literally true what is merely a cultural convention and then refusing to open their position to discussion. Since their views are to them so self-evident, they are even tempted on occasion to force them on others.

Yet however influential therapeutic and modern individualist views have become in our society, they have not, as we have seen, been able to replace social practices and commitments that are rooted in older views. Traditional modes of relating—familial, religious, and civic—persist in our society and cannot be wholly subjected to therapeutic reformulation. The search for common moral understandings continues even in the face of the assertion that they are impossible. We will be returning in subsequent chapters to a consideration of the continuing vitality of traditional forms of relationship and moral discourse. But it is time now for us to deal directly with the reigning ideology of individualism, to understand its roots and its tendencies, and to see that it is perhaps closer in its real aspirations to aspects of the older religious and political traditions than its proponents have imagined. Indeed it may be only in terms of those older traditions that the deeper meaning of our individualism and the aspirations it embodies can be salvaged at all.

□

6 Individualism

The Ambiguities of Individualism

Individualism lies at the very core of American culture. Every one of the four traditions we have singled out is in a profound sense individualistic. There is a biblical individualism and a civic individualism as well as a utilitarian and an expressive individualism. Whatever the differences among the traditions and the consequent differences in their understandings of individualism, there are some things they all share, things that are basic to American identity. We believe in the dignity, indeed the sacredness, of the individual. Anything that would violate our right to think for ourselves, judge for ourselves, make our own decisions, live our lives as we see fit, is not only morally wrong, it is sacrilegious. Our highest and noblest aspirations, not only for ourselves, but for those we care about, for our society and for the world, are closely linked to our individualism. Yet, as we have been suggesting repeatedly in this book, some of our deepest problems both as individuals and as a society are also closely linked to our individualism. We do not argue that Americans should abandon individualism—that would mean for us to abandon our deepest identity. But individualism has come to mean so many things and to contain such contradictions and paradoxes that even to defend it requires that we analyze it critically, that we consider especially those tendencies that would destroy it from within.

Modern individualism emerged out of the struggle against monarchical and aristocratic authority that seemed arbitrary and oppressive to citizens prepared to assert the right to govern themselves. In that struggle, classical political philosophy and biblical religion were important cultural resources. Classical republicanism evoked an image of the active citizen contributing to the public good and Reformation Christianity, in both Puritan and sectarian forms, inspired a notion of government based on the voluntary participation of individuals. Yet both these traditions placed individual autonomy in a context of moral and religious obligation that in some contexts justified obedience as well as freedom.

In seventeenth-century England, a radical philosophical defense of individual rights emerged that owed little to either classical or biblical sources. Rather, it consciously started with the biological individual in a "state of nature" and derived a social order from the actions of such individuals, first in relation to nature and then in relation to one another. John Locke is the key figure and one enormously influential in America. The essence of the Lockean position is an almost ontological individualism. The individual is prior to society, which comes into existence only through the voluntary contract of individuals trying to maximize their own self-interest. It is from this position that we have derived the tradition of utilitarian individualism. But because one can only know what is useful to one by consulting one's desires and sentiments, this is also ultimately the source of the expressive individualist tradition as well.

Modern individualism has long coexisted with classical republicanism and biblical religion. The conflict in their basic assumptions was initially muted because they all, in the forms commonest in America, stressed the dignity and autonomy of the individual. But as modern individualism became more dominant in the United States and classical republicanism and biblical religion less effective, some of the difficulties in modern individualism began to become apparent. The therapeutic ethos to which we have devoted so much attention is suggestive of these because it is the way in which contemporary Americans live out the tenets of modern individualism. For psychology, as Robert Coles has written, the self is "the only or main form of reality."[1]

The question is whether an individualism in which the self has become the main form of reality can really be sustained. What is at issue is not simply whether self-contained individuals might withdraw from the public sphere to pursue purely private ends, but whether such individuals are capable of sustaining either a public *or* a private life. If this is the danger, perhaps only the civic and biblical forms of individualism—forms that see the individual in relation to a larger whole, a community and a tradition—are capable of sustaining genuine individuality and nurturing both public and private life.

There are both ideological and sociological reasons for the growing strength of modern individualism at the expense of the civic and biblical traditions. Modern individualism has pursued individual rights and individual autonomy in ever new realms. In so doing, it has come into confrontation with those aspects of biblical and republican thought that accepted, even enshrined, unequal rights and obligations—between husbands and wives, masters and servants, leaders and followers, rich and poor. As the absolute commitment to individual dignity has condemned those inequalities, it has also seemed to invalidate the biblical and republican traditions. And in undermining these traditions, as Tocqueville warned, individualism also weakens the very meanings that give content and substance to the ideal of individual dignity.

We thus face a profound impasse. Modern individualism seems to be producing a way of life that is neither individually nor socially viable, yet a return to traditional forms would be to return to intolerable discrimination and oppression. The question, then, is whether the older civic and biblical traditions have the capacity to reformulate themselves while simultaneously remaining faithful to their own deepest insights.

Many Americans would prefer not to see the impasse as starkly as we have put it. Philosophical defenders of modern individualism have frequently presumed a social and cultural context for the individual that their theories cannot justify, or they have added ad hoc arguments that mitigate the harshness of their theoretical model. As we saw in chapter 5, therapists see a need for the social ties that they cannot really comprehend—they cry out for the very community that their moral logic undercuts. Parents advocate "values" for their children even when they do not know what those "values" are. What this suggests is that there is a profound ambivalence about individualism in America among its most articulate defenders. This ambivalence shows up particularly clearly at the level of myth in our literature and our popular culture. There we find the fear that society may overwhelm the individual and destroy any chance of autonomy unless he stands against it, but also recognition that it is only in relation to society that the individual can fulfill himself and that if the break with society is too radical, life has no meaning at all.

Mythic Individualism

A deep and continuing theme in American literature is the hero who must leave society, alone or with one or a few others, in order to realize the moral good in the wilderness, at sea, or on the margins of settled society. Sometimes the withdrawal involves a contribution to society, as in James Fenimore Cooper's *The Deerslayer*. Sometimes the new marginal community realizes ethical ends impossible in the larger society, as in the interracial harmony between Huckleberry Finn and Jim. Sometimes the flight from society is simply mad and ends in general disaster, as in *Moby Dick*. When it is not in and through society but in flight from it that the good is to be realized, as in the case of Melville's Ahab, the line between ethical heroism and madness vanishes, and the destructive potentiality of a completely asocial individualism is revealed.

America is also the inventor of that most mythic individual hero, the cowboy, who again and again saves a society he can never completely fit into. The cowboy has a special talent—he can shoot straighter and faster than other men—and a special sense of justice. But these characteristics make him so unique that he can never fully belong to society. His destiny is to defend society without ever really joining it. He rides off alone into the sunset like Shane, or like the Lone Ranger moves on accompanied only by his Indian companion. But the cowboy's importance is not that he is isolated or antisocial. Rather, his significance lies in his unique, individual virtue and special skill and it is because of those qualities that society needs and welcomes him. Shane, after all, starts as a real outsider, but ends up with the gratitude of the community and the love of a woman and a boy. And while the Lone Ranger never settles down and marries the local schoolteacher, he always leaves with the affection and gratitude of the people he has helped. It is as if the myth says you can be a truly good person, worthy of admiration and love, only if you resist fully joining the group. But sometimes the tension leads to an irreparable break. Will Kane, the hero of *High Noon*, abandoned by the cowardly townspeople, saves them from an unrestrained killer, but then throws his sheriff's badge in the dust and goes off into the desert with his bride. One is left wondering where they will go, for there is no longer any link with any town.

The connection of moral courage and lonely individualism is even tighter for that other, more modern American hero, the hard-boiled detective. From Sam Spade to Serpico, the detective is a loner. He is often unsuccessful in conventional terms, working out of a shabby office where the phone never rings. Wily, tough, smart, he is nonetheless unappreciated. But his marginality is also his strength. When a bit of business finally comes their way, Philip Marlowe, Lew Archer, and Travis McGee are tenacious. They pursue justice and help the unprotected even when it threatens to unravel the fabric of society itself. Indeed, what is remarkable about the American detective story is less its hero than its image of crime. When the detective begins his quest, it appears to be an isolated incident. But as it develops, the case turns out to be linked to the powerful and privileged of the community. Society, particularly "high society," is corrupt to the core. It is this boring into the center of society to find it rotten that constitutes the fundamental drama of the American detective story. It is not a personal but a social mystery that the detective must unravel.[2]

To seek justice in a corrupt society, the American detective must be tough, and above all, he must be a loner. He lives outside the normal bourgeois pattern of career and family. As his investigations begin to lead him beyond the initial crime to the glamorous and powerful center of the society, its leaders make attempts to buy off the detective, to corrupt him with money, power, or sex. This counterpoint to the gradual unravelling of the crime is the battle the detective wages for his own integrity, in the end rejecting the money of the powerful and spurning (sometimes jailing or killing) the beautiful woman who has tried to seduce him. The hard-boiled detective, who may long for love and success, for a place in society, is finally driven to stand alone, resisting the blandishments of society, to pursue a lonely crusade for justice. Sometimes, as in the film *Chinatown,* corruption is so powerful and so total that the honest detective no longer has a place to stand and the message is one of unrelieved cynicism.

Both the cowboy and the hard-boiled detective tell us something important about American individualism. The cowboy, like the detective, can be valuable to society only because he is a completely autonomous individual who stands outside it. To serve society, one must be able to stand alone, not needing others, not depending on their judgment, and not submitting to their wishes. Yet this individualism is not selfishness. Indeed, it is a kind of heroic selflessness. One accepts the necessity of remaining alone in order to serve the values of the group. And this obligation to aloneness is an important key to the American moral imagination. Yet it is part of the profound ambiguity of the mythology of American individualism that its moral heroism is always just a step away from despair. For an Ahab, and occasionally for a cowboy or a detective, there is no return to society, no moral redemption. The hero's lonely quest for moral excellence ends in absolute nihilism.[3]

If we may turn from the mythical heroes of fiction to a mythic, but historically real, hero, Abraham Lincoln, we may begin to see what is necessary if the nihilistic alternative is to be avoided. In many respects, Lincoln conforms perfectly to the archetype of the lonely, individualistic hero. He was a self-made man, never comfortable with the eastern upper classes. His dual moral commitment to the preservation of the Union and the belief that "all men are created equal" roused the hostility of abolitionists and Southern sympathizers alike. In the war years, he was more and more isolated, misunderstood by Congress and cabinet, and unhappy at home. In the face of almost universal mistrust, he nonetheless completed his self-appointed task of bringing the nation through its most devastating war, preaching reconciliation as he did so, only to be brought down by an assassin's bullet. What saved Lincoln from nihilism was the larger whole for which he felt it was important to live and worthwhile to die. No one understood better the meaning of the Republic and of the freedom and equality that it only very imperfectly embodies. But it was not only civic republicanism that gave his life value. Reinhold Niebuhr has said that Lincoln's biblical understanding of the Civil War was deeper than that of any contemporary theologian. The great symbols of death and rebirth that Lincoln invoked to give meaning to the sacrifice of those who died at Gettysburg, in a war he knew to be senseless and evil, came to redeem his own senseless death at the hand of an assassin. It is through his identification with a community and a tradition that Lincoln became the deeply and typically American individual that he was.[4]

The Social Sources of Ambivalence

As we saw in chapter 2, individualism is deeply rooted in America's social history. Here the bondservant became free, the tenant became a small landowner, and what Benjamin Franklin called the self-respecting "middling" condition of men became the norm. Yet the incipient "independent citizen" of colonial times found himself in a cohesive community, the "peaceable kingdoms" that were colonial towns, where ties to family and church and respect for the "natural leaders" of the community were still strong.[5] Individualism was so embedded in the civic and religious structures of colonial life that it had not yet found a name, even though John Locke's ideas about individual autonomy were well known. It took the geographical and economic expansion of the new nation, especially in the years after 1800, to produce the restless quest for material betterment that led Tocqueville to use the word "individualism" to describe what he saw.[6] The new social and economic conditions did not create the ideology of modern individualism, most of whose elements are considerably older than the nineteenth century, but those conditions did make it possible for what we have called utilitarian and, later, expressive individualism to develop their own inherent tendencies in relative independence from civic and religious forms of life, important though those still were.

Tocqueville was quick to point out one of the central ambiguities in the new individualism—that it was strangely compatible with conformism. He described the American insistence that one always rely on one's own judgment, rather than on received authority, in forming one's opinions and that one stand by one's own opinions. We have already heard many examples of this attitude in the conversations recorded in earlier chapters—in the assertion, for example, that compromise with others is desirable, but not if you sacrifice your own "values." But, as Tocqueville observed, when one can no longer rely on tradition or authority, one inevitably looks to others for confirmation of one's judgments. Refusal to accept established opinion and anxious conformity to the opinions of one's peers turn out to be two sides of the same coin.[7]

There has been a long-standing anxiety that the American individualist, who flees from home and family leaving the values of community and tradition behind, is secretly a conformist. Mark Twain depicted the stultifying conformity of the mid-nineteenth-century town of his youth in recounting the adventures of boys who tried to break free of it and never quite succeeded. As late as the 1920s, Sinclair Lewis identified a classic American type in his portrait of *Babbitt*, the small town businessman too afraid of censure from neighbors and family to develop his political convictions or pursue his own happiness in love. The advice Babbit gives his son not to make the mistake he has made is typical: "Don't be scared of the family. No, nor all of Zenith. Nor of yourself, the way I've been."

In the past hundred years, individualism and its ambiguities have been closely linked to middle-class status. As pointed out in chapter 5, the "middle class" that began to emerge in the later part of the nineteenth century differed from the old "middling condition." In the true sense of the term, the middle class is defined not merely by the desire for material betterment but by a conscious, calculating effort to move up the ladder of success. David Schneider and Raymond Smith usefully define the middle class as a "broad but not undifferentiated category which includes those who have certain attitudes, aspirations, and expectations toward status mobility, and who shape their actions accordingly." Status mobility has increasingly depended on advanced education and competence in managerial and professional occupations that require specialized knowledge. For middle-class Americans, a calculating attitude toward educational and occupational choice has been essential and has often spilled over into determining criteria for the choice of spouse, friends, and voluntary associations. From the point of view of lower-class Americans, these preoccupations do not necessarily seem natural. As one of Schneider and Smith's informants put it, "To be a square dude is hard work, man."[8]

For those oriented primarily to upward mobility, to "success," major features of American society appear to be "the normal outcome of the operation of individual achievement." In this conception, individuals, unfettered by family or other group affiliation, are given the chance to make the best of themselves, and, though equality of opportunity is essential, inequality of result is natural. But the ambiguities of individualism for the middle-class person arise precisely from lack of certainty about what the "best" we are supposed to make of ourselves is. Schneider and Smith note that "there are no fixed standards of behavior which serve to mark status. The only clearly defined cultural standards against which status can be measured are the gross standards of income, consumption, and conformity to rational procedures for attaining ends." Middle-class individuals are thus motivated to enter a highly autonomous and demanding quest for achievement and then left with no standard against which achievement is to be measured except the income and consumption levels of their neighbors, exhibiting anew the clash between autonomy and conformity that seems to be the fate of American individualism.[9]

But perhaps Schneider and Smith's third cultural standard, "rational procedures for attaining ends," offers a way of asserting individual autonomy without the anxious glance at the neighbor. In the case of middle-class professionals whose occupation involves the application of technical rationality to the solution of new problems, the correct solution of a problem or, even more, an innovative solution to a problem, provides evidence of "success" that has intrinsic validity. And where such competence operates in the service of the public good—as, for example, in medical practice at its best—it expresses an individualism that has social value without being conformist.[10]

But to the extent that technical competence is enclosed in the life pattern that we have designated "career," concern for rational problem solving (not to speak of social contribution) becomes subordinated to standards of success measured only by income and consumption. When this happens, as it often does to doctors, lawyers, and other professionals, it raises doubts about the intrinsic value of the work itself. These doubts become all the more insistent when, as is often the case, the professional must operate in the context of a large public or private bureaucracy where much ingenuity must be spent, not on solving external problems, but on manipulating the bureaucratic rules and roles, both in order to get anything done and in order to move ahead in one's career. Anxieties about whether an "organization man" can be a genuine individual long predate William H. Whyte's famous book *The Organization Man*.[11] The cowboy and the detective began to appear as popular heroes when business corporations emerged as the focal institutions of American life. The fantasy of a lonely, but morally impeccable, hero corresponds to doubts about the integrity of the self in the context of modern bureaucratic organization.

The irony of present-day middle-class American individualism derives from the fact that while a high degree of personal initiative, competence, and rationality are still demanded from individuals, the autonomy of the successful individual and even the meaning of "success" are increasingly in doubt. It is as though the stress on the rationality of means and on the importance of individual wants, the primary emphases of utilitarian and expressive individualism, have come loose from an understanding of the ends and purposes of life, in the past largely derived from the biblical and republican traditions. One response to this situation is to make occupational achievement, for so long the dominating focus of middle-class individualism, no longer an end in itself, but merely an instrument for the attainment of a private lifestyle lived, perhaps, in a lifestyle enclave. Yet this solution, as we saw in chapters 3 and 5, is subject to doubt. The same inner contradictions that undermined occupational success as a life goal also threaten to deprive private life of meaning when there is no longer any purpose to involvement with others except individual satisfaction.

The ambiguity and ambivalence of American individualism derive from both cultural and social contradictions. We insist, perhaps more than ever before, on finding our true selves independent of any cultural or social influence, being responsible to that self alone, and making its fulfillment the very meaning of our lives. Yet we spend much of our time navigating through immense bureaucratic structures—multiversities, corporations, government agencies—manipulating and being manipulated by others. In describing this situation, Alasdair MacIntyre has spoken of "bureaucratic individualism," the form of life exemplified by the manager and the therapist.[12] In bureaucratic individualism, the ambiguities and contradictions of individualism are frighteningly revealed, as freedom to make private decisions is bought at the cost of turning over most public decisions to bureaucratic managers and experts. A bureaucratic individualism in which the consent of the governed, the first demand of modern enlightened individualism, has been abandoned in all but form, illustrates the tendency of individualism to destroy its own conditions.

But in our interviews, though we saw tendencies toward bureaucratic individualism, we cannot say that it has yet become dominant. Rather we found all the classic polarities of American individualism still operating: the deep desire for autonomy and self-reliance combined with an equally deep conviction that life has no meaning unless shared with others in the context of community; a commitment to the equal right to dignity of every individual combined with an effort to justify inequality of reward, which, when extreme, may deprive people of dignity; an insistence that life requires practical effectiveness and "realism" combined with the feeling that compromise is ethically fatal. The inner tensions of

American individualism add up to a classic case of ambivalence. We strongly assert the value of our self-reliance and autonomy. We deeply feel the emptiness of a life without sustaining social commitments. Yet we are hesitant to articulate our sense that we need one another as much as we need to stand alone, for fear that if we did we would lose our independence altogether. The tensions of our lives would be even greater if we did not, in fact, engage in practices that constantly limit the effects of an isolating individualism, even though we cannot articulate those practices nearly as well as we can the quest for autonomy.

The Limits of Individualism

We have pointed out the peculiar resonance between middle-class life and individualism in America. We have also stressed the special nature of the middle class, the fact that it is not simply a "layer" in a "system of stratification" but rather a group that seeks to embody in its own continuous progress and advancement the very meaning of the American project. To a large extent, it has succeeded in this aspiration. It so dominates our culture that, as Schneider and Smith put it, "middle-class values can be said to encompass both lower- and upper-class values." This is true for the lower class in that not only are middle-class values understood and respected but "lower-class people explain their inferior position in terms of circumstances that have prevented them from behaving in a middle-class fashion." The upper class sometimes takes comfort in its special sense of family and tradition, but it does not try to substitute its values for the dominant ones. On the contrary, its members praise middle-class rationality and achievement as the values on which our society is based, even when they do not choose to follow them.[13]

The nature of middle-class individualism becomes even clearer when we contrast it to lower-class and upper-class culture. Schneider and Smith describe the contrast very suggestively when they say that the middle class sees "individual and social behavior as predominantly determined by the application of technical rules to any situation that arises," whereas the lower class (and, interestingly enough, the upper class) have a more "dramaturgical view of social action." By "dramaturgical" they mean action that takes on meaning because of a particular history of relationships. Abstract rules are less important than the examples set by individuals. Schneider and Smith argue, for example, that it is in the lower class that ethnicity, as a specific pattern of cultural life, survives in America, and that as individuals enter the middle class, ethnicity

loses distinctive social content even when it is symbolically emphasized.[14] The point is not that lower- and upper-class Americans are not
individualistic, but rather that their individualism is embedded in specific
patterns of relationship and solidarity that mitigate the tendency toward
an empty self and empty relationships in middle-class life. The contrast
is expressed by middle-class Americans themselves when they entertain
envious fantasies about more "meaningful community" among lower-
class racial and ethnic groups or among (usually European) aristocracies.

Important though the distinctions we have been drawing are, we
should not overemphasize the degree to which rationality and technical
rules govern middle-class life. Children do not grow up through abstract
injunctions. They identify with their parents, they learn through role
modeling, and they are influenced by the historic specificity of their family, church, and local community. It is the middle-class orientation toward
technical education, bureaucratic occupational hierarchies, and the market economy that encourages the greater emphasis on universal rules and
technical rationality. The upper and lower classes can maintain greater
cultural specificity (though in the United States that specificity is only
relative) because they are less oriented to these rationalizing institutions.

Since middle-class people, too, are embedded in families, churches,
and local communities, they also experience conflict between the more
rational and the more dramaturgic spheres of life. The tensions that divide middle-class Americans from other Americans also exist within the
middle class itself. Much is said about the cultural diversity and pluralism of American life. But perhaps what divides us most is not that diversity, but the conflict between the monoculture of technical and bureaucratic rationality and the specificity of our concrete commitments.[15]

Communities of Memory

In chapter 3 we discussed at length the process by which a primary emphasis on self-reliance has led to the notion of pure, undetermined
choice, free of tradition, obligation, or commitment, as the essence of
the self. We pointed out that the radical individualist's sincere desire to
"reconnect" with others was inhibited by the emptiness of such an "unencumbered" self. It is now time to consider what a self that is not empty
would be like—one that is constituted rather than unencumbered, one
that has, let us admit it, encumbrances, but whose encumbrances make
connection to others easier and more natural. Just as the empty self
makes sense in a particular institutional context—that of the upward

mobility of the middle-class individual who must leave home and church in order to succeed in an impersonal world of rationality and competition—so a constituted self makes sense in terms of another institutional context, what we would call, in the full sense of the word, community.

Communities, in the sense in which we are using the term, have a history—in an important sense they are constituted by their past—and for this reason we can speak of a real community as a "community of memory," one that does not forget its past. In order not to forget that past, a community is involved in retelling its story, its constitutive narrative, and in so doing, it offers examples of the men and women who have embodied and exemplified the meaning of the community. These stories of collective history and exemplary individuals are an important part of the tradition that is so central to a community of memory.[16]

The stories that make up a tradition contain conceptions of character, of what a good person is like, and of the virtues that define such character. But the stories are not all exemplary, not all about successes and achievements. A genuine community of memory will also tell painful stories of shared suffering that sometimes creates deeper identities than success, as we saw when Ruth Levy recognized her own identity with a community of shared love and suffering in the number on her babysitter's arm. And if the community is completely honest, it will remember stories not only of suffering received but of suffering inflicted—dangerous memories, for they call the community to alter ancient evils. The communities of memory that tie us to the past also turn us toward the future as communities of hope. They carry a context of meaning that can allow us to connect our aspirations for ourselves and those closest to us with the aspirations of a larger whole and see our own efforts as being, in part, contributions to a common good.[17]

Examples of such genuine communities are not hard to find in the United States. There are ethnic and racial communities, each with its own story and its own heroes and heroines. There are religious communities that recall and reenact their stories in the weekly and annual cycles of their ritual year, remembering the scriptural stories that tell them who they are and the saints and martyrs who define their identity. There is the national community, defined by its history and by the character of its representative leaders from John Winthrop to Martin Luther King, Jr. Americans identify with their national community partly because there is little else that we all share in common but also partly because America's history exemplifies aspirations widely shared throughout the world: the ideal of a free society, respecting all its citizens, however diverse, and allowing them all to fulfill themselves. Yet some Americans also remember the history of suffering inflicted and the gap between promise and realization, which has always been very great. At some times, neighborhoods, localities, and regions have been communities in America, but that has been hard to sustain in our restless and mobile society. Families can be communities, remembering their past, telling the children the stories of parents' and grandparents' lives, and sustaining hope for the future—though without the context of a larger community that sense of family is hard to maintain. Where history and hope are forgotten and community means only the gathering of the similar, community degenerates into lifestyle enclave. The temptation toward that transformation is endemic in America, though the transition is seldom complete.

People growing up in communities of memory not only hear the stories that tell how the community came to be, what its hopes and fears are, and how its ideals are exemplified in outstanding men and women; they also participate in the practices—ritual, aesthetic, ethical—that define the community as a way of life. We call these "practices of commitment" for they define the patterns of loyalty and obligation that keep the community alive. And if the language of the self-reliant individual is the first language of American moral life, the languages of tradition and commitment in communities of memory are "second languages" that most Americans know as well, and which they use when the language of the radically separate self does not seem adequate.

The empty self, as we said in chapter 3, is an analytic concept, a limit toward which we tend, but not a concrete reality. A completely empty self could not exist except in the theory of radical individualism. It is theoretically imaginable but performatively impossible. The constituted self is also an analytic concept, a limit that is never quite reached. It is true that we are all children of specific parents, born in a particular locality, inheritors of those group histories, and citizens of this nation. All of these things tell us who we are in important ways. But we live in a society that encourages us to cut free from the past, to define our own selves, to choose the groups with which we wish to identify. No tradition and no community in the United States is above criticism, and the test of the criticism is usually the degree to which the community or tradition helps the individual to find fulfillment. So we live somewhere between the empty and the constituted self.

The tension can be invigorating, helping to keep both individual and community vital and self-critical. But the tension is also anxious and sometimes leads to the potentially explosive conflicts between technical rationality and concrete commitments we mentioned earlier. Liberal intellectuals, in their own minds devoted to individual freedom, sometimes caricature regional or religious groups whose traditions and communities they find ignorant and potentially authoritarian. And since liberal intellectuals have considerable influence on public policy, both through the courts and through legislation, they have on occasion forced their own enlightened views on their fellow citizens. On the other hand, some conservative groups, dismayed by rapid social change and by the social consequences of radical individualism, simplify and objectify their traditions with fundamentalist inflexibility and then condemn those of their fellow citizens who hold differing views, sometimes joining political action committees in the attempt to legislate their convictions. We have used the terms *liberal* and *conservative* here because they are frequently used in this context, but they do not serve well. The conflict is cultural more than political, though it can have serious political consequences. Another way of speaking of these antagonists is to call them "modernists" and "antimodernists," but this, too, is of only limited utility. Rather than relying on simplistic labels, we should recognize that some of our deepest cultural conflicts arise from differing understandings of our common individualism.

For a long time, our society was held together, even in periods of rapid change, by a largely liberal Protestant cultural center that sought to reconcile the claims of community and individuality. Rejecting both chaotic openness and authoritarian closure, representatives of this cultural center defended tradition—some version of the civic republican and biblical traditions—but not traditionalism. They sought to reappropriate the past in the light of the present, mindful of the distortions that mar the past of every tradition. That task has become increasingly difficult, as we shall see in later chapters, but it has by no means been abandoned. In the rest of this chapter, we will consider a few examples of those who have attempted to articulate a socially responsible individualism within the context of communities of memory and the second languages and practices of commitment they carry. We will see that this is no easy task in a society in which the first language of modern individualism, fusing utilitarian and expressive components, and the practices of separation that go with it, are so dominant that alternatives are hard to understand. Yet as the ambivalence that we have repeatedly noticed in this chapter indicates, even those most exclusively caught in the first language seem to be yearning for something more.

Community, Commitment, and Individuality

Les Newman, very much a middle-class American, has found a home in the church, one that allows him to take a critical view of the environing society. He says that "American society is becoming very self-oriented, or very individual-oriented: what's in it for me, how much do I get out of it, am I getting everything I'm entitled to in my life? It is tearing down a lot that is right about the country. People don't look at the repercussions of their individual actions outside of themselves."

For this evangelical Baptist, reared in the South, just graduated from a well-known business school, and now working as an executive in the California suburbs, such sweeping criticism becomes more specific in characterizing his fellow-alumni. Most of them "felt they didn't need God, didn't need religion. There was a strong impression in business school, the self-made individual, being able to do it all yourself if you just work hard enough and think hard enough, and not having to rely on other people." It is precisely because such self-made individuals don't appreciate their need for God that they don't appreciate their need for other people, Les Newman observes. He experiences both needs in the active life of his church congregation. Its members aren't "the standard go-to-church-Sunday-morning people" who practice "a ritual as opposed to a lifestyle." For them religion is more than just saying "Here's a set of morals to live by and here's this great example of 2,000 years ago." The heart of their shared life and teaching "is that Jesus Christ is a person. He's alive today, to relate to today. He works in your life today, and you can talk to Him through the week in prayer." Church for this believer, therefore, "isn't just a place, it's a family" that has given him the closest friends he has. Despite leaving home, moving to California, and entering the competitive world of business, he has found a new family-like anchor for his life, a new bond to other people through the shared celebration of a "personal relationship with Jesus Christ."

In this traditional Christian view, what connects one self to another is the objectively given reality of their creation as God's children and God's own continuing presence in the world in Jesus Christ. This reality is one each person freely accepts, thus establishing the bonds of the Christian congregation while affirming individual identity. Reflecting on this process of self-integration, the Baptist businessman testifies, "I got my personal Christian relationship with Jesus and that has sort of been the ongoing thing that has tied together a whole bunch of different things. That relationship with Christ has changed me somewhat as an individual when it comes to my outlook on the world. He is the person who has steadied my emotion. Before, I was kind of unstable, and I've had some pretty good lows, and now I find that doesn't happen. It has strengthened my commitment in my marriage, and it's had a great deal of impact on the way I relate to other people at work. My life is such a combination of disjointed events. My childhood was just a whole series of moves." Relating oneself to Christ, even in the disjointed course of social uprooting and cultural conflict, yields an experience of the self's integrity.

His church community has helped Les Newman find a language and a set of practices that have strengthened his marriage, aided him in dealing with his work situation, and given him a more coherent sense of self, as well as providing him with some critical distance from the environing society. Ted Oster, whom we met in chapter 4, has no such community and seems much more at ease in the first language of modern individualism, a language he uses to explain most of what goes on around him. Yet when pressed to explain why he remains in a long marriage, his several attempts to do so in cost /benefit terms finally break down. His happiness with his wife comes from "proceeding through all these stages of life together. . . . It makes life meaningful and gives me the opportunity to share with somebody, have an anchor, if you will, and understand where I am. That for me is a real relationship." Here Ted Oster seems to be groping for words that could express his marriage as a community of memory and hope, a place where he is not empty, but which essentially defines who he is. It is as though he had to invent a second language out of the failing fragments of his usual first language.

Although we did not see it in the case of Ted Oster, and only tentatively in the case of Les Newman, communities of memory, though often embedded in family experiences, are an important way in which individuals are led into public life. Angelo Donatello, a successful small businessman who has become a civic leader in a suburb of Boston, tells how a reluctant concern for the ethnic heritage rooted in his family finally led him into public life: "One of the important things that got me into politics was that I was a confused individual. I came from a real old-fashioned Italian family in East Boston. We spoke both languages at home, but I was more Americanized than my brothers or sisters, so to speak. We were forgetting our heritage—that meant becoming more free, more liberal, being able to express myself differently. Thirteen or fourteen years ago, there was a group of people in town who talked about forming a chapter of the Sons of Italy. I would not have been one of the first ones to propose such a thing. My wife was Irish—I was one of the first ones in my family to marry out. But I went to these meetings. Before I had gotten into this I had forgotten my heritage." What catalyzed Angelo's involvement was the unexpected appearance of prejudice when the group tried to buy a piece of land for the Sons of Italy hall. In fighting the opposition, which seemed to focus on the belief that Italians are drunken and rowdy, Angelo became involved with the town government. Remembering his heritage involved accepting his origins, including painful memories of prejudice and discrimination that his earlier efforts at "Americanization" had attempted to deny.

The experience of ethnic prejudice helped Angelo see that there is more to life than leaving behind the past, becoming successful on his own, and expressing himself freely. But as he became more involved with the community he had tried to forget—more active, that is, in the Sons of Italy—he also became more involved with his town. Elected a selectman, he saw it his duty to represent not only Italian-Americans but also the welfare of the town as a whole. Abandoning one kind of individualism, he was led toward a civic individualism that entailed care for the affairs of his community in both the narrower and wider senses. While leaving behind "Americanization," he became American.

Marra James provides an interesting contrast to Angelo Donatello. Born in a small town in West Virginia, she has lived for some years in a Southern California suburb, where she has become active in a variety of causes focussing around environmental issues such as saving wild land from development. Marra was raised in the Catholic church and was active in her parish when she first came to California. She does not go to church anymore as she has gone beyond what she calls "structural religion." Yet she has carried a sensitivity to ritual over into her new concerns. She dates her involvement in the environmental movement from the celebration of the first Earth Day at a local college, and she was, when interviewed some ten years later, actively planning the local tenth anniversary celebration.

Marra has a strong and explicit understanding of the importance of community: "Many people feel empty and don't know why they feel empty. The reason is we are all social animals and we must live and interact and work together in community to become fulfilled." But she sees serious impediments to the realization of community in America: "Most people have been sold a bill of goods by our system. I call it the Three C's: cash, convenience, consumerism. It's getting worse. The reason you don't feel a part of it is that nobody is a part of it. Loneliness is a national feeling." But Marra has not reacted to this realization with despair. She is intensely active and returns to the fray whether she wins or loses. In her years as city council member and chair of a county planning commission, she has suffered plenty of defeats. "I sometimes describe myself as a rubber ball," she says. "I've been pushed down sometimes to where I've almost been pressed flat, but I've always been able to bounce back." For Marra, politics is a worthwhile educational endeavor, win or lose, perhaps especially when you lose.

Marra James is remarkable in the scope with which she defines her community: "I feel very much a part of the whole—of history. I live in a spectrum that includes the whole world. I'm a part of all of it. For what I do impacts the whole. So if I'm going to be wasteful, misuse resources— that will impact the whole world." Marra identifies herself as a moderate Republican, but her politics go beyond any such label. For her, the "whole world" is a community of memory and hope and entails practices of commitment that she assiduously carries out. Undoubtedly, there has been involvement in many communities along the way, each one important in constituting her as the person she is—her family, the church, the network of her fellow environmental activists. In trying to give substance to what is as yet an aspiration by defining her community as the whole world, she runs the risk of becoming detached from any concrete community of memory.

Finally, let us consider the example of Cecilia Dougherty, in whose life a series of communities of memory have played a part in leading to her present political commitment in ways even clearer than in the case of Marra James. Cecilia lives in a part of Santa Monica whose landscape is shaped by shade trees, schools, and churches. She, like Wayne Bauer, is an active member of the Campaign for Economic Democracy. At present she works for a local attorney involved in progressive causes, and in addition serves as an elected official of city government. Despite these rather daunting commitments, Cecilia is the single mother of four teenagers, her husband having died several years ago, an event that was for her at once traumatic and transformative.

Cecilia Dougherty began her political activism in her forties following the great break caused in the continuity of her life by her husband's death. She started out by working on the congressional campaign of a local candidate, in part because his opponent supported many things she opposed, but also to try out her capacities to engage in political life on her own. Cecilia had begun to think about taking more public initiative while her husband was living.

The critical event was meeting a colleague of her husband, a woman of their age, who told Cecilia that having heard good things about her from her husband, she was eager to learn more about her. Cecilia says that she began, "I have four children . . ." but the woman persisted, saying, "Wait just a minute. I didn't ask about your children, I asked about you. Where are *you* coming from?" At this Cecilia was stunned. "I mean, my role was a housewife and I didn't quite grasp what she was really talking about." But the woman told her: "I'm not talking about your identity as Greg's wife. I'm concerned with your identity as a human being, as a person, and as an individual, and as a woman." She invited Cecilia to join a consciousness-raising group, "a turning point in my life, a real change for me."

Once into the consciousness-raising group, Cecilia Dougherty experienced herself as waking up as if from a sleep, reaching back to hopes and aspirations she had had as a girl, before becoming a wife and mother. Cecilia rediscovered that she had wanted to become a teacher, and at first thought about going to college to fulfill that dream. She was already working as a clerk for a labor union, however, and she decided to tailor her educational aspirations around that. "I decided that I would work with what I had already." Whatever earlier "gut feelings" Cecilia may have discovered in consciousness raising, her decision to build on the past, on what she "had already," is characteristic of the way she has acted on her new sense of freedom and efficacy.

In fact, for all their importance as catalysts, contact with feminist consciousness raising and discovering her identity "as a person and as an individual" have not been the determining factors in Cecilia Dougherty's activist commitments. Rather, as she describes it, the new sense of efficacy that she learned from consciousness raising in a real sense returned her to earlier commitments and an identification with the cause of the dignity of working people that was deeply rooted in her family's experience. Her sense of purpose in political involvement is not based simply on radical individualism but grounded in the continuity of generations: "I want to see the have-nots have power that reflects their numbers, and I want to protect the future of my children and my grandchildren. I feel a historical family responsibility for continuing to be working for progressive causes."

When Cecilia was asked to explain her commitment to activism, she responded, characteristically, with the story of how her ideals of self developed through the experience of her family. That is, she employed a "second language" that organizes life by reference to certain ideals of character—virtues such as courage and honor—and commitments to institutions that are seen as embodiments of those values. For example, Cecilia's feminism is in part emulation of her mother in a different context. Her mother was an Italian immigrant who married at eighteen and did not go to college, but became the first woman in her county to be elected chair of the state Democratic Central Committee. "So," commented Cecilia, "she made me realize a commitment at a very early age. By eight years old, I was working in party headquarters, licking stamps and answering the phone."

But the paradigmatic event that gave Cecilia a deep sense of identity with the labor movement and its goals of a more just and inclusive society involved her father. When Cecilia was fourteen, her father, an Irish Catholic immigrant working for an energy corporation, went on strike. This was shortly after World War II. Cecilia vividly recalls the weeks of the strike, especially the union solidarity that got the family through it. "We went every night to the town where the union hall was," she recounted, "for dinner in the soup kitchen kind of thing, and my mother would help cook." However, the decisive event occurred six weeks into the strike, when her father was arrested on charges of throwing rocks at strikebreakers.

The shock was that Cecilia's father "who'd been such a good citizen; so honest, and so conscientious, the American-way type person" should be not only arrested, but attacked in court as a communist and rabble-rouser. The revelation of the low tactics of the corporation's lawyers had a strong impact on her, resulting in a sense of moral outrage that continues to frame her political concerns. She was also deeply impressed by her father's courage and sense of honor under attack by the "company attorneys, with their suits and everything." Most of all, she was impressed by the strength of the solidarity in the labor movement. "I realized then the value of the union and how we were utterly dependent on the union for our very sustenance."

Thus when Cecilia Dougherty returned to politics in the Democratic party, and when she decided to become heavily involved in local activism, she could, and did, draw upon a considerable heritage. She describes her transition from working wife and mother to her present, much more public involvements not so much as a choice—in the sense that one might choose to take up painting versus taking up bowling—but as a response to part of her identity, as fulfilling a responsibility to which her life, her heritage, and her beliefs have called her.

Asked what she sees her activism achieving, Cecilia responded by saying that she hopes to "bring people away from concern only about their own lives, to a sense of much, much broader, greater responsibility. It sounds very grandiose! Probably the most I'm going to be able to do is sustain and build better community in Santa Monica, you know, and that's certainly a life's work." The image of community contained in Cecilia's account of the strike is quite different from the association of like-minded individuals advocated by others we talked to.

The fundamental contrasts between Cecilia Dougherty's self-understanding and the first language of modern individualism can be narrowed to three. First, Cecilia articulates her sense of self by reference to a narrative illustrative of long-term commitments rather than desires and feelings. While she sees certain breaks with her past as crucial "turning points" in her life, she interprets the resulting freedom as an opportunity for new commitments, often "working from what I had already." Thus, unlike the radical individualistic notion of a life course based on leaving home in order to become a free self, Cecilia's self-image is rooted in a concept of the virtues that make an admirable life, especially those exemplified in the lives of her mother and father. This is the second contrast: that her sense of self is rooted in virtues that define a worthwhile life and have been passed on and modeled by others who have shared that tradition, not in a contentless freedom attained by leaving concrete commitments behind.

The third distinguishing feature of Cecilia's "second language" is her notion that community means a solidarity based on a responsibility to care for others because that is essential to living a good life. She describes her solidarity with working people and "the have-nots" as an expression of a concern for human dignity, the violation of which sparked her first anger at the abuse of power. This sense of a community of solidarity recalls the classical civic contrast between the private person who thinks first of himself alone and the citizen who knows himself to be a participant in a form of life through which his own identity is fulfilled. The civic vision is quite different from the image of a gathering of like-minded individuals whose union depends entirely on their spontaneous interest. Indeed, thinking about this contrast tends to confirm Tocqueville's claim that public order and trust cannot spring from individual spontaneity alone, but require the kind of cultivation that only active civic life can provide.

The lived source of the civic language in Cecilia Dougherty's life is not hard to identify: it was her and her parents' lifelong commitments to the labor movement. It was probably reinforced by a similar emphasis on solidarity in the Catholicism she shared with parents and husband. It is this that she has been able to expand into a general concern for "economic democracy."[18]

It is characteristic of Cecilia Dougherty and the others we have just considered that they define themselves through their commitments to a variety of communities rather than through the pursuit of radical autonomy. Yet Cecilia, like the others, exhibits a high degree of self-determination and efficacy. She exemplifies a form of individualism that is fulfilled *in* community rather than against it. Conformism, the nemesis of American individualism, does not seem to be a problem for Cecilia and the others. Their involvement in practices of commitment makes them able to resist pressures to conform. On occasion, they show great resilience in so doing, as when Marra James bounces back after being "pressed flat." Our examples suggest that Tocqueville was probably right in believing that it was isolation, not social involvement, that led to conformism and the larger danger of authoritarian manipulation.

There are authoritarian groups in the United States, sometimes devoted to destructive ends. What makes them different from genuine communities is the shallowness and distortion of their memory and the narrowness of what they hope for. A radically isolating individualism is not a defense against such coercive groups. On the contrary, the loneliness that results from isolation may precipitate the "hunger for authority" on which such groups feed.

Private and Public

Sometimes Americans make a rather sharp dichotomy between private and public life. Viewing one's primary task as "finding oneself" in autonomous self-reliance, separating oneself not only from one's parents but also from those larger communities and traditions that constitute one's past, leads to the notion that it is in oneself, perhaps in relation to a few intimate others, that fulfillment is to be found. Individualism of this sort often implies a negative view of public life. The impersonal forces of the economic and political worlds are what the individual needs protection against. In this perspective, even occupation, which has been so central to the identity of Americans in the past, becomes instrumental— not a good in itself, but only a means to the attainment of a rich and satisfying private life. But on the basis of what we have seen in our observation of middle-class American life, it would seem that this quest for purely private fulfillment is illusory: it often ends in emptiness instead. On the other hand, we found many people, some of whom we introduced earlier in this chapter, for whom private fulfillment and public involvement are not antithetical. These people evince an individualism that is not empty but is full of content drawn from an active identification with communities and traditions. Perhaps the notion that private life and public life are at odds is incorrect. Perhaps they are so deeply involved with each other that the impoverishment of one entails the impoverishment of the other. Parker Palmer is probably right when he says that "in a healthy society the private and the public are not mutually exclusive, not in competition with each other. They are, instead, two halves of a whole, two poles of a paradox. They work together dialectically, helping to create and nurture one another."[19]

Certainly this dialectical relationship is clear where public life degenerates into violence and fear. One cannot live a rich private life in a state of siege, mistrusting all strangers and turning one's home into an armed camp. A minimum of public decency and civility is a precondition for a fulfilling private life. On the other hand, public involvement is often difficult and demanding. To engage successfully in the public world, one needs personal strength and the support of family and friends. A rewarding private life is one of the preconditions for a healthy public life.

For all their doubts about the public sphere, Americans are more engaged in voluntary associations and civic organizations than the citizens of most other industrial nations. In spite of all the difficulties, many Americans feel they must "get involved." In public life as in private, we can discern the habits of the heart that sustain individualism and commitment, as well as what makes them problematic.   □

Part Two □ Public Life

Getting Involved 7

"What would you want me to tell my students about how to fulfill their responsibilities as citizens?" one of us used to ask at the conclusion of his interviews with community leaders. Almost always the characteristically American answer was "Tell them to get involved!" The United States is a nation of joiners.[1] Recent research confirms what Tocqueville said 150 years ago:

> Americans of all ages, all stations in life, and all types of disposition are forever forming associations. There are not only commercial and industrial associations in which all take part, but others of a thousand different types—religious, moral, serious, futile, very general and very limited, immensely large and very minute. . . . In every case, at the head of any new undertaking, where in France you would find the government or in England some territorial magnate, in the United States you are sure to find an association.[2]

Implicit in this penchant for "getting involved" is the peculiarly American notion of the relationship between self and society. Individuals are expected to *get* involved—to choose for themselves to join social groups. They are not automatically involved in social relationships that impose obligations not of their choosing, and social institutions that are not the product of the voluntary choice of the individuals who constitute them are perceived as illegitimate. Most people say they get involved in social institutions to achieve their self-interests or because they feel an affinity with certain others.[3] Given such assumptions about the purposes of involvement, what kind of vision can one have of the public good? What would lead such individuals to sacrifice their self-interests to the public good and consciously link their destinies to those of their ancestors, contemporaries, and descendants?

The Free and Independent Township

Tocqueville thought that the experience of getting involved in local voluntary civic associations was in itself capable of generating a sense of responsibility for the public good. He thought he saw a vivid example of how this happened in the New England township. It was, in the first place, individual self-interest that led the residents of such towns to get involved in local civic associations. But the experience of local self-government transformed them—gave them an understanding of public responsibility that transcended individual self-interest and thus turned them into "orderly, temperate, moderate, and self-controlled citizens." The New Englander, said Tocqueville, "invests his ambition and his future" in his town. "[I]n the restricted sphere within his scope, he learns to rule society; he gets to know those formalities without which freedom can advance only through revolutions, and becoming imbued with their spirit, develops a taste for order, understands the harmony of powers, and in the end accumulates clear, practical ideas about the nature of his duties and the extent of his rights."[4] But how, exactly, could getting involved in the civic associations of a small town transform self-interested motives into public commitment? And can getting involved in the voluntary associations of a large city do the same for Americans today? Before we attempt to answer these questions, let us first hear some of the civic leaders of a town that once resembled those Tocqueville visited: Suffolk, Massachusetts, the home of Joe Gorman, whose story we heard in chapter 1.

Suffolk began as a voluntary association incorporated in 1730 by an act of the Great and Central Court of Massachusetts upon petition by the residents. The expressed motive for the petition was the desire to set up a separate Congregational Church, the neighboring churches being too far away for easy travel to public worship. From its beginning, the town has been governed by an open meeting that all registered voters are eligible to attend. Held as a matter of course once a year and throughout the year if need demands, the town meeting acts as a kind of legislative assembly empowered to debate and vote on changes in the bylaws and budget. The agenda for a town meeting is called a "warrant" and specific agenda items are called "articles"—the same terminology used by the Congregational Church in its annual governing assemblies. The executive branch of the town consists of committees elected by the town's voters—a five-member board of selectmen, a finance committee, and a school board. The members of these committees serve without pay. All these political institutions resemble those studied by Tocqueville.[5] Only now, unlike in Tocqueville's time, day-to-day management of the town's affairs is carried out by paid managers responsible to the appropriate executive committee.

The traditional institutions of the town express a classic vision of what such a community is and what it must continually strive to become: a self-reliant congregation created and maintained by the voluntary cooperation of self-reliant individuals living in self-reliant families. At the same time, forming a fading background to this voluntaristic vision, there is appreciation of the town as a community of memory linking the destiny of its citizens with their ancestors and descendants. A steep-spired, whitewashed Congregational church still stands beside the town common, a few hundred feet from where the original church once stood. Across from the church is the town hall, a small whitewashed building built about two hundred years ago. Behind the town hall is the town cemetery. The gravestones of the earliest residents still stand there, and to this day any resident is entitled to free burial in the cemetery. Many local civic leaders can still successfully enhance their status by referring to how many generations their families have lived in the town. As we saw in chapter 1, when we described the local reaction to the town's 250th anniversary, many of the townspeople take pride in carrying on a venerable, but still living, tradition.

In early American history, the natural citizen of such a town was the self-employed producer of goods and services—the owner of a family farm, the self-employed craftsman, the independent retailer—people for whom the demands of work, family, and community involvement converged in the context of the town. In the eighteenth and early nineteenth centuries, when the town was populated mostly by such people, the classic vision of the nature of the community's life may, indeed, have fitted the realities of its dominant economic and social relationships.[6] But the self-employed producers of goods and services who were the main carriers of that vision are mostly gone now. As late as the 1950s, one would still have found some family-owned farms in the town, but by now all the farms have been sold and their land turned into industrial parks or subdivided into housing developments. Few self-employed craftsmen remain. But there are still many residents—like Joe Gorman—who use the classic vision of community life to give meaning to their lives. You can see them at the meetings of the town's Rotary, Lions and Kiwanis clubs; they belong to the local chamber of commerce; and some of them sit on the boards and committees through which local citizens continue to govern their town. Such individuals are often called "town fathers."

The Town Father

The town father* can be thought of as the contemporary incarnation of the character ideal of the independent citizen, which, as we have seen, summed up the spirit of nineteenth-century America for Tocqueville. The contemporary town father orients himself toward the same vision of public life represented by the independent citizen, but must be distinguished from the independent citizen because he is not truly independent. Unlike the Tocquevillian independent citizen, the town father advocates ideals that are in the end unable to guide him through the maze of economic interdependence and political conflict that defines his social world.

The nineteenth-century independent citizen lived in a community in which the demands of work, family, and neighborliness were intersecting. The contemporary town father lives in a community in which these demands still converge enough to provide a surface plausibility for the vision of public responsibility once brought to life by the independent citizen.[7] Thus Joe Gorman can see himself being a successful public relations man for his company by serving the small town where his family grew up and most of his relatives and friends still live. But insofar as he is part of a large national corporation that is likely to be committed to Suffolk only as long as its factory there is profitable, Joe could some day be forced to choose between being successful in his work and being of service to the "big family" of Suffolk. Indeed, only a few employees of a corporation such as the one Joe works for could afford to be so deeply involved in the life of their home town. Most people who espouse Joe's town father ideal, in fact, do not draw salaries from large corporations, but rather are self-employed businessmen, usually owners of commercial enterprises whose clientele is drawn mainly from the town and its immediately surrounding area. They are accordingly more preoccupied

---

*As the name "town father" implies, this character type is typically a man. This is partly because of the simple fact that the local business establishments of small towns are dominated by men, but it is also a reflection of the pattern of moral sentiments that guides the local small businessman in thinking about how to reconcile his personal drive for success with his concern for his community. It is the ideal of the traditional American family that provides the basic metaphor for structuring those sentiments: the husband enters the public world while the wife specializes in being a "homemaker." Within the family, the husband provides authority, the wife emotional support. The role played within the community by the town father is modeled on this kind of moral and emotional division of labor. The town father serves his community not so much by openly showing affection for it—that would be considered unduly "sentimental"—but by furthering its economic well-being and providing authoritative leadership. His wife assists by joining clubs that with the help of funds raised by the town fathers' "service clubs" deliver personal charitable help to the "truly needy"—usually children and old people—of the community.

than Joe with the economic "bottom line" of their community involvements. Like the yeoman farmers and self-employed craftsmen who made up the bulk of Tocqueville's independent citizens, these small businessmen—more explicitly than Joe—think of their love for their community as intertwined with what Tocqueville would have called "self-interest properly understood."[8]

A good example of a vision of community service as enlightened self-interest can be found in an interview with Howard Newton, who owns a Chrysler dealership in Suffolk established in the 1930s by his father. Howard's oldest son—Howard, Jr.—works in the dealership and seems destined to take over the business. Howard's main business competition in town comes from Suffolk Chevrolet, a dealership that is much larger than Howard's and very prominently advertised throughout the Boston area. Howard speaks of his competition in a barely hidden tone of moral disapproval: "Suffolk Chevrolet has been in town only about twenty years. It is owned by people who don't live here. They are much bigger than we are in size and volume. We live here in town and have a different approach. We do our business in a personal way." Earlier in our conversation, Howard contrasted "doing business in a personal way" with being concerned simply about maximizing profits. "There are some people for whom nothing will satisfy them. It's the same in business. There are different ways you can carry on business. We do business in a personal way."

The "personal way" of doing business involves paying attention to the "basics": "Getting to know your customers, being good to your customers." It was clear from the conversation that Howard would include being completely honest in his business dealings among the "basics." His "personal way of doing business" also involves an attitude toward the rewards to which he or anyone else is entitled from work. One should be rewarded, he strongly feels, simply and directly on the basis of the contribution one makes to a socially worthwhile undertaking. Thus, he insists on the moral value, as well as the practical utility, of giving his employees piece rates. "Jobs have to have incentives. The mechanic that works here—he's the best mechanic I've got. He has twelve dependents and he commutes in here from Boston. The way he gets paid, he has a special incentive to get work done in, say, two hours. If he does that, he gets paid extra. Well, he does that work, and you can bet that he'll be done in two hours if he says so. But then, there are other mechanics who get paid just by the hour. And you cannot count on them getting that work done in two hours like the mechanic from Boston does. That's the trouble with our business, our industry. People don't have incentives to get the jobs done. They get paid if they work for eight hours whether they do anything in those eight hours or not." "It's never any good," says

Howard, "when you give people something they don't earn and don't work for."

This "personal" approach to doing business carries over into Howard's appreciation of the value of getting personally involved with the life of his town. "Some people, in places like California, move out of their house on the average of once every five years or so: always trying to move to a different place, a better place." His criticism of this restlessness is in line with his criticism of businessmen who will be satisfied only by ever-increasing profits, even if this means that they have to treat their customers in an impersonal and manipulative way. Howard has lived in Suffolk all his life except for a couple of years spent in the military. "I love Suffolk. I have always enjoyed Suffolk's people. When I go to the post office on Monday morning, there's always someone I know that I see there, and there are always people who want to stand and talk to you. These are some of the benefits that a small town offers: continuity, the fact that everybody knows everybody else, and my children know about the community and become involved in it. For instance, my daughter who is now fifteen is involved in the basketball team and the Girl Scouts and in things at her school. Getting involved is something that you can do in a small town. Being involved in this way brings a lot of satisfaction. You get a lot of enjoyment out of it. It's simply that you are doing things for the town and for yourself. For instance, the Rotary Club is a service organization and is always doing stuff for themselves and for the citizens of Suffolk. Besides the Rotary, the Lions and the Kiwanis are also very active. All these service organizations do a lot of little things that add up to a lot. Help for the senior citizens' center, help for the recreational program, and so forth. The Knights of Columbus and the Masons also do a lot. People get involved in a town like Suffolk and they enjoy it. It's a lot of fun. You don't get monetary value. But you get the satisfaction from giving the effort."

Howard Newton thus sees a natural harmony between his self-interest and the public good of his community. In the long run, his prosperity depends on the prosperity of the community as a whole. And he deserves a share in its prosperity by doing his part to provide for the needs of its members. He earns his livelihood by directly providing a valuable service to individuals in his community—good cars at a fair price. He is not like the mechanics who receive an hourly wage but feel no obligation to do an hour's worth of work in return. He believes in the mutuality between his interests and those of his customers not simply because of some faith in the "invisible hand" of an impersonal market but because of his personal knowledge of many of his satisfied customers. On the basis of such personalized commercial relationships, he builds a general picture of his relationship to the town as a whole. His business success depends on the support of his community. But this support has not been gratuitously given. He has earned it by providing charity to its members. He and other local businessmen do this mainly through "service clubs," such as the town Rotary Club. The charity consists mostly of "little things that add up to a lot"—personal gestures of help to individuals, such as the very old and very young, who clearly need help but cannot provide it for themselves and thus have no moral responsibility to do so.

Howard sees himself as a self-reliant individual whose enlightened self-interest is neatly congruent with the interests of his community. His ideas about the harmony between his and the community's interests flow into his understanding of town politics. The town government should provide an efficient framework within which self-reliant individuals can earn their livelihood by providing useful things to individuals in the community. The town government basically does "a pretty good job. There are a lot of things that they do that they don't get credit for. The civic duty type of deal. It may be over-manpowered—but that's universal. Maybe we don't need quite so many people doing all those jobs, and maybe we could cut back some." In such a moral vocabulary, the highest kind of civic duty is "doing things you don't get credit for." And the worst kind of political irresponsibility is getting credit for something that you don't do—as is the case with the people who supposedly occupy sinecures in an "over-manpowered" government.

One of the major problems with town politics nowadays, according to Howard, is that "special interest groups" have too much influence at the town meeting. Such groups are "interested just in one thing. They all organize among themselves and show up for the meeting. They push for just one thing." The kinds of people who do this are usually the "new people in town," who try to use political organizing tactics to wrest benefits from the town that they have not individually earned. A good example of a special interest group is the school teachers, who often pack the town meeting with their friends and supporters to push through allocations for higher school budgets and to sell the town on educational services it does not need. Echoing Joe Gorman, Howard says, "Nowadays in the school system you have all these highly skilled people—all these specialists—wanting to teach these special courses. Well, they say these are wonderful persons, but I don't think they are well worthwhile. I think in the schools we have to get back to the basics." Howard would say that it is legitimate for a group like the chamber of commerce to organize vigorously to promote town meeting decisions that would make it easier to do business in town. Such policies would merely assure a framework of regulations that would enable individual businesses to make a contribution to the community by providing products or jobs needed by individual community members. If individual businesses fail to provide desired products, they will go out of business. Groups like the school teachers, however, are using their organizations to gain higher salaries for the same work they have been doing all along, or to create new jobs that will provide services for which there is no natural demand in the town—services the value of which is appreciated only by educated experts. That is what makes them "special interest groups" rather than "community service organizations."

Howard sums up his outlook on politics by declaring: "It's never any good when you give people something they don't earn and work for. The people don't realize what it means to take money from the government. For instance, once I was sitting in the statehouse in Boston, sitting in on a hearing on the auto industry, and an aide came up to one of the senators and I heard him say, 'Excuse me, Senator, we should vote to approve this bill. It isn't costing us anything; it's coming from the federal government.' But the federal government—it's everyone of us sitting in our own homes, paying our own bills."

In the vocabulary of the town father, the public good is thus defined in terms of the long-range ability of individuals each to get what they have paid for, no more and no less. One's contribution to the community—in time and taxes—is not thought of as a duty but as a voluntary investment. One of the most important problems facing the community is, therefore, the problem of "free riders"[9] who take more than they contribute and thus keep the investments of good citizens from yielding their rightful return. Tocqueville thought that such a vision of the public good founded in enlightened self-interest was "the best suited of all philosophical theories to the wants of men in our time." It did "not inspire great sacrifices, but every day it prompts some small ones; by itself it cannot make a man virtuous, but its discipline shapes a lot of orderly, temperate, moderate, careful, and self-controlled citizens"[10]—citizens, one would imagine, very much like Howard Newton and Joe Gorman. But as Tocqueville noted, such civic virtues were not purely and simply the product of interest calculations. Enlightened self-interest established "habits" that "unconsciously" turned the will toward such virtues. "At first it is by necessity that men attend to the public interest, afterward by choice. What had been calculation becomes instinct. By dint of working for the good of his fellow citizens, he in the end acquires a habit and taste for serving them."[11] One can see this "habit and taste" at work in the consciousness of Howard Newton and even more vividly in that of Joe Gorman. Buried within their language of individual self-interest is what we have called a second language of social commitment. Howard finds it "fun" to be involved in the town, even though he doesn't get "monetary value." Joe Gorman worked so hard on the town anniversary festival because Suffolk is like a family to him and "I love being a part of it." Such "natural citizens" of a community such as Suffolk experience little conflict between their self-interest and the community's public interest precisely because a long-term involvement in the community has led them to define their very identity in terms of it. Insofar as one defines oneself as a "natural citizen" of the town, to harm the town would be to harm oneself.

In the twentieth century, however, the social basis of this process of moral identification, in which a conception of the community's interest comes to shape one's conception of self-interest, is fragile. Contemporary town fathers no longer inhabit the homogeneous, well-integrated towns Tocqueville described. As pointed out in chapter 1, Suffolk is now a suburb of Boston, part of the social life of the metropolis and the economic life of national and international markets. To maintain their moral balance, town fathers have to pretend they live in a kind of community that no longer exists.

Howard Newton's impassioned speech at a Suffolk Rotary Club meeting in 1981 justifying the federal government's $1.2 billion guaranteed loan to Chrysler to bail the corporation out of its economic distress is a vivid example of the conflict thrust upon the contemporary town father by the diversity and interdependence of complex national and international political systems.

Howard began by pulling a little American flag out of his pocket and waving it at the audience. "A lot of people have been saying things during our meetings criticizing the government for giving this loan, and today I'd like to say my piece about this," he announced. He told his fellow Rotarians how Chrysler had become a great corporation in the 1920s and 1930s by coming up with one engineering breakthrough after another—the floating engine, hydraulic brakes, and so forth. The company, he implied, had truly earned its stature.

In the 1950s, when he was his son's age, Howard had gone to Detroit and actually visited one of the Chrysler plants. "Now I'm not against unions," he said, "but those workers there weren't putting in a full day's work. They wanted to get paid for not working. It finally got to the point where they had no pride in their work. Not enough pride even to buy the cars they had made. They say you can go to the Chrysler parking lot nowadays and see that half the cars are foreign cars. The unions have funds so that you'll not only get paid when you work, but you'll get paid when you don't work. So now Chrysler is several billions of dollars in the red, Ford is in the red, and even GM is hurting."

And then came the most poignant part of his speech. "Now, if the government doesn't give that loan, people like me who have worked hard all my life will be out of work and the sixty people we employ will be out of work, and so will thousands and thousands of people all over the country. And you know how much money it will take in welfare, unemployment, and so forth to take care of them—$22 billion!" He ended up by stressing that if such a tragedy were to come to pass, it would be the fault of the unions who have forced the corporations to give wages to people who do not work and of "Ralph Nader and other do-gooders" who have insisted on government regulations that are uneconomical. He waved the American flag again: "I ask you to take pride in the country. Buy American products. Take pride in being an American and pride in what you make."

The Rotary Club members gave Howard a very polite reception. It was clear that most of them deeply respected him as an individual. But many of them were nevertheless skeptical about the loan to Chrysler. They thought that if a company, like an individual worker, failed through its own fault to produce things the public wanted to buy, it should not expect public assistance; and, unlike Howard, they seemed to think that the Chrysler Corporation's management, and not just its workers, shared the blame for the corporation's troubles.

One might reasonably suspect that if Howard had been, say, a General Motors dealer, he would have agreed with his fellow Rotarians that the government should not have bailed out Chrysler. His ideas about individual responsibility for success and failure through work were fully in tune with those of his fellow Rotarians and, indeed, of most of the rest of the local small businessmen represented in the Suffolk Chamber of Commerce. Given those ideas, it required considerable mental gymnastics for him to argue for the Chrysler loan. But this is not to say that his new ideas about the need for massive government help for a failing industry were simply a rationalization of his own economic interest. They were the result of the conflict created by the fact that he was being forced to recognize his dependence on a complicated national and international political economy. In much of their daily working lives, Suffolk's small businessmen are insulated from that vast system. To the extent that they can take for granted a steady supply of the things they sell, their success in business feels as though it depends on their personal salesmanship, which in turn depends on the extent to which they are willing to work and on how much they are trusted in the community. For most practical purposes, they live in a local economic world that is a remnant of the past. Their thinking about the moral meaning of work, family, and community makes sense out of the patterns of life lived within that remnant. But that thinking runs into painful anomalies when and if they are forced, like Howard, to cope directly with the more complex realities of the present. Honest, hardworking men who have owned businesses that have served the community all their lives should not suddenly have to lose their jobs because a large corporation, headquartered far away, goes bankrupt. One common response to an inexplicable anomaly is to ignore it. That is what most of Howard's fellow small businessmen seemed to prefer to do. That is likely what Howard himself would have preferred to do if he had not been in the painful position of being unable to afford to ignore it.

From Town to Metropolis

The moral language of the town father was the dominant language of the era Tocqueville described—the eighteenth and early nineteenth centuries, when the moral imagination of Americans was nurtured by practices of commitment in the interlocking social, economic, and political life of "strong and independent" small towns. The language of the contemporary town father remains vital to the extent that it remains embedded in remnants of the interlocking, localized patterns of work, family, and community that once shaped the social landscape of that bygone era. But since the end of the nineteenth century, the American landscape has been forever changed by urbanization and industrialization.

Though urban Americans still get involved in an astounding variety of voluntary associations, the associational life of the modern metropolis does not generate the kinds of second languages of social responsibility and practices of commitment to the public good that we saw in the associational life of the "strong and independent township." The metropolitan world is one in which the demands of work, family, and community are sharply separated and often contradictory, a world of diverse, often hostile groups, interdependent in ways too complex for any individual to comprehend. Unlike the town father, the metropolitan resident's work is carried on in large, private corporations that produce commodities for a national or international market or in large government bureaucracies that deliver a range of services in response to the pressures generated by conflicting interest groups. The urbanite's family and community relations are carried on in homogeneous circles of individuals with whom he feels a personal affinity because they share similar beliefs, values, and styles of life. The separation between the worlds of work and of family and community is often expressed and realized by a daily commute between factory or office and residential neighborhood.

In such circumstances, what positive meaning can public life have for a private individual? What responsibilities does one have for the long-term social effects of the work one does? What duties does one have toward the vast agglomeration of anonymous individuals that surrounds the circles of family and friends with whom one is personally involved? Can the impersonal metropolis be a community of memory?

One characteristic response to the scale and complexity of metropolitan life is that which Tocqueville predicted: "As the extent of political society expands, one must expect the sphere of private life to contract. Far from supposing that the members of our new societies will ultimately come to live in public, I am more afraid that they will in the end only form very small coteries."[12] The social landscape then comes to consist, in Robert Park's words, of "little worlds that touch but do not interpenetrate."[13]

The life course of Ted Oster (the California lawyer who sometimes talks of life as a "big pinball game") is a good example of this process of privatization. In college he was class president and a political activist deeply concerned with America's Indochina war policy. Just before he got married, he led the student strike at his college in protest against the U.S. invasion of Cambodia. Since he got married and became a lawyer, however, he has "left all that kind of stuff. I don't feel the need for it now." His work as a lawyer gives him a great deal of satisfaction, but the amount of time he must spend at work makes him "very, very much value whatever time I have to spend at home." Now his circle of friends has narrowed from the days when he was a student leader, but it is a "more closely developed circle of friends and maybe I get a lot of satisfaction in being with my friends and having them like me and the numbers are relatively insignificant." With the narrowing of his circle of friends has come a transformation of his political views. He has become a registered Republican, firmly against government interference in free enterprise, and very concerned about fraud and waste in the welfare system—political views that "ten years ago would have really shocked me." This change in political ideology, however, "has nothing whatsoever to do with my views about people. In other words, because I'm a registered Republican doesn't mean that I don't think we all have a responsibility to each other in the sense of society and looking out for each other. I still have a view toward my fellow man, a charitable view, and that sort of thing." But when asked what it would mean to exercise his sense of social

responsibility, he speaks about becoming a "scoutmaster with my kids."
He is not interested in exerting a lot of energy getting involved in national political causes. "I have a big problem with identifying with hundreds of millions of whatever—people, flowers, cars, miles. I can see the
community around me."

When thinking of the imperative to "love thy neighbor," many metropolitan Americans like Ted thus consider that responsibility fulfilled
when they love those compatible neighbors they have surrounded themselves with, fellow members of their own lifestyle enclave, while letting
the rest of the world go its chaotic, mysterious way.

Urban Localism

Just who those neighbors are and how compatible they may be depends
upon the dynamics of social class as well as the voluntary choices of
individuals. People who can afford it often tend to move into enclaves
where they will be literally surrounded by people with similar tastes. An
extreme example of this is the Southern California community of Santa
Eulalia—a place of rolling hills, graceful eucalyptus trees, luxuriant
flowering bushes, and large mansions. Within those homes, protected
behind elaborate security systems, live the heads of some of this country's largest corporations. But life in this community shows little trace of
the hectic, competitive activity that characterizes the boardrooms of
those corporations. Here all the emphasis is on relaxed sociability—for
the men, friendly banter on the community's golf course or relaxed
luncheons in the casual atmosphere of its major restaurant; for the
women, a busy round of activities in social clubs that organize benefits
for charity. There are no street numbers on the houses here, as if it were
beneath the residents' dignity to be reduced to units in the postal service's bureaucratized delivery system. Everything about Santa Eulalia is
set up to assure its residents that they are unique individuals who interact
with the other unique individuals in their community not as anonymous
competitors but as personal friends. It is not uncommon to hear residents of such wealthy Southern California enclaves say that they have
fully satisfied their social responsibilities by generously participating in
the various charitable benefits—dinner dances, fashion shows, art exhi-
bitions, and so on—sponsored by the clubs in the community, while
frankly maintaining a "public be damned" stance in their business dealings. Thus, Tom Clay, a real estate investor who is one of the most convivial members of the Santa Eulalia social scene, admits with pride: "I

have managed to make a fair amount of money in my life, and everything I have done, I have done for my own ego."

Few of those we talked to could afford to live in an exclusive residential community such as Santa Eulalia, but they often made considerable financial sacrifices to escape from inner city neighborhoods, where they had been surrounded with "undesirables," and move into "decent" suburbs, from which they commuted to work in the central city. Like Steve Johnson, a city high school teacher who lives in a middle-class suburb near Santa Eulalia, they see their choice of suburban living in terms that are as much moral as practical. "When we lived in the city, we felt hemmed in. The crowds near the ocean. All the people. I don't want drunk drivers driving like crazy down my street. It was just too crowded, too noisy. What's important to us is the sky, the quiet, and the space."

What distinguishes this quiet environment from the fast-paced life of the central city is its guiding ethic: "It's different. It's a sense of community. We're not out there making bucks, trying to get contracts, trying to sell something, to buy something. We're working for the community. *And we're meeting people*" (said with great emphasis). According to Steve, such a sense of community "makes for a particular kind of personality— calm, slow-paced." This kind of personality is not distinguished by the amount of energy it has, but by the intention of that energy. It is an energy directed toward expressing itself in communion with other people, not in using other people as means to its personal goals. It is a personality directed by an expressive, rather than utilitarian, ethic. And suburban life allows one the opportunity to retreat from the utilitarian world of work into an expressive world of friendly community. "At work I have five hours of tense human contact. I can only take so much. I have so much emotional energy and it gets drained away," Steve says.

For many of our suburbanites, however, it is becoming less and less possible to use residential mobility to find a private haven from the problems of the public world. Many of them worried that the quality of their neighborhoods was deteriorating. Some were trying to escape from this by moving to more "exclusive" neighborhoods, but the inflation of housing prices and the limitations of transportation systems were making this increasingly difficult. Meanwhile state and federal governments were trying to levy more taxes from suburbanites to pay for the costs of maintaining the facilities and social services required by the central city—a move the suburbanites often resented. Thus Steve Johnson and his wife were fighting desperately to slow down the development of their suburban community—to "keep it from becoming like Los Angeles."

"If I had my way," said an ally of Steve's in this local battle, "I would like this place to be like it was in 1959, before we even came here—even though this would mean that we would not even be there. I wish we could have bought twenty acres back then—twenty acres in the back country—and put a moat around it with alligators in it. A good community is when you have a complete mixture—enough shopping to take care of your needs, but not large shopping centers that would bring people in from outside the community. I would want to see our community develop as if it were an island."

The Concerned Citizen

With their private sanctuaries threatened, such people often feel the need to get involved in politics. Unlike the town father, they experience such participation not as the routine fulfillment of the duties of citizenship, but as a heroic enterprise. They often begin their political careers in trepidation—fear of speaking in public, fear of being humiliated by the distant, powerful people who inhabit City Hall. They see their involvement in self-sacrificial terms, as a giving up of the real joys of a good life—the joys of staying at home, at peace with family, neighbors, and friends. They often call themselves "concerned citizens."* Implicit in this designation is the idea that one can be a good citizen simply by being passively law abiding, and that one need become actively involved in public issues only when one becomes concerned about threats to the interests of one's self and one's community.

Steve Johnson and many of his beleaguered neighbors in Southern California think of themselves as concerned citizens; but our most vivid example of this character ideal is Mike Conley, a retired machinist who, like town fathers Joe Gorman and Howard Newton, happens to live in Suffolk, Massachusetts. Mike is part of an influx of migrants from the central city to Suffolk that began before World War II and has continued down to the present. Most of these are blue-collar workers who, as a town official puts it, "came from places like Somerville and Chelsea where they lived in very high-density situations—triple decker apartments, etc. They are going to make their final stand here. They have

---

*Unlike the town father, the concerned citizen is as likely to be a woman as a man—in some contexts even more likely because housewives have more free time to get involved in political activism than their working husbands.

shot their wad in coming from Somerville or Chelsea and there's no place to go." A primary concern of Mike and his blue-collar friends and neighbors is that nothing disrupt the quality of life they are trying to create in their single-family homes.

Mike got involved in local politics when he banded together with some neighbors to petition the town for improvements in the neighborhood's sidewalks. As for many of our politically involved citizens, his first experiences in public life were terrifying. "When I would stand up in front of the town meeting and speak, I had a nerve in the side of my mouth that would twitch because I was so full of nervousness about speaking in public." But he forced himself to learn, attending night courses at local schools in speaking and public administration. Eventually, he became an effective speaker and a local leader to be reckoned with. He has recently become a leader of a group that calls itself the Concerned Citizens of Suffolk.

This group was formed to block a proposed HUD-sponsored project that would have provided housing for the town's elderly—and also for some low-income (probably black and Hispanic) families from Boston. Mike is bluntly bitter about what this would do to his community. "You know what low-cost housing is like. You put in so many houses and you will take people who are destitute, so called, and within a year they will tear the wallpaper out. They will tear the copper pipes out to sell them and buy booze, and if you are within a mile of the place they will rob you and beat you up and rape you. These people have no sense of values. They will go to bed with anyone who puts his bucks in their pockets. All they care about is booze. I don't say that they are wrong—but I don't want them living near me, causing trouble for me."

But it is not just people below him who are immoral. People above him are just as bad, only their cardinal sins are greed and avarice rather than lust and drunkenness. "Because of the things I see, I don't have respect for educated people"—especially for lawyers who manipulate the law to serve the interests of the rich. Big businessmen are just as bad: "The oil companies, they have a monopoly. All the heads of these big companies work together and they are going to keep jacking the price up. I agree with Reagan—things have to be deregulated. But now these oil companies are going to get together and they're going to keep the price way up. Hard times are coming." He tends to distrust local small businessmen because they are in favor of opening the town to more industry and to apartment buildings. "As a planner I have always fought apartments in Suffolk. I came from Somerville. I came out here, my father came out here because of wanting to have a single family residence." And he distrusts most politicians, national, state, and local.

"Look at those things in Egypt [the pyramids]. Look at the vast number of people that they buried in building those things. That's what politics is like. It's the same way today, but they're somewhat more sophisticated about it. Look at the Roman Empire. It fell apart because of lust and booze. What we've got today—is it any better than that? Where is the Christianity in all of this?"

What remains of "Christianity" in this country seems to be identified with good, family-oriented people such as Mike and his neighbors—people who at times have been so afraid of being robbed or vandalized that "you couldn't go to Mass together on Sunday morning. One person had to stay behind in the house or if you didn't by the time you got back, the house would be broken into." One neatly focussed glimpse of the moral ideals that govern the social relations of such good people comes not from Mike's discussion of religion, but from his description of his favorite recreation, square dancing. Mike and his wife belong to a square dance club that has chapters throughout New England. They love square dancing. According to Mike, you mix partners during the dancing, hold hands with other women, other people's wives—and yet "it's all very clean fun." Every summer for the past four years, the Conleys have had a big gathering at their house for everyone in the square dance club. About a hundred people picnic in their large yard, and even though there is not much room for parking, they all manage to park their cars very neatly so that no one gets in anyone else's way. The square dancers all bring their children to the picnic. Mike considers that important. They start out with each family sitting on its own individual blanket, but then they end up going around, sharing some of their food and drink and mixing in. It's a very good time. Mike's ideas about square dancing seem to correspond with his ideas about good community living. Each family should provide for itself. When Mike's family grew up during the depression, "We worked like dogs to get along. But we never took a penny from anyone. And we made it." This self-reliance should not make one antisocial. Families should get involved with other families to enjoy life together. But such sociability must be orderly and "clean." And for it to be so, the individual participants must be self-reliant and self-controlled.

A good society thus depends in the last analysis on the goodness of individuals, not on the soundness of institutions or the fairness of laws. Accordingly, Mike Conley believes that one cannot rely on the legal system to give justice to decent people such as himself, because laws are too easily manipulated by the selfish rich and too frequently broken with impunity by the immoral poor. True justice is a matter of giving people what they deserve; and knowledge of what people deserve comes out of the common sense of good people.

Typically, Mike illustrates these ideas by giving a series of concrete examples, rather than formulating them in general terms. He tells how he handled two cases of nepotism that he discovered when he was elected to a post in the town government. The first case emphasizes the importance of fairness in politics. The son of a local official had been given a make-work job in the town hall because of his father's influence. "I said, 'Fire him right now. I don't want anybody taking a job for patronage.' Then I got a call a little later from the assistant town manager. He told me the guy was still there. He was suing the town for having gone back on its contract with him. Well, I said, 'I don't know'—and I didn't care." In the end, the young man was laid off and there were no legal problems.

The second case modifies the demand for fairness with a call for sympathy. Immediately after telling the story about firing the young man, Mike talked about another case of nepotism, toward which he had a more positive attitude. This was a story about another son of a local official—a "brilliant kid" who unfortunately had a drinking problem and marital difficulties. With the help of his father, he was able to get a job working for the town. Mike was sympathetic because the job provided this young man with stability and gave him the opportunity to solve some of his problems. So he did not make a fuss about the appointment.

But how is one to know exactly when to temper a commitment to fairness with feelings of sympathy? Mike does not answer this by referring to absolute principles but rather by appealing to the quality of his character. "I'm telling you this," he says, "because it shows you what kind of person I am. I have a firm set of convictions and I speak my mind. I will compromise. Hell, when you get up in the morning and say your prayers, you've already started to compromise. But it's the part where my values go away that I won't compromise." Mike is convinced that he is a person of courage and integrity and that it is because of this that his actions are right, even though, as illustrated by his handling of the two nepotism cases, they might seem to be based on contradictory principles.

But how is one to tell if someone is truly a person of courage and integrity? In the end, Mike appeals to the common sense of "decent people"—hardworking, self-controlled people of modest means who struggle heroically to resist the blandishments of a corrupt society. Such convictions have, of course, an extremely powerful resonance in American culture. They are constantly affirmed and reaffirmed by our most popular literary genres—the stories of the tough, courageous cowboy and the hardboiled, incorruptible detective. Consider, for example, *The Verdict*, one of the most popular films of 1982. The hero in this movie is a Boston lawyer whom bad luck has forced to the fringes of the legal establishment. He argues the case of a victim in a medical malpractice suit and in the course of the movie finds out that the major institutions in the city are riddled with corruption—the hospitals, the hierarchy of the Catholic Church, and the law courts are all controlled by unprincipled people who manipulate the letter of the law to suit their interests. With little to go on but his own personal resourcefulness and courage, he withstands a series of attempts by the leaders of these institutions to destroy him and his client. When he finally appears to triumph, his opponents try to snatch away his victory by invoking a legal technicality. But he emerges victorious by convincing a panel of jurors, decent people like himself, that they should follow not the letter of the law but their own innate sense of what is right.

But if the major religious and legal institutions of our society are so untrustworthy, where can ordinary, decent people get their sense of what is right, their appreciation of the public good? Neither popular works of fiction such as *The Verdict* nor the beliefs of people such as Mike Conley provide any convincing answer to this question. One nurtures public virtue, they suggest, only by withdrawing into *private* life, by associating with people who share one's own standards of decency, familiar others uncorrupted by the public world. One gets involved in public life only to protect one's hearth and home and one's decent friends and neighbors from the evils of a mysterious, threatening, complicated society composed of shadowy, sinister, immoral strangers. There is no rationale here for developing public institutions that would tolerate the diversity of a large, heterogeneous society and nurture common standards of justice and civility among its members.

Urban Cosmopolitanism

There are, of course, many urban Americans who would reject Mike Conley's moralism as crude and primitive. Many of them would rather sympathize with Brian Palmer's view that "if you've got the money, honey, you can do your own thing as long as your thing doesn't destroy someone else's property, or interrupt their sleep, or bother their privacy." A sophisticated person, they would say, is one who tolerates and, indeed, positively enjoys diversity and uses reason rather than passion to resolve conflicts with others. The style of reasoning that leads to such conclusions finds its natural home among people whose family background, education, and good luck have given them a wider range of opportunities for mobility than Howard Newton and Mike Conley—among cosmopolitan professionals rather than localized entrepreneurs or wage workers.

The modern professional's identity is bound up with the possession of certain specialized skills, developed, certified, and evaluated by a national system of educational institutions and professional associations. The application of these skills typically requires resources that can only be provided by large-scale organizations and commits one to a career path that entails moving from job to job and place to place. A professional must be ready to move to wherever the best opportunities for professional advancement open up. Being tied to one particular job in one particular location is tantamount to being stuck, trapped, denied the opportunity for personal fulfillment. You must, as one person we know put it, constantly be ready to "grow your own roots." The life situation of professionals, then, leads them to view the reconciliation of individual ambition with the need to find joy in a human community in a different way from the small town businessman and the locally rooted wage earner. Professionals see themselves as providing a kind of service to others by doing well the very things that will make them a success. Thus, for instance, doctors are able to see their personal success in their profession as taking place because they have made a general contribution to the quality of medical care.

If the only way one makes a contribution to the community's good is through specialized application of a professional skill, one gets lonely. The company of family and friends remains important. While mobile professionals in the United States do indeed engage themselves in complicated networks of intimate relationships, these networks are often not tied to a particular place. One may maintain close friendships with a host of peo| scattered all across the country. The members of these "radial" friendship networks tend, moreover, to be very diverse. The friends one makes at work may be very different from the friends one makes through a recreation club or a church, and they are not likely to know one another. Indeed, the professional often considers it a major virtue to be able to accept a wide range of people with different values and styles of life as friends.[14]

But this moral tolerance often makes it extremely difficult for professionals to give any justification for the sacrifice of private interests to the public good. We saw this difficulty vividly exemplified in many of the therapists discussed in chapter 5, who use therapeutic self-awareness to fulfill some of the functions home ownership fulfills for Mike Conley: to manage the conflicts of the harsh, impersonal public world and provide refuge in a community of like-minded friends. The therapist's "circle of friends, formed after his own taste" has the advantage of much more flexibility than the urban or suburban neighborhood enclave. It is not confined to a particular space, and it is based not on rigid similarities in lifestyle but on negotiated compatibilities of felt needs. It tends to take the shape of a wide array of dyadic relationships between oneself and a host of other people, many unknown to one another. Since it has no fixed values, it does not engender an angry program to impose its values on the rest of the world. It produces, rather, a bewilderment in the face of the problems of modern politics. As therapist Ellen Schneider puts it: "The complexity is what astounds me. It's just overwhelming how many aspects of the situation there are, but there's no one solution."

The therapeutic ethos is not the only way of thinking about the public good for modern cosmopolitans. Since the beginning of this century, professionals have been actively engaged in "good government" reform movements. Although the moral reasoning of such civic-minded professionals encourages much greater concern for the public welfare than the discourse of the therapist, it shares a fundamental weakness with the latter: it sees moral concerns as matters of personal preference and is thus unable to give any substantive definition of the public good.

The Civic-Minded Professional

Consider, for example, Eleanor Macklin, a graduate of the school of public administration at Yale who works in both therapy and management—she is the manager of a mental health center and spends much of her leisure time involved in the League of Women Voters. She also happens to be a resident of Suffolk and has spoken out on the same issues that worry Mike Conley and his fellow concerned citizens. Yet Eleanor frames those issues in a very different way. Where Conley sees evil and corruption, she sees differences in values, interests, and opinions. Where Conley would condemn, she would educate. Where he would fight, she would mediate. For instance, regarding the dispute between the Suffolk Housing Authority and the townspeople over public housing that might have brought poor blacks and Hispanics into the town, she says: "The Housing Authority should say: we need to provide housing for people, even for some poor people who would come from Boston. It's the humanitarian thing to do. The Housing Authority could have presented this and then begun working with people to develop common ideas about exactly how this could be accomplished. But no, they didn't do that. They just went out and made their plans, and they tried to push those plans onto everybody else. I would love to see them buy some houses scattered throughout the community and subsidize them and allow low-income people to live there without advertising the fact that they were low-income. The problem with HUD and the federal government is that they force you to take certain things, take it or leave it. So I supported the formation of the Concerned Citizens of Suffolk. I supported their right to make their objections. That's not to say that I would agree with everything that they have said. But they must have some opportunity for public expression of their concerns. You have to deal with the concerns of these people." As it happened, the town became polarized, and "when things get polarized, everybody loses."

The discourse of such a civic-minded professional denies that in most cases one can make a valid public judgment about the relative legitimacy of different conceptions of life goals. Privately, one might not agree with the demands of blue-collar whites to keep poor blacks and Hispanics out of their neighborhood, but one must respect the right of these people to be heard, just as one must presumably respect the right of the urban poor to be heard. This assumes, however, that such competing claims can be resolved peacefully by the creation of neutral technical solutions that are beyond debate. Eleanor recalls that "at Yale during one of my seminars we had a long discussion about our professor's contention that business and government have to get together. One person raised his hand and asked, 'If that happens, who is going to protect the public interest?' That's an important question. The local chamber of commerce—and other groups in this town and across this country—they are exercising tremendous control over the affairs of the community and causing damage. And the problem is that government officials aren't caring about the public interest. You see one of the problems with this adversarial relationship in the case of the elderly /low-cost family housing controversy of last year. I think the approach to be taken to things like this is the one advocated by one of my professors. In a democratic society, he says, the only way to go is to get different groups involved and to have an honest broker mediating between them; and to have all the groups involved in comprehensive research on the issue, from the economic, sociological, and political points of view."

The public good is thus defined in terms of a utilitarian individualism that differs from the utilitarianism of the town fathers in that it disagrees that the good will arise naturally—as if by an invisible hand—out of the spontaneous interplay among local businessmen whose individual self-interest is tempered by concern for social respectability and affection for their community. The utilitarianism of the civic-minded professional asserts that individuals can know their long-term interests in today's complex world only by careful research into the consequences of different courses of action. "Once all the facts are known then a good decision can be made," Harry Reynolds, a civic-minded professional from Southern California, believes. A broad range of citizen participation is desirable to obtain information so that a decision can be made in the best interests of each. Ideally, one's political leaders should not primarily be moral exemplars, as Mike Conley would demand, but well-educated experts: "more intelligent, better educated, brighter, and more dedicated than the average person"—the type to develop comprehensive formulae for individuals realistically to pursue their various interests in a community. "A good leader needs to have a basic sense of justice," Harry says. This is not thought of as a good in itself but as a means to effective mobilization of constituents: "In a way, you are trying to get as broad a constituency as possible. And that works only if people on the periphery think you are a fair and honest and honorable person."

Such hopes for achieving community peace through neutral technical solutions are, however, based on problematic hidden assumptions. First of all, one must assume that, in the long run, the interests of the parties to political conflict are not fundamentally incompatible—so that one contending group does not permanently have to sacrifice its welfare for the good of another or for the good of society as a whole. This might be plausible if politics were being conducted in the context of a steadily expanding economy that would enable all to regularly increase their standards of living so long as a general peace and harmony prevailed. But the assumption obviously loses its plausibility in a stagnant, "zero-sum" economy[15] such as ours keeps threatening to become, in which one group becomes richer only at the cost of making others poorer. And even in an expanding economy, one can assume a fundamental compatibility of long-term interests only if all contending interests are, at bottom, based on economic concerns and not, as one finds in the debate over abortion, on contradictory beliefs about moral values.

Secondly, the civic-minded professional's hopes for a technical solution to political conflict assume that technical expertise—the ability to carry out comprehensive research "from the economic, sociological, and political points of view"—uncontestably qualifies one to be a leader. This might be so if the techniques available to social scientists for gathering data were highly reliable and if the accepted procedures for analyzing that data usually produced unambiguous conclusions—and if the experts could be generally trusted to be so impartial that their work was never influenced by personal ambition or greed. But social science journals are full of debates about the validity of various kinds of research, and people such as Mike Conley retain a healthy skepticism about the motives of experts. It is no surprise, then, that the arguments of the civic-minded professional often fall upon deaf ears.

Consider the way in which Eleanor Macklin participated in the Suffolk town meeting called to vote on the public-housing proposal opposed so vehemently by Mike Conley and the other concerned citizens. After a number of speakers had fulminated against accepting any HUD-sponsored public housing ("HUD is a socialist, revolutionary government organization that wants to overthrow the fabric of this country and its towns. If HUD ran this country we would be in alliance with the Soviet Union and with Castro"), Eleanor rose to speak. All she asked was a simple procedural question: was it absolutely certain that the old-age housing project and the low-cost family project had to be accepted together in the form in which they were being proposed? Was there any way to separate them? It was a question that tried to suggest a compromise that all parties might rationally agree was in their best interest. But the official answer was "No"—current HUD regulations forbade such an arrangement. And the emotional tone of the meeting also shouted a resounding "No"—the angry, fearful whites were terrified of having their safety endangered and their families corrupted by the alien mores of poor ethnic minorities. The one-sided debate moved toward its angry conclusion.

The Professional Activist

The civic-minded professional provides cosmopolitan Americans with what is perhaps their dominant language for thinking about public commitment. There is, however, a kind of dialect of this language to be found among cosmopolitans committed to more radical kinds of social change, the language of the professional activist. Our conversation with Wayne Bauer, the Campaign for Economic Democracy activist whom we introduced in chapter 1, provides a good example of this language.

Wayne would criticize the thinking of civic-minded professionals such as Eleanor Macklin for being too optimistic about the possibilities of negotiating compromises and too naive about the harshness of power politics. He would say they ignore the fact that people's interests may be so fundamentally opposed that there is no way to develop a compromise acceptable to all. They also ignore the fact that the poor and the powerless always seem to lose out in such arrangements. What is needed above all is to empower the poor so that they will be able to achieve a fair share of their interests. That is what he has been doing in his tenant-organizing work: "I organize tenants to take care of an immediate crisis that they have. But really what I do is give them a sense of power about their own lives." But what will they do once they get that power? They will be able to participate in a vital way in the kind of process the civic-minded professional speaks of—a process in which citizens of equal power reach reasonable compromises about how they are to achieve their various interests under a given set of circumstances.

The language of the professional activist thus has the same basic structure and shares the same basic inadequacies as that of the civic-minded professional: needs and wants are relative and justice is a fair chance to get what one wants. The only difference is that professional activists insist that a fair chance can only come about when all groups have equal power, which they are convinced is not now the case. But the language of professional activists contains its own paradox: it cannot account for the moral commitments underlying their behavior. As long as one has the power to get what one wants, why should one care about others who do not? What justifies the hardships and frustrations faced by a dedicated professional activist? The relativistic moral language used by many of the professional activists we interviewed gives no real answer to such questions. Sometimes they speak of commitment simply in terms of personal preference; for others, politics is a thrilling kind of game in which they test themselves in the heat of power struggles. But often in the lives of professional activists—and for that matter, of civic-minded professionals as well—one senses a deeper and more positively defined commitment to the public good than their language can usually articulate.

"Getting involved" for most of those we have met so far in this chapter has two fundamental meanings. It expresses a genuine concern for one's local community, a concern expressed in working for its betterment and caring for those in need within it. This form of getting involved implies an extension of the notion of family to include the local community, as when Joe Gorman speaks of Suffolk as "a big family." The second meaning of getting involved has to do with the protection of one's interests, so vivid in the consciousness of the concerned citizen, but never far from the consciousness of the town father either.

The civic-minded professional and the professional activist are often motivated by community concern, but they see the community largely in terms of a variety of self-interested individuals and groups. However else they differ, they tend to view the community as a context in which a variety of interests should be expressed and adjudicated. It seemed particularly hard for those we interviewed to articulate a language of citizenship based neither on the metaphor of extended kinship nor on a conflict of interests. It was difficult for them to conceive of a common good or a public interest that recognizes economic, social, and cultural differences between people but sees them all as parts of a single society on which they all depend. We have nonetheless found more than one example of how getting involved can lead to a deepened conception of society and the role of citizenship within it.

From Volunteer to Citizen

In chapter 6 we met Angelo Donatello, an Italian-American concerned citizen who was led first to reestablish his identity with his own traditional community and then to engage in politics concerned for the welfare of the town as a whole. We also met Cecilia Dougherty, a professional activist whose concern to create a society that will genuinely include the have-nots is rooted in her own family experience of the union movement.

In our conversations with Mary Taylor, a member of the California Coastal Commission, we found a civic-minded professional who was able to move from the cosmopolitan value of relativistic tolerance toward the kind of commitment to the common good that is necessary to assure the integrity of a community. A housewife married to a literature professor, Mary became involved in politics by volunteering in the League of Women Voters and has since moved on to work in a number of organizations concerned with a broad range of environmental issues in California, particularly the Friends of the Earth. In line with the thinking of other civic-minded professionals, Mary lays great stress on the need to tolerate the fact that different individuals have very different interests and viewpoints, and she stresses the need to establish fair procedural rules within which such individuals can negotiate their differences. "It's very important to realize that other people have other values, but they are to be respected. That is what freedom is all about."

Notice how, for Mary, "what freedom is all about" concerns mutual respect among members of a society. This respect for the values of others does not, then, really imply that all values are equally good; rather it presupposes that respect for the dignity of others and concern for the welfare of society as a whole are more important than selfish interests. "What makes me angriest [about government officials] is that they are not for the public good. They have been given a public trust. But they are just out for the pocketbook of the people in front of them. So long as we can be upset about that, we can be healthy. I rebel against the self-serving things I see in government," Mary says. Individuals cannot achieve success or happiness simply by serving themselves: "It is important for all people to live as happy persons. The way to do that is to recognize that you have a debt to society." Mary says she learned this sense of social responsibility from the example of her grandfather, who was a member of the socialist Wobblies (Industrial Workers of the World) and of the Catholic Worker movement. To be aware of one's debt to society means to recognize the need to limit one's desires. "I feel that people should never have lots of money. It's dangerous for people to have more money than they can be comfortable living on. We all have to learn: it's a pie, a limited pie, and when you take all the pieces out of it, then it all will be gone. Decision makers should be conscious of their responsibilities toward future generations."

But what exactly are those responsibilities? What is the content of the public good? "I don't pretend that I know the public good. I would need a monstrous ego to pretend that." But such professions of agnosticism do not mean that Mary is totally without any substantive conception of the public good. At the back of what she says is a sense that the public good is based on the responsibility of one generation to the next, and that an awareness of such a responsibility is a sine qua non for any understanding of the public good. "To try to find out the public good, I would try to ask questions about how this or that would affect the community twenty-five years from now. Not whether such and such a regulation will affect somebody else's pocketbook. The biggest problem we have in all areas of government is that people look to the immediate present rather than to the future. Why? Because we are human. We are great spoilers. That's the American tradition, isn't it?"

Though Mary neither thinks it easy to determine the long-term public good nor claims any certainty about it, her political experience has convinced her that that is what we must seek to do. The pursuit of short-term interests is what is killing us. After she became a member of the Coastal Commission, she says, "I came to realize that we were looking not only at a whole state, but at a whole continent. What the hell were we going to do about it?" In carrying out her responsibilities, Mary has taken some strong stands and made some bitter enemies. In particular, her commitment to carrying out the mandate of the law to provide mixed-income housing in coastal areas has irked her opponents. She has been unhappy with what she calls the "incestuous relationship" between government leaders and economic interest groups. She has been concerned to provide access to public processes to those usually excluded and unable to take part. Like most Americans, she does not enjoy the conflict that ensues when she takes a strong stand. She does not even enjoy the task of persuading others of the rightness of her views, a routine aspect of her political work. Yet even though she has a strong sense of public obligation, Mary is not a martyr, and does not believe you should do political work unless you get satisfaction out of it. In the end, it is her commitment to the longer run and the wider vision that keeps her going.

Thus Mary Taylor protests against that part of the American cultural heritage that, as Tocqueville noted, makes "men forget their ancestors . . . clouds their view of their descendants and isolates them from their contemporaries." But whence comes her sense that she is a part of a larger social and historical whole? Part of it may come from religion—the example of her grandfather in the Catholic Worker movement. But in her mind, at least, religion is no longer important to her. Although raised a Catholic, she does not go to church any more because she thinks religion is "too sentimental." The main source of her sense of social responsibility seems to be the experience of caring and being cared for in the course of her volunteer work. "How much impact the work I've done will have, I don't know. But it's been such a big part . . . has made such a big impact on my own life. I do it not just for intellectual reasons but for emotional ties. I have deep ties with people all over the state. I think there is a kind of caring network of which I am a part that extends all throughout the state. But to become a part of such a network you have to be willing to give." One does not, however, give simply in order to get. One's reward for such giving is not simply a good feeling, not simply the company of like-minded friends. It is an experience that enfolds and somehow makes meaningful a tremendous amount of pain, frustration, and indeed loneliness. "Of course I feel lonely. I would be lying if I said I didn't. People who are willing to love are always going to be lonely—that's what you are going to have to cope with. I'm lonely all the time. It goes with the territory. My husband feels lonely. We've supported one another even when that means sharing our lonely feelings. We are a very close, supportive family, private about certain things. But this ability to support one another is something that I, my husband, my kids, and only a few other people I know have—a generosity of spirit in which you are willing to invest emotional commitment in other people and other things. A lot of people can't live that way. That doesn't mean that I don't respect them or love them less for it. You will find this spirit in most people involved in community work—and in some politicians."

Generosity of spirit is thus the ability to acknowledge an interconnectedness—one's "debts to society"—that binds one to others whether one wants to accept it or not. It is also the ability to engage in the caring that nurtures that interconnectedness. It is a virtue that everyone should strive for, even though few people have a lot of it—a virtue the practice of which gives meaning to the frustrations of political work and the inevitable loneliness of the separate self. It is a virtue that leads one into community work and politics and is sustained by such involvements. As

Mary Taylor seems to recognize, it is a virtue that goes against the grain of much of the American cultural tradition. ("We're great spoilers. That's the American tradition, isn't it?") Yet it remains a powerful element within that tradition, even though it is most often found among civic-minded professionals as a second language that expresses the civic ideal of friends who sustain one another in pursuit of the common good.

Mary Taylor's remarkable strengths—her courage, vision, and commitment—show us a conception of citizenship that is still alive in America. But we did not meet many Mary Taylors. In the next chapter we will explore some of the difficulties of articulating a language of citizenship and why the political sphere is so intimidating to most Americans.

□

8 Citizenship

Success and Joy

Looking back over his volunteer fund raising for a local branch of the YMCA, Jim Reichert, a bank manager in Southern California, calls it "a real joy—success-oriented joy." The intertwined themes of success and joy sum up the way his work life and his community involvement began to flow together. He had been personally successful in rising to a top executive position in his bank, and because of this, he was called upon to play a key role in raising funds for the "Y" to be used for extensive new recreation facilities, mainly for young Mexican-Americans whose numbers in the community were growing and who lacked a constructive outlet for their energies.

This charitable work was a new kind of challenge for Jim—it involved making a great number of personal appeals to potential benefactors in his locality—and he had been apprehensive about his ability to meet it. Success heightened his self-confidence, but his joy came more from the feeling that he had unselfishly contributed something of real value to the community.

Practically all of those we talked to would agree with Jim Reichert that two of the most basic components of a good life are success in one's work and the joy that comes from serving one's community. And they would also tend to agree that the two are so closely intertwined that a person cannot usually have the one without having the other. "I have worked hard," says the California banker, summarizing an account of a life well lived. "I haven't shirked my employer, I haven't shirked my community."

And yet for Jim Reichert, as for most of those with whom we talked, there is something very fragile about the happy coincidence of success in work and joy in community service. These two elements of a good life are not organically unified but exist in a constant state of tension that could always result in their dissolution. "I have lost some of my desire to be committed," Jim felt as he approached the age of forty. One thing that affected his attitude was an offer from his boss to go back to school for an MA in banking. "I think it will help me tremendously in my career. I'm fat, dumb, and happy right now. My job is easy now. It was hard learning it, but it's gotten after a while to be pretty easy. It's not a challenge to me anymore. I've gotten bored. But now, if I get the degree at banking school, I'll be in line for a promotion. But I don't really want to go anywhere. I would have to uproot eleven years of work here. . . . But if I don't move, I'm afraid that I'll become so stale here that it'll hurt my job. So I feel there are reasons that I should move. It's not really for the money, though I would feel the freeze in my salary if I don't move upward and be promoted."

"Leaving home" for the professional middle class is not something one does once and for all—it is an ever-present possibility. Thus the pressure to keep moving upward in a career often forces the middle-class individual, however reluctantly, to break the bonds of commitment forged with a community. Mary Taylor, the ecological activist we met in the preceding chapter, might seem to be immune to these pressures. As a housewife, she lacks a career to compete with her political concerns; or, we might say, politics has become her career. But she, too, is vulnerable to the pressures affecting Jim Reichert. Her husband's career vicissitudes could conceivably uproot her from her deep embeddedness in her community. The individual's need to be successful in work becomes the enemy of the need to find the meaning of one's work in service to others. It is such an experience that is behind Jim Reichert's anguished comment that "I'm afraid that nowadays we're becoming a selfish nation. Our whole thinking process is behind trying to stay alive financially." Work does not integrate one into the public household but estranges one from it. It becomes hard to do good work and be a good citizen at the same time.

Besides saying that he is losing his sense of social commitment because of the pressure to leave his community for a higher echelon job in his bank, Jim also muses that his loss of commitment is "probably caused by too much government. The government's like a domineering mother. It takes away all the people's incentive and tries to do everything for them. You know what it's like for children who have been dominated all their lives by a strong, powerful mother. They become damn near vegetable cases. It's the same way with government." Jim's experience at work, typical of the American middle class, and his attitudes toward government are linked. The paternalism and pressure to "stay alive financially" that he criticizes in the public sphere is exactly what he is experiencing in his own work life under pressure to abandon his community commitments in spite of their deep meaning for him.

Americans define success in terms of the outcome of free competition among individuals in an open market. One is a success to the extent that one personally comes out ahead in a fair competition with other individuals. Most of those we talked to emphasized that they attained their present status in life through their own hard work, seldom mentioning the part played by their family, schooling, or the advantages that came to them from being middle class to start with. It is not that they would deny the contributions others have made to their success in life; what they deny is the moral relevance of those contributions. It is only insofar as they can claim that they have succeeded *through their own efforts* that they can feel they have deserved that achievement.

The achievement of happiness or joy that comes not from calculating competition but from giving oneself to the service of others without counting the cost is a very different matter from success. Truly to deserve this joy, one has to make a personal, voluntary effort to "get involved." But one of the greatest sources of unhappiness for most Americans is the sense of being involuntarily involved—"trapped"—in constraining social relationships. Those with whom we talked tend to think of themselves as deserving joy only if they make such a commitment beyond their having to do so. Thus when Howard Newton mentions the joy that comes from helping needy people in his town through the Rotary Club, he does not take into account the fact that for all practical purposes a successful businessman in a small American town *has* to join some such "service club." Happiness, satisfaction, and joy are earned by making a free individual decision to join such an organization, to accept its discipline, and to participate in its charitable work. One earns joy on the basis of one's own individual effort.

Although both success and joy are in this view legitimately earned only through individual effort, their pursuit actually embodies two contrasting types of individualism. When those we talked with think of a world composed of individuals bent on pursuing success, they quite naturally imagine a utilitarian market system of producers and consumers: buyers and sellers exchanging goods and services with one another for mutual benefit. By contrast, they tend to associate joy with the expressive ideal of a union of similar individuals bound together by spontaneous ties of love: a world of harmonious unanimity that exists more in the realm of hope than in everyday reality. The world of individualistic competition is experienced every day; the world of harmonious unanimity is fully realized only in sporadic flashes of togetherness, glimpses of what might be if only people would cooperate and their purposes reinforce, rather than undercut, one another.[1]

Thus success and joy both complement and counterbalance each other. One is not much good without the other and, in the eyes of many, one cannot very well be achieved without at least a modicum of the other. The self-interest demanded by the individualistic pursuit of success needs to be balanced by voluntary concern for others. Without the joyful experience of support in such a community of concern, an individual would find it difficult to make the effort to be a success, and success achieved would likely turn to ashes. On the other hand, without some individually deserved success, an individual would have little voluntarily to contribute to his chosen community.

It is, of course, no easy task to strike a balance between the kind of self-interest implicit in the individualistic search for success and the kind of concern required to gain the joys of community and public involvement. A fundamental problem is that the ideas Americans have traditionally used to give shape and direction to their most generous impulses no longer suffice to give guidance in controlling the destructive consequences of the pursuit of economic success. It is not that Americans have today become less generous than in the past, as many recent social critics have claimed. Practically all of those we talked with are convinced, at least in theory, that a selfish seeker after purely individual success could not live a good, happy, joyful life. But when they think of the kind of generosity that might redeem the individualistic pursuit of economic success, they often imagine voluntary involvements in local, small-scale activities such as a family, club, or idealized community in which individual initiatives interrelate to improve the life of all. They have difficulty relating this ideal image to the large-scale forces and institutions shaping their lives. This is what creates the pathos underlying many of the conversations about work, family, community, and politics we recounted in the last chapter. Many of those we talked with convey the feeling that sometimes their very best efforts to pursue their finest ideals seem senseless.

Of course, some, particularly the activists, only occasionally see their participation in political and social movements as senseless, while others, often professionals and managers, have definite ideas about why efforts at community involvement turn out to be frustrating. It is rarely "getting involved" as a moral act that is thought to be senseless. Instead, the difficulty has to do with the realm of politics. For a good number of those we talked to, *politics* connotes something morally unsavory, as though voluntary involvement were commendable and fulfilling up to the point at which it enters the realm of office holding, campaigning, and organized negotiating. Their judgments of public involvement and responsibility turn negative when they extend beyond the bounds of their local concerns.

Three Types of Politics

Like other key concepts in American moral discourse, *politics* and *citizenship* have a variety of meanings, not all of which are compatible with one another. At least three distinct conceptions of politics, with attendant notions of the meaning of citizenship, emerged from our interviews. For those who hold them, these understandings serve both to orient action and to explain it. One or more of them are conscious conceptions for some, and they seem to be implicit in the way of living of others. The three understandings are quite distinct, yet in practice they are often held simultaneously.

In the first understanding, politics is a matter of making operative the moral consensus of the community, reached through free face-to-face discussion. The process of reaching such a consensus is one of the central meanings of the word *democratic* in America. This understanding idealizes an individualism without rancor. Citizenship is virtually coextensive with "getting involved" with one's neighbors for the good of the community. Often Americans do not think of this process as "politics" at all. But where this understanding is seen as a form of politics, it is the New England township of legend, the self-governing small town singled out by Tocqueville, that remains the ideal exemplar. We call this first type "the politics of community."

In sharp contrast to the image of consensual community stands the second understanding, for which politics means the pursuit of differing interests according to agreed-upon, neutral rules. This is the realm of coalitions among groups with similar interests, of conflicts between groups with opposing interests, and of mediators and brokers of interests—the professional politicians. We call this second type the "politics of interest." It is sometimes celebrated by political scientists as "pluralism," but for ordinary Americans the connotation is often negative. The politics of interest is frequently seen as a kind of necessary evil in a large, diverse society, as a reluctantly agreed-to second best to consensual democracy.

One enters the politics of interest for reasons of utility, to get what one or one's group needs or wants, rather than because of spontaneous involvement with others to whom one feels akin. To the extent that many of those we talked to see *politics* as meaning the politics of interest, they regard it as not entirely legitimate morally. Hence the generally low opinion of the politician as a figure in American life. Politics suffers in comparison with the market. The legitimacy of the market rests in large part on the belief that it rewards individuals impartially on the basis of fair competition. By contrast, the politics of negotiation at local, state, and federal levels, though it shares the utilitarian attitudes of the market, often exposes a competition among groups in which inequalities of power, influence, and moral probity become highly visible as determinants of the outcome. At the same time, the politics of interest provides no framework for the discussion of issues other than the conflict and compromise of interests themselves. Visibly conducted by professionals, apparently rewarding all kinds of inside connections, and favoring the strong at the expense of the weak, the routine activities of interest politics thus appear as an affront to true individualism and fairness alike.

Citizenship in this second understanding of politics is more difficult and discordant for the individual than in the ideal of community consensus. It means entering the complicated, professional, yet highly personal, business of adversarial struggles, alliance building, and interest bargaining. It requires dealing with others from quite different consensual communities. For most people, it lacks the immediacy of everyday involvement unless urgent interests are at stake. Supporting candidates by voting is the typical expression of this understanding of politics for most people, keeping politics at arm's length.

Yet in the crazy quilt of conflicting and overlapping interests, Americans have traditionally, through their legislators and elected officials, been able to discover enough common interest across the discontinuities of region, class, religion, race, and sex to order and regulate the affairs of a giant industrial society. The chief vehicle for this task has been the national political party, a party more of allied interests than, as in Europe, of ideology, led by the person who has been sufficiently adept as an interest broker to become the presidential candidate. Once elected to office, however, the party's candidate, himself a professional politician, becomes at least partly transformed in public understanding into a very different figure, the president, symbol and effective author of national unity. To some extent the members of the United States Senate and the Supreme Court also share this role as representatives not of factions but of national order and purpose. They become exemplars of the revered Constitution.

There thus emerges the third understanding we call "the politics of the nation," which exalts politics into the realm of statesmanship in which the high affairs of national life transcend particular interests. If the politics of community is seen as the realm of "natural" involvement and the politics of interest as that of semilegitimate bargaining, the politics of the nation is the sphere of impartial governance according to law and, above all, of "leadership" in the sense of uniting a disparate people for action. While in the second vision politics is the "art of the possible," the politics of the nation can on occasion be expressed in a very different language, the language of "national purpose."

Despite the erosion of public trust in governmental institutions that has been going on for two decades, Americans continue to express a degree of patriotism that is remarkable when compared to most other industrial societies.[2] The increase in the number of "independent" voters not aligned with any party that has occurred in the same period, suggests that the politics of interest, with which parties are associated, has suffered more than the politics of the nation from a "legitimation crisis."[3] The citizenship that attends the third type of politics is experienced more symbolically and less in the practices of everyday life than citizenship of the first two sorts. In a variety of public rituals, in foreign relations, and above all in war, the sense of being part of a living national community colors the meaning of life.

The politics of the nation is a positive image for most citizens. It is a notion that bypasses the reality of utilitarian interest bargaining by appealing for legitimacy to the first type of politics—the vision of consensual, neighborly community. But even in the actualities of the first type of politics, the politics of community, when the local school board confronts differences with respect to curriculum content or the town council must decide about permits for developers, it is the politics of interest, as the citizens of Suffolk uncomfortably realized, that has emerged. And it is in situations such as these that even local officials can be accused of "playing politics"—that is, acting more in terms of interests than consensus. Often groups that seem exceptionally able to work their way with boards, officials, and legislatures become branded as "special interests." Perhaps this is rightly so, but it is a usage that besmirches the notion of "interests" or "interest politics" altogether. Indeed, one of the most abusive epithets an opponent can hurl at a national political figure such as the president is that he is simply playing "partisan politics," meaning that the person accused is using the prerogatives of office to advance the interests of his own party as opposed to standing virtuously "above politics" to seek the general good.

But periodically presidents have been seen as rising above politics and expressing a sense of the national community. Franklin Delano Roosevelt, a master of coalition politics, was superbly able to embody a sense of national purpose in response to the challenges of the Great Depression and World War II. It is the notion of the politics of the nation as the politics of a consensual community that helps us understand the general willingness of Americans to pay their taxes and serve in the military. But it is also this understanding of the politics of the nation that makes sense of the recurrence in the United States of social movements that insist on a new level of public morality. Major social movements from Abolition to Civil Rights to the opposition to the Vietnam War have appealed, with more than a little success, to a sense that justice and the common good can be addressed at the level of national consensus. But social movements quickly lose their moral edge if they are conceived as falling into special pleading, as when the Civil Rights movement was transformed into "Black Power." Then we are back in the only semilegitimate realm of the politics of interest.

What is paradoxical in this picture of the three types of American politics is that in an individualistic culture that highly values diversity and "pluralism," it is consensus that is appreciated and the conflict of interests that is suspect. There is something baffling and upsetting in the actual differences that divide us. We need to explore further why this is the case.

Politics and the Culture of Individualism

In chapter 5 we saw that the therapeutically inclined believe that discussion between those whose "values" are different is apt to prove futile. Where moral views are seen as rooted only in subjective choice, there is no way of deciding among them except through coercion or manipulation. Even those not inclined to a therapeutic view distrust all responsibilities and agreements that have not been explicitly negotiated for purposes of mutual advantage or arisen from the conjunction of deeply held personal values. In this cultural context, politics is not impossible so much as severely limited in scope. The fear is that where the interests involved are incommensurable and therefore almost impossible to adjudicate, interest politics must inevitably break down into coercion or fraud. This may lead to the conclusion that the only morally legitimate and worthwhile politics is our first type, the politics of consensual community. Legitimacy can also extend to certain features of the politics of the nation, our third type, when it can be understood by analogy with an idealized politics of local consensus. But politics of the second type means conflict among various groups that are quite unlike one another in their "values" and styles of life, and since there is no way to discuss or evaluate the relative merits of values and lifestyles in the culture of individualism, a generalized tolerance, dependent on strict adherence to procedural rules, is the best that can be expected. But tolerance, despite its virtues, is hardly adequate to deal with the conflict and interdependence among different groups in a complex society.

What the individualist vision of politics is least able to account for are the sources of the conflicting interests themselves. There is no generally understood account of how the divergent interests of regions, occupational groups, races, religious groups, and genders actually arise, or why they contest with very unequal power to effect their wills. The realm of interest politics seems to float disconnected from the sources of interests. Divergences make moral sense so long as they can be explained as the result of individual agency. Hence, the liberal individualist idealizing of the free market is understandable, given this cultural context, since, in theory, the economic position of each person is believed to derive from his or her own competitive effort in an open market.

The extent to which many Americans can understand the workings of our economic and social organization is limited by the capacity of their chief moral language to make sense of human interaction. The limit set by individualism is clear: events that escape the control of individual choice and will cannot coherently be encompassed in a moral calculation. But that means that much, if not most, of the workings of the interdependent American political economy, through which individuals achieve or are assigned their places and relative power in this society, cannot be understood in terms that make coherent moral sense. It further suggests why, in order to minimize "cognitive dissonance," many individuals tend not to deal with embedded inequalities of power, privilege, and esteem in a culture of self-proclaimed moral equality.

Lacking the ability to deal meaningfully with the large-scale organizational and institutional structures that characterize our society, many of those we talked to turned to the small town not only as an ideal but as a solution to our present political difficulties. Nostalgia for the small town and the use of its image in political discussion was common regardless of political views. A major reason why many who voted Republican wanted to "get government off our backs" was that if "big government" were reduced in size and less intrusive in our lives, the healthier voluntary participation of the face-to-face community might return as the most prominent mode of our political life. But those on the left who wanted "decentralization" and "citizen participation" did so for much the same reasons.

For Suffolk town father Howard Newton, the small town ideal, however attenuated, is still alive and in need of defense. Howard Newton speaks for many more Americans than his fellow small businessmen when he says that the mores of community life should foster strong desires to achieve self-respect and a measure of success in work, as well as a sense of concern and compassion for others. It is a widely held middleclass—and American—view that through work one gains self-respect and the ability to control, at least in part, one's environment. In this understanding, compassion takes the form of "helping others to help themselves." But Howard's version of the small town ideal is vulnerable on two scores. It did not help him, as we saw, make sense of the faltering of the Chrysler Corporation, on whose existence his livelihood depends, except through the conclusion that its failures were due to the lack of small town virtues among its employees. But not only does he lack the resources to understand the vicissitudes of our national political economy, he also cannot explain why so many other Americans lack his happy conjunction of economic position and community ties, the conjunction that gives his life meaning and fulfillment.[4] As in the case of the Chrysler Corporation, he can only explain the relative failure of others as due to their lack of self-discipline and failure to work hard, for the structural factors that affect individual outcomes remain opaque to him.

For concerned citizens such as Mike Conley, lacking Howard's abiding sense of security and self-confidence, the survival of the town as a community is more precarious and, if anything, more precious. For Mike the town is a place where good, clean, hard-working people, people who are "in the same boat," can take care of themselves and their own and lead a decent life. For him the threats to the viability of the town as a good community come from poor people who have never learned any self-restraint on the one hand and from selfish power holders who would sacrifice people of his kind for their own profit on the other. For Mike, too, the small town ideal provides no resources for thinking about the larger society and the forces that threaten the town as he understands it, except a highly personal and moralistic rhetoric with no clue to the understanding of large-scale structures and institutions.

But even for Eleanor Macklin, a civic-minded professional with a Public Administration degree and a much better understanding of the national society and economy than Howard or Mike, nostalgia for the idealized small town is strong. She wants Suffolk to become like an old-fashioned New England town again, a place in which people harmoniously work together on the basis of "old-fashioned patriotic values." But the values she is thinking of are not the rigid values of a town dominated by a single religious belief and a unified political vision. She ignores these aspects of the past and focuses on the warm ties of friendship she presumes (against much historical evidence) predominated in such a community. She thinks of a traditional New England town as a localized version of the kind of widely extended, loose-knit friendship networks common among middle-class professionals. Such a town would be composed of voluntarily chosen friends who, though different in many ways, shared particular interests or experiences, a mutuality understood and appreciated through extensive personal dialogue with one another. Eleanor Macklin knows better than Howard Newton and Mike Conley about the structural factors of class and race that prevent many Americans from attaining her status in life or being realistic candidates for citizenship in her idealized small town. But her solution to the larger question is in its own way as individualistic and limited as that of Howard and Mike. She would concentrate on the provision of educational resources to, and the protection of the individual rights of, members of relatively deprived groups. This would enable them to enter the middle class and so qualify, in becoming more like her, for membership in her ideal town.

Nor is it clear that our professional activists are fundamentally different. The Campaign for Economic Democracy has a conception of needed institutional changes in the larger society, but, as we saw in the interview reported in chapter 1, Wayne Bauer is far from clear about that larger view. His imagination is caught up in his tenant-organizing work, where he is essentially engaged in helping people, such as Mexican-Americans, become autonomous, efficacious political individuals, capable of dealing with landlords and governmental procedures. Thus he is, in an important sense, educating them in middle-class skills. Cecilia Dougherty, a member of the same group, for all her breadth of vision, defines her task as essentially to "sustain and build better community in Santa Monica." For both Wayne and Cecilia, it is the tangibility of local community that inspires their political commitment. And their conception of community as a voluntary gathering of autonomous individuals is not radically different from the views of the others we have just discussed.

Americans, it would seem, feel most comfortable in thinking about politics in terms of a consensual community of autonomous, but essentially similar, individuals, and it is to such a conception that they turn for the cure of present ills. For all the lip service given to respect for cultural differences, Americans seem to lack the resources to think about the relationship between groups that are culturally, socially, or economically quite different. Writing from the context of a very different culture, Octavio Paz, the Mexican poet, has pointed out that hierarchical societies often do better than egalitarian ones at including culturally different groups in a common moral order because they can accept and give moral meaning to different levels and degrees of wealth and power.[5] Some groups are poor and weak, but all are included in a common social body where the strong and the rich have special obligations to look out for the others. Of course, this view has often been used to rationalize exploitation and oppression. But the radical egalitarianism of an individualist society has its own problems. For such a society is really constituted only of autonomous middle-class individuals. Those who for whatever reason do not meet the criteria for full membership are left outside in a way unknown in a hierarchical society. The very existence of groups who do not meet the criteria for full social participation is anomalous. There should be no such groups. Their existence must be someone's fault, either their own—perhaps because their culture is defective, and they lack a "work ethic" or there is something wrong with their family system—or someone else's: economic or political elites perhaps oppress them and prevent their full participation. Whatever explanation is accepted, it is difficult to give moral meaning to differences that are considered fundamentally illegitimate.

If the culture of individualism has difficulty coming to terms with genuine cultural or social differences, it has even more difficulty coming to terms with large impersonal organizations and institutions. Politicians are always tempted to personalize and moralize complex problems. The media are much more interested in the charisma of politicians and the dramatic conflicts between them than in their positions on policy issues. Understanding a complex modern society is indeed not easy, particularly when we cannot relate its problems to immediate lived experience.

Invisible Complexity

The tremendous growth of the social sciences in this century, especially economics and sociology, testifies to the widespread desire to understand the complexity of modern social relations. Whatever the achievements of social science (largely, after all, a realm of "experts"), the Americans with whom we talked had real difficulty piecing together a picture of the whole society and how they relate to it. We call this the problem of invisible complexity.

Since, as we have seen, we lack a way of making moral sense of significant cultural, social, and economic differences between groups, we also lack means for evaluating the different claims such groups make. The conflict of interests is troubling when we do not know how to evaluate those interests. In this moral vacuum, it has been tempting to translate group claims and interests into the language of individual rights, a language that makes sense in terms of our dominant individualistic ideology. But if large numbers of individuals and groups or categories of individuals begin to insist, as they have in recent years, that they are owed or are entitled to certain benefits, assistance, or preference as a matter of right, such claims are not readily accepted as matters of justice. They begin to be treated instead as simply competing wants. And since wants cannot be evaluated in terms of the ideology of individualism, the outcome of the political struggle is widely interpreted in terms of power. Wants are satisfied not in terms of their justice but in terms of the power of the wanters. Too many demands can even begin to threaten the legitimacy of the logic of individual rights, one of the few bases for making morally legitimate claims in our society. A conception of society as a whole composed of widely different, but interdependent, groups might generate a language of the common good that could adjudicate between conflicting wants and interests, thus taking the pressure off of the overstrained logic of individual rights. But such a conception would require coming to terms with the invisible complexity that Americans prefer to avoid.

As we have noted before, the image of society as a marketplace of fair competition among roughly equal competitors is an appealing resolution to the problems of understanding the larger society, one that complements the moral balance of consensual voluntary community. But though this model continues to have wide appeal, most Americans know that it is far from descriptive of what really happens. Most are aware to some degree of things that do not fit the market model: large corporations that dominate whole sectors of the market; massive efforts to influence consumer choice through advertising; government programs that subsidize various sectors, such as agriculture; contracts for defense industries that escape reliable cost accounting; technologies that extend and intensify the centralized control of finance, production, and marketing; and so forth.

One long-standing American reaction to such facts is to suspect all groups powerful enough to avoid the operation of the free market. It is not only big government but big business and big labor that have suffered declining levels of public confidence in the past two decades.[6] Such groups in one way or another "go too far" in interfering with market mechanisms for the benefit of special interests. But at the same time, many Americans are aware that large-scale organizations, however distasteful, are part of social reality in the late twentieth century and that trust-busting, union-busting, and the dismantling of government regulative agencies are not really desirable. With that realization, the quandary deepens and leads many to believe that only effective "leadership," with the assistance of technical expertise, can meet the problems of our invisible complexity.

Citizenship and Professional Rationality

If, as we noted, the growth of invisible complexity has called forth special professions to try to understand it, it has also called forth special professions to run it: administrators, managers, and a variety of technical specialists and applied scientists. From early in the nineteenth century, the emergence of managerial and technical specialists has been viewed, with hope or with fear, as having major political implications, leading either to a new kind of politics or to the replacement of politics altogether by enlightened administration. Claude Saint-Simon and Auguste Comte were hopeful that a society directed by managers and scientists would be more efficient, humane, and harmonious than a society wracked by the conflict of interests. Tocqueville was one of the first to warn that this solution could be dangerous.

Tocqueville thought that the rise of "administrative despotism," or what he sometimes paradoxically called "democratic despotism," would be one way in which modern societies might lose their freedom. He defined administrative despotism as a kind of "orderly, gentle, peaceful slavery which . . . could be combined more easily than is generally supposed, with some of the external forms of freedom and . . . there is a possibility of getting itself established even under the shadow of the sovereignty of the people." Tocqueville feared that the inherent tendency of large-scale government toward centralization and the emergence of large-scale industry would lead to administrative despotism, especially where the citizens were divided by the individualistic pursuit of material interest. He emphasized the relative benevolence of this form of despotism. It is a form of government that erects over its citizens "an immense protective power which is alone responsible for securing their enjoyment and watching over their fate." Such a government "does not break men's will, but softens, bends, and guides it; it seldom enjoins, but often inhibits, action; it does not destroy anything, but prevents much from being born; it is not at all tyrannical but it hinders, restrains, enervates, stifles, and stultifies." He wrote, "I do not expect their leaders to be tyrants, but rather schoolmasters." Nor would such a system abolish voting: "Under this system the citizens quit their state of dependence just long enough to choose their masters and then fall back into it."[7]

While the fears articulated by Tocqueville are not far below the surface in the minds of many Americans, we should remember that the small scale and decentralized state that Tocqueville described as existing in the America of his day, actually continued well into the twentieth century. The early proponents of national planning in the hands of professional administrators were attempting to bring order to the chaos of rapid industrialization and urbanization that had occurred under the aegis of a weak central government. These were the largely Protestant, middle-class reformers of the early twentieth century known as the Progressives. Faced with the class conflicts, tensions over immigration, and disturbances arising from the development of the corporate industrial economy, the Progressives sought through "good government" reforms to achieve a more humane public life by taking the heat out of the clash of interests. They sought to smooth the politics of interest into a well-ordered community by applying expert technical knowledge.

The ideal of planning received a major push in the New Deal era when another, more collectively minded group of trained experts sought to repair the ravages of a corporate economy in disarray by creating a large national administrative state that would, for the first time, take responsibility for bringing a measure of order and compassion into economic life on a large scale, an effort that was only partially successful.

It is worth noting that both Progressives and New Dealers had, in more than a few instances, commitments to civic or religious "second languages" and hoped to enhance the possibility of democratic citizenship by making politics more rational. But they were never able to formulate a vision of the national polity that would legitimate their efforts in terms of a moral discourse of the common good and provide an alternative to the culture of individualism. Subsequent advocates of administrative centralization opted for a less ambitious strategy, arguing that their responsibility was merely to carry out the public mandate. This strategy is not without its dangers.

Administrative centralization is now an integral part of American life and will undoubtedly stay that way for the foreseeable future. For many highly educated professionals, this is not only the way it should be, it is taken for granted. For such professionals, the experience of community is not primarily local, and their sense of citizenship is not linked to a city or town. Their outlook is cosmopolitan, shaped by higher education and linked to others of similar training and skills or to those of similar tastes in networks of friends, often widely dispersed geographically. They are closely tied to the priorities of the corporate and governmental worlds, in which expertise must struggle to master and reconcile competing goals, while at the same time their personal contacts are mostly with those whose jobs and income allow a great deal of personal choice in private matters of consumption and leisure. Carefully worked out expert solutions applied in an atmosphere of tolerance bred of easy mobility appear the natural way to make life better for everyone.

A professionalism without content is widespread among those in the higher echelons of American society, since in the struggle to excel, the practices of separation often seem to win out over the practices of commitment. The danger is that, without ever quite intending to, such professional managers and experts may become the benevolent "schoolmasters" of Tocqueville's administrative despotism. Apparently responding, even in their own eyes, to popular "needs" as summed up in ritualized and plebiscitary elections, they are, in fact, prepared to administer much of the lives of our vast population. If the productivity "pay-off" is adequate, they need, to think neither of the massive disparities of wealth and power in our society nor of the efforts of communities of memory to nurture ethical individuality and citizenship. The professional vision tends to assume the validity of a trade-off between utilitarian efficiency in work and individual expressive freedom within private lifestyle enclaves. The policies pursued as a result become a self-fulfilling prophecy. It is a further irony that many Americans who would recoil from Tocqueville's picture of administrative despotism if they heard it described in his words are actually living it out under the illusion that they are contributing to a "free society." But to

Tocqueville it is axiomatic that a private freedom purchased at the price of public despotism is finally no freedom at all. Consequently, the first step in defending ourselves against a form of despotism that is already well advanced in American society is to analyze and criticize what has been happening to us. But the next step is not a knee-jerk reaction to "get big government off our back" or to "decentralize our economy," neither of which in any absolute sense is going to happen. What we must do, in line with Tocqueville's argument, is to strengthen all those associations and movements through which citizens influence and moderate the power of their government, thus revitalizing a politics that can withstand the pull toward administrative despotism. (We will turn to that strategy in the last part of this chapter.) We cannot simply write off "big government" as the enemy. Reducing its powers where appropriate and decentralizing authority, both political and economic, can be pursued as far as practical. But the effective power of citizens in their associations and movements will only be guaranteed in the long run if we succeed in transforming the spirit of centralized administration itself.

The transformation of the state, however complex that process would be, should focus on bringing a sense of citizenship into the operation of government itself. Such a spirit is not entirely lacking today, but it is severely weakened by suspicion of government and politics on the one hand and the idea of impersonal efficient administration on the other. In order to limit the danger of administrative despotism, we need to increase the prestige of government, not derogate it.[8] That prestige should be based on substantive commitments, not formal efficiency. We need to discuss the positive purposes and ends of government, the kind of government appropriate for the citizens we would like to be. Among other things, we need to reappropriate the ethical meaning of professionalism, seeing it in terms not only of technical skill but of the moral contributions that professionals make to a complex society. We undoubtedly have much to learn from the Progressives and the architects of the early New Deal, who still thought of professionalism partly in terms of the ethic of the calling. To change the conception of government from scientific management to a center of ethical obligations and relationships is part of our task.

However uncomfortable it makes us feel, all of us in the modern world depend on one another for our economic survival and for the avoidance of nuclear destruction. That delicate dependence is mediated by powerful governments that are not going to disappear. We will either humanize them or they will tyrannize over us. It is still possible for the action of citizens to determine whether we will have administrative despotism or a responsible and responsive state.

Forms of Citizenship

In his persistent search for social forces that could control and limit the tendency toward administrative despotism, Tocqueville was interested in whatever filled the gulf between the individual and the state with active citizen participation: the family, religious bodies, and associations of all sorts. These he saw as moderating the isolating tendencies of private ambition on the one hand and limiting the despotic proclivities of government on the other. We have already had much to say about such intermediate groups in this book. We have paid particular attention to those groups that are able to elicit deep and lasting commitments, what we have called communities of memory, and we will have more to say about such groups in the next chapter when we discuss religion. We have had much to say about local communities and how they involve people in group activities. We have touched on the importance of voluntary associations as foci of civic life. Vigorous citizenship depends on the existence of well-established groups and institutions, including everything from families to political parties, on the one hand, and new organizations, movements, and coalitions responsive to particular historical situations, on the other. The social movement has been of particular importance as a form of citizenship in the United States.

In times of national difficulty, when the existing order of things appears unequal to its challenges, Americans have often sought new visions of social life. But when new visions have appeared, they typically have done so not through political parties, as in many European societies, but in the form of social movements. The social movement has a long history in the United States, reaching back to the agitation for independence itself. As an expression of political involvement and citizenship, it operates in the undefined middle ground between the private power of the market on the one hand and the public power of government on the other. American social movements have been of very various types, from Abolition to Prohibition, from organized labor to Civil Rights. They have developed in the relatively unstructured public spaces in which opinion is formed but have often drawn leadership and support from churches and other established groups. Energetic social movements have frequently led to the creation of new public institutions, sometimes powerfully changing the course of national life.

Given the difficulties presently facing the nation, one strand in the history of social movements deserves special attention. It is perhaps the only alternative we as a nation have ever had, or are likely to discover, to the dominance of business leaders or the rule of technical experts. This is the tradition of democratic reform that arose in response to the emerging industrial capitalist order. This reforming impulse flourished in various embodiments during the great transitional period at the beginning of the century. The motive force of these movements of democratic reform was a fundamentally similar political understanding. It animated the agrarian populism of the Midwest and Southwest, the socialism of eastern industrial workers and western labor, some aspects of Progressivism, and the upsurge of industrial unionism in the 1930s. Suspicious both of the massive private power that was undercutting the basis for independent citizenship and of government without popular control, these movements sought to use government at all levels to bring a degree of public responsibility to the new technologies and the wealth they generated. They strove to adapt the old Jeffersonian republican sense of democratic citizenship to twentieth-century conditions.[9] Politically, of course, the movements failed to do more than place limits, often fragile, on the exercise of private power. But they left a considerable legacy of experience, symbols, and the exemplary type of the movement organizer.

The political legacy of these earlier movements for democratic reform was revived again in the Civil Rights movement of the 1950s and 1960s. Like these earlier movements, the struggle for civil rights was more than a lobby for a special interest group. Under the leadership of Martin Luther King, Jr., it explicitly aimed at broadening and strengthening effective membership in the national community, invoking biblical and republican themes and emphasizing the economic and social dimensions of full citizenship on an international as well as national level. The power of the movement was sufficient to galvanize widespread political action, particularly among college youth, for reforms in various quarters of the society.

The impact of the Civil Rights movement and its attendant political upsurge has not yet died away. As the ideological and political ferment of the 1960s faded, the 1970s saw the development of new kinds of political activity aiming at democratic reform on the local level, sparked in many cases by activists formed through the experiences of the 1960s. Since the contemporary movement is largely local in focus and geographically scattered, it does not represent the kind of massive linkage of local to national concerns typical of earlier movements of similar purpose.[10] Yet it may provide us with some useful examples of how a renewal of democratic citizenship at the national level might be achieved. Viewed as experiments, the efforts of the members of the California Campaign for Economic Democracy and the Institute for the Study of Civic Values in Pennsylvania illustrate the problem of developing institutions, practices, and understandings that can foster an effective sense of the public good.

The Citizens' Movement: An Example

In our conversations with Wayne Bauer and Cecilia Dougherty, we have seen how the Campaign for Economic Democracy has attempted to combine local organizing on the specific issue of rent control with a larger vision of citizen participation in the control of the economy. In Philadelphia the Institute for the Study of Civic Values has tried since 1973 to develop an effective, practical answer to similar issues, focussing not on rent control but on rebuilding the economic life of depressed neighborhoods, and raising the larger issues as well. Both of these groups are trying to bring a clear sense of responsible citizenship to our second type of politics, the politics of interest, drawing on the positive conceptions that people have of our first and third types, the politics of community and the politics of the nation. As both have found, this is no easy task.

Unlike the Campaign for Economic Democracy, the Institute for the Study of Civic Values has based its efforts at local organizing and political education on an explicit sense of the biblical and republican traditions of American citizenship. Its program speaks of a notion of justice that is not just procedural but has substantive content. Significantly, it draws leadership and support from churches and labor unions as well as other established community groups.

Edward Schwartz has for a decade been both an effective leader of the Institute for the Study of Civic Values and a national advocate of what he terms "citizen education." In the fall of 1983, he was elected to the Philadelphia City Council as councilman-at-large. Schwartz argues that genuine education for citizenship has never been more crucial for the survival of the United States as a democratic society than during the present crisis of what he calls the "antipolitical system." By this he means "the network of large corporations that controls most of the wealth of the country, that employs a large percentage of our people, but disparages politics and tries to insulate itself against governmental control." Schwartz started his critique of the privatizing of politics as a leader in the student movement in the 1960s. He thinks the indictment of corporate hegemony advanced in those years was fundamentally correct, despite the excesses and misguided efforts of some of the student leaders.

"This antipolitical system," according to Schwartz, "elevates individual achievement in the quest for wealth and power above the collective effort of communities to determine common destinies. Yet it is this antipolitical system that decides most important matters for us—where we work, where we can live, even how we can live, and competes with political parties, and government itself for our allegiance and support." The point of political organization for Schwartz is not simply individual or group empowerment to succeed better in increasingly ruthless competition. Rather, politics creates a certain kind of character in a certain kind of context.

As its name suggests, the Institute for the Study of Civic Values was begun to promote the understanding of politics in the civic sense. In effect, the institute has sought to find a practically compelling answer to the question the Campaign for Economic Democracy and the citizens' movement as a whole confronts: empowerment for what ends? The long-standing theory of grass-roots political organizing, made an article of faith by Saul Alinsky's school for organizers, has been that people become politically involved to advance particular interests, and that out of this essentially instrumental involvement will come a sense of citizenship, if not at once, at least after oppressive conditions have been eliminated. The institute's particular contribution has been to question the wisdom of this old axiom of political organizing, arguing that a more positive understanding of politics must inform organizational work from the start.

The context in which the institute has tried to develop a new articulation of civic politics at the grass roots is in many ways very different from suburbanizing cities such as Suffolk or Santa Monica. Philadelphia is a large metropolitan center that has endured decades of industrial decay, attendant on a shift toward a commercial-service economy, and struggled with severe racial tensions and divisions. Like many cities of the Northeast and Midwest, large-scale economic and social trends, including the emergence of the city's black community as a major electoral power, have unbalanced older political arrangements, while making dependence on shifts in the national and international economy painfully visible. Thus from its inception in 1973, the institute's efforts to organize political participation around "civic values" have confronted not growth but the agonies of contraction and intense rivalries among racial, neighborhood, and occupational groups for whatever lifelines they could secure to private or governmental resources.

The institute has sought to provide research and civic understanding for grass-roots political action. Beginning with neighborhood organizing projects that needed political and technical skills, the institute built ties with labor educational programs, church groups, and college and university faculty concerned about the decline of Philadelphia's neighborhoods. As industry departed and the expanding commercial-service economy looked to a more educated, generally suburban workforce, the institute supported the creation of a citywide umbrella council of neighborhood organizations to act as advocate for city services and federal aid. At the same time, the institute pioneered a program of locally run credit unions to stimulate housing renewal and local economic activity throughout the city. While in many ways successful, the credit union and technical assistance programs illustrate the political difficulties of the citizens' movement.

Creating local institutions of self-help in poor and working-class neighborhoods draws previously uninvolved citizens not only into the politics of community, but into the larger arena of interest politics on the citywide level and beyond as well. It does to some degree empower people. The head of the institute's organizing efforts in this area is Ed Schwartz's colleague and wife, Jane Shull. Her assessment of these efforts goes beyond the usual discussions of organizing strategy and tactics. According to Shull, "People become involved because institutions do real things, enable them to improve their lives. To this degree traditional organizing is right." But "in fact, economic skills and knowing about how to organize and lobby effectively don't add up in any direct fashion to citizenship as a cooperative form of life. If you don't start from things like equity, you'll never get there. And that is what we're all about here." For Jane Shull, it is people's political understanding and moral character as a whole, developed through practical experience, that condition their abilities to participate politically.

As Schwartz put it talking to an audience of activists on the West Coast, to transform interest politics into a form of civic politics is to begin not from a desire for power, but from "concerns for security, for justice and for fellowship." Schwartz argued that the purposes for which an institution or a life practice is established determine its outcome. For this reason, like Jane Shull, he sees political organizing as more than a utilitarian means to the end of power. It is also a context in which to nurture a form of moral development on which democratic self-government depends: the practice of citizenship.

But Schwartz also insists that genuine civic politics must be "reflective," by which he means patterns of involvement in which people can come to think about their lives in relation to the larger good of the local and national society. He believes that civic politics finds its grounding through "going behind the language of self-interest to the specific content of people's interests, which center on concern for personal dignity." But dignity is only achieved by becoming a respected member of a community knit together by mutual trust. Schwartz sees justice in the civic sense as securing the dignity of citizens through their participation in social and economic life as well as politics. "There is a basis for progressive coalitions on a wider and more enduring ground than self-interest," Schwartz contends, "and that basis is the historical fact that because of the American civic tradition, American churches, labor, neighborhood and community organizations do have much in common." For Schwartz the common basis is the civic notion that justice is the guiding end of citizenship.

Judged by their own aims, the achievements of Ed Schwartz, Jane Shull, and their colleagues are impressive, if limited. The institute has succeeded in empowering citizens across racial lines in large enough numbers to create an effective "neighborhood presence" in Philadelphia's political and economic life, a presence reflected in Ed's recent electoral victory. Institute members have injected considerable awareness and sophistication into local political discussion. The institute has worked hard to develop forums and institutional contexts within which to shape political perspectives wider than immediate interests. Despite formidable obstacles, the institute has frequently raised the root question of the ends of political action and cooperation, answering that justice, not power, is the true end of politics.

This process is vividly illustrated in an incident that occurred in 1980. Schwartz's organization held a forum to discuss City of Philadelphia plans for public-private ventures in the economic development of the city's poorer neighborhoods. The city's position was advanced by an official who enjoyed a reputation as a reform-minded liberal businessman. He argued that the private corporate sector and government social services share many similar problems of "human services delivery" that could be greatly alleviated by economic undertakings in poorer neighborhoods resulting in "job development."

In response, Ed Schwartz objected that the city's plan focussed on "jobs" in isolation from questions about the kinds of work to be done, how it was to be organized, and by whom. The city was thus tacitly directing economic development into channels of purely individual success, in effect promoting the hegemony of the very "antipolitical system"—the corporate economy—that had for so long ignored the needs of the city's poorer neighborhoods. Instead, Schwartz contended that "people's political development—their capacity to organize their common life—is both an end and a means. It fundamentally conditions their ability to participate in other development, including economic development." Job creation should take place through locally based, cooperative organizations such as community development corporations "and not corporate-directed Enterprise Zones" both "to create jobs to meet the neighborhood's needs and to help neighborhoods to meet society's needs. It is a matter of justice."

But justice with respect to jobs and distributive justice in the larger sense have different meanings depending on whether one views work—and politics—in an instrumental way, as utilitarian individualism does, or as cooperative forms of moral life, as the civic republican tradition has done. In fact, Ed Schwartz argues, there have been in American life not one but three competing notions of justice regarding work. "The first is the corporate capitalist view, typical of the private sector. Here jobs are determined exclusively by what the market will bear. The end of work is consumption and private satisfaction." The second notion of justice is advocated by welfare liberalism as represented by the later New Deal, Social Security, and Great Society programs. It is embodied in affirmative action and varying programs of governmental assistance to the private economy. Here the aim is not to challenge or supplant the individualist view but to use governmental agencies to enable everyone to compete with roughly equal chances of success and to aid those who lose out. Schwartz distinguishes a third "civic-religious conception of justice" from these by noting that it sees work "as a calling, contributing to the common good and responding to the needs of others as these needs become understood" through public discussion about the economic and social interrelationships among different groups.

Clearly caught off-guard by these arguments, the city's representative responded with a revealing objection to Schwartz's scheme for development through locally based, cooperative organizations. Such diversified development would be an "administrative nightmare" and possibly "less efficient" in return on venture capital than a corporate strategy, he said. And there, for the moment, the matter stood. Two images of American life confronted each other: the efficient organizational society of private achievement and consumption versus the civic vision of work as a calling and a contribution to the community, binding individuals together in a common life.

The fullest conception of civic politics that emerges from the citizens' movement proposes to link local participation to a national dialogue. Politics in this view is a forum within which the politics of community, the politics of interest, and the politics of the nation can be put into a new context of wider possibilities for accommodation and innovation. This view of politics depends upon a notion of community and citizenship importantly different from the utilitarian individualist view. It seeks to persuade us that the individual self finds its fulfillment in relationships with others in a society organized through public dialogue. The necessary dialogue can be sustained only by communities of memory, whether religious or civic, and it is symptomatic of the present state of American society that this vision remains sporadic and largely local in scope, though the larger implications are clear. These local initiatives may, however, be the forerunners of social movements that will once again open up spaces for reflection, participation, and the transformation of our institutions.   □

Religion

9

Religion is one of the most important of the many ways in which Americans "get involved" in the life of their community and society. Americans give more money and donate more time to religious bodies and religiously associated organizations than to all other voluntary associations put together.[1] Some 40 percent of Americans attend religious services at least once a week (a much greater number than would be found in Western Europe or even Canada) and religious membership is around 60 percent of the total population.[2]

In our research, we were interested in religion not in isolation but as part of the texture of private and public life in the United States. Although we seldom asked specifically about religion, time and again in our conversations, religion emerged as important to the people we were interviewing, as the national statistics just quoted would lead one to expect.

For some, religion is primarily a private matter having to do with family and local congregation. For others, it is private in one sense but also a primary vehicle for the expression of national and even global concerns. Though Americans overwhelmingly accept the doctrine of the separation of church and state, most of them believe, as they always have, that religion has an important role to play in the public realm. But as with every other major institution, the place of religion in our society has changed dramatically over time.

Religion in American History

America itself had religious meaning to the colonists from the very beginning.[3] The conjunction of the Protestant Reformation and the discovery and settlement of a new world made a profound impression on the early colonists. They saw their task of settlement as God-given: an "errand into the wilderness," an experiment in Christian living, the founding of a "city upon a hill."⁴ Many early settlers were refugees from persecution in England. They sought religious freedom, not as we would conceive of it today, but rather to escape from a religious establishment with which they disagreed in order to found a new established church. They were seeking religious uniformity, not religious diversity. Of course there were some, even in the seventeenth century, who had ideas of religious freedom that we would more readily recognize, and down through the centuries, America has been a "promised land" to immigrants in part because it has allowed them to practice their religion in their own way. But religion had been part of the public order for too long in the history of the West for the colonists quickly or easily to give up the idea of an established church.

Indeed, a pattern of establishment characterized most of the American colonies throughout their history. There was one publicly supported church even when others were tolerated. In some states, establishment continued even after the Revolution (the First Amendment only forbade establishment at the federal level), and it was not until 1833 that Massachusetts gave up the last vestiges of establishment. Once religion is disestablished, it tends to become part of the "private sphere," and privatization is part of the story of American religion. Yet religion, and certainly biblical religion, is concerned with the whole of life—with social, economic, and political matters as well as with private and personal ones. Not only has biblical language continued to be part of American public and political discourse, the churches have continuously exerted influence on public life right up to the present time.

In colonial New England, the roles of Christian and citizen, though not fused, were very closely linked. The minister was a public officer, chosen by the town and not only by church members. Even when dissent gradually came to be tolerated, the established Congregational church was the focus of community life and its unifying institution. Sermons were preached annually on election day. What has been called New England "communalism" valued order, harmony, and obedience to authority, and these values centered on the figure of the "settled minister." Such a minister was "both the keeper and purveyor of the public culture, the body of fundamental precepts and values that defined the social community, and an enforcer of the personal values and decorum that sustained it."⁵

Today religion in America is as private and diverse as New England colonial religion was public and unified. One person we interviewed has actually named her religion (she calls it her "faith") after herself. This suggests the logical possibility of over 220 million American religions, one for each of us. Sheila Larson is a young nurse who has received a good deal of therapy and who describes her faith as "Sheilaism." "I believe in God. I'm not a religious fanatic. I can't remember the last time I went to church. My faith has carried me a long way. It's Sheilaism. Just my own little voice." Sheila's faith has some tenets beyond belief in God, though not many. In defining "my own Sheilaism," she said: "It's just try to love yourself and be gentle with yourself. You know, I guess, take care of each other. I think He would want us to take care of each other." Like many others, Sheila would be willing to endorse few more specific injunctions. We will return to Sheila later in this chapter, for her experience and belief are in some ways significantly representative. But first we must consider how it came about that "Sheilaism" somehow seems a perfectly natural expression of current American religious life, and what that tells us about the role of religion in the United States today. How did we get from the point where Anne Hutchinson, a seventeenth-century precursor of Sheila Larson's, could be run out of the Massachusetts Bay Colony to a situation where Anne Hutchinson is close to the norm?

The tight linkage of religion and public life that characterized the early New England "standing order" was challenged long before the Revolution, although at the local level it survived with remarkable resiliency all through the eighteenth century. The sheer diversity of religious groups, the presence of principled dissenters, and the fact that even those who believed in establishment found themselves dissenters in colonies where another church than their own was established were obstacles to establishment. Diversity of opinion was compounded by a small, but very influential, group of deists and rationalists scattered through the colonies. It would be a mistake to think of them as atheists—they almost all believed in God—but some of them did not accept the authority of biblical revelation and believed that one's religious views could be derived from reason alone. Some of the dissenters opposed establishment on principle, believing that religion involved a direct relationship to God with which no political authority could interfere. Many of the deists believed that religion, while salutary with respect to private morals, was prone to fanaticism and should be kept out of the public sphere except where it converged with beliefs based on reason, such as that "all men are created equal."

It was undoubtedly pressure from the dissenting sects, with their large popular following, on the one hand, and from that significant portion of the educated and politically effective elite influenced by Enlightenment thought on the other, that finally led to the disestablishment of religion in the United States. Yet the full implications of disestablishment were not felt immediately. In the early decades of the republic, American society, particularly in small towns, remained stable and hierarchical, and religion continued to play its unifying public role. George Washington, whatever his private beliefs, was a pillar of the Episcopal church. He was a frequent attender and long served as a vestryman, though he was never observed to receive communion. It was religion as part of the public order that he was thinking of when, in his Farewell Address, he called "religion and morality" the "indispensable supports [of] political prosperity." He doubted that "morality can be maintained without religion" and suggested that these two are the "great pillars of public happiness" and the "firmest props of the duties of men and citizens."

By the early decades of the nineteenth century, the older communal and hierarchical society was rapidly giving way in the face of increasing economic and political competition, and religious change accompanied social change. Even in the longer-settled areas, ministers could no longer count on the deference due to them as part of a natural elite, while in the newer and rapidly growing western states no such hierarchical society had ever existed. With rapid increase in the numbers of Baptists and Methodists, religious diversity became more pronounced than ever. By the 1850s, a new pattern of religious life had emerged, significantly privatized relative to the colonial period, but still with important public functions.

In the preceding chapter, we spoke of the importance of local consensual politics, though we noted that consensus often partly obscures discordant and conflicting realities. The mid-nineteenth-century town, though considerably more consensual than the suburban town today, was nonetheless very different from the colonial township. No longer unified religiously and politically around a natural elite of "the wise and the good," it was much more publicly egalitarian. For religion to have emphasized the public order in the old sense of deference and obedience to external authorities would no longer have made sense. Religion did not cease to be concerned with moral order, but it operated with a new emphasis on the individual and the voluntary association. Moral teaching came to emphasize self-control rather than deference. It prepared the individual to maintain self-respect and establish ethical commitments in a dangerous and competitive world, not to fit into the stable harmony of an organic community.[6] Religious membership was no longer unified. Even in the smaller communities, it had become highly segmented.

The unity that the old township had sought was now seen as a property of the segmented church community, and so in important respects privatized. Together with segmentation came a sharper distinction between spheres. The religious and secular realms that had appeared so closely intertwined in colonial America were now more sharply distinguished. Churches, no longer made up of the whole community but only of the like-minded, became not so much pillars of public order as "protected and withdrawn islands of piety." Sermons turned more "to Christ's love than to God's command."[7] They became less doctrinal and more emotional and sentimental. By the middle of the nineteenth century the "feminization" of American religion that Ann Douglas has described was fully evident. Religion, like the family, was a place of love and acceptance in an otherwise harsh and competitive society.[8]

It was largely this new, segmented and privatized religion that Tocqueville observed in the 1830s. If Washington's analysis of religion was nostalgic for the old hierarchical society, Tocqueville's analysis recognized its value in the new individualistic one. Tocqueville saw religion primarily as a powerful influence on individual character and action. He suggested that the economic and political flux and volatility of American society was counterbalanced by the fact that "everything in the moral field is certain and fixed" because "Christianity reigns without obstacles, by universal consent." Tocqueville was fully aware of and applauded the separation of church and state, and yet, while recognizing that religion "never intervenes directly in the government of American society," he nevertheless considered it "the first of their political institutions."[9] Its political function was not direct intervention but support of the mores that make democracy possible. In particular, it had the role of placing limits on utilitarian individualism, hedging in self-interest with a proper concern for others. The "main business" of religion, Tocqueville said, "is to purify, control, and restrain that excessive and exclusive taste for well-being" so common among Americans.

Tocqueville saw religion as reinforcing self-control and maintaining moral standards but also as an expression of the benevolence and self-sacrifice that are antithetical to competitive individualism. He said that Christianity teaches "that we must do good to our fellows for love of God. That is a sublime utterance: man's mind filled with understanding of God's thought; he sees that order is God's plan, in freedom labors for this great design, ever sacrificing his private interests for this wondrous ordering of all that is, and expecting no other reward than the joy of contemplating it." Here Tocqueville expressed the hope that the destructiveness of utilitarian individualism could be countered with a generalized benevolence, rooted in sublime emotions "embedded in nature,"[10] that is, in an expressive individualism. His generalized analysis of religion kept him from noticing within some of the religious traditions those "second languages" that we have argued provide better alternatives to utilitarian individualism than expressive individualism alone can do. But with respect to second languages, Tocqueville offers us little guidance. He is better at posing the problem of individualism and showing us where to look for alternatives than at close analysis of the alternatives themselves.

American religion has always had a rich treasury of second languages in the Bible itself and the lived traditions descending from it. Yet the relegation of religion to the private sphere after disestablishment tended to replace the specificity of those second languages with a vague and generalized benevolence. Privatization placed religion, together with the family, in a compartmentalized sphere that provided loving support but could no longer challenge the dominance of utilitarian values in the society at large. Indeed, to the extent that privatization succeeded, religion was in danger of becoming, like the family, "a haven in a heartless world," but one that did more to reinforce that world, by caring for its casualties, than to challenge its assumptions. In this respect, religion was a precursor of therapy in a utilitarian managerial society.

Yet therapeutic privatization, the shift from casuistry to counseling, was not the whole story. In the very period in which the local church was becoming a "protected and withdrawn island," evangelical Protestantism was spawning an array of institutions and organizations that would have a major impact on public life. The early nineteenth century saw a great expansion in the numbers of the Protestant clergy as many new functions besides the parish ministry opened up. New educational institutions, both colleges and divinity schools, were central to this wave of expansive influence. The clergyman as professor exerted influence not only in the classroom but on the lecture circuit and in periodicals and books. Numerous societies were established to distribute bibles and tracts, carry on missionary activities at home and abroad, work for temperance and Sabbath observance, and combat slavery. All of these raised money, hired functionaries, issued publications, and spoke to a national audience about the public meaning of Christian ideals. After bitter dissension over the issues of temperance and slavery early in the nineteenth century, most local congregations opted for unity and harmony, either excluding those who differed or suppressing controversial issues. But this was not just privatization; it also involved a division of labor. Through societies and voluntary associations, the Christian clergy and laity could bring their concerns about temperance and slavery, or whatever, to the attention of their fellow citizens without disturbing the warm intimacy and loving harmony of the local congregation.

Nor did the churches have a monopoly over religious language in the nineteenth century any more than in the eighteenth. Abraham Lincoln was known to be skeptical of church religion, yet he found in biblical language a way to express the most profound moral vision in nineteenth-century America. He articulated both the moral justification for emancipation and the grounds for reconciliation with unrivaled profundity in prose that drew not only from biblical symbols but from the rhythms of the Authorized Version. In his writings, we can see that biblical language is both insistently public and politically demanding in its implications.

Religious Pluralism

The American pattern of privatizing religion while at the same time allowing it some public functions has proven highly compatible with the religious pluralism that has characterized America from the colonial period and grown more and more pronounced. If the primary contribution of religion to society is through the character and conduct of citizens, any religion, large or small, familiar or strange, can be of equal value to any other. The fact that most American religions have been biblical and that most, though of course not all, Americans can agree on the term "God" has certainly been helpful in diminishing religious antagonism. But diversity of practice has been seen as legitimate because religion is perceived as a matter of individual choice, with the implicit qualification that the practices themselves accord with public decorum and the adherents abide by the moral standards of the community.

Under American conditions, religious pluralism has not produced a purely random assortment of religious bodies. Certain fairly determinate principles of differentiation—ethnic, regional, class—have operated to produce an intelligible pattern of social differentiation among religious groups, even though there remains much fluidity. Most American communities contain a variety of churches, and the larger the community the greater the variety. In smaller towns and older suburbs, church buildings draw significant public attention. They cluster around the town square or impressively punctuate the main streets. Local residents know very well who belongs where: the Irish and Italians go to the Catholic church and the small businessmen to the Methodist church, whereas the local elite belong to the Presbyterian and, even more likely, Episcopal churches.

Hervé Varenne has beautifully described the pattern in a small town in southern Wisconsin. Each congregation emphasized its own cultural style, often with implications about social class. Though the Protestant churches tended to be ranked in terms of the affluence and influence of their members, Varenne discovered, it was a relatively small core group that gave them their identity and their actual membership was often diverse. Small fundamentalist sects appealed to the poorest and most marginal townspeople, and the Catholic church had the most diverse membership in terms of class background. Varenne gives an example of the social differentation of religion in "Appleton" in the following paragraph:

> As perceived by many people in Appleton, the Presbyterian church, for example, was supposed to be "intellectual" and "sophisticated"; the Methodist was the church both of older, established small farmers and younger, "up-and-coming" businessmen in the town. Indeed, the Presbyterian church appealed mainly to professionals and high-level civil servants, the Methodist to merchants. The school board was dominated by Presbyterians, the town council by Methodists. There was clearly a feeling of competition between these two churches, the most important ones in Appleton. For the time being, the advantage appeared to lie with the Presbyterian church for the top spot in the ranking system.[11]

In the communities we have studied, all of them larger than Appleton, the relationship between the churches and the social structure was even looser, though the same general principles of differentiation applied.

Most Americans see religion as something individual, prior to any organizational involvement. For many, such as Sheila Larson, it remains entirely individual. Where it does involve organizational commitment, the primary context is the local church. Larger loyalties are not missing, but a recent study indicates that even American Catholics, for whom *church* necessarily has a larger meaning, identify their faith primarily with what goes on in the family and local parish and are much less influenced religiously by the pronouncements of the bishops or even the teachings of the pope than by family members and the local priest.[12]

Yet important as the local church is to many Americans, it is not identical with what is understood by *religion*, which has a meaning that transcends the individual and the local congregation. It is one of those differentiated spheres into which modern life is divided and which is largely handed over to "experts" who profess to understand it. We have already noted the development of a body of religious specialists beyond the local parish ministry in the nineteenth century. Today there are not only denominational bureaucracies and clerical hierarchies, a wide variety of educational and charitable religious institutions, and numerous religious organizations oriented to social and political action, but also religious intellectuals who command the attention of segments of the general public, not to mention media stars of the electronic churches. However private religion may be at the levels of the individual and the local church, at this third, or cultural, level religion is part of public life, even though the way in which it is public and the appropriate content of its public message are subject to controversy.

The Local Congregation

We may begin a closer examination of how religion operates in the lives of those to whom we talked by looking at the local congregation, which traditionally has a certain priority. The local church is a community of worship that contains within itself, in small, so to speak, the features of the larger church, and in some Protestant traditions can exist autonomously. The church as a community of worship is an adaptation of the Jewish synagogue. Both Jews and Christians view their communities as existing in a covenant relationship with God, and the Sabbath worship around which religious life centers is a celebration of that covenant. Worship calls to mind the story of the relationship of the community with God: how God brought his chosen people out of Egypt or gave his only begotten son for the salvation of mankind. Worship also reiterates the obligations that the community has undertaken, including the biblical insistence on justice and righteousness, and on love of God and neighbor, as well as the promises God has made that make it possible for the community to hope for the future. Though worship has its special times and places, especially on the Sabbath in the house of the Lord, it functions as a model or pattern for the whole of life. Through reminding the people of their relationship to God, it establishes patterns of character and virtue that should operate in economic and political life as well as in the context of worship. The community maintains itself as a community of memory, and the various religious traditions have somewhat different memories.

The very freedom, openness, and pluralism of American religious life makes this traditional pattern hard for Americans to understand. For one thing, the traditional pattern assumes a certain priority of the religious community over the individual. The community exists before the individual is born and will continue after his or her death. The relationship of the individual to God is ultimately personal, but it is mediated by the whole pattern of community life. There is a givenness about the community and the tradition. They are not normally a matter of individual choice.

For Americans, the traditional relationship between the individual and the religious community is to some degree reversed. On the basis of our interviews, we are not surprised to learn that a 1978 Gallup poll found that 80 percent of Americans agreed that "an individual should arrive at his or her own religious beliefs independent of any churches or synagogues."[13] From the traditional point of view, this is a strange statement—it is precisely within church or synagogue that one comes to one's religious beliefs—but to many Americans it is the Gallup finding that is normal.

Nan Pfautz, raised in a strict Baptist church, is now an active member of a Presbyterian congregation near San Jose. Her church membership gives her a sense of community involvement, of engagement with issues at once social and moral. She speaks of her "commitment" to the church, so that being a member means being willing to give time, money, and care to the community it embodies and to its wider purposes. Yet, like many Americans, she feels that her personal relationship to God transcends her involvement in any particular church. Indeed, she speaks with humorous disdain of "churchy people" such as those who condemn others for violations of external norms. She says, "I believe I have a commitment to God which is beyond church. I felt my relationship with God was O.K. when I wasn't with the church."

For Nan, the church's value is primarily an ethical one. "Church to me is a community, and it's an organization that I belong to. They do an awful lot of good." Her obligations to the church come from the fact that she has chosen to join it, and "just like any organization that you belong to, it shouldn't be just to have another piece of paper in your wallet." As with the Kiwanis or any other organization, "you have a responsibility to do something or don't be there," to devote time and money, and especially to "care about the people." It is this caring community, above all, that the church represents. "I really love my church and what they have done for me, and what they do for other people, and the community that's there." Conceived as an association of loving individuals, the church acquires its value from "the caring about people. What I like about my church is its community."

This view of the church as a community of empathetic sharing is related to another aspect of Nan's thought. Despite her fundamentalist upbringing, her religiousness has developed a mystical cast. She sees the Christian tradition as only one, and perhaps not even the best, expression of our relationship to what is sacred in the universe. It is this mysticism and her sense of empathy with others, rather than any particularly Christian vision, that seems to motivate Nan's extraordinary range of social and political commitments. "I feel we have a commitment to the world, to animals, to the environment, to the water, to the whole thing. It all, in my opinion, is the stewardship of what God has loaned us. The American Indian religion is so fantastic, I think. All those Bible-pounding people came and told them that they were pagans, when they have such a better concept of what religion is all about." For Nan, empathy creates a sense of responsibility because she feels kinship, equality, perhaps even a kind of fusion with all others in the world, and so she suffers for their suffering. Her credo is, "We're all on this earth. Just because I was fortunate to be born in America and white doesn't make me any better than someone that's born in Africa and is black. They deserve to eat just as much as I deserve to eat. The boat people have the same feelings that I do. The same feelings—how can we say no to them?"

In talking to Art Townsend, the pastor of Nan's church, we found views quite consonant with hers. Art is not unaware of the church as a community of memory, though he is as apt to tell a story from the Maharishi or a Zen Buddhist text as from the New Testament. But what excites him are the individuals themselves: "The church is really a part of me and I am a part of the church, and my shift professionally has gone from 'how can I please them and make them like me so that I can keep my job and get a promotion' to 'how can I love them, how can I help these beautiful, special people to experience how absolutely wonderful they are.'" It is the self—both his and those of others—that must be the source of all religious meaning. In Art's optimistic vision, human beings need to learn to "lighten up" as "one of the steps to enlightenment." His job in turn is to "help them take the scales from their eyes and experience and see their magnificence." Difficulties between people are misunderstandings among selves who are ultimately in harmony. If a couple who are angry or disappointed or bored with each other really share their feelings, "you get into a deeper level, and what happens is that feelings draw together, and you actually, literally feel the feeling the same way the other person feels it. And when you do, there is a shift, there is a zing, and it is like the two become one."

For Art Townsend, God becomes the guarantee of what he has "experienced in my life, that there is nothing that happens to me that is not for the fulfillment of my higher self." His cheery mysticism eliminates any real possibility of sin, evil, or damnation, since "if I thought God were such a being that he would waste a human soul on the basis of its mistakes, that would be a little limiting." In consonance with this primarily expressive individualist ethos, Art's philosophy is remarkably upbeat. Tragedy and sacrifice are not what they seem. "Problems become the playground of consciousness" and are to be welcomed as opportunities for growth.

Such a view can justify high levels of social activism, and Art Townsend's church engages in a wide variety of activities, volunteering as a congregation to care for Vietnamese refugee families, supporting broader understanding of the homosexual minority, and visiting the sick or distressed in the congregation. A member such as Nan Pfautz carries her sense of responsibility further, participating through the church in a range of activities from environmental protection to fighting multinational corporations marketing infant formula in the Third World. But it is clear for her, as for Art Townsend, that the ultimate meaning of the church is an expressive-individualist one. Its value is as a loving community in which individuals can experience the joy of belonging. As the church secretary says, "Certainly all the things that we do involve caring about people in a loving manner, at least I hope that we do." She puts it succinctly when she says, "For the most part, I think this community is a safe place for a lot of people."

Art Townsend's Presbyterian church would be viewed as theologically liberal. A look at a nearby conservative church brings out many differences but also many similarities. Pastor Larry Beckett describes his church as independent, conservative, and evangelical, and as neither liberal nor fundamentalist. At first glance, this conservative evangelical church is more clearly a community of memory than Art Townsend's. Larry Beckett indicates that its central beliefs are the divinity of Christ and the authority of scripture. A great deal of time is given to the study and exposition of scripture. Larry even gave a brief course on New Testament Greek so that the original text would be to some degree available to the congregation. While Larry insists that the great commandment to love God and one's neighbor is the essence of biblical teaching, his church tries to follow the specific commandments as much as possible. It is, for example, strongly against divorce because of Jesus' injunction (Matt. 19:6) against putting asunder what God has joined together. The firm insistence on belief in God and in the divinity of Christ, the importance of Christ as a model for how to act, and the attempt to apply specific biblical injunctions as far as possible provide the members of this church with a structure of external authority that might make the members of Art Townsend's congregation uneasy. Not so different socially and occupationally from the nearby Presbyterian church, and subject to many of the same insecurities and tensions, the members of this evangelical church have found a faith that is secure and unchanging. As Larry Beckett says, "God doesn't change. The values don't change. Jesus Christ doesn't change. In fact, the Bible says He is the same yesterday, today, and forever. Everything in life is always changing, but God doesn't change."

Despite his religious conservatism, Larry Beckett mixes a liberal dose of humanistic psychology with his strong biblical imagery, telling church members that God's love can be a source of "self-worth." Because God has created them in his image, because he loves them and sent his son to redeem them, they have infinite worth and value. "No matter how a person is performing, no matter how many friends they have, no matter how handsome or ugly, or no matter how much money they have, they have an inherent value base that cannot be changed or altered." But this attempt to make people feel good about themselves is only a first step in persuading them to enter an exclusive Christian community. He distances himself from the view that "basically everybody in America and everybody in Western culture is Christian. That's not what Evangelicals mean. It is that I have made a personal identification with the historic person of Christ in a very simple way. I did that about ten years ago, and before that I was non-Christian."

The community of Larry Beckett's church is a warm and loving one. There is freshly baked zucchini bread sitting out on the counter of the church's modest kitchen, and the whole community has the feeling of a family. Here members practice the virtues of their biblical ethic, learning to put the needs of others before their own. For Larry Beckett and the members of his congregation, biblical Christianity provides an alternative to the utilitarian individualist values of this world. But that alternative, appealing precisely because it is "real clear," does not go very far in helping them understand their connection to the world or the society in which they live. The Bible provides unambiguous moral answers about "the essential issues—love, obedience, faith, hope," so that "killing or, say, murdering is never right. Or adultery. A relationship outside of your marriage is never right. The Bible says that real simple." To "follow the Scriptures and the words of Jesus" provides a clear, but narrow, morality centered on family and personal life. One must personally, as an individual, resist temptation and put the good of others ahead of one's own. Christian love applies to one-to-one relationships—I may not cheat my neighbor, or exploit him, or sell him something I know he can't afford. But outside this sphere of personal morality, the evangelical church has little to say about wider social commitments. Indeed, the sect draws together those who have found a personal relationship to Christ into a special loving community, and while it urgently seeks to have everyone make the same commitment, it separates its members off from attachment to the wider society. Morality becomes personal, not social; private, not public.

Both Larry Beckett's conservative church and Art Townsend's liberal one stress stable, loving relationships, in which the intention to care outweighs the flux of momentary feelings, as the ideal pattern in marriage, family, and work relationships. Thus both attempt to counter the more exploitative tendencies of utilitarian individualism. But in both cases, their sense of religious community has trouble moving beyond an individualistic morality. In Art Townsend's faith, a distinctively religious vision has been absorbed into the categories of contemporary psychology. No autonomous standard of good and evil survives outside the needs of individual psyches for growth. Community and attachment come not from the demands of a tradition, but from the empathetic sharing of feelings among therapeutically attuned selves.

Larry Beckett's evangelical church, in contrast, maintains a vision of the concrete moral commitments that bind church members. But the bonds of loyalty, help, and responsibility remain oriented to the exclusive sect of those who are "real" Christians. Direct reliance on the Bible provides a second language with which to resist the temptations of the "world," but the almost exclusive concentration on the Bible, especially the New Testament, with no larger memory of how Christians have coped with the world historically, diminishes the capacity of their second language to deal adequately with current social reality. There is even a tendency visible in many evangelical circles to thin the biblical language of sin and redemption to an idea of Jesus as the friend who helps us find happiness and self-fulfillment.[14] The emphasis on love, so evident within the community, is not shared with the world, except through missionary outreach.

There are thousands of local churches in the United States, representing an enormous range of variation in doctrine and worship. Yet most define themselves as communities of personal support. A recent study suggests that what Catholics look for does not differ from the concerns of the various types of Protestants we have been discussing. When asked the direction the church should take in future years, the two things that a national sample of Catholics most asked for were "personal and accessible priests" and "warmer, more personal parishes."[15] The salience of these needs for personal intimacy in American religious life suggests why the local church, like other voluntary communities, indeed like the contemporary family, is so fragile, requires so much energy to keep it going, and has so faint a hold on commitment when such needs are not met.

Religious Individualism

Religious individualism, evident in these examples of church religion, goes very deep in the United States. Even in seventeenth-century Massa-

chusetts, a personal experience of salvation was a prerequisite for acceptance as a church member. It is true that when Anne Hutchinson began to
draw her own theological conclusions from her religious experiences and
teach them to others, conclusions that differed from those of the established ministry, she was tried and banished from Massachusetts. But
through the peculiarly American phenomenon of revivalism, the emphasis on personal experience would eventually override all efforts at church
discipline. Already in the eighteenth century, it was possible for individuals to find the form of religion that best suited their inclinations. By the
nineteenth century, religious bodies had to compete in a consumers' market and grew or declined in terms of changing patterns of individual religious taste. But religious individualism in the United States could not be
contained within the churches, however diverse they were. We have noted
the presence of individuals who found their own way in religion even in
the eighteenth century. Thomas Jefferson said, "I am a sect myself," and
Thomas Paine, "My mind is my church." Many of the most influential
figures in nineteenth-century American culture could find a home in none
of the existing religious bodies, though they were attracted to the religious
teachings of several traditions. One thinks of Ralph Waldo Emerson,
Henry David Thoreau, and Walt Whitman.

Many of these nineteenth-century figures were attracted to a vague
pantheistic mysticism that tended to identify the divine with a higher self.
In recent times, what had been a pattern confined to the cultural elite has
spread to significant sections of the educated middle class. Tim Eichelberger, a young Campaign for Economic Democracy activist in Southern
California, is typical of many religious individualists when he says, "I feel
religious in a way. I have no denomination or anything like that." In 1971,
when he was seventeen, he became interested in Buddhism. What attracted him was the capacity of Buddhism to allow him to "transcend" his
situation: "I was always into change and growth and changing what you
were sort of born into and I was always interested in not having that control me. I wanted to define my own self." His religious interest involved
the practice of yoga and a serious interest in leading a nonviolent life. "I
was into this religious purity and I wanted the earth around me to be pure,
nonviolence, nonconflict. Harmony. Harmony with the earth. Man living
in harmony with the earth; men living in harmony with each other." His
certainty about nonviolence eventually broke down when he had to acknowledge his rage after being rejected in a love relationship. Coming to
terms with his anger made him see that struggle is a part of life. Eventually, he found that involvement in CED gave an expression to his ideals as
well as his understanding of life as a struggle. His political concern with
helping people attain "self-respect, self-determination, self-realization"

continues his older religious concern to define his own self. But neither his religion nor his politics transcend an individualism in which "self-realization" is the highest aspiration.

That radical religious individualism can find its own institutional form is suggested by the story of Cassie Cromwell, a suburban San Diego volunteer a generation older than Eichelberger, who came to her own religious views in adolescence when she joined the Unitarian church. She sums up her beliefs succinctly: "I am a pantheist. I believe in the 'holiness' of the earth and all other living things. We are a product of this life system and are inextricably linked to all parts of it. By treating other living things disrespectfully, we are disrespectful of ourselves. Our very survival depends on the air 'god,' the water, sun, etc." Not surprisingly, she has been especially concerned with working for ecological causes. Like Eichelberger, she began with a benign view of life and then had to modify it. "I used to believe that man was basically good," her statement of her philosophy continues. "I didn't believe in evil. I still don't know what evil is but see greed, ignorance, insensitivity to other people and other living things, and irresponsibility." Unlike most of those to whom we talked, Cassie is willing to make value judgments about religion and is openly critical of Christianity. She believes that "the Christian idea of the superiority of man makes it so difficult to have a proper concern for the environment. Because only man has a soul, everything on the earth can be killed and transformed for the benefit of man. That's not right."

Commoner among religious individualists than criticism of religious beliefs is criticism of institutional religion, or the church as such. "Hypocrisy" is one of the most frequent charges against organized religion. Churchgoers do not practice what they preach. Either they are not loving enough or they do not practice the moral injunctions they espouse. As one person said, "It's not religion or the church you go to that's going to save you." Rather it is your "personal relationship" with God. Christ will "come into your heart" if you ask, without any church at all.[16]

In the cases of Tim Eichelberger and Cassie Cromwell, we can see how mystical beliefs can provide an opening for involvement in the world. Nonetheless, the links are tenuous and to some extent fortuitous. Both had to modify their more cosmic flights in order to take account of evil and aggression and work for the causes they believe in. The CED provides a focus for Eichelberger's activities, as the ecology movement does for Cassie. But their fundamental views were formed outside those contexts and their relation to the respective groups, even Cassie's longstanding connection with the Unitarians, remains one of convenience.

As social ideals, neither "self-realization" nor the "life system" provide practical guidance. Indeed, although both Tim and Cassie value "harmony with the earth," they lack a notion of nature from which any clear social norms could be derived. Rather, the tendency in American nature pantheism is to construct the world somehow out of the self. (Again, Emerson is a clue.) If the mystical quest is pursued far enough, it may take on new forms of self-discipline, committed practice, and community, as in the case of serious practitioners of Zen Buddhism. But more usually the languages of Eastern spirituality and American naturalistic pantheism are employed by people not connected with any particular religious practice or community.

Internal and External Religion

Radically individualistic religion, particularly when it takes the form of a belief in cosmic selfhood, may seem to be in a different world from conservative or fundamentalist religion. Yet these are the two poles that organize much of American religious life. To the first, God is simply the self magnified; to the second, God confronts man from outside the universe. One seeks a self that is finally identical with the world; the other seeks an external God who will provide order in the world. Both value personal religious experience as the basis of their belief. Shifts from one pole to the other are not as rare as one might think.

Sheila Larson is, in part, trying to find a center in herself after liberating herself from an oppressively conformist early family life. Her "Sheilaism" is rooted in the effort to transform external authority into internal meaning. The two experiences that define her faith took a similar form. One occurred just before she was about to undergo major surgery. God spoke to her to reassure her that all would be well, but the voice was her own. The other experience occurred when, as a nurse, she was caring for a dying woman whose husband was not able to handle the situation. Taking over care in the final hours, Sheila had the experience that "if she looked in the mirror" she "would see Jesus Christ." Tim Eichelberger's mystical beliefs and the "nonrestrictive" nature of his yoga practices allowed him to "transcend" his family and ethnic culture and define a self free of external constraint.

Conversely, cosmic mysticism may seem too threatening and undefined, and in reaction a religion of external authority may be chosen. Larry Beckett was attracted to Hinduism and Buddhism in his countercultural stage, but found them just too amorphous. The clarity and authority that he found in the New Testament provided him with the structure that till then had been lacking in his life.[17]

Howard Crossland, a scientist and a member of Larry Beckett's congregation whom we met in chapter 4, finds a similar security in his religion. He tends to view his Christianity as a matter of facts rather than emotion: "Because I have the Bible to study, it's not really relying on your emotions. There are certain facts presented and you accept the facts." Not surprisingly, Crossland is concerned about his own self-control and respects self-control in others. He never went through a countercultural phase, but he does have memories of a father who drank too much—an example of what can happen when control gets lost. In his marriage, in relation to his children, and with the several people who work under him, Crossland tries to be considerate and put the good of others ahead of his own. As he sees it, he is able to do that because of the help of God and His church: "From the help of other members of the congregation and with the help of the Holy Spirit, well, first of all you accept God, and then He gives you help to do good to your fellowman, to refrain from immorality, to refrain from illegal things."

Ruth Levy, the Atlanta therapist we met in chapter 5, comments on what she calls "born-again Jews," who are in many ways similar to born-again Christians. They come from assimilated families who haven't kept kosher in three generations, yet "incredibly, they do stuff that my grandparents may not even have done." What these born-again Jews are doing is "instilling structure, discipline, and meaning." They have found that "to be free to do anything you want isn't enough. There isn't anything you want to do."

Since these two types of religion, or two ways of being religious, are deeply interrelated, if our analysis is correct, some of the obvious contrasts between them turn out to be not quite what they seem. It is true that the first style emphasizes inner freedom and the second outer control, but we cannot say that the first is therefore liberating and the second authoritarian, or that the first is individualistic and the second collectivist. It is true that the first involves a kind of radical individualism that tends to elevate the self to a cosmic principle, whereas the second emphasizes external authorities and injunctions. But the first sees the true self as benevolent and harmonious with nature and other humans and so as incompatible with narrow self-seeking. And the second finds in external authority and regulation something profoundly freeing: a protection against the chaos of internal and external demands, and the basis for a genuine personal autonomy. Thus, though they mean somewhat different things by freedom and individuality, both hold these as central values. And while the first is clearly more focussed on expressive freedom, the second in its own way also allows important opportunities for expressive freedom in intensely participatory religious services and through emphasis on love and caring. Finally, though conservative religion does indeed have a potential for authoritarianism, particularly where a magnetic preacher gathers inordinate power in his own hands, so does extreme religious individualism. Where a guru or other religious teacher is thought to have the secret of perfect personal liberation, he or she may gain excessive power over adherents.

The limitation for millions of Americans who remain stuck in this duality in one form or another is that they are deprived of a language genuinely able to mediate among self, society, the natural world, and ultimate reality. Frequently, they fall back on abstractions when talking about the most important things. They stress "communication" as essential to relationships without adequately considering what is to be communicated. They talk about "relationships" but cannot point to the personal virtues and cultural norms that give relationships meaning and value. It is true that religious conservatives go further in specifying content than the others we have discussed, but they, too, not infrequently revert to the popular language of therapy, and even when they are specific, there are often little more than the idealized norms of "traditional morality," accepted unreflectively, to fall back on.

The Religious Center

For a long time what have been called the "mainline" Protestant churches have tried to do more than this. They have offered a conception of God as neither wholly other nor a higher self, but rather as involved in time and history. These churches have tried to develop a larger picture of what it might mean to live a biblical life in America. They have sought to be communities of memory, to keep in touch with biblical sources and historical traditions not with literalist obedience but through an intelligent reappropriation illuminated by historical and theological reflection. They have tried to relate biblical faith and practice to the whole of contemporary life—cultural, social, political, economic—not just to personal and family morality. They have tried to steer a middle course between mystical fusion with the world and sectarian withdrawal from it.

Through the nineteenth century and well into the twentieth, the mainline churches were close to the center of American culture. The religious intellectuals who spoke for these churches often articulated issues in ways widely influential in the society as a whole. But for a generation or more, the religious intellectuals deriving from the mainline Protestant churches have become more isolated from the general culture. This is in part because they, like other scholars, have become specialists in fields where only specialists speak to one another. Their isolation also derives in part from the long pressure to segregate our knowledge of what is, gained through science, from our knowledge of what ought to be, gained through religion, morality and art. Finally, the religious intellectuals have themselves lost self-confidence and become vulnerable to short-lived fads. For some years now, they have failed to produce a Tillich or Niebuhr who might become the center of fruitful controversy and discussion. Without the leavening of a creative intellectual focus, the quasi-therapeutic blandness that has afflicted much of mainline Protestant religion at the parish level for over a century cannot effectively withstand the competition of the more vigorous forms of radical religious individualism, with their claims of dramatic self-realization, or the resurgent religious conservatism that spells out clear, if simple, answers in an increasingly bewildering world.[18]

But just when the mainline Protestant hold on American culture seemed decisively weakened, the Roman Catholic church after Vatican II entered a much more active phase of national participation. Though never without influence in American society, the Catholic church had long been more concerned with the welfare of its own members, many of them immigrants, than with moulding the national society.[19] The period 1930–60 was a kind of culmination of a long process of institution building and self-help. The church, still a minority, but long the largest single denomination, grew in confidence as the majority of its constituents attained middle-class respectability. An educated and thoughtful laity was thus ready to respond to the new challenges the Second Vatican Council opened up in the early 1960s. The unprecedented ecumenical cooperation that brought Catholics together with Protestants and Jews in a number of joint endeavors from the period of the Civil Rights movement to the present has created a new atmosphere in American religious life.[20] With the American Catholic bishops' pastoral letter of May 3, 1983, on nuclear warfare, the promise of Vatican II began to be fulfilled.[21] The Catholic church moved toward the center of American public life, invigorating the major Protestant denominations as it did so.

Recently Martin Marty, in the light of this new situation, has attempted to describe the religious center as what he calls "the public church."[22] The public church, in Marty's sense, includes the old mainline Protestant churches, the Catholic church, and significant sectors of the evangelical churches. It is not a homogeneous entity but rather a "communion of communions" in which each church maintains the integrity of its own traditions and practices even while recognizing common ground with the others. Without dissolving its Christian particularity, the public church welcomes the opportunity for conversation, and on occasion joint action, with its Jewish, other non-Christian, and secular counterparts, particularly where matters of the common good are concerned. The public church is not triumphalist—indeed it emerges in a situation where Christians feel less in control of their culture than ever before—but it wishes to respond to the new situation with public responsibility rather than with individual or group withdrawal. The public church and its counterparts in the non-Christian religions offer the major alternative in our culture to radical religious individualism on the one hand and what Marty calls "religious tribalism" on the other.

It is possible to look at Art Townsend's liberal Presbyterian congregation, Larry Beckett's conservative evangelical church, and Ruth Levy's "community that's rooted in a synagogue" as examples of the public church or analogous to it. All reject the radical self-seeking of utilitarian individualism and none of them is content to be only a lifestyle enclave of warm mutual acceptance. For all of them, religion provides a conception, even if rudimentary, of how one should live. They all share the idea that one's obligations to God involve one's life at work as well as in the family, what one does as a citizen as well as how one treats one's friends. Yet, as we have seen, each of these communities has suffered to some degree from a therapeutic thinning out of belief and practice, a withdrawal into the narrow boundaries of the religious community itself, or both. As a result, continuity as a community of memory and engagement in the public world are problematic for each of them.

Let us turn, then, to another religious community, St. Stephen's Episcopal Church, which, while suffering from the same problems, seems to be able to combine a sense of continuity with the past and an engagement with the public world of the present. Like Art Townsend's and Larry Beckett's churches, St. Stephen's is in the San Francisco Bay area and has a largely middle-class membership. For a congregation of only a few hundred members, St. Stephen's is the center of a surprising amount of activity. There are prayer groups and bible study groups that meet weekly or more often. There is a pastoral care team to assist the rector, the only full-time cleric, at a variety of tasks such as visiting the sick, the shut-ins, those in convalescent hospitals, and so on. There are a number of people active in a local mission that consists mainly in feeding, clothing, and caring for the hungry and the homeless in the city where St.

Stephen's is located. The church supports an Amnesty International group and a number of parishioners are involved in antinuclear activities. St. Stephen's has joined a local consortium of churches in a Sanctuary Covenant whereby they provide sanctuary for Salvadoran refugees.

But for all the parish's many activities, it is the life of worship that is its center. The Book of Common Prayer provides a pattern of liturgy that is continuous with the practices of worship from the early centuries of the church. Holy Communion is celebrated daily and three times on Sunday, with more than half the parish attending at least once a week. The liturgical year is taken seriously, with the Lenten and Easter seasons having a particular salience. Father Paul Morrison, rector of St. Stephen's, believes that for those who come regularly, worship "becomes a genuine source of life and of focussing what they do during the week." The rector, a modest but articulate man of fifty, speaks with conviction balanced by self-searching. He attributes the effectiveness of worship not to the preaching but to the Eucharist, which "draws people in and somehow informs them of the source of life that is present at the heart of worship." In administering the sacraments, he finds he must keep some detachment in order not to be overwhelmed by the poignancy of all the individual lives he knows so well, of his people who "have brought their life, the heart of their life," to the communion rail and "they hold it up and find healing and comfort and walk away somehow renewed, restored, and fit for another week in a pretty tough world." In the Episcopal tradition, the sermon is less central than in most Protestant denominations, but Father Morrison's sermons are effective, sometimes moving, interpretations of the biblical readings and applications of them to contemporary personal or social problems.

When asked whether his parishioners view the church as a necessary condition of their faith or as an organization that is optional for the Christian, the rector replied, "It's a constant uphill battle." He finds that contemporary American life "places enormous pressures on people to marginalize and isolate them and force them away from community," pressures that run absolutely contrary to the biblical understanding of life. When people can genuinely "hear scripture" and "experience community," he says, they realize that the church is a necessity, not an option. Concomitantly, Father Morrison finds that the idea of valid authority does not come easily: "The concept that a community can set standards, adopt values, capture conscience, and become authoritative in the life of human beings is not obvious in our culture, and it falls apart without it." When individuation is more important than community, "people are not together enough to take on the responsibilities of authority." He foresees a possible clash between the authority of the church and that of the state over the parish's participation in providing sanctuary for Salvadoran refugees, and he worries how people will react: "We will need to hang together with a very close fabric if we are to survive, and if people go to jail we will need to understand very clearly what we think and believe."

Although the Episcopal church relaxed its absolute prohibition of divorce over twenty-five years ago, Father Morrison finds that marriage is currently in high esteem. The number of babies has doubled in the past three years and is in the process of redoubling, so the parish must find expanded facilities for infant care. He speaks of "the seriousness with which people are taking marriage and family and are attempting consciously to establish a family pattern." He suggests that the young people who come to his parish "might have been screened out somewhere along the line" because, in spite of the prevalence of divorce in American society, "they're very serious about lifelong vows" and are more genuinely prepared to make them than was sometimes the case in previous generations.

Another challenge that faces the rector in "an urban mixed parish" is "how to deal with homosexual unions, both male and female" in a way that will be supportive of the Christian character of these commitments while faithful to tradition. Such unions, Father Morrison says, "are part and parcel of all parishes and always have been, but are now quite out in the open."

The one thing he finds missing in the young people who come to him for marriage counseling, who are otherwise quite mature, is "any conception that their happiness and fulfillment depends on their moving from the nurture of each other to the self-giving of the couple to those around them. I mean we have all of the channels for service available for anybody and particularly for young couples who are already in the church to begin to live beyond themselves and to find that kind of fulfillment."

In discussing the occupational involvements of his parishioners, Father Morrison noted that the major criticism of him that had come out of a recent parish evaluation was that he was perhaps too quick to assume that Christian commitment meant taking some organizational or committee responsibility within the parish. "They said," he reports, "we are in difficult places in the world and we think we should be here. Support us where we are. That was their criticism of me, which I took very much to heart." He finds that "strong lay people" are "working in banks, in corporations, or at the university where they find it is very difficult to live out the Christian life and they're very lonely and they musn't be." The rector believes that "politics, law, and other professions" that are often looked down upon today are "potentially Christian areas of service" and that church people must be helped to fulfill "their vocations and calling and ministry effectively and nobly in those areas."

But Father Morrison believes that only a spiritually strong parish can really support individuals in their difficult worldly callings. They need workshops and discussions, but they also need inner resources. The rector has encouraged the development of individual and group prayer, bible study, and meditation within the parish, so that something close to half of the congregation engages in some form of regular spiritual discipline. The Book of Common Prayer has adapted and simplified the monastic daily office for the use of the laity and the parish encourages its use during Lent and at other times.

When asked whether an emphasis on therapeutic self-realization has replaced the traditional Christian teaching about sin and redemption, Father Morrison laughed and said, "I'm realizing how traditional we are." It is true, he said, that when people who have had miserable childhoods or "have it beaten into them that they are inferior, perhaps because of sexual orientation, . . . have come to the church and found that they really are not, that they are loved and that they have unlimited potential, it's very difficult to go back and say 'I'm a miserable sinner.'" Yet he finds on the basis of his conversations with those who come to him for counseling or confession, as well as the attendance at lenten and Holy Week services, that most people in the congregation understand the relationship between sin and forgiveness and have not lost either aspect of the traditional teaching.

When asked whether the Episcopal church, which has traditionally stood close to the centers of power in our society and attempted to influence the power structure from within, should continue that policy or perhaps take a position closer to the margins of society, protesting against it, Father Morrison replied, "I wish I knew the answer to that." He often speaks in his sermons about people, not only in the United States but in Central America or southern Africa, who are on the margins and the edges and how the church must stand with them. He reminds his congregation that Christianity itself began among a peasant people at the margins of the Roman Empire. Yet he does not want to "abandon the world or undercut lay vocations." He sums up his view by saying, "If we recover to any extent our support of our people in their vocations and ministries in the world, then maybe one would have enough confidence to say 'yes, from the inside we certainly can take responsibility, because our best people are there and they are nourished and succored by the church and ready to do the job.' Right now it seems almost accidental if there is any relationship between Episcopalians in power and the Gospel."

Church, Sect, and Mysticism

In his comments on the relationship between the church and secular power, Father Morrison seems to be wavering between two conceptions of the religious community—what Ernst Troeltsch called "church" and "sect." Whereas the church enters into the world culturally and socially in order to influence it, the sect stands apart from the secular world, which it sees as too sinful to influence except from without. Troeltsch's third type, which he called "mysticism" or "religious individualism," is one in which the focus is on the spiritual discipline of the individual, however he or she relates to the world.[23] Religious organization is important to both church and sect, but to mystics or religious individualists organization, being inessential, may be casual and transient. St. Stephen's, with its emphasis on individual spiritual discipline, seems to contain an element of mysticism as well as elements of church and sect. What this example suggests is that Troeltsch's types are dimensions of Christian (and often non-Christian) religious community. Individual congregations or denominations may emphasize one dimension more than another—St. Stephen's, for example, and the Episcopal church generally are predominantly of the church type—but examples of pure types will be rare. Nevertheless, by looking at American religion in terms of Troeltsch's types, we may gain a better understanding of how religion influences our society.

We may briefly characterize the church type as an organic conception of the religious institution for which the defining metaphor is the Pauline image of the body of Christ. The church is seen as the living presence of Christ on earth—as, in Karl Rahner's terms, itself the fundamental sacrament from which all the sacraments are derived.[24] The church has a temporal and even ontological priority over the individual. There is a givenness, a reality, in the church that allows the individual to count on it, to take it for granted in a positive sense. Through the sacraments and the word, the church takes all individuals where they are and nurtures, educates, and supports them in whatever degree of Christian life they are capable of attaining. The church is inevitably in one sense hierarchical, even elitist, for some are recognized as more learned or more spiritually advanced than others. The church puts forth role models—saints, those in religious orders, priests, teachers—from whom others have much to learn. All are one in Christ, but the organic metaphor allows a hierarchical differentiation of function. Along with this organic model goes a partial willingness to accept the world as it is, to compromise with the world in the service of Christian pedagogy, to stay close to power in hopes of Christianizing it to some degree. The church tends to be comprehensive and flexible with respect to society and culture, accepting and attempting to transform social forms and also art, science and philosophy. The characteristic distortions of the church are a temptation to authoritarianism, on the one hand, and too-easy compromise with, and even cooptation by, the powers of this world on the other. But when the church sets itself against worldly powers, it can mobilize tremendous resources of resistance.

The church type has been present in America from the beginning of European settlement, but it has never been dominant in pure form. Early New England Puritanism embodied much of the church type but with a strong admixture with the spirit of the sect. The more purely sectarian forms of Protestantism that were already present in the seventeenth century and grew markedly in the eighteenth century strongly colored all of subsequent American culture. The Roman Catholic church, even after massive immigration made it a significant force in the United States, remained a minority church. As it absorbed ever more of American culture, it too was affected by sect ideals. Indeed, in the United States, the church type has become harder and harder to understand. Our ontological individualism finds it hard to comprehend the social realism of the church—the idea that the church is prior to individuals and not just the product of them.

The sect type has been present in America virtually from the beginning, includes the Protestant denominations with the largest numbers, and has in many ways been the dominant mode of American Christianity. The sect views a church as primarily a voluntary association of believers. The individual believer has a certain priority over the church in that the experience of grace is temporally prior to admission to membership, even though, once admitted, collective discipline in the sect can be quite strong. The sectarian church sees itself as the gathered elect and focusses on the purity of those within as opposed to the sinfulness of those without. Whereas the church type, with its ideal of communion, includes everybody in its hierarchical organic structure at some level or other, the sect with its ideal of purity draws a sharp line between the essentially equal saints within and the reprobates without.[25] The strong sectarian emphasis on voluntarism and the equality of believers—the sect is anti-elitist and insists on the priesthood of all believers—is congenial to democratic forms of organization and congregational autonomy.

There is a tendency for grace to be overshadowed by "the law of Christ" and for the sacraments to be less central than a moralism that verges on legalism. As Troeltsch pointed out, the sectarian group is often, especially in its beginnings, found primarily among lower income groups and the less educated. It is tempted toward a radical withdrawal from the environing society and a rejection of secular art, culture, and science. As Troeltsch also observed, the sect is especially close to the spirit of the synoptic gospels. Christianity began as a lower-class religion of people of no great education, although the urban churches founded by St. Paul in the Greco-Roman cities already had elements of the church type in New Testament times.[26]

In looking at the potentialities for distortion in the sect type, we may note the fragility of the sect organization. Society, particularly religious society, is secondary to individuals and depends on their continued purity and constant effort to maintain it. The emphasis on purity leads to splits with those felt to be impure, whereas the stress on the objectivity of the sacraments in the church type can operate to maintain the unity of the more pure and less pure in a united body.

Even though in their early stages, and potentially thereafter, sects have sometimes been radically critical of the world and have sometimes experimented with utopian alternatives to it—one thinks of the Anabaptists and their many successors—they have their own form of compromise with the world. Moderate sectarianism, remaining aloof from the world, has nevertheless been highly congenial to capitalism, liberalism, and democracy. The tightly structured sect has released the energy of autonomous enterprise in the secular world. Though highly intolerant within and quick to expel deviants, sectarians have often collaborated with secular liberals in support of civil liberties as against the pressures of a coercive church. Perhaps unintentionally, the sects have played into the liberal drive to privatize and depoliticize religion.

In any case, the influence of the sects on American society has been enormous. They are a major source of our individualism and of the pervasive American idea that all social groups are fragile and in need of constant energetic effort to maintain them. There is a deep, though also ironic, relationship between the spirit of the sects and the utilitarian individualism that has been so important in the American past. The world that the sects find so uncongenial today is in part their creation.

The mystical type is also not new in America—we have mentioned Anne Hutchinson in the seventeenth century and Emerson, Thoreau, and Whitman in the nineteenth—but it has developed into a major form in the late twentieth century. Troeltsch's mystical type is not necessarily mystical in the traditional sense of the word, though Americans of this type have been open to a wide variety of influences from genuine mystics both Eastern and Western. Contemporary religious individualists often speak of themselves as "spiritual" rather than "religious," as in "I'm not religious but I'm very spiritual." It is worth remembering that Troeltsch sees mysticism, too, at least in its moderate forms, as rooted in the New Testament, particularly the Johannine writings.

Mysticism has a social appeal almost opposite to sectarianism, though it shares the latter's individualism, indeed radicalizes and absolutizes it. For mysticism is found most often among prosperous, well-educated people, perhaps one reason why it flourishes in our affluent society. Mysticism lacks any effective social discipline—which, as we noted, is present in the sect. Mysticism is probably the commonest form of religion among those we interviewed, and many who sit in the pews of the churches and the sects are really religious individualists, though many more never go to church at all.

Radical religious individualism has played a role in the life of the Christian peoples from the beginning, and it still has much to contribute today. Much of the freshness and vitality of American religion can be found in forms of "new consciousness," which are not without their social contributions.[27] The cultural revolution of the 1960s was in part an upwelling of mystical religious feeling and the issues to which it made us sensitive—ecology, peace, opposition to nuclear weapons, internationalism, feminism—are still very high on our agenda. Yet the particular distortions to which the mystical type is prone are also more than evident: its inner volatility and incoherence, its extreme weakness in social and political organization, and, above all, its particular form of compromise with the world—namely, its closeness to the therapeutic model in its pursuit of self-centered experiences and its difficulty with social loyalty and commitment.

If there is to be an effective public church in the United States today, bringing the concerns of biblical religion into the common discussion about the nature and future of our society, it will probably have to be one in which the dimensions of church, sect, and mysticism all play a significant part, the strengths of each offsetting the deficiencies of the others. We are not suggesting homogenization—there is little danger of that. Each religious community will continue to speak in its own voice and will in some ways be incompatible with others, whether Christian or non-Christian. Strongly held differences do not undermine the debate about our common future as long as it is pursued through civil discourse and we seek to persuade, rather than coerce, our fellow citizens.

The great contribution that the church idea can make today is its emphasis on the fact that individuality and society are not opposites but require each other. It was perhaps necessary at a certain stage in the development of modern society for individuals to declare their independence from churches, states, and families. But absolute independence becomes the atomism Tocqueville feared, a condition for a new despotism worse than the old. The church idea reminds us that in our independence we count on others and helps us see that a healthy, grown-up independence is one that admits to healthy grown-up dependence on others. Absolute independence is a false ideal. It delivers not the autonomy it promises but loneliness and vulnerability instead. Concomitantly, the church idea reminds us that authority need not be external and oppressive. It is something we can participate in—as Father Morrison puts it, we have to be "together enough to take on the responsibilities of authority." A church that can be counted on and that can count on its members can be a great source of strength in reconstituting the social basis of our society. Such a church may also, through its social witness, have the influence to help move our society in a healthier direction. To be effective, however, the church tradition in the United States would have to be revitalized by taking seriously the criticisms of it by sectarian and mystical religion.

The sects at their best have attempted, by being as genuinely Christian as they know how, to bring their witness to the larger society in hopes of converting and reforming it. The Quakers and the Mennonites, for example, have persisted in upholding a clear Christian pacifism that speaks to our society with a new urgency in the nuclear age. The unwillingness of the sects to compromise with the world has on occasion made them marginal or even irresponsible. But the sectarian insistence on purity has an enormous contribution to make, particularly in calling church and mystical religion to examine the nature of their compromises and to try to discern when they are strategic retreats and when they are betrayals of what must not be betrayed.

Religious individualism is, in many ways, appropriate in our kind of society. It is no more going to go away than is secular individualism. Ours is a society that requires people to be strong and independent. As believers, we must often operate alone in uncongenial circumstances, and we must have the inner spiritual strength and discipline to do so. Objecting to its authoritarianism and paternalism, religious individualists have often left the church or sect they were raised in. Yet such people often derive more of their personal strength than they know from their communities of origin. They have difficulty transmitting their own sense of moral integrity to their children in the absence of such a community, and they have difficulty sustaining it themselves when their only support is from transient associations of the like-minded. It would seem that a vital and enduring religious individualism can only survive in a renewed relationship with established religious bodies. Such a renewed relationship would require changes on both sides. Churches and sects would have to learn that they can sustain more autonomy than they had thought, and religious individualists would have to learn that solitude without community is merely loneliness.

Religion and World

Throughout this chapter, we have seen a conflict between withdrawal into purely private spirituality and the biblical impetus to see religion as involved with the whole of life. Parker Palmer suggests that this apparent contradiction can be overcome:

> Perhaps the most important ministry the church can have in the renewal of public life is a "ministry of paradox": not to resist the inward turn of American spirituality on behalf of effective public action, *but to deepen and direct and discipline that inwardness in the light of faith* until God leads us back to a vision of the public and to faithful action on the public's behalf.[28]

Palmer seems to be asserting with respect to religious individualism something similar to what we argued in chapter 6—namely, that American individualism is not to be rejected but transformed by reconnecting it to the public realm.

Toward the end of the previous chapter, we discussed the social movement as a form of citizenship and pointed out how often in our history religion has played an important role in such movements. Time and again in our history, spiritually motivated individuals and groups have felt called to show forth in their lives the faith that was in them by taking a stand on the great ethical and political issues of the day. During the Revolution, the parish clergy gave ideological support and moral encouragement to the republican cause. Christian clergy and laity were among the most fervent supporters of the antislavery cause, just as Christians involved in the Social Gospel movement and its many ramifications did much to ameliorate the worst excesses of early industrial capitalism. Of course, the churches produced opponents of all these movements—the American religious community has never spoken with one voice. On occasion, a significant part of the religious community has mounted a successful crusade that the nation as a whole later came to feel was unwise—for example, the Temperance movement that led to a constitutional amendment prohibiting the sale of alcoholic beverages in the United States. But without the intervention of the churches, many significant issues would have been ignored and needed changes would have come about much more slowly.

To remind us of what is possible, we may call to mind one of the most significant social movements of recent times, a movement overwhelmingly religious in its leadership that changed the nature of American society. Under the leadership of Martin Luther King, Jr., the Civil Rights movement called upon Americans to transform their social and economic institutions with the goal of building a just national community that would respect both the differences and the interdependence of its members. It did this by combining biblical and republican themes in a way that included, but transformed, the culture of individualism.

Consider King's "I Have a Dream" speech. Juxtaposing the poetry of the scriptural prophets—"I have a dream that every valley shall be exalted, every hill and mountain shall be made low"—with the lyrics of patriotic anthems—"This will be the day when all of God's children will be able to sing with new meaning, 'My country 'tis of thee, sweet land of liberty, of thee I sing'"—King's oration reappropriated that classic strand of the American tradition that understands the true meaning of freedom to lie in the affirmation of responsibility for uniting all of the diverse members of society into a just social order. "When we let freedom ring, when we let it ring from every village and hamlet, from every state and every city, we will be able to speed up the day when all of God's children, black men and white men, Jews and Gentiles, Protestants and Catholics, will be able to join hands and sing the words of that old Negro spiritual. 'Free at last! Free at last! Thank God almighty, we are free at last!'" For King, the struggle for freedom became a practice of commitment within a vision of America as a community of memory. We now need to look at that national community, our changing conceptions of it, and what its prospects are.

□

10   The National Society

Conceptions of the Public Order

So far we have examined some of the ways in which middle-class people in our society understand and live out their involvements in personal and domestic life, in work, in religion, and in politics. We now need to examine the connection between what we have learned from our interviews and observations and the larger conception of American society more closely. Since a conversation cut off from past and future necessarily loses its bearings, we seek to reconnect the personal stories we have narrated with the enduring national conversation and the public voices that still continue it.

In our interviews, it became clear that for most of those with whom we spoke, the touchstones of truth and goodness lie in individual experience and intimate relationships. Both the social situations of middle-class life and the vocabularies of everyday language predispose toward private sources of meaning. We also found a widespread and strong identification with the United States as a national community. Yet, though the nation was viewed as good, "government" and "politics" often had negative connotations. Americans, it would seem, are genuinely ambivalent about public life, and this ambivalence makes it difficult to address the problems confronting us as a whole.

A difficulty so pervasive must involve fundamental aspects of how people understand themselves and their society. As we have seen, ours is a society in which the language of individualism allows people to develop loyalties to others in the context of families, small communities, religious congregations, and what we have termed lifestyle enclaves. Even in these relatively narrow contexts, reciprocal loyalty and understanding are frequently precarious and hard to maintain. It is thus natural that the larger interdependencies in which people live, geographically, occupationally, and politically, are neither clearly understood nor easily encompassed by an effective sympathy. As we saw in chapter 8, the enormous complexity of our society remains to most of us elusive and almost invisible. When people do express a general concern for their fellow citizens as members of the national society, it is usually inspired by a hope that their more personal moral understanding can be extended to the scale of a genuinely public good.

The problem of articulating the public good in the contemporary United States was evident in the two preceding chapters on citizenship and religion. In this respect, religious life seems strikingly similar to political life. Many with whom we spoke prized their civic and religious activities as vital to their lives, providing ways to share the joy of love and caring that the utilitarian world of work often seemed to inhibit. Yet, as we have seen, pursuit of the joys of involvement is always a precarious venture, subject to derailment from frustration or "burnout" because of the fragility of voluntary expressive community. The commercial dynamism at the heart of the ideal of personal success also undermines community involvement. California banker Jim Reichert found his "desire to be committed" waning as possibilities for career advancement put pressure on him to relocate—and so sever his ties with the voluntary organization in whose service he had found so much fulfillment.

The American search for spontaneous community with the like-minded is made urgent by the fear that there may be no way at all to relate to those who are too different. Thus the tremendous nostalgia many Americans have for the idealized "small town." The wish for a harmonious community we heard from a variety of sources is a wish to transform the roughness of utilitarian dealings in the marketplace, the courts, and government administration into neighborly conciliation. But this nostalgia is belied by the strong focus of American individualism on economic success. The rules of the competitive market, not the practices of the town meeting or the fellowship of the church, are the real arbiters of living.

Yet the public realm still survives, even though with difficulty, as an enduring association of the different. In the civic republican tradition, public life is built upon the second languages and practices of commitment that shape character. These languages and practices establish a web of interconnection by creating trust, joining people to families, friends, communities, and churches, and making each individual aware of his reliance on the larger society. They form those habits of the heart that are the matrix of a moral ecology, the connecting tissue of a body politic.

At moments, such an understanding becomes truly national in scope. As we saw at the end of the preceding chapter, the movement for civil rights led by Martin Luther King, Jr., demonstrated the strength and vitality still latent in the sense of the public good Americans have inherited. King's articulation of the biblical and republican strands of our national history enabled a large number of Americans, black and white, to recognize their real relatedness across difference. King characterized legal disenfranchisement, poverty, and unemployment as institutionalized denials of personal dignity and social participation—glaring failures of collective national responsibility. The powerful response King elicited, transcending simple utilitarian calculations, came from the reawakened recognition by many Americans that their own sense of self was rooted in companionship with others who, though not necessarily like themselves, nevertheless shared with them a common history and whose appeals to justice and solidarity made powerful claims on their loyalty.

On a more local scale, we found similar resources for reappropriating a sense of the public good among some of those to whom we talked. We found people like Cecilia Dougherty, Mary Taylor, Ed Schwartz, and Paul Morrison, whose second languages have enabled them to link their hopes and their sufferings with larger communities of memory. What emerged from these conversations was the understanding that becoming one's own person, while always a risky, demanding effort, takes place in a community loyal to shared ideals of what makes life worth living. Sharing practices of commitment rooted in religious life and civic organization helps us identify with others different from ourselves, yet joined with us not only in interdependence and a common destiny, but by common ends as well. Because we share a common tradition, certain habits of the heart, we can work together to construct a common future. Yet what concrete shape and direction the public good might take in our present historical circumstances is difficult for most Americans to envision. Even the most articulate of those to whom we talked found it difficult to conceive of a social vision that would embody their deepest moral commitments.

The Public Good: The Uncompleted American Quest

The search for an adequate vision of the public good has a long history in the United States, reaching back to the founders of the republic. Perhaps our best hope for gaining perspective on our present situation is to connect our contemporary reflections with the reflections of those who began the nation. Despite agreement that they were establishing a republic, the leaders of the revolutionary generation differed in important ways about the kind of republic best suited to the conditions they confronted. John Adams, for example, argued that government should represent in its institutions the major social groups in the society. Thomas Jefferson and Thomas Paine from the beginning of the Revolution pressed vigorously for widespread democratic participation both as a check on the ambitions of leaders and as vital education in the spirit of republicanism. By contrast, Alexander Hamilton and James Madison feared that without strong leadership and central direction, a territorially extended and commercially oriented republic such as they contemplated would dissipate itself in endless factional battles. Yet all were agreed that a republic needed a government that was more than an arena within which various interests could compete, protected by a set of procedural rules. Republican government, they insisted, could survive only if animated by a spirit of virtue and concern for the public good.

It is perhaps most instructive to listen closely to James Madison on this topic. Madison, the Constitution's chief architect and joint author with Alexander Hamilton and John Jay of *The Federalist Papers*, has often been presented as the hard-headed advocate of the political machinery of checks and balances against the republican idealism of Jefferson and Paine. Yet it was Madison who warned in *The Federalist Papers* that "the public good, the real welfare of the great body of the people, is the supreme object to be pursued; and that no form of government whatever has any other value than as it may be fitted for the attainment of this object" (*Federalist* No. 45). Madison was here drawing on the tradition of civic republicanism as he had come to understand it through years of struggle with Great Britain and through the painful emergence of a new nation moving in an irresistibly democratic and commercial direction.

Mobilized through the revolutionary experience, the "great body of the people"—that is, white, male freeholders, and not only men of Madison's own gentry class—were the actual as well as legal source of sovereignty. And despite misgivings about the dangers of easily swayed masses that had been the commonplaces of aristocratic arguments against democracy, Madison agreed with Hamilton that "it is a just observation that the people commonly intend the PUBLIC GOOD" (*Federalist* No. 71, emphasis in original). Madison confided in another, less public writing that, "I go on this great republican principle, that the people will have virtue and intelligence to select men of virtue and wisdom." The basis of this "great republican principle" was the proposition that the citizens of a republic are capable of recognizing and acting on what the eighteenth century called virtue. "Is there no virtue among us?" asked Madison. "If there be not, no form of government can render us secure.

To suppose that any form of government will secure liberty or happiness without any virtue in the people is a chimerical idea."[1]

The notion of public virtue, as Gary Wills has recently reminded us, bulked very large for the revolutionary generation, with "a heft and weightiness unknown to us." Virtue was to them not an abstraction but a visible quality exemplified by contemporary men of virtue: by George Washington, the modern Cincinnatus, forming the new nation, ruling without excess, and returning to ordinary life, or by Nathan Hale becoming the American Cato in his last moments.[2] The notion of virtue described an ideal of character made concrete not just in the works of the ancient writers but in the stories of the revolutionaries themselves. It depended upon the belief that besides the grimly self-focussed passions, there was in human beings a capacity to apprehend and pursue the good and to recognize in the character of others the qualities of integrity, grace, and excellence. Madison and his contemporaries thought of the pursuit of virtue as the way to reconcile the desire to be esteemed by one's peers with publicly beneficial ends.

Yet as Madison, Hamilton, Jefferson, Adams, and the others knew, aristocratic republics had been both more numerous historically and more enduring than democracies. As students of the Enlightenment philosopher Montesquieu, they also knew the explanation for this discomfiting fact, which set the problem the new democratic republic had to solve. Montesquieu had defined a republic as a self-regulating political society whose mainspring is the identification of one's own good with the common good, calling this identity civic virtue. For Montesquieu, the virtuous citizen was one who understood that personal welfare is dependent on the general welfare and could be expected to act accordingly. Forming such character requires the context of practices in which the coincidence of personal concern and the common welfare can be experienced. For a specialized ruling group, an aristocracy, this conjunction of private and public identity is, other things being equal, more likely than it is in a democracy whose citizens spend most of their time in private affairs, taking part in government only part-time. This, according to Montesquieu, accounts for the relatively greater stability and endurance of aristocratic as compared with democratic republics.

Both conviction and political necessity, however, committed Madison and the other framers to a regime that was ultimately democratic in spirit. The special challenge facing the founding generation was thus historically unique. They were attempting to establish republican institutions of democratic cast in an expansive commercial society. They needed to develop public virtues in democratic citizens. To achieve this end, the Constitution of 1787 organized a machinery of national government consciously adapted to the social reality of expanding capitalism and the attendant culture of philosophic liberalism. However, the instrumentality of checks and balances has as its positive aim to so offset the centrifugal and anarchic tendency of competitive individual and local self-interest as to foster what Madison called the "*permanent* and aggregate interests of the community" (*Federalist* No. 10). The founders were not expecting the common good to result mechanically, as though by the automatic workings of interests, or at least they did not expect it to happen unaided. Madison designed the elaborate constitutional mechanism to filter and refine popular passions in hopes that in the main it would be men of vision and virtue who would reach office at the national level.

The premise of the system was that the virtue of the people would lead them to choose for their officials and representatives men who would be great-spirited enough to place the public good above their own, or their local region's, special advantage. Such men would constitute a genuine aristocracy of merit. Ruled by leaders whose public stewardship was subject to frequent popular review through elections, the United States would secure the advantages Montesquieu had ascribed to aristocratic republics but with a democratic constitution.

The revolutionary leaders trusted the people to continue to recognize the claims to political leadership of an educated and cultivated stratum of which they themselves were examples. They thus saw little need actively to shape the political culture of the populace, already shaped by religious, personal, and political ties in local communities. Yet ironically, the Revolution, which had brought notions of public virtue and proven wisdom to the fore, also unleashed an egalitarian spirit and a drive for individual success that soon swamped this first, fragile pattern in a torrent of territorial and economic expansion, ending dreams of secure leadership by a national civic-minded elite in close touch with popular feeling.

In the new climate that dominated the nineteenth century, Americans' minds turned to private advancement and local economic growth, leaving the weak and distant national government in the hands of a new breed of professional politicians who specialized in the accommodation of interests rather than in civic virtue. The first republican vision of national life receded before a more individual dream of enterprise. But this made the coherence of the national society a continuing problem. The role of guiding the nation, which the founders had originally cast for the proven aristocracy of merit, was partially assumed by political parties that attempted to articulate an accommodation of interests in law and national policy. The life of the relatively small-scale local community was heavily shaped by a religious and civic morality that generally worked to channel and transform private ambition into the public concerns of the independent citizen and town father, but the economic and social interests of the local communities were frequently in conflict with one another, and at the national level, the brokerage system was hardpressed to accommodate mounting stresses. It finally broke down altogether in the traumatic Civil War of 1861 to 1865.

The war and its aftermath temporarily galvanized a renewed sense of dedication to democratic and republican purposes, particularly in the North, but this sense dissipated rapidly in territorial and commercial expansion, which continued through the turn of the century. Spurred by vast untapped resources, new industrial technology, and waves of immigrant labor, American capitalism was by the 1890s developing an integrated national market centered on the industrial cities of the Northeast and Midwest. This new industrial and commercial system decisively subordinated the life of the local community to nationwide economic development. The result was a new class of economic leaders, who established new institutions of private power, along with new conditions of work and living that were national in reach and impact. Those old patterns of local life that resisted these tendencies survived only in an attenuated form.

The turn-of-the-century economic and social transformation into an interdependent national society was never complemented by new political institutions to foster Madison's "permanent and aggregate interests" of the national society. Thus the founders' problem of developing an effective, democratic civic spirit in a commercial republic was postponed, not resolved.

Six American Visions of the Public Good

The tension between self-reliant competitive enterprise and a sense of public solidarity espoused by civic republicans has been the most important unresolved problem in American history. Americans have sought in the ideal of community a shared trust to anchor and complete the desire for a free and fulfilled self. This quest finds its public analogue in the desire to integrate economic pursuits and interrelationships in an encompassing fabric of national institutional life. American culture has long been marked by acute ambivalence about the meshing of self-reliance and community, and the nation's history shows a similar ambivalence over the question of how to combine individual autonomy and the interrelationships of a complex modern economy.

Six distinct visions of the public good have arisen in the United States in the past hundred years. They each have their specific histories, but all have developed as responses to the need for citizens of a society grown increasingly interdependent to picture to themselves what sort of a people they are and where they should be heading. These visions of the public good have, in fact, been different proposals for how best to make sense of that basic American tension between individualism and the common good as this tension has grown in the industrial age.

Historically, the six visions have arisen in pairs, each pair emerging in a period of institutional breakdown and subsequent reintegration of the national economic order. But since these economic upheavals have also been times of social and political ferment, visions of the public good have been concerned not just with the narrowly economic but with the meaning of the United States as a national society.

The first, perhaps most fundamental and enduring, pair of alternative visions arose in the last decades of the nineteenth century to shape national consciousness until after World War I. We will call this the opposition of the Establishment versus Populism. The radically changed circumstances that followed the collapse of the private corporate economy in 1929 gave rise to a second debate, pitting a revived defense of private capital, or Neocapitalism, against the vision gradually evolving out of the various, largely ad hoc, policies of the New Deal, which we will term Welfare Liberalism. While the unsettled economic conditions of the 1980s have resulted from the gradual unravelling of the economic settlement of 1933–45, the political debate continues to be conducted largely in terms of Neocapitalism versus Welfare Liberalism. But the novel features of our present difficulties with inherited corporate-governmental arrangements have brought two other competing visions to the fore, though to date mostly among political and economic specialists. These new, only partially articulated rivals we will call the Administered Society versus Economic Democracy.

We shall briefly consider these six visions in turn, two at a time, asking how they have functioned as forms of political imagination, and then how they resonate with the themes of American culture we encountered in our conversations. The first pair of visions, the competing claims of the Establishment versus Populism, arose as a response to new industrial conditions in the 1880s and 1890s, but it was a conflict that continued earlier American debates. As notions of the public good, of what the national community should be like, both the Establishment and Populist visions touched the basic sources of the American cultural imagination. Thus these first two visions provide the underlying themes for the following two pairs as well.

The Establishment versus Populism

The extraordinary scope and speed of the changes American society underwent between the 1880s and World War I stirred national awareness and debate to a new intensity. To observers at the time, it seemed that the very patterns of American life were being remade. At the dramatically staged World's Columbian Exposition at Chicago in the summer of 1893, the historian Frederick Jackson Turner presented his famous paper arguing that the great western frontier had finally closed, and that with its closing, the strength and optimism of nineteenth-century America was threatened with constriction. The journalist Walter Lippmann was only one of many who responded shortly thereafter to Theodore Roosevelt's aggressive evocation of the "strenuous life" as the beginning of a much-needed national renewal. "The days of easy expansion had come to an end," wrote Lippmann, explaining Roosevelt's appeal. T.R. was "the first President who realized clearly that national stability and social justice had to be sought deliberately and had consciously to be maintained . . . turning the American mind in the direction it had to go in the Twentieth Century."[3]

Thus the context of political discourse by the turn of the century had begun to shift away from the ideologically unadorned competition of interests typical of the nineteenth century, a politics many came to see as having failed to confront the new economic and social situation. "Reform" came to mean seeking "national stability and social justice" by deliberate means. The issue was how and on what terms Americans were to shape the emerging industrial order into a viable and morally decent national society.

One answer was the Establishment vision. It was primarily associated with those segments of the industrial and financial elites who at the end of the nineteenth century created and endowed a network of private institutions such as universities, hospitals, museums, symphony orchestras, schools, churches, clubs, and associations alongside their new corporations. What is interesting is that these new institutions, whether metropolitan, regional, or national in scope, were based on the principle of voluntary association, as was the corporation itself. Their strength correlated with a relatively weak state in America. Indeed, even to this day, institutions such as great research universities and museums of international reputation, which would be run by government in most other societies, are still "private" institutions here, a legacy of the Establishment vision of institution building.

The creators of these institutions sought to spread a cosmopolitan ethic of *noblesse oblige* and public service to give local magnates a sense of national responsibility. The Establishment vision clearly had affinities with religion of the church type. In contrast to the ethics of town fathers, the Establishment vision accepted large institutions and the bargaining politics of interest, while seeking to guide and harmonize social conflicts toward fruitful compromise through personal influence and negotiation. As given theoretical formulation by thinkers such as Walter Lippmann in the first decades of the century, the Establishment vision was cosmopolitan, flexible, striving to reconcile interests in larger national purposes. Theodore Roosevelt was perhaps its classic embodiment in political life.

Against the high-minded, genteel image of the Establishment, the Populist vision accented the egalitarian ethos in the American tradition, often proposing Thomas Jefferson as its founding hero and Alexander Hamilton as its representative villain. The Populist vision asserted the claims of "the people," ordinary citizens, to sufficient wisdom to govern their affairs. Like the Establishment vision, Populism was rooted in the ideal of the politics of face-to-face community. But because Establishment ideals from the beginning appealed to the controllers of the commanding heights of the new national institutions, Populist rhetoric often had an oppositional cast. Yet in the program of the People's party of 1896, Populism sought to expand government power over economic life for the common good. Populism's great themes of the dignity and importance of ordinary citizens frequently involved biblical language. Populism had affinities with both the antinomian, mystical aspects of American religion and the fervent commitment of the religious sect. If the Establishment vision rearticulated important aspects of the republican ideal of the common good in turn-of-the-century America, Populism was the great democratizer, insisting on the incompleteness of a republic that excluded any of its members from full citizenship.

Despite their vast disagreements, the Establishment and the Populist visions were alike in their insistence on the need to encompass the emerging industrial and corporate economic society within a public moral order. Moreover, this order was seen in both cases as the reassertion of the authority of a civic and religious moral ecology felt to be endangered by the radically instrumental mores of the market. Advocates of Establishment leadership no less than Populist democrats spoke in the strong accents of a common tradition concerning the ends of public life, ends they feared were being betrayed by the new economic and technological developments of the age.

In 1889, for instance, Andrew Carnegie, the prototypical self-made magnate, spoke in his "Gospel of Wealth" of the need for captains of industry to think of themselves not as owners but as trustees of the nation's wealth, bound to administer it for general betterment. "The problem of our age," Carnegie wrote, "is the proper administration of wealth, that the ties of brotherhood may still bind together the rich and poor in harmonious relationship."[4] Henry Lee Higginson, a leading member of Boston's business establishment, wrote in 1911, "I do not believe that, because a man owns property, it belongs to him to do with as he pleases. The property belongs to the community, and he has charge of it, and can dispose of it, if it is well done and not with the sole regard to himself or to his stockholders." Higginson, who considered himself a Progressive in politics, joined Charles W. Eliot, president of Harvard, and other leading Bostonians in believing "that the best solution to the problem of national order lay in the education of individuals to ideals of service, stewardship, and cooperation."[5]

The advocates of the Populist vision spoke in similar language. "The spirit of fraternity abroad in the land [counters] the mad chase for the 'almighty dollar,'" wrote labor leader Eugene Debs in 1890. Fraternity, he argued, grows out of "the ties and bonds and obligations that large souled and large hearted men recognize as essentials to human happiness." Later, as a socialist, Debs continued to speak in familiar republican and biblical terms, stressing the obligations of contemporaries to the brave precursors who suffered in their "struggle to leave the world better for us." The proper response, Debs urged, was to discharge one's obligation to those heroic forebears "by doing the best we can for those who come after us. . . . [Then] you will know what it is to be a real *man* or *woman* . . . to find yourself—to really know yourself and your purpose in life."[6]

The Populist vision thus shared with the Establishment ideal an understanding that work, welfare, and authority are tightly interrelated and embedded in community life. For Populism, this pattern often resembled the ideals of small town life we have found strongly alive in the United States today, whereas the Establishment image was less egalitarian and emphasized paternal relationships of reciprocal, though unequal, duties. However, both visions shared a larger perspective and saw work as a contribution to a public household held together by mutual ties. Justice required public efforts to repair the collapse of these social relationships. The Establishment vision was large-scale—national and international in scope—and Populism was often suspicious of size, but both saw politics, like work, as a matter of public trust and, ultimately, of personal relationships. This common understanding led to a second major agreement—that a national society requires not only fair procedures regulating the individual pursuit of happiness but a substantive conception of just institutions and virtuous citizens. This substantive concern about the ends of social life differentiates the Populist and Establishment visions from the dominant political visions of our own time, which offer conceptions of procedural rules and effective means but have less to say about common ends.

Debs's language of public ends was built on a conception of a just society as one whose citizens shared both the economic position needed to take active part in social life and an understanding of its duties and rights. Indeed, Debs's fundamental argument for socialism was that there is a moral substance to justice that overrides the principles of market exchange, a substance grounded in the solidarity of citizens who share an understanding of what human dignity requires. Thus Debs could argue that as industrial development had undermined the nineteenth-century independent citizen's basis for dignity, which was in his labor on his own property, a new conception of social property and economic participation was needed to provide substance to citizenship under industrial conditions.

The political reform movements of the early twentieth century that we group together loosely as "Progressive" borrowed from both the Establishment and the Populist visions yet led finally in a direction different from either. Like the proponents of the Establishment vision, the Progressives wanted to create a national community, but, like the Populists, they wanted a national community that would be genuinely democratic and inclusive. To the reformers of the Progressive era, as Michael Sandel has put it, "If a virtuous republic of small-scale, democratic communities was no longer a possibility, a national republic seemed democracy's next best hope." Still believing in a politics of the common good, these reformers "looked to the nation, not as a neutral framework for the play of competing interests, but rather as a formative community, concerned to shape a common life suited to the scale of modern social and economic forms."[7]

Yet there was another side to the thought of the Progressive reformers. This was their commitment to "rationality" and "science" as the chief means for attaining the new national community. They developed an enthusiasm for public administration as a sort of social engineering able to heal political and social divisions and promote a more "efficient" and "rational" national society. Progressives often embraced the goals of better public services, health, and education along with the governmental regulation of big business in the public interest. This desire for a more "rational" politics, standing above interest but based on expertise rather than wisdom and virtue, moved American political discourse away from concern with justice, with its civic republican echoes, toward a focus on progress—a progress defined primarily as material abundance. Thus, ironically, given its original intentions, the reform movement shifted the goal of political action away from the realization of a democratic republic and toward the creation of an administrative system that could "deliver the goods." The new political goal was summed up by Walter Lippmann as the growth of "mastery." The hopes of that age seemed about to be fulfilled in 1928 with the election to the presidency of Herbert Hoover, himself an engineer, hailed by the press as "the most commanding figure in the modern science of 'engineering statesmanship' . . . 'the dynamics of mastery.'"[8]

Neocapitalism versus Welfare Liberalism

Whereas the opposing visions of Populism and the Establishment sought to subordinate the competition of interests in the economic and political arenas to a national life based on relationships of reciprocity, the visions that emerged from the dislocations of the corporate economy after 1929, Neocapitalism and Welfare Liberalism, have appealed to a different common aspiration. The Great Depression seemed like nothing so much as a loss of mastery, but as a problem of means rather than ends. Both Neocapitalism and Welfare Liberalism agree about the primary aim of modern society. It is twofold: to provide physical security and material well-being for its citizens and at the same time encourage as much individual choice as possible regarding the goals of activity. Though with differing conceptions of how it should be directed and by whom, both visions have inherited the Progressives' enthusiasm for scientific and technological advance, as well as a belief in the necessity and value of specialization of function.

Welfare Liberalism finds its beginnings in Franklin D. Roosevelt's New Deal, when the resources of government were brought massively, but with only partial success, to bear on the solution of the problems created by the Great Depression. World War II greatly expanded the capacities of the American state, and from 1950 to 1970, in a period of unparalleled economic growth, Welfare Liberalism scored its greatest successes and created something close to a national consensus. Neocapitalism, an effort to revive older free-market ideas in contemporary form, developed as the major critique of Welfare Liberalism, gaining plausibility and adherents as a consequence of the economic difficulties of the 1970s. Since 1970 Neocapitalism has entered into a serious contest for hegemony in the American political consciousness.

The Neocapitalist vision has, of course, been the basis of the rhetoric of Ronald Reagan. From the time he accepted his party's nomination as a candidate for the presidency in 1980, Reagan has eloquently defined his mission as one of building "a new consensus with all those across the land who share a community of values embedded in these words: family, work, neighborhood, peace and freedom." In Reagan's rhetoric, however, such words, charged with moral resonance, are evocations of private, rather than public, virtues. Work is an economic activity pursued by self-reliant individuals in the interests of themselves and their families. In his inaugural address, Reagan said that "we the people" are "a special interest group" that is "made up of men and women who raise our food, patrol our streets, man our mines and factories, teach our children, keep our homes and heal us when we're sick." By defining us by our occupations, Reagan sees us not as a polity but as an economy, in which the population is an all-inclusive "interest group," chiefly concerned with "a healthy, vigorous, growing economy that provides equal opportunity for all Americans." The primary aim of government is to safeguard the peace and security necessary to allow self-reliant individuals to pursue their largely economic aims in freedom. "Work and family are at the center of our lives, the foundation of our dignity as a free people."

According to Reagan, a government that attempts to provide more than such essentials is "overgrown and overweight" and "should go on a diet." Although there is some need for the government to provide a "safety net" for those individuals who fail in their quest for self-sufficiency, such government assistance must be reduced to the minimum necessary to protect the "truly needy," and, if possible, restore them to self-reliance. Concern for the poor should be encouraged, but as a private virtue, not a public duty. "It's time to reject the notion," Reagan said in a speech in early 1984, "that advocating government programs is a form of personal charity. Generosity is a reflection of what one does with his or her resources—and not what he or she advocates the government do with everyone's money."[9] The implication of such remarks is that community is a voluntary association of neighbors who personally know one another and freely express concern for one another, an essentially private, rather than public, form of association.

This Neocapitalist vision of national life has its origins in the economic and social transformation of the late nineteenth century. It derives from the creed of business, particularly corporate business, which was able in that era to emancipate itself from the strictures of local communities and explicitly to celebrate the flourishing of business as the principal means toward a better future. In an interview published in the *Los Angeles Times* in 1982, President Reagan's longtime friend and "kitchen cabinet" member, the late multimillionaire businessman Justin Dart, articulated the classic moral justification for this vision in franker terms than Reagan himself: "I have never looked for a business that's going to render a service to mankind. I figure that if it employs a lot of people and makes a lot of money, it is in fact rendering a service to mankind. Greed is involved in everything we do. I find no fault with that."[10] Whereas entrepreneurs have often been indifferent to social issues—what Dart calls "these crappy issues like equal rights"—the Neocapitalist vision has frequently been allied with religious and cultural currents that seek, in the words of Jerry Falwell, to "bring back decency to America," by promoting the traditional family and conservative forms of Christianity, though remaining largely positive about scientific technology and material progress as the means toward individual prosperity. Neocapitalism has thus retained continuity in some respects with the culture of the nineteenth-century town, though it accepts that culture only as the foundation for a local, private life and perceives the dynamics of the free market as the sole effective means of integrating the national society.

Neocapitalism developed its present form in opposition to the contrasting vision of Welfare Liberalism, which in turn developed as a response to the breakdown of the private corporate economy in the Great Depression. The hallmark of Welfare Liberalism has been administrative intervention by the government to balance the operations of the market in the interests of economic growth and social harmony. Like Neocapitalism, Welfare Liberalism has accepted the capitalist market and its private economic institutions as the core mechanism for growth in material abundance, while promoting the application of expertise and functional organization to both economic and social life. Welfare Liberalism views the market as in more or less permanent need of intervention by the national state through a variety of institutions designed to regulate or assist market exchange.

This emphasis on governmental intervention in the market leads to Welfare Liberalism's conception of politics. The public good is defined as national harmony achieved through sharing the benefits of economic growth. It is the purpose of activist government to promote economic growth and to guarantee individuals a fair chance to benefit from it. This intervention in economy and society has moral purposes: to provide all citizens with an "equal opportunity" to engage in economic competition, to prevent economic exploitation, and, since the early 1970s, to conserve environmental resources. The most eloquent, unabashed recent statement of the Welfare Liberal vision has come not from the Democratic aspirants in the 1984 election, but from Senator Edward Kennedy. In the speech he gave while conceding the presidential nomination of the Democratic party to Jimmy Carter in 1980, Kennedy gave a ringing call for a government based on fairness and compassion: "The commitment I seek is not to outworn values but to old values which will never wear out. Programs may sometimes become obsolete, but the ideal of fairness always endures. Circumstances may change but the work of compassion must continue. It is surely correct that we cannot solve problems by throwing money at them, but it is also correct that we dare not throw out our national problems onto a scrap heap of inattention and indifference. . . . The demand of our people in 1980 is not for smaller government or bigger government but for better government."

Kennedy went on to call for government spending to provide full employment, promote worker safety, "reindustrialize" America, and protect the environment. He demanded that the "full power of the government" be invoked to control inflation. He called for tax reforms that would increase the taxes paid by the wealthy. And he insisted that the government control the rising cost of medical treatment and make government-sponsored health insurance available to all. All of this would ensure a fair government, one that would be based on our willingness as a people to "give back to our country in return for all it has given us" and on the principle that "whatever sacrifices must be made will be shared—and shared fairly." And it would ensure a compassionate government that would maintain a commitment to "the cause of the common man and the common woman."

Yet despite all of its contrasts with Neocapitalist policies on tax reform, government intervention in the market, and the provision of social services to the poor, the Welfare Liberal vision articulated by Kennedy shares with Neocapitalism a fundamental assumption about the relationship between public and private life. The purpose of government is to give individuals the means to pursue their private ends. Welfare Liberals believe that this can be done only if the economy is managed by bureaucratic agencies guided by experts and if those who have historically suffered from disadvantages are given government assistance to enable them to compete on an equal basis with more privileged individuals. But the disagreement with the Neocapitalists is about the *means* by which to foster individual self-reliance, not about the ultimate value of fostering it. The debate is over procedures to achieve fairness for each, not about the substantive meaning of justice for all.

For those who might fail to achieve individual self-sufficiency even in a fair competition, Welfare Liberalism offers only what Neocapitalists such as Reagan offer: "compassion," the subjective feeling of sympathy of one private individual for another. Unlike Neocapitalists, of course, Welfare Liberals argue that compassion toward the losers in the social competition is best administered by government agencies staffed by experts from the "helping professions." But such agencies gain their legitimacy only as the social expression of compassion. When the price of government welfare programs becomes high, or when they seem to increase the dependency of their clients rather than foster self-reliance, Welfare Liberals are vulnerable to the charge of being "bleeding hearts" who are imprudently compassionate—or, as President Reagan put it, all too willing to express their personal feelings of generosity with someone else's money. They lack a language to express their own deep moral commitment to justice in a way that would be persuasive to their fellow citizens.

In the decades after World War II, Welfare Liberalism continued to be the basis for a national consensus only so long as its prescriptions for government intervention in the economy actually worked to provide rising standards of living for the majority and only so long as the cost of the bureaucratic agencies of compassion seemed less for most people than the benefits of rising affluence. And then, in the 1970s, the economic growth machine began to falter seriously, with unfortunate, but predictable, results. If the great pie would no longer grow very fast, then the whole optimistic vision of Welfare Liberalism became less and less credible. The American electorate grew increasingly volatile and resistant to party appeals. The stage was set for the resurgence of Neocapitalism, a vision that, for many, promised a more effective means than Welfare Liberalism to continue the individual pursuit of private goods allowing for the expression of personal compassion for the unfortunate, but at less cost.

If the Welfare Liberal vision is in trouble in an "era of limits," the Neocapitalist vision is also on shaky ground in pretending that the links between government and the private market can be dissolved in a complex modern society. The huge military-industrial complex ardently espoused by the Neocapitalists refutes their own claims, and there is the critical problem of providing convincing and effective substitutes for active management of the political economy and "compassionate government," given the persistent structural problems of poverty and unemployment in modern capitalism.

To cope with these difficulties, contemporary adherents of both Neocapitalism and Welfare Liberalism borrow rhetorically from the earlier images of community ties and concern for the common good found in the Populist and Establishment traditions. Yet the growth of unprecedented deficits, a deeply troubled world economy, and other economic, social, and political uncertainties have led some to suggest that the time is fast approaching when neither Welfare Liberalism nor Neocapitalism will be able to cope with our mounting difficulties. These concerns have given rise to yet another pair of contrasting visions of how to pursue the public good.

The Administered Society
versus Economic Democracy

The Administered Society and Economic Democracy represent the two boldest efforts to imagine a next step beyond the stalemated efforts of Welfare Liberalism and Neocapitalism to solve the problems of our society. The advocates of these new visions strongly reject the notion that the United States can return to anything like the situation that prevailed before 1929. In accepting the interpenetration of private and public power, they represent a crucial break with the assumption that fundamental economic interests can be effectively integrated either through the market alone or through informal alliances among interest groups. Rather, these two visions declare the need to go beyond exclusive reliance on voluntarist strategies for integrating major sectors of society such as business, labor, and government. They propose a more visible, public institutionalization, expanding the linkages between sectors and placing them in a more encompassing national framework.

There is a similarity between the proponents of these still inchoate visions. Both announce that something new to American politics is required because of the failure of older visions. Proponents of these new views join others in a widespread criticism of Neocapitalism and Welfare Liberalism as alike sacrificing the general welfare to "special interests." Welfare Liberals such as Walter Mondale are thought to give too much attention to labor, ethnic and racial minorities, and other special constituencies, and Neocapitalists such as President Reagan are criticized as agents of the corporations and the selfish rich. The proponents of the Administered Society and Economic Democracy present their visions as efforts to incorporate and transcend contending interests. Like earlier reformers, they do so with confidence in expertise as the way to extricate our society from its apparent impasse.

As yet, major politicians have embraced only fragments of these new visions as they seek to update fundamentally older conceptions. For coherent expression of these visions we must turn to theorists rather than politicians. We may consider first a vocal advocate of an administratively more integrated national society, the well-known investment banker Felix Rohatyn. In the 1970s, Rohatyn figured prominently in the rescue of New York City from bankruptcy, a rescue carried out by placing fiscal authority in the hands of an appointed board of the city's creditors, employees, bondholders, and bankers, operating outside ordinary legislative channels. Rohatyn proposed in the early 1980s that the United States, confronting an increasingly competitive international economy, needed a similar rescue that would produce "stable growth, low unemployment, reasonably balanced budgets, and reasonably valued currency." Such a policy would need to be "committed to maintaining our social gains by promoting economic growth and full employment," which Rohatyn argued could not be realized by the kinds of political compromises characteristic of congressional politics. "Only institutions that can take the long view and act accordingly will be able to bring about the kinds of changes that are required," he contended.

In arguing for the necessity for such new institutional arrangements, Rohatyn spoke in a language strong in technical economic and administrative terms, as Welfare Liberals and Neocapitalists have done for a long time, but with a weaker evocation of the moral tradition of American politics than even these long-dominant positions usually contain. Rohatyn's specific proposal was for a "tri-partite economic development board," made up of representatives of "business, labor and government," appointed by the president and the Congress, in order to intervene in the economy to promote the economic goals described above. The board, the centerpiece of Rohatyn's "industrial policy," was modeled after the New York City rescue board and drew inspiration from the Reconstruction Finance Corporation designed by Herbert Hoover to fight the 1929 depression. To bring so massive a reorganization into being, Rohatyn called for strong national leadership by a "bipartisan administration in which a Republican or Democratic president would include opposition leaders in his cabinet" and which would select members of the economic board in a similar spirit.[11]

The Administered Society is above all a vision of social harmony among different and unequal groups cooperating for the goals of improved individual security and widely shared economic growth. To accomplish these ends, it would link private groups, especially business and labor, with governmental agencies to steer economic development through this period of technological and international change. At the same time, traditional Welfare Liberal programs such as improved opportunity and assistance for those dislocated by major change would be continued. One key to this vision is the idea of "partnership" among various sectors of the economy and society, brought together through governmental boards, commissions, and agencies.[12] Such a policy would depend heavily on the administrative structure of government, rather than on popular representation, and would thus bring technical and managerial experts to increased prominence. Yet the basic understanding of work as a means toward private goals would remain the same as in Neocapitalism and Welfare Liberalism. The "permanent and aggregate interests" of the nation would receive more focused and perhaps

more expert attention, but presumably only by those at or near the sum-
mits of their respective institutions. The ironic result of the Administered Society is very likely to be an increase of privatized attitudes for the
many, now more securely provided for.

Unlike the proponents of the Administered Society, advocates of Economic Democracy consciously worry about how to empower citizens to
take part in the array of new integrating institutions that they, too, see as
necessary to a more humane, as well as a more abundant future. An important voice of this developing position in the early 1980s was Michael
Harrington, a long-time advocate of what he has termed "democratic socialism." To Harrington, neither Welfare Liberalism nor Neocapitalism
will do: "We have entered a decade of decision, a crisis of the system,
whether we like it or not." As an alternative to the failed policies of the
past, Harrington endorses a part of Rohatyn's logic on the grounds that
conscious centralization in economic policy is the precondition for more
citizen participation in economic decisions—for "decentralization." Seeing corporate domination of the economy as the chief obstacle, Harrington proposes an active government role to bring about a "democrati-
zation of the investment function." Such a policy would lead eventually to
"introducing democracy from the shop floor to the board room."

While a planner such as Rohatyn can be sanguine about the benevolence of centralized institutions, Harrington thinks the situation requires more ingenuity. Rohatyn defends his proposals as ultimately
likely to enhance democracy, saying that "far from being undemocratic,
the work of such a board could add to the democratic process an element
of consultation with the major forces of our society." In contrast, Harrington sees public as well as private bureaucracies as threats to freedom.
But, he asks, "What if there were legal provisions of funds for any significant group of citizens who wanted to hire their own experts to put
together a counter-plan?" For Harrington, the element that divides Economic Democracy and the Administered Society is the notion of citizen
empowerment.[13]

Yet Harrington shares the same universe of discourse with Rohatyn to
such an extent that he turns to the provision of funds to citizens "to hire
their own experts" as the major defense of the democratic nature of his
proposed reforms. But experts, no matter how "democratic" in spirit,
are neither moral exemplars nor prophets nor political leaders, and the
politics of competing experts sounds like a "high tech" version of the
politics of interest. Harrington's vision of Economic Democracy intends
to evoke a political vision greater than the sum of competing interests,
and it recognizes that this vision would require the support of a widespread social movement. Harrington even recognizes something Roha-

tyn gives no hint of—that the new vision requires a major cultural transformation as well as institutional innovation. But when it comes to suggesting the substance of that cultural transformation, Harrington's vision falls as silent as Rohatyn's. They mutely reveal the lack of a moral basis for their political purposes, the end point of a discourse of means without ends.

This is not to say that there is no difference between these two most recent visions, any more than it could be said that there is no difference between Welfare Liberalism and Neocapitalism. Though Rohatyn may not intend it, it is certainly possible that the Administered Society as he envisions it would only tighten the hold of corporate business on our collective life and result in the administrative despotism that Tocqueville warned against. The vision of Economic Democracy continues the long struggle to bring the corporate economy under democratic control that we alluded to in chapter 8. But can we not imagine that without a cultural and moral transformation, the experts—on whom the Economic Democrats, too, rely—would succeed in bringing about an administrative despotism, or what Tocqueville also called a "democratic despotism," just as surely under Economic Democracy as under the Administered Society?

The Unresolved Tension

Earlier in this chapter, we spoke of the belief of Madison and the other founders that our form of government was dependent on the existence of virtue among the people. It was such virtue that they expected to resolve the tension between private interest and the public good. Without civic virtue, they thought, the republic would decline into factional chaos and probably end in authoritarian rule. Half a century later, this idea was reiterated in Tocqueville's argument about the importance of the mores—the "habits of the heart"—of Americans. Even at the end of the nineteenth century, when Establishment and Populist visions were the chief antagonists in the continuing argument about the shape of our society, Madisonian ideas were still presupposed. The tension between private interest and the public good is never completely resolved in any society. But in a free republic, it is the task of the citizen, whether ruler or ruled, to cultivate civic virtue in order to mitigate the tension and render it manageable.

As the twentieth century has progressed, that understanding, so important through most of our history, has begun to slip from our grasp.

As we unthinkingly use the oxymoron "private citizen," the very meaning of citizenship escapes us. And with Ronald Reagan's assertion that "we the people" are "a special interest group," our concern for the economy being the only thing that holds us together, we have reached a kind of end of the line. The citizen has been swallowed up in "economic man."

Yet this kind of economic liberalism is not ultimately liberating, for, as became quite clear with the final two visions of the public good described, when economics is the main model for our common life, we are more and more tempted to put ourselves in the hands of the manager and the expert. If society is shattered into as many special interests as there are individuals, then, as Tocqueville foresaw, there is only the schoolmaster state left to take care of us and keep us from one another's throats.

But if the fears of Madison, Tocqueville, and Debs seem today to be becoming alarmingly true, then perhaps their hopes can speak to us as well. They believed that the survival of a free people depends on the revival of a public virtue that is able to find political expression. The way a free society meets its problems depends not only on its economic and administrative resources but on its political imagination. Political vision thus plays an indispensable role in providing understanding of the present and of the possibilities for change. Is it possible that we could become citizens again and together seek the common good in the post-industrial, postmodern age?

□

Conclusion

Transforming American Culture

As we saw in the preceding chapter, much of the thinking about our society and where it should be going is rather narrowly focussed on our political economy. This focus makes sense in that government and the corporations are the most powerful structures in our society and affect everything else, including our culture and our character. But as an exclusive concern, such a focus is severely limited. Structures are not unchanging. They are frequently altered by social movements, which grow out of, and also influence, changes in consciousness, climates of opinion, and culture. We have followed Tocqueville and other classical social theorists in focussing on the mores—the "habits of the heart"—that include consciousness, culture, and the daily practices of life. It makes sense to study the mores not because they are powerful—in the short run, at least, power belongs to the political and economic structures—but for two other reasons. A study of the mores gives us insight into the state of society, its coherence, and its long-term viability. Secondly, it is in the sphere of the mores, and the climates of opinion they express, that we are apt to discern incipient changes of vision—those new flights of the social imagination that may indicate where society is heading.

A Change of Eras?

In the course of this book, we have documented the latest phase of that process of separation and individuation that modernity seems to entail. John Donne, in 1611, at the very beginning of the modern era, with the prescience that is sometimes given to great poets, vividly described that process:

> 'Tis all in peeces, all cohaerence gone;
> All just supply, and all Relation:
> Prince, Subject, Father, Sonne, are things forgot,
> For every man alone thinkes he hath got
> To be a Phoenix, and that then can bee
> None of that kinde, of which he is, but hee.[1]

Donne lived in a world where the ties of kinship and village and feudal obligation were already loosening, though only a few perceived how radical the consequences would be.

America was colonized by those who had come loose from the older European structures, and so from the beginning we had a head start in the process of modernization. Yet the colonists brought with them ideas of social obligation and group formation that disposed them to recreate in America structures of family, church, and polity that would continue, if in modified form, the texture of older European society. Only gradually did it become clear that every social obligation was vulnerable, every tie between individuals fragile. Only gradually did what we have called ontological individualism, the idea that the individual is the only firm reality, become widespread. Even in our day, when separation and individuation have reached a kind of culmination, their triumph is far from complete. The battles of modernity are still being fought.

But today the battles have become half-hearted. There was a time when, under the battle cry of "freedom," separation and individuation were embraced as the key to a marvelous future of unlimited possibility. It is true that there were always those, like Donne, who viewed the past with nostalgia and the present with apprehension and who warned that we were entering unknown and dangerous waters. It is also true that there are still those who maintain their enthusiasm for modernity, who speak of the third wave or the Aquarian Age or the new paradigm in which a dissociated individuation will reach a final fulfillment. Perhaps most common today, however, is a note of uncertainty, not a desire to turn back to the past but an anxiety about where we seem to be headed. In this view, modernity seems to be a period of enormously rapid change, a transition from something relatively fixed toward something not yet clear. Many might find still applicable Matthew Arnold's assertion that we are

Wandering between two worlds, one dead,
The other powerless to be born.[2]

There is a widespread feeling that the promise of the modern era is slipping away from us. A movement of enlightenment and liberation that was to have freed us from superstition and tyranny has led in the twentieth century to a world in which ideological fanaticism and political oppression have reached extremes unknown in previous history. Science, which was to have unlocked the bounties of nature, has given us the power to destroy all life on the earth. Progress, modernity's master idea, seems less compelling when it appears that it may be progress into the abyss. And the globe today is divided between a liberal world so incoherent that it seems to be losing the significance of its own ideals, an oppressive and archaic communist statism, and a poor, and often tyrannical, Third World reaching for the very first rungs of modernity. In the liberal world, the state, which was supposed to be a neutral nightwatchman that would maintain order while individuals pursued their various interests, has become so overgrown and militarized that it threatens to become a universal policeman.

Yet in spite of those daunting considerations, many of those we talked to are still hopeful. They realize that though the processes of separation and individuation were necessary to free us from the tyrannical structures of the past, they must be balanced by a renewal of commitment and community if they are not to end in self-destruction or turn into their opposites. Such a renewal is indeed a world waiting to be born if we only had the courage to see it.

The Culture of Separation

One of the reasons it is hard to envision a way out of the impasse of modernity is the degree to which modernity conditions our consciousness. If modernity is "the culture of separation," Donne characterized it well when he said " 'Tis all in peeces, all cohaerence gone." When the world comes to us in pieces, in fragments, lacking any overall pattern, it is hard to see how it might be transformed.

A sense of fragmentariness is as characteristic of high intellectual culture as of popular culture. Starting with science, the most respected and influential part of our high culture, we can see at once that it is not a whole, offering a general interpretation of reality, as theology and philosophy once did, but a collection of disciplines each having little to do with the others. As Stephen Toulmin recently put it:

> From the early seventeenth century on, and increasingly so as the centuries passed, the tasks of scientific inquiry were progressively divided up between separate and distinct "disciplines." . . . Every independent scientific discipline is marked by its own specialized modes of abstraction: and the issues to be considered in each discipline are so defined that they can be investigated and discussed independently—in abstraction from—the issues belonging to other disciplines. . . . As a result of this first kind of abstraction, the broad and general questions about "cosmic interrelatedness" which were the focus of the earlier debates about nature have been superseded by other, more specialized, disciplinary questions. . . . In its actual content (that is to say) the science of the nineteenth and early twentieth centuries became an aggregate, rather than an integration, of results from its component disciplines.[3]

What Toulmin has pointed out for the natural sciences is equally true of the social sciences and, indeed, of all the "disciplines" and "fields" into which contemporary intellectual culture is divided. As the French anthropologist Louis Dumont has observed:

> [I]n the modern world each of our particular viewpoints or specialized pursuits does not know very well—or does not know at all—what it is about and the reason for its existence or distinctness, which is more often a matter of fact than of consensus or rationality. Just as our rationality is mostly a matter of the relation of means and ends, while the hierarchy of ends is left out, so also our rationality manifests itself within each of our neatly distinct compartments but not in their distribution, definition and arrangement.[4]

The poet and critic Wendell Berry has described the consequences for the place of poetry in a culture of separation and specialization. Since science specializes in the external reality of the world, the poet is consigned to speak about his own feelings. He is himself his chief subject matter and "the old union of beauty, goodness and truth is broken." Such poets can no longer be public persons, so that even when, as of late, some of them have turned to protest, it is a private protest. As Berry puts it, "In his protest, the contemporary poet is speaking publicly, but not as a spokesman; he is only one outraged citizen speaking *at* other citizens who do not know him, whom he does not know, and with whom he does not sympathize."[5] One recent poet who tried to integrate the world—politics, economics, culture—into one vast poem, taking

Dante as his model, only showed how impossible such an integration is under modern conditions. According to Helen Vendler, Ezra Pound's huge *Cantos* are a "jumble of detail," a "mound of potsherds," of which Pound himself finally said, "I cannot make it cohere."[6]

These developments in the realm of high culture have had devastating consequences for education. Here, particularly in higher education, students were traditionally supposed to acquire some general sense of the world and their place in it. In the contemporary multiversity, it is easier to think of education as a cafeteria in which one acquires discrete bodies of information or useful skills. Feeble efforts to reverse these trends periodically convulse the universities, but the latest such convulsion, the effort to establish a "core curriculum," often turns into a battle between disciplines in which the idea of a substantive core is lost. The effort is thus more symptomatic of our cultural fracture than of its cure.

When we turn from intellectual culture to popular culture, particularly the mass media, the situation is, if anything, even more discouraging. Within the disciplinary and subdisciplinary "compartments" of intellectual culture, though there is little integration between them, there is still meaning and intensity in the search for truth. In popular culture, it is hard to say even that much. To take an extreme example, television, it would be difficult to argue that there is any coherent ideology or overall message that it communicates. There is a sense in which the broadcasters' defense of their role—that they are merely mirroring the culture—has a certain plausibility. They do not support any clear set of beliefs or policies, yet they cast doubt on everything. Certainly, they do not glorify "the power structure." Big business is not admirable: its leaders are frequently power-hungry bullies without any moral restraints (J. R. Ewing, for example). Government is under a cloud of suspicion: politicians are crooks. Labor is badly tarnished: labor leaders are mobsters. The debunking that is characteristic of our intellectual culture is also characteristic of the mass media. While television does not preach, it nevertheless presents a picture of reality that influences us more than an overt message could. As Todd Gitlin has described it,

[T]elevision's world is relentlessly upbeat, clean and materialistic. Even more sweepingly, with few exceptions prime time gives us people preoccupied with personal ambition. If not utterly consumed by ambition and the fear of ending up as losers, these characters take both the ambition and the fear for granted. If not surrounded by middle-class arrays of consumer goods, they themselves are glamorous incarnations of desire. The happiness they long for is private, not public; they make few demands on society as a whole, and even when troubled they seem content with the existing institutional order. Personal ambition and consumerism are the driving forces of their lives. The sumptuous and brightly lit settings of most series amount to advertisements for a consumption-centered version of the good life, and this doesn't even take into consideration the incessant commercials, which convey the idea that human aspirations for liberty, pleasure, accomplishment and status can be fulfilled in the realm of consumption. The relentless background hum of prime time is the packaged good life.[7]

Gitlin's description applies best to daytime and prime-time soaps. It does not apply nearly so well to situation comedies, where human relations are generally more benign. Indeed, the situation comedy often portrays people tempted to dishonesty or personal disloyalty by the prospect of some private gain, who finally decide to put family or friends ahead of material aggrandizement. Yet, finally, both soaps and situation comedies are based on the same contrast: human decency versus brutal competitiveness for economic success. Although the soaps show us that the ruthlessly powerful rich are often unhappy and the situation comedies show us that decent "little people" are often happy, they both portray a world dominated by economic competition, where the only haven is a very small circle of warm personal relationships. Thus the "reality" that looms over a narrowed-down version of "traditional morality" is the overwhelming dominance of material ambition.

Of course, in television none of these things is ever really argued. Since images and feelings are better communicated in this medium than ideas, television seeks to hold us, to hook us, by the sheer succession of sensations. One sensation being as good as another, there is the implication that nothing makes any difference. We switch from a quiz show to a situation comedy, to a bloody police drama, to a miniseries about celebrities, and with each click of the dial, nothing remains.

But television operates not only with a complete disconnectedness between successive programs. Even within a single hour or half-hour program, there is extraordinary discontinuity. Commercials regularly break whatever mood has built up with their own, often very different, emotional message. Even aside from commercials, television style is singularly abrupt and jumpy, with many quick cuts to other scenes and other characters. Dialogue is reduced to clipped sentences. No one talks long enough to express anything complex. Depth of feeling, if it exists at all, has to be expressed in a word or a glance.

The form of television is intimately related to the content. Except for the formula situation comedies (and even there, divorce is increasingly common), relationships are as brittle and shifting as the action of the camera. Most people turn out to be unreliable and double-dealing.

Where strong commitments are portrayed, as in police dramas, they are only between buddies, and the environing atmosphere, even within the police force, is one of mistrust and suspicion.

If popular culture, particularly television and the other mass media, makes a virtue of lacking all qualitative distinctions, and if the intellectual culture, divided as it is, hesitates to say anything about the larger issues of existence, how does our culture hold together at all? The culture of separation offers two forms of integration—or should we say pseudo-integration?—that turn out, not surprisingly, to be derived from utilitarian and expressive individualism. One is the dream of personal success. As Gitlin has observed, television shows us people who are, above all, consumed by ambition and the fear of ending up losers. That is a drama we can all identify with, at least all of us who have been (and who has not?) exposed to middle-class values. Isolated in our efforts though we are, we can at least recognize our fellows as followers of the same private dream. The second is the portrayal of vivid personal feeling. Television is much more interested in how people feel than in what they think. What they think might separate us, but how they feel draws us together. Successful television personalities and celebrities are thus people able freely to communicate their emotional states. We feel that we "really know them." And the very consumption goods that television so insistently puts before us integrate us by providing symbols of our version of the good life. But a strange sort of integration it is, for the world into which we are integrated is defined only by the spasmodic transition between striving and relaxing and is without qualitative distinctions of time and space, good and evil, meaning and meaninglessness. And however much we may for a moment see something of ourselves in another, we are really, as Matthew Arnold said in 1852, "in the sea of life enisled . . . / We mortal millions live *alone*."[8]

The Culture of Coherence

But that is not the whole story. It could not be the whole story, for the culture of separation, if it ever became completely dominant, would collapse of its own incoherence. Or, even more likely, well before that happened, an authoritarian state would emerge to provide the coherence the culture no longer could. If we are not entirely a mass of interchangeable fragments within an aggregate, if we are in part qualitatively distinct members of a whole, it is because there are still operating among us, with whatever difficulties, traditions that tell us about the nature of the world, about the nature of society, and about who we are as people. Primarily biblical and republican, these traditions are, as we have seen, important for many Americans and significant to some degree for almost all. Somehow families, churches, a variety of cultural associations, and, even if only in the interstices, schools and universities, do manage to communicate a form of life, a *paideia,* in the sense of growing up in a morally and intellectually intelligible world.

The communities of memory of which we have spoken are concerned in a variety of ways to give a qualitative meaning to the living of life, to time and space, to persons and groups. Religious communities, for example, do not experience time in the way the mass media present it—as a continuous flow of qualitatively meaningless sensations. The day, the week, the season, the year are punctuated by an alternation of the sacred and the profane. Prayer breaks into our daily life at the beginning of a meal, at the end of the day, at common worship, reminding us that our utilitarian pursuits are not the whole of life, that a fulfilled life is one in which God and neighbor are remembered first. Many of our religious traditions recognize the significance of silence as a way of breaking the incessant flow of sensations and opening our hearts to the wholeness of being. And our republican tradition, too, has ways of giving form to time, reminding us on particular dates of the great events of our past or of the heroes who helped to teach us what we are as a free people. Even our private family life takes on a shared rhythm with a Thanksgiving dinner or a Fourth of July picnic.

In short, we have never been, and still are not, a collection of private individuals who, except for a conscious contract to create a minimal government, have nothing in common. Our lives make sense in a thousand ways, most of which we are unaware of, because of traditions that are centuries, if not millennia, old. It is these traditions that help us to know that it does make a difference who we are and how we treat one another. Even the mass media, with their tendency to homogenize feelings and sensations, cannot entirely avoid transmitting such qualitative distinctions, in however muted a form.

But if we owe the meaning of our lives to biblical and republican traditions of which we seldom consciously think, is there not the danger that the erosion of these traditions may eventually deprive us of that meaning altogether? Are we not caught between the upper millstone of a fragmented intellectual culture and the nether millstone of a fragmented popular culture? The erosion of meaning and coherence in our lives is not something Americans desire. Indeed, the profound yearning for the idealized small town that we found among most of the people we talked to is a yearning for just such meaning and coherence. But although the yearning for the small town is nostalgia for the irretrievably lost, it is worth considering whether the biblical and republican traditions that small town once embodied can be reappropriated in ways that respond to our present need. Indeed, we would argue that if we are ever to enter that new world that so far has been powerless to be born, it will be through reversing modernity's tendency to obliterate all previous culture. We need to learn again from the cultural riches of the human species and to reappropriate and revitalize those riches so that they can speak to our condition today.

We may derive modest hope from the fact that there is a restlessness and a stirring in the intellectual culture itself. Stephen Toulmin tells us that "our own natural science today is no longer 'modern' science." It is a "postmodern" science in which disciplinary boundaries are beginning to appear as the historical accidents they are and the problems that are necessarily "transdisciplinary" are beginning to be addressed. This recognition is based on the realization that we cannot, after all, finally separate who we are from what we are studying. As Toulmin puts it, "We can no longer view the world as Descartes and Laplace would have us do, as 'rational onlookers,' from outside. Our place is within the same world that we are studying, and whatever scientific understanding we achieve must be a kind of understanding that is available to participants within the processes of nature, i.e., from inside."[9] Perhaps nature as perceived by the poet, the theologian, and the scientist may be the same thing after all. At least there is now room to talk about that possibility. And there are parallel developments in the social sciences. There, too, it appears that studying history and acting in it are not as different as we had thought. If our high culture could begin to talk about nature and history, space and time, in ways that did not disaggregate them into fragments, it might be possible for us to find connections and analogies with the older ways in which human life was made meaningful. This would not result in a neotraditionalism that would return us to the past. Rather, it might lead to a recovery of a genuine tradition, one that is always self-revising and in a state of development. It might help us find again the coherence we have almost lost.

Social Ecology

Stephen Toulmin gives an illuminating and suggestive example of a transdisciplinary development in natural science that has a deep relationship to changes in social practice. The study of ecology draws on numerous disciplines to ask the general question, How do living things, including human beings, exist in relation to one another in their common habitat? Since human beings are presently having an enormous impact on the planet earth, which is their habitat and also the habitat of all other living things, ecology as a science has close connections to ecology as a philosophy and as a social movement. Toulmin is not saying that ecological science and ecological social philosophy are identical. He is only saying that there is no way to keep them separate, since every ecological "fact" has ethical significance.[10]

It is only a step beyond Toulmin's argument to suggest that there is such a thing as "social ecology"—what we have referred to earlier in this book as "moral ecology"—that raises questions related to, and parallel with, natural ecology. Human beings and their societies are deeply interrelated, and the actions we take have enormous ramifications for the lives of others. Much of social science serves to shed light on these ramifications.

Without derogating our modern technological achievements, we now see that they have had devastatingly destructive consequences for the natural ecology. We are engaged in an effort to mitigate and reverse the damage and regain an ecological balance whose complete loss could prove fatal. Modernity has had comparable destructive consequences for social ecology. Human beings have treated one another badly for as long as we have any historical evidence, but modernity has given us a capacity for destructiveness on a scale incomparably greater than in previous centuries. And social ecology is damaged not only by war, genocide, and political repression. It is also damaged by the destruction of the subtle ties that bind human beings to one another, leaving them frightened and alone. It has been evident for some time that unless we begin to repair the damage to our social ecology, we will destroy ourselves long before natural ecological disaster has time to be realized.

For several centuries, we have been embarked on a great effort to increase our freedom, wealth, and power. For over a hundred years, a large part of the American people, the middle class, has imagined that the virtual meaning of life lies in the acquisition of ever-increasing status, income, and authority, from which genuine freedom is supposed to come. Our achievements have been enormous. They permit us the aspiration to become a genuinely humane society in a genuinely decent world, and provide many of the means to attain that aspiration. Yet we seem to be hovering on the very brink of disaster, not only from international conflict but from the internal incoherence of our own society. What has gone wrong? How can we reverse the slide toward the abyss?

In thinking about what has gone wrong, we need to see what we can learn from our traditions, as well as from the best currently available knowledge. What has failed at every level—from the society of nations to the national society to the local community to the family—is integration: we have failed to remember "our community as members of the same body," as John Winthrop put it. We have committed what to the republican founders of our nation was the cardinal sin: we have put our own good, as individuals, as groups, as a nation, ahead of the common good.

The litmus test that both the biblical and republican traditions give us for assaying the health of a society is how it deals with the problem of wealth and poverty. The Hebrew prophets took their stand by the *'anawim,* the poor and oppressed, and condemned the rich and powerful who exploited them. The New Testament shows us a Jesus who lived among the *'anawim* of his day and who recognized the difficulty the rich would have in responding to his call. Both testaments make it clear that societies sharply divided between rich and poor are not in accord with the will of God. Classic republican theory from Aristotle to the American founders rested on the assumption that free institutions could survive in a society only if there were a rough equality of condition, that extremes of wealth and poverty are incompatible with a republic. Jefferson was appalled at the enormous wealth and miserable poverty that he found in France and was sanguine about our future as a free people only because we lacked such extremes. Contemporary social science has documented the consequences of poverty and discrimination, so that most educated Americans know that much of what makes our world and our neighborhoods unsafe arises from economic and racial inequality.[11] Certainly most of the people to whom we talked would rather live in a safe, neighborly world instead of the one we have.

But the solution to our problems remains opaque because of our profound ambivalence. When times are prosperous, we do not mind a modest increase in "welfare." When times are not so prosperous, we think that at least our own successful careers will save us and our families from failure and despair. We are attracted, against our skepticism, to the idea that poverty will be alleviated by the crumbs that fall from the rich man's table, as the Neocapitalist ideology tells us. Some of us often feel, and most of us sometimes feel, that we are only someone if we have "made it" and can look down on those who have not. The American dream is often a very private dream of being the star, the uniquely successful and admirable one, the one who stands out from the crowd of ordinary folk who don't know how. And since we have believed in that dream for a long time and worked very hard to make it come true, it is hard for us to give it up, even though it contradicts another dream that we have—that of living in a society that would really be worth living in.

What we fear above all, and what keeps the new world powerless to be born, is that if we give up our dream of private success for a more genuinely integrated societal community, we will be abandoning our separation and individuation, collapsing into dependence and tyranny. What we find hard to see is that it is the extreme fragmentation of the modern world that really threatens our individuation; that what is best in our separation and individuation, our sense of dignity and autonomy as persons, requires a new integration if it is to be sustained.

The notion of a transition to a new level of social integration, a newly vital social ecology, may also be resisted as absurdly utopian, as a project to create a perfect society. But the transformation of which we speak is both necessary and modest. Without it, indeed, there may be very little future to think about at all.

Reconstituting the Social World

The transformation of our culture and our society would have to happen at a number of levels. If it occurred only in the minds of individuals (as to some degree it already has), it would be powerless. If it came only from the initiative of the state, it would be tyrannical. Personal transformation among large numbers is essential, and it must not only be a transformation of consciousness but must also involve individual action. But individuals need the nurture of groups that carry a moral tradition reinforcing their own aspirations. Implicitly or explicitly, a number of the communities of memory we have discussed in this book hold ethical commitments that require a new social ecology in our present situation. But out of existing groups and organizations, there would also have to develop a social movement dedicated to the idea of such a transformation. We have several times spoken of the Civil Rights movement as an example. It permanently changed consciousness, in the sense of individual attitudes toward race, and it altered our social life so as to eliminate overt expressions of discrimination. If the Civil Rights movement failed fundamentally to transform the position of black people in our society, it was because to do that would have required just the change in our social ecology that we are now discussing. So a movement to transform our social ecology would, among other things, be the successor and fulfillment of the Civil Rights movement. Finally, such a social movement would lead to changes in the relationship between our government and our economy. This would not necessarily mean more direct control of the economy, certainly not nationalization. It would mean changing the climate in which business operates so as to encourage new initiatives in economic democracy and social responsibility, whether from "private" enterprise or autonomous small- and middle-scale public enterprises. In the context of a moral concern to revive our social ecology, the proposals of the proponents of the Administered Society and Economic Democracy that we discussed in the preceding chapter could be considered and appropriate ones adopted.[12]

To be truly transformative, such a social movement would not simply subside after achieving some of its goals, leaving the political process much as it found it. One of its most important contributions would be to restore the dignity and legitimacy of democratic politics. We have seen in earlier chapters how suspicious Americans are of politics as an area in which arbitrary differences of opinion and interest can be resolved only by power and manipulation. The recovery of our social ecology would allow us to link interests with a conception of the common good. With a more explicit understanding of what we have in common and the goals we seek to attain together, the differences between us that remain would be less threatening. We could move to ameliorate the differences that are patently unfair while respecting differences based on morally intelligible commitments. Of course, a political discourse that could discuss substantive justice and not only procedural rules would have to be embodied in effective political institutions, probably including a revitalized party system.

It is evident that a thin political consensus, limited largely to procedural matters, cannot support a coherent and effective political system. For decades that has become ever clearer. We have been afraid to try for a more substantial consensus for fear that the effort may produce unacceptable levels of conflict. But if we had the courage to face our deepening political and economic difficulties, we might find that there is more basic agreement than we had imagined. Certainly, the only way to find out is to raise the level of public political discourse so that the fundamental problems are addressed rather than obscured.[13]

If we are right in our stress on a revitalized social ecology, then one critically important action that government could take in a new political atmosphere would be, in Christopher Jencks's words, to reduce the "punishments of failure and the rewards of success."[14] Reducing the inordinate rewards of ambition and our inordinate fears of ending up as losers would offer the possibility of a great change in the meaning of work in our society and all that would go with such a change. To make a real difference, such a shift in rewards would have to be a part of a reappropriation of the idea of vocation or calling, a return in a new way to the idea of work as a contribution to the good of all and not merely as a means to one's own advancement.

If the extrinsic rewards and punishments associated with work were reduced, it would be possible to make vocational choices more in terms of intrinsic satisfactions. Work that is intrinsically interesting and valuable is one of the central requirements for a revitalized social ecology. For professionals, this would mean a clearer sense that the large institutions most of them work for really contribute to the public good. A bright young lawyer (or a bright old lawyer, for that matter) whose work consists in helping one corporation outwit another is intelligent enough to doubt the social utility of what he or she is doing. The work may be interesting— even challenging and exciting—yet its intrinsic meaninglessness in any larger moral or social context necessarily produces an alienation that is only partly assuaged by the relatively large income of corporate lawyers. Those whose work is not only poorly rewarded but boring, repetitive, and unchallenging are in an even worse situation. Automation that turns millions of our citizens into mere servants of robots is already a form of despotism, for which the pleasures of private life—modest enough for those of minimum skill and minimum wage—cannot compensate. The social wealth that automation brings, if it is not siphoned into the hands of a few, can be used to pay for work that is intrinsically valuable, in the form of a revival of crafts (that already flourish in supplying goods for the wealthy) and in the improvement of human services. Where routine work is essential, its monotony can be mitigated by including workers in fuller participation in their enterprises so that they understand how their work contributes to the ultimate product and have an effective voice in how those enterprises are run.

Undoubtedly, the satisfaction of work well done, indeed "the pursuit of excellence," is a permanent and positive human motive. Where its reward is the approbation of one's fellows more than the accumulation of great private wealth, it can contribute to what the founders of our republic called civic virtue. Indeed, in a revived social ecology, it would be a primary form of civic virtue. And from it would flow a number of positive consequences. For one thing, the split between private and public, work and family, that has grown for over a century, might begin to be mended. If the ethos of work were less brutally competitive and more ecologically harmonious, it would be more consonant with the ethos of private life and, particularly, of family life. A less frantic concern for advancement and a reduction of working hours for both men and women would make it easier for women to be full participants in the workplace without abandoning family life. By the same token, men would be freed to take an equal role at home and in child care. In this way, what seemed at first to be a change only in the nature of work would turn out to have major consequences for family life as well.

Another consequence of the change in the meaning of work from private aggrandizement to public contribution would be to weaken the motive to keep the complexity of our society invisible. It would become part of the ethos of work to be aware of our intricate connectedness and interdependence. There would be no fear of social catastrophe or hope of inordinate reward motivating us to exaggerate our own independence. And with such a change, we might begin to be better able to understand why, though we are all, as human beings, morally deserving of equal respect, some of us begin with familial or cultural advantages or disadvantages that others do not have. Or perhaps, since we would not conceive of life so much in terms of a race in which all the prizes go to the swiftest, we might begin to make moral sense of the fact that there are real cultural differences among us, that we do not all want the same thing, and that it is not a moral defect to find other things in life of interest besides consuming ambition. In short, a restored social ecology might allow us to mitigate the harm that has been done to disadvantaged groups without blaming the victims or trying to turn them into carbon copies of middle-class high achievers.

It should be clear that we are not arguing, as some of those we criticized in chapter 10 have done, that a few new twists in the organization of the economy would solve all our problems. It is true that a change in the meaning of work and the relation of work and reward is at the heart of any recovery of our social ecology. But such a change involves a deep cultural, social, and even psychological transformation that is not to be brought about by expert fine-tuning of economic institutions alone. On the contrary, at every point, institutional changes, educational changes, and motivational changes would go hand in hand. For example, part of our task might well involve a recovery of older notions of the corporation. As Alan Trachtenberg has written:

> The word [corporation] refers to any association of individuals bound together into a *corpus*, a body sharing a common purpose in a common name. In the past, that purpose had usually been communal or religious; boroughs, guilds, monasteries, and bishoprics were the earliest European manifestations of the corporate form. . . . It was assumed, as it is still in nonprofit corporations, that the incorporated body earned its charter by serving the public good. . . . Until after the Civil War, indeed, the assumption was widespread that a corporate charter was a privilege to be granted only by a special act of a state legislature, and then for purposes clearly in the public interest. Incorporation was not yet thought of as a right available on application by any private enterprise.[15]

As late as 1911, as we saw in chapter 10, a leading Boston businessman, Henry Lee Higginson, could say, following earlier Protestant notions of stewardship, that corporate property "belongs to the community."

Reasserting the idea that incorporation is a concession of public authority to a private group *in return for* service to the public good, with effective public accountability, would change what is now called the "social responsibility of the corporation" from its present status, where it is often a kind of public relations whipped cream decorating the corporate pudding, to a constitutive structural element in the corporation itself. This, in turn, would involve a fundamental alteration in the role and training of the manager. Management would become a profession in the older sense of the word, involving not merely standards of technical competence but standards of public obligation that could at moments of conflict override obligations to the corporate employer. Such a conception of the professional manager would require a deep change in the ethos of schools of business administration, where "business ethics" would have to become central in the process of professional formation. If the rewards of success in business management were not so inordinate, then choice of this profession could arise from more public-spirited motives. In short, personal, cultural, and structural change all entail one another.

Signs of the Times

Few of those with whom we talked would have described the problems facing our society in exactly the terms we have just used. But few have found a life devoted to "personal ambition and consumerism" satisfactory, and most are seeking in one way or another to transcend the limitations of a self-centered life. If there are vast numbers of a selfish, narcissistic "me generation" in America, we did not find them, but we certainly did find that the language of individualism, the primary American language of self-understanding, limits the ways in which people think.

Many Americans are devoted to serious, even ascetic, cultivation of the self in the form of a number of disciplines, practices, and "trainings," often of great rigor. There is a question as to whether these practices lead to the self-realization or self-fulfillment at which they aim or only to an obsessive self-manipulation that defeats the proclaimed purpose. But it is not uncommon for those who are attempting to find themselves to find in that very process something that transcends them. For example, a Zen student reported: "I started Zen to get something for myself, to stop suffering, to get enlightened. Whatever it was, I was doing it for myself. I had hold of myself and I was reaching for something. Then to do it, I found out I had to give up that hold on myself. Now it has hold of me, whatever 'it' is."[16] What this student found is that the meaning of life is not to be discovered in manipulative control in the service of the self. Rather, through the disciplined practices of a religious way of life, the student found his self more grasped than grasping. It is not surprising that "self-realization" in this case has occurred in the context of a second language, the allusive language of Zen Buddhism, and a community that attempts to put that language into practice.

Many Americans are concerned to find meaning in life not primarily through self-cultivation but through intense relations with others. Romantic love is still idealized in our society. It can, of course, be remarkably self-indulgent, even an excuse to use another for one's own gratification. But it can also be a revelation of the poverty of the self and lead to a genuine humility in the presence of the beloved. We have noted in the early chapters of this book that the therapeutically inclined, jealous though they are of their personal autonomy, nonetheless seek enduring attachments and a community within which those attachments can be nurtured. As in the case of self-cultivation, there is in the desire for intense relationships with others an attempt to move beyond the isolated self, even though the language of individualism makes that sometimes hard to articulate.

Much of what is called "consumerism," and often condemned as such, must be understood in this same ambiguous, ambivalent context. Attempts to create a beautiful place in which to live, to eat well and in a convivial atmosphere, to visit beautiful places where one may enjoy works of art, or simply lie in the sun and swim in the sea, often involve an element of giving to another and find their meaning in a committed relationship.[17] Where the creation of a consumption-oriented lifestyle, which may resemble that of "the beautiful people" or may simply involve a comfortable home and a camper, becomes a form of defense against a dangerous and meaningless world, it probably takes on a greater burden than it can bear. In that case, the effort to move beyond the self has ended too quickly in the "little circle of family and friends" of which Tocqueville spoke, but even so the initial impulse was not simply selfish.

With the weakening of the traditional forms of life that gave aesthetic and moral meaning to everyday living, Americans have been improvising alternatives more or less successfully. They engage, sometimes with intense involvement, in a wide variety of arts, sports, and nature appreciation, sometimes as spectators but often as active participants. Some of these activities involve conscious traditions and demanding practices, such as ballet. Others, such as walking in the country or jogging, may be purely improvisational, though not devoid of some structure of shared meaning. Not infrequently, moments of intense awareness, what are sometimes called "peak experiences," occur in the midst of such activities. At such moments, a profound sense of well-being eclipses the usual utilitarian preoccupations of everyday life. But the capacity of such experiences to provide more than a momentary counterweight to pressures of everyday life is minimal. Where these activities find social expression at all, it is apt to be in the form of what we have called the lifestyle enclave. The groups that form around them are too evanescent, too inherently restricted in membership, and too slight in their hold on their members' loyalty to carry much public weight. Only at rare moments do such largely expressive solidarities create anything like a civic consciousness, as when a local professional sports team wins a national championship and briefly gives rise to a euphoric sense of metropolitan belongingness.

Many of those with whom we talked were locked into a split between a public world of competitive striving and a private world supposed to provide the meaning and love that make competitive striving bearable. Some, however, were engaged in an effort to overcome this split, to make our public and our private worlds mutually coherent—in a word, to recover our social ecology. Cecilia Dougherty, Mary Taylor, Ed Schwartz, and Paul Morrison, whom we met near the end of chapters 6, 7, 8, and 9, are examples of those engaged in such efforts. Cecilia Dougherty is working for a society in which the "have-nots" can have voice and participation, and in which her children and grandchildren can safely lead their lives. Mary Taylor is trying to think about the long haul, at least the next twenty-five years and not just the next one or two years that preoccupy most politicians. She is concerned to repair the damage that has been done both to our natural ecology and to our social ecology. Ed Schwartz is concerned with the dehumanizing aspect of the way we organize work and is trying to bring the moral concerns of the biblical and republican traditions into our economic structures. Paul Morrison is attempting to build a strong parish life so that the members of his congregation can carry out vocations in the world that will really make a difference.

All of these people are drawing on our republican and biblical traditions, trying to make what have become second languages into our first language again. We have spoken of "reappropriating tradition"—that is, finding sustenance in tradition and applying it actively and creatively to our present realities. These people give us specific examples of what that means. We may ask what help they receive in their reappropriation of traditions from the major cultural institutions of our society. Here the story is mixed. In spite of the fragmentation of our intellectual culture, work done in the universities did provide assistance to some of those to whom we talked. For example, Ed Schwartz has been influenced significantly by one strand of contemporary American political philosophy that is trying to rethink the republican tradition. Paul Morrison draws on contemporary theology and theological ethics for help in thinking through his positions. It may not always be easy to find, but among the fragments of our intellectual culture there is clearly significant work being done.

And while our universities are under greater pressure than ever to emphasize pragmatic results—technological achievements and career-oriented skills—there are voices calling for a reaffirmation of the classic role of education as a way to articulate private aspirations with common cultural meanings so that individuals simultaneously become more fully developed people and citizens of a free society. Eva Brann has recently given an eloquent defense of this understanding of education in her *Paradoxes of Education in a Republic*. She argues that in education at present, the choice is either tradition or technique, and that technique has become far too dominant.[18] The result is that in the multiversities of today, it is hard to find a single book, even a single play of Shakespeare's, that all the students in a large class know. When education becomes an instrument for individual careerism, it cannot provide either personal meaning or civic culture. And yet, somehow, the tradition does get transmitted, at least to students who seek it out.

Tradition gets transmitted because there are still teachers who love it and who cannot help transmitting it. Helen Vendler, in her 1980 presidential address to the Modern Language Association, took as her text a passage at the end of Wordsworth's *The Prelude*:

> What we have loved,
> Others will love, and we will teach them how.

She sums up her argument by saying:

> It is not within our power to reform the primary and secondary schools, even if we have a sense of how that reform might begin. We do have it within our power, I believe, to reform ourselves, to make it our own first task to give, especially to our beginning students, that rich web of associations, lodged in the tales of majority and minority cultures alike, by which they could begin to understand themselves as individuals and as social beings. . . . All freshman English courses, to my mind, should devote at least half their time to the reading of myth, legend and parable; and beginning language courses should do the same. . . . We owe it to ourselves to show

our students, when they first meet us, what we are: we owe their dormant appetites, thwarted for so long in their previous schooling, that deep sustenance that will make them realize that they too, having been taught, love what we love.[19]

If college education, and probably more than a few secondary schools as well, are still providing us with some of the help we need to make tradition a vital resource in our lives, it is hard to see how that other great cultural institution, television, which competes with the schools for the education of our youth and for the continuing education of adults, succeeds in doing so. Except for some notable contributions from public television, most programming is devoid of any notion of coherent tradition.

On the basis of our interviews, and from what we can observe more generally in our society today, it is not clear that many Americans are prepared to consider a significant change in the way we have been living. The allure of the packaged good life is still strong, though dissatisfaction is widespread. Americans are fairly ingenious in finding temporary ways to counteract the harsher consequences of our damaged social ecology. Livy's words about ancient Rome also apply to us: "We have reached the point where we cannot bear either our vices or their cure." But, as some of the more perceptive of the people to whom we talked believe, the time may be approaching when we will either reform our republic or fall into the hands of despotism, as many republics have done before us.

The Poverty of Affluence

At the very beginning of the modern era, Thomas Hobbes painted a picture of human existence that was to be all too prophetic of the society coming into being. He compared "the life of man" to a race and said, "But this *race* we must suppose to have no other *goal*, nor other *garland*, but being foremost, and in it [to give only a few of his many specifications]:

> To consider them behind, is *glory*,
> To consider them before, is *humility*.
> To fall on the sudden, is disposition to *weep*.
> To see another fall, is disposition to *laugh*.
> Continually to be out-gone, is *misery*.
> Continually to out-go the next before, is *felicity*.
> And to forsake the course, is to *die*.[20]

In *Leviathan*, Hobbes summed up his teaching about human life by arguing that the first "general inclination of mankind" is "a perpetual and restless desire of power after power, that ceaseth only in death."[21] But we are beginning to see now that the race of which he speaks has no winner, and if power is our only end, the death in question may not be merely personal, but civilizational.

Yet we still have the capacity to reconsider the course upon which we are embarked. The morally concerned social movement, informed by republican and biblical sentiments, has stood us in good stead in the past and may still do so again. But we have never before faced a situation that called our deepest assumptions so radically into question. Our problems today are not just political. They are moral and have to do with the meaning of life. We have assumed that as long as economic growth continued, we could leave all else to the private sphere. Now that economic growth is faltering and the moral ecology on which we have tacitly depended is in disarray, we are beginning to understand that our common life requires more than an exclusive concern for material accumulation.

Perhaps life is not a race whose only goal is being foremost. Perhaps true felicity does not lie in continually outgoing the next before. Perhaps the truth lies in what most of the world outside the modern West has always believed, namely that there are practices of life, good in themselves, that are inherently fulfilling. Perhaps work that is intrinsically rewarding is better for human beings than work that is only extrinsically rewarded. Perhaps enduring commitment to those we love and civic friendship toward our fellow citizens are preferable to restless competition and anxious self-defense. Perhaps common worship, in which we express our gratitude and wonder in the face of the mystery of being itself, is the most important thing of all. If so, we will have to change our lives and begin to remember what we have been happier to forget.

We will need to remember that we did not create ourselves, that we owe what we are to the communities that formed us, and to what Paul Tillich called "the structure of grace in history," that made such communities possible. We will need to see the story of our life on this earth not as an unbroken success but as a history of suffering as well as joy. We will need to remember the millions of suffering people in the world today and the millions whose suffering in the past made our present affluence possible.

Above all, we will need to remember our poverty. We have been called a people of plenty, and though our per capita GNP has been surpassed by several other nations, we are still enormously affluent. Yet the truth of our condition is our poverty. We are finally defenseless on this earth. Our material belongings have not brought us happiness. Our military defenses will not avert nuclear destruction. Nor is there any increase in productivity or any new weapons system that will change the truth of our condition.

We have imagined ourselves a special creation, set apart from other humans. In the late twentieth century, we see that our poverty is as absolute as that of the poorest of nations. We have attempted to deny the human condition in our quest for power after power. It would be well for us to rejoin the human race, to accept our essential poverty as a gift, and to share our material wealth with those in need.

Such a vision is neither conservative nor liberal in terms of the truncated spectrum of present American political discourse. It does not seek to return to the harmony of a "traditional" society, though it is open to learning from the wisdom of such societies. It does not reject the modern criticism of all traditions, but it insists in turn on the criticism of criticism, that human life is lived in the balance between faith and doubt. Such a vision arises not only from the theories of intellectuals, but from the practices of life that Americans are already engaged in. Such a vision seeks to combine social concern with ultimate concern in a way that slights the claims of neither. Above all, such a vision seeks the confirmation or correction of discussion and experiment with our friends, our fellow citizens.

□

Appendix: Social Science as Public Philosophy

Tocqueville was following precedent when he wrote in the introduction to volume I of *Democracy in America*, "A new political science is needed for a world itself quite new."[1] Someone in almost every generation during the past several centuries has announced that such a new social science has begun or is about to begin. Often this claim meant that the social sciences were about to attain the status of the natural sciences. Yet those who expected social science to attain the same kind of cumulativeness, agreement on paradigms, and obsolescence of predecessors as natural science have been perennially disappointed.

Although Tocqueville's contemporary and fellow countryman Auguste Comte was one of the most ardent disseminators of what we might call the myth of social science—the idea that social science is soon to become like natural science—there is no reason to believe that Tocqueville shared that idea. Indeed, Tocqueville's argument for a new science rested specifically on the notion that the object of study—namely, society in a new world—was new and therefore required a new approach. Tocqueville returned throughout his life to several major figures in the tradition of French social thought: Pascal, Montesquieu, and Rousseau. He did not believe them outmoded or prescientific. Yet Tocqueville saw that the task of appropriating and applying their insights to a new historical situation could not be automatic but was so demanding as to require the invention of something like a new science. In that sense, each generation, no matter how much it learns from tradition or how much it is aware that, unlike natural science, it cannot forget its founders, must still create a new social science for new realities.

If we, too, have had to find a new way to deal with new realities, we have done so not by imagining that with us a truly scientific social science has at last arrived but by consciously trying to renew an older conception of social science, one in which the boundary between social science and philosophy was still open. During the century and a half since Tocqueville wrote *Democracy in America,* a "hard" social science has not emerged, but certainly a "professional" social science with significant achievements has. So much is this the case that many of our colleagues may look askance at the credence we give to Tocqueville and his work. Isn't Tocqueville merely a brilliant "humanistic amateur" whose work has long been outdated by the technical accomplishments of professional social science? It is certainly true that in many areas we have data of a sort entirely unavailable to Tocqueville. (It is even true that Tocqueville did not always utilize the best available data in his own day.) And it is also true that we understand many particular social processes better than anyone did in the 1830s. Yet Tocqueville's sense of American society as a whole, of how its major components—family, religion, politics, the economy—fit together, and of how the character of Americans is affected by their society, and vice versa, has never been equaled. Nor has anyone ever better pointed out the moral and political meaning of the American experiment. It is that synoptic view, at once philosophical, historical, and sociological, that narrowly professional social science seems not so much incapable of as uninterested in. It is in order to reappropriate that larger view that we must try to restore the idea of social science as public philosophy. Such a social science does not need to be "reinvented," for the older tradition has survived side by side with narrowly professional social science and requires only to be encouraged and strengthened.[2] To see how we might revive that older view, we should first consider the conditions under which narrowly professional social science first emerged.

When we look at the history of our own disciplines and their professionalization, it turns out to be the same history that has preoccupied us throughout this book. We have repeatedly had to notice that during the nineteenth century, the social world changed from being a community, a cosmos of callings, into an industrial-corporate society organized around competing professional careers. Educational institutions were transformed in ways comparable to the transformation of other institutions. The American college through much of the nineteenth century was organized on the assumption that "higher learning constituted a single unified culture." The purpose of college education was to produce a "man of learning" who would have "an uplifting and unifying influence on society." Literature, the arts, and science were regarded as branches of a single culture of learning. It was the task of moral philosophy, a required course in the senior year, usually taught by the college president, not only to integrate the various fields of learning, including science and religion, but even more importantly to draw the implications for the living of a good life individually and socially. Interestingly, most of what we now call the social sciences was taught, so far as it was taught at all, under the heading of moral philosophy.[3]

It was only late in the nineteenth century that the research university replaced the college as the model for higher education—contemporaneously with the rise of the business corporation. The two institutions were manifestations of the same social forces. Graduate education, research, and specialization, leading to largely autonomous departments, were the hallmarks of the new universities. The prestige of natural science as the model for all disciplined knowing and the belief that the progress of science would inevitably bring social amelioration in its wake partially obscured the fact that the unity and ethical meaning of higher education were being lost.[4]

The early social sciences were caught up in this transformation. While they were concerned with establishing professional specialities providing useful knowledge about an increasingly complex society, many social scientists still felt the older obligations of moral philosophy to speak to the major ethical questions of the society as a whole. This tradition has never died, but it has been driven to the periphery by an ever more specialized social science whose subdisciplines often cannot speak to one another, much less to the public. The early nineteenth-century "man of learning" became the twentieth-century "scientist."

There were great positive achievements in this transformation of higher education. The new educational system prepared vastly larger numbers of people for employment in an industrial society, and it included as students those who, because of class, sex, or race, were almost completely excluded in the early nineteenth century. The authors of this book and, in all probability, most of its readers, are beneficiaries of this great change. Yet we must be aware of the costs. One of the major costs of the rise of the research university and its accompanying professionalism and specialization was the impoverishment of the public sphere. As Thomas Haskell has put it, the new man of science had to "*exchange general citizenship in society for membership in the community of the competent. Within his field of expertise, the worth of his opinions henceforth would be judged not by open competition with all who cared to challenge him, but by the close evaluation of his professional colleagues.*"[5] If we may again take Tocqueville as our example, we may note that he was read by the leading intellectuals of his time—John Stuart Mill, for example— but he was also intelligible to any educated reader. Today's specialized academics, with notable exceptions, write with a set of intellectual assumptions and a vocabulary shared only by their colleagues. We do not intend to forget the achievements of a specialized and professionalized social science. It is a necessary enterprise in a complex modern society, and we have gratefully used many of its findings in this book. But we refuse to believe that the choice as Haskell put it is final. The competent social scientist does not have to cease to be a "general citizen of society." Specialization requires integration; they are not mutually exclusive. A professional social science that loses concern for the larger society cannot do even its professional job, for there is too much of reality with which it cannot deal. And if we remember that "calling" or "vocation," with the implication of public responsibility, is the older meaning of "profession," then we would see that a really "professional social scientist" could never be only a specialist. He would also see social science as, in part, public philosophy.

Let us consider how such a social science differs from much current work. It is of the nature of a narrowly professional social science that it is specialized and that each specialized discipline disavows knowledge of the whole or of any part of the whole that lies beyond its strictly defined domain. It is the governing ideal of much specialized social science to abstract out single variables and, on the natural science model, try to figure out what their effects would be if everything else were held constant. Yet in the social world, single variables are seldom independent enough to be consistently predictive. It is only in the context of society as a whole, with its possibilities, its limitations, and its aspirations, that particular variables can be understood. Narrowly professional social science, particularly in its most reductionist form, may indeed deny that there is any whole. It may push a radical nominalism to the point of seeing society as a heap of disparate individuals and groups lacking either a common culture or a coherent social organization. A philosophical social science involves not only a different focus of attention but a different understanding of society, one grounded, as we will see, in commitments to substantive traditions.[6]

Being concerned with the whole does not mean a mere adding together of facts from the various specialized disciplines. Such facts become relevant only when interpreted in terms of a frame of reference that can encompass them and give form and shape to a conception of the whole. It is not likely that such a conception will arise from research that is simply interdisciplinary in the usual sense of the word—that is, involving the cooperation of several disciplinary specialists. For knowledge of society as a whole involves not merely the acquisition of useful insights from neighboring disciplines but transcending disciplinary boundaries altogether.

The most important boundary that must be transcended is the recent and quite arbitrary boundary between the social sciences and the humanities. The humanities, we are told, have to do with the transmission and interpretation of cultural traditions in the realms of philosophy, religion, literature, language, and the arts, whereas the social sciences involve the scientific study of human action. The assumption is that the social sciences are not cultural traditions but rather occupy a privileged position of pure observation. The assumption is also that discussions of human action in the humanities are "impressionistic" and "anecdotal" and do not really become knowledge until "tested" by the methods of science, from which alone comes valid knowledge.

It is precisely that boundary between the social sciences and the humanities that social science as public philosophy most wants to open up. Social science is not a disembodied cognitive enterprise. It is a tradition, or set of traditions, deeply rooted in the philosophical and humanistic (and, to more than a small extent, the religious) history of the West. Social science makes assumptions about the nature of persons, the nature of society, and the relation between persons and society. It also, whether it admits it or not, makes assumptions about good persons and a good society and considers how far these conceptions are embodied in our actual society. Becoming conscious of the cultural roots of these assumptions would remind the social scientist that these assumptions are contestable and that the choice of assumptions involves controversies that lie deep in the history of Western thought. Social science as public philosophy would make the philosophical conversation concerning these matters its own.

Tocqueville and John Stuart Mill (and Marx and Weber and Durkheim, not to mention George Herbert Mead) knew that what they said had philosophical implications and took conscious responsibility for their philosophical positions in a way that most social scientists today do not. But fortunately we still have more than a few exemplars: Louis Dumont, Alasdair MacIntyre, and Jürgen Habermas among others.[7] We cannot classify such scholars simply by their "discipline," any more than we could the pre-professional social thinkers of the past.

Social science as public philosophy, by breaking through the iron curtain between the social sciences and the humanities, becomes a form of social self-understanding or self-interpretation.[8] It brings the traditions, ideals, and aspirations of society into juxtaposition with its present reality. It holds up a mirror to society. By probing the past as well as the present, by looking at "values" as much as at "facts," such a social science is able to make connections that are not obvious and to ask difficult questions. In this book, for example, we have tried to disclose the nature of American individualism, its historical and philosophical roots as well as its present reality, and we have asked whether individualism, as the dominant ideology of American life, is not undermining the conditions of its existence. That question is simultaneously philosophical and sociological, and an answer to it requires not just an evaluation of arguments and evidence but ethical reflection.

A social science concerned with the whole of society would, as we have said, have to be historical as well as philosophical. Narrowly professional social science has given us valuable information about many aspects of contemporary society, but it often does so with little or no sense of history. Social historians have been ingenious in giving us information about the past that is often only slightly less rich than that discovered by social scientists about the present. Yet what we need from history, and why the social scientist must also, among other things, be a historian, is not merely comparable information about the past, but some idea of how we have gotten from the past to the present, in short, a narrative. Narrative is a primary and powerful way by which to know about a whole. In an important sense, what a society (or a person) is, is its history. So a Habermas or a MacIntyre gives us his story about how modern society came to its present pass. Such stories can, and must, be contested, amended, and sometimes replaced.[9]

The social scientist as public philosopher also seeks to relate the stories scholars tell to the stories current in the society at large and thus to expose them both to mutual discussion and criticism. In this book, we have been continuously concerned with the way in which the largely agrarian and small-town society of early nineteenth-century America was transformed, especially in the period 1880 to 1920, into the bureaucratic industrial society of today. We feel that any effort to draw on our formative traditions to meet our present needs will fail if it does not understand that transformation. In chapter 6, we pointed out how many of the myths in our fiction and popular culture have avoided coming to terms with that transformation. Instead, they have romanticized individualism and ignored those traditions that might help us today. Our argument, then, relates to getting the story right for scholarship but also for popular consciousness.

Social science as public philosophy cannot be "value free." It accepts the canons of critical, disciplined research, but it does not imagine that such research exists in a moral vacuum. To attempt to study the possibilities and limitations of society with utter neutrality, as though it existed on another planet, is to push the ethos of narrowly professional social science to the breaking point. The analysts are part of the whole they are analyzing. In framing their problems and interpreting their results, they draw on their own experience and their membership in a community of research that is in turn located within specific traditions and institutions. For instance, when our research group studied individualism in America, we were studying something that is as much a part of us as it is of the people we interviewed. Furthermore, we brought to our study a set of assumptions about the personal and social implications of individualism that have been developed by previous social scientists, such as Tocqueville, assumptions that are simultaneously evaluative and analytical. What we learned as a result of our study is a contribution to our own self-understanding as well as to social self-understanding. It is impossible to draw a clear line between the cognitive and the ethical implications of our research, not because we cannot make an abstract distinction between the analysis of evidence and moral reasoning, but because in carrying out social research both are simultaneously operative. We cannot deny the moral relationship between ourselves and those we are studying without being untrue to both.

We have argued that if the analyst is within the society he is studying, he is also within one or more of its traditions, consciously or not. There is no other place to stand. Even if the analyst is studying a different society, he is still within the traditions of his own society and will have to come to terms with traditions in the society he is studying, so the problem is inescapable. We have tried to make it clear where we stand in regard to the traditions of modern society generally and American society in particular. Our society has been deeply influenced by the traditions of modern individualism. We have taken the position that our most important task today is the recovery of the insights of the older biblical and republican traditions. The authors of this book are grounded in a social scientific tradition that has insisted on an idea of society as a reality in itself, not as something merely derived from the agreement of individuals. We do not see public social science as unitary or monolithic. We have argued that any living tradition is a conversation, an argument in the best sense, about the meaning and value of our common life. We expect that our interpretations will be contested by others with other views, and we expect that, on occasion, we will be shown good reasons to change our minds.

Social science as public philosophy is public not just in the sense that its findings are publicly available or useful to some group or institution outside the scholarly world. It is public in that it seeks to engage the public in dialogue. It also seeks to engage the "community of the competent," the specialists and the experts, in dialogue, but it does not seek to stay within the boundaries of the specialist community while studying the rest of society from outside. We conceived of our research from the beginning as a dialogue or conversation with fellow citizens about matters of common interest.

We did not come to our conversations empty-handed. We did not, as in some scientific version of "Candid Camera," seek to capture their beliefs and actions without our subjects being aware of us. Rather, we sought to bring our preconceptions and questions into the conversation and to understand the answers we were receiving not only in terms of the language but also, so far as we could discover, in the lives of those we were talking with. Though we did not seek to impose our ideas on those with whom we talked (as should be clear from the many articulate voices in this book, we could not have done that had we tried), we did attempt to uncover assumptions, to make explicit what the person we were talking to might rather have left implicit. The interview as we employed it was active, Socratic.

For example, Tipton, in interviewing Margaret Oldham, tried to discover at what point she would take responsibility for another human being:

Q: So what are you responsible for?
A: I'm responsible for my acts and for what I do.
Q: Does that mean you're responsible for others, too?
A: No.
Q: Are you your sister's keeper?
A: No.
Q: Your brother's keeper?
A: No.
Q: Are you responsible for your husband?
A: I'm not. He makes his own decisions. He is his own person. He acts his own acts. I can agree with them or I can disagree with them. If I ever find them nauseous enough, I have a responsibility to leave and not deal with it any more.
Q: What about children?
A: I . . . I would say I have a legal responsibility for them, but in a sense I think they in turn are responsible for their own acts.

Or, as another example, Swidler, trying to get Brian Palmer to clarify the basis of his moral judgments, responded to his statement that "lying is one of the things I want to regulate" by asking, "Why?"

A: Well, it's a kind of thing that is a habit you get into. Kind of self-perpetuating. It's like digging a hole. You just keep digging and digging.
Q: So why is it wrong?
A: Why is integrity important and lying bad? I don't know. It just is. It's just

so basic. I don't want to be bothered with challenging that. It's part of me. I don't know where it came from, but it's very important.

Q: When you think about what's right and what's wrong, are things bad because they are bad for people, or are they right and wrong in themselves, and if so how do you know?

A: Well some things are bad because . . . I guess I feel like everybody on this planet is entitled to have a little bit of space, and things that detract from other people's space are kind of bad . . .

Without much longer excerpts, it is not possible to show how, in our interviews, we were able to attain a degree of common understanding with those we were interviewing without necessarily ending up in agreement. Much of what we heard, even when it made us think in new ways, we still wanted to argue with, and have argued with in this book.

These considerations should make it clear why the active interview is a primary method for social science as public philosophy, whereas the survey questionnaire, while generating useful data (which we have frequently used in this book), often remains secondary. Poll data, generated by fixed questions that do not begin any conversation, give us findings that appear as a kind of natural fact, even when successive questionnaires reveal trends over time. This is true even when there are open-ended questions, for there is still no dialogue between interviewer and interviewee. Poll data sum up the *private* opinions of thousands of respondents. Active interviews create the possibility of *public* conversation and argument. When data from such interviews are well presented, they stimulate the reader to enter the conversation, to argue with what is being said. Curiously, such interviews stimulate something that could be called public opinion, opinion tested in the arena of open discussion. "Public opinion polling" does not and might better be called "private opinion polling."

This public and dialogical nature of our study helps to explain why we carried it out as we did and how it is similar to, and differs from, many other social scientific studies. There is no methodological innovation in this book. We have used some of the oldest and most fundamental social scientific methods: participant observation and the interview. There are certainly other valid uses of these methods. We could have sought a sample of people to interview that would be as representative as possible of the larger population and of the major variations within it. Or we could have attempted to situate those we studied, whether they were representative or not, in the richest possible understanding of their local culture and community in all its ethnographic specificity. We did not entirely ignore these sorts of considerations. We did not want to study highly aberrant people, and we carried out our interviews in a number of places on both coasts. We read excellent field studies of communities in the Middle West, such as Varenne's *Americans Together* and the Middletown III studies,[10] and found that the themes we were discovering were common there as well. We also wanted to know something of the context of the lives of those we interviewed. In many cases, and this is particularly true of Madsen's and Sullivan's studies of the politically involved, we saw the people we talked to in real-life contexts other than the interview situation.

But what we were interested in above all was the language people used to think about their lives and the traditions from which that language comes. We believe, for reasons argued earlier in the book, that the mobile middle classes define reality for most of us in the United States, and it was on those groups that we concentrated, choosing, in particular, people who would exemplify involvement in public life or withdrawal from it, as that was our central problem. We believed before we started that there are variations in how Americans think about social and personal life, but that those variations are finite, and our study has confirmed us in this belief. We think our interviews have allowed us to describe the most influential forms of middle-class language and moral reasoning about private and public life in America today.

But in talking to our contemporaries, we were also talking to our predecessors. In our conversations, we were listening not only to voices present but to voices past. In the words of those we talked to, we heard John Calvin, Thomas Hobbes, and John Locke, as well as Winthrop, Franklin, Jefferson, Emerson, and Whitman. Often enough, we also heard the words of recent and contemporary professional social scientists. So our book is a conversation not only with those we interviewed but with representative figures of the various traditions, including the traditions of social science. The book is an interpretive reading of, and an argument with, those figures. In one case that concern has been central. Our book is, explicitly and implicitly, a detailed reading of, and commentary on, Tocqueville, the predecessor who has influenced us most profoundly in thinking about life in America.[11]

Though this may not be apparent to the reader, our book has also involved more than five years of dialogue among ourselves. Although each of us has had specific responsibilities and four of us have carried out independent field studies, we have worked together from the beginning in a way that is not common in scholarly collaboration today. As an expression of our way of working, we wrote *Habits of the Heart* together rather than assigning particular chapters to individuals. This way of working made some of our colleagues nervous. How can you write a book *together*?

We wrote a book together by becoming a group that shared a common culture.[12] Particularly during the summers, we had frequent opportunities for group discussion. We read and discussed a number of classical and contemporary works related to our project. Even more important, we spent many hours going over the early interviews of each of the fieldworkers. During these sessions, we worked out a common interpretive framework, which in turn influenced each field worker in his or her subsequent interviews.

When we began to think about the book that would report our work, we discussed its organization as a whole and what would go into each chapter before we began writing. Chapters or parts of chapters had to be drafted by individuals, but these drafts were in turn intensively discussed and rewritten on the basis of group discussion.[13] Bellah has been responsible for the final rewriting of the whole book, so that it will have a unity of style and argument. The book is the product of all of us, and none of us could have done it alone. But, as subsequent individual monographs should make clear, we have not been homogenized. Each of us has learned to speak better in his or her own voice. Our experience together has confirmed for us one of the central arguments of our book, that the individual and society are not in a zero-sum situation; that a strong group that respects individual differences will strengthen autonomy as well as solidarity; that it is not in groups but in isolation that people are most apt to be homogenized.

Finally, this book, based on conversations with ourselves, our ancestors, and several hundred of our fellow citizens, is now intended to open a larger conversation with our fellow citizens, to contribute to the common dialogue. We know we will be subject to the judgments of the academic "community of competence," but we hope the reader will not respond passively to our book, awaiting expert judgment as to whether we have got our data or our methods right. Anyone who has spent a lifetime in this society knows a great deal about the subject matter of this book. Even the social scientist may know more about our society from the common experience of living in it than from any number of monographic studies. We hope the reader will test what we say against his or her own experience, will argue with us when what we say does not fit, and, best of all, will join the public discussion by offering interpretations superior to ours that can then receive further discussion. Without a public, social science as public philosophy will certainly wither away. We hope our book will merit discussion by fellow citizens in their voluntary associations, their churches, and even in political debate. A free society needs constantly to consider and discuss its present reality in the light of its past traditions and where it wants to go. We will be happy if we have contributed in however small a degree to that discussion. □

Notes

PREFACE

1. Alexis de Tocqueville, *Democracy in America,* trans. George Lawrence, ed. J. P. Mayer (New York: Doubleday, Anchor Books, 1969), p. 287.
2. Three of the field researchers and Bellah, who undertook one interview for chapter 9, used tape recorders. Madsen followed the practice of dictating his interviews into a tape recorder immediately after their completion, trying to remember verbatim as much of the conversation as possible. We have used the language of our informants as it was transcribed from the interviews without change except for very light editing to make spoken language intelligible in writing. Madsen's interviews, which are not quite as verbatim as those taped directly, may be recognized as deriving from "Suffolk," Massachusetts, or as from Southern California, with the exception of those identified with the Campaign for Economic Democracy. We have changed personal characteristics of those we interviewed in a way that will disguise their identity without distorting culturally relevant information, and given them pseudonyms, except for Wayne Bauer in chapter 1 and Edward Schwartz and Jane Shull in chapter 8, who asked that we use their correct names. Other than the light disguise for those who preferred anonymity, we have not fictionalized or conflated individuals. The eloquence with which many people in this book speak is their own.

CHAPTER 2

1. Alasdair MacIntyre has recently emphasized the idea that tradition is an argument: "A living tradition then is an historically extended, socially embodied argument, and an argument precisely in part about the goods which constitute that tradition. . . . Traditions, when vital, embody continuities of conflict" (*After Virtue* [South Bend, Ind.: University of Notre Dame Press, 1981], pp. 207, 206). See also Edward Shils, *Tradition* (Chi-

cago: University of Chicago Press, 1981), and Jaroslav Pelikan's forthcoming Jefferson Lectures on religious tradition.

2. Alexis de Tocqueville, *Democracy in America*, trans. George Lawrence, ed. J. P. Mayer (New York: Doubleday, Anchor Books, 1969), p. 279. Cotton Mather's Life of John Winthrop, "Nehemias Americanus" ("The American Nehemiah"), is conveniently printed as an appendix to Sacvan Bercovitch, *The Puritan Origins of the American Self* (New Haven, Conn.: Yale University Press, 1975), pp. 187–205. Tocqueville quotes Winthrop on p. 46 of *Democracy in America*, ed. Mayer. Perry Miller speaks of Winthrop as standing "at the beginning of our consciousness" in *Nature's Nation* (Cambridge, Mass.: Harvard University Press, 1967), p. 6. See also Miller's many references to Winthrop in *Errand into the Wilderness* (Cambridge, Mass.: Harvard University Press, 1956) and elsewhere.

3. John Winthrop's "A Model of Christian Charity" is found in many collections of Puritan documents. A convenient one is *Puritan Political Ideas, 1558–1794*, ed. Edmund S. Morgan (Indianapolis: Bobbs-Merrill, 1965), where the above quotation will be found on p. 92. A short biography of Winthrop is Edmund S. Morgan's *The Puritan Dilemma: The Story of John Winthrop* (Boston: Little, Brown, 1958).

4. *Puritan Political Ideas*, ed. Morgan, p. 139. Tocqueville quotes this same passage with a significant omission on p. 46 of *Democracy in America*, ed. Mayer.

5. Bercovitch, *Puritan Origins*, appendix, pp. 190, 193.

6. Morgan, *Puritan Dilemma*, chapter 8.

7. Tocqueville considered Jefferson "the greatest democrat ever to spring from American democracy" (*Democracy in America*, ed. Mayer, p. 203).

8. Winthrop D. Jordan in his scholarly book *White Over Black: American Attitudes Toward the Negro, 1550–1812* (Chapel Hill: University of North Carolina Press, 1968) considers Jefferson's views on the Negro to be inconsistent (pp. 475–81). Gary Wills in chapters 15 and 22 of *Inventing America: Jefferson's Declaration of Independence* (Garden City, N.Y.: Doubleday, 1978) sets the record straight, showing the absolute consistency of Jefferson's antislavery views and also why he did not view immediate emancipation as a solution.

9. Thomas Jefferson, *The Complete Jefferson*, ed. Saul K. Padover (New York: Duell, Sloan and Pearce, 1943), *Notes on the State of Virginia* (1785), query 19, p. 678.

10. See Jefferson, *Complete Jefferson*, ed. Padover, letter to John Cartwright, June 5, 1824, pp. 293–97, and letter to John Adams, October 28, 1813, pp. 282–87.

11. Jefferson, *Complete Jefferson*, ed. Padover, *Notes on Virginia*, query 17, p. 676.

12. See Wills, *Inventing America*, part 3.

13. Jefferson, *Complete Jefferson*, ed. Padover, First Inaugural Address, March

4, 1801, p. 386; *Notes on Virginia*, query 18, p. 677.

14. Benjamin Franklin, *The Autobiography of Benjamin Franklin*, ed. Leonard W. Labaree (New Haven, Conn.: Yale University Press, 1964), p. 150.

15. Benjamin Franklin, *The Political Thought of Benjamin Franklin*, ed. Ralph Ketcham (Indianapolis: Bobbs-Merrill, 1965), p. 341.

16. Franklin, *Political Thought of Benjamin Franklin*, ed. Ketcham, p. 134.

17. For all the utilitarian aspects of Franklin's conception of individual self-improvement, it was nevertheless linked to the themes of public spirit and social responsibility. See John G. Cawelti, *Apostles of the Self-Made Man: Changing Concepts of Success in America* (Chicago: University of Chicago Press, 1965), pp. 13–24.

18. F. O. Matthiessen, *The American Renaissance* (London: Oxford University Press, 1941). For the attack on the "self-made man" by Francis Parkman and James Fenimore Cooper and the new synthesis of the "self-culture" ideal by Whitman and Emerson see Cawelti, *Apostles of the Self-Made Man*, pp. 77–98.

19. Walt Whitman, *Complete Poetry and Collected Prose* (New York: Library of America, 1982), p. 188.

20. Whitman, *Poetry and Prose*, p. 537.

21. Whitman, *Poetry and Prose*, p. 297.

22. Whitman, *Poetry and Prose*, pp. 929–94. Phillip Rieff has developed a typology similar to ours. He speaks of "religious man, political man, economic man and psychological man." He tends to believe, however, that his "psychological man" (our expressive individualist) has "triumphed" more completely than we believe: "Americans no longer model themselves after the Christians or the Greeks. Nor are they such economic men as Europeans believe them to be. The political man of the Greeks, the religious man of the Hebrews and Christians, the enlightened economic man of eighteenth-century Europe, has been superseded by a new model for the conduct of life. Psychological man is, I suggest, more native to American culture than the Puritan sources of that culture would indicate" (*The Triumph of the Therapeutic* [New York: Harper and Row, 1966], p. 58).

23. J. Hector St. John de Crèvecoeur, *Letters from an American Farmer* (New York: Penguin Books, 1981), p. 83.

24. Crèvecoeur, *Letters*, p. 70. Emphasis in original.

25. Crèvecoeur, *Letters*, p. 67.

26. Louis Hartz, *The Liberal Tradition in America* (New York: Harvest, 1955); Daniel Boorstin, *The Americans: The National Experience* (New York: Random House, 1965), and *The Americans: The Democratic Experience* (New York: Random House, 1973). On the limitations of the interpretation of American culture as exclusively liberal see Dorothy Ross, "The Liberal Tradition Revisited and the Republican Tradition Addressed," in *New Directions in American Intellectual History*, ed. John Higham and Paul K. Conkin (Baltimore: Johns Hopkins University Press, 1979), pp. 116–31; and

Robert E. Shallope, "Toward a Republican Synthesis: The Emergence of an Understanding of Republicanism in American Historiography," *William and Mary Quarterly* 29 (1972): 49–80.

27. Tocqueville, *Democracy in America*, ed. Mayer, pp. 305–8.

28. Tocqueville, *Democracy in America*, ed. Mayer, p. 287. Xavier Zubiri, commenting on the concept of the "heart" in Pascal, sheds light on Tocqueville's usage, since Tocqueville was a lifelong student of Pascal: "In Pascal we are witness in part to one of the few fully realized attempts to apprehend philosophical concepts which are capable of encompassing some of the important dimensions of man. For example, his concept of 'heart,' so vague, is true but on account of its vagueness badly understood and poorly used. It does not mean blind sentiment as opposed to pure Cartesian reason, but the knowledge constitutive of the day-to-day and radical being of man" (Zubiri, *Nature, History, God*, trans. Thomas B. Fowler, Jr. [Lanham, Md.: University Press of America, 1981], p. 123). *Heart* in this sense is ultimately biblical. Both the Old and the New Testaments speak of the heart as involving intellect, will, and intention as well as feeling. The notion of "habits of the heart" perhaps goes back ultimately to the law written in the heart (Rom. 2:15; cf. Jer. 31:33 and Deut. 6:6). It is interesting that both Confucianism and Buddhism have a notion of the heart that is somewhat comparable.

29. Tocqueville, *Democracy in America*, ed. Mayer, p. 506

30. Tocqueville, *Democracy in America*, ed. Mayer, p. 508

31. Tocqueville, *Democracy in America*, ed. Mayer, p. 510.

32. On the importance of the local community in mid-nineteenth-century America see Thomas Bender, *Community and Social Change* (New Brunswick, N.J.: Rutgers University Press, 1978), and Richard Lingeman, *Small Town America* (New York: Putnam, 1980).

33. On representative characters see MacIntyre, *After Virtue*, pp. 26–29.

34. On the independent citizen see Marvin Meyers, *The Jacksonian Persuasion* (Palo Alto, Calif.: Stanford University Press, 1960) and James Oliver Robertson, *American Myth, American Reality* (New York: Hill and Wang, 1980).

35. On the cult of domesticity see Carl Degler, *At Odds: Women and the Family in America from the Revolution to the Present* (New York: Oxford University Press, 1980), pp. 26–51; Barbara Welter, "The Cult of True Womanhood, 1820–1860," *American Quarterly* 18 (1966): 151–74; Richard Sennett, *Families Against the City: Middle Class Homes of Industrial Chicago, 1872–1890* (Cambridge, Mass.: Harvard University Press, 1970); and Kirk Jeffrey, "The Family as Utopian Retreat from the City: The Nineteenth Century Contribution," *Soundings* 55 (1955): 21–40.

36. Carey Wilson McWilliams describes the decline of the old town democracy in New England (Boston abolished its town meeting in 1822) and the failure of the western towns and cities to replicate the New England institutions, so that "the individual was left to his own devices" (*The Idea of*

Fraternity in America [Berkeley and Los Angeles: University of California Press, 1973], p. 228).

37. See Tocqueville, *Democracy in America*, ed. Mayer, vol. 1, part 2, chapter 10.

38. See Tocqueville, *Democracy in America*, ed. Mayer, vol. 2, part 2, chapter 20.

39. See Peter Dobkin Hall, *The Organization of American Culture, 1700–1900: Private Institutions, Elites, and the Origins of American Nationality* (New York: New York University Press, 1982); and Burton J. Bledstein, *The Culture of Professionalism: The Middle Class and the Development of Higher Education in America* (New York: Norton, 1976).

40. See Alfred D. Chandler, *The Visible Hand: The Managerial Revolution in American Business* (Cambridge, Mass.: Harvard University Press, 1977). For the broader cultural implications see Alan Trachtenberg, *The Incorporation of America: Culture and Society in the Gilded Age* (New York: Hill and Wang, 1982).

41. The link to the ideology of individualism, now in its relatively unadorned utilitarian form, was still strong: "Admiration for the great mythical corporation grew because Americans assumed that at the center of the octopus was the single controlling brain—the greedy and ambitious, hard-working and independent, single American individual" (Robertson, *American Myth, American Reality*, p. 177). But see the section on the establishment ideology in chapter 10 below for a discussion of the way in which the corporation was placed in a moral context.

42. Businessmen criticized their early critics as "moss-backs left behind in the march of progress"; such people were seen as coming from "scrubby little towns" (Robertson, *American Myth, American Reality*, p. 178).

43. "Even before the Civil War demonstrated that ideology could not by itself hold the country together, another system of integration was emerging. The new pattern was one of technical unity. . . . Technical unity connects people by occupational function rather than general beliefs" (John Higham, "Hanging Together: Divergent Unities in American History," *Journal of American History* 61 [1974]: 19).

44. On the new professional middle class see, especially, Bledstein, *Culture of Professionalism*.

45. On the managerial type see MacIntyre's development of themes from Max Weber (*After Virtue*, pp. 24–31, 70–75, 81–83). For an empirically grounded discussion of managerial types see Michael Maccoby, *The Gamesman* (New York: Simon and Schuster, 1976).

46. For a discussion of efficiency as the essence of the managerial role see Samuel Haber, *Efficiency and Uplift: Scientific Management in the Progressive Era, 1890–1920* (Chicago: University of Chicago Press, 1954). For a broad discussion of the problem of social cohesion in the period of the decline of the independent local community and the rise of the segmental society see Robert Wiebe, *The Segmented Society: An Historical Preface to the Meaning of America* (New York: Oxford University Press, 1975).

47. On the therapist as a type see MacIntyre, *After Virtue*, pp. 29, 70–71. On

the cultural context within which therapy first arose in America see, especially, T. J. Jackson Lears, *No Place of Grace: Antimodernism and the Transformation of American Culture, 1880–1920* (New York: Pantheon, 1981).

48. Robert S. Lynd and Helen Merrell Lynd, *Middletown: A Study of Contemporary American Culture* (New York: Harcourt, Brace, 1929), especially pp. 496–502; Robert S. Lynd and Helen Merrell Lynd, *Middletown in Transition: A Study in Cultural Conflicts* (New York: Harcourt, Brace, 1937); and Robert S. Lynd, *Knowledge for What? The Place of Social Science in American Culture* (Princeton, N.J.: Princeton University Press, 1939).

49. David Riesman, with Nathan Glazer and Reuel Denney, *The Lonely Crowd: A Study of the Changing American Character* (New Haven, Conn.: Yale University Press, 1950).

50. Compare Joseph Featherstone, "John Dewey and David Riesman: From the Lost Individual to the Lonely Crowd," in *On the Making of Americans: Essays in Honor of David Riesman*, ed. Herbert Gans (Philadelphia: University of Pennsylvania Press, 1979).

51. Hervé Varenne, *Americans Together: Structured Diversity in a Midwestern Town* (New York: Teachers College Press, 1977).

52. We received Richard M. Merelman's *Making Something of Ourselves: On Culture and Politics in the United States* (Berkeley and Los Angeles: University of California Press, 1984), after this book was mostly written. We were struck, however, by the parallels to our analysis. Merelman analyzes the cultural form and content of television, advertising, and public education, which he finds to varying degrees exemplify the increasing dominance of what he calls "loosely bounded culture." Older American culture, he argues, was more tightly bounded and came in Puritan, democratic, and social-class forms. He connects the dominance of loose-boundedness to the rise of individualism.

CHAPTER 3

1. The best-documented study of some of the changes to which we are referring is Joseph Veroff, Elizabeth Douvan, and Richard A. Kulka, *The Inner American: A Self-Portrait from 1957 to 1976* (New York: Basic Books, 1981). This study is based on two large-scale national sample surveys some twenty years apart. Some of the changes they document as having occurred between 1957 and 1976 are a shift toward "a more *personal* or *individuated* paradigm for structuring well-being" and *"an increase in Americans' self-expressive and self-directive reactions to their adjustment"* (pp. 529–30). Emphasis in original.

2. Thomas Jefferson, *The Complete Jefferson*, ed. Saul K. Padover (New York: Duell, Sloan and Pearce, 1943), p. 33.

3. Ralph Waldo Emerson, *Essays and Lectures* (New York: Library of America, 1983), pp. 261, 262.

4. Daniel Calhoun, *The Intelligence of a People* (Princeton, N.J.: Princeton University Press, 1973), pp. 143–47.

5. For Locke's views see his *Some Thoughts Concerning Education* in John Locke, *Educational Writings*, ed. James L. Axtell (London: Cambridge University Press, 1968). It is worth remembering that Locke's *First Treatise of Government* was a refutation of Robert Filmer's *Patriarcha*, a defense of monarchy as continuous with patriarchy. See John Locke, *Two Treatises of Government*, ed. Peter Laslett (London: Cambridge University Press, 1963). The pattern of American child-rearing influenced by Locke is close to what Philip Greven calls the "moderate Protestant temperament" in *The Protestant Temperament: Patterns of Child-Rearing, Religious Experience, and the Self in Early America* (New York: Knopf, 1977), part 3.

6. Hervé Varenne, *Americans Together: Structured Diversity in a Midwestern Town* (New York: Teachers College Press, 1977), pp. 185–86.

7. Varenne, *Americans Together*, chapters 8 and 9.

8. Emerson, *Essays and Lectures*, pp. 259, 260.

9. Gallup Opinion Index, *Religion in America* (Princeton, N.J.: American Institute of Public Opinion, 1981).

10. Alasdair MacIntyre, *After Virtue* (South Bend, Ind.: University of Notre Dame Press, 1981), chapter 10.

11. See Daniel J. Levinson, *The Seasons of a Man's Life* (New York: Ballantine Books, 1978), chapters 13, 16, 18, 20; especially pp. 201–8, 245–51, 330–40. Compare George Vaillant, *Adaptation to Life* (Boston: Little, Brown, 1977), pp. 215–30.

12. Gail Sheehy, *Passages: Predictable Crises of Adult Life* (New York: Bantam Books, 1977), chapter 20.

13. See MacIntyre, *After Virtue*, chapter 14.

14. Sheehy, *Passages*, p. 364.

15. Frances FitzGerald, "Sun City Center," *New Yorker*, April 25, 1983, pp. 61, 90–93.

16. Sheehy, *Passages*, p. 364.

17. Michael Sandel, *Liberalism and the Limits of Justice* (New York: Cambridge University Press, 1982). For a philosophical critique of a conception of the self emptied of specific moral character, sentiments, and ends, as entailed by both utilitarian and Kantian ethics, including John Rawls's contractarianism, see Bernard Williams, "Persons, Character, and Morality" in *The Identity of Persons*, ed. Amélie O. Rorty (Berkeley and Los Angeles: University of California Press, 1976), pp. 197–216, and his "A Critique of Utilitarianism" in J. J. C. Smart and Bernard Williams, *Utilitarianism: For and Against* (Cambridge: Cambridge University Press, 1973). See also Charles Taylor, "Responsibility for Self" in *Identity of Persons*, ed. Rorty, pp. 281–99.

18. John Locke, *An Essay Concerning Human Understanding*, ed. Peter H. Nidditch (Oxford: Oxford University Press, 1975), book 2, chapter 27, paragraph 6, pp. 331–32.

19. Erving Goffman, *The Presentation of Self in Everyday Life* (New York: Doubleday, Anchor Books, 1959). See also Phillip Rieff, *The Triumph of the*

Therapeutic (New York: Harper and Row, 1966), on this point and on the argument of this chapter in general.

20. FitzGerald, "Sun City Center," p. 90.

CHAPTER 4

1. "When, finally, individual happiness becomes the criterion by which all things are measured, when the ability to withstand, strength of character, position in a community, the good of the group, exemplary and responsible adult behavior, and / or the welfare of one's children are all subjugated to individual happiness and 'self-realization,' then social arrangements weaken. . . . Fullness of life—the satisfactory experience and performance of all the roles available to an adult in one's society—loses significance. . . . In fact, role and status designations have become objects of suspicion, as though they were different from—even contradictory to—the core self, the essential person" (Joseph Veroff, Elizabeth Douvan, and Richard A. Kulka, *The Inner American: A Self-Portrait from 1957 to 1976* [New York: Basic Books, 1981], pp. 140–41).

2. Alexis de Tocqueville, *Democracy in America*, trans. George Lawrence, ed. J. P. Mayer (New York: Doubleday, Anchor Books, 1969), p. 603.

3. Tocqueville, *Democracy in America*, ed. Mayer, p. 291.

4. Carl N. Degler, *At Odds: Women and the Family in America from the Revolution to the Present* (New York: Oxford University Press, 1980), chapter 1, especially p. 8. Theodore Caplow, *Middletown Families: Fifty Years of Change and Continuity* (Minneapolis: University of Minnesota Press, 1982), shows how strong this pattern remains in contemporary Muncie, Indiana.

5. See Nancy F. Cott, *The Bonds of Womanhood: "Woman's Sphere" in New England, 1780–1835* (New Haven, Conn.: Yale University Press, 1977), on "female academies," pp. 114–25; on voluntary associations, pp. 141–57.

6. David M. Schneider and Raymond T. Smith, *Class Differences and Sex Roles in American Kinship and Family Structure* (Englewood Cliffs, N.J.: Prentice-Hall, 1973), pp. 14, 103.

7. Cott, *Bonds of Womanhood*, pp. 58–59.

8. Cott, *Bonds of Womanhood*, p. 61.

9. Cott, *Bonds of Womanhood*, p. 71.

10. See Tocqueville, *Democracy in America*, ed. Mayer, vol. 2, part 3, chapter 9.

11. See Cott, *Bonds of Womanhood*, pp. 80–83.

12. See Cott, *Bonds of Womanhood*, pp. 127–29.

13. Edmund S. Morgan, *The Puritan Family: Religion and Domestic Relations in Seventeenth-Century New England* (New York: Harper Torchbooks, 1966), p. 47.

14. See Veroff, Douvan, and Kulka, *Inner American*, on the increased acceptability of remaining unmarried, p. 147; on increased acceptability of divorce, p. 151. See also Daniel Yankelovich, *New Rules: Searching for Self-*

Fulfillment in a World Turned Upside Down (New York: Random House, 1981), for similar trend data, pp. 92–99.

15. Yankelovich, *New Rules,* pp. 252, 98.
16. Yankelovich, *New Rules,* pp. 103–5.
17. Veroff, Douvan, and Kulka, *Inner American,* p. 147.
18. Veroff, Douvan, and Kulka, ibid., p. 192, find marriage and parenthood to be "a more central source of value realization" than work or leisure. They find most Americans happy with their marriages and happier in 1976 than in 1957, the dates of their two surveys. They comment that the increase in the rate of divorce and the acceptance of divorce that also occurred between 1957 and 1976 could actually be part of the reason why marriages are happier: unhappy marriages have been dissolved.
19. Tocqueville, *Democracy in America,* ed. Mayer, pp. 567, 587–89.
20. Veroff, Douvan, and Kulka, *Inner American,* p. 178.
21. Carol Gilligan, *In a Different Voice: Psychological Theory and Women's Development* (Cambridge, Mass.: Harvard University Press, 1982); Sara Ruddick, "Maternal Thinking," in *Rethinking the Family: Some Feminist Questions,* ed. Barrie Thorne (New York: Longman, 1982), pp. 76–94.

CHAPTER 5

1. See Joseph Veroff, Richard A. Kulka, and Elizabeth Douvan, *Mental Health in America: Patterns of Help-Seeking from 1957 to 1976* (New York: Basic Books, 1981), and *The Inner American: A Self-Portrait from 1957 to 1976* (New York: Basic Books, 1981). The therapy that is the focus of interest in this chapter is "nondenominational." Tipton interviewed therapists of many different persuasions and clients of a wide variety of therapists, from psychoanalysts to behaviorists, although the middle-class focus of his research led most often to neo-Freudian, Rogersian, Gestalt, interactionist, and humanist therapists. Many of these practitioners described themselves as "eclectic" and emphasized that their own outlook, and often their training, was more oriented to achieving "practical results" than to theoretical consistency or allegiance. Our interest was not primarily in psychological theory or psychic disorders. We were interested chiefly in therapy as a cultural form, a language for thinking about self and society. We are aware that there are exceptions to almost every statement we make in this chapter about "therapy," "therapists," and "the therapeutically inclined." What struck both Tipton and the other three interviewers, who were not primarily interested in therapy, was the frequency of certain expressions and ways of thinking that Americans have adopted from a loose and eclectic therapeutic culture. It is this common coin as used and understood by ordinary Americans, in which we are interested. The large-scale survey research of Veroff, Kulka, and Douvan demonstrates the wide diffusion of this culture and the representativeness of those with whom we talked.

What we report should not be interpreted as representing the views of influential psychologists or personality theorists, analysts, or therapists, but it may have something to do with how they are popularly understood.

2. Robert Frost, "The Death of the Hired Man" (1914).

3. Aristotle, *Nichomachean Ethics*, books 7 and 9; Cicero, *De amicitia*; Thomas Aquinas, *Disputations: De caritate*.

4. Lester J. Cappon, ed., *The Adams-Jefferson Letters: The Complete Correspondence Between Thomas Jefferson and Abigail and John Adams* (Chapel Hill, N.C.: University of North Carolina Press, 1959), 2:562–63.

5. Alexis de Tocqueville, *Democracy in America*, trans. George Lawrence, ed. J. P. Mayer (New York: Doubleday, Anchor Books, 1969), pp. 565, 536, 538.

6. George M. Beard, *American Nervousness* (1881; New York: Arno Press and the *New York Times*, 1972), pp. 26, 171–72.

7. Beard, *American Nervousness*, pp. 122–23.

8. Burton J. Bledstein, *Culture of Professionalism: The Middle Class and the Development of Higher Education in America* (New York: Norton, 1976), pp. 105–20 and passim.

9. Bledstein, *Culture of Professionalism*, pp. 172, 176.

10. William James, *Psychology: Briefer Course* (New York: Henry Holt, 1892), p. 149. See also William James, *On Vital Reserves: The Energies of Men, The Gospel of Relaxation* (New York: Henry Holt, 1911), pp. 25, 66, 78; and E. Brooks Holifield, *A History of Pastoral Care* (Nashville, Tenn.: Abingdon Press, 1984), pp. 184–90.

11. Veroff, Kulka, and Douvan, *Mental Health in America*, pp. 6–7.

12. Ibid., pp. 166–67, 176–77.

13. See Arlie R. Hochschild, *The Managed Heart: Commercialization of Human Feeling* (Berkeley and Los Angeles: University of California Press, 1983).

14. See Guy E. Swanson, "A Basis of Authority and Identity in Post-Industrial Society," in *Identity and Authority*, ed. Roland Robertson and Burkart Holzner (New York: Saint Martin's Press, 1980), pp. 196–204.

15. See Steven M. Tipton, *Getting Saved from the Sixties* (Berkeley and Los Angeles: University of California Press, 1982), chapter 4; also Hochschild, *Managed Heart*.

16. Compare Richard Sennett, *The Fall of Public Man* (New York: Random House, Vintage Books, 1978), pp. 3–5, 257–68, 337–40; also Phillip Rieff, *The Triumph of the Therapeutic* (New York: Harper and Row, 1966), pp. 1–28, 232–61.

17. We would put less stress on the influence of a radically competitive market model for personal life than would Russell Jacoby, *Social Amnesia* (Boston: Beacon Press, 1975), pp. xvii, 46–72, 103–16, or Christopher Lasch, *The Culture of Narcissism* (New York: Norton, 1978), pp. 3–70, especially p. 30.

18. See David Lyons, *Forms and Limits of Utilitarianism* (Oxford: Clarendon Press, 1965); also Charles Taylor, "The Diversity of Goods," in *Utilitarianism and Beyond*, ed. Amartya Sen and Bernard Williams (Cambridge: Cambridge University Press, 1982), pp. 129–44.

19. Robert Coles, "Civility and Psychology," *Dædalus* 109 (Summer 1980), p. 140. For an example of an organized effort to personalize politics inspired by human potential psychology see Tipton, *Getting Saved from the Sixties*, pp. 267–70, on Self-Determination, "a personal / political network" founded by California Assemblyman John Vasconcellos. For criticism of psychological theories of politics see, for example, Philip Rieff, *Freud: The Mind of the Moralist* (Chicago: University of Chicago Press, 1959), pp. 220–56. According to Rieff, Freud saw politics as an irrationally authoritarian projection formed by individuals within domestic institutions, and, as such, lacking coherent reference to objective reality. On the fragility of a psychologized politics of authenticity see Russell Jacoby's attack on "The Politics of Subjectivity" among the American New Left, in *Social Amnesia*, pp. 101–18. On the cultural roots of such politics in radical liberalism see Marshall Berman, *The Politics of Authenticity* (New York: Atheneum, 1980), especially pp. xv–xxiv, 311–25.

20. Dale Carnegie, *How to Win Friends and Influence People* (1936; New York: Simon and Schuster, 1981), p. 25.

21. Assessed in such psychological terms as "self-esteem" and "self-accept-ance," Americans feel better about themselves now than twenty years ago. Because they are "more likely to think of personality characteristics than moral stereotypes or role designations" and to judge themselves less by general rules or standards, they feel less guilt at falling short of the moral mark. On the other hand, as social roles and practices lose their moral coherence, Americans experience more doubt about who they "really" are and more difficulty in finding an authentic self. Thus over time guilt de-clines but anxiety increases. See Veroff, Douvan, and Kulka, *Inner American*, pp. 19–25, 115–22.

22. Jaroslav Pelikan, Jefferson Lectures on religious tradition, forthcoming.

23. See Veroff, Douvan, and Kulka, *Inner American*, pp. 115–18.

CHAPTER 6

1. Robert Coles, "Civility and Psychology," *Dædalus* (Summer 1980), p. 137.

2. On individualism in nineteenth-century American literature see D. H. Lawrence, *Studies in Classic American Literature* (1923; Garden City, N.Y.: Doubleday, Anchor Books, 1951). On the image of the cowboy see Will Wright, *Sixguns and Society: A Structural Study of the Western* (Berkeley and Los Angeles: University of California Press, 1975). On cowboys and detec-tives see John G. Cawelti, *Adventure, Mystery, and Romance: Formula Stories as Art and Popular Culture* (Chicago: University of Chicago Press, 1976).

3. On the hero's avoidance of women and society see Leslie Fiedler, *Love and Death in the American Novel* (New York: Stein and Day, 1966), and Ann Swidler, "Love and Adulthood in American Culture," in *Themes of Work*

and Love in Adulthood, ed. Neil J. Smelser and Erik H. Erikson (Cambridge, Mass.: Harvard University Press, 1980), pp. 120–47.

4. The best book on Lincoln's meaning for American public life is Harry V. Jaffa, *Crisis of the House Divided: An Interpretation of the Lincoln-Douglas Debates* (Garden City, N.Y.: Doubleday, 1959). Reinhold Niebuhr's remarks appear in his essay "The Religion of Abraham Lincoln," in *Lincoln and the Gettysburg Address,* ed. Allan Nevins (Urbana, Ill.: University of Illinois Press, 1964), p. 72.

5. See, particularly, Michael Zuckerman, *Peaceable Kingdoms: New England Towns in the Eighteenth Century* (New York: Random House, 1970). The phrase "peaceable kingdom" is, of course, eschatological in its reference. It is what the New Englanders aspired to be, not what they claimed they were.

6. On the introduction of the term individualism by Tocqueville and the American response see Yehoshua Arieli, *Individualism and Nationalism in American Ideology* (Cambridge, Mass.: Harvard University Press, 1964), pp. 183–210, 246–76. On the emergence of the term in the European context see Koenraad W. Swart, "Individualism in the Mid-Nineteenth Century," *Journal of the History of Ideas* 23 (1962): 77–90.

7. Alexis de Tocqueville, *Democracy in America,* trans. George Lawrence, ed. J. P. Mayer (New York: Doubleday, Anchor Books, 1969), vol. 2, part 1, chapters 1 and 2.

8. David M. Schneider and Raymond T. Smith, *Class Differences and Sex Roles in American Kinship and Family Structure* (Englewood Cliffs, N.J.: Prentice-Hall, 1973), pp. 19, 20.

9. Ibid., p. 24.

10. Ibid., p. 46.

11. William H. Whyte, *The Organization Man* (New York: Simon and Schuster, 1956).

12. Alasdair MacIntyre, *After Virtue* (South Bend, Ind.: University of Notre Dame Press, 1981), p. 33.

13. Schneider and Smith, *Class Differences,* p. 27.

14. Ibid., pp. 107, 39. "The direct experience of our field research was that, while consciousness of ethnic identity persists at all levels of society, it is of rapidly decreasing significance as a factor affecting the behavior of those who are middle class. In fact, one aspect of becoming middle class is the abandonment of most of the behavioral characteristics of ethnicity, a process considerably aided by orientation toward individual achievement, the rational control of events and things, and looking to the future rather than to the past" (pp. 35–36).

15. Richard M. Merelman in *Making Something of Ourselves: On Culture and Politics in the United States* (Berkeley and Los Angeles: University of California Press, 1984) defines this conflict as between loose-boundedness and tight-boundedness. He sees it as the major conflict in American life today.

16. See MacIntyre, *After Virtue,* chapter 15.

17. On the memory of suffering and the importance of keeping such memories alive see Johann Baptist Metz, *Faith in History and Society: Toward a Practical Fundamental Theology* (New York: Seabury, 1980). Freud, in "Mourning and Melancholia," (1917) *Collected Papers* (London: Hogarth Press, 1956), 4:152–70, points out that if the memory of suffering is suppressed it continues to dominate a person in unhealthy ways. This suggests a dialectic of forgetting and remembering: only by remembering can we be free to act without being dominated by unconscious memory.

18. Cecilia Dougherty might be surprised to know that the early twentieth-century Catholic social thinker Monsignor John A. Ryan, author of *Distributive Justice* (New York, 1927), was already using the term "economic democracy."

19. Parker J. Palmer, *The Company of Strangers: Christians and the Renewal of America's Public Life* (New York: Crossroad, 1981), p. 31.

CHAPTER 7

1. James Curtis, in "Voluntary Association Joining: A Cross-National Comparative Note," *American Sociological Review* 36 (1971): 872–80, finds that voluntary association membership in Canada and the United States is significantly higher than in Great Britain, Germany, Italy, and Mexico. If multiple memberships are taken into account, the differences are even more striking. David Horton Smith, in "Voluntary Action and Voluntary Groups," *Annual Review of Sociology* 1 (1975): 247–51, finds that Scandinavians are as higher or higher than Canadians and Americans in voluntary association membership, but that other industrial nations are significantly lower. Sidney Verba, Norman H. Nie, and Jae-on Kim, in *Participation and Political Equality: A Seven Nation Comparison* (New York: Cambridge University Press, 1978), add a useful perspective to the understanding of these consistent differences. They find Americans highest in active membership in "organizations engaged in solving community problems" but relatively low in membership in political parties, clubs, and organizations. This fits with our findings in chapters 7 and 8 that Americans prefer voluntary community organizations to "politics." Verba, Nie, and Kim also find that the correlation between participation and levels of income and education is higher in the United States than in other industrial countries. Alex Inkeles in "The American Character," in *The Center Magazine,* a publication of the Center for the Study of Democratic Institutions, November/December, 1983, pp. 25–39, reports continuity in community involvement from Tocqueville's time to the present. He finds many other continuities, including self-reliance and a sense of individual efficacy. He also notes some significant differences, the chief of which are increased tolerance of diversity, a decline in regard for work and frugality, and erosion of political confidence.

2. Alexis de Tocqueville, *Democracy in America*, trans. George Lawrence, ed. J. P. Mayer (New York: Doubleday, Anchor Books, 1969), p. 523.

3. Hervé Varenne, *Americans Together: Structured Diversity in a Midwestern Town* (New York: Teachers College Press, 1977), pp. 150–59.

4. Tocqueville, *Democracy in America*, ed. Mayer, p. 70.

5. Tocqueville, *Democracy in America*, ed. Mayer, pp. 63–70.

6. Thomas Bender, *Community and Social Change in America* (New Brunswick, N.J.: Rutgers University Press, 1978), pp. 61–108.

7. For valuable recent summaries and interpretations of the literature on this subject see Bender, *Community and Social Change*; Robert H. Wiebe, *The Segmented Society: An Introduction to the Meaning of America* (New York: Oxford University Press, 1975); and Morris Janowitz, *The Last Half-Century: Societal Change and Politics in America* (Chicago: University of Chicago Press, 1978), especially pp. 264–319.

8. Tocqueville, *Democracy in America*, ed. Mayer, pp. 525–30.

9. See Mancur Olson, *The Logic of Collective Action* (Cambridge, Mass.: Harvard University Press, 1965), for an analysis of the "free rider" problem within the logic of utilitarian individualism.

10. Tocqueville, *Democracy in America*, ed. Mayer, p. 527.

11. Tocqueville, *Democracy in America*, ed. Mayer, pp. 512–13.

12. Tocqueville, *Democracy in America*, ed. Mayer, p. 604.

13. Robert E. Park, "The City: Suggestions for the Investigation of Human Behavior in the Urban Environment" (1925), in *The City*, ed. Robert E. Park and E. W. Burgess (Chicago: University of Chicago Press, 1967), p. 40.

14. See Edward O. Laumann, "Interlocking and Radial Nets: A Formal Feature with Important Consequences," in his *Bonds of Pluralism: The Form and Substance of Urban Social Networks* (New York: Wiley, 1973), pp. 111–30; Paul Craven and Barry Wellman, "The Network City," *Sociological Inquiry* 43 (1974): 57–88; Barry Wellman et al., "Community Ties and Support Systems: From Intimacy to Support," in *The Form of Cities in Central Canada: Selected Papers*, ed. L. S. Bourne, R. D. MacKinnon, and J. W. Simmons (Toronto: University of Toronto Press, 1973), pp. 152–67; Claude S. Fischer et al., *Networks and Places* (New York: Free Press, 1977); and Claude S. Fischer, *To Dwell Among Friends* (Chicago: University of Chicago Press, 1982).

15. Lester C. Thurow, *The Zero-Sum Society: Distribution and the Possibilities for Economic Change* (New York: Basic Books, 1980).

CHAPTER 8

1. Hervé Varenne, *Americans Together: Structured Diversity in a Midwestern Town* (New York: Teachers College Press, 1977), chapter 11.

2. Morris Janowitz, *The Reconstruction of Patriotism* (Chicago: University of Chicago Press, 1983), p. 193.

3. On the increase in voter nonalignment see Norman Nie, Sidney Verba, and John Petrocik, *The Changing American Voter* (Cambridge, Mass.: Harvard University Press, 1976); and Walter D. Burnham, "American Politics in the 1970s: Beyond Party?" in *The Future of Political Parties,* ed. Louis Maisel and Paul Sacks (Beverly Hills, Calif.: Sage, 1975), pp. 238–77, and "American Politics in the 1980s," *Dissent* 27 (Spring 1980): 149–60. On a possible "legitimation crisis" see Seymour Martin Lipset and William Schneider, *The Confidence Gap: Business, Labor and Government in the Public Mind* (New York: Free Press, 1983), chapter 12. See also James House and William Mason, "Political Alienation in America, 1952–1968," *American Sociological Review* 68 (1974): 951–72; and Daniel Yankelovich, "A Crisis of Moral Legitimacy?" *Dissent* 21 (Fall 1974): 526–33.

4. On the relation between economic position and community involvement see Sidney Verba and Norman Nie, *Participation in America: Political Democracy and Social Equality* (New York: Harper and Row, 1972). See also Lee Rainwater, *What Money Buys: Inequality and the Social Meanings of Income* (New York: Basic Books, 1974).

5. Octavio Paz, "Mexico and the United States," *New Yorker,* September 17, 1979, pp. 136–53.

6. See Lipset and Schneider, *Confidence Gap,* chapters 6–10.

7. Alexis de Tocqueville, *Democracy in America,* trans. George Lawrence, ed. J. P. Mayer (New York: Doubleday, Anchor Books, 1969), pp. 691–93.

8. "It is not the exercise of power or habits of obedience which deprave men, but the exercise of a power they consider illegitimate and obedience to a power which they think usurped and oppressive" (Tocqueville, *Democracy in America,* ed. Mayer, p. 14).

9. See particularly Nick Salvatore, *Eugene V. Debs: Citizen and Socialist* (Urbana, Ill.: University of Illinois Press, 1982) for the sense in which Debs and the movements with which he was associated—labor, populism, socialism—attempted to maintain the notion of republican citizenship under conditions of rapid industrialization.

10. On some of these movements see Harry C. Boyte, *The Backyard Revolution: Understanding the New Citizen Movement* (Philadelphia: Temple University Press, 1980).

CHAPTER 9

1. A 1982 Gallup poll reported in *Patterns of Charitable Giving by Individuals: A Research Report* (Washington, D.C.: Independent Sector, 1982) found that 71 percent of Americans gave to churches and religious organizations whereas only 32 percent gave to educational organizations and 24 percent

to hospitals. Furthermore, the amounts given to religious groups were much larger than to any other type of association. Out of an average charitable contribution by individuals of $475 in 1982, $313 was given to churches and religious organizations.

2. A convenient recent summary of national religious statistics can be found in Theodore Caplow et al., *All Faithful People: Change and Continuity in Middletown's Religion* (Minneapolis: University of Minnesota Press, 1983), pp. 20–30. Weekly church attendance was about 40 percent in 1950, rose to almost 50 percent in the late 1950s and declined to about 40 percent in the early 1970s. Since then it has remained nearly constant at about 40 percent. Religious membership has remained close to 60 percent since 1950 with only minor fluctuations. When asked whether they "believe in God or a universal spirit" about 95 percent of Americans from 1950 to the present say "Yes." Affirmative answers to the same question in Western Europe are 15 to 30 percent lower. What that belief means receives more detailed treatment in Robert S. Bilheimer, ed., *Faith and Ferment: An Interdisciplinary Study of Christian Beliefs and Practices* (Minneapolis: Augsburg, 1983), a study of churches in Minnesota.

3. See Robert N. Bellah, *The Broken Covenant: American Civil Religion in Time of Trial* (New York: Seabury, 1975), chapter 1.

4. See Perry Miller, *Errand Into the Wilderness* (Cambridge, Mass.: Harvard University Press, 1956).

5. Donald M. Scott, *From Office to Profession: The New England Ministry, 1750–1850* (Philadelphia: University of Pennsylvania Press, 1978), p. 12.

6. Paul Boyer, *Urban Masses and Moral Order in America, 1820–1920* (Cambridge, Mass.: Harvard University Press, 1978), part 1.

7. Scott, *From Office to Profession*, pp. 149, 139.

8. Ann Douglas, *The Feminization of American Culture* (New York: Knopf, 1977).

9. Alexis de Tocqueville, *Democracy in America*, trans. George Lawrence, ed. J. P. Mayer (New York: Doubleday, Anchor Books, 1969), p. 292.

10. Tocqueville, *Democracy in America*, ed. Mayer, pp. 529, 535.

11. Hervé Varenne, *Americans Together: Structured Diversity in a Midwestern Town* (New York: Teachers College Press, 1977), pp. 99–100.

12. Joan L. Fee et al., *Young Catholics: A Report to the Knights of Columbus* (Los Angeles: Sadlier, 1981), pp. 229–30.

13. Dean R. Hoge, *Converts, Dropouts, Returnees: A Study of Religious Change Among Catholics* (Washington, D.C.: United States Catholic Conference; New York: Pilgrim Press, 1981), p. 167.

14. James Davison Hunter has documented an important shift in conservative evangelical piety through a study of books published by the eight largest publishers of evangelical literature. He finds a phenomenon he calls "psychological Christocentrism" beginning in the 1960s and reaching dominance in the 1970s. This literature consists of many variations on such statements as "Jesus meant for the Christian life to be an exciting, abun-

dant adventure." Suffering and sacrifice are downplayed and happiness, fulfillment, and "a new zest for living" are promised. Hunter summarizes: "Subjectivism has displaced the traditional asceticism as the dominant attitude in theologically conservative Protestant culture. There is some variability, but in mainstream contemporary American Evangelicalism, an austere instrumentalism has been replaced by a malleable expressivity" (James Davison Hunter, *American Evangelicalism* [New Brunswick, N.J.: Rutgers University Press, 1983], 91–101).

15. Hoge, *Converts, Dropouts, Returnees,* p. 171.

16. Fee et al., *Young Catholics,* p. 242.

17. A more extreme example of the need for "structure" is provided by a member of the very conservative Living Word Fellowship on the San Francisco Peninsula who complained that all through school he had been expected to "decide what is right and wrong and why I was alive and what I was living for. . . . That's the worst thing to do to a man—make him decide everything himself, because he can't. It's a Satanic trap." A Christian, on the contrary, "doesn't have to decide what is right or wrong. He just has to decide to *do* right or wrong" (Steven M. Tipton, *Getting Saved from the Sixties* [Berkeley and Los Angeles: University of California Press, 1982], p. 44).

18. On the extent to which higher education has operated as a missionary outpost of secular culture weaning the younger generations of the mainline churches away from their tradition see Dean R. Hoge and David A. Roozen, eds., *Understanding Church Growth and Decline, 1950–1978* (New York: Pilgrim Press, 1979), especially chapter 8, written by Hoge.

19. See Jay Dolan, *The Immigrant Church* (Baltimore: Johns Hopkins University Press, 1975).

20. David J. O'Brien, *The Renewal of American Catholicism* (New York: Oxford University Press, 1972), and John A. Coleman, *An American Strategic Theology* (New York: Paulist Press, 1982), especially part 3.

21. National Conference of Catholic Bishops, *The Challenge of Peace: God's Promise and Our Response,* A Pastoral Letter on War and Peace, May 3, 1983 (Washington, D.C.: United States Catholic Conference, 1983).

22. Martin E. Marty, *The Public Church: Mainline-Evangelical-Catholic* (New York: Crossroad, 1981).

23. Ernst Troeltsch, *The Social Teachings of the Christian Churches* (1911), trans. Olive Wyon (London: George Allen, 1931); see especially volume 1, pp. 328–82, and volume 2, conclusion.

24. Karl Rahner, *The Church and the Sacraments* (1963), trans. W. J. O'Hara (London: Burns and Oates, 1974), p. 11.

25. Octavio Paz, "Mexico and the United States," *New Yorker,* September 17, 1979, pp. 136–53.

26. See Wayne A. Meeks, *The First Urban Christians: The Social World of the Apostle Paul* (New Haven, Conn.: Yale University Press, 1983).

27. See Charles Y. Glock and Robert N. Bellah, *The New Religious Conscious-*

ness (Berkeley and Los Angeles: University of California Press, 1976).

28. Parker J. Palmer, *Company of Strangers: Christians and the Renewal of America's Public Life* (New York: Crossroad, 1981), p. 155. Emphasis in original.

CHAPTER 10

1. Quoted in Theodore Draper, "Hume and Madison: The Secrets of *Federalist Paper* No. 10," *Encounter* 58 (February 1982): 47.

2. Garry Wills, *Explaining America: The Federalist* (New York: Penguin Books, 1982), p. 268. Nathan Hale's reputed last words, "I regret that I have but one life to give for my country," are similar to a line in Joseph Addison's play *Cato*.

3. Quoted in Ronald Steel, *Walter Lippmann and the American Century* (Boston: Little, Brown, 1980), p. 64.

4. Andrew Carnegie, "The Gospel of Wealth" (1889), in *The Gospel of Wealth and Other Timely Essays*, ed. Edward A. Kirkland (Cambridge, Mass.: Harvard University Press, 1962), p. 14.

5. Peter Dobkin Hall, *The Organization of American Culture, 1700–1900: Private Institutions, Elites, and the Origins of American Nationality* (New York.: New York University Press, 1982), pp. 266, 268.

6. Nick Salvatore, *Eugene V. Debs: Citizen and Socialist* (Urbana, Ill.: University of Illinois Press, 1982), pp. 88, 293.

7. Michael Sandel, "The Procedural Republic and the Unencumbered Self," *Political Theory* 12 (1984): 93.

8. Quoted in John Kenneth Galbraith, *The Great Crash, 1929* (Boston: Little, Brown, 1972), p. 143.

9. Ronald Reagan, address to the Annual Concretes and Aggregates Convention, January 31, 1984, as quoted in the *Los Angeles Times*, February 1, 1984. Recent efforts to give Neocapitalism a broad cultural as well as economic defense are George Gilder, *Wealth and Poverty* (New York: Basic Books, 1982) and Michael Novak, *The Spirit of Democratic Capitalism* (New York.: Simon and Schuster, 1983). George F. Will, however, exposes many of the fallacies of his fellow conservatives in *Statecraft as Soulcraft: What Government Does* (New York.: Simon and Schuster, 1983).

10. Justin Dart, as quoted in an interview in the *Los Angeles Times*, February 6, 1982. Dart was reported as saying, "You gotta look at me as a big-issues guy. I'm interested in the national economy and our defense ability, not all these crappy issues like equal rights."

11. Felix G. Rohatyn, "Time for a Change," *New York Review of Books*, August 18, 1983, pp. 46–49.

12. The Administered Society has a certain affinity to the "Japanese model" optimistically described by Ezra F. Vogel in *Japan as Number One: Lessons for America* (Cambridge, Mass.: Harvard University Press, 1979). The Administered Society is also related to what is called "corporatism" in Eu-

rope, about which much has been written recently. Representative works include: Philippe Schmitter and Gerhard Lehmbruch, eds., *Trends Toward Corporate Intermediation* (Beverly Hills, Calif.: Sage, 1979); Suzanne Berger, ed., *Organized Interests in Western Europe* (New York.: Cambridge University Press, 1981); and Gerhard Lehmbruch and Philippe Schmitter, eds., *Corporatism and Public Policy Making* (Beverly Hills, Calif.: Sage, 1982).

13. Michael Harrington, *Decade of Decision: The Crisis of the American System* (New York.: Simon and Schuster, 1980), pp. 320, 325. Another useful recent discussion of the Economic Democracy position is Martin Carnoy and Derek Shearer, *Economic Democracy: The Challenge of the 1980s* (White Plains, N.Y.: M. E. Sharpe, 1980). Although we do not identify Economic Democracy exclusively with the position taken by the California Campaign for Economic Democracy, that position is well expressed in Tom Hayden, *The American Future: New Visions beyond Old Frontiers* (Boston: South End, 1980). Mark E. Kann analyzes the relationship of these new developments to the recent history of the left and argues for what he calls "radical democracy" in Mark E. Kann, *The American Left: Failures and Fortunes* (New York: Praeger, 1982).

CHAPTER 11

1. John Donne, "An Anatomie of the World: The First Anniversary."
2. Matthew Arnold, "Stanzas from the Grand Chartreuse" (1855).
3. Stephen Toulmin, *The Return to Cosmology: Postmodern Science and the Theology of Nature* (Berkeley and Los Angeles: University of California Press, 1982), pp. 228–29, 234.
4. Louis Dumont, *From Mandeville to Marx: The Genesis and Truimph of Economic Ideology* (Chicago: University of Chicago Press, 1977), p. 20.
5. Wendell Berry, *Standing by Words* (San Francisco: North Point Press, 1983), pp. 5, 20.
6. Helen Vendler, "From Fragments a World Perfect at Last," *New Yorker,* March 19, 1984, p. 143.
7. Todd Gitlin, *Inside Prime Time* (New York: Pantheon, 1983), pp. 268–69. Conversations with Todd Gitlin and Lisa Heilbronn were helpful in clarifying our views of television.
8. Matthew Arnold, "To Marguerite." Emphasis in original.
9. Toulmin, *Return to Cosmology*, pp. 254, 209–10.
10. Toulmin, *Return to Cosmology*, pp. 265–68.
11. Lee Rainwater, *What Money Buys: Inequality and the Social Meanings of Income* (New York: Basic Books, 1974).
12. On many of these issues, an approach refreshingly free of ideological narrowness is provided by recent Catholic social teaching. See the collection of documents from Vatican II and after: *Renewing the Earth: Catholic Documents on Peace, Justice and Liberation,* ed. David J. O'Brien and Thomas A. Shannon (Garden City, N.Y.: Image Books, 1977). See also Pope John Paul

II's 1981 encyclical letter *Laborem Exercens*, contained in Gregory Baum, *The Priority of Labor* (New York: Paulist Press, 1982), which provides a useful commentary. Charles K. Wilber and Kenneth P. Jameson use these teachings to reflect about the American economy in their *An Inquiry into the Poverty of Economics* (Notre Dame, Ind.: University of Notre Dame Press, 1983).

13. On the modern fear of politics and the need to connect politics and vision see Sheldon Wolin, *Politics and Vision: Continuity and Innovation in Western Political Thought* (Boston: Little, Brown, 1960), especially chapter 10. For a helpful consideration of some of these issues see Michael Walzer, *Spheres of Justice: A Defence of Pluralism and Equality* (New York: Basic Books, 1983). For a critique of the dangers of too thin a moral consensus see Daniel Callahan, "Minimalist Ethics," *Hastings Center Report* 11 (October 1981): 19–25.

14. Christopher Jencks et al., *Inequality: A Reassessment of the Effect of Family and Schooling in America* (New York: Basic Books, 1972), p. 8. On pp. 230–32 Jencks discusses the various ways, preferably indirect, in which this could be done. Daniel Yankelovich criticizes Jencks for being wildly out of touch with popular American consciousness in making his suggestion about limiting income (*New Rules: Searching for Self-Fulfillment in a World Turned Upside Down* [New York: Random House, 1981], pp. 137–39). But he in no way answers Jencks's argument.

15. Alan Trachtenberg, *The Incorporation of America: Culture and Society in the Gilded Age* (New York: Hill and Wang, 1982), pp. 5–6.

16. Steven M. Tipton, *Getting Saved From the Sixties* (Berkeley and Los Angeles: University of California Press, 1982), p. 115.

17. The differences between private vacations and public holidays, or holy days, illustrate the moral limits of expressive alternatives to traditional civic and religious forms of enacting our social solidarity. The vacation began its short, century-long history as a stylish middle-class imitation of the aristocrat's seasonal retreat from court and city to country estate. Its character is essentially individualistic and familial: "Everyone plans his own vacation, goes where he wants to go, does what he wants to do," writes Michael Walzer. Vacations are individually chosen, designed, and paid for, regardless of how class-patterned vacation behavior may be or how many vacation spots depend on public funds for their existence. The experience vacations celebrate is freedom—the freedom to break away from the ordinary places and routines of the workaday world and "escape to another world" where every day is "vacant" and all time is "free time." There we have "our own sweet time" to do with as we will and empty days to fill at our own pace with activities of our own choosing. Public holidays, by contrast, were traditionally provided for everyone in the same form and place, at the same time, to celebrate together by taking part in the fixed communal rites, meals, and celebrations that already filled them. In ancient Rome, the *dies vacantes*, in a telling reversal of meaning, were those ordinary working days devoid of religious festivals or public games. Public

holy days such as the Sabbath are the common property of all. "Sabbath rest is more egalitarian than the vacation because it can't be purchased: it is one more thing that money can't buy. It is enjoined for everyone, enjoyed by everyone," Walzer observes. The Sabbath requires a shared sense of obligation and solemnity, backed not only by a shared impulse to celebrate but by a common mechanism of enforcement. God created the Sabbath for everyone and *commanded* all of the faithful to rest, although in our society today individuals are free to choose to respect it or not. Nonetheless, the Sabbath signifies a freedom interwoven with civic equality and unity under an ultimate authority that is not merely a man-made social idea. (Walzer, *Spheres of Justice*, pp. 190–96.)

18. Eva T. H. Brann, *Paradoxes of Education in a Republic* (Chicago: University of Chicago Press, 1979), p. 111.

19. Helen Vendler, "Presidential Address 1980," *PMLA* 96 (1981): 350. Vendler's aim is not to create more literature majors but to save us from going through life "unaccompanied by a sense that others have also gone through it, and have left a record of their experience." We need to be able to think about Job, Jesus, Antigone, and Lear "in order to refer private experience to some identifying frame or solacing reflection," to the classic stories of our culture's traditions that show us what it means to be a good person in practical relationships to others in particular situations (p. 349). More than laws or philosophical arguments, such stories shape the habits of our hearts by guiding us through example.

20. From Thomas Hobbes, "Human Nature," in *Body, Man and Citizen*, ed. Richard S. Peters (New York: Collier, 1962), pp. 224–25.

21. Thomas Hobbes, *Leviathan* (1651), ed. C. B. MacPherson (Harmondsworth, England: Penguin Books, 1968), p. 161.

APPENDIX: SOCIAL SCIENCE AS PUBLIC PHILOSOPHY

1. Alexis de Tocqueville, *Democracy in America*, trans. George Lawrence, ed. J. P. Mayer (New York: Doubleday, Anchor Books, 1969), p. 12.

2. A recent effort to revive the tradition of public philosophy that has been especially influential on our research group is William M. Sullivan, *Reconstructing Public Philosophy* (Berkeley and Los Angeles: University of California Press, 1982).

3. Douglas Sloan, "The Teaching of Ethics in the American Undergraduate Curriculum, 1876–1976," in *Ethics Teaching in Higher Education*, ed. Daniel Callahan and Sissela Bok (New York: Plenum Press, 1980), pp. 1–57, quotations from p. 4.

4. See Burton J. Bledstein, *The Culture of Professionalism: The Middle Class and the Development of Higher Education in America* (New York: Norton, 1976), for an analysis of the emergence of the research university in its cultural and social context.

5.   Thomas L. Haskell, *The Emergence of Professional Social Science: The American Social Science Association and the Nineteenth-Century Crisis of Authority* (Urbana, Ill.: University of Illinois Press, 1977), p. 67. Emphasis added.

6.   For a discussion of these issues see Alasdair MacIntyre, *After Virtue* (South Bend, Ind.: University of Notre Dame Press, 1981), chapter 8, "The Character of Generalisations in Social Science and their Lack of Predictive Power."

7.   For representative works see Louis Dumont, *From Mandeville to Marx: The Genesis and Triumph of Economic Ideology* (Chicago: University of Chicago Press, 1977), and "On Value," 1980 Radcliffe-Brown Lecture, *Proceedings of the British Academy* 66 (1980): 207–41; MacIntyre, *After Virtue;* and Jürgen Habermas, *Knowledge and Human Interests* (1968), trans. Jeremy J. Shapiro (Boston: Beacon Press, 1971), and *The Theory of Communicative Action,* vol. 1, *Reason and the Rationalization of Society* (1981), trans. Thomas McCarthy (Boston: Beacon Press, 1984).

8.   On social science as social self-understanding see especially Edward Shils, "The Calling of Sociology," in *The Calling of Sociology and Other Essays on the Pursuit of Learning* (Chicago: University of Chicago Press, 1980), pp. 3–92.

9.   Thus Richard J. Bernstein seeks to amend MacIntyre's story by changing the valence given to the Enlightenment in the account of modern society and its problems. He argues that MacIntyre has suppressed an important actor in the modern story, Hegel, and shows how the form of the drama changes if we give him a central role. See his discussion "Nietzsche or Aristotle? Reflections on MacIntyre's *After Virtue,*" *Soundings* 67 (1984): 6–29; also his *Beyond Objectivism and Relativism: Science, Hermeneutics and Praxis* (Philadelphia: University of Pennsylvania Press, 1983), pp. 226–29.

10. We have seen the first two Middletown III volumes: Caplow, *Middletown Families: Fifty Years of Change and Continuity* (Minneapolis: University of Minnesota Press, 1982) and Caplow et al., *All Faithful People: Change and Continuity in Middletown's Religion* (Minneapolis: University of Minnesota Press, 1983), referred to in earlier chapters.

11. Hans-Georg Gadamer has provided us with valuable guidance in our understanding of our work as always involving a dialogue with the tradition out of which we come. He reminds us also that our conversation with contemporaries or predecessors is never closed on itself but is always *about something.* See particularly his *Truth and Method* (1960) (New York: Seabury, 1975) and *Reason in the Age of Science* (1976), trans. Frederick G. Lawrence (Cambridge, Mass.: MIT Press, 1981). See also the discussion of Gadamer in Bernstein, *Beyond Objectivism and Relativism.*

12. Some of the germinal ideas for our work derived from Robert N. Bellah, *The Broken Covenant: American Civil Religion in Time of Trial* (New York: Seabury, 1975) and Bellah's conclusion to Bellah and Charles Y. Glock, *The New Religious Consciousness* (Berkeley and Los Angeles: University of California Press, 1976). Sullivan's *Reconstructing Public Philosophy* gave an important theoretical background and Steven M. Tipton's *Getting Saved from the Sixties* (Berkeley and Los Angeles: University of California Press,

1982) was our methodological exemplar. With respect to issues of social science and ethics see Norma Haan, Robert N. Bellah, Paul Rabinow, and William M. Sullivan, *Social Science as Moral Inquiry* (New York: Columbia University Press, 1983), especially the introduction by Bellah and the chapters by Bellah and Sullivan; and Robert N. Bellah, "Social Science as Practical Reason," in *Ethics, The Social Sciences, and Policy Analysis,* ed. Daniel Callahan and Bruce Jennings (New York: Plenum Press, 1983), pp. 37–64.

Writings that contributed to the culture of the research group are signalled only in part in the above footnotes. Many that were influential for us in some stage of our work have not found their way into notes on specific points. For instance, we read Ralph H. Turner's "The Real Self: From Institution to Impulse," *American Journal of Sociology* 81 (1976): 989–1016, early on, and it helped to shape the argument of chapters 3 through 5. Robert Lane's *Political Ideology: Why the American Common Man Believes What He Does* (New York: Free Press, 1962) was a model for our fieldwork and contributed to our thinking about individualism and inequality. Daniel Bell's *The Cultural Contradictions of Capitalism* (New York: Basic Books, 1976), particularly the chapter on "the public household," contributed to our ideas about state and society. Charles Taylor's *Hegel and Modern Society* (Cambridge, Eng.: Cambridge University Press, 1979) helped us to see the illusions of a private expressiveness and the emptiness of formal freedom. Our indebtedness far exceeds these examples.

13. Madsen and Swidler drafted chapter 1. Bellah and Sullivan drafted chapter 2. Tipton drafted chapter 3, with contributions from Madsen and Swidler, and Bellah substantially revised it. Swidler drafted chapter 4, and Bellah added new material in the final revision. Tipton drafted chapter 5, which Bellah substantially revised. Sullivan drafted chapter 6, which Bellah substantially revised, incorporating a section of Swidler's and material from Madsen and Tipton. Madsen drafted chapter 7 with help from Swidler. Sullivan drafted chapter 8, which Bellah revised, incorporating material from Madsen. Bellah drafted chapter 9, with Swidler adding a section. Sullivan drafted chapter 10 with contributions from Madsen and Tipton. Bellah drafted chapter 11 as well as the preface and the appendix, incorporating suggestions from the other members of the research group. In addition, each member of the group made significant contributions to the book as a whole. For example, Madsen provided a rich sense of the communities in which our respondents lived and of the social setting that grounds moral life. Sullivan developed a number of practical philosophical concepts such as "moral ecology," "communities of memory," and "practices of commitment." Swidler attended to the organization of the book's argument as a whole, pressing us not to lose sight of the positive meaning of American individualism, and in the drafting and revision of each chapter she continually suggested how to keep the book thematically on track. Tipton provided a model of how to integrate moral dialogue with social inquiry, shaping our approach to interviewing and suggesting many of the questions we asked.

Glossary of Some Key Terms

Biblical tradition. The tradition that originates in biblical religion and, though widely diffused in American culture, is carried primarily by Jewish and Christian religious communities. Though certain elements, such as belief in God, are widely shared, there are numerous versions of this tradition. In the Colonial period, Puritanism, a form of Protestantism, was particularly influential. In the eighteenth century, Protestant sects increased in numbers, and in the nineteenth century, large numbers of Catholics and Jews immigrated to America. Church, sect, and mystical or individualistic forms of Christianity have all played an important role in American history. (See chapter 9)

Community, community of memory. *Community* is a term used very loosely by Americans today. We use it in a strong sense: a *community* is a group of people who are socially interdependent, who participate together in discussion and decision making, and who share certain *practices* (which see) that both define the community and are nurtured by it. Such a community is not quickly formed. It almost always has a history and so is also a *community of memory,* defined in part by its past and its memory of its past. (See *Lifestyle enclave;* also pp. 153–54)

Culture. Those patterns of meaning that any group or society uses to interpret and evaluate itself and its situation. *Language* (which see) is an important part of culture. Since culture always has a history, it frequently takes the form of *tradition* (which see). In this book, because we are especially interested in history, we frequently refer to tradition where other social scientists would refer to culture. We take culture to be a constitutive dimension of all human action. It is not an epiphenomenon to be explained by economic or political factors.

Expressive individualism. A form of individualism that arose in opposition to *utilitarian individualism* (which see). Expressive individualism

333

holds that each person has a unique core of feeling and intuition that should unfold or be expressed if individuality is to be realized. This core, though unique, is not necessarily alien to other persons or to nature. Under certain conditions, the expressive individualist may find it possible through intuitive feeling to "merge" with other persons, with nature, or with the cosmos as a whole. Expressive individualism is related to the phenomenon of romanticism in eighteenth- and nineteenth-century European and American culture. In the twentieth century, it shows affinities with the culture of psychotherapy. (See *Individualism;* see also pp. 33–35)

Individualism. A word used in numerous, sometimes contradictory, senses. We use it mainly in two: (1) a belief in the inherent dignity and, indeed, sacredness of the human person. In this sense, individualism is part of all four of the American traditions we have described in this book—biblical, republican, utilitarian individualist, and expressive individualist; (2) a belief that the individual has a primary reality whereas society is a second-order, derived or artificial construct, a view we call *ontological individualism.* This view is shared by utilitarian and expressive individualists. It is opposed to the view that society is as real as individuals, a view we call *social realism,* which is common to the biblical and republican traditions.

Justice. As we use it, *justice* has three senses: (1) *procedural justice,* which is a matter of the fairness of the rules under which society operates and disputes are adjudicated; (2) *distributive justice,* which is a matter of the fairness of the society's system of rewards, of its distribution of goods and opportunities; (3) *substantive justice,* which is a matter of the institutional order of society as a whole and its justice or fairness. People can agree on the norms of procedural justice even when they disagree about the purposes or ends of life, which is why such agreement is sometimes called a *thin consensus.* More than such a thin consensus is usually required for agreement about distributive justice and always for agreement about substantive justice.

Language. We do not use *language* in this book to mean primarily what the linguist studies. We use the term to refer to modes of moral discourse that include distinct vocabularies and characteristic patterns of moral reasoning. We use *first language* to refer to the individualistic mode that is the dominant American form of discourse about moral, social, and political matters. We use the term *second languages* to refer to other forms, primarily biblical and republican, that provide at least part of the moral discourse of most Americans.

Lifestyle enclave. A term used in contrast to *community* (which see). A lifestyle enclave is formed by people who share some feature of private life. Members of a lifestyle enclave express their identity through shared patterns of appearance, consumption, and leisure activities, which often serve to differentiate them sharply from those with other lifestyles. They are not interdependent, do not act together politically, and do not share a history. If these things begin to appear, the enclave is on the way to becoming a community. Many of what are called *communities* in America are mixtures of *communities* in our strong sense and *lifestyle enclaves.* (See pp. 71–75)

Moral ecology. The web of moral understandings and commitments that tie people together in community. Also called *social ecology.*

Practices, practices of commitment. Practices are shared activities that are not undertaken as means to an end but are ethically good in themselves (thus close to *praxis* in Aristotle's sense). A genuine community—whether a marriage, a university, or a whole society—is constituted by such practices. Genuine practices are almost always practices of commitment, since they involve activities that are ethically good. In the strict sense, *practices of separation* is a contradiction in terms, since such activities are undertaken in the interest of the self at the expense of commitments to others. (See p. 154)

Public good. In the individualist tradition, the public good is usually identified with the sum of private benefits. In the republican tradition, the public good is that which benefits society as a whole and leads to what the founders of the American republic called *public happiness.* It includes everything from adequate public facilities to the trust and civic friendship that makes public life something to be enjoyed rather than feared. Also called the *common good.*

Republican tradition. The tradition that originated in the cities of classical Greece and Rome, was expressed in the civic humanism of late medieval and early modern Europe, and contributed to the formation of modern Western democracies. It presupposes that the citizens of a republic are motivated by civic virtue as well as self-interest. It views public participation as a form of moral education and sees its purposes as the attainment of *justice* and the *public good* (both of which see). In much of American history, the republican tradition has been closely linked to the biblical tradition. (See pp. 30–31)

Tradition. A tradition is a pattern of understandings and evaluations that a community has worked out over time. Tradition is an inherent dimension of all human action. There is no way of getting outside of tradition altogether, though we may criticize one tradition from the point of view of another. *Tradition* is not used in contrast to *reason*. Tradition is often an ongoing reasoned argument about the good of the community or institution whose identity it defines. (See pp. 27–28)

Utilitarian individualism. A form of individualism that takes as given certain basic human appetites and fears—for Hobbes, the desire for power over others and the fear of sudden violent death at the hands of another—and sees human life as an effort by individuals to maximize their self-interest relative to these given ends. Utilitarian individualism views society as arising from a contract that individuals enter into only in order to advance their self-interest. According to Locke, society is necessary because of the prior existence of property, the protection of which is the reason individuals contractually enter society. Utilitarian individualism has an affinity to a basically economic understanding of human existence. (See *Individualism, Expressive individualism;* also pp. 32–33)

Index

(continued)

Eastern Europe

THE WORLD'S LANDSCAPES
Edited by Dr J. M. Houston

Dean S. Rugg
University of Nebraska

with a Foreword by

J. M. Houston
Chancellor of Regent College, Vancouver

Eastern Europe

Longman London and New York

Longman Group Limited
Longman House, Burnt Mill, Harlow
Essex CM20 2JE, England
Associated companies throughout the world

*Published in the United States of America
by Longman Inc., New York*

© Longman Group Limited 1985

First published 1985

British Library Cataloguing in Publication Data
Rugg, Dean S.
　　Eastern Europe. – (The World's landscapes)
　　1. Europe, Eastern – Description and travel
　　I. Title　II. Series
　　914.7　DJK18

　　ISBN 0-582-30019-3

Library of Congress Cataloging in Publication Data
Rugg, Dean S.
　　Eastern Europe.
　　4.5 (The World's landscapes)
　　Bibliography: p.
　　Includes index.
　　1. Europe, Eastern – History.　2. Europe, Eastern –
Historical geography.　I. Title.　II. Series.
DJK 38.R84　1985　　947　　84–20131
ISBN 0-582-30019-3

Set in Linotron 202 10/12 pt Bembo

Produced by Longman Singapore Publishers (Pte) Ltd.
Printed in Singapore

To the Memory of My Parents

Contents

Contents

Contents

List of photos

List of figures

xiv

Foreword

by Dr J. M. Houston, Chancellor of Regent College, Vancouver, BC.

Despite the multitude of geographical books that deal with differing areas of the world, no series has before attempted to explain man's role in moulding and changing its diverse landscapes. At the most there are books that study individual areas in detail, but usually in language too technical for the general reader. It is the purpose of this series to take regional geographical studies to the frontiers of contemporary research on the making of the world's landscapes. This is being done by specialists, each in his own area, yet in non-technical language that should appeal to both the general reader and to the discerning student.

We are leaving behind us an age that has viewed nature as an objective reality. Today, we are living in a more pragmatic, less idealistic age. The nouns of previous thought forms are the verbs of a new outlook. Pure thought is being replaced by the use of knowledge for a technological society, busily engaged in changing the face of the earth. It is an age of operational thinking. The very functions of nature are being threatened by scientific takeovers, and it is not too fanciful to predict that the daily weather, the biological cycles of life processes, as well as the energy of the atom will become harnessed to human corporations. Thus it becomes imperative that all thoughtful citizens of our world today should know something of the changes man has already wrought in his physical habitat, and which he is now modifying with accelerating power.

Studies of man's impact on the landscapes of the earth are expanding rapidly. They involve diverse disciplines such as Quaternary sciences, archaeology, history and anthropology, with subjects that range from pollen analysis to plant domestication, field systems,

xvi

settlement patterns and industrial land use. But with his sense of place, and his sympathy for synthesis, the geographer is well placed to handle this diversity of data in a meaningful manner. The appraisal of landscape changes, how and when man has altered and remoulded the surface of the earth, is both pragmatic and interesting to a wide range of readers.

The concept of 'landscape' is of course both concrete and elusive. In its Anglo-Saxon origin, *landscipe* referred to some unit of area that was a natural entity, such as the lands of a tribe or of a feudal lord. It was only at the end of the sixteenth century that, through the influence of Dutch landscape painters, the word also acquired the idea of a unit of visual perceptions, of a view. In the German *Landschaft*, both definitions have been maintained, a source of confusion and uncertainty in the use of the term. However, despite scholarly analysis of its ambiguity, the concept of landscape has increasing currency precisely because of its ambiguity. It refers to the total man-land complex in place and time, suggesting spatial interactions, and indicative of visual features that we can select, such as field and settlement patterns, set in the mosaics of relief, soils and vegetation. Thus the 'landscape' is the point of reference in the selection of widely ranging data. It is the tangible context of man's association with the earth. It is the documentary evidence of the power of human perception to mould the resources of nature into human usage, a perception as varied as his cultures. Today, the ideological attitudes of man are being more dramatically imprinted on the earth than ever before, owing to his technological capabilities.

Professor Rugg has made an important contribution to the series, *The World's Landscapes*, in this study of Eastern Europe. Few areas of the world have witnessed more cultural and political upheaval. It well deserves its name as 'The Shatter Belt of Europe'. Bearing this in mind, the author sees the landscapes of the area more as a historical than as a geographical reality, although the two dimensions are always together. The landscapes therefore represent a unique palimpsest of five stages: medieval colonization; belated feudalism; early multinationalism; recent nationalism; and contemporary socialism. He also identifies five elements of landscape change: the relics of the past; prevailing cultures; the process of change; ideologies associated with changes; and the social changes themselves, initiated or assisted.

Although considerable geographical and historical research has been published in German and other languages of Eastern Europe on landscape changes, this author has produced the first book of its kind

in English, to account systematically for the vast body of literature on this subject. He has done much personal field work, travelled extensively in the area, and added significantly to our methodological understanding of landscape trends. The maps he has compiled are an original and significant contribution. This book should be of great value to all students of landscape change, as well as of general interest to those now living in the West, whose ancestry came from Eastern Europe.

J. M. Houston

Acknowledgements

We are indebted to the following for permission to reproduce copyright material:

Academy of Political Science, New York for fig 5.2 from article 'European Political Boundaries' by S. Columb Gilfillan pp 458–84 *Political Science Quarterly* 1924; the author, Dr. F. W. Carter for fig 7.10 (F. W. Carter 1973); the Editor, Geographica Polonica for fig 7.6 (Misztala Kaczolowski 1980); VEB Hermann Haack for figs 7.4 (Harke & Dischereit 1979), 7.7 (Barthel 1962), 7.11 (Kohl et al 1979); Verlag Ferdinand Hirt for figs 5.4–5.6 (Peterson et al 1983); Akadémia Kiadó for fig 7.5 (Petri 1971); Longman Group Ltd for figs 3.2 (C. T. Smith 1978), 7.5 (Wilczewski et al 1978); Oxford University Press for fig 4.6, p 39 (Yates & Warriner 1943); B. G. Teubner for photo 3.2 (Krebs II 1930); Sport i Turystyka & the author, Jan Hattowski for photo 6.1 (Poland 1977); George Westermann Verlag GmbH & the authors, for figs 7.13 (Schöller 1974), 7.14 (Richter 1974); the author, Marianne Van Valkenburg Carey for fig 4.7 from Map A (Van Valkenburg & Huntingdon 1935); John Wiley & Sons Inc for fig 7.8 from fig 16.6 (Compton 1979).

We have unfortunately been unable to trace the copyright holders of fig 4.8, photos 3.3, 4.3, 5.3, 6.3 and would appreciate any information which would enable us to do so.

Preface

Twenty-five years ago, when I first traveled deep into Eastern Europe, I remember thinking how different the landscape appeared from that in the western part of the continent. Here the institution of feudalism had persisted longer as reflected in the ubiquitous peasant villages and in the lag of economic development. In the intervening period, I have been obsessed with an attempt to trace the connections between the many landscape relics of this area and the different social orders that produced them. However, these connections are blurred by the new landscape system of socialism that is responsible for considerable progress in modernization throughout the area. These landscapes, old and new, tell many stories, but to me they reflect, above all, the continuous influence of large external powers on a Shatter Belt of small cultural groups. This perception became a central theme of landscape change that I have used in this book.

My primary problem in planning the book was organization. From the beginning I felt that, although each country of Eastern Europe is unique in some way, the landscape tells a story of a common historical background distinct from that of Western Europe. Therefore, I make no attempt to write separate chapters on the different countries but instead focus on the processes that I feel affected all of them, albeit to different degrees. This book, then, deals with Eastern Europe as a distinct area, and regional differences by country emerge within the chapters dealing with the processes of landscape change. Some may object to this emphasis on historical process over regional description, but I feel that this approach is essential to the understanding of the landscape of this complex area.

Several constraints affected this book. First, the normal restrictions placed on researchers in socialist countries hindered me. For geographers, this can be serious in terms of access to maps and data and additionally in opportunities to take pictures of 'strategic' objects. Second, the variety of languages in Eastern Europe makes competency in even a few of them a rarity for most specialists. My knowledge of these languages is limited to German, which proved very useful as a lingua franca in the area and in using primary sources, especially for East Germany. Actually, I considered the landscape itself a primary source as I carried out field work in all countries except Albania, investigating personally the many relics mentioned in the text. Finally, the landscape analysis was limited by the prescribed length of the books in the World Landscape Series, although the publisher has been generous in allowing me some leeway.

In Eastern Europe, place names present a complex problem. As I explain in the text, the region has a multinational background. Many places, especially in the northern part, were settled under German law and had high percentages of German colonists. Later, the percentage of Slavs or Hungarians surpassed the number of Germans, but the towns at times came under Germanic administration. For example, the present Poznań in Poland was called Posen (German) in the early period and later during the nineteenth century. In general, in Chapters 3 to 5 the Germanic names are used, followed by the present names in parentheses. In Chapters 6 and 7, which deal with the recent eras, and in the index, present names only are given.

On a work of this nature, researched and written over an extended period, various forms of assistance, suggestions, advice, and encouragement were offered to me, and I wish to acknowledge these. I am grateful to the University of Nebraska for providing me two grants for research in the area. I benefited immeasurably by the comments of several people who read the final draft: Leslie Dienes, Stephen Fischer-Galati, George Hoffman, György Ránki, and Ivan Volgyes. In the field, the hours spent with the East European geographers are especially memorable: East Germany – H. Reinhard and E. Wegner; Poland – L. Kosiński, J. Kostrowicki, M. Koter, E. Kwiatkowska, S. Leszczycki, T. Lijewski, M. Rośeiszewski, L. Straszewicz, A. Werwicki; Czechoslovakia – K. Ivanička; Hungary – G. Enyedi; Romania – V. Cucu and H. – D. Schmidt; Bulgaria – B. Manev; Yugoslavia – I. Crkvenčić, M. Friganović, V. Klemenčić, B. Milojević, Z. Pepeonik, A. Pushka, M. Radovanović, J. Roglić, R.

Rsumović, and J. Trifunovski. In Vienna, long conversations with Hans Bobek produced inspiration and valuable information about cultural geography in Eastern Europe; J. Breu and E. Lichtenberger also provided ideas. In West Germany, W. Tietze of Wolfsburg offered helpful suggestions about relics to investigate, especially in Romania. I profited from the hospitality of American embassies and consulates in the area and even traveled with Foreign Service officers including especially Glenn Schweitzer in Yugoslavia. In London I benefited from talks with Doreen Warriner and Ian Hamilton. Here in the United States, many geographers and other colleagues made useful suggestions; I recall notably those by Bill Berentsen, George Demko, Jack Fisher, Chauncy Harris, Les Heathcote, Dave Hoosen, Doug Jackson, Karel Kansky, Robert Knoll, Richard Lonsdale, Don Meinig, Jerry Petr, Jacek Romanowski, and Witold Saski. Finally, the editor, James Houston, recommended pertinent changes that have improved the book. Help from all of these sources proved important and beneficial, but in the end the responsibility for the material remains mine.

Unless otherwise cited, the maps and photographs are also mine. In this regard I wish to acknowledge the cartographic assistance of Les Howard. For the typing of the manuscript, I am grateful to Mildred Kohler for her patience and skill.

Without the support of my wife, June, who not only did line-by-line editing of the manuscript but also gave much moral support, this work could never have been completed.

Dean S. Rugg
Lincoln, Nebraska, 1984

1
The problem: development of a landscape methodology

The origins of the idea

The seeds of this book go back to 1954, when I first observed the contrasts between the large, block, enclosed fields of England and the open strips so common in the western part of the European continent. This sharp visual difference in field patterns intrigued me and prompted me to investigate the factors that lie behind this contrast. Since research indicates that both enclosure and strip types of fields had common roots in the medieval open-field system, I carried out field work at Laxton, near Nottingham, England, examining the relic of the three-field pattern that exists there. This analysis of field patterns – patterns so different from those in the United States – led me to the work of W. C. Hoskins, who had been a pioneer in analyzing *The Making of the English Landscape* (1957, 1973). I became excited about the possibilities the landscape offers to understand the spatial and environmental impacts of historical processes.

During a period of six years from 1957 to 1963 while a Foreign Service Officer assigned to the American Embassy in Bonn, Germany, I had additional opportunities to apply the landscape approach. I utilized it indirectly in my doctoral dissertation – a comparison between a German and an American city. During these years in Germany, my official duties often took me to Eastern Europe, where I found the landscape particularly revealing in that historic relics have been less erased by modernization than in many other areas. It seemed to me that these relics represented the marks of earlier social orders that were responsible for geographical change in the area. For example, deep in the mountains of southwestern

Romania is a Baroque spa established by the Austrian imperial government. Visiting it is like stepping back in history a century and viewing a social order that has been preserved indelibly in the landscape. After many travels and observations, therefore, I hypothesized that the East European landscape consists of a palimpsest or a series of cultural layers which, if unraveled, would tell a story of historical, spatial organization in the area. The most recent layer, of course, is the social order of socialism.

These thoughts resulted in a paper, 'Aspects of Change in the Landscape of East-Central and Southeast Europe' (Rugg 1971), which was presented at a geographical conference on this area held in Austin, Texas, in 1969 (Hoffman 1971). The paper created considerable discussion because it raised the question as to whether or not such a thing as a 'socialist landscape' exists. The landscape components analyzed in the paper were traced to processes of nationalism, modernization through industrialization, and socialism. Basically, however, this 1969 paper represented just a starting point in the analysis of East European historical geography, and I began to ask myself what fundamental processes had operated in this area throughout time to transform the landscape. Answers to this question form the main headings to chapters in this book.

Before examining the nature of the landscape concept and the methodology of my approach, however, I must discuss briefly the importance of Eastern Europe, its limits, and the cultures present.

Eastern Europe as a region

The area vaguely referred to as Eastern Europe has no easily defined boundaries and geographically means the eastern portion of the continent (see Fig. 1.1). But how far? Does it include the western part of Russia east to the Urals? As a political notion, the term often is applied to the tier of countries that emerged after the First World War. Personally, with Berend and Ránki (1974a: 1–2), I feel that Eastern Europe is primarily a historical concept, evolving from the peculiar course of its development.

In pursuing this idea, I deal with two somewhat conflicting themes regarding the geographical position of Eastern Europe. First, I emphasize that during the period of German medieval colonization from 950 to 1350 many aspects of Western European civilization – including Christianity, techniques of agriculture and mining, and town law – were diffused into the eastern portion of the continent,

Fig. 1.1   The countries and major cities of Eastern Europe.

creating what Barraclough (1970: 9–10) calls a single European civilization. Second, I point out that during the fifteenth and sixteenth centuries the two portions of Europe diverged as feudalism – especially serfdom – made a belated rise in the east while it was disappearing in the west. The Elbe River became a significant dividing line of economic and social demarcation that has persisted. In this book, I attempt to explain the implication of this paradox – one Europe or two – in terms of the landscape and social change. Little doubt exists in my mind that one of the primary criteria

3

separating Eastern Europe from the rest of the continent was the long persistence of feudal characteristics in this area.

Eastern Europe as a historic concept can be illustrated also by its importance in the modern period (Rugg 1978). Seeds of trouble existed in this zone in the nineteenth century not only because of the nationalistic aims of cultures dominated by imperial powers – Germany, Russia, Austro-Hungary, and Turkey – but also because of the expansionist policies of these states and the conflict with other Great Powers. The most important locus of imperialism was the Balkans where the 'Eastern Question' was paramount: who was going to control the area given up by Turkey, the 'sick man' of Europe? Both Austria and Russia had designs on the Balkans, the latter using its ethnic base to portray itself as a defender of Pan Slavism. Great Britain in its attempts to block both powers was forced to support Turkey. A conflict between the nationalist aspirations of the Serbs and the imperialistic aims of the Austrians eventually set off the First World War. When the Austrian Archduke Ferdinand was assassinated by a Serbian nationalist in Sarajevo, the Austrian ultimatum to Serbia was backed by Germany, while Russia, allied to Britain and France, supported Serbia. Thus, the Great Powers were drawn into a global conflict that started in a relatively unknown city in the Balkans. The First World War thus served to emphasize the geopolitical importance of Eastern Europe.

As early as 1905, a British geographer, Halford Mackinder (1904), pointed out the dangers posed by one or more powers controlling the 'heartland' of Eurasia with its vast resources and space (see Fig. 1.2). Hall (1955: 112) explains that Germany, because of its recent industrialization, seemed to have had more potential for controlling the Heartland, either alone or allied with Russia; the latter power, however, although well located in the center of Eurasia, had appeared to be rather weak at the turn of the century, an evaluation that was confirmed by its defeat by Japan in 1905. Even with the defeat of Germany in the First World War and the weakness of Russia after the Revolution, Mackinder continued to point to the possibilities of German and/or Russian domination of Eurasia. According to him, Eastern Europe, now composed of a tier of independent states, was the key to the control of the vast area because access into it was easiest from this direction – through the German-Slav borderlands.

This prognosis proved a reality in 1939 when Eastern Europe – this time Poland – again became the origin for a world war. The possibility of joint Nazi-Communist control of the Heartland materi-

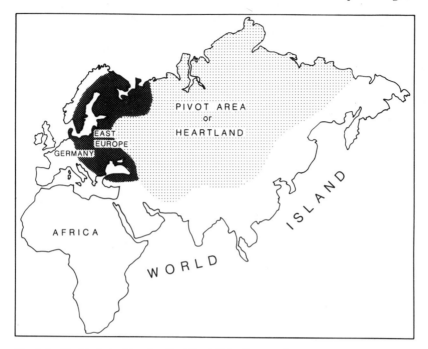

Fig. 1.2 Mackinder's 'Heartland' of the 1920s. Eastern Europe became a key for access from the West after the First World War when a new tier of countries separated Russia from Germany.

alized in 1939 when these two powers became allies. Later, when the Germans broke this pact and invaded Russia, it appeared that the Heartland would become Nazi. After the Second World War, however, the Soviet Union established control of the Heartland including the western approaches, which were secured by supporting communist governments in Eastern Europe. The Iron Curtain, descending on Europe, divided Germany and the rest of the continent, separating western and eastern parts and forcing a Cold War with the West. Thus, Mackinder's warning had come true, although the domination was not by Germany, as he had feared, but by the Soviet Union.

Eastern Europe, therefore, has played an important role in the political development of the world, especially in the twentieth century, which has witnessed the start of two world wars here; in addition, for several decades now, this area has served as a meeting place of two vastly different ideological systems. Europe, which

5

exhibited signs of unity in the Middle Ages when German colonists from the west had established patterns of continental spatial organization, is now divided by the Iron Curtain in a manner new to history. Perhaps most significant of all is the continued influence of an outside power over small states. Eastern Europe poses a question now found in other parts of the world – Southeast Asia, the Near East, Africa, and Central America: can small states exist in a world without being catspaws between the Great Powers (Wanklyn 1941: 27)?

Having established the general importance of Eastern Europe as a historical concept, I must now define the area more precisely for purposes of this study. The definitions of the region are many and varied. Topographically, the grain runs east and west in the northern portion of the area complicating north–south demarcation. Because European Russia is sometimes called Eastern Europe, the term East-Central Europe was, and is, used; most often, however, the term Eastern Europe has been applied to the area where ethnic groups have been most mixed, leading to use of the term 'Shatter Belt' (East 1961). Just after the First World War, Unstead (1923) called it the 'zone of political change', largely because of the new political states that had shattered the old imperial map. In 1941, Wanklyn referred to the area as the 'Eastern Marchlands', which she defined as a borderland region of small states sandwiched between large ones. This is the area to which I devote my attention in this book. Specifically, I include the eight communist states west of the Soviet Union: Albania, Bulgaria, Czechoslovakia, East Germany, Hungary, Poland, Romania, and Yugoslavia. At the present time, they remain clearly separated from states in Western Europe by an Iron Curtain, although admittedly this curtain has rusted a bit in the case of Yugoslavia. Seven of these states emerged in this area after the First World War, when the prewar empires were carved up. I add East Germany because its orientation now is to the East, but I omit Greece in the south and the Baltic states – Estonia, Latvia, and Lithuania – in the north; Greece's orientation has always been western, while the Baltic states played only a short role as independent states before the Second World War.

Eastern Europe as defined is a zone of about 500,000 square miles inhabited by some 135 million people. In comparable terms, it is about the size of the tier of seven Great Plains-Midwest states composed of North and South Dakota, Nebraska, Kansas, Minnesota, Iowa, and Missouri. However, the American area includes less

than 20 million people. A much higher population density, then, characterizes Eastern Europe, and, indeed, rural overpopulation there has been a persistent problem.

In confining Eastern Europe to eight communist states located west of the Soviet Union, I must consider that part of Russia has historically been viewed as East European. Although I realize that many people hold to the somewhat deterministic idea of Europe extending to the Urals (Parker 1960), I feel that the cultural frontier of the Soviet state holds much more significance than the physical barrier of the Urals, since the latter only separates two parts of one state. Anyone who has visited this part of the world cannot help sensing a different atmosphere when crossing the Soviet frontier; to the west is Europe, to the east is Asia. The difference is more than religion where Catholics in areas like Poland are contiguous to the Orthodox Church of Russia. The difference is also more than language, for Slavic is shared except in Hungary and Romania. Although the change in railroad gauge – from 4ft 8½in in the west to 5ft in the Soviet Union – appears to be a minor inconvenience, the secrecy to which the Russians have resorted in disguising this transition at the fifteen or so transloading stations along their frontier symbolizes an attitude or way of thinking that is very unusual.[1]

However, even beyond these differences between the Soviet Union and Eastern Europe is the matter of orientation: the countries west of this line have long looked westward. German is a common *lingua franca* in the area, and French and Italian are used in places like Romania and Albania, respectively. Many intellectuals of the past studied or resided in the west, for example, Chopin, Liszt, Paderewsky, and the stimuli for many of their cultural contributions came from this area. The East European states, moreover, have strong ties to America through the millions of emigrants. Although Russia has had long contacts with cultures to their west, especially now through a common ideology, a suspicion of the West – whether under czar or commissar – remains strong. To me, therefore, Europe extends from Brest (France) to Brest or Brześć (Poland)!

Having delimited the area, I also wish to mention the variety of cultures responsible for the term 'Shatter Belt'. Table 1.1 shows twenty-four different ethnic groups associated historically with the area. Of these, only the Jews lacked a territorial base with which they have been linked, e.g. Poles with the Vistula-Warta River valleys or Hungarians with the Middle Danube. As frontiers between these groups have expanded and contracted over 2000 years, the number

7

Table 1.1 Eastern Europe: Matrix of cultural contacts

	L	R	B	U	P	P-G	J	Cz	Sl	A	H	I	Slo	Cr	Se	Bos	T	Ro	Mo	Ma	Al	Bu	Gr	By
Lithuanians																								
Russians	X																							
Belorussians	X																							
Ukrainians	X	X																						
Poles	X	X	X																					
Prussians–Germans	X	X	X	X																				
Jews	X	X	X	X	X																			
Czechs	X			X	X	X																		
Slovaks		X	X	X	X	X																		
Austrians		X	X	X	X	X	X	X	X															
Hungarians		X		X	X	X		X	X	X														
Italians						X				X		X												
Slovenians						X				X	X	X												
Croats					X	X		X	X	X	X	X	X	X										
Serbs					X	X				X	X	X	X	X	X									
Bosnians						X				X	X	X	X	X	X									
Turks		X		X		X	X			X	X	X		X	X	X	X							
Romanians		X		X	X	X				X	X	X		X	X	X	X	X						
Montenegrins						X						X			X		X		X					
Macedonians						X					X	X			X		X		X	X				
Albanians						X				X		X			X		X		X	X	X			
Bulgarians						X	X			X	X			X	X	X	X	X	X	X	X			
Greeks		X													X		X			X	X	X		
Byzantines		X				X						X			X					X		X	X	
	7	11	5	8	8	16	3	3	3	10	8	10	3	5	9	3	6	2	3	4	2	2	1	

of contiguous contacts between groups obviously has been responsible for considerable interaction, much of which resulted in conflict. In measuring these *contiguous* contacts by finding common boundaries in historical atlases, I discovered 132 between the 24 groups. These contacts are ranked and, unsurprisingly, 7 of the top 8 represent imperial powers external to the area, for example, Austria. Forty-one of these contacts represent absorption of one culture by another – the Turks and Austrians being most important as 'absorbers'. Indeed, the existence of a 'multinational environment' throughout the region for much of its history forms the theme of Chapter 5. After Hungary, Serbia ranks second as the indigenous group with the most contacts, and Poland is third. The mosaic of twenty-four cultures is further intensified if languages and religions are included. Twelve of the groups speak languages significantly different from any of the others, a fact that certainly has hindered interaction. Several lines of religious cleavage run through the area to further fragment it – most especially Orthodox-Catholic and Catholic-Protestant, while Islam further confuses the pattern.

This fragmentation of cultures and the political instability that has accompanied it account for the common use of the term 'Shatter Belt' for Eastern Europe. Since 1945, however, the domination of the area by the Soviet Union has provided an era of stability that contrasts with that of the past. Nevertheless, fragmentation, including nationalism, still exists.

Having discussed the importance of Eastern Europe, delimited the region, and mentioned some of its characteristics of fragmentation, we now turn to the landscape concept and my methodology in this book.

Applying the landscape concept to Eastern Europe

The landscape represents the tangible imprint of human spatial and ecological processes on the earth. This concept has had a long history of use in geography because it fits easily into three of the main paradigms of the field: (1) the landscape reflects the *relationships* between people and their environment, one of the traditions of geography since the time of the Greeks; (2) the landscape also refers to a *region*, either a unique portion of the earth's surface or one that repeats itself in other areas, e.g. an Alpine landscape; and (3) the landscape can portray the components of a *spatial* system. In all of these approaches, the focus remains on the paradigm itself, although

9

variations can occur as shown by the examples given in the table below.

People-land relations	Region	Space
Imprint of central authority: Whittlesey (1935).	Regional impact of a religion: Bjorklund (1964).	Landscape as system: Curry (1964).
Landscape assessment for recreation: Leopold (1969).	Perception through mental maps: Lynch (1960).	Diffusion of the court-house square: Price (1968).
Landscape tastes: Lowenthal and Prince (1965).	Relics and social change in Nova Scotia: Watson (1959).	Chance and the landscape: Curry (1967).

Only one serious attempt was made to make the landscape itself a main paradigm in geography. Around the turn of the twentieth century, a German geographer, Otto Schlüter (1906: 24, 27) led a group of 'landscape purists' who, in trying to isolate research objects unique to geography, focused on material forms perceptible to the physical senses. Although this approach exerted considerable influence on the field of geography in the early part of this century, it remains a subparadigm largely because the narrow scope excludes studies unrelated to perceptible form, e.g. a political territory, social group, or traffic movement.

Any current landscape, of course, is actually a historical document, and it is this characteristic that fascinates me. The landscape holds an accumulation of relics from different periods. In some areas, many of these relics have been erased, while in others, like Eastern Europe, they are numerous enough to tell a story if only we can read the code. I began to look on the East European landscape as a palimpsest of culture layers – in the words of Wagner (1972: 102) 'preserving the traces of untold assertions of human will and spirit, one inscription on another, half illegible' – with the feeling that such relics offer the opportunity to understand the spatial and environmental impacts of historical processes in this part of Europe.

In developing a workable methodological model, I started with the landscape itself, using visible relics as keys to the understanding

of Eastern Europe. I rejected the sequent occupance approach – a standard method used by historical geographers – because cross-sections in time interrupt what I feel were continuous historical processes that overlapped in time. But what processes should I use? It seemed logical that a listing of the major landscape relics would permit the isolating of the historical processes that caused them. In other words, my classification emerges from the data, i.e. the relics. Using this approach, I selected four processes whose environmental and spatial impacts contributed to the making of the East European landscape. Superimposed on this palimpsest of four landscapes is the present one of socialism. Although one may argue that these processes are not exactly parallel, I feel that they allow me to explain better the historical changes in spatial organization and the landscape.

German medieval colonization

Among the most impressive series of relics from the Middle Ages in Eastern Europe are the forms of settlement – villages, mining communities, churches and monasteries, towns – established by German colonists in the years 950–1350. These colonists moved into the area as corporate groups, often at the invitation of Slavs or Hungarians, bringing with them innovations in agriculture, mining, commerce, industry, and town law. German colonization, then, represents the first process of spatial organization that transformed the landscape.

Feudalism

Feudalism actually comprised a social order based on precise and reciprocal obligations between crown, lord, vassal, and peasant. The manorial system functioned as a related institution. After 1350, feudalism in Eastern Europe became dominated by serfdom. The lord helped to restrict social change in the area for some 600 years, leaving his indelible mark on the landscape. The ubiquitous landscape relics of manor house, peasant village and urban palace (of the nobility) in Eastern Europe serve as keys to this second process of spatial organization.

Multinationalism

Overlapping the processes of German colonization and feudalism is the process of political organization. Study of the historical spatial pattern of this organization reveals that for some 2000 years the political environment of Eastern Europe has been multinational.

11

Within the restricted confines of this area, twenty-four cultural groups intermixed, creating the inevitable situation that whichever political units emerged would be multinational. Even today, Yugoslavia is composed of several national groups. Obviously, within such an environment some cultures, especially the more powerful ones that were external to the region like Austria and Turkey, came to dominate others. Indeed, these multinational states – empires, kingdoms, or feudal oligarchies – controlled spatial organization and influenced the landscape of Eastern Europe for much of its history.

Nationalism

This process of landscape change is recent, since ethnic aspects of nationalism only emerged in the nineteenth century in Eastern Europe, a time when individual cultures within empires began to think of themselves as collective groups with similar characteristics of language and custom. The nation–state as a concept began to break out of multinational frameworks in the nineteenth century when the Poles created the Congress state and when certain Balkan nations achieved degrees of independence from the Turkish Empire. Nationalism in Eastern Europe reached new heights after 1918 when the entire area became organized on the basis of nation–states, causing some cities to be transformed as they became capitals and new spatial patterns of economic organization to be developed. National states, therefore, began to transform the landscape and certain relics remain to tell the story.

Socialism

The most recent process of landscape transformation occurred after the Second World War with the establishment of socialist regimes in Eastern Europe and the reorganization of agriculture, industry, and settlement in line with Marxist-Leninist principles. Although arguments exist as to the actual influence of this communist ideology on economy and landscape, there is no doubt that the landscape has changed drastically during the long post-1945 period of stability provided by the influence of the Soviet Union.

A time model (Fig. 1.3) illustrates the varying ways in which space was organized politically in Eastern Europe as a result of four of the processes – feudalism, multinationalism, nationalism, and socialism. This model attempts to show the diversity of cultural groups represented within political units at different times. During much of

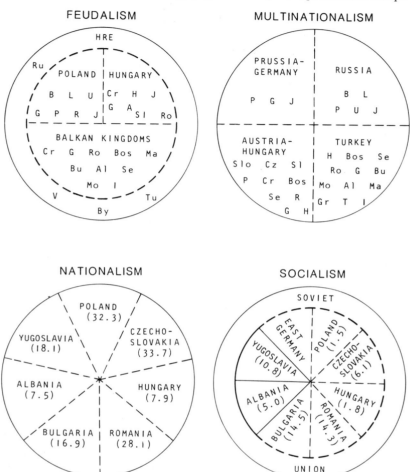

Fig. 1.3 Four major periods of political organization and the diversity of cultural groups represented within each. This diversity has led to the term Shatter Belt. Abbreviations are clarified in Table 1.1. The numbers in parentheses indicate the percentages of the national populations that are minorities.

the early feudal period, Poland, Hungary, and some Balkan powers exhibited degrees of independence in the face of pressure from German, Byzantine, Venetian, Russian, and Turkish empires. Later, the multinational empires of Prussia-Germany, Austria, Russia, and Turkey absorbed the different cultural groups. Only in the nineteenth century did nationalism really appear, as nation-states broke from the

13

old imperial molds; this process continued more dramatically after the First World War, when a new tier of states emerged in Eastern Europe. Finally, today, these states exhibit varying degrees of resistance to pressure from the newest external power, the Soviet Union.

An example of the changes in political organization of space is provided by Poland: this state exhibited considerable power in the Middle Ages before being partitioned by three empires in the latter part of the eighteenth century; after 1918 the state reappeared, only to be partitioned again during the Second World War; finally, as a communist state, Poland tries to preserve its independence in the face of Soviet dominance.

These historical processes overlap in time. For example, multi-nationalism extends through some 2000 years of the region's history, while feudalism overlaps with German colonization and nationalism. Even today nationalism extends into the socialist era, as Poland, Romania, and Yugoslavia illustrate. Thus, I feel that the processes selected permit me to deal with the relics encountered in East Europe, regardless of their position in time. The methodological model for the book now includes three categories; Landscape relics→Cultures→Processes.

This model is still incomplete, however, unless it also takes into account the ideologies that lie behind the processes of landscape change. I define ideology in a broad sense as Knight (1971: 386) does: the complex of values, beliefs, and sentiments that bind together members of a society and so differentiate them from other societies. An ideology provides the behavioural framework for the manner in which a cultural group perceives its environment, the resources it develops from this environment, and the kinds of spatial organization it involves. A few geographers, like Kniffen (1936), focus on the role of ideology, but for the most part this factor in landscape analysis has been slighted. Kniffen, for example, feels that culture is composed of historical ideas which are expressed geographically in the landscape, e.g. regional variation of house types in Louisiana. I am motivated in turn to find, if possible, some of the ideas or ideology that were behind the decision-makers in Eastern Europe – German colonist, feudal lord, multinational ruler, nationalist group, and socialist party – who were responsible for the five processes of landscape change. This concept, therefore, should even include the perceptions of these decision-makers. As Mikesell (1968: 578) emphasizes, the features of a landscape may be explained most adequately not by their form or function, but by the idealized images

14

and visual prejudices of human groups or individuals. Ideology, then, becomes an additional component to the model: Landscape relics→Cultures→Ideology→Processes.

However, this model still lacks one other component. My strong feeling is that the landscape relics not only reflect the ideology of decision-makers in different eras, but also the social change that was initiated or resisted. Social change is defined by Rogers and Shoemaker (1971: 7) as the process by which alteration occurs in the structure and function of a social system. Explaining social change seems to be one of the common denominators of the social sciences and even of the humanities. As a social scientist/geographer, my particular interest concerns the relationship between a society's spatial-ecological organization and social change. Also, like Jackson (1980: 115) I feel that one of the significant aspects of the landscape is that it makes visible the social order of the time. Thus, the relics of manor houses in Eastern Europe today show not only the former presence of a feudal social order, but also the degree to which such an order resisted social change. Under socialism, Marxist ideology and social change are closely linked as seen in the transformation of peasants into peasant-workers, a process that is visible in the landscape. As a consequence, a final component – social change – is added to the model, which now appears as: Landscape relics→Cultures→Ideology→Processes→Social Change→Landscape. The model actually has gone full cycle, for it starts with the relics as clues to processes that cultures with particular ideologies have used to transform society and produce the present landscape.

One other aspect of the landscape concept remains to be clarified – the notion of system. For the most part, the starting point of landscape studies is an individual form – the farm house, village structure, city boulevard, and so forth. Yet, these forms are parts of settlement systems designed by a variety of cultural groups throughout time. The geographer, however, can see only certain forms within the system and never all of them at one time. Still, in my mind, the overall system – its components and their spatial relationship to each other – must be considered in a study focused on the landscape. In Eastern Europe, an absolute state like Austria organized an imperial system that is still recognizable from relics left in the landscape. In contrast, a communist state like Czechoslovakia has been responsible for not only the mass transformation of the landscape through collectivization, but also attempts to manipulate greater balance between regions and settlement components. A geographer has an obligation to look

at landscape elements as part of a system and this includes not only the structure of the individual components, but also their locational interrelationships.

The challenge posed in this study, therefore, is immense, especially in the restricted length of books in the 'World Landscape' series. However, I feel that a focus on the five processes, each examined in a separate chapter, gives the most satisfactory framework for an analysis of the East European landscape. In the first part of each chapter, I examine the background of the process in terms of cultures, ideologies, and social changes. Of necessity, such background includes considerable history, at least enough to explain the effects of the processes on spatial organization. Then in the last part of each chapter I analyze those relics that still remain in the landscape to reflect this process. Although these relics serve as clues to the processes of landscape change and thus stand first in my model, I analyze them last as components of a series of complete landscapes that evolved under these processes.

Notes

1. At the frontier, individual cars of each train are uncoupled, lifted, and fitted with the proper undercarriage. In the 1960s, window blinds in passenger cars were closed and locked to prevent observation of this procedure; whether this is still the case is uncertain.

2
Physical geography and cultures

As a Shatter Belt of cultures, Eastern Europe has exhibited degrees
of weakness that led to exploitation by external powers. In addition,
conflicts existed between cultures within the region. We should now
try to fix these cultures in place, that is, examine the nature of their
habitat. To do this, the physical geography of the area is analyzed
as a setting for these cultures, which, in organizing space in Eastern
Europe, left their mark on the landscape.

According to Whittlesey (1944: 2), each state crystallizes around
a core area that fosters integration with other areas. This core
generally possesses fertile agricultural land, resources, and accessibility to other regions. Such an area may persist for hundreds of years
as the ecumene or center of settlement or it may shift with time as
historical forces affect the particular culture. For example, the historic
core area of France is the Paris basin, which remains as such today.
In the United States, however, the original core lay along the
Atlantic coast where the thirteen colonies developed, but today the
ecumene is a large manufacturing-agricultural region extending from
New York to Chicago. Although the delimiting of core areas for
different states can be an intriguing exercise, political geographers
point out that it often leads to rather sterile results unless it is utilized
to analyze the regionalization of cultures within a physical environment. I shall use the concept in this way for Eastern Europe. Certain
cultures here remained associated with regional habitats for hundreds
of years, while others shifted their locales in response to historical
circumstances.

The map depicts both the primary terrain features of Eastern
Europe and (by number) a primary city, often the capital, within the

17

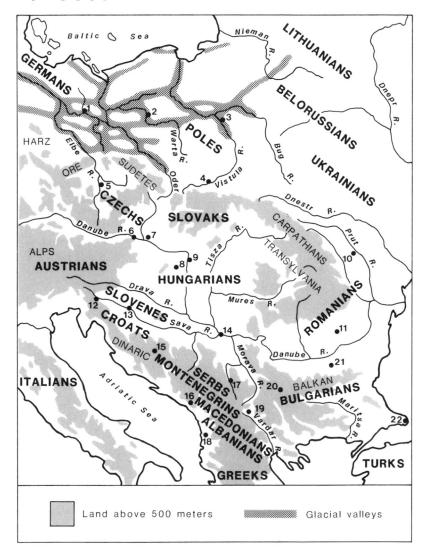

Fig. 2.1 The terrain regions of Eastern Europe and their associations with the core areas of cultural groups. Numbers refer to major cities mentioned in the text.

core area of different cultural groups (see Fig. 2.1). It is obvious that little correlation exists between terrain and cultural groups. In the north, the European plain is a dominant feature of the landscape and the homeland of several groups; barriers aligned north–south are

lacking and Germans contested with Slavs for living space. In the south, mountains and basins compartmentalized the region and either facilitated dominance of one group over another or separated members of the same group; thus, Hungary has prevailed in the central Danube basin while the Carpathian Mountains separate Romanians. The primary gateways into Eastern Europe are related to the Danube River and its tributaries. Vienna (No. 6 on the map) stands at the western entry point, while the gorges of the Danube above the Iron Gate reef form an eastern portal where the river cuts through extensions of the Carpathian Mountains. On the north, the upper portion of the Oder River provides a route between the Sudetes and the Carpathians. Finally, on the south, the Morava–Vardar routeway witnessed invasions of Byzantine and Turkish forces into the heart of Eastern Europe.

The coastline of the Baltic Sea shows a differentiation between west and east. To the west (now the area of East Germany), a *Bodden* or inlet coast exists where offshore islands linked by sandspits protect the shoreline and ports like Rostock and Szezecin (Stettin). To the east, a *Haff* or lagoon coast is present where ocean currents have formed long sandbars that protect ports like Gdánsk (Danzig) and Kaliningrad (Königsberg).

The regions

North European plain

The north European plain in Eastern Europe varies in width from 200 to 300 miles (322–483 km). Although most of the plain is less than 300 ft (91 m) above sea level, it is far from level or uniform. The terrain features are largely of glacial origin and consist of four north – south zones (see Fig. 2.1). In the Middle Ages, a dense forest covered all of these zones, but today much of the original cover is gone; the dominant vegetation now consists of planted pine trees.

Behind the Baltic coast lies the first zone, a broad belt of ground and terminal moraines made up of unstratified glacial deposits of marginal fertility. The chief feature is the Baltic Ridge, a series of hills that extends in an arc from Denmark to Lithuania. In the north-east area of Poland, these morainic deposits have blocked the drainage, creating the Masurian Lake district.

South of this morainic zone is a second zone of stratified deposits of sand and gravel (called *Geest*) laid down by melt water draining

Photo 2.1   The sandy glacial soils in East Germany and Poland are often used for the cultivation of rye and potatoes.

from the glaciers to the north (see Photo 2.1). These infertile deposits are often associated with crops of rye and potatoes that do well on soils derived from these parent materials. Pine trees and heath are also characteristic. The margravate or principality of Brandenburg, which became an electorate of the Holy Roman Empire and later the core area of Prussia, is located in this area. Not for nothing was it derisively called 'the sand-box of the Empire'.

These areas of *Geest* are cut up into low islands of sandy terrain by the *Urstromtäler* or great valleys, a third glacial feature of this north European plain (see Fig. 2.1). These broad but shallow valleys represent the locale of great rivers of melt water that flowed along the front of the glacial lobes as they advanced and retreated in Eastern Europe over a period of a million years. At the close of this period, north-flowing rivers re-established themselves, often following portions of these valleys. In other places, the rivers are only broad, marshy troughs which have been transformed to canals linking the rivers – Elbe, Oder, Warta, Vistula, and Niemen. These poorly drained valley soils are often used as pasture for livestock.

Finally, a fourth zone north of the Ore, Sudetes, and Carpathian

Mountains is only indirectly related to glaciation. This zone is the Börde, a fertile plain bordered by mountains where fine wind-blown material called *loess* was deposited at the end of the glacial period. Soils derived from this water-retentive material are the most fertile in Eastern Europe and are often marked by crops of wheat and sugar beets.

Two of the major cultures of Eastern Europe – the Germans and the Poles – had core areas that developed on this plain. To the west is Brandenburg, the core area of Prussia and later of a unified Germany in the nineteenth century. In the medieval period, Brandenburg was a *Mark* (march), a frontier province established by the Holy Roman Empire as a bastion against Slavic groups to the east. The *Mark* was called Brandenburg, the same name as the capital and major town in the district; later, however, the capital was shifted to Berlin (1 on Fig. 2.1) as a result of the latter's superiority as a focus of natural routes. Berlin's site lies where the sandy uplands of *Geest* most closely approach each other, providing both an easier crossing of the damp valleys and well-drained locations for later expansion of the city.

The Hohenzollern rulers made Berlin their capital in the sixteenth century, utilizing its possibilities as a transport focus to form a great empire. Note on Fig. 2.1 how the glacial valleys focus in the vicinity of Berlin. First, Berlin intercepted north – south road traffic between Silesia and the port of Hamburg and between Thuringia and the port of Stettin. Second, the opening of the Havel – Spree canal along a glacial valley in the seventeenth century linked Berlin with the Elbe and Oder River systems. Third, the expanding railroad network focused on Berlin when Prussia incorporated Silesia, Pomerania, and West Prussia. Finally, the belt of minerals and rich *loess* soils to the south of Berlin contributed to its growth.

The Poles are a second cultural group of Eastern Europe with a rather large core in the north European plain. Unlike the Germans, however, the Poles utilized several centers, reflecting the importance of regionalism in Polish history and competition between the principalities of Great Poland, Little Poland, and Masovia. The Polish core area is linked with the Vistula River, a chief organizing force in the thousand-year history of Poland. The words of the Polish national anthem embody this focus: 'We shall cross the Vistula, the Warta . . . We shall remain Poles.'

The earliest Polish centers were in Wielkopolska or Great Poland, with the seat of kings and archbishops at Gniezno. The political

capital was later shifted to nearby Poznań (2 on Fig. 2.1), located on the Warta River but accessible to the Vistula by the glacial valley of the Notec River. Later, the capital shifted to Cracow (4) in Malopolska or Little Poland, a district on the upper Vistula River. This site, marked by a great castle on the bluff overlooking the river, was well suited to control the movement of people through the Moravian Gate between the Sudetes and Carpathian Mountains. However, Cracow's location became increasingly unsuitable as a capital when Poland's territorial expansion, blocked by the Germans to the west, became oriented to the east. When Poland and Lithuania joined as one state in the sixteenth century, Warsaw (3) in Masovia on the middle Vistula River was chosen as a new capital, well situated as a crossing point on the main route from central Europe to Moscow.

Bohemian uplands

Bohemia, the core area of the Czech culture in Eastern Europe, is a basin surrounded on all sides by uplands: the Ore and Sudetes Mountains on the north and the Bohemian Forest and Moravian Uplands to the south and east (see Fig. 2.1). These forested uplands are termed *Mittelgebirge* or middle mountains (2500–4500 ft [762–1372 m]), a generic type of forested upland that is found throughout central Europe. They represent older mountains that were worn down by erosion over long periods and then uplifted as blocks along fault lines. In the center of the basin is Prague (5), the thousand-year-old capital of the Czechs. The city benefited early from a location on routes from Nürnberg to Cracow and from Vienna to Leipzig. Furthermore, the northern part of the basin possesses fertile loessial soils. Bohemia is drained by the navigable Elbe River which provides a direct link with Germany. Protected by the encircling mountains, the Czechs formed the westermost bastion of Slavs in Europe, a location that allowed considerable western influence to penetrate into the area. Czech history has been linked over centuries with that of Germanic peoples. With its minerals and coal, it was (with Moravia) the chief industrial district of the Holy Roman Empire and later of the Austrian Empire. Yet, the Czechs frequently tried to separate themselves from this Germanic influence. For instance, the famous composer, Bedřich Smetana, actually left Prague for a time to rid himself of the Germanized atmosphere, but later returned to write his famous 'Moldau', symbolizing the river

of Prague and national feeling. The piece could be called 'Vltava', the Czech name of this river.

Basins associated with the Danube River and its tributaries

In the north, the European plain and the Bohemian uplands are well demarcated physical regions in Eastern Europe. However, to the south the basis for classification of landforms becomes complex. I will utilize a series of basins associated with the Danube River as it flows from west to east through the area (see Fig. 2.1).

The first of these basins is the Alföld or Great Hungarian Plain, which occupies the heart of Eastern Europe. Bordered by mountain ranges on all sides, the Alföld has been occupied by Hungarian settlement for a thousand years. Although a plain, it is far from uniform in its physical characteristics with four major types of terrain, each of which is reflected in the type of land use observed today. One type of terrain consists of fertile *loess* deposits similar to those found in southern Poland. In contrast, however, is a second type – the infertile areas of sand. At the close of the glacial period, the Danube River, heavily swollen by glacial melt water, deposited large areas of sand on the plain. These deposits were later re-formed by the wind into a series of dunes elongated northwest to southeast in the area between the Danube and the Tisza Rivers. Another sandy area occurs along the upper Tisza River in the vicinity of Nyíregyháza.

The other two terrain types of the Plain consist of *puszta* wastelands and scattered areas of poor drainage, both related to microrelief differences in the plain. From volcanic source rocks at the margins of the plain, sodium and chlorine salts are introduced into the ground water of the area drained by the Tisza River. Because of the low gradient of this stream, the concentration of salts is high and the water table is relatively close to the surface. Where this water table is less than two meters below the surface, the dry climate of this enclosed basin causes capillary action to precipitate the salts to the surface where they harden to become a cement-like surface incapable of cultivation (a *puszta*). This low gradient also produced many areas of poor drainage which were corrected in part through reclamation schemes carried out on the Tisza system in the nineteenth century. Such schemes led to the straightening of channels and the lowering of water tables, thereby improving the overall drainage.

Numerous oxbows, however, were cut off, leaving areas of poor drainage as relics of an earlier hydrologic system.

A fascinating aspect of the Alföld today is the pattern of land use which reflects these micro-terrain differences. The *loess* areas are dominated by crops of wheat, corn, and sugar beets, which require the fertile soils that are generated on this parent material. On the other hand, the sterile sands are utilized for rye, potatoes, or fruit trees. The salt-encrusted areas are grazed by sheep or cattle as evidenced in the famous Hortobágy *puszta* west of Debrecen (see Photo 2.2). Finally, the damp areas of poor drainage are mostly in meadow, pasture, forest, or marsh. This rapid spatial change in the landscape of the Alföld provides great interest for the geographer because it illustrates geographic aspects of hydrologic processes.

Two other major areas of Hungary consist of Transdanubia to the west of the Danube River and portions of the Carpathian Mountains that lie to the north of the Great Hungarian Plain. Transdanubia is an area of plateaus, hills, and valleys, where remnants of beech and oak forests are common. The highest portion is the east – west Bakony ridge north of Lake Balaton that includes the famous bauxite deposits. In the extreme northwest lies the Little Alföld, a *loess*-covered alluvial plain adjacent to the Danube River. The second major area – Carpathian outliers north of the Great Hungarian Plain – includes a series of higher ridges, often forested, that contain coal and iron resources supporting heavy industry near the city of Miskolc. Nearby are volcanic hills like the Tokaj whose lower slopes are covered with vineyards. The interdependence of mountain and plain, formerly facilitated by Hungarian control of the upper courses of the rivers flowing into the Alföld, is now hindered by the national frontiers with Czechoslovakia and Romania.

The Hungarians moved into the plain of the middle Danube River in the ninth century, dislodging Slavic groups in the process, and since then have dominated the heart of Eastern Europe. Much of Hungarian culture reflects its association with this Danubian region. The early core area was in the hilly region west of the Danube with a capital located at Székesfehérvár (8) and the religious center at the town of Esztergom. Three centuries later the capital was moved to Buda (9), a defensive site on the western bluffs overlooking the Danube. The islands in the river served as defensive features as well as crossing points. From this location the Hungarians extended their control eastward across the Alföld to include the bordering mountain or plain areas of what are now Slovakia, Romania, and Croatia.

Photo 2.2   The sweep well and *Csikós* (cowboy) are still to be seen on the Great Hungarian Plain, as shown here in the Hortobágy *puszta*.

Indeed, much of Hungarian history is marked by the attempts to coordinate the complementary activities of mountain and plain, regions which were occupied by a variety of cultural groups. As the eastern part of the Alfold became more secure, the city of Pest arose opposite Buda as a commercial collecting and distributing point. During the Turkish occupation the capital was moved to Pozsony (Bratislava) (7), an area to the north near Vienna that remained free. Finally, in the nineteenth century Buda and Pest merged as the capital of the Hungarian nation and later a state.

The second series of basins associated with the Danube River includes the Wallachian plain and the Moldavian tablelands. The former was a Black Sea gulf that is now entirely filled by river deposits from the Transylvanian Alps to the north. Near these mountains, the Wallachian plain is cut up by rivers, but to the south near

the Danube River it is quite flat. Moving east into the rolling steppe of Moldavia, one encounters an increasingly semiarid climate. *Loess* covers both Wallachia and Moldavia, which have constituted the core areas and granaries of the Romanian culture group. Both were principalities in the Middle Ages with capitals at Tîrgovişte, and Bucharest (11) for Wallachia and Iaşi (10) for Moldavia. Eventually, Bucharest became the capital of a united country because the city was best situated for access over low passes of the Carpathian Mountains to Transylvania, where Romanians also lived.

The mountains bordering the Hungarian and Romanian plains have played a significant role because they have been controlled by cultures based in the plains. In the north and east the Carpathian Mountains constitute a long arc of forested ridges (3500–7500 ft [1067–2286 m]) that extend from Vienna to the Iron Gate of the Danube River, a distance of over 1000 miles (1609 km). The forests range from oak on the lower slopes to beech on middle levels and to conifers at highest elevations. Extensive glaciation similar to that of the Alps has occurred only in the Tatra Mountains, whose general elevation is lower than the Alps (see Photo 2.3). In the north the Carpathians have served as the homeland or core area of the Slovaks, although their major cities of Nitra and Bratislava (7) are located on the southwestern margins. To the east, within the bend of the Carpathians, lies the forested hill region of Transylvania, where Romanian, German, and Hungarian cultures have interacted. Partly from the orientation of drainage to the west, however, the Hungarians have dominated the area for long periods. The cities of Kolozsvár (Cluj) and Marosvásárhely (Tîrgu Mureş) have relics of Hungarian origin.

Mountains and plains of the Balkans

The mountainous Balkan Peninsula forms the fourth major physical region of Eastern Europe. The main ranges are the Dinaric Mountains that parallel the coast of the Adriatic Sea and the Balkan – Rhodope complex that dominates the present country of Bulgaria. Between these two ranges lie the lower mountains of Serbia (see Fig. 2.1).

The Dinaric chain, world famous because of extensive land forms (karst) associated with the solution of limestone, extends as an unbroken barrier for 350 miles (563 km) between Italy and Albania and has been a strong factor in the history of the Balkan Peninsula.

Photo 2.3 The Tatra Mountains of northeastern Czechoslovakia, part of the Carpathian range, exhibit the sharp peaks and other features of glaciation in contrast to the generally forested ridges of adjacent sections.

These mountains present an imposing sight when approaching the Adriatic coastline by sea, for they rise abruptly from the water, leaving little flat land. Instead, terraces built over hundreds of years cover the slopes in many areas and produce corn, olives, and grapes.

This mountain range, composed of a series of high limestone ridges called *planina*, varies in elevation from 4000 to 6500 ft. (1219–1981 m). Despite high precipitation, the landscape appears barren because water quickly seeps underground and is not available to support vegetation. The water dissolves the karst to create small sinkholes (*dolina*) or larger depressions (*uvala*) on the surface, while, underneath, the water excavates large caverns like Postojna near Ljubljana and forms a subterranean drainage system (see Photo 2.4) The primary valleys are called *polja* (singular *polje*) – broad, flat-

27

Photo 2.4 A sinkhole (*doline*) in the karst (limestone) topography of western Yugoslavia. Note the use of terraces to hold soil and crops of cabbage, corn, and potatoes.

floored depressions caused by tectonic forces and modified by solution. The *polje* is floored with a red soil, called *terra rossa*, which represents the insoluble material in the limestone that is deposited by the underground streams as they emerge to traverse the basins before going below ground again. In addition to the Croatians, the only cultural group directly associated with the Dinaric Mountains is the Montenegrins, whose core area historically has been the *polje* in which the ancient capital of Cetinje (16) is located.

Farther south along the Adriatic coast, the mountains change to a north – south orientation and the coastal plain widens. This stretch of mountainous coast comprises the homeland of the Albanians whose capitals have shifted from places like Shkodër (Scutari) and Krujë to Tirana (18). This plain was once a fertile granary for classical Rome, but hundreds of years of timber cutting on the adjacent mountains for fuel and ships plus overgrazing by livestock led to loss of cover. Gradually, the streams silted up, overflowed, and created marshes. This unhealthy environment became a wasteland and malaria became endemic. After the Second World War the communist government successfully undertook reclamation projects.

On the inner margins of the Dinaric chain the limestone topography gives way to hills and mountains of different structure where forests are more prevalent. In this belt of rugged topography several Slavic groups had their original homelands. In the north the Slovenes settled in Carniola, a former *Mark* of the Holy Roman Empire, that is centered on the Ljubljana basin (12) of the Austrian Alps. To the east in the hill country flanking the upper Sava River is Zagreb (13), the capital of the Croatians. Farther south in the heart of the mountains lies the core area of the Bosnians, who had capitals at Jajce and Sarajevo (15).

The original core area of the Serbs also lay in the inner mountains of the Balkans, specifically at Raš (17) in the rough country of the upper Ibar River. This site was located close to the important north – south route of the Morava – Vardar Rivers and just north of the Kosovo and Metojiha basins – major settlement areas of the southern Balkans – which are connected to the Adriatic coast via the Drin River gap. Later in the Middle Ages the Serbian capital was moved to Skopje (19) in Macedonia. However, in the fourteenth century Serbia came under Ottoman Turk domination, which lasted until the nineteenth century. As the Turks were pushed south in the Balkans, the Serbs were forced to develop a new capital and core area around Belgrade (14) on the Danube River because the Turks still occupied the medieval core area. Today, the old Raška area retains an important place in Serbian historical tradition as seen in the monasteries located deep in these mountains.

A similar shift of capital site between medieval and modern periods took place in Bulgaria. The medieval Bulgarian empires originated on a fertile *loess*-covered platform of land between the Danube River and the Balkan Mountains. In this region, Pliska, Preslav, and Trnovo (21) served as capitals of empires that extended

far west and south in the Balkan peninsula. The last Bulgarian Empire, after being weakened by wars with Serbia and Byzantium, eventually succumbed to the Turks, who occupied the territory for almost five hundred years. Upon liberation in 1878, the new Bulgarian state transferred the capital from Trnovo to the more accessible Sofia (20). The latter location, an important nodal point in the Balkans since Roman times, stands near the point where the Iskur, Maritsa and Struma rivers originate. Sofia occupies perhaps the optimum location in the country for controlling both northern and southern Bulgaria, which are separated by the east – west barrier of the Balkan Mountains. Once again, the concept of core area illustrates the regional advantages of different areas for organizing space within a political unit.

Climate

The climate of Eastern Europe represents a transition between the moderate patterns of maritime Western Europe and the greater extremes of the continental Soviet Union. The difference in temperature between the warmest and coldest months is only 59 °F (15 °C) in West Germany but rises to 77 °F (25 °C) in the western portions of Russia. The range in Eastern Europe, therefore, is around 62.6°–71.6 °F (17°–22 °C) in most places, although in the Hungarian plain, Wallachia, and northern Bulgaria it is over 77 °F (25 °C).

The northerly location of Eastern Europe reinforces the importance of cold winter temperatures and reduces the influence of summer insolation. For example, winter temperatures over much of the region decrease eastwardly owing to the persistence of the high pressure cell over Eurasia. Thus, average January temperatures decrease from 32 °F (0 °C) in Berlin to 26.6 °F (–3 °C) in Warsaw and from 30.2 °F (–1 °C) in Prague to 24.8 °F (–4 °C) in Banská Bystrica, Czechoslovakia; this represents a change from west to east of a month of below-freezing temperatures to three months. On the other hand, average summer temperatures are similar along given latitudinal lines but increase southwardly, although the presence of mountains there tends to lower means in many locations. In both Berlin and Warsaw, therefore, the average July temperature is 64.4 °F (18 °C), while in both Prague and Banská Bystrica it is close to 66.2 °F (19 °C). Even in Budapest and Belgrade average July temperatures are only 71.6 °F (22 °C) and 73.4 °F (23 °C), respectively. In the mountains of the Balkans, however, average July

temperatures vary from 53.6 °F (12 °C) to 60.8 °F (16 °C).

Actually, the common division of Eastern Europe into two humid continental variations – cool summer to the north and warm summer to the south – is a bit misleading. The dividing line between the two is a temperature of 71.6 °F (22 °C) for the warmest month. From the Baltic coast to central Serbia or Bucharest the July temperature only varies from 62.6 °F (17 °C) to 73.4 °F (23 °C). Thus, in general, the summers of continental Eastern Europe do not vary greatly from north to south. However, there is little doubt that summer days can become hot in the Hungarian basin or on the Moldavian steppe.

Perhaps the greatest deviation from the climate patterns just described occurs in the areas near the Mediterranean Sea, where summer average temperatures are much warmer but winter readings depend on the influence of the Eurasian high. Dubrovnik, on the central Adriatic coast, averages 48.2 °F (9 °C) in January and 77 °F (25 °C) in July. However, January temperatures can drop suddenly along this coast when the cold bora wind breaks over the Alps. Skopje, an inland location in Macedonia, averages 35.6 °F (2 °C) in January and 73.4 °F (23 °C) in July; in this case, the Mediterranean influence is greater in summer.

Eastern Europe is not as wet in all seasons as Western Europe, and except for the Mediterranean area, precipitation tends to be concentrated in the summer-half year. Drought does not present a widespread problem. The driest places are the Hungarian plain and Moldavian steppe with 20–25 inches (500–625 mm) of annual precipitation, but in some years lower amounts can affect crop production. Much of Eastern Europe receives 20–30 inches (500–750 mm), while the mountains can have 30–50 inches (750–1250 mm). In the Dinaric Mountains, precipitation averages over 60 inches (1500 mm). The dividing line for snow cover runs east and west through Eastern Europe: in the north it is over 30 days but is less in the south; however, in the Carpathians and the mountains of the Balkans, snow cover lasts for several months. Ice hampers navigation on rivers in the northern plain from 30 to 60 days but is not a barrier in the south.

Summary

In this chapter, we examine the locational relationships between the numerous cultures of Eastern Europe and the physical geography of the area. The primary terrain zones are described and the concept

of core area is utilized to illustrate the focal points of settlement within the physical setting. In this way, the process of regionalization by the various cultures in different habitats is clarified. The regional pattern of climates is also analyzed. Now our attention turns to the primary processes of spatial organization in Eastern Europe, starting with German colonization.

3

Landscapes of German medieval colonization

From northern Poland to Transylvania in Romania, a distance of 700 miles, there exists a series of landscape relics that are derived from a single process – the colonization of Eastern Europe during the Middle Ages by German-speaking peoples. This broad arc of settlement affected especially Bohemia – a Slavic Kingdom within the Holy Roman Empire – and the kingdoms of Poland and Hungary (see Fig. 3.1)[1]. The process lasted about 400 years (950–1350) and took place at different rates and with varying degrees of intensity. It would be a mistake to call it an imposed German colonization because Slavs and Hungarians participated as well. Yet, it was essentially one process and has been described as the greatest single transformation of the East European landscape. The Germans transformed the economy of Eastern Europe by clearing and settling the land, opening up mines, and creating networks of trade and urbanization. More significantly, the ensuing interaction between east and west initiated significant social change among the Slavs and Hungarians, giving all of Europe for the first time a common civilization (Barraclough 1970: 9–10). In the steady expansion of a frontier or settlement to the east, this East European colonization resembled that of the American frontier, but differed in important aspects, too.

The locations of selected landscape relics of this process of colonization are shown on the map (see Fig. 3.1). What do these relics tell us? Mainly, they illustrate that this colonization brought innovations from the west: the three-field system of agriculture, which actually was preserved in its medieval form until the 1960s in eastern Poland; new village forms of settlement like the *Strassendorf* (street village); Christianity, primarily through monasteries of the Cistercian

33

Fig. 3.1 Eastward colonization by German settlers between 950 and 1350. Note the three major prongs: along the Baltic coast, up the Oder River, and down the Danube River to Vienna.

Order; mining technology transmitted through a series of towns extending from Freiberg through Bohemia and Slovakia to Romania; and early commercial activities as reflected in the gabled architecture of Danzig (Gdańsk) and in the Zips (Spiš) town of Leutschau (Levoča) in Slovakia. Finally, the planned towns of this colonization, exemplified by Thorn (Toruń) and Cracow in Poland and Hermannstadt (Sibiu) and Schässburg (Sighişoara) in Romania illustrate not only an increase in urban activity but also the diffusion of town law into Eastern Europe. Although separated in space, these relics collectively tell a story of the early stages in the making of the East European landscape, the ideology of the settlers, and the role that colonization played in social change within the area.

How were these innovations from Western Europe transmitted to the east? In general, the colonization process exhibited degrees of

similarity, but certain differences existed as well. The primary territories involved were the eastern portions of imperial Germany and the Kingdoms of Poland, Bohemia (within the Empire), and Hungary.

The geographical background to colonization

Political organization and colonization

During the Middle Ages, the eastern frontier of the Germanic Holy Roman Empire remained relatively unstable in response to conflicts between Teutons and Slavs or Hungarians. Before the tenth century, the Slavs in the north and the Hungarians farther south had pushed westward. German defense against these incursions took the form of *Marken* (marches) or fortified frontier provinces. The best known were from north to south, Billung, North, East (of Saxony), Meissen, East (of Bavaria), Styria, and Carinthia. Gradually, German pressure increased, and the frontier was pushed eastward so that the marches served as points of departure for colonization. As shown on the map, the pattern of advance took the form of three major prongs extending along the Baltic coast, up the Oder River, and down the Danube River, areas which became consolidated and transformed as the imperial principalities of Pomerania, Silesia, and Austria (see Fig. 3.1). Farther south, Styria and Carinthia became German imperial principalities as well. Later the Billung, North, East (of Saxony), and Meissen marches were consolidated as the Mark Brandenburg, a province that was to play a strong role in the rise of Prussia–Germany under the Hohenzollern rulers.

On the eastern borders of the Holy Roman Empire, German colonization took place within marchlands and the principalities or kingdoms farther east. The marches represented frontier provinces of the Empire, which was itself a loose political organization with a core area in the Rhine River region near Frankfurt. Because of distance from this core and the strength of individual lords, the marches operated rather independently of the Empire. The colonists came directly under the lords or bishops who had been granted land. However, in Poland, Bohemia, and Hungary, differences in political organization and regional authority existed and affected colonization accordingly. In Poland, regionalism was strong in the medieval period because the kings had difficulty establishing control over the historic provinces. Pomerania and Silesia, for example, were

marginal to the Polish kingdom and thus became Germanized by colonization, eventually becoming principalities in the German Empire. On the other hand, colonization was less important in the principality of Great Poland, which with its centers of Gnesen (German Gniezno) and Posen (German Poznań), became an early core area for the Polish state. In the fourteenth century, the principality of Little Poland to the south developed as a core area where Cracow was the royal capital. However, these Polish principalities operated rather independently of the king, and German settlers came directly under the prince, while the lord did not serve as an intermediate authority (Aubin 1966: 469). In Bohemia and Hungary, on the other hand, the colonists were responsible to the king, who in both cases had encouraged German settlers as border guards, miners, and traders; thus, regionalism was less of a factor in these kingdoms, although it must be remembered that Bohemia was a component of the Empire.

German colonization, therefore, took place within several frameworks – marches and principalities of the Empire, principalities of Poland, and kingdoms of Bohemia and Hungary. In all of these areas, the Germans operated under town law that gave them degrees of independence they had not possessed in the Empire. However, they owed certain obligations in taxes and other duties to respective authorities.

An additional territorial element that developed as a part of medieval German colonization was the region dominated by the Teutonic Knights, a military/religious order. After earlier colonization activity in what is now Transylvania, this order was invited by Polish princes in the thirteenth century to conquer and Christianize the heathen Prussians who occupied the eastern Baltic region. Upon carrying out this mission, however, the Order remained in the area as a colonizing force, operating from its capital in the great fortress of Marienburg (Malbork) and from towns like Thorn (Toruń) and Danzig (Gdańsk) (see Fig. 3.1). This exclave of German settlement, centred just east of the lower Vistula River, restricted Polish access to the Baltic and in the long run served as a core area for what much later became German East Prussia. The relationships between the Knights and settlers differed from those found in other colonial areas because the German colonists were often segregated from the Prussians – a policy of expediency, not prejudice (Carsten 1954: 65). Later, however, as the supply of German colonists declined, mixing of populations occurred. In addition, the Knights restricted the

powers of Church and town. In the Polish principalities, on the other hand, Aubin (1966: 481) states that Germans and Slavs lived side by side:
Supplementing the political territories of German imperial marches (later principalities), Polish principalities, Bohemian and Hungarian kingdoms, and region of the Teutonic Knights, was the Hanseatic League (Hansa). Actually, this League was a voluntary association of some eighty commercial towns around the Baltic and North Seas for the purpose of promoting and even monopolizing trade. The League was dominated by German towns, and eastern colonization helped its development by spreading German population and commercial ideas along the southern Baltic coast. Each Hansa town owed some allegiance to the lay or ecclesiastical prince in whose territory it was located. In the thirteenth and fourteenth centuries the wealth of the towns enabled them to make loans to the princes and to obtain in return a degree of sovereignty that included the right to levy tolls and market dues, to fortify the towns, and to exercise criminal jurisdiction. Only in League towns within the territory of the Teutonic Knights were these elements of sovereignty missing. In a real sense, then, the Hanseatic League was not a sovereign power but an amorphous organization, lacking legal status, having at its disposal neither finances of its own nor an army and fleet. Nevertheless, the League was an important late medieval power in the maritime area of northern Europe because of the trade sanctions it could levy against a town that refused to follow its policy. A primary historical function of the League was to control the commerce of northeastern Europe – providing fish, furs, grain, timber, hemp, and amber to Western Europe in return for many products, but especially cloth, wine, and salt (Dollinger 1970: 217–23). Eventually decline set in. In the fifteenth century, Dutch and British competition increased, especially as the heavy shoals of herring left the Baltic Sea for the North Sea. Hansa problems reflected an overall deterioration of urban power in Eastern Europe after the fifteenth century that was related to agrarian crises and the establishment of serfdom.

The map shows the spatial pattern of German colonization that occurred within the political framework previously described (see Fig. 3.1) It is evident that various aspects of this settlement went on simultaneously along a broad front from the Baltic Sea to Transylvania. The leading prong of settlement was Bavaria and its Ostmark, where German settlement existed along the Danube to Vienna by

1100. By the end of the twelfth century, German settlers had crossed the Elbe River and their settlements also had begun to appear in the mountainous rim of Bohemia. The first half of the thirteenth century witnessed the crossing of the Oder River and the extension of a prong of settlement into Silesia; in addition, further penetration of the Bohemian mountain rim was evident, and early outliers of settlement were found in the Carpathian Mountains of Hungary. Finally, the period 1250–1350 saw the expansion of a third prong of German colonization along the Baltic Coast, including Pomerania and the area controlled by the Teutonic Knights, and additional settlement into northern Bohemia and mountainous areas of eastern Hungary. However, the colonization process slowed with the Black Death of the mid-fourteenth century and with military battles such as the defeat of the Teutonic Knights at Tannenberg in 1410.

By 1350, then, the pattern of German settlement in Eastern Europe was established, a geographical phenomenon that featured three major prongs in Pomerania–Prussia, Silesia, and Austria separated by areas of Slav settlement in Great Poland and Bohemia. Thus, the colonization tended to follow borderlands around the Polish and Bohemian core areas. To the south, the Hungarians made up a strong wedge of population. However, to the east of these groups of German colonization were hundreds of scattered German settlements, the most noteworthy being the frontier and mining colonies found in the eastern mountains of Hungary. Blum (1957: 816) reports that some idea of the size of this eastward movement is gained by estimates that 1400 villages with a total population of about 150 000 were established in East Prussia; another 150 000 to 180 000 settled in Silesia. This medieval settlement, together with later private and state colonization after 1500, accounted for the presence of a large German ethnic element in the population of Eastern Europe, an element that was to affect its history and landscape.

Terrain and colonization

German colonization took place in two general types of terrain – the north European plain, dominated by glacial landforms, and the basins and forested mountains of Bohemia and Hungary. In Chapter 2 we mentioned the characteristics of this plain (see Fig. 2.1). For the most part, the morainic and outwash areas are infertile in contrast to the Börde or *loess* zone to the south. Germans and Poles – the chief cultural groups of the area – had core areas in the zone of *Geest* and

glacial valleys that dominates the central portion of the plain: Berlin, Posen, and Warsaw. In addition, the Poles developed the core area of Cracow in the Börde.

A second major area of German colonization was Bohemia, a basin protected on all sides by low, forested mountains – Ore (Erzgebirge or Krušné hory), Sudetes, and Bohemian Forest (Böhmerwald or Šumava) (see Fig. 3.1)[2]. Although these mountains served to protect the Czech core area of settlement in the basin from German political encroachment, minerals present there began to attract colonists in the Middle Ages. The hearth area for the development of mining technology was the Harz Mountains, now straddling the Iron Curtain between West and East Germany. As Thompson (1928: 524–5) mentions, the richest gold, silver, and copper deposits in medieval Europe lay in these mountains, and Goslar became the principal mining center. Gradually, the Germans, and especially the Saxons, came to monopolize the development of mining technology and law in Europe. In the second half of the twelfth century, silver was discovered in the Ore Mountains (Erzgebirge) – a name reflecting the presence of minerals – and gave rise to German mining communities both on the northern flanks where Germans dominated the settlement pattern and on the south in the midst of Czech population. The most important town on the north was Freiberg, where a mining school was established; it became a center for the spread of mining technology and law into central Bohemia and the mountainous areas of Hungary. In Bohemia, this influence was reflected in the importance of towns like Kuttenberg (Kutná Hora), where royal Czech silver mines existed, and Iglau (Jihlava). Other German colonists moved into the mountainous rim of Bohemia, establishing farming and commercial settlements to supplement those of mining. Certain towns, like Gablonz (Jablonec), specialized in artisan work in glass. All of these medieval German settlements, relics of which are still visible, provided the early basis for the Sudeten German population that became such an issue in the 1930s. Within the Bohemian basin, Czech settlement remained predominant, a wedge of Slav population between German prongs in Silesia and Austria. However, in the large cities of Bohemia like Prague and Pilsen (Plzeň), German influence was strong. By the end of the fourteenth century, for example, the German community in Prague occupied an important segment of the Old Town, and the university had taken on a German character.

To the east, German settlement in Hungary was even more notice-

ably clustered in the mountains and basins of the Carpathian Mountains of Slovakia and Transylvania. Kuhn (1937: 812–14) has grouped these settlements into two rings which he calls *Grenzer- und Bergbausiedlungen* (frontier and mining settlements) (see Fig. 3.1). Most of these settlements were royal free towns established by the Hungarian kings and settled by Germans. The outer ring of *Grenzersiedlungen* was made up of German towns established on the frontier in the twelfth century to defend against the Tartar groups to the east and to bring in mining and commercial technology; here they complemented the Szeklers, a Hungarian cultural group settled very early in eastern frontier regions. The primary relics of the outer ring of German settlements are the twenty-four Zips (Spiš) trading towns of Slovakia and the seven 'Saxon' towns of Siebenbürgen (Transylvania). Leutschau (Levoča) is the leading relic of the Zips groups, while Hermannstadt (Sibiu), Schässburg (Sighişoara) and Kronstadt (Braşov) are relics of the latter group[3]. A special territory within the *Grenzer* ring near Kronstadt is marked today by the villages of Tartlau (Prejmer) and Honigberg (Hărman), relics of the frontier district of Burzenland (Hungarian Barcza) developed by the Teutonic Knights after 1211 on the invitation by Andrew II of Hungary; in these settlements, a huge church, surrounded by a wall, stands in the center and dominates the skyline from miles away. The inner ring of German settlements (*Bergbausiedlungen*) was composed of mining towns like Kremnitz (Kremnica), Schemnitz (Banská Štiavnica), and Ofenberg (Baia de Arieş).

Kuhn (1937: 810) emphasizes that these German frontier and mining settlements collectively represent the connection between *Boden und Volk* (land and cultural group) commonly found on the frontier: in these mountains, colonists found areas that not only met their needs in terms of agriculture and resources, but also were separated by terrain from other ethnic groups; over a period of time these became *Volksräume* (folk areas) that represented long-term adjustments to the environment. Perhaps it is this process of people–land relationships that helps to explain the persistence of German *Volksräume* in Eastern Europe for hundreds of years.

Routes for colonization and trade

By 1500, a well-defined network of trade routes extended across the northern part of Eastern Europe in contrast to the Balkans where only two long-distance lines to Constantinople existed. The total

network developed over a period of several hundred years. Originally, the routes were designed to serve colonization, but gradually they evolved into a full-fledged network of trade, connecting Western and Eastern Europe. In this way the network illustrates the effects of German colonization on social change in this part of Europe.

Details of the network before 1500 are sketchy, but apparently Halle was an early clearing house for eastern commerce, because by 1125 an important route led from the eastern part of the Empire to this city and then along the Saale, Elbe, Havel, and Peene Rivers to Stettin (Szczecin) on the Baltic. In the fourteenth century, four major east–west routes connected Germany with Poland (see Fig. 3.1). The first route followed the Baltic coast north of the Baltic glacial moraine, connecting Lübeck with Stettin, Danzig (Gdańsk), and Königsberg (Kaliningrad). The second one followed the glacial valley zone but kept to the dry and higher *Geest*, avoiding the damp meadowlands, as it connected Braunschweig, Magdeburg, Berlin, Posen (Poznań), and Thorn (Toruń). A third one – the famous *Hohe Strasse* – paralleled the fertile *loess* zone and, in part, the Oder River as it extended through Erfurt, Leipzig, Görlitz, Breslau (Wrocław) and Lublin. Finally, the fourth left Nürnberg to cross the Böhmerwald into Bohemia and through Prague, Olmütz (Olomouc), and the Moravian Gate between the Sudetes and Carpathian Mountains to Cracow.

North–south connections existed between these east–west routes, particularly along the major rivers as exemplified by the one along the Elbe River from Saxony to Prague. The three medieval fair towns of Leipzig, Posen, and Breslau are indicative of the importance of the intersections of major routes with rivers.

The development of routes in Hungary differed from that to the north in Poland. Because Austria, as an early march of the Empire, was responsible for generating a trade policy with Hungary, a charter granted in 1231 guaranteed Vienna a monopoly of this commerce with cloth and other articles moving east in return for gold and silver products plus cattle. In general, the backward nature of the Balkans curbed transportation through southeast Europe. Nevertheless, two major routes, which traversed the Balkans from Vienna to Constantinople, allowed both German and Byzantine cultures to affect medieval Hungary. The more northerly one, which has survived as a main road and rail route, crossed the Hungarian plain from Ofen (Buda) – now Budapest – through Grosswardein – today Oradea –

before cutting through Transylvania via the German fortified towns of Klausenberg (Cluj), Hermannstadt (Sibiu) and Kronstadt (Braşov). The other stayed west of the Danube River from Ofen before striking southeast to Belgrade, Sofia, and Constantinople.

However, the duties and charges levied by Vienna restricted trade between west and east Europe. In 1325, this pattern changed when Bohemia, Poland, and Hungary jointly eliminated Vienna as a transshipment point and decreed commercial letters of guarantee for German and French exporters (Tihany 1976: 57). This action provided the stimulus for new trade connections into Hungary via Brünn (Brno) and Kaschau (Košice). Kaschau became a trans-shipment point, and the route from the Baltic via this city to Ofen was called the *Kupferweg* (copper road) because of the minerals of the Slovakian Ore Mountains. This route passed through the group of German trading towns known collectively as the Zips (Spiš), which served as useful commercial intermediaries between German, Polish, and Hungarian cities (Wanklyn 1954: 199).

The colonization process

German medieval colonization in Eastern Europe took place within the environment of feudalism, which is defined as a social order based on precise obligations between ruler, lord, vassal, and peasant. The lord held his land in fief from the crown and was obliged in return to serve the king. The lord in turn let out parts of the land to vassals, generally mounted fighting men or knights, whose services were available to him in fulfilling his military obligations. This grant of land gave a vassal the right to receive an income from a particular estate or manor. The vassal had the duty of maintaining order on the estate and of collecting various fees or feudal dues from dependents. These dependents were the peasants who cultivated the vassal's land and were assured of a number of defined liberties and rights. The essence of feudalism, then, was the reciprocity of obligations. A chain of responsibility, loyalty, and obligation extended from peasant to king. Related to feudalism was the manorial system, which represented the economic process in medieval society and which was characterized by the communal working of land in a village in which the peasants not only cultivated communal strips in open fields but also worked the lord's land or demesne in return for protection.

Feudalism and the manor system, therefore, provided a degree of

order in a medieval world characterized by the breakdown of central authority and by self-sufficiency of the economy. As Pounds (1973: 225) says, feudalism in a political sense consisted of the delegation of the functions of government to, or their assumption by, the aristocracy. The system predominated in Western Europe when colonization in Eastern Europe was initiated. In fact, the nature of feudalism in the west affected its form in the east. Postan (1970: 167–8) calls the latter *de facto* feudalism because the system was less rigid – the duties, obligations, and local powers of the lords and vassals were based less on a contract and more on their *de facto* position in the colonial areas as soldiers, owners of the land, and colonizing entrepreneurs. The status of the peasants, too, was different in the east from that in the west: it was freer, more prosperous, and seemingly more promising. What was the nature of this *de facto* feudalism of the east as it developed as a part of the German colonization process?

Gerhard (1959: 220) emphasizes that German colonization in Eastern Europe was carried out by communal groups, a process that stands in contrast to the more individualistic settlement of the American West. Aubin (1928: 192) further clarifies this movement by stating: 'Beyond the Elbe all corporate groups moved in simultaneously, nobles and peasants, merchants, craftsmen, and miners. The whole economy of the mother country was extended to the east.' These different groups cooperated in transferring the institutions of the German Empire to the east. Thus, it was a widespread movement to the east on the part of many groups – *Drang nach Osten* – and not a process of settlement by individuals as in the American West.

The scale of this colonization required some means of coordination, a task that was provided by the so-called 'locator', in reality what we in America might call a promoter. This official, often a merchant with money to invest, was responsible for the recruitment and eventual placement of the settlers. He had to take the land, whether purchased or secured by grant, divide it among the settlers, handle the legal problems that arose, and deal with Slavonic princes who had issued invitations to German settlers. Success in recruiting colonists resulted largely from the cooperation that existed among the locators. In turn, the migrant, knowing that he would be a part of a community rather than an isolated figure and that he himself could select the final location of the homestead, had considerable confidence in the locator.

For this organizational work, the locator could expect considerable

rewards from the lord who hired him, i.e. a large amount of land, often free of dues, and the position of judge with legal jurisdiction over the colonists including the right to retain fines. Sometimes the locator received not only a monopoly right to trade in the area, including the establishment of mills, smithies, inns, and so forth, but also a part of the revenue in dues and taxes from the colonists.

Feudal obligations of the colonists in connection with land holdings were quite different in the east from what they had been in the west. Originally, land was acquired in the east by conquest or grant. Under the latter, the colonists received their holdings from the sovereign, Church, or lay lords on free hereditary tenure. Rental obligations of the colonists were simple and fixed, while labor services amounted to only a few days a year. Moreover, these dues and services were exempt for as long as twenty years after the settlers arrived. The colonists could sell their land and also could move from their village at will. As the competition for settlers increased, these rights also were extended to the Slavic and Hungarian peasants, a trend that was enforced by the German law that increased seigneural power at the expense of indigenous princes. Thus, as Blum (1957: 817) remarks, serfdom, which had held so many of the native peasantry before the Germans arrived, gradually disappeared; the same was true of slavery. Even the Prussians enserfed by the Teutonic Order eventually were assimilated with the German peasantry.

Spatial organization under the colonization process was dominated by the coupling of rural and urban life. Where forests existed, clearing the land was the first step in laying out a whole group of villages with a central town and accompanying land for agriculture. Although this small regional system was self-contained in terms of support, it was eventually linked to a pattern of trade that was widespread in Eastern Europe. In the villages, permanent farming with regular field systems and with emphasis on grain culture replaced the more primitive agriculture of the indigenous population which had been dominated by cattle raising and by slash-burn with no regular form of rotation. Intensive crops like beans, hops, flax, vegetables, fruit, and grapes supplemented grain. The towns served as markets and distributing points for this new agriculture. In addition, many of the town burghers owned villages or farms and gained rents from them. This colonial pattern of spatial organization had the disadvantage of concentrating craft and trade functions in the town, leaving the villages purely agricultural; this latter characteristic, according to Aubin (1966: 474), left the village especially vulnerable to subjugation

by the lords when serfdom made a delayed but strong entry on the East European scene after the fifteenth century (see next chapter). Ecclesiastical services existed within this network of town and surrounding villages. Normally each new village built its church on land set aside for this purpose, and the parish established relationships with the diocese. Each colonist gave a small offering to the parish priest in addition to required tithes to the Church. Perhaps the most influential clerical nodal point, however, was the monastery whose founding was an act of colonization. Monasteries like Oliva (Oliwa) in Poland (founded in 1186) kept in close communication with their mother monasteries in Germany (and France) and spread improved methods in agriculture and industry among the people of their districts, e.g. the consolidation of land in large granges and the building of mills.

The founding of towns subject to German law was central to the entire colonization process. Several aspects of town establishment, which with local variations were characteristic of the process, are noteworthy. Upon invitation from a local (non-Germanic) lord or prince, a town was located near a fortified place of an existing village. Almost immediately it received a code or Germanic law which granted to the citizens not only the rights of judicial and administrative self-government but also the right to hold a market and the replacement of dues in kind to the feudal lord by payment in money (Ostrowski 1966: 11). Representation on town councils was often split among wealthy merchants, guilds, and common people. Citizenship was generally reserved for German colonists, e.g. the town charter granted in 1257 by Duke Boleslav to the German colonists in Cracow withheld this right to Poles for more than fifty years. However, this restriction may be too broad, for settlements with town character apparently existed in Poland before the colonists arrived; later, German law was applied to them despite few German colonists in the region.

In Hungary, the towns and mining areas were exempted by the King from seigneurial control. These royal free towns, inhabited mostly by Germans and protected by charters which enabled them to deny nobles even the right to settle on their territory, formed the chief centers of Hungary's trade and industry.

The perceptions and ideologies of the colonizing forces

Territorial and organizational aspects of the German colonization

45

process in Eastern Europe have been outlined. Now some perceptions and ideologies that influenced this movement are presented. A variety of 'push' and 'pull' factors probably influenced all segments of the population – lords, clergy, merchants, and peasants – involved in this migration. The 'push' factors were dominated by the dual effects in western Germany of population pressure on the land and feudal oppression on the people. Thompson (1915: 136–9) gives some of the essential reasons for these effects: pressure of people on the land increased as cultivation expanded into forests which formerly had been the 'poor man's refuge'; land pressure also came from newer, more intensive methods of agriculture, which allowed the estates to expand; as the lords and clergy cultivated land, freeholds were split or even abolished as peasants were forced into greater dependency; in addition, the peasants could not sell their land or pass it on to their heirs. Therefore, available land to the east acted as a pull factor to all groups, especially the peasant, and was perceived as a solution to the population pressure on land in the west.

Accompanying this pressure on land was a change in feudal status of the peasant farmers in western Germany. Peasant obligations became increasingly difficult as freeholds frequently were abolished, forcing the peasants into serfdom. As such they were bound to the lord personally and could be moved about at his will. Manorial rights were also extended to mills, bake ovens, wine presses, breweries, and other village functions; and tithes were extended from grain and wine to small produce like vegetables and poultry. Thus, feudal oppression supplemented population pressure as a 'push' factor for individual colonists. As Blum (1957: 815) relates, they could be persuaded to come 'only if they received assurances that they would be rid of princely and seigneurial burdens that weighed upon them at home'. Although the prosperity of the twelfth and thirteenth centuries in western Germany improved the status of the peasants, the 'push' factors were apparently reinforced by rapid population growth.

The 'pull' factors represented attractive aspects of the Slav and Hungarian lands. In the case of the Slavs, a proclamation of the bishops and princes of Saxony expressed the inducements used for colonization (Kötzschke 1912: 9–10):

> They [the Slavs] are an abominable people, but their land is very rich in flesh, honey, grain, birds, and abounding in all products of the fertility of the earth, when cultivated, so that none can be compared unto it. So they say who know. Wherefore, O Saxons, Franks,

Lotharingians, men of Flanders most famous – here you can both save your souls, and if it please you, acquire the best of land to live in.

The 'pull' factors, therefore, represented the antithesis to 'push' factors: land was available for peasants, and feudal obligations were reduced. These new farmers could pass on or sell their land, and they were protected by town law. The clergy, on the other hand, was motivated by the goals of converting the heathen Slavs and establishing Christianity in Eastern Europe; in addition, of course, increased tithing was a great incentive. Finally, the German princes and lords promoted colonization on their newly acquired lands with the intent of increasing rents and developing grain and forest resources. In the twelfth century, for example, Albert, Margrave of Brandenburg, imported Dutch and Flemish colonists who were accustomed to deep plowing, ditching, and draining in the Low Countries of northwest Europe and who therefore could develop the marshy region around medieval Berlin.

Supplementing this general behaviour were the attitudes of the Slav and Hungarian rulers in the east. Above all, they were interested in reforming the economic and social structure of their areas and, according to Bosl (1970: 61–2), they perceived that German law – by which the status of farmer, miner, trader, and artisan was raised – was a means to this transformation. Furthermore, they knew that the German system of colonization – including field systems, agricultural and mining technology, village forms, and town law – had been tried and tested within the eastern portions of the Empire. For example, Smith (1967: 176) reports that the German immigrants possessed heavy, wheeled plows with coulter and mouldboard and also heavy felling axes for clearing the thicker forests. Other settlers, like the Flemish, were expert in reclaiming marshy land. The name Fläming, for hills south of Berlin, indicates a Dutch source area.

Such a colonization system was well adapted to move into Slav and Hungarian areas which exhibited definite signs of economic weakness. In the years before colonization a large portion of the Slavic or Hungarian peasantry had lost their freedom and either owed obligations or were slaves. In Poland, the agricultural system existed largely to produce tribute from peasant to prince or lord; the fortresses became collecting centers rather than headquarters of agriculture as in Germany. The compulsory services inhibited peasant motivation from a maximum production of cereals or from opening new land and extending arable farming. This attitude

contrasted with that of the German freeman who prized regularly tended fields as a part of his normal way of life. The recognition by Slav princes of this discrepancy between east and west helps to account for their frequent invitations to Germans for settlement. They were aware of the possibility of increasing a district's monetary yield by adopting German innovations. It is important, therefore, to point out that (1) the colonization process was not necessarily accompanied by conflict between German and Slav, but was more often accomplished peacefully and in cooperation, and that (2) much of the progress initiated in Eastern Europe by German colonists was the result of a flexible social environment provided by the rulers, an environment that did not exist in Western Europe at this time.

The hearth areas of the colonization were originally located within the German Empire itself. However, later sources were the early areas of colonization (e.g. the marches) where children, numerous in a frontier environment, were hungry for as much land as their fathers had had.

In Bohemia and Hungary the attitudes of people fostering colonization were both similar to and different from those in Poland. First of all was the desire to promote foreign immigration so as to introduce innovation in trade and agriculture from the more advanced west. Thompson (1928: 532, 535) quotes Stephen, the first Christian king of Hungary, as saying, 'Hold the guests (*hospites*) in honor, for they bring foreign learning and arms into the country.' Thompson also emphasizes the need for defense and mining and commercial technology as an attitude generating German colonization. Kuhn (1937: 812–14), too, emphasizes the role of Germans in filling the defensive gaps along the Hungarian eastern frontier and in extending mining activities from the Ore Mountains source area. He also states that, even though the colonists were liable to military service, their legal position was advantageous since they were often treated as royal guests with retention of their own law in towns that were extraterritorial. Such a situation undoubtedly acted as a pull factor on the colonists coming from Germany. Still another force was the image, spread by crusaders returning from the Holy Land in the latter part of the eleventh century, of vast, fertile, uninhabited areas in Hungary.

The ideologies of the colonization movement are not easy to ascertain. As mentioned in Chapter 1, ideology is defined by Knight (1971: 386) as the complex of values, beliefs, and sentiments that bind

together members of a society and so differentiate them from other societies. Ideologies are recognized as stable and persistent elements in all social systems and, therefore, not only can work toward fostering social change but also can obstruct or resist it.

In the feudalism of the West, men were legally categorized into three estates – clergy, nobility, and people. These distinctions were closely related to a religious and social ideology that justified the legal supremacy of the bishops, knights, and land-holding groups; it was also an ideology that disparaged economic or productive functions and groups. Thus, for a long time, the existing ideology helped medieval society to resist the incorporation of merchants and artisans, thereby obstructing social change. These legal estates, however, cut across social groups in medieval society. Two men who were legally similar could occupy different places in the social system of stratification, e.g. a village priest versus a city bishop.

It was this type of society – legally and socially stratified – which migrated eastward. The peasant settler from western Germany could look forward to the possibility of rising within the social system to a free landholder or even a merchant, although he had no hope of moving out of the third estate. An ideology existed, then, which supported separate legal and social systems of stratification. Movement across the legal lines of stratification was much more difficult than across the social ones. However, as mentioned previously, these lines of stratification were less rigid in the *de facto* feudalism of the East. Furthermore, as production of agricultural, mineral, and artisan groups increased in Eastern Europe and as trade expanded, especially within the Hanseatic League, economic and social change created need for a higher evaluation of these commercial groups. In this way, the medieval ideology was altered somewhat in Eastern Europe.

Effects of colonization on the landscape

The primary effect of medieval German colonization in Eastern Europe was the complete transformation of society. German developments in agriculture, mining, commerce, religion, architecture, and law were diffused into this area and accepted by the Slavonic and Hungarian populations: 'the assimilation of Western institutions shaped the cultural face of central and eastern Europe from that time down to the present day' (Bosl: 1970, 63–4). These effects are both visible and invisible. In the following section the visible effects of

colonization on the present-day landscape are discussed, while the invisible ones are analyzed in the section on 'Colonization and social change'.

The visible landscape forms resulting from colonization include village patterns, open-field strips, town layouts and individual buildings, monasteries, and the remains of mining activities. The uniformity of these relics is related not only to the common Germanic culture but also to a similar colonization process. Even the physical environment was more like the source area than the West was for American settlers.

Village forms

The most obvious, visible feature resulting from the colonial movement was the establishment over much of this area of Germanic villages which were standardized in terms of size, layout, and field pattern. Today the contrast between the irregular villages of western Germany and the more regular ones of Eastern Europe is one of the most apparent regional differences in the landscape. Schröder and Schwarz (1969), who have compiled a comprehensive map of settlement forms in Europe, show this contrast very vividly. A portion of a map by Smith (1978: 266) also portrays this (see Fig. 3.2). Although it cannot be proved that the *Strassendorf* (street village) and other linear forms are the result of diffusion from west German hearth areas during the colonization era, Mayhew (1973: 79) states that the evidence supports this conclusion. Nucleated villages in regular form, especially the *Strassendorf*, were easy to plan; therefore, 'locators' favoured them. These forms facilitated laying out the communal three-field system of agriculture which became dominant throughout the area and which survived until the 1960s in parts of eastern Poland. In addition, these regular forms facilitated a type of regional planning practiced in colonial areas in which a series of villages surrounded a market town. For example, in 1253 the 'locator' of Posen was given seventeen adjacent Polish holdings which the grand duke of Great Poland wished to have colonized by Germans (Aubin 1966: 473).

The German land system, as the basis of colonial settlement, affected the field patterns and the forms of the village. The system was organized around a *Hufe*, an allotment of varying size depending on its origin. For example, the Flemish *Hufe* was 42 acres, whereas the Frankish was 60 acres. Considered an area of farmland

Fig. 3.2   The pattern of settlement forms in Central and Eastern Europe. *A.* irregular forms: (1) villages (*Haufendörf*); (2) hamlets (*Weiler*); (3) scattered farmsteads; *B.* regular forms: (4) small villages and hamlets including the round village (*Runddorf*) and Prussian estates; (5) round villages; (6) street villages (*Strassendorf*) and villages with elongated greens (*Angerdorf*); (7) forest or heath villages (*Waldhufendorf* or *Hagenhugendorf*); (8) marsh villages (*Marschhufendorf*); *C.* postmedieval planned forms; (9) geometric villages of the eighteenth century; (10) villages on poorly drained (*Moor*). Note the shift from irregular to regular forms east of the Elbe River. (Source: Smith 1978: 266.)

necessary for the support of a farmer and his family, this allotment could be distributed in different ways. Aubin (1966: 464–5) relates that two types of field systems dominated – *Gewanne* and *Gelänge* which totally made up the *Flur* or field pattern of a village, e.g. *Gewannflur* or *Gelängeflur*. Under the *Gewanne* (furlong) system, each peasant had his parcels allotted as strips in the three-field system (rotation of grain, feed, and fallow). This approach was more common in flat areas, but in mountain or hill country the *Gelänge* (long lot) form was more rational. In the latter arrangement, each allotment was kept intact as a long narrow strip oriented away from the road with a homestead followed by a succession of land uses – meadow, orchard, arable and grazing land, or forest – up the side of the slope. The furlong and long lot were obviously related to both terrain and layout of the village. Today, relics of strips from these two forms are most evident in Poland and Yugoslavia, the two communist countries which have resisted collectivization and in which the field strips remain (see Photo 3.1).

The village forms corresponding to these two variations of the German land system are predominant today over much of Eastern Europe as a legacy of the Middle Ages (see Fig. 3.3). The types associated with the furlong were the *Strassendorf* (street village) and *Angerdorf* (green village), both apparently related to three-field agri-culture in the northern plain, especially as the forest was cleared. The former, in which two series of farmsteads face each other across a road, is by far the more widely distributed in Eastern Europe. The author has noted it in street villages in the Hungarian plain as well, although these villages were established during a later period. The green village is similar except that the road separates to form a green or common space for grazing or for public buildings (see Photo 3.2). Smith's map of settlement shows that both types are widely distributed over Eastern Europe (see Fig. 3.2). The difference in distribution between the two forms is felt by some to be related to the absence or presence of livestock – with the common grazing of the green being a key feature.

The village types associated with the long lot are the *Waldhufendorf* (forest-lot village) and the *Marschhufendorf* (marsh-lot village). These two types feature farms arranged along a forest or dike road, like beads on a string, with land uses extending away from the road in succession – garden, orchard, cultivated fields, pasture, and forest (see Fig. 3.3). Since each long lot occupies space along the road, these forest and marsh villages are less compact than the street

Photo 3.1 Open-field strips in eastern Czechoslovakia near Poprad were evident in this 1959 scene. Collectivization of the 1960s replaced these strips with large fields.

villages, but they have a similar linear pattern. Naturally, the forest-lot village is more common in forested areas, especially in the mountains of the *Mittelgebirge* – in Silesia, Thuringia, Saxony, and Bohemia – and the Carpathians. Szulc (1972: 95) presents evidence that the distinction made in the Middle Ages between the open-field villages and the forest-lot village type are still apparent in the landscape. On the other hand, the marsh-lot village is seen in the reclaimed regions of the lower Oder and Vistula Rivers or along the Baltic coast. The marsh-lot village may have originated and spread eastward from the Low Countries by Dutch or Flemish settlers who were recruited for their experience in draining these damp areas.

All of these linear village forms were ideal for colonization because they could be laid out quickly along a single road. More restricted in its distribution is the *Rundling* or *Runddorf* (round village), a Slav

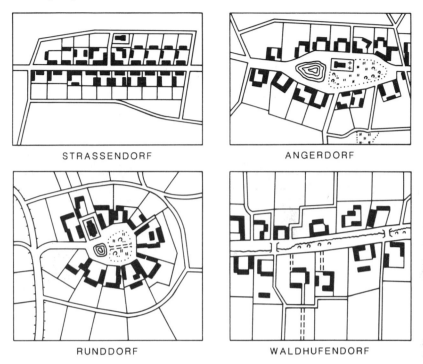

STRASSENDORF

ANGERDORF

RUNDDORF

WALDHUFENDORF

Fig. 3.3 Plans of the typical street village (*Strassendorf*), green village (*Angerdorf*), round village (*Runddorf*), and forest village (*Waldhufendorf*).

settlement form located today along the lower Elbe River (see Figures 3.2 and 3.3). It is possible that the Germans adopted the round form from the Slavs but changed its size, layout, field system, and social structure. These adaptations may explain its location along the early German–Slav border area. Its origin is open to question, but the most common theories involve a circular plan either for defense or for maximizing access to arable and pasture land. The central space also may have been a form of common land or green.

All of these settlement forms are fairly regular in layout as a result of systematic planning by 'locators', but when local lords were responsible for founding settlements, the forms were often irregular because the colonists were left to organize them as they wished. In this way, one may speculate that hamlets evolved, often with the farms spread at low density over a wide area and with numerous isolated farms. The fields were more compact than in the furlong

Photo 3.2 Heiligensee, an *Angerdorf* located on the outskirts of Berlin, was founded in the thirteenth century. This picture dates from the 1930s, but the village layout is similar today. (Source: Krebs, II 1930: p. 96.)

system, as the colonists were able to keep them in a single block. Mayhew (1973: 60) hypothesizes that many of the Slav settlements were irregular before colonization and were later occupied by Germans with little change.

Today, all of these village forms are still recognizable as relics of the early colonization process. In many cases, they have been altered through time but, in others hardly at all. For example, Marxwalde (formerly Quilitz), a village also discussed in Chapter 7 as a model of socialist rural planning in East Germany, is a green village.

Open-field strips of the medieval three-field system

In Poland and Yugoslavia, agricultural land is still, for the most part, privately owned with holdings in the form of narrow strips without fences (see Photo 3.1). These fields are a legacy of the Middle Ages and of the three-field system of agriculture that was introduced by the Germans in many colonial areas of Eastern Europe. Along with

the larger estates of the noble class, a feature of the later feudalization process (discussed in the next chapter), these strips comprised an element of the field-system landscape of Eastern Europe until after 1945, when collectivization in six of the countries erased them.

The three-field system of agriculture, which originated in the Middle Ages as a means of maximizing production of crops while minimizing loss of soil fertility, utilized three fields – one for a food crop (wheat or rye), one for a feed crop (oats or beans), and one for fallow (no crop). By rotating the fields each year, the fallow permitted all land over a three-year period to be rested in terms of plant minerals and moisture. Each peasant of the village possessed land in all of the fields, but, to insure equality, parcels were distributed on the basis of quality and accessibility. Thus, a farmer might have fifty parcels scattered in the three fields while his neighbor, also living in the village, might have fifty similar parcels. The parcels were in strip form because normally only one plow per village existed, and a long, narrow strip required fewer turns and thus less space wasted at the end of fields. Finally, animals grazed on common land, often meadows or forests, or on the stubble of the fields after harvest. It is important to stress that the three-field system was a communal one in which the rye and bean fields were planted and harvested as units, even though different strips existed there. Thus, crops were harvested at the same time, permitting the grazing of animals on the stubble of the entire field.

The three-field system of agriculture was diffused into Eastern Europe by colonists from the west and served them well. However, its later evolution varied between east and west. After the close of the Middle Ages in Western Europe, the peasants were gradually freed from feudal obligations and began to claim ownership of what had been the lord's property but farmed in a communal way. Then the peasants began to farm the strips individually and gradually developed rotations that eliminated the need for fallow; for example, a seed grass like lucerne adds nitrogen to the soil while a root crop enables hoeing of weeds. Such individual peasant farms evolved slowly in Eastern Europe, however, because large estates owned by the nobility tended to prevail (see next chapter). Nevertheless, various stages of three-field development existed in the area for hundreds of years, and in 1960 I viewed a three-field system (with fallow) in operation in eastern Poland at the village of Borysówska. Although this relic of the past, which was investigated by Biegajto

(1965: 29–60) has since disappeared, the open-field strips remain all over Poland and Yugoslavia as relics of the past.

Town distribution and form

The establishment and planning of regular towns parallel the repetition of German village forms as one of the most ubiquitous relics of German colonization in Eastern Europe. Indeed, the two were frequently laid out together by a 'locator', with the town serving as a market center for the surrounding villages. The residents of the villages relied on the town for legal security because the jurisdiction of the court of justice extended to these settlements. As stated previously, the retention by the town of all the nonagricultural functions weakened the villages and facilitated their take-over later by the lords when serfdom made a delayed appearance in Eastern Europe.

The regular distribution of the medieval towns under German law is a feature of the East European landscape that is still recognizable. Aubin (1934) calls this phenomenon a *Stadtrechtslandschaft* (city-law landscape). These towns held charters that granted them considerable autonomy, whether they were located within the eastern Marches of the German Empire or within the jurisdiction of Slavic or Hungarian princes or lords. Some were entirely new and dominated by German settlers, and others were Slavic with Germanic law[4]. Dickinson (1942: 48) reports that over 1500 towns were established in this area between 1200 and 1400. Only a few – notably Magdeburg, Danzig (Gdańsk), Cracow, Prague, and Brünn (Brno) – reached a population of over 10 000 during the Middle Ages (Pounds 1971: 63). Most of them were established north and west of the Carpathian Mountains, and the Magdeburg form of German law predominated. The dates of their founding, as shown in Westermann (1956: 75), illustrate this advance with the Oder River serving as a limit before 1250 and the Vistula River as a limit a hundred years later. The burghers, or citizens of these towns, had certain rights of representation and justice, reflected in building forms such as the *Rathaus* (city hall) and *Gildehaus* (guild hall). These towns received a great influx of merchants and were regarded as outposts of German commerce, civilization, and political influence of the Empire. In addition to German town law, German silver money became the prevalent currency; the German language was even used for municipal records. Although the merchants dominated the decision-making, the artisans were

important as well, and political struggles existed between these two groups as the guilds tried to acquire political rights and representation.

Most of the German colonial towns were located north of the Carpathian Mountains. To the south of these mountains, the towns were less numerous. The two rings of *Grenzer* (boundary) and *Bergbau* (mining) settlements referred to previously were perhaps most significant as they included Leutschau and the other Zips towns, mining towns like Kremnitz, and the seven Saxon cities of Transylvania (see Photos 3.3 and 3.4). In addition, Germans made

Photo 3.3 The old medieval German town of Leutschau in eastern Czechoslovakia is today known as Levoča. The town, colonized in the thirteenth century, was located on major trade routes between Poland, Silesia, and Hungary; this led to trade leadership among the Zips (Spiš) towns. Shown in the picture are the main square, town hall, and Church of Saint James. (South: Vasiliak 1970: p. 98.)

Photo 3.4 Schassburg, now Sighişoara in Romania, is one of the seven fortified towns settled by Germans in the Middle Ages in the area known as Siebenbürgen (today Transylvania). Shown here is the clock tower dating from the 14th century.

up significant percentages of population in larger cities like Prague and Cracow, where German 'quarters' developed. Thompson (1928: 536) reports that by the thirteenth century the German community of Prague occupied almost all of the old town; this legacy is visible in the architecture today.

The morphology or internal structure of these towns is a strong, visible effect of this urban colonization. Very apparent in the landscape is the protective wall or at least portions thereof. In addition, there is a planned layout of streets in rectangular form, a contrast with western Germany where a more irregular pattern of narrow, crooked streets had evolved slowly. Marburg in West Germany and cities like Danzig (Gdańsk), Breslau (Wrocław), Cracow, and Prague exemplify this contrast (see Fig. 3.4). The central portions of these four cities have retained the rectangular layout, a reflection of the adaptability of this plan to a colonial environment where many buildings were laid out quickly. Even more, the old city center (*Altstadt*) of each retains buildings that illustrate the three major groups vying for power when the new towns were introduced from the west. The castle and cathedral represented the impact of (1) the prince or lord and (2) the clergy, respectively; and the market square and town hall reflected the (3) middle class of traders and artisans who gained the right to have market days and to elect representatives.

These municipal rights were laid down in a charter, one of the great contributions of medieval town development to modern times. Pounds (1971: 59–60) emphasizes that this institution of town law, rather than the rectangular layout, represents the peculiar German contribution to urban development in Eastern Europe during the Middle Ages; the layout seems to be a feature of all cities in a frontier environment, even where the German population was not necessarily predominant. For example, Kuhn (1955: I, 105) states that in 1400 Cracow's population was 90 per cent German but that by 1500 this had fallen to 10 per cent. So, although the original town impetus was Germanic, the Slav or Hungarian influence in early towns of Eastern Europe must be recognized.

The towns of the Teutonic Knights, while religious in origin, were somewhat different in other respects. In addition to their mission of Christianizing the Prussians, the Knights created cities, actually fortresses, which spread Germanic civilization within their territory on the eastern shores of the Baltic Sea. Two of the most imposing relics are the castles at Marienburg (Malbork), which served as the headquarters of the Order, and at Thorn (Toruń) on

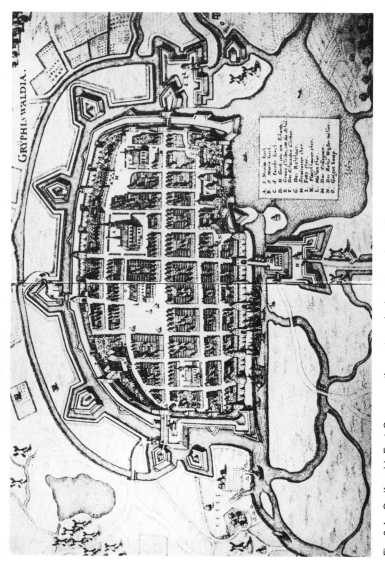

Fig. 3.4 Greifswald, East Germany: the rectangular layout as shown by a seventeenth-century map. Today the plan remains but only portions of the walls still stand. (Source: Stadt Archiv, Greifswald.)

the Vistula River. These castles exemplify the red-brick architecture in Gothic style, called *Backstein* (brick), which was characteristic of buildings in Teutonic Knight cities and which was diffused in the Middle Ages from Flanders through Lübeck to the eastern Baltic region. These huge brick structures together with the plain exterior devoid of decoration convey a sense of power. Many of the Teutonic Knight cities, like Thorn (Toruń), later became members of the Hanseatic League, thus superimposing a commercial function on earlier military-religious activity. In Danzig (Gdańsk), the medieval core of the city has been restored, including the famous Lang Gasse (ulica Długa) and the granaries overlooking the Mottlau (Motława) River. Steep and narrow gables as seen on the burgher houses, a legacy of the late Gothic period but with the addition of later Renaissance forms, abound in this city as well as in cities from Ghent in Belgium to Riga in Latvia (now in the Soviet Union). The gabled façade reflects a functional unity to the core of the town represented by the artisans and merchants.

Monasteries

Relics of monasteries and churches remain in Poland, Bohemia, and Hungary to illustrate the role of religion in German colonization. These relics are best represented by particular Cistercian monasteries that functioned as components of a system of religious spatial organization. This religious order, whose hearth area was France, spread its influence through the German Empire where daughter monasteries existed. Knox (1971: 22) shows that Morimond in Burgundy was the point of origin for many Polish monasteries. Outstanding relics at Jędrzejów, or Maly Morimond (1140), and Trebnitz (Trzebnica) (1218) reflect the French-German influence in architecture, especially the vertical proportions. The other major starting point was Clairvaux, also in Burgundy, which had links to two well-known abbey relics at Kolbatz (Kolbacz) (1175) and Oliva (Oliwa) (1186). One of the best-preserved Cistercian monasteries in East Germany today is Chorin (1272), located northeast of Berlin near the Elbe River. Coming upon it accidentally in 1980, I was astonished at its vertical size (see Photo 3.5). Knox (1971: 86–7) calls Pelplin (1276) the prince of such abbey-churches in Poland; the large transepts of this brick building seemingly illustrate the imperial influence, for they resemble those of the mother church at Doberan in Germany. This great brick abbey at Pelplin, whose tall silhouette is visible for miles across the landscape, was the clerical counterpart of

Photo 3.5   Chorin, a well-preserved Cistercian monastery located northeast of Berlin, was constructed in the thirteenth century. This structure illustrates the brick (*Backstein*) architecture that extends from Lübeck to Riga (Latvia).

Marienburg in the area of the Teutonic Knights.

The Cistercians also were important in the colonization process in Hungary where the tie to France was much more direct. In the twelfth century King Bela III of Hungary had ties to France through marriage and court advisors. In his attempt to graft French institutions upon Hungarian ones, perhaps as a counterweight to German influence, he invited Cistercians to establish monasteries within the kingdom. The ones located at Pilis (1184) and Egresch (Igris) (1179) have disappeared, while that at Zircz (Zirc) (1182) has been rebuilt. The most impressive relic is Kerz (1202), now Cîrta in Romania, near the city of Hermannstadt (Sibiu). This monastery is referred to by Romanian authorities as the oldest Gothic building in the country.

An interesting relic or offshoot of the Church in Poland is the production of grapes in the middle Oder River region near Grünberg (Zielona Gora). The vine was introduced in the Middle Ages to provide wine for Holy Communion. Today production continues, even though the area lies on the northern margin of grape-vine production in Europe.

Mining   The last visible group of landscape relics dating from the German colonization process in Eastern Europe is the chain of mining settlements that stretched across medieval Bohemia and Hungary. As mentioned previously, mining was a German monopoly in the Middle Ages, and the technology was diffused from Goslar in the Harz Mountains through Freiberg in the Ore Mountains, where a mining school existed, to settlements like Kuttenberg (Kutná Hora), Iglau (Jihlava), Kremnitz (Kremnica), Schemnitz (Banská Štiavnica), and Ofenberg (Baia de Arieş). The last three were part of the ring of *Bergbausiedlungen* (mining settlements) founded in the Carpathian Mountains.

Today, all of these towns exhibit their German heritage. Kutná Hora, for example, although small (12 000 inhabitants) still reflects its importance as a source of silver for the Bohemian kings. The most famous relics are the Gothic Saint Barbara Cathedral, dating from the late fourteenth century, and the Vlaśský dvôr, a former royal residence and silver mint. Farther east, Kremnica also is a jewel as a historic relic of early mining in Hungary. The royal mint, now producing coins for Czechoslovakia from the few mines operating in the surrounding mountains, still stands on the fourteenth-century square. A visit to this city is like stepping back in time some five hundred years.

Colonization and social change

The visible effects of German colonization on the landscape of Eastern Europe have been analyzed. These effects, however, are the outward manifestation of deeper changes that occurred in society as a result of this process. Thus, a study of colonization with its geographical effects on the landscape provides a key to social change in an area. In general, the German settlers brought innovations in economic development, law, and technology that had a tremendous impact on society in Eastern Europe.

Economic development

According to Blum (1957: 818), 'The German colonists deserve most of the credit for promoting the economic development of the lands to which they migrated.' The introduction of town life by the Germans gave the eastern areas a permanent, market-controlled economy with a division of labor. This economy replaced the Slav monopolies, which were based on a certain degree of personal-service obligations by peasants. Under the German system, both German and Slav settlers were relieved of these services; for the Slavs, this allowed a casting off of all bonds of former dependencies, perhaps one of the most apparent indications of the social changes initiated by colonization. The agricultural rent produced by the colonists, either in cash or in kind, was used by the lords as capital for economic purposes. The towns served as market centers for agricultural surpluses like grain and wool which could be exported abroad in return for salt, wine, cloth, and spices. For example, Smith (1978: 181) reports that Brandenburg was beginning to export grain to England and Flanders by 1250. The trade of the Hanseatic League represented the culmination of this new commercial activity. In addition, developments in mining were evident.

Town law The Germans brought with them a form of municipal law that established new relationships between the feudal lord and the colonists, thereby creating favorable conditions for economic development. According to Ostrowski (1966: 11), 'the most important changes introduced by German law were the replacement of the payment of dues in kind to the feudal lord by payment in money, and the granting to the burghers of quite extensive judicial

65

and administrative self-government'. This law, as set forth in charters giving rights of representation and justice to the people, made the towns and often their surrounding villages independent of laws that existed in the areas controlled more directly by the lords or princes. Therefore, German law as an institution represents one of the most significant aspects of civilization that was diffused from west to east across Europe in the Middle Ages. Unlike the earlier medieval towns, which were administrative, military or religious centres, these towns were urban in an economic and social sense because they possessed corporate rights and manifested a spirit of collective association that facilitated manufacture and trade.

Technology

A third contribution of the German colonists was the technology that accompanied this settlement by corporate groups, e.g. the wheeled plows and the large felling axes described earlier. Aiding cultivation were completely new systems of village and field patterns. Dutch and Flemish settlers, who sometimes accompanied the German colonists, brought techniques of reclamation and drainage. In the towns, German rectangular plans were omnipresent, and German architectural style, reflected in the use of brick, was diffused along the Baltic coast from Flanders. Mining technology was a German monopoly. Finally, certain crafts like glassmaking represented just one example of a continuous transfer of skills from west to east.

These innovations in economic development, law, and technology served to Germanize the Slavic population. The German economy of Western Europe was transferred *in toto* to the east, where it was utilized by both colonizers and Slavic or Hungarian populations. Such innovations brought by colonization, however, were not evenly spread over Poland, Bohemia, and Hungary. German influence was strongest in Silesia and Bohemia, although in the latter area and in most of Poland the effects varied by region (Thompson 1928: 535). For example, the Ore Mountains and Prague were Germanized, but most Bohemian Slavs never lost their identity. In Hungary, the German towns were isolated clusters within the Carpathian Mountains. However, the Germanic cultural influence extended into those Slav or Hungarian areas where Germanization did not take place – a process that Aubin (1966: 457) calls 'colonization under German law'. It is important to stress that linguistic differences were of little significance. Nationalism had not yet raised its ugly head, and

political boundaries based on language were not important. This Europe created by German colonization was indeed much closer to a 'one Europe' than it was during later periods. The communal, corporate structure of colonization operated as a full-fledged spatial system, something that was completely new to the region.

The colonization process completely altered the structure of society in Eastern Europe. Before colonization, Slavic society was highly stratified with sovereign prince at the top, upper-class lords of the soil in their various grades next, and a mostly soil-bound, or completely unfree, population of peasants on the bottom. Fortresses, which served as collecting places for produce paid as tribute from peasant holdings, were the focal points of spatial organization. The most striking characteristic of this Slavonic social system was the obligation of personal services from peasant to lord. The economic system was self-sufficient and only a few objects – slaves, furs, beeswax – went to distant markets. The colonists replaced this medieval Slavonic system with a less stratified society. The farmers, while paying rent, owed few personal services to the lord and could pass on or sell their land. The rights of the Slav farmers, therefore, resembled those of the Germans who had left the Empire to escape a feudal system of obligations. The Slavs shook off all bonds of former dependence and took part as settlers in the foundation of villages under German law, side by side with the Germans. Only in areas controlled by the Teutonic Knights did elements of separation between German and Slav remain. Finally, the monasteries imported and exploited some labor from Germany since their grants did not always include the right to reduce the local population to serfdom (Thompson 1928: 537).

The German and American frontiers in perspective

Gerhard (1959) has provided an interesting perspective on the frontier in general and how the process of German settlement in the east differed from the American West. In doing so, he makes reference to Turner's (1893) concept of the frontier as a force influencing society. In other words, the frontier represents a continuous settlement function rather than a defensive one. Although both German and American expansions were marked by the 'pull' of empty land and the 'push' of a surplus population, certain differences can be discerned:

1. *Relationship to indigenous population* Unlike the American settler, who had to deal with nomadic Indian groups of relatively small numbers, German colonists advanced into areas of sedentary population. Relationships with the numerous Slav or Hungarian groups had to be established. As we have seen, these relationships varied from pure domination in the area controlled by the Teutonic Knights to actual assimilation and Germanization in many other regions.

2. *Role of corporate groups* Gerhard feels that a corporate structure involving territorial princes, lords, clergy, merchants, craftsmen, miners, and peasants was a dominating feature of German colonization. Whole groups moved in simultaneously, transferring the economy of the mother country to the east. Although corporate groups like the Mormons settled the American West, the role of individual settlers was much more significant. However, the importance of land speculators and the railroads in establishing towns in the American West should not be minimized.

3. *Religious components* Ecclesiastical initiative and missionary endeavors were basic forces in the German eastward movement. A common crusading spirit of Christianity, which bore resemblance to the Spanish conquest in the New World, existed and contrasted with the development of individual religious denominations on the American frontier.

4. *Role of authorities* The various authorities, both ecclesiastical and secular, sometimes cooperating and sometimes competing, influenced the eastward colonization in Europe in a much more significant way than did the federal government in America. These authorities were on the spot in their individual East European territories and utilized an intermediate authority – the 'locator' – to coordinate the spatial organization of communal–corporate groups.

5. *Pattern of land survey* The pattern of land survey and settlement was fundamentally different on the two frontiers. The Germans used authority and communal society to establish villages around which irregular strips evolved in furlong or long-lot form. Equality was not necessarily the rule. This pattern was completely different from the American homestead located on a part of a rectangular township. In superimposing a uniform and artificial survey system on a nonuniform environment, one may argue that the American settlers were less in harmony with nature than the German colonizers were.

6. *Role of cities* The role of cities perhaps most sharply differentiates the German and American colonization movements. In contrast to the American cities, which were not deliberately planned as focal points of colonization, the German cities were a constituent part of the entire process. Regions were colonized at one time with the city in each case forming a node from which the corporate features of western Germany were transmitted. The spread of German town law and the commercial activity were basic results of this colonization, and they remain important to the present. On the other hand, American cities of the interior, although developing as early commercial centers (e.g. Saint Louis), were never parts of regional colonization schemes.

Summary

As Barraclough (1970: 9–10) states, the Middle Ages period marks a time when a common civilization began to characterize Europe – a period of cultural interchange and assimilation during which institutions of Western Europe were diffused into Eastern Europe by German colonists within a social environment that was less confining than that of Western Europe. These colonists brought with them the three-field system, city law, Christianity, commercial enterprises, and mining technology. Such innovations not only produced aspects of social change but also altered the landscape in ways that have lasted to the present.

Unfortunately, however, this common civilization was not to last. The reciprocal aspects of feudalism, which had been allowed in Eastern Europe during the Middle Ages by colonization, were altered so that serfdom of peasants became predominant. For a variety of reasons, the power of the lords increased and the peasants became increasingly tied to the soil. The so-called *Gutsherrschaft* (estate property) developed in Eastern Europe in lands dominated by Prussia-Germany, Austria-Hungary, and Russia. Large estates were also characteristic of the Turkish Empire. All of this took place while Western Europe moved on through the commercial and industrial revolutions. A division, therefore, developed between commercial-industrial Western Europe and feudal-backward Eastern Europe. This cleavage, still apparent in the landscape, lasted until World War II in some countries like Germany, Poland, and Hungary. The relics of a landscape dominated by castle, palace, large estate, and peasant

village and strip fields were the products of the feudalization process. This process is the subject of the next chapter.

Notes

1. On the map, German names for places are used. In the text of this chapter, German names are used, and, if different today, are followed in parentheses by the present spelling.
2. These ranges are all uplifted blocks of an ancient massif which in central Europe generally are termed *Mittelgebirge*. The Sudetes Mountains represent a collective term for a series of ranges of which the most important is the Giant Mountains (Riesengebirge or Krkonoše). Unfortunately, the term Sudeten has a political significance in terms of German influence in the area. The word Sudetes is used for these mountains by Demek and Střida (1971) in their *Geography of Czechoslovakia*.
3. Although the German towns of Transylvania are labelled 'Saxon', most of the settlers came from the Rhine area of Germany. Tihany (1976: 49) goes so far as to state that the German migrations into Transylvania probably provided the historical background for the Pied Piper of Hamelin folk story.
4. Towns with 'zig' or 'in' endings (Leipzig or Berlin) seem to have been of Slav origin (Thompson 1928: 525). An actual Slavic enclave is Bautzen in Saxony, which is today the center of a small island of Sorb culture in East Germany. This town, seemingly doomed to extinction by German pressure and by separation from the others, was preserved by the interest which Germans like Georg Körner took in it and its folkways. Today, one sees the traditional Sorb costumes in the streets.

4
Landscapes of feudalism

One of the most impressive geographical characteristics of Europe from the Middle Ages to the present has been the social and economic contrast between the western and eastern portions of the continent, a contrast coinciding with a dividing line separating Germanic peoples in the west from Slavic and Hungarian groups in the east. In the early nineteenth century, the cleavage gained prominence with tales from travelers who crossed the Hungarian plain (Alföld), an area comprising a wilderness of swamp and steppe given over to livestock. The malevolent remark of a Viennese diplomat holds some truth: 'Behind the garden of my house, Asia begins.' The contrasts between west and east were very evident as late as the 1930s when Eastern Europe was largely peasant with only a few scattered regions of industry and a general lack of urban development. Although these differences between west and east in Europe are being reduced considerably under communist efforts at modernization, the landscape still tells this story of cleavage through the middle of the continent.

According to many scholars, a major factor in this contrast is that Eastern Europe retained feudal characteristics much longer than Western Europe did. Today, the landscape reflects the imprint of this social order by the persistence of relics of both the nobility – castles, palaces, or estates – and the peasants – strip fields, cottages of laborers, and villages. For six hundred years – 1350 to 1945 – the lord was an important decision-maker in Eastern Europe, and feudalism, although varying in its characteristics and in its impact on different periods, was a persistent process affecting spatial organization. The feudal lord had to contend with the rising influence of multinational

rulers and nationalistic peoples. The process of feudalism, therefore, was interwoven with the processes of multinationalism and nationalism, which are subjects of the next two chapters. The feudal era, which lasted from the fourteenth century right up to the First World War in most cases and even to the Second World War in a few places, is paradoxical because it was preceded by a period of progress dominated by German colonization (950–1350). What happened, then, to change this pattern of historical development and to reverse the progress of social change? The answer to this question lies in the persistent roles of lord and peasant in Eastern Europe.

The role of the lord in forming the East European landscape

The rise of serfdom in Eastern Europe

Perhaps the primary factor explaining this social and economic cleavage that developed between the two halves of Europe was the rise of serfdom – one aspect of feudalism – in the east as it began to decline in the west. Although feudalism is a broad term, we defined it as a social system of rights and obligations between lords and vassals; the latter held land on the condition that military and other services would be rendered to the lord in return for protection and use of the land. However, the system of feudalism established in Eastern Europe in the years 950–1350 and to which the German colonists contributed, constituted a less confining social environment than existed in the west, where society was hierarchical and where the position of the lord was dependent upon a feudal contract between him and his sovereign. Peasants in Western Europe were serfs or unfree laborers because they were bound to the lord and land by institutional ties – rather than contractual – which were degrading; the lord had jurisdiction over the peasants to the exclusion of the state in terms of their movement and obligations. In Eastern Europe, however, the environment was less hierarchical and rigid. The status of the lord was less dependent upon a feudal contract with the ruler than upon his *de facto* position as soldier, owner of land, and colonizing entrepreneur. The legal and material position of the peasant, also, was better: although obligations existed, labor dues and rents were low; farms were larger and more prosperous; land could be sold or handed down to heirs; and, finally, freedom to move was possible.

With such a start, the eastern part of Europe should have forged ahead of the west or at least have kept up with it. Such was not to

be. The paths of political, economic, and social development diverged in the fourteenth and fifteenth centuries, producing a serious cleavage which has persisted to the present. A variety of factors explain this divergence in development, but an important one was the *late* rise of serfdom in Eastern Europe and its role in restricting social change. Thus, as the position of the peasant improved in Western Europe, it worsened in Eastern Europe. Gradually, strong rulers in Western Europe, acting independently of the nobility, established norms for the obligations a lord could demand of the peasants. Work obligations were converted to rent payments and serfs eventually became free. In the east, however, the rulers became more dependent on the lords and thus allowed them to increase their powers over the peasant class, especially as a means of producing grain for export; the bond between lord and serf ceased to be one of mutual obligation, degenerating into one-sided exploitation or serfdom.

What are the reasons for this belated rise of serfdom in Eastern Europe? Jerome Blum, in an article entitled 'The Rise of Serfdom in Eastern Europe' (1957: 807–36), feels that four interrelated factors explain this phenomenon and the strong geographical contrasts that arose between eastern and western parts of the continent: (1) the increase in the political power of the nobility; (2) the growth of seigneurial jurisdictional powers over the peasantry living on their manors; (3) the shift by the lords from being rent recipients to being producers for the market; and (4) the decline of the cities and of the urban middle class. I now examine these factors briefly.

The *first* factor, a rise in the power of the nobility at the expense of rulers in Eastern Europe (except for Russia and Byzantium), occurred at the very time when strong monarchs were establishing centralized power in the west. The series of wars, epidemics, and financial crises of the period from 1350 to 1650 caused the rulers of the east to look to the noble groups for political and economic support. Postan (1970: 167–71) indicates that the structure of state economy and society in the east can be called 'feudal' because the landowners continued to perform military and administrative functions long after Western European rulers had ceased to be dependent on the nobility for these functions and relied, instead, on hired soldiers and civil servants. Eastern rulers, therefore, continued to be dependent on the lords, a situation that had arisen out of the *de facto* position of the lords, who operated from the beginning rather freely without a feudal contract.

In return for this support, the lords were given land and greater control over their peasants, the *second* factor in the late rise of serfdom in Eastern Europe. The economic and political rights of the peasants, formerly guaranteed by German law and supported by the rulers, were transferred to the noble class. This transfer was facilitated because these rights were not anchored in legal codes as in western Germany (Mayhew 1973: 135). In the sixteenth century in Poland, for example, royal courts no longer could hear cases between peasants and their lords. Coupled with this was the loss of municipal rights as the lords gained power over mayors of towns and thereby the villages under them. Perhaps most important were laws passed in the sixteenth and seventeenth centuries binding peasants to the land by abolishing the right of migration in Prussian, Russian, and Hungarian territories (Berend and Ránki 1974a: 5). By the end of the fifteenth century, Blum (1957: 826) states that 'the noble had become the government so far as the peasants who lived on his land were concerned. He was their judge, their police chief, their jailor, their tax collector, and sometimes he chose the clergymen in their church.'

This power of the noble class over the peasant was an important factor when the export markets for grain opened up in the sixteenth century, a *third* factor that Blum mentions for the divergent development of Eastern Europe. These western markets developed when the price of grain rose substantially in Western Europe (e.g. rye increased sixfold in the sixteenth century) from a shortage generated by population increase and the enclosure of land for pasture. Those lords in Eastern Europe occupying land accessible to the Baltic Sea, therefore, took steps to plant more grain for export by expanding their demesnes. In some cases, this expansion occurred in the fifteenth century by taking over land abandoned by peasants (*Wüstungen*) as a result of epidemics, wars, soil erosion, and economic depressions. Gutkind (VII, 1972: 6) remarks, for example, that at the beginning of the sixteenth century 30 per cent of the cultivable land in Poland was abandoned. In other cases, the lords expanded demesnes by expropriating peasant land – the so-called *Bauernlegen* (laying of peasants). Dispossessed peasants, lacking support, were forced to work as laborers on the estates. Peasants who retained some land had their services increased, a situation which often caused them to leave and seek better conditions elsewhere; their loss of legal rights made this move difficult, however. In essence, they were tied to the land and became serfs.

This change in the nature of estates in Eastern Europe was a

fundamental one that requires additional comment. Basically, the change was from a rental system (*Grundherrschaft*) to a large-scale proprietor cultivation (*Gutsherrschaft*) (Hitze 1914: 499–500; Abel 1962: 187–93). The German terms are generic in the sense that the changes occurred in a large area of northern Eastern Europe including Prussia, Poland, Hungary, and Bohemia-Moravia. The first term represents the type of feudalism, mentioned in the previous chapter, that was transmitted by German colonists to Eastern Europe. Rent was paid by the peasant to the lord partly in produce and partly in cash. The burden of the peasantry was not great because manual labor played a small role in this type of estate. The lord was not a large-scale producer, only needing enough food for his household and his soldiers to play his role in society. Thus, his *demesne* was small and the peasants needed to spend less than twenty days a year laboring there. In fact, much of the lord's land was distributed among the peasants who tilled it in common. Above all, this type of feudalism was characterized by a series of mutual relationships between the lord and his peasants in terms of protection, rent, labor, and other functions.

This *Grundherrschaft* gradually gave way to a large-scale feudal operation for profit known as the *Gutsherrschaft*. Such a change was influenced especially by the growing of grain for export, as evidenced today by the landscape relics of medieval granaries in Gdańsk and Kazimierz Dolny (on the middle Vistula River) (see Photo 4.1). In addition, the export of timber, flax, and hemp took place in the Baltic region. In Hungary, the export of cattle supplemented that of grain. The outstanding characteristic of these estates was serfdom in which peasants, dispossessed of their land, were tied to the lord and forced to perform compulsory service. The condition of these peasant laborers represents one of the worst examples of human exploitation in the history of European agriculture. This situation did not change after the serfs were freed in the nineteenth century: peasants continued to be exploited by having to work as farm laborers on estates, especially in Prussia, Poland, and Hungary.

These three factors explaining the late rise of serfdom in Eastern Europe – increase in political power, jurisdiction over the peasants, and increased exports – are supplemented by a *fourth* factor which is related to the other three, namely, the decline of the towns. Although towns were important during the period of German colonization, they began to lose ground to the nobility in the sixteenth century. The chief reasons for their decline were trade

Photo 4.1   An enormous *Zuraw* (crane), now a leading relic and symbol of the early trading functions of Danzig (Gdańsk), was built in the fifteenth century, well after the original German settlement. The crane was reconstructed after the damage of the Second World War.

contraction within Eastern Europe caused by break-up of the Hanseatic League, defeat of the Teutonic Order, and war and strife throughout much of the area. These factors helped to isolate Eastern Europe from changes generated in Western Europe by the Commercial Revolution that included the rise of a middle class of traders and artisans in cities. The Ottoman Turks blocked changes from the south and even controlled the Mediterranean Sea for a period. At the same time, the nobility in all parts of Eastern Europe was following an anti-urban policy that sought, from rulers, economic concessions which would promote their own interests at the expense of cities. Above all, the nobles wanted to break the urban monopolies in

foreign and domestic trade. The noble class, therefore, came to bypass the towns by selling their grain to foreign merchants directly from their estates; gained tariff advantages over the urban merchants in the sale of goods; secured rights to the sale of certain products like beer; and, finally, stopped the cities from taking in runaway peasants.

This decline of the cities is of fundamental importance in explaining why Eastern Europe remained a backward, agrarian society in which an institution like serfdom, rejected in the West, was able to flourish. The nature of towns in Eastern Europe became quite different from that in Western Europe. In the former, noble influence caused towns to stagnate into provincial market places with few functions of handicrafts or regional commerce. In addition, Volgyes (1980: 95) points out that urban areas frequently were viewed as 'illegitimate', for in Poland, Hungary, and Bohemia they were dominated by foreign princes and dynasties. At the same time, the cities of Western Europe were entering a new period of commercial expansion that contributed to the transformation of society there. This contrast between towns in Europe was based on differences in political development of the eastern nobility, who came to dominate both town and countryside, a situation that was not true in the west. These events affected the landscape: the east became a land dominated by large estates with the towns exhibiting only limited commercial and industrial development.

The four factors previously cited to explain the late rise of serfdom in Eastern Europe are focused on the fifteenth and sixteenth centuries when the nobles gained power at the expense of the political rulers. In the seventeenth and eighteenth centuries, however, this situation changed as strong rulers arose in Prussia, Austria, and Russia to challenge the independence of the noble class. These rulers are called 'absolute' because they answered to no one in developing strong centralized states into which the nobility was integrated. Although the effect of the absolute ruler on the landscape is treated in the next chapter, it is mentioned here because of the overlap with feudalism. In part, absolutism in Eastern Europe was a reaction to a need for defense against aggressive states such as Sweden, France, and the Ottoman Turks. To survive, the rulers of Prussia, Austria, and Russia (in Poland control was always in the hands of the nobility, and in Turkey the power of the sultan was diminished after the sixteenth century as oligarchic factions took over) had to establish strong centralized states, a step which required the help of the nobility.

The nobility, however, had historically opposed the rulers, so a trade-off was arranged: the lords were integrated increasingly into the state apparatus as military men and civil servants – a sort of service nobility – in return for trade advantages over towns and for complete control over the countryside including help in binding peasants to the land. In this way, where absolute rulers were in control, serfdom as an aspect of feudalism was prolonged until the modern era. As the mobility of peasants increased during the wars, depressions, and other changes of the sixteenth and seventeenth centuries, the nobles in particular faced the problem of a labor shortage on their estates; however, the concessions by the absolute rulers to the nobles gave the latter a means of controlling this mobility especially through laws prohibiting peasant migration. Serfdom-feudalism in Eastern Europe, then, arose in a period of weak rulers but continued well into a period of strong rulers, i.e. absolutism.

Serfdom in different areas

Prussia exemplified how the noble class preserved its power in Eastern Europe through all the changes of absolutism, industrializ-ation, and liberal reforms – thereby influencing the landscape. This class became known as the Junkers or *junk-herre*, a term originally designating a young nobleman but later a synonym pertaining to any person claiming noble status and privilege. The original landowners had developed grain very early for exporting purposes and in the sixteenth century had forced a weak Elector to transfer from the cities to them the exclusive right to perform this function. This early form of capitalistic agriculture was supported by increasing bondage of the peasants as the Junkers altered the peasants' obligations from money dues to services. After a long period of uncontested rule over the provincial areas of Prussia, however, the Junkers were finally forced to compromise with the strong Hohenzollern rulers who were developing a centralized, militaristic state (Goodwin 1953: 83–101). Frederick William I, the Elector, worked out an agreement in 1653 in which the Junkers renounced degrees of political independence and accepted an active role in supporting a standing army. The Junker rights of patrimonial jurisdiction over their feudal tenants, however, were left undisturbed and the lords retained a secure hold on the day-to-day administration of the country districts. More significantly, the alliance of 1653 broke down the provincial isolation of the Junkers

and opened avenues to new careers for them as professional army officers and salaried government employees.

Even in the nineteenth century, the Junkers managed to survive the changes of liberalism and industrialization. The laws of 1807, 1811, and 1816 (the Stein-Hardenberg Reforms), although emancipating the serfs, actually furthered the economic interests of the lords by permitting them to enlarge their estates by claiming peasant land as indemnification. The laws, therefore, restricted social change by forcing the small peasants into work as landless day laborers. Dunman (1975: 129) points out that from 1811 to 1848 more than one million hectares – one-third of the agricultural area in the provinces of East and West Prussia, Brandenburg, Pomerania, and Silesia – were transferred from peasants to large estate owners. In this way, the landscape of agrarian dualism in Germany between large estates to the east of the Elbe River and small farms to the west was considerably intensified. In the nineteenth century, the Junkers also participated as entrepreneurs in industry and together with positions as civil servant and military officers made a continuing contribution to the rise of Prussia-Germany. Muncy (1944: 35) says that 'the Junkers' most fundamental principle was to fight to conserve in all its aspects a social order of which they were the chief beneficiaries'. Today, through estate residences and day-laborer quarters, the landscape still reflects the role of this class.

In Austria, as well, the noble classes retained power for a lengthy period and thereby preserved the institution of serfdom that stabilized landscape change. Schenk and Macartney (1953: 102–35) explain that although the situation differed in the Bohemian and Hungarian portions of the Empire, the result was the same. In Bohemia, the nobility became truly multinational after 1620 when most of the Czech aristocracy was forced into exile. The new nobility of Bohemia, recruited from different parts of Europe, tended to support the Habsburgs and even occupied important posts in the court in return for retention of their privileges. In Hungary, the great magnates or large land holders – but not the gentry or lesser nobility – also were devoted to the Habsburgs and their interests. Although the nobilities of Bohemia and Hungary cannot necessarily be lumped together, they did show similarities, because they tended to be multinational in origin and supported the imperial court. Their palaces in the city and their estates in the country continued to dominate the landscape.

Still another country in Eastern Europe in which the nobility

preserved their power and way of life, thereby influencing the land-scape, was Poland. The lords, called the *Szlachta*, were of varied origin – Polish, Lithuanian, Ukrainian – but were thoroughly Polonized in culture. They enjoyed a monopoly of power exceeding that described for Prussia and Austria. This nobility elected the king – who after 1370 was mainly of foreign origin – and, in return for votes, exacted from him the assurance that he would be nothing but a figurehead. Poland, therefore, was a loose federation of fifty or so small noble oligarchies without any effective central authority. The *Szlachta* used its political power to exempt itself from compulsory military service and from most taxes and to give itself a monopoly of land ownership over the peasantry and of all high offices in Church and state. However, its internal weakness eventually contributed to partition in the latter part of the eighteenth century. Even though the state of Poland disappeared from the map of Europe for over a hundred years, the *Szlachta* survived, and some of their town and country residences remain to tell a story of oligarchy in Poland. After 1918, this class re-emerged to wield considerable power up to the Second World War. For example, in 1921, 2000 noble families owned an average of 3000 hectares of land (Dunman 1975: 162).

In the Balkans, feudalism as a process is not nearly so evident in the landscape. Seton-Watson (1946: 56, 60) mentions that neither the Byzantine Empire nor the Ottoman Empire was a feudal state as in the previously described sense. From Roman times the Byzantine Empire had preserved a centralized monarchical system, which never allowed the lord magnates to build great power. During the centuries of Ottoman rule, land ownership was concentrated in the hands of the state but administered by landlords appointed by the sultan. Thus, the landlord – serf relationship was of a special nature and the peasants were actually subject to the state. The landlord was only a state official without ownership. Throughout much of the Balkans, therefore, no real aristocracy existed in the sense that it did in the northern part of Eastern Europe. In Bosnia and Albania, certain Moslem converts held land and constituted a special aristocracy under Turkish rule. Some Wallachian families in Romania were landowners, but most of the aristocracy were Phanariots, Greek princes from Constantinople who ruled the principalities of the area for a price.

As the Balkan lands were freed from Turkish control in the eighteenth and nineteenth centuries, the pattern of land tenure changed. In the north, in areas taken from the Turks by Austria, large estates

controlled by Austrian and Hungarian lords appeared; by 1905, for example, a mere 209 owners held a quarter of the agricultural land in Croatia and Slavonia (Allcock 1977: 543–4). Farther south in Serbia and Bulgaria, however, the peasants gained control of the land, an event that was to influence the landscape up to the socialist period.

Carsten (1954: 276) feels that the influence of the nobility was the most important factor in the social history of Eastern Europe, creating a boundary line between social systems of the two parts of the continent. As he states, 'The nobility preserved serfdom as the condition of the majority of the population, it monopolized the key positions in state and army, and it effectively prevented the carrying through of any reforms which could have curtailed its power and influence.'

Some characteristics of the nobility

The two major classes of the nobility – the great magnates and the gentry – differed in their place in society, in their ideology, and in their effect on the landscape (Knapp 1976: Ch. 1).

The great magnates, who were the few great families dominating the noble class in the different countries, owed their position in society to birth, for most of them traced their ancestry to a knightly class of the Middle Ages. The basis of their power was land in the form of large estates that provided a steady income and that were worked by peasants bound to the lords. Except in Prussia, these estates were characterized by low production per unit of land. Their large size was perpetuated by two legal devices – primogeniture or inheritance by the oldest son, and 'entail' or prohibition on selling estate land. These estates dominated large parts of the landscape of Eastern Europe. In Bohemia in the seventeenth century the aristocracy and the Church controlled three-quarters of the land. In Hungary in the nineteenth century, 46 of about 200 great families owned more than 3600 square miles (9320 sq. km) of territory – an area somewhat smaller than the state of Connecticut. The greatest landowner was Prince Eszterházy, who owned 29 estates, 160 market towns, and 414 villages; he was followed by Baron von Sica with 19 estates; Count Karolyi, also 19; and Count Széchenyi, 18 (Blum 1948: 36). The percentages of land held by the noble class were equally high in Prussia and Poland. In the latter country, the estates were geographically more significant in the eastern areas of Lithuania and the

81

Ukraine – the home of great families like Radziwiłł, Potocki, Sapieha, Pac, Ogiński, and Sanguszko (Boswell 1953: 167–9). In all of these areas – Bohemia, Hungary, and Poland – palaces built on these estates still stand as relics of this social order.

As explained earlier in this chapter, the great magnates represented a cosmopolitan group. Their ties were to the ruler and to other members of their class in place of loyalty to a particular nationality. For example, the nobility of Lithuania had more in common with the Polish nobility than they did with the Lithuanian peasants with whom, in fact, they might not have been able to converse. However, the most extreme example of a cosmopolitan nobility was that of Bohemia. Schenk (1953: 106) remarks that the Protestant majority of the old Bohemian nobility had been forced into exile after the battle of the White Mountain in 1620, leaving in the seventeenth century only eight of the ancient Czech aristocratic families: Čzernín, Kinsky, Kolovrat, Lobkovic, Wallenstein, Schlick, Sternberg, and Kaunitz. Toward the end of the century, only about 15 per cent of the nobility in this area was of Bohemian origin; the remainder consisted of families recruited from other countries – for example, Trautmannsdorf, Auersperg, and Sternegg from Austria; and the Schwarzenberg, Fürstenberg, and Rottenhaus from Germany. Other families were from France, England, and Ireland. The map shows the geographical distribution of these families in Bohemia in the seventeenth century and their cosmopolitan nature (see Fig. 4.1). All of these families had offered their services to the Emperor and, during and after the Thirty Years' War, were richly rewarded in terms of land. In the middle of the eighteenth century, this denationalized noble class of Bohemia was welded to Austria by a series of administrative actions. Czech was hardly spoken by the landowners, thereby widening the cleavage between nobles and peasants.

Although their basis for wealth and power lay in the countryside, the great magnates actually spent much time in the cities. During the seventeenth and eighteenth centuries, these landowners became urbanized and thereby absentee rural landlords. In most cases, they were members of the court and supported the imperial rulers. The magnates also assumed an increasing role in state government as they penetrated the military, Church, and civil service. Their privileged position in urban society is reflected in the elaborate urban palaces which complemented their rural ones. Capital cities – like Berlin, Warsaw, Prague, and Budapest – and even regional centers – like

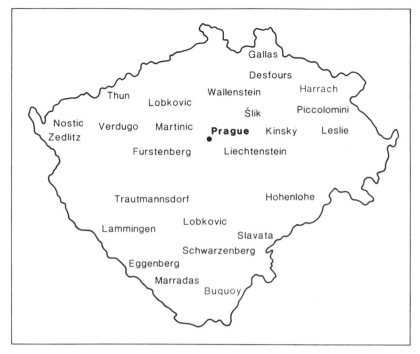

Fig. 4.1 Bohemia: distribution of aristocratic families about 1650. (Source: *Školní Atlas Československých Dějin* [Prague: Kartografie, 1959], p. 19.)

Poznań, Bratislava, and Zagreb – retain the palace as an important component of the present-day urban landscape.

What kind of person was the great magnate? He dominated national institutions like the royal court, legislative bodies, judicial offices, civil service, military, and even the Church; was well educated, often in foreign cities for a long period which ended with a 'Grand Tour'; sought cultural enlightenment in Italy, which often was reflected in the architecture of the palace he built; was also a patron of the arts, establishing sizeable collections for the public and sponsoring musicians as Eszterházy sponsored Haydn; and, lastly, in a political sense, served to limit the despotic power of the crown.

In contrast to the great magnates, who were relatively few in number but possessed enormous power, the more numerous lesser nobility or gentry occupied a lower position within Eastern European society. In many cases, like Hungary, they owed their position to birth but had lost status with time. In other cases, they were not true

aristocracy, but generally had been elevated to this position by the monarch who attempted to offset the magnates by creating a loyal group of supporters. However, the gentry often resisted the rulers as those of Hungary resisted the Habsburgs. This class remained rural-oriented, based on small estates from which they received rent, in cash or kind, from servile labor. Knapp (1976: 14) mentions that the Hungarian gentry often owned two homes, one in the local village and one a few miles out in the countryside; in comparison with the homes of the magnates, these residences were rather unpretentious, yet they remain today to portray social structure in this area during the eighteenth and nineteenth centuries.

In Prussia, Poland, and Hungary, the nobility gradually developed a 'tradition' that legitimated the subordination of the peasant masses and provided a model of behavior that included values of elitism, heredity, and social acceptance, a dislike for manual work, and an anti-urban and anticommercial mentality. The attitude of the nobility is expressed by the Hungarian poet, Petöfi (1845: 340), when he writes: 'Serf, repair that road! Your horse has to carry me, of course. Walking's not for me – and why? A Magyar nobleman am I!'

Above all, the nobility's perception of society was narrow not only in terms of their own bias against investment, payment of taxes, and commercial activity, but also in any extension of opportunities to other groups or classes. In turn, this narrow view led to a restriction on social change evidenced at both the local and national levels. Locally, noble wealth was based on land, yet the nobles did not really invest in this resource very extensively, e.g. through practices such as rotation, use of fertilizer, and drainage projects. In most parts of Eastern Europe, however, the estate, where it existed, was extensive in nature. Warriner (1939: 12) notes that, except in Prussia, where the lord ran his estate on modern lines, the feudal landlord did not function as an entrepreneur investing capital in his estate or even in processing of products. The large estates were often tilled by the peasants for the benefit of absentee owners, generally with the peasant's animals and plows and often with their seed. Any increase in the productivity of estates did not result from economic superiority but from the landed class exploiting the prevailing economic social conditions with all their abuses.

On the national level, the lord also restricted social change. Macartney (1953: 133–4) has emphasized the debit side of the ledger in Hungary when he writes that 'the nobles' tenacious defense of their privileges undoubtedly prevented the evolution of Hungary into a

modern state'. The nobles not only refused to accept taxation but also resisted any attempt at reducing the peasant socage obligations, which included rent or work for the lord. This resistance, of course, was directed against the Habsburgs, who in retaliation (especially on the taxation issue) refused their assistance in developing Hungary economically by applying discriminatory tariffs against the state, deliberately keeping it a colonial market for Austrian industrial products. The present-day cleavage between Austria and Hungary in their economic landscapes goes back, in part, to this period. Exceptions existed, of course, for enlightened elements among the magnates reclaimed and settled marsh areas, introduced modern methods of agriculture, and even formed industrial enterprises.

Relics of the nobility from the feudal period

The relics of the nobility that survive in the landscape from the long period of feudalism consist of the rural and urban residences and a few towns planned and built by them. The land holdings, including the field patterns, of the nobility no longer exist in exactly the same form, although some of the large collective or state farms bear a striking similarity in terms of size. In addition, certain relics of economic activity by the nobility remain, such as industrial factories and drainage projects. The most ubiquitous relics, however, are the residences – castles, palaces, or manor houses – which are so impressive in both rural and urban landscapes. It should be noted that the geographical distribution of these residences, more than anything, reflects political as well as other factors. Warriner (1939: 13–17), for example, shows that large estates were located in both advanced Prussia and backward Hungary, thereby reflecting the persistence of the lords' political power. If large estates really indicated a higher degree of efficiency, they should have been found in the most economically advanced countries where agricultural technique was high. Instead, they were found in all types of areas and, therefore, represent relics of a social system (feudalism) rather than relics of advanced technology.

Rural residences

A rural residence of the nobility in Eastern Europe was either a castle or a palace. The castle, characteristic of the Middle Ages when security was lacking in rural areas, was of necessity a fortified resi-

dence often situated on an inaccessible hilltop. The palace, on the other hand, came later when absolute rulers had created greater security through standing armies and when gunpowder had made the castle obsolete. Both forms are omnipresent in Europe today despite the destruction by many intervening wars. Frenzel (1970: 11) estimates that between 100 000 and 200 000 castles exist in Europe, but he feels that these figures are probably on the conservative side. I cannot find any figures for palaces, but the number is equally high. Certainly the two together dominate the rural historical landscape of Europe. Many of these structures were built by rulers of state, but only those constructed by the nobility, whose ideology and social change they reflect, concern us here.

The major noble-class residences that are preserved today in the Czechoslovakian landscape are shown on the map, which is taken from *Města Hrady a Zámky* (Prague 1970) (see Fig. 4.2). I have included not only the castle and palace but also the city, because the noble class was associated with its development as well. As is apparent from the map, these residences are located in all portions of Bohemia and Moravia as well as Slovakia. This map complements the earlier one which shows the widespread distribution of the cosmopolitan nobility of Bohemia (see Fig. 4.1).

Some of the earlier residences in Czechoslovakia were constructed during the Middle Ages in Gothic style as fortified castles; many are

Fig. 4.2 Major relics of the nobility in Czechoslovakia. The locations demonstrate that they are ubiquitous features of the landscape. (Source: adapted from *Města Hrady a Zámky*, 1970, endcover map)

now either in ruins or in a different form as the result of reconstruction. One example is Hrad Hasištejn (Burg Hassenstein) in northwest Bohemia. A plan of this castle shows the primary elements of outer and inner walls with gates, keep or inner fortress, chapel, and residential apartments. Since fortresses of this type generally were constructed in hilly terrain for defense, they adapted to fit the contour of the site. As defense against the cannon became a factor, battery towers and barbicans jutting from the walls were added; outstanding examples of these features are evident at Frýdlant and Pernštejn. The Hungarian connection with Slovakia is shown in castles at Krásná Horka and Smolenice, which were built by the Hungarian noble families of Mariassy and Pálffy, respectively.

In the late Middle Ages and during the period of absolutism, the fortress elements were de-emphasized while the residential or palace features increased in importance. The courtyard, therefore, increased in size, and the apartments expanded to include variety such as banquet halls, galleries for art objects, and even dance salons. Some of the noble residences in Czechoslovakia fall into the category of a castle-palace, i.e. an original castle modified into a palace-type residence. One of the best examples of such an edifice dominates the town of Krumau (Český Krumlov), which is located on a bend of the Moldau Vltava River in southern Bohemia (see Photo 4.2). As a Gothic castle, it passed through the hands of the Vitkovec and Rožmberk families. The latter began to transform the castle into a Renaissance residence, and this transformation continued under the Eggenbergs and the Schwarzenbergs during the seventeenth and eighteenth centuries. Today, the residence contains three hundred rooms including a chapel, numismatics chamber, picture galleries, and halls for other purposes. However, it is hard to think of the castle-palace without including the surrounding town, which evolved with it and, indeed, is considered a historical relic as an entity. However, the Český Krumlov residence was the seat of power of various noble families in the countryside and cannot be called an urban residence similar to those which will be mentioned later in connection with Prague.

In the eighteenth century the palace began to dominate the rural landscape of northern Eastern Europe just as the castle had done earlier. This development was, of course, tied in with the increasing security provided by the armies of absolutist states like Prussia and Austria (including Bohemia and Hungary) and even nonabsolute Poland before the partitions. If a noble family chose not to retain and

Photo 4.2   The castle of Krumau (Česky Krumlov), located in southern Bohemia on a bend of the Moldau (Vltava) River, is an example of a well-preserved relic of a noble residence.

expand its castle into a residence, it established new palaces in both rural and urban areas. This move was particularly true of the great magnates, who, as mentioned previously, became attached to the court and the developing urban life. These great nobles, therefore, tended to become urban residents and, as absentee landowners, to utilize the rural estates only occasionally.

Very little was spared in making the rural palaces reflect the power of the social class. Often times the prototype for the larger residences was the Palace of Versailles outside Paris, but only absolute kings like Frederick the Great or the wealthiest noble families could match this model. Nevertheless, certain similarities differ only in scale. The architecture was international rather than national, and, therefore, showed elements of uniformity regardless of location. Italian architects often were brought in, and their influence is evident. Both Renaissance and Baroque styles were used, depending on the date. However, Baroque style dominated because it was associated with absolutism: 'It was the social soil from which it sprang' (Frenzel 1970: 13). This architectural style emphasizes outer effect by giving façades plasticity and depth using boldly projected or recessed features with

pediments and huge colonnades. Individual architectural forms were overstated to appeal to the sensibilities of the beholder and to influence the emotions. Individual palaces exhibited these features to a greater or lesser extent.

Perhaps even more characteristic of the country palace was the elaborate site planning. All of the buildings were arranged symmetrically in a horseshoe shape around the palace while the entire ensemble was surrounded by geometric gardens. Avenues and paths converged on the palace in axial fashion and sometimes water bodies were incorporated. These gardens were elaborately landscaped and often included small buildings of a symbolic nature like a Greek temple.

In Czechoslovakia, outstanding examples of planned palaces, and the aristocratic families who built them, are at Roudnice (Lobkowic), Slavkov (Kaunitz), Chroustovice (Kinský), and Kozel (Čzerín). The Austrian family Trautmannsdorf constructed a palace at Jemniště, while the German family of Harrach was associated with Červený Hrádek. The international origin of these palaces is further illustrated by the one built by the Hungarian Serényi family at Milotice. The palace at Dobříš with its formal gardens is one of the most typical in terms of planned layout (see Photo 4.3).

Relics of the gentry illustrate the lower position of this group in Eastern Europe: hundreds of modest manor houses persist – either in villages or out in the country – as relics of a period of feudalism when the lesser nobility preserved a measure of power in the countryside against the rule of strong monarchs. These relics are especially well represented in Hungary, where the gentry was so numerous, and in parts of Prussia (now East Germany), where many of the Junkers were often of the gentry class, particularly in the nineteenth century when some of their powers were curtailed. My visit to outstanding examples of manor houses of the gentry at Stresow and Bandelin in Kreis Greifswald confirms their modest appearance in comparison to palaces of the great magnates (see Photo 4.4). Obenaus (1975: 175) provides details of a Prussian estate as it existed in 1937 in Leezen in the Schwerin area of Mecklenburg. The top map shows the original estate, while the bottom one illustrates the transformation that has occurred under socialism (see Fig. 4.3). As shown, some of the old buildings including the manor house, barn, stables, and residences of workers are still present as relics; however, their actual use today may vary from what it was in the past. Nevertheless, the overall impression from travels through Mecklenburg and

Photo 4.3   The Dobříš palace of Bohemia illustrates the elaborate architecture and site planning of the feudal era. (Source: *Města Hrady a Zámky* 1970: p. 189.)

Vorpommern (Lower Pomerania) is of a landscape of collective and state farms utilizing many of the old estate facilities. In other words, the feudal landscape is still apparent.

Today, these estates located in the countryside, whether a palace of the great magnate or a manor house of the gentry, generally are utilized by the communists for some functional purpose, usually agricultural, although other uses are encountered. Several years ago when I visited an estate in Poland, I was given three interpretations of that relic revealing how the Party relates history to a Marxist ideology: (1) the owner of the estate exploited the peasants in the past; (2) the architectural merits of the building deserve display; and (3) the building – now a health institute – should serve a functional

Photo 4.4   Prussian manor house in Bandelin, East Germany, is now the headquarters of a collective farm.

purpose in a socialist society. All of these views are ideological. The first explains in Marxist terms the role of the relic in the past. The second justifies the use of the building as a tourist sight in a nationalistic sense, i.e. that the Poles in an earlier era were capable of producing works of art. This view is interesting because the residence itself is not necessarily Polish in appearance, many estates being the product of foreign architects. Finally, the third view stresses the need for all structures to play a social role in a Marxist-Leninist society.

Therefore, function does not follow form in historic structures within socialist countries, for the old residences of the nobility today serve a variety of functions that vary with their form – farm headquarters, museum, hospital, hotel, restaurant, and government institute. Analysis of the use of historic buildings in such societies reveals that Marxist settlement patterns are, in part, preconditioned by the existing environment, since wiping out the old and creating a totally new pattern is impossible.

The feudal estate is much more important as a relic in the northern part of Eastern Europe than in the Balkans, because in the latter most of the Ottoman land was controlled directly by the Turkish government or was in the hands of military or civil officials as fiefs for

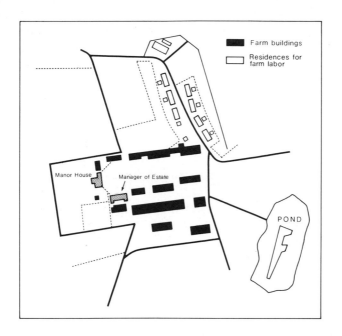

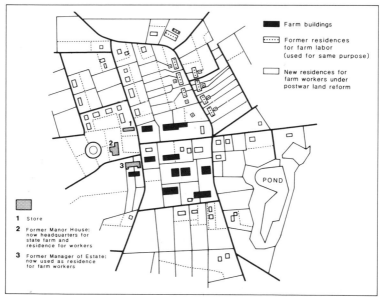

Fig. 4.3 Transformation of a Prussian estate at Leezen in Mecklenburg. Top, as it existed in 1937; bottom, as a state farm today. Former manor house and manager residence are now used for administration. (Source: Obenaus, 1975, 175.)

service. Only in the nineteenth century did some of this land become private estates under certain officials who had it worked by non-Moslem subjects. These estates, known as *čifliks* of which only a few traces exist today in Serbia and Bulgaria, varied in size and appearance but usually contained a mansion in the form of a tower (*külle*) whose windowless upper stories were inaccessible to outsiders. Grouped around the mansion in no particular form were residences for the women, living quarters for the workers, and stalls, barns, and sheds (Gutkind, VIII 1972: 18–19). In some cases, the *čiflik* was a village composed of buildings around one or more squares – sometimes walled – within which the homesteads of the peasants were arranged more like contiguous cells than houses. The village of Slivnica, west of Sofia, Bulgaria, was once a *čiflik*; portions of others are scattered through the southern Balkans.

Urban residences

The great magnates were really urban dwellers although they retained castles or palace residences in the countryside. Many of the Bohemian noble families possessed houses in both Vienna and Prague.

> In 18th Century Prague, the typical setting would be provided by the *palais* Čzernín, Lobkowic, and Fürstenberg, as well as by the delightful gardens surrounding these splendid town residences. On the outskirts of the city, Count Michna's miniature Villa Amerika, designed by that great architect Kilian Ignaz Dientzenhofer, and Count Sternberg's picturesque Castle Troja, deserve more than a passing interest (Schenk 1953: 113).

The importance of the nobility in the urban landscape of Prague is illustrated by a map that shows the ever-present palace (see Fig. 4.4). This landscape of palaces is preserved today as an outstanding laboratory of East European history and architecture.

In Prague, many of these palaces are located in the Malá Strana (Lesser Town), which was originally a second town of Prague (after the Staré Město or Old Town), founded by royal charter in 1257. Its special character as the residential district of the nobility developed in the seventeenth and eighteenth centuries. After the Battle of the White Mountain in 1620, the whole area, which lies in the shadow of the Prague castle, was rebuilt, the palaces of the important noble families forming the largest component. For the building of the

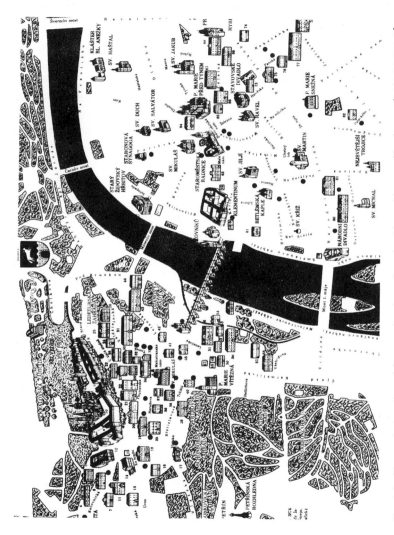

Fig. 4.4 The central portion of Prague showing relics of noble residences. Numbers refer to names of noble families (not listed). (Source: 'Praga Bohemiae Metropolis', Prague, 1954 [map]).

Wallenstein palace alone, twenty-three houses, a brick kiln, and three gardens were demolished to provide the site. The majority of the palaces are of Baroque architecture; however, one of the Schwarzenberg palaces is in Renaissance style, while a Kinsky palace exemplifies Rococo style. On the slopes of the hills behind Mala Strana, impressive terraced gardens were fashioned so as to add considerable charm to the district. Despite later decline in the fortunes of the noble class, this district remains almost untouched. The visitor, therefore, sees a fine historical presentation of Baroque palaces, gardens, picturesque squares, and quaint houses – a place where the romance of the past lingers on, a delightful oasis in the hustle and bustle of modern life. The palaces themselves are used by the communist government in a functional way as state offices, museums or art galleries, or embassies. An outstanding example is the Čzernín palace, the largest in Prague, now housing the Czech Ministry of Foreign Affairs.

Prague serves as an ideal laboratory for studying the urban palaces of the nobility because the city was relatively undamaged in the Second World War. Yet other cities, although partially destroyed, have been reconstructed according to original plans with noble palaces included. Dresden, Warsaw, Cracow, and Budapest are perhaps most outstanding because they were centers of court life for relatively long periods. In Bucharest and other Balkan capitals, palaces appear on a smaller scale. In all of Eastern Europe, one of the most impressive streets reflecting the nobility is Krakowska Przedmieście in Warsaw. This street with the fine palaces of Kazanowski, Koniecpolski, Potocki, Kazimierzowski, Czapski, and Uruski illustrates that the nobility, or *Szlachta*, dominated the urban landscape (see Photo 4.5).

Town planning

The nobles' contribution to the historical landscape of Eastern Europe was primarily through individual residences in city and country. Rarely did they engage in substantial town building as a whole, a function usually handled by the state. However, several outstanding examples exist in which towns were developed almost entirely by a noble family. In one important case, a town was planned by an individual bishop of the Church.

Jičín in eastern Bohemia is one of the better examples of an East European town whose landscape is largely the result of input by a member of the nobility. Although the original town was laid out in

Photo 4.5 The former urban palace of the Koniecpolski and Radziwiłł families on Krakowska Przedmieście Street in Warsaw, Poland, is now used by the Council of Ministers.

the thirteenth century, the greatest construction took place immediately after the Thirty Years' War when Albrecht von Wallenstein, leader of the imperial armies, made Jičín the center of his feudal dukedom. A wonderful square, laid out under his sponsorship, is distinguished by its arcades and by the Wallenstein palace, in early Baroque style, which fronts on one side of the square. His plans also were responsible for numerous town houses and for a nearby summer residence.

Certain other towns in Czechoslovakia owe their present-day character to various degrees of noble input, e.g. Český Krumlov, mentioned earlier as the site of an important castle-palace in southern Bohemia. Others include Pardubice, Jindřichův Hradec, Litomyšl, Náchod, Telč, and Nové Město and Metují. In addition, Kroměříž, a town in Moravia, deserves mention (Gutkind, VII 1972: 262–3); here, instead of a noble family involved in urban planning, another

aspect of feudalism – the Church – was involved. In this case, Bishop Bruno von Schaumburg in the thirteenth century established his residence in a Gothic episcopal palace situated on one corner of the main square in the town. The close association of palace and town led to considerable input by later bishops into the planning of Kroměříž itself. The present-day landscape of palace, gardens, and town is due mostly to Baroque reconstruction carried out by Bishop Charles of Liechtenstein after the destruction of the Thirty Years' War. The flower garden, situated away from the palace, includes elaborate colonnades; its scale makes it unique among early European Baroque gardens. Formal gardens, whose relics are numerous throughout the European landscape, were artificial environments designed to give visibility to the rulers or nobles (Jackson 1980: 51–2).

One must turn to Poland, however, to view perhaps the most outstanding example of a town planned and built as a unit by a great landowner (Gutkind, VII 1972: 56–59). The town of Zamość in eastern Poland was built in the last part of the sixteenth century by Jan Zamoyski, who represented one of the great noble families of Poland. While standing high in the favor of the king, Zamoyski acquired a huge complex of hereditary estates in an area south of Lublin. Altogether he owned twenty-three cities and over eight hundred villages. Zamość, founded as the center of the Fee Tail estates, served not only as the family residence but also as a commercial trading community between east and west.

The town was built according to town planning principles then advocated in Italy, and, indeed, the architects were Italian. The landscape today still reveals the unity of the seventeenth-century plan, which is marked by a uniform and deliberately intended Renaissance character, only slightly altered in later centuries. Inside the fortifications, a symmetrical city was laid out along two axes that intersected in a large square (see Fig. 4.5). The east–west axis was the main traffic artery with the Zamoyski palace located at one end. The four corners of the town, in following town planning theory, were reserved for public buildings – in this case, collegiate church, academy, a Franciscan monastery, and an Armenian church. The town hall was located on the square. Today, relics of these buildings remain. The unity of the town plan is evident in layout and in the architecture, especially the arcades that front on the square and main streets.

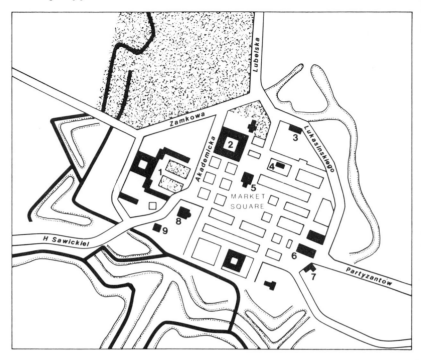

Fig. 4.5   Zamość, Poland: a planned town built by the noble and political leader, Jan Zamoyski, in the sixteenth century. Numbers indicate (1) palace of Zamoyski family; (2) Academy; (3) Lublin gate; (4) synagogue and hostel; (5) city hall; (6) Franciscan church; (7) Lwów gate; (8) Collegiate Church; (9) Szczebrzeska Gate.

Industrial development

A lack of entrepreneurial initiative generally characterized the nobility in Eastern Europe in terms of either investment in industry or intensive agriculture. Consequently, the effect on the landscape was mostly negative, i.e. a lack of factories or progressive farms. However, there were the exceptions in which the nobility produced a positive effect on the landscape. The most important of these are remnants of early developments in the linen, coal, and iron industries in Silesia. Other examples include the Lauchhammer ironworks in Saxony and the textile, glass, and mining enterprises in Bohemia.

Among the outstanding relics, however, are those in Hungary that are derived from the feudal entrepreneur Istvan Széchenyi. Henderson (1969: 116–20) provides details on his work, explaining

that Széchenyi in the early part of the nineteenth century was a recognized leader of those who wished to create a new Hungary. His most important accomplishments were the Chain Bridge over the Danube River, an engineering marvel when constructed in the 1840s to link Buda and Pest; development of a railway along the right bank of the Danube River from Vienna to Budapest; formation of the famous Ganz engineering firm; and drainage improvements along the Tisza River. The results of these promotions of public utilities and industries are still visible. The Chain Bridge, for example, although destroyed in the Second World War, was reconstructed in similar form (see Photo 4.6).

The role of the nobility in developing industry in upper Silesia is described by Pounds (1958), who emphasizes that they owned much of the coal area in the eighteenth century when mining and smelting began. Today, pinpointing specific relics of this early economic activity is difficult. One notable relic is the large park, which was part of the early estate of the Donnersmarck family, located at the village of Świerklaniec, just south of Tarnowskie Góry in upper Silesia. This family was one of the early leaders in the industrialization of this district. The vast park (now a national reserve) of some 400 acres with 'guest house' and monuments of fighting animals serves as a landscape relic illustrating a somewhat different role of the nobility in Eastern Europe than has been described in other parts of this chapter. Hartshorne (1934: 437), in his well-known analysis of upper Silesia between the wars, emphasizes the contrast between feudal estate and poor residences of the factory workers. This contrast, he feels, indicates a rather direct transformation, with no intermediate commercial period, from the feudal agricultural structure of the past into a feudal industrial structure. Today the Donnersmarck park and existing urban tenements of workers from the nineteenth century still illustrate this transformation. Furthermore, the support of Silesian industrial development by Prussian rulers indicates the colonial nature of this province.

The role of the peasant in forming the East European landscape

Considerable attention has been given in the preceding sections to the role of the lord in transforming the East European landscape and to the role which shows his residences in rural and urban areas.

Photo 4.6 The Lánchid or Chain Bridge of Budapest, one of the earliest of its kind in Europe, was initiated by Count Széchenyi and completed in 1849.

However, the role of the peasant is equally important and should be considered.

The subjects of the lord were known by various terms depending on the obligations owed to him. As Blum (1960: 12) reiterates, the serf was a peasant bound to the lord as a part of legal and social structures of tenure rather than as a result of any contract between lord and peasant. This meant that the lord had legal jurisdiction over his peasant to the complete, or nearly complete, exclusion of the state. Although today the term peasant often refers to a subsistent farmer producing only enough food for himself, this type of farmer in Western Europe often produced surpluses for sale; however, such production was based on hand labor since very little capital was available. For hundreds of years in Europe the word 'peasant' was a synonym for a rude and uncouth person and still is in some circles. Sanders (1958: 24–48) explains that soil, family, and village provided elements of security in a world dominated by the lord. Thus, the

term peasant has both economic and social connotations. Owing to the historical importance of the peasant in Eastern Europe, this area has been one of the great laboratories for the study of peasant farming. Perhaps the best known of these studies is Doreen Warriner's classic, *The Economics of Peasant Farming*, published in 1939 following the land reforms of the interwar period.

Just as the noble landscape was dominated by various rural and urban residences, the peasant landscape consisted of villages, housing provided on estates for day laborers, and small fields. The peasant village remains ubiquitous throughout Eastern Europe and, despite modernization introduced by the communists, reflects much from the past. The residences of day laborers are especially visible in former Prussian areas and in Hungary. Excluding Poland and Yugoslavia, the strips in open fields, which were important in all of these countries in the 1930s except the eastern part of Germany, have largely disappeared under collectivization programs.

Three agricultural maps from the 1930s help to explain the background of peasant landscapes as they exist in Eastern Europe today (see Fig. 4.6). The top map, which shows the density of farm population, illustrates that most of Eastern Europe had over fifteen active workers in agriculture per 100 acres of farm land. Only in Czechoslovakia, Hungary, and parts of Germany was the density lower (12–15); France, on the other hand, averaged nine to twelve per 100 acres, while the British Isles had less than six. The other two maps – output per acre and output per worker – show strong correlations with population density. Several factors – industry, capital, and environment – help to explain this correlation.

In Western Europe, growing industry in the cities attracted peasants in the nineteenth century and thereby reduced rural population densities. Capital, which increased for the peasant through sale of products to the cities, was applied to farms in the form of animals, thus providing manure and increasing yields. Similarly, a moderate climate with a well-distributed yearly precipitation facilitated the growing of seed grasses and root crops, which could be adapted to rotations and thereby increase the production of animal products.

The situation in Eastern Europe was quite different, for little industry existed in the towns to attract rural migrants or to provide markets for agricultural products. Population density, therefore, remained high; in addition, most acreage was utilized for food grains, feed restricting even if capital had been available. The lack

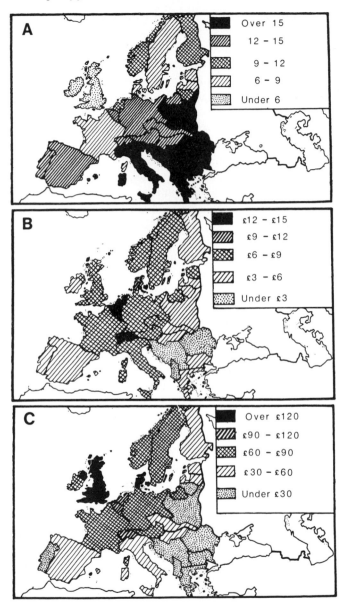

Fig. 4.6   Europe: agricultural population and economics. *A* – density of agricultural population per 100 acres; *B* – farm production in £ per acre; *C* – net production per active worker in £. Figures are for 1937. (Source: Yates and Warriner 1943: p. 39.)

of capital also was reflected in the absence of tractors which caused a reliance on inadequate, primitive plows – a major defect in Eastern European agriculture; Berend and Ránki (1974a: 293) report that in Poland in the 1930s the ratio of tractor to acreage was 1:20 000 vs. 1:1000 in Italy, or 1:350 in England. Furthermore, the climate, characterized by dry periods especially in the Danube basin and Balkan areas, hindered the growth of seed grasses which, barring the establishment of expensive irrigation facilities, might have been used for increased animal production. Warriner (1939: 100) shows, for example, that cattle per acre in the 1930s were only nine in Hungary as against 26 in the British Isles. Finally, the rugged topography, especially in the Balkans, reduces the land availability per worker. The overall result of this system of agriculture in Eastern Europe was to perpetuate high population densities and low output per worker and per acre, as revealed in the maps. Underemployment (or overpopulation) was the great evil in Eastern Europe before the Second World War.

This spatial characteristic of rural overpopulation was the product of a long period of feudal development, a process explained early in the chapter. From the sixteenth century, the East European peasant became increasingly tied to the land as serfdom came to dominate the social order of feudalism. Even in the nineteenth century when the peasants were emancipated, lack of opportunities in the cities left them dependent on the lords as day laborers on the estates. Finally, the land reforms of the interwar period allowed the peasants to possess land, but this beneficial social change only led to increased population density and decreased *per capita* production. Furthermore, the peasants, who made up some 60 million or 60 per cent of the total East European population, never were able to generate successful political movements because their conservative, rural-centered ideology was incompatible with the more progressive, town-centered socialist movement.

Not even the export of grain to the west during the interwar years could be considered a sign of strength in Eastern Europe (Durand 1922: 176–7). This grain came primarily from the Danubian countries and represented surpluses from peasant labor on large inefficient estates, or from peasant plots, in the form of taxes, rent, or loan payments. A small number of wealthy people were able to import luxuries, largely through these exports. Certain essential items used by the peasant also had to come from abroad and were paid for by

grain exports. But the proportion of these exports to total grain production in the East European countries between the wars was generally small.

After the Second World War, these exports declined as a result of several factors. Population in the cities increased under communist programs of industrialization, and the consumption of wheat bread replaced that of corn bread formerly so important on peasant farms of the Danubian countries. In addition, agricultural production stagnated as a result of priorities placed on industry and early difficulties with collectivization. This decline in grain exports is reflected in the landscape today, e.g. the Bega Canal, a former outlet for grain from the Banat of Romania, is now unused, a relic of the interwar period (see Photo 4.7).

Today, the peasants' attitudes are changed as they become peasant-workers, a process explained in the chapter on socialism. Parochial-

Photo 4.7 The Bega Canal crosses the Banat plain of Romania and Yugoslavia. Before the Second World War, it was used for the export of grain to Western Europe via the Danube River. Unused today, it remains as a relic of past economic activity.

ism has been reduced as many peasants migrate to the cities and return on weekends or commute on a daily basis. The movement of these commuters by bus is one of the most evident aspects of landscape change in Eastern Europe during the communist era. Yet, to a certain extent, the old peasant attitudes still prevail and include resistance to central authority, a village tradition, or a *nie ma* mentality (Time-Life, *Eastern Europe* 1965: 107). For example, communist central authorities are baffled by the continued refusal of German minority groups to intermarry with Romanians. Peasant tradition is evident in the landscape in costumes and in the periodic celebrations in villages (see Photo 4.8). Finally, a general attitude that visitors see today in both town and country is the *nie ma* syndrome – a shrugging of the shoulders while raising the palms of both hands upwards. The literal translation of *nie ma* – 'there is none!' – sometimes becomes the figurative, 'What can I do?' The term and gesture seem to reflect a general attitude of helplessness in the face of an omnipresent government. Although it may have originated among the peasants in the days of serfdom, it now persists in the communist society marked by scarcities of goods and services.

The economic backwardness of Eastern Europe reflects the concept of three cultural zones of Europe (A–B–C) created by Van Valkenburg and Huntington (1935: Ch. 1), a concept apparently an outgrowth of Delaisi's (1929) separation of Europe into a western industrial portion and an eastern agricultural one (see Fig. 4.7). Although sometimes criticized as being deterministic in an environmental sense, the concept represents one attempt to clarify and account for a geographical gradient of decreasing economic development from west to east across the continent. Certain indicators are used including national and farm income per capita, percentage of labor force in industry versus agriculture, yields of crops, foreign trade per capita, death rates, illiteracy, railroad density, and automobile ownership. The map showing population density, and output per acre and per worker also illustrates this concept (see Fig. 4.6). There is little doubt that in the 1930s the East European countries, with some exceptions, were part of the C area.

Peasant relics of the feudal period

The peasant also affected the East European rural landscape through the patterns of field and village, both now altered in form. For example, collectivization programs have obliterated peasant fields in

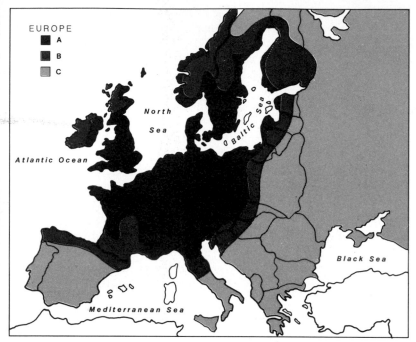

Fig. 4.7   The A–B–C zones in Europe. (Source: Van Valkenburg and Huntington, p. 7.)

all countries except Poland and Yugoslavia, where the strips remain as relics of this group. Strips are also found in all countries where the topography prevents collectivization. Finally, strips in the form of private plots are allowed in all countries as supplements to collectives. Although villages are still ubiquitous, their character has been partially altered under the influence of communism. Both of these relics, field and village, are discussed briefly here in terms of what has persisted from the past; in the later chapter on socialism, recent alterations to field and village are discussed.

Farming strips

The traditional pattern of fragmented strips, which along with the

Photo 4.8   The clothes of the woman on the right illustrate that peasant costumes are still worn in Eastern Europe. This scene is from Macedonia in Yugoslavia.

large estate has dominated the East European landscape for so long, is derived from the land allocation policy of the Middle Ages. The last chapter discussed this policy because it was introduced by German colonists as the three-field system featuring mandatory communal rotation and a fallow to allow the land to rest. In a few parts of Eastern Europe, this three-field system lasted until the Second World War and I actually observed one relic as late as 1963 in eastern Poland.

The transformation of this three-field system differed in Western Europe in comparison to Eastern Europe. In the former area, the feudal system disappeared and the peasants took control of the communal strips. However, only in England did consolidation of these strips occur, and in much of Western Europe the old tenure system prevailed with the pattern of noncontiguous strips lasting until the present. However, the use of rotations involving seed grasses (e.g. alfalfa) and root crops permitted the elimination of the fallow. Thus, the strips today show different uses, though in the Middle Ages they were similar as part of communal mandatory rotation.

In Prussia, Poland, and Hungary, the transformation of the old three-field system was quite different than it was in Western Europe. As explained previously peasant land farmed in three fields during the late Middle Ages was absorbed into large estates, and the peasants themselves became serfs. Maps of the village of Stresow in East Germany show a typical change in tenure: the three-field system existed in 1694 but the large estates dominated the village for the next two hundred years (see Fig. 4.8). Thus, even the emancipation laws of the nineteenth century in Prussia did not result in land reform, and the peasants continued to work as day laborers on the estates. Only in the post-Second World War years did the peasants receive land as the communists attempted to gain support in the countryside. However, in the 1950s, full-scale collectivization began and the fields became large. In other parts of Eastern Europe, the transformation was similar, with large estates replacing three-field systems after the sixteenth century. However, land reforms may have taken place in the nineteenth century or between the wars. Thus, by the 1930s, the large estates existed in Germany (East), Poland, and Hungary. Elsewhere, strips dominated the landscape as they did in most of Western Europe.

This entire system of strip farming was wiped out by the collectivization programs instituted by the communist party in all eight

countries of Eastern Europe in the 1950s. Such programs, which involved the creation of large fields suitable for mechanization, have continued to the present in six of the countries. In Poland and Yugoslavia, however, the party's attempt to collectivize land was successfully resisted for reasons explained in the chapter on socialism. As a result, private farms in strip form still dominate the landscape in both countries.

The peasant strips which survive in the landscapes of Poland and Yugoslavia, therefore, are the product of a long history. These strips are discussed in this chapter because they are inseparable from the process of feudalism as it persisted in Eastern Europe. The strips are also mentioned briefly in the chapter on nationalism to point up the connection between this political process, as it emerged in the nineteenth century, and land reform.

Hamilton (1968: 170–9) has provided some details about this field pattern as it existed in Yugoslavia in the 1960s – a pattern that in general prevails to the present. He indicates that Yugoslavia is still predominantly a land of peasant farmers, e.g. in 1963, some 2.6 million private landowners held 71 per cent of all farmland, 85.8 per cent of all cultivated land, and 91 per cent of all livestock. These farmers produced 70–75 per cent of total farm output, but marketed only 55–60 per cent of the net surpluses, facts that indicated the importance of subsistence farming. Farms were very small – 72 per cent were under 12 acres; most were worked with draft animals instead of modern machinery; and yields and incomes were low. The primary obstacle, according to Hamilton, is farm fragmentation. In 1960, 2.6 million peasants worked 20.8 million scattered strips of farmland or an average of eight to nine per farm. Although arable land is most fragmented in the mountainous areas of the west and south, it is also broken up in the flat, broad Vojvodina (Danube area) but consolidation in state farms has occurred in places. In the rugged karst areas of Dalmatia, farms of 7–25 acres might be divided into 35–65 plots (15–25 arable). Over much of Yugoslavia, therefore, noncontiguous strips make mechanization, specialization, and mixed farming with livestock very difficult.

In Poland, fragmentation into strips is most evident in the east and southeast of the country, a pattern related to both the influence of the partition powers in the nineteenth century and political changes in boundaries after the Second World War (see Photo 3.1). In Polish areas previously under Austrian and Russian control, manor and peasant properties were seldom consolidated into larger parcels; land

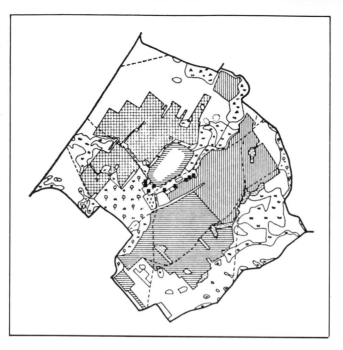

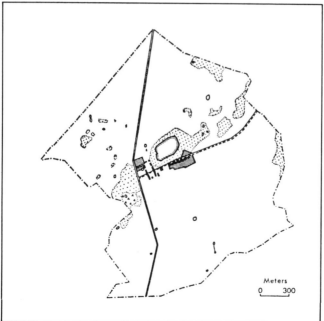

Fig. 4.8   The evolution of Stresow, a village in the former Prussian area, now East Germany. Top left, the three-field system of 1694; bottom left, large fields of the estate in 1900; top right, the strips created after the land reform of 1945; bottom right, large fields created by collectivization in 1960. (Source: Benthien 1963.)

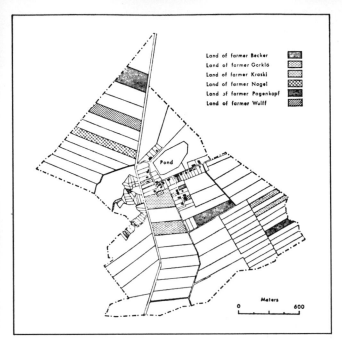

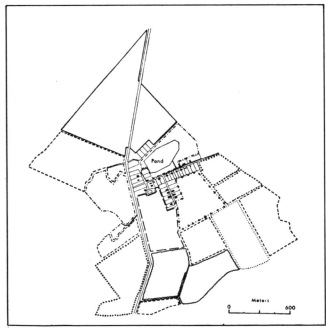

111

division among sons caused further fragmentation. In the Polish lands formerly under Prussian rule, however, the situation was different: consolidation did occur and hereditary division was not important. After the Second World War, of course, the western and northern areas were depopulated of Germans, and the large estates of these areas were either left intact for state farms or were only partially fragmented.

Villages

The second major relic of the peasant landscape of Eastern Europe is the village, which exhibits considerable cultural variation in layout and architectural style. Although many villages have been altered by the processes of modernization introduced by communist regimes, certain aspects of this relic of feudalism are still apparent.

Historically, the village is ubiquitous as a settlement form in Eastern Europe because in feudal times a nucleated settlement near the lord's fortress provided not only protection and water, but also the communal aspects of open-field cultivation discussed previously. In the Balkans, nucleation was furthered by the presence of extended families (*Zadruga*) who lived in one village. Finally, the social climate of a village has long been favored in Europe instead of a dispersed pattern so characteristic of the frontier in North America.

The layout of villages in Eastern Europe varies considerably: irregular, wherever settlement took place over a long period, a feature especially evident in mountainous regions; regular in those areas where German colonization took place, because linear villages were easily established. The *Strassendorf, Angerdorf, Waldhufendorf,* and *Marschhufendorf* (discussed in Ch. 3), therefore, are more characteristic of Eastern Europe than they are of Western Europe where irregular forms dominate (see Fig. 3.2). However, this regular layout has been modified through time. Nevertheless, research by Kiełczewska-Zaleska (1965) shows that in Poland villages of feudal origin are still evident.

The dominant house type in linear villages is the elongated courtyard dwelling, a feature which has led to its generic name of *Streckhof* (extended court) (see Fig. 4.9). This settlement form of Frankish origin appears as the norm throughout the area of southeastern Europe where Germans have settled – from Vienna eastward to the border of Wallachia (Schimscha 1939: 80). But it is more than just a German form. I have seen variations of it in all parts of Eastern

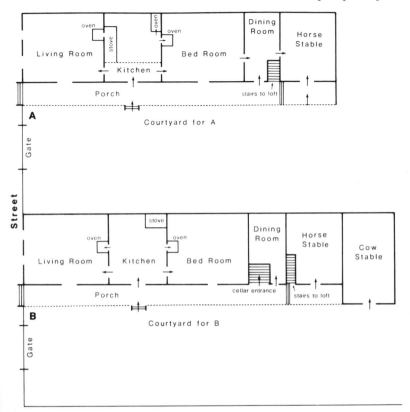

Fig. 4.9   A model of the *Streckhof* (extended court), a type of settlement ubiquitous in Eastern Europe in areas east and south of Vienna. In orienting the buildings on a line away from the street and in separating them from each other by a courtyard, the settlement is economical in use of space and in reducing fire possibilities. (Source: Petersen 1933: p. 243.)

Europe, and the Austrian *Kozenn Atlas* (1961: 53) shows it as predominant in the rural landscape east of Vienna. What is the *Streckhof*? As shown on the plan, this house type is distinguished by a line of buildings oriented at right angles to the street so that the *end* of the house fronts on the street itself. Farm house, granary, and stables as a connected unit front on a long, narrow courtyard. This arrangement provides a maximum concentration of settlement along a street, an important consideration for the establishment of villages in areas where only a single road existed. The pattern also restricts the spread of fire by requiring space between adjacent farms.

113

The East European village landscape tells a variety of stories: one, of course, is the establishment of linear settlements, often under Germanic influence, in a pioneer region where crossroads were lacking and where crowding houses together (*Streckhof* style) was necessary; a second is the persistence of folk customs, expressed, for example, in the wooden crosses found in the cemetery of Detva in western Slovakia – the wood symbolizing, I was told, man's close tie to the earth; a third is the poverty of many of these villages, reflecting a long period of exploitation, especially in the Balkans where the Turks were in control for centuries. Today, these villages remain throughout Eastern Europe – some still resembling those so vividly portrayed by Warriner (1939), others reflecting improvement through the influence of the communist party and from income earned by commuting peasant-workers. Finally, a fourth story tells of social changes that occurred after emancipation in some parts of Eastern Europe when the peasants expressed their new freedom through architecture.

This last story is particularly evident in the area of south Bohemia where a group of Czech villages has been preserved as an example of popular architecture. These elaborate villages, although not necessarily linear, include variations of the *Streckhof* idea in their plan. The gable end of the line of farm buildings fronts on the street, while a long, massive wall with an arched gateway extends along the street, shutting off the courtyard. The more elaborate farms have a granary fronting on the street at the opposite end of the wall. The gable end and the wall are often embossed with the farmer's or builder's name and the date of construction. Sometimes referred to as peasant Baroque, these elaborate façades express the newly found freedom of the peasant class. Sanda and Weatherall (1951: 255–61) quote a peasant of the nineteenth century: 'I am my own master and can live in houses just as stately as those of the town and country gentry.' The masons, bricklayers, and carpenters formerly had worked for the aristocracy and the clergy, acquiring an idea of the motifs of the Baroque without necessarily understanding their functional and social meaning. I took the photograph of the village of Záluží as representative of those in the area (see Photo 4.9). The farmers of the villages are members of a collective farm but receive a stipend for maintaining the farmsteads in their old style.

While emphasizing the physical characteristics of the villages that survive in the landscape, the human aspects should not be ignored. Although the communist party has affected local folklore, certain

Photo 4.9   This farm house in the village of Záluží south of Prague represents a relic of peasant Baroque architecture, now preserved as a form of national art.

customs continue. For example, villagers still dance the 'kolo' on Sunday afternoons in Yugoslavia. As shown previously, costumes characteristic of individual regions are still worn on holidays and days of celebration.

Dwellings on estates

Although most peasants in Eastern Europe formerly lived in villages, some were forced to reside on estates in their own dwellings or in those provided by the lords. The condition of such dwellings reflects the role of the nobility in restricting social change. The early part of this chapter relates that the status of many Prussian peasants changed very little before and after their release from serfdom in the early part of the nineteenth century. Before this event, they were tied to the estates by service obligations, while afterwards they were unable to acquire land, thereby being forced to work on the same estates at low wages. Relics of the housing provided for these day laborers still

115

remain in Vorpommern, Mecklenburg, and in other parts of East Germany. Others exist in Poland and Hungary where the estates lasted in some regions until 1945. On Prussian estates, housing existed for three types of day laborers: (1) *Kotter* or day laborers living in row dwellings provided by the lord; (2) *Hävsler* or day laborers with their own small dwelling; and (3) *Büdner* or day laborers with some few acres of their own on which a dwelling stood. The photograph of a *Kotter* residence in the village of Bandelin, south of Greifswald, was taken in 1980 (see Photo 4.10). As is evident, the building is still occupied by workers (on a collective farm), but such housing, I was told, is gradually being replaced.

In Hungary, the homes of day-laborers were part of a complex of buildings that also included a school, church, stables, sheds, and granaries on the estates. This complex, often the size of a village, is called a *puszta* and has been graphically described by Gyula Illyés in his classic called *People of the Puszta* (1936). This type of estate village, which is found west of the Danube River in Transdanubia, is to

Photo 4.10   Old row houses for day laborers on a Prussian estate at Bandelin, East Germany, are still used as residences on a present-day collective farm.

be differentiated from the use of the word *puszta* or wasteland of the Hungarian plain to the east. Illyés (1936: 9) relates that almost half the arable land in Hungary was cultivated by the farm-servants living in the *pusztas*. He paints a vivid picture of these settlements, their isolation from society, their rural poverty, and the repression of their people who were not considered a part of the Hungarian nation. Today examples of these *pusztas* remain as described by Uren (1969: 34–5, 43–4), who includes a picture of a dwelling in the village of Keszthely – a long, low single-story house, which in Illyés's day was subdivided into single rooms for separate families and was provided with a common kitchen. This house resembles that of the *Kotter* dwelling shown above.

Summary

We have now examined two layers in the palimpsest of culture that makes up the landscape of Eastern Europe. The progress brought to the area by German colonists was halted by the power of the lords. Growth of cities and commercial activity was stifled as the nobility began to control the countryside and, through agreements with rulers, to reduce the functions of urban settlements. For six hundred years the nobility had a strong voice in the landscape of Eastern Europe, especially in rural areas where the peasants were reduced to an indentured class. Today, the ubiquitous presence of country estates, peasant villages, and fields together with palaces in the larger cities tells a story of the great influence of the aristocracy on the landscape. On the other hand, industrial relics are few. The impression portrays Europe as separated into two parts – an Eastern, agrarian one where modernization is only now becoming important and a Western, industrial portion where the effects of commercial and industrial revolutions together with liberalism had a greater effect on social change.

However, the roles of German colonists and feudal lords are interwoven with those of political rulers in Eastern Europe, making it necessary to turn to a third process of landscape change – multinationalism.

5
Landscapes of multinationalism

The material in the preceding chapters focuses on two early historical processes – German colonization and feudalism – that affected spatial organization and left certain relics in the landscape of Eastern Europe. These two processes operated within a *political* framework of spatial organization that was also responsible for social change and other landscape relics: capital cities, administrative centers or military fortresses, state-supported colonies and factories, and religious buildings. How can these relics be classified to sort out the frameworks of state organization within which they were created? After some testing, I came to the conclusion that the relics reflect two different political environments which dominated the landscape of Eastern Europe for over two thousand years – multinationalism and nationalism.

Multinationalism vs. nationalism

For the greater part of this long period, multinational states dominated the environment of Eastern Europe. With twenty-four cultures interacting within the rather restricted area of Eastern Europe, political units inevitably became multinational, with many of the cultures existing in a dependent relationship to others. Although these units have disappeared, the relics remain to tell a fascinating story, especially for the geographer, of past spatial organization and the ideologies of state leaders who affected social change and the landscape within their domains. For example, relics of the Austrian Empire – now scattered from Vienna to Lemberg (L'vov in the

Soviet Union) and from Karlsbad (Karlovy Vary, Czechoslovakia) to Sarajevo, Yugoslavia – persist to illustrate how this large political unit dominated parts of Eastern Europe for so long.

The national state – dominated by one nationality and the ideology of nationalism – represented a later political environment of Eastern Europe. Hayes (1926: 3–6) clarifies these terms:

> State: a sovereign political territory
> Nation: the population of a sovereign political territory
> Nationality: a group of people speaking the same language and observing the same customs. They do not all necessarily live within the same territory. Therefore, 'nation' (or citizenship) is not the same as nationality.
> Nationalism: a condition of mind or ideology among members of a nationality in which loyalty to this group and its eventual political unification is paramount.

When these four definitions are clearly understood, confusion about them is clarified. France is a good example of a national state: the French nationality dominates and nationalism is characteristic of the peoples' behavior, i.e. a loyalty to the nationality or to a common heritage of language and custom is basic to most members of the state. Switzerland, on the other hand, is a multinational state, populated by a nation composed of three nationalities – French, German, and Italian – who, of course, extend beyond the boundaries of Switzerland. The loyalty of these three groups within Switzerland, however, is greater to that nation than to the individual nationalities, e.g. the Italians of Switzerland have no desire to join the Italians in Italy.

Hayes (1926:6, 24) goes further by stating that nationalism represents the modern fusion of two very old phenomena – nationality and patriotism. Nationality rests on loyalty to a group with the same language and customs. Patriotism, on the other hand, is broad in that it implies a loyalty to a person, territory, or nationality. A nationality, therefore, is one type of patriotism or loyalty. Historically in Europe, patriotism changed from local sentiment into imperial pride without passing through an intermediate national stage. In neither case – small region or large empire – did patriotism coincide with a particular nationality. Although nationality and patriotism are old, the fusion of the two, in which patriotism focuses on nationality above all, i.e. nationalism, is recent. Keeping the ideologies of patri-

otism and nationalism separate helps to avoid confusion. In Switzerland, the German, Frenchman, or Italian who is loyal to the Swiss nation is a patriot and not a nationalist, for otherwise loyalty to a nationality (e.g. French) would come before loyalty to a nation-state (e.g. Switzerland). In the same way, a Polish friend of mine in Warsaw insists he is a patriot rather than a nationalist because his loyalty is to Poland and not just to the Polish nationality. This loyalty to a territory helps explain the historical importance of eighteenth-century Jagellonian Poland to Poles, despite its fragmented structure of nationalities. Thus, nationality and patriotism have geographical foundations.

Why did nationalism develop so slowly in Europe? Up to the sixteenth century, nationalities had little opportunity to realize their common attributes, because the social and geographical aspects of a multinational environment prevented it. One factor included the fragmentation of common nationalities by class: nobility, peasant, and a restricted middle class. The nobility of a territory, whatever their nationality, considered themselves members of one class. Another factor concerned language, for the educated people used Latin, Greek, French, or German. Even when their written language had the same origin as the vernacular, it differed from the spoken language (Kohn 1942: 72). As a result, the nobility and peasants, even of the same nationality, could not communicate easily. Perhaps the greatest disadvantage, however, was that no literary form existed in the vernacular language for preserving national traditions. In addition, the problem of parochialism, i.e. overcoming distances, compounded class and language differences in splitting nationalities. The residents of a territory were familiar with only the local area to which they could be loyal and not to the area occupied by a nationality. Furthermore, nationalities adhered to various international religions that tended to hinder the expression of national feelings. Lastly, political organization which might have focused national feeling did not correspond to nationality. For a long time, therefore, multinational states dominated in Europe because the forces of patriotism to territory or ruler were stronger than loyalty to national group. Cohesion between members of a nationality became fragmented by factors of class, language, distance, religion, and political organization. The influence of these factors began to lessen earlier in Western Europe than in Eastern Europe as nationalism became a significant ideology. This process is described in more detail in the next chapter.

Political organization of multinational states

How were states organized in the multinational environment of Eastern Europe where a large number of cultures competed for space and resources? Although the primary *political units* were empires, kingdoms, and principalities, the nature of each *government* varied and this in turn affected the landscape. For example, an absolute government in which the ruler possessed enormous power frequently affected spatial organization and the landscape more completely than less authoritative types of government such as a feudal oligarchy. One should also point out the dominant characteristic of a multinational environment: certain cultures or national groups existed in a *dependent* relationship to others within the political units, whatever their form. In many cases, the dominating group had its base outside Eastern Europe; indeed, external influence has been a basic spatial characteristic of history in this region.

The primary forms of political organization were empires, kingdoms, and principalities. The term empire usually indicated the larger states that dominated political organization of space, but certain smaller kingdoms like Poland, Hungary, Serbia, and Bulgaria behaved in an imperialistic fashion. These groups and others in Eastern Europe – Czechs, Slovaks, Romanians, Slovenes, Croats, Montenegrins, Macedonians, and Albanians – found themselves absorbed within large empires for extensive periods. On the other hand, these same groups at various times formed kingdoms and on those occasions incorporated other cultural groups within their borders. For example, the Croatians formed a medieval kingdom before being absorbed into Hungary and Turkey. The Montenegrins resisted incorporation within imperial Turkey for hundreds of years, yet they were part of the Serbian Empire in the Middle Ages. The Romanians have lived under Roman, Byzantine, Turkish, Austrian, and Hungarian rule for much of their history, but when they finally emerged as a national state in the nineteenth century, it was first as principalities (Wallachia and Moldavia) and later as a kingdom. Finally, the Macedonians have not really formed a separate state since the days of Alexander, but as a multinational territory have been split between states controlled by Bulgaria, Serbia, and Greece. Truly, Eastern Europe represents the epitome of a multinational environment. Today a geographer takes interest in the landscape relics of the past which are located within a national political framework but which serve as clues to the earlier multinational environment.

The empire emerges as a major type of political unit in Eastern Europe for two thousand years. The term comes from the Latin word 'imperator', or commander, which refers to dictatorial power, centralized government, and arbitrary administration. The word also implies expansion beyond one's borders through economic penetration and the acquisition of colonial territory. Kohn (1942: 111–42) emphasizes the difference between a universal imperialism like Rome, which covered the known world, and the more recent period of plural imperialism, dominated by competing empires such as Russia, Austria, and Turkey. The problem with both these terms is that they are too narrow. Cohen (1973: 15) presents a more comprehensive definition of imperialism as an *asymmetrical* relationship between the components of a territory. This relationship is one of dominance and dependence between these components with the dependent ones in direct or indirect subjugation. This definition of imperialism thereby focuses on extension of a people or a government over alien peoples or alien lands.

Empires have been an indisputable part of the political landscape of Eastern Europe, the best known being those of Rome, Byzantium, Holy Rome, Turkey, Austria, Russia, and Prussia-Germany. All were multinational and incorporated elements of dominance and dependence between the components; all were externally based, yet left their mark on landscapes within Eastern Europe proper. Some historians have even called Athens an empire because of its colonies established along the coastlines of the Mediterranean Sea including the Black and Adriatic Seas. Relics of these colonies still exist and, therefore, Greek influence should be included as part of the multinational environment, although the dominance was not similar to the other externally based empires.

Grounds exist for considering the Polish, Hungarian, Bulgarian, and Serbian multinational states of the Middle Ages as empires. Seton-Watson (1946: 320) supports this idea by remarking that

> historical Poland was not a national state but a multinational empire which arose in the course of centuries when the dogma of nationalism, as understood in modern times, did not exist . . . The fact that the true political aim of the Polish ruling class was not nationalist, that it involved the domination of Poles over large numbers of people of origin other than Polish, has never been sufficiently understood in Western Europe, and this failure to understand it has been responsible for errors in the policy of the Western Powers toward Poland

Seton-Watson (1946: 341–2) continues with similar statements about the Hungarians and the Balkan states: 'Like Poland, Hungary was never during its long history a national state, and until very recent times its rulers were not nationalists . . . Hungarian policy was aimed at the defense of a territory which was always admitted to be greater than that occupied by people of Hungarian speech'; finally (1946: 351), the 'Balkan Peninsula is the scene of imperialisms less continuously held and less firmly rooted in public opinion than those of Poland or Hungary, but in no way inferior to them in violence and extravagance'. In this light, many internally based cultures of Eastern Europe exhibited imperialistic tendencies, a fact which explains the location today of landscape relics of those states in areas dominated by other cultures.

Not every specialist on Eastern Europe holds this view. Halecki (1952: 4–5), in a penetrating analysis of the persistence of Russian imperialism, argues that Poland even at the height of its Jagellonian dimensions was based on voluntary agreements, and, therefore, was not an empire. Nevertheless, following our definition, Poland constituted a multinational environment in the eighteenth century by incorporating dependent cultural groups. The same is true of Hungary, Serbia, and Bulgaria in the Middle Ages. Thus, when nationalism arose as a doctrine in Eastern Europe, these states, lacking a political framework for national development, were forced into a type of cultural nationalism or patriotism in which loyalty was to the multinational state of the past rather than to the ruling nationality.

Three recent empires – Prussia, Austria, and Russia – were called absolute states because of their type of government. The importance of these three states in affecting the spatial organization and landscape of Eastern Europe requires comment about the special characteristics of this political phenomenon. The absolute state originated in France where Louis XIV (1638–1715) fended off restraints on his power and centralized authority in his own person: 'I am the state'. Above all, the absolute state was centralized around the monarch with the administrative apparatus, the Church, and a standing army dependent on his will; its economic policy was mercantilistic – aimed at making the state as self-sufficient as possible to force other states into economic dependence on it. Thus, the rulers not only built up their own industries and curtailed imports but also monopolized the sources of raw materials, transport, and technical skill. Above all was

an emphasis on military power. Absolute rulers, therefore, had the capacity to influence social change and the landscape. Absolutism, however, differed between Western Europe – where the nobility's power was eroded by the loss of traditional institutions in an environment of a rising middle class – and Eastern Europe – where the absolutist monarch made an arrangement in which the nobility was pressed into military and administrative service in exchange for degrees of control over the peasant, i.e. serfdom. Absolutism reached perhaps its greatest heights in Prussia under Frederick the Great and in Austria under Maria Theresa and Joseph II.

Turkey, the fourth nineteenth-century empire, was in no sense an absolute state, because the power of the sultan, who was often the puppet of oligarchic factions, declined after the sixteenth century. Nevertheless, Turkey remained a power in southeastern Europe until the First World War and as a multinational state affected the spatial organization and landscape of the Balkans. In fact, the 'Eastern Question' – what to do with the void in the Balkans as Turkey retreated – was basic to international politics because the geopolitical aims of Britain, Austria, and Russia came into direct conflict here.

Until the partitions of the eighteenth century, Poland occupied a large space on the map of Europe. This state, Jagellonian Poland, formed a commonwealth with Lithuania that extended far into what is now Russia. Although sometimes designated an empire because of its multinational characteristics, Poland's government consisted of an oligarchy dominated by the noble class with power concentrated in provincial assemblies of the lords who elected representatives to the diet. A single lord could force the dissolution of this body by exercise of the *liberum veto*. This noble class, in effect, had the greatest impact on the landscape.

Characteristics of empires dominating the multinational environment in the nineteenth century

Even though landscape relics exist to illustrate the impact of ancient and medieval states on the landscape of Eastern Europe, the remains after 1800 are most numerous. In the nineteenth century, four empires dominated the spatial organization of this area: the absolute states of Prussia, Russia, and Austria (including Hungary), and the empire of Turkey (see Fig. 5.1). Let us examine some of the characteristics of these empires in order to understand better their capacity for transformation of the landscape.

Fig. 5.1 Political boundaries of Eastern Europe in 1914. In the nineteenth century, four empires – Prussia/Germany, Austria-Hungary, Russia and Turkey – dominated the multinational environment of Eastern Europe. The Turkish Empire was the first to break up as new national states appeared.

Absolutism was often linked to militarism and the need for states to survive in an environment of aggression. In Eastern Europe during the early modern period, aggressor states, i.e. France, Sweden, and Turkey, prompted Prussia, Russia, and Austria to respond by devel-

oping centralized structures based on a strong army. However, to do this restructuring, the latter states needed the help of the nobility and for this reason institutionalized serfdom. In the previous chapter, we looked at this process in terms of the lord and his effects on the landscape; now we look at it in terms of the ruler's imprint. The primary process was a trade-off between lord and ruler. The lords were integrated into the state administration as military men and civil servants in return for trade advantages over the towns and complete power over the countryside, including the peasants. With their participation, therefore, the lords became a sort of 'service nobility' on a permanent basis. Such service to the state insured the ruler's assistance with their primary problem – the binding of peasant labor to the land in an era of wars, depressions, and epidemics. Thus, the state 'stopped at the gates of the manor house'.

The absolute states of Prussia-Germany, Russia, and Austria reflected this trade-off between rulers and lords. In Prussia, the famous Pact of 1653 between the Great Elector and the nobility included support by the latter for taxes to be used for a standing army and for ordinances binding the peasants to the land. Similar pacts were signed in Russia and Austria. In the latter, the elimination of the Czech nobility after 1648 had made the task easier in Bohemia: the *Verneuerte Landesordnung* concentrated all executive power in Vienna at the expense of nobles and towns. A new cosmopolitan aristocracy from foreign areas was established which, for the most part, remained loyal to the crown. In the countryside, serfdom was institutionalized with the labor services constituting half of the working week, and feudal dues, tithes, and taxes involving two-thirds of the peasant's product. Strong measures were invoked to prevent flight of the peasants from the land in an era of depopulation following the Thirty Years' War. This shortage of labor during the seventeenth century required the domestic policing of a centralized state to guarantee the stability of serfdom in view of peasant revolts. One function of the absolute state in the east, therefore, was to defend the class position of the feudal nobility, thereby restricting social change.

This absolute state in Eastern Europe was closely tied to warring – more characteristic of Prussia-Germany than Austria but nevertheless affecting the landscape in both. In the former area, state militarization was reflected in the importance of the *Generalkriegskomissariat* (General War Commission), which formed the basis of the Hohenzollern war machine. The entire tax structure, civil service, and local

administration emerged as subdepartments of this organization, which dominated most state activities including the regulation of industry. As we shall see, the importance of Silesia to Prussia as a strategic province is reflected in the landscape today. In Austria, the centralization was never as great but the military influence was evident. For example, in the sixteenth century the *Hofkriegsrat* was the only administrative body with jurisdiction throughout the Habsburg territories. To maintain civil jurisdiction along the Turkish frontier, it established the *Militärgrenze* (military frontier), a string of fortresses north of the Sava River. The supreme war council organized systematic colonization along the depopulated Turkish frontier, using Germans as a reliable counterpart to Hungarians. Imperial organization along this military frontier, therefore, was responsible for social change and landscape relics that are visible today. However, the multinational nature of the Austrian Empire not only prevented the degree of militarism and centralization found in Prussia, but also led eventually to weaknesses based on nationalist aspirations of the separate groups.

The three absolute empires mentioned previously – Prussia-Germany, Austria, and Russia – must be separated from the fourth empire of Eastern Europe – the Ottoman. This fourth empire which ruled over portions of the Balkans for periods of up to five hundred years, had political, economic, and social characteristics markedly different from those of the other three. These characteristics help to explain why the Balkans evolved in a divergent way from the rest of Eastern Europe. The Ottoman Empire represented a military state supported by Islamic faith. Its structure rested on perpetual military conquest because the administrative and military bureaucracies were drawn from slaves, mostly conscripted in the Christian areas of the Balkans. Supplementing this group was a native Islamic military class that was given landed estates (*timars*) from which they drew revenues in exchange for providing military services. However, they did not constitute a noble class in the European sense, for all land in the Ottoman Empire belonged to the Sultan. The primary goal of the state was the fiscal exploitation of the imperial possessions except beyond the Danube River – in Wallachia, Moldavia, and Transylvania – where a native landholding class was allowed to remain. Elsewhere, the existing nobilities were eliminated.

This goal of exploitation helps to explain the economic backwardness of the Balkans under Turkish rule, a condition, of course, reflected in part in the landscape: without a noble class of land-

owners, the land was not cultivated in any systematic way, and large areas of uncultivated land existed throughout the Balkans because many Christian peasants were driven into mountain areas or to large towns. An indirect result of Turkish exploitation, therefore, was the depopulation of certain areas; for example, village settlement on the Hungarian plain declined as people fled to the towns for protection. Old pre-Ottoman units of social organization like the *Zadruga*, or extended family, persisted because they had never been ruptured through feudalism as in areas farther north. Towns lost their commercial importance as the craft and trade functions became secondary to military and administrative ones. Actually, the commercial functions, where they existed, fell on minority communities like the Greeks, Jews, or Armenians. Thus, although considerable personal freedom, including religion, existed among the Christians under the Turks, the occupation actually interrupted economic and social development of a more advanced feudal order such as was taking place in the northern part of Eastern Europe. Christians paid larger taxes than Moslems, which often prompted conversions to the Islamic faith. Today, Moslems still dominate the population in areas where conversions were greatest, e.g. Bosnia.

The foregoing statements indicate that the environment of the multinational empires of Eastern Europe restricted social and landscape change. In the northern empires of Prussia-Germany, Russia, and Austria, absolute rulers, to gain the nobles' support in their objective of territorial aggrandizement, gave them power over the towns and countryside, thereby insuring the perpetuation of feudalism. In the Balkans, on the other hand, the Turkish Empire, while not absolute in nature, exploited the area in terms of manpower and tribute. The cleavage in economic development, therefore, between the eastern and western parts of Europe is attributed in great part to the exploitation of the former area by both rulers and lords for hundreds of years. In addition, as Wanklyn (1944: 111–16) points out, the eastern areas suffered isolation from artisan and trade activity initiated in the western part of Europe by the Commercial Revolution.

Not all the aspects of social change in Eastern Europe were negative. On the positive side, certain absolute rulers in Prussia and Austria incorporated ideas of the Enlightenment – humanism, reason, liberalism, and science – to support policies that benefited many people despite an archaic social structure. The enlightened absolute ruler thought of himself as a state official whose function

was to promote the welfare of the people. The best known in Eastern Europe were Joseph II of Austria and Frederick II (the Great) of Prussia. The former introduced education in the vernacular language and religious tolerance, both of which helped to create cultural elites among the subject peoples of Austria and to foster ideas of nationalism (Seton-Watson 1975: 7). In Prussia, Frederick the Great combined absolutist expansion with enlightened reforms such as the acceptance of religious refugees and restrictions on confiscation of peasant land. However, his policy of economic revitalization had perhaps the largest impact on social change, an impact visible in the landscape of the present. Silesia, Frederick's greatest conquest, proved invaluable with its coal, iron, and lead resources. The industrial foundation that was established in this province was important to the policies of later rulers of Prussia and imperial Germany.

These Prussian absolute rulers also introduced agricultural changes – farming techniques like elimination of the fallow by the introduction of root crops (e.g. potato) and seed grasses, land drainage projects along the rivers of the east, and colonization schemes that drew some 300 000 settlers (Mayhew 1973: 121, 172). For example, relics of reclamation in the bog areas along the Oder (Odra), Warthe (Warta), and Netze (Notec) valleys, and colonial villages in upland Silesia are still visible, all representing substantial capital undertakings.

The Enlightenment in Eastern Europe was a short-lived era. Although later rulers of Prussia and Austria exhibited some liberal tendencies, their overriding ideology was one of tradition and conservatism. Thus, the absolute rulers of Prussia, Russia, and Austria with their supporters – the feudal lords – lasted longer than those in the west where the liberal forces released by the French Revolution and the Industrial and Commercial Revolutions created a middle-class society with political liberties. In the east, a feudal and multinational environment prevailed.

Some ideologies of states within the multinational environment

The states that dominated the long period of a multinational environment in Eastern Europe were influenced strongly by ideologies that in turn affected the landscape. These ideologies in effect have geographical implications, because they lie behind the policies of leaders who, in organizing space within the area, transformed the landscape. This creates the need to give some attention to them. The

most evident ideologies consisted of territorial aggrandizement which perpetuated a multinational environment; unification of the state, which involved policies promoting patriotism and assimilation of multinational subjects; economic intervention in an environment where capital was lacking; and regional politics favoring different portions of states over others. All of these were characteristic of absolutism which itself could be called an ideology.

Territorial aggrandizement

Territorial expansion has been a persistent spatial characteristic of political organization in Eastern Europe. Gilfillan's map of 1924 illustrates the multiplicity of boundaries which reflect territorial change in a multinational environment (see Fig. 5.2). Some of these changes were initiated within Eastern Europe, but most of them came from external powers and perpetuated this environment. The motives for territorial expansion varied, but common ones included security, resources, strategic location, and defense against an alien race and religion. Prussia, Russia, and Austria exemplified all of these behavioral ideas. The first, Prussia, acquired Silesia not only for strategic reasons in its rivalry with Austria, but also for the great mineral and coal resources there. Prussia later supported the partition of Poland so as to unite East Prussia with Pomerania and Silesia. Austria was influenced, along with the normal motives of strategy and resources in its campaigns against Turkey, by a 'crusader' feeling of warfare with the infidel. On the other hand, at least one of Russia's imperial motives in the Balkans was Pan Slavism or an attempt to become the protector of Slav cultural groups caught in the Turkish–Austrian conflict.

These factors, therefore, made it possible to ascribe several different motives to the territorial behavior of imperial states in or on the margins of Eastern Europe. This behavior led to social change and landscape alteration in the territories concerned. For example, the presence today of Prussian-style architecture in Poland, an Austrian imperial spa in Romania, and the Turkish mosques in Yugoslavia reflect territorial boundaries of the past which seldom correspond to those of today.

Closely related to the ideology of territorial expansion by the rulers of multinational states within Eastern Europe was these rulers' desire for political grandeur. The splendor of imperial rulers is

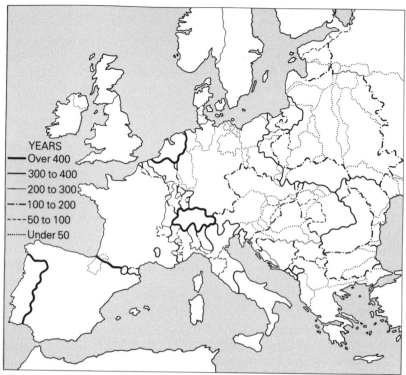

Fig. 5.2 Gilfillan's map of European boundaries. This illustrates the variety of spatial interaction that has occurred historically in Eastern Europe. (Reprinted with permission of the Academy of Political Science, New York.)

reflected in large capital cities like Berlin, Vienna, Saint Petersburg (Leningrad), Constantinople (Istanbul), Athens, and Rome. Only one of these – Berlin – lies in Eastern Europe as defined in this book but policies set in the others were important. Internal capitals like Dresden, Budapest, Warsaw, Prague, and Trnovo were also associated with past multinational environments. In Berlin, the predominant ideology employed grandiosity to reflect the power of both the ruler and his state, e.g. the triumphant Hohenzollern rulers' entrance into Berlin was through the Brandenburg Gate and down Unter den Linden. Each of these rulers left his mark of grandeur on the capital in some way, and many of these relics remain today. Some effects of this political-grandeur attitude on the development of a city like Berlin are provided later in this chapter.

Unification of a multinational state

Multinational states faced a primary problem in unification when they tried to promote patriotism or loyalty among the different classes such as nobles, churchmen, and peasants while simultaneously assimilating various national groups. As mentioned before, a primary force of cohesion was loyalty to local, regional, or royal institutions. Thus, a person could be loyal to a local priest, town, or territory and at the same time to the emperor or the Catholic Church; however, loyalty to a nationality only emerged in the nineteenth century. The Greek colonist, settled in what is now Eastern Europe, exhibited this loyalty transition – local to imperial – by focusing on both his own place and Athens or other mother state. On the other hand, the imperial loyalty of Rome was much more artificial with the subjects exhibiting a loyalty to the Pax Romana, which was supplementary to local loyalties rather than a substitute for them. In the Middle Ages, loyalties to class supplemented those of local place and regional institutions.

The Austrian Empire, where the basis of legitimacy was *Kaisertreu*, or loyalty to the Habsburg Emperor, serves as a good example of loyalties in an absolute state. Crankshaw (1963: 26) quotes Franz Joseph as asking, when a servant of the Austrian Empire was recommended to him as a sterling patriot, 'But is he a patriot for me?' This loyalty to the emperor in Austria, as in other empires, gave subjects the important benefit of protection, regardless of their station in life or of ethnic background. The armed forces and the bureaucracy, whose members were drawn from all nationalities, also served as important cohesive forces and symbols of the supranational character of the Empire. The throne had close ties to the Roman Catholic Church, to which three-quarters of the Empire's peoples belonged, and Catholicism acted as another supranational unifying force. Similarly, the denationalized aristocracy, with its close links to the throne and its monopoly in social, political, and military leadership, helped to hold the Empire together. Even the Hungarian magnates, although not Germanized, were Habsburgists. Finally, the geographical interdependence between industrial north and west versus agricultural south and east was a factor in unity, especially in terms of the central route of the Danube River and its tributaries. Relics in the landscape illustrate this unity of the Empire.

Certain other aspects of loyalty within a multinational environment are related to social class structure. This structure was domi-

nated by the nobles and peasants because the urban centers with a growing middle class had been weakened by most East European rulers in their attempts to build strong absolute states. In return for power over the peasants, the nobility of the large East European states, except Poland, gave their loyalty to the ruler. This nobility made up one class, regardless of ethnic background. Thus, as Kolarz (1946: 13) remarks, the Slovak and Romanian nobles were part of the Hungarian nobility, while the Lithuanian, White Russian, and Ukrainian nobility were part of the Polish nobility.

Large numbers of Jews also affected the multinational states. During the Middle Ages, they had settled in Eastern Europe, especially in Polish and Russian areas to escape persecution in other parts of Europe and to utilize commercial possibilities in the east. Up to the nineteenth century, they tended to settle in rural areas where they performed urban operations, e.g. tax and grain collecting for the landowners or money lending. At the time of the first partition of Poland (1772), the Jews were responsible for an estimated 75 per cent of the country's export trade. In the nineteenth century, however, population increases in Eastern Europe placed severe burdens on resources, helping to cause anti-Semitism. In Russia, including Russian Poland, Jews were restricted in their places of residence. This gradually led to the creation of large ghetto areas in the cities. Discrimination was less severe in Austrian Poland, but ghettos existed in Cracow and Lemberg (Polish Lwów). Pressure in these partition areas caused thousands of Jews to emigrate to America. However, in Prussian Poland, Jews were often assimilated into cultural and economic life, especially in commerce and industry. Until the Second World War period, Jews unquestionably made up an important part of the multinational environment of Eastern Europe. Today, only a few landscape relics remain to remind us of this group. These relics are discussed later in the chapter.

Supplementing the cohesive forces of loyalty to the ruler and lord was another form of consolidation within the multinational environment of Eastern Europe known as forced cultural assimilation. In Hungary, this policy – called Magyarization – had both imperialist and liberal motives. For example, the Hungarian rulers wanted to reduce the influence of nationalities located outside Hungarian territory by making certain that minorities of these nationalities within the country – especially Romanians and Croats – were acculturated. Supplementing this imperialist motive was what Seton-Watson (1975: 10) calls a liberal motive – the idea that only through strong

centralized government with one dominant language could the subject nationalities receive a higher culture. In the latter part of the nineteenth century, therefore, the Hungarian language became mandatory for use in public, while other languages could be used in private. In practice, however, the use of non-Hungarian languages became more and more difficult, even though this privilege was protected by the Nationality Law of 1867. The result created even more resentment toward the Magyars by non-Hungarian subjects and hastened the spread of nationalism. Similar programs of forced assimilation of subject nationalities within an imperial environment occurred in Prussia-Germany and Russia with the same results.

Thus, strong attempts were made to unify multinational states by centralizing authority and erasing cultural differences. For example, Crankshaw (1963: 332–3) phrases it well when he says that Vienna was the hub of the entire Austrian imperial system and that each city in the monarchy, even Cracow and Prague, owed much of its appearance and culture to Habsburg rule. This carried over to include even the designation of color – 'Maria Theresa Yellow' – for public buildings, a feature familiar to tourists today. However, despite these policies, the imprint of national groups within a multinational environment was perceptible in the landscape. To cite one case, in northeastern Romania a group of Orthodox monasteries, through their external frescoes, bear the mark of this nationality regardless of previous Byzantine efforts at unification.

State intervention

For a variety of reasons, intervention by the state in economic activity represents still another ideology of the multinational environment. Early intervention by states like Rome with its mining in the Balkans and medieval Hungary with its encouragement of colonization by German miners and craftsmen left only scattered relics; state intervention by the rulers of absolute states, being more recent and pronounced, left a greater imprint. In some cases, this intervention reflected a policy of mercantilism, a system by which a government regulates its economic activity to create a favorable balance of trade, using quotas and tariffs to protect domestic goods from foreign competition. State intervention also included ownership of factories or railways and certain incentives aimed at encouraging domestic industry. The most significant measures, perhaps, sought to attract foreign capital. Such policies of intervention were furthered

by the multinational environment in which many areas of Eastern Europe were not only militarily unstable but also were agrarian and lagging in economic development.

In analyzing this role of the state in the multinational government of Eastern Europe, the statements of Berend and Ránki (1974a: 83, 92) provide insight. They stress that although state intervention was not a role unique to Eastern Europe, since it occurred in all parts of Europe, it was later and more direct in the east. However, they point out that the import of foreign capital promoted by state activity is the feature that most distinguishes this part of the continent. This foreign capital, attracted in the latter part of the nineteenth century by better conditions and by guarantees on interest, was imperative because domestic capital failed to materialize for developing these relatively backward areas. In the first place, except in Bohemia the socio-economic structure lacked an urban-based middle class anxious to invest in manufacturing. Second, the aristocracy was not entre-preneurial, e.g. the Hungarian noble could not be induced to think of any career worthy of him except that of landowner. Foreign capital, therefore, became important and left its mark on the landscape.

An ideology of state economic intervention was most evident in Prussia in the years between the accession of Frederick the Great (1740) and the founding of a united Reich (1871). Henderson (1958: xix) provides considerable information that supports this state role, i.e. that the functions of a paternal state included taking an active part in fostering the agrarian and industrial expansion of the country. This ideology, tied to the preindustrial notion that Prussia was a vast estate to be managed by the king and his advisors, survived into the era of steam engines and railways. The eastern portions of Prussia especially showed this influence, for they reflected the added factor of defense. The scattered nature of Prussia's territories, which extended from Cologne to Königsberg, prompted the consolidation of these areas and the development of resources in frontier areas like Silesia. Ideology favoring a state role was influenced by people like von Reden, director of the Prussian mining administration in the early nineteenth century. He believed that the state was in a more advantageous position than private persons to finance and administer new industrial undertakings in relatively remote parts of the kingdom.

The role of the state in Prussian spatial organization for industrial purposes is shown in the network of state railroads in the mid-

nineteenth century. The pattern resembles a wheel: Berlin at the hub with spokes to Königsberg, Upper Silesia, Leipzig, and Hamburg. This network served both defense needs and separate economic development. The maintenance of the royal foundry in Berlin, the establishment of iron and armament works at Malapane (Ozimek) in Silesia, and the opening of lead mines in Silesia were, to some extent, measures dictated by military needs.

The role of the state government in organizing political and economic space in the Austrian Empire – and thereby influencing social change and the landscape – was not as direct as that in Prussia-Germany and was complicated later by the importance of a partner, Hungary. Bohemia-Moravia, because of location, resources, and favorable political factors, became the industrial base of the Austro-Hungarian Empire. Private Viennese banking firms (e.g. Rothschild) controlled heavy industry like the Skoda armament plant at Pilsen (Plzeň) or the iron works at Witkowitz (Vítkovice) in Moravia. On the other hand, some of the scattered iron and steel factories in the Empire were state owned, e.g. the Austrian State Railway Company owned the Reschitza (Reşiţa) ironworks in the Banat, and the Hungarian government developed the iron and steel works at Zolyombrezó (Podbrezová).

The Habsburg role in railroad construction perhaps had the greatest overall locational influence on the organization of political (administrative), economic, and military space in the Empire. Gross (1973: 260–1) summarizes this role by noting that an imperial decree of 1841 reserved for the state both the planning of the network and the construction, operation, and acquisition of any specific line. Even between 1854 and 1881, when private construction was encouraged, the state not only subsidized the companies but also had a say in the alignment of routes. By 1913, the Austrian rail system was essentially state owned (19 000 of 23 000 total km); in Hungary, a somewhat lower proportion was either state-owned or operated. Moodie (1945: 116–23) describes how the railroad to Trieste (the *Südbahn*) was built by the Austrian government and users were given concessions, an arrangement that served not only to strengthen the position of this primary imperial port, but also to cover the high cost of constructing and maintaining the railroad through alpine topography. The Austrian government indirectly had a role in the development of the spa-resort of Abbazia (Opatija) near Fiume (Rijeka) since this port was linked to the *Südbahn*, which reportedly

constructed the large hotel Humler (later called Quanero and now Kvarner). Even today this hotel and the resort of Opatija retain a distinct Austrian image. However, the state in its role of economic planner and developer also used foreign capital, as exemplified by the railroad line across Transylvania built by British money.

In the two other external empires controlling parts of Eastern Europe, the role of state intervention in organizing space, especially economic, varied. Turkey had little interest in industry and thus contributed in a negative way to the heritage of backwardness. As Serbia, Romania, and Bulgaria became independent in the nineteenth century, they intervened in supporting economic development, including especially laws to stimulate foreign investment, e.g. oil in Romania and minerals in Serbia. Russian aid to its puppet state – Congress Poland – in the form of railroad construction and the lowering of tariffs was encouraged by the demand for manufactured goods which the latter could supply to the Empire. Industrialization in Congress Poland actually reflects Polish nationalism (or patriotism) and is discussed in the next chapter.

What can one conclude about the industrialization of Eastern Europe before 1914? Actually, the absolute amount was fairly small. Although comparative statistics are lacking, Berend and Ránki (1974a: 130–3) point out that Great Britain, Germany, and France before the First World War produced 72 per cent of Europe's industrial output. The percentage of Germany's production that came from eastern portions of the country, while important, was not as large as that of the west. The Austro-Hungarian Monarchy with 15.6 per cent of Europe's population produced 6.3 per cent of the industrial output; over one-half came from the East European portion with 60 per cent of this from Bohemia. These figures demonstrate that Eastern Europe before the First World War was not heavily industrialized except in parts of Prussia and Bohemia-Moravia. Nevertheless, the impact of the changes in the last third of the nineteenth century affected the entire economy of the area, transforming all its branches including agriculture, banking, transport, and industry. Eastward diffusion of the Industrial Revolution, then, clearly affected social change by initiating alterations in occupational and social structure and in the degree of urbanization. Although comparative figures on such change are difficult to obtain, one table for Hungary shows the changes in occupations between 1870 and 1910 (Berend and Ránki 1974b: 74).

	1870 (%)	*1910* (%)
Agriculture	80.0	64.5
Industry	8.6	17.1
Transport and trade	2.9	6.5
Others	8.5	11.9

Geographically, the distribution of this social change was unequal: in terms of the A–B–C concept, only Prussia and Bohemia-Moravia were zone A, while a narrow corridor through Poland, western Slovakia, central Hungary, and Slovenia was zone B (see Fig. 4.7). The rest of Eastern Europe, including eastern Poland, Slovakia, and Hungary plus almost all of the Balkans, was zone C. These regional differences are still apparent although modified under communism.

Regional politics

A final ideology that affected social change and the landscape in the multinational environment of Eastern Europe involved two types of regional politics practiced by state rulers. In one type, differing external state policies of imperial powers had varying impacts on areas which now are joined as one state. The second type involved internal state policy favoring one or more regions over others.

The policies of three empires in partitioned Poland illustrate the first type. Each imperial ruler tended to force the orientation of his part of Poland toward the respective capitals of Berlin, Vienna, and Moscow, although actually the Russian area received the least attention. Former imperial alignment patterns of railroads were difficult to consolidate after the First World War in the new state of Poland; even the gauge was different – 5ft (1.5 m) in the Russian area instead of 4 ft 8½ in (1.4 m). Furthermore, differences existed in development within the three areas. For example, the Prussian-Germans invested much more in agriculture than did the Russians and Austrians (Wandycz 1974: 229). Fertilizer was used as the German response to barren, sandy soils, and large fields, which replaced the small plots, contrasted with the fragmented pattern in Russian and Austrian Poland. But investment in the cities also wrought changes, e.g. Poznań (Posen) assumed a German face, still seen today in the opera house. A Polish friend remarked to me that a characteristic mark of late nineteenth century Prussian-German rule in western Poland is the distinctive large, brick post office building still found in many

cities. Posen also served as one of several centers of Germanization in this former Polish territory, i.e. use of the German language was required, and the Catholic Church was harassed by the government. This Germanization policy led to increased nationalistic feeling by Polish residents, a situation that was also found in Russian Poland, where Russification policies were employed and little was done to help the populace. Polish culture was allowed its greatest expression in Austrian Poland through use of the Polish language and representation in political bodies. Even the landscape that exists from this period shows a mixture of Austrian and Polish input.

A second type of regional politics is exemplified by Austria, where policy was aimed at not only protecting the Empire but also consolidating and conserving the economic and cultural supremacy of the western 'hereditary' provinces over the eastern ones. Bohemia-Moravia benefited because of a German medieval tradition in craftsmanship, its large resources of coal, and access to the Elbe River; these provinces, therefore, became the industrial 'workshops' of the empire. Hungary was not favored because the imperial government saw no reason to encourage industrial growth to compete with Bohemia – Moravia. Instead, Hungary became a 'colonial market' for Austrian industrial products and a producer of raw materials. Thus, Austria practiced regional discrimination in both industry and agriculture. A tariff line, which separated Austria and Hungary until the middle of the nineteenth century, protected industrial and agricultural producers in the western provinces. Even after the *Ausgleich* of 1867, Hungary's customs union with Austria did not protect its domestic industry, and a series of laws, e.g. tax exemptions, had to be passed to remedy this problem. In the nineteenth century, the Magyars practiced regional politics against the Slovaks and other cultural groups on the edges of the kingdom, continually favoring Budapest as a focus of development. These regional policies within Austria-Hungary consequently left a legacy of uneven development that persisted for decades and is still apparent.

Austrian regional politics also were applied to Bosnia and Hercegovina, border provinces occupied, and later annexed, by Austria before the First World War. Here Habsburg state intervention was more direct, and considerable economic development occurred under the Austrians and Hungarians with the exploitation of coal, iron, oil, salt, and wood products. Nonetheless, Sugar (1963: 77–80) shows that the rivalry between the dual powers prevented the railroad expansion that was necessary in this backward area. This regional

policy, as with the others within the Empire, left an important negative legacy in social change and the landscape.

In Eastern Europe, these different ideologies created a multinational environment that was unstable and immature economically. Territorial expansion by the strong powers pervaded the entire region. Loyalty to nationalities began to replace patriotism to emperor or church, while forced cultural assimilation only strengthened national feelings among the smaller cultural groups. Although state intervention attempted to make up for the lack of private development, such intervention often hinged on regional politics which tended to perpetuate backwardness and imbalance. The multinational environment of Eastern Europe in 1914, therefore, was not a favorable one for the formation of new states after the First World War.

Relics of the multinational environment

In contrast to the previous environments of landscape change – German colonization and feudalism – this multinational environment was, above all, political. The primary decision-maker was the ruler – emperor, king, prince, or duke; but he made decisions within what was essentially a multinational environment where a variety of cultural groups interacted within political units. What effects did this person have on the landscape?

I have chosen to focus on four types of relics that can be separated from later developments under nationalism and socialism. The first type includes the relics found in *political centers* established as capitals in states such as those of the Hohenzollern rulers in Berlin. The second type concerns relics of *settlement* outside the centers, which often were controlled by decisions made in places either external to Eastern Europe, like Vienna, Constantinople, Moscow, or Venice; or internal, such as Berlin, Budapest, Warsaw, or Prague. Various relics in the landscape today, e.g. the Greek colony, Roman provincial center and road, Byzantine fortress, Austrian colonial settlement and frontier fortress, Turkish *caravanserai*, and Italian cities in Dalmatia fall into this category. The third type involves the relics of *religious systems* – Catholic, Orthodox, Protestant, Uniate, Jewish, and Moslem – for religious groups played a strong role in these states, often sharing power with the rulers. Finally, the fourth type consists of *industrial* relics, many of which were originally part of state promotion programs. At the end of the chapter, the Habsburg

imperial system serves as an example to illustrate how these relics combine today to reflect the total impact of the system on the landscape. Reference is made throughout the chapter to the relationships between the relics, the ideology of the decision-maker, and social change. Before discussing the four types of relics, however, the process of urbanism in Eastern Europe must be examined, because, in contrast to the feudal period when the nobility had its basis of power in the countryside, the rulers within a multinational environment operated from cities and many of the relics are located in urban areas.

As mentioned in Chapter 3, early Slavic or Hungarian towns in Eastern Europe emphasized administrative, military, and religious functions, but the arrival of German medieval colonists brought the institution of municipal law, which allowed for urban autonomy. In time, the towns developed corporate rights, which related to and even facilitated the expansion of artisan production and long-distance trade. Pounds (1971: 62) shows that towns in the northern parts of Eastern Europe, where this German town-forming process went on, contrasted with the paucity of them in the Balkans. He feels that this difference in pattern between north and south represents a reversal from the classical period when Rome produced East Europe's first real urban network of which only a few scattered relics remain today. The reasons for this reversal related to the inability of cities in the Balkans to recover from their devastation during the invasions of Slavic tribes. Pounds' map, therefore, shows the importance of large northern towns like Danzig (Gdańsk), Prague, Brünn (Brno), Breslau (Wrocław), Cracow, Kaschau (Košice), and Ofen (Budapest). Urban life in the Balkans was restricted to German towns of Transylvania (Siebenbürgen) such as Hermannstadt (Sibiu), certain mining towns like Srebrenica or Novo Brdo, a few regional centers such as Laibach (Ljubljana), and the trading towns of the Adriatic like Ragusa (Dubrovnik).

This late medieval pattern of urbanism did not change much between the mid-fourteenth and nineteenth centuries as urban stagnation set in all over Eastern Europe. In the north, feudalism as a social and economic system dominated Eastern Europe as the aristocracy infringed on the earlier-initiated municipal rights and functions. Even the influence of absolute rulers had little effect until the eighteenth century. Towns were characterized by administrative-military functions including the ruler's court. When these courts in Poland, Hungary, and Bohemia were controlled by dynasties of foreign origin,

141

the towns became even more alien to the population. In the south, where the Turkish Empire dominated political organization for five centuries, cities became islands of foreign Turks, Jews, and Germans in a peasant countryside. The map of urbanization, therefore, illustrates as well as anything how feudalism, absolutism or autocracy, and imperialism restricted social change in the eastern half of Europe – especially in the Balkans – leading to a cleavage that lasted until the twentieth century. The pattern of urban development changed slightly in the nineteenth century as absolute rulers like the Hohenzollerns and Habsburgs initiated industrialization programs. However, real urban growth based on an expanding middle class only began on a limited scale in the late nineteenth century. Hence, the cleavage between Western and Eastern Europe persisted.

We now examine four types of relics that are characteristic of the multinational environment in Eastern Europe: political centers, settlements outside the centers, religious structures, and industrial establishments.

Political centers

The relics of political centers in Eastern Europe vary greatly, but I feel that they fall logically into two groups according to time – medieval or Renaissance-Baroque. Premedieval towns were mostly administrative centers for Athens, Rome, or Constantinople and are treated separately later on. Hajdu (1978) draws a distinction between *Altstadt* (old town) and *Residenzstadt* (residence town), which fits this medieval-Renaissance and Baroque classification. Although Hajdu is really focusing on the German town, his two-fold designation seems appropriate for Eastern Europe because of its German heritage of municipal development. Cities of Eastern Europe had their old towns and residence towns, which may have had Germanic input, especially in town law; but later these urban districts acquired other cultural characteristics. Relics of both are preserved today and illustrate the impact of political forces on social change and the landscape.

1. Medieval centers

The medieval political center in Eastern Europe displayed several characteristics. First, it was associated with a wall and castle or fortress, an essential in the insecure environment of feudalism. In this sense, the fortified castle symbolizes the medieval period just as the unfortified palace symbolizes the Renaissance–Baroque period.

142

Second, the medieval center was known as the old town to differentiate it from later urban developments. This old core is equally recognizable by two features that indicate Germanic background: (1) a planned rectangular layout which reveals its colonization origin and (2) a market square and town hall which reflect the privileges gained from diffusion of town law from the west. However, as stated in Chapter 2, German law did not necessarily mean Germanic population. Consequently, many East European towns, where Slavic, Hungarian, or Romanian populations dominated, had their own terms for this medieval city. For example, the *Staré Město*, meaning old town, in Prague was dominated in the thirteenth century by Germanic settlement. Later it became largely Czech populated, although it also had a large Jewish section. As towns expanded, a *Neustadt*, or new town (in Czech *Nové Město*) developed. Like Prague, other towns such as Dresden, Warsaw, Cracow, Budapest, Agram (Zagreb), had (and have) their 'old town' and 'new town'.

The medieval political center reflected three groups of people, each with its own ideology. The castle and cathedral exemplify the first two – the ruler and the clergy – who together dominated society until challenged by the third group – the middle class – that demanded a share of the power. This compromise, legalized in a municipal charter, is reflected by the town hall and market square, which symbolized the privileges of citizen representation and the right to hold a market. Thus, the relics of the old town today can illustrate two somewhat anomalous symbols: a castle, which represented the insecurity of the early feudal environment, and a market place, which reflected the growing security of long-distance trade.

Possibly the finest relics of medieval political rule within a multinational environment in Eastern Europe are found in Prague and Cracow. These two cities fortunately escaped serious damage during the Second World War, leaving the primary architectural monuments intact. Both cities have the two focal points mentioned – castle (Hradčany in Prague and Wawel in Cracow) and old town. Both castles stand on bluffs overlooking rivers associated with the cities' histories – the Moldau (Vltava) and Vistula, respectively. Both castles have famous cathedrals within their walls that illustrate the links between political ruler and clergy. Both cities were prominent in the histories of their respective states. Prague, for most of its history, was the political center of Bohemia, an important component of the Holy Roman Empire (later Austrian). Cracow, the capital of multinational Poland during the late Middle Ages, has always been

143

viewed as the most Polish of cities. Both castle and old town in these cities include a historical abundance of architectural styles ranging from Romanesque to Baroque. As a result, both castles, although of medieval origin, were central factors in the later period of the *Residenzstadt* (residence town), when Renaissance planning was important. Indeed, Dziewoński (1943: 34) writes that Cracow became a primary center of Renaissance culture north of the Alps. Two of the most beautiful portions of the castle complexes are the Renaissance Belvedere garden in the Hradčany and the Renaissance courtyard in the Wawel (see Photo 5.1). The old towns of both cities are virtually relic storehouses of medieval urbanism – town halls, market squares, cloth hall (Cracow), historic churches, town gates, and walls. Clock towers in the squares of both cities still sound their chimes while providing images from the medieval past – the Apostles gesture while a cock crows (Prague) and the bugler sounds the alarm of the Mongol attack (Cracow). Truly, the old town relics of Prague and Cracow present a picture of life and social change in medieval Eastern Europe – again the anomaly of castle and market square.

In the area comprising medieval Hungary, no city retains the variety of early urban relics that Prague or Cracow does. In an unstable multinational environment, the capital changed five times – Stuhlweissenburg (Székesfehérvár), Gran (Esztergom), Visegrád, Pressburg (Pozsony), and Ofen (Budapest). In the first three cities only a few relics of royal castles remain. Pressburg (Pozsony), today known as Bratislava in Czechoslovakia, was aligned with Hungary in medieval times; its fortress, which overlooks the Danube River and the old town, is a dominating landmark. The city also served for over two centuries as a capital of Hungary during the Turkish occupation of Budapest. The latter, known in the medieval period as Ofen (Buda), was not the capital until the late fifteenth century. Once again, the spatial focus of the medieval city was Castle Hill on the Buda side of the Danube River. Besides providing a wonderful panoramic view of the entire city bisected by the Danube, this hill location contains Dísz Square, which was the site of the medieval market place; the remains of the royal palace; and the famous Coronation Church. Pounds (1971: 56) feels that the frequent association of palace and cathedral in Europe is no accident: 'Prince and bishop could thus broaden the territorial basis of their authority in the closest association with one another.' This same connection pertains to Prague and Cracow.

Photo 5.1   Within the Hradčany castle of Prague is one of the outstanding
Renaissance buildings in Eastern Europe – the royal summer residence
(Belvedere). Built in the sixteenth century, this palace reflects the multinational
environment that dominated Prague and Bohemia for so long.

In the Balkans, the fortified castle also survives as a primary relic
of medieval centers within a multinational environment, but its
relationship with particular cultures is less clear because of successive
occupation by different powers. Hence, these fortresses represent
links not only to the empires of Bulgaria and Serbia, but also to the
kingdoms, principalities, or duchies of Carniola (Slovenia), Croatia,
Bosnia, Montenegro, Wallachia, Moldavia, and Albania. These

citadels served as political centers of power for these internal groups and for longer periods as strong points of the externally based empires of Byzantium or Turkey.

Albania has two outstanding examples of such medieval political centers, Shkodër and Krujë. Although both served as capitals of feudal Albanian states, Byzantine, Venetian, and Ottoman forces also utilized them at different times. At Shkodër a large fortress crowns a hill that rises above Lake Shkodër. Just as famous is the fortress at Krujë, located on a peninsula of rock overlooking the plain where the great Albanian hero George Castrioti or Skanderbeg held off the Turks on three different occasions in the fifteenth century.

Although the fortress remains an ubiquitous political symbol of a multinational environment in the Balkans, other relics survive. For example, remnants of two palaces exist at Cetinje, the former capital of Montenegro, located in a *polje* (basin) surrounded by barren and forbidding limestone mountains. At the sites of Preslav and Pliska, former capitals of the Bulgarian Empire, only excavated foundations are visible.

2. The Renaissance and Baroque center

Post-medieval towns that were the product of transformation by either absolute or petty rulers have been grouped together under the architectural terms that dominated their design – either Renaissance or Baroque. Hajdu (1978) has called this type of city a *Residenzstadt* (residence town) because it served as the residence of a ruler, whose ideology, as explained earlier, often involved a feeling of absolute power. This authority was translated into a desire to create a city, often the capital, that in representing power and grandeur could be considered an 'extension' of the ruler. In those days of the sixteenth to nineteenth centuries, when gunpowder had made the fortified castle obsolete, the palace became the symbol of the Renaissance-Baroque city. Planning as directed by these rulers constituted civic projects on a grand scale with entire sections of cities being re-designed. Such transformation occurred most in the capital city of an empire or large kingdom. As Lichtenberger (1970: 47–52) says, the influence of absolutism on cities represents the impact of the state rather than of municipal bodies as had been the case in the chartered cities of the Middle Ages. The absolute state superimposed its administration on that of the city, which lost its former autonomy in the areas where German town law had been important.

In Eastern Europe, Baroque is the predominant architectural style.

The term means 'odd-shaped', and was initially applied to the architecture of Italy from the mid-sixteenth century onwards because that architecture was characterized by unusual, extravagant shapes. The main features of the style portray movement and tension, attained by the use of undulating curves, sculptured figures, and large, overly colorful paintings. The style, accompanied by city planning based on geometrical patterns, spread over much of Eastern Europe. The grand boulevard, a straight line flanked by impressive buildings – barracks, theater and opera, museum, university – and leading to the palace, anchored the geometric design. This avenue, used by the carriages of the rulers and nobility, had intersections which were developed as squares adorned with buildings, fountains, or statues. Formal gardens and parks, with the latter often providing royal hunting grounds, complemented the palaces.

The size and scale of this urban design, especially the grand boulevard axis, reflected the ideology of 'political grandeur' that served as a motivating force for the rulers. This ideology included the collecting of foreign art objects for the glory of the realm and the storing of them in a museum. Certain art historians (*Christian Science Monitor*, 9 June 1978, 27) feel that this idea was born in the *Kunstkammer* (chamber of art treasures) of Dresden in the sixteenth century. Finally, the ideology of grandeur was related to the large residential town as a center of royal court activity. The nobility, referred to in the previous chapter as representatives of persistent feudal tradition, contributed to this city through their urban residences; they not only became a part of the bureaucracy but also supported the arts by sponsoring a group of artisans serving the court.

The most outstanding examples of smaller residential towns in Eastern Europe are the German cities of Potsdam and Dresden. Both reflect the contrast between a rather severe Baroque style and a more lavish Rococo with an emphasis on delicate detail in decoration. The Rococo style represented the attempt by absolute rulers to gain privacy in smaller palaces adjacent to the main public ones. Thus, in Potsdam, Frederich the Great constructed the new palace in classic Baroque style, while using pure Rococo in the smaller palace of Sanssouci; the latter style illustrated the ruler's ties to France where this type of architecture originated (Hamlin 1953: 476–81). The same contrast between two architectural styles is evident in Dresden, where the Saxon kings emphasized Baroque values of dynamic power, great scale, and overall plan conception in the major part of

Photo 5.2 The Baroque Zwinger palace in Dresden represents the grandeur of the Saxon kings and this impressive capital city.

the royal complex, but utilized Rococo delicacy in the Zwinger palace. Built as an addition to the residential palace for entertainment purposes, the Zwinger consists of a series of lavish pavilions and halls whose unity is not easily comprehended at first glance (see Photo 5.2). Both Potsdam and Dresden today transplant the visitor to this absolutist era and project the political grandeur of these rulers. The influence of the Saxon kings on the landscape is also evident in other palaces and in the royal porcelain works at Meissen.

Of the four imperial capitals that exercised great influence on Eastern Europe in the nineteenth century, three – Vienna, Moscow, and Istanbul – lie outside the area as defined earlier. The fourth, Berlin, does not. It is this city whose landscape best reflects the monumental power of the multinational absolute state (see Fig. 5.3). A leisurely walk down Unter den Linden, Berlin's most famous boulevard, provides the best way of sensing the aura of former imperial strength (see Photos 5.3 & 5.4).

Each of the Hohenzollern rulers contributed to this feeling of power that still radiates from the inner city, now a part of communist East Berlin: the wife of the Great Elector laid out the boulevard to connect the royal palace with the Brandenburg Gate; Frederick II

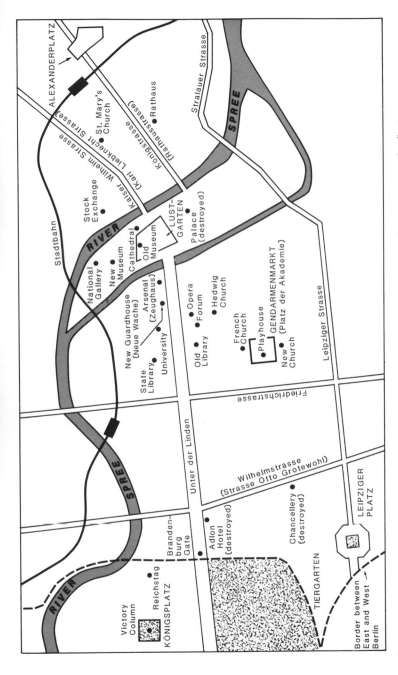

Fig. 5.3　The major existing relics in East Berlin. These developed under the Hohenzollern dynasty and reflect the power of the multinational absolute state.

created not only the adjacent Forum Fredericianum, one of the great eighteenth-century squares of Europe, but also the enormous Gendermenmarkt (now called the Platz der Akademie) which is dominated by two large churches that bear the marks of the Second World War; Frederick William II was responsible for the newer Brandenburg Gate; under Frederick William III, the famous architect Schinkel continued the tradition of monumentality with the Altes Museum; William I established the City Hall (Rotes Rathaus) and three large railway stations; finally, William II was responsible for the completion of the Reichstag building, the Dom or cathedral, and the other buildings on Museum Island in the Spree River.

What was common to this input by a series of strong rulers over a period of some 250 years? Willis (1973: II, 781, 808) feels (and I agree) that two forces directed the development of Berlin. The first was military; Prussia, later Germany, was a militaristic state and Berlin a garrison city. This function is best represented by the Neue Wache or Watch House on Unter den Linden. This low, grey building, resembling a Roman temple, originally housed a permanent guard available on a moment's notice for any emergency, but now serves as a monument to the victims of fascism. The Neue Wache along with these other monumental structures just mentioned symbolizes a second force in the development of Berlin – the attempt to make the city a synthesis of Greece and Rome. This force corresponded to the various rulers' beliefs, especially in the nineteenth century, that Berlin could represent a combination of spirit (*Geist*) and strength (*Macht*). Thus, the Brandenburg Gate became a Doric version of a Roman triumphal arch and the Old Museum a long basilica, like Caesar's in Rome, masked by a façade of Ionian columns.

The Hohenzollern rulers employed two additional forces, art and industry, to express their ideology. The former is symbolized by the emergence on an island in the Spree River of one of the greatest

Photo 5.3   This scene from Hohenzollern Berlin captures the ideology of militarism, Greek–Roman symbolism, and political grandeur that is still visible today through relics in the landscape. (Source: *Spaziergang durch die Geschichte Berlins* Berlin–Information 1978: p. 43; from Märkisches Museum, Berlin, GDR.)

Photo 5.4   The Neue Wache or Watch House, built in 1818, originally housed a permanent guard of Prussian soldiers but now serves as a monument to the victims of fascism. This building, as much as any on Unter den Linden, illustrates the Hohenzollern ideology of power.

complexes of museums in the world. These buildings embody the attempt to gather archaeological remains from the Near East and include, for example, the Pergamon Altar, a large Greek temple transported from Turkey. The arts are also symbolized by the opera, Humboldt University, and the state library – all on Unter den Linden. The second force, the rapid industrialization of Germany in the late nineteenth century, is evidenced by three large railway stations, today in East Berlin – Friedrichstrasse, Alexanderplatz, and Ostbahnhof (formerly Silesian Bahnhof). These stations illustrate Berlin's rise after 1871 to the status of a *Weltstadt* (world city), the result not only of its role of *Hauptstadt* (capital) for a unified empire but also of its importance as an industrial city. As already noted, Berlin under Prussia became the center of a vast network of railroads that was expanded under Bismarck to all parts of the empire. Population in the city rose from one million in 1870 to four million in 1914.

The large number of imposing structures which still stand in Berlin clearly tell a story of Hohenzollern ideology – a combination of militarism, Greek–Roman symbolism, and the nineteenth-century influences of art and industry (see Fig. 5.3). The relics also recount attitudes of political grandeur and state intervention on the part of the Hohenzollern rulers who, in creating this capital of a powerful absolute state, were responsible for social change – the spread of industrialization which allowed the average German's real income to more than double. These relics also symbolize the rise of Germany as a center of European and even world politics. At the present, these relics of former power stand alongside new monuments of power – the rather imposing structures of the communist party in East Berlin. This landscape is treated in Chapter 7.

Poland, of course, was not an absolute state. Yet Warsaw possesses one relic that illustrates civic planning in a capital city by a ruler – the Saxon axis, a park in the central portion of the city, is the sole fragment of a once-great palace and garden complex in Baroque style. Built in the years 1713–63 by Augustus II, the new Saxon king of Poland, the layout represents the cultural influence of this Germanic state on Polish city planning (Gutkind, VII 1972: 78–82).

As indicated, the internal pattern in the political centers of East European states is a product of several processes. In Chapter 3, I point out the role of German colonization in establishing the old town of these cities including regular layout, city hall, and market

square. Chapter 4 illustrates the input of the noble class as they built urban residences (palaces) throughout the cities. Finally, this chapter has added the impact of the rulers in multinational environments by combining castles or palaces with considerable civic planning. The total association of these three processes – colonization, feudalism, and multinationalism – is demonstrated best in Prague, but is also evident in most of the large cities. In the next two chapters the added influence of the processes of nationalism and socialism to the total urban landscape is examined.

Settlement relics

Supplementing the landscape relics found in *political* centers are those that existed as components of *settlements* away from the centers. These relics occurred as parts of multinational environments, and they still reflect this legacy despite now being located within a completely different pattern of spatial organization dominated by nation-states. Control of these settlements often emanated from the political centers, referred to in the previous section, that were located both in Eastern Europe and outside the area. At the same time, the religious and industrial structures mentioned in following sections are discussed separately because they are found in both political centers and other settlements. Only a few isolated settlement relics remain from the classical and medieval systems (e.g. Roman and Byzantine), while many more exist from nineteenth-century multinational systems (e.g. Austrian or Prussian). In the latter instances, the railroad became an important means of interaction, serving to hold each empire together. On the other hand, the road served this purpose in the Turkish Empire.

To illustrate and discuss the most typical examples of settlement relics in the East European landscape, I have chosen seven examples which reflect early multinational systems of spatial organization: Greek colony, Roman settlement, imperial fortress, Turkish *caravanserai* or hotel, imperial colony, Hungarian *tanya* or isolated farm, and Italian settlement along the Adriatic coast.

1. The Greek colony

Today only a few relics along the Black Sea and Adriatic coasts show the extent of early Greek colonial settlement. Should these relics be called multinational in the sense of the term as it is being used here?

Ferguson (1941: 30) considers the unification of city-states and colonies under Athens' domination as an empire. Although this empire did not include large numbers of non-Greeks – an aspect of a multinational state – the environment in which the colonies were established was certainly multinational. Although the Greek city-states traded with the Slavic hinterlands, they seldom penetrated very deeply on a permanent basis. The Westermann *Atlas zur Weltgeschichte* (1956: 16) shows three cities along the Black Sea coast – Mesembria (Nesebǎr), Odessos (Varna), and Kallatis (Mangalia) – as tied to Athens in 431 BC (the names in parentheses indicate present-day sites, the first two in Bulgaria and the last in Romania). Today, a portion of a rampart in Nesebǎr indicates Greek influence, but later Roman, Byzantine, and Turkish relics in the town give a clue to the commercial and strategic importance of this city.

The Romanian *Atlas Istoric* (1971: plate 11) shows two other sites of Greek colonies in Romania – Tomi and Istros. The former was the early settlement of present-day Constanța, the major port for the country. An open-air museum includes excellent Greek remains. Istros, today called Histria, lies farther north and, with no modern city occupying this point, represents a complete archaeological site.

Along the Adriatic coast, the degree of linkage between Greek colonies and Hellenic city-states is obscure. Perhaps the best known is Epidamnos, today the port of Durrës, Albania. Farther south is Apollonia, a Greek city located inland from the sea near the town of Fier, Albania, which as the *Tourist Guide Book of Albania* (1969: 110–18) explains is the largest archaeological site in the country. Its importance apparently rivaled that of Epidamnos, perhaps at a later time, as Cicero called it *magna urbs et gravis* (great and significant city). The excavations have unearthed the most complete set of relics of a Greek colony in the Balkans: walls, arched gates, assembly hall, library, theater, and a house with mosaics. Unfortunately, because Albanian policies create so many restrictions to visiting the country, historical sites like Apollonia are virtually inaccessible to foreigners.

Can the Greek colony be linked to the ideologies of multinational states mentioned in the first part of this chapter? The existence of relics along the Black Sea and Adriatic coastlines obviously indicates the social change that was taking place through the extension of settlement and trade in these areas. Furthermore, the Greek colonies illustrate the ideologies of state intervention and regional politics on the part of the mother states which were sponsoring this expansion of the Hellenic world. Hence, Greek relics in areas that are today

Bulgarian, Romanian, or Albanian illustrate an early type of spatial organization within a multinational environment.

2. The Roman settlement

Ancient Rome subjected the Balkan Peninsula to its rule from the third century BC until the end of the first century AD and divided the area into the provinces of Pannonia, Dalmatia, Moesia, Dacia, Thrace, and Macedonia. A primary purpose of the conquest was military but the economic aspect, in terms of mineral and grain production, was also involved. By a network of roads, resembling in part the modern pattern covering the Balkan Peninsula, Latin civilization spread over the area and Romanized the Illyrian people, often through military service. Five natives of Illyria actually became Roman emperors. Social change, therefore, was introduced into the Balkan multinational environment from an outside source and was most pronounced in the settlements established along the Roman road system. These settlements varied according to the stage of development which already existed. For example, along the Dalmation coast the Romans discovered existing towns such as Epidamnos and Apollonia with developed urban structures; in other areas, such as the frontier along the Danube, they found few existing settlements and proceeded to establish their own, lining the road system at intervals with forts, towers, way stations for sleeping or changing horses, and fortified camps. These diverse establishments understandably produced a varying degree of actual urbanization.

Škrivanić (1977: 115–45) has provided a detailed description of the Roman road system of the Balkans and of the relics that remain along it. The pattern does not exactly agree with the modern network. For example, there are scattered relics from a road along the south bank of the Danube River from Singidunum (Belgrade) to the mouth where today there is no important road. On the other hand, several important nodal points in the Roman system are now principal cities: Singidunum (Belgrade), Scobre (Shkodër), Dyrrachium (Durrës), Scopis (Skopje), Naissus (Niš), Serdica (Sofia), Philippopolis (north of Plovidiv), Odessos (Varna), Thessolonika, and Konstantinopolis (Istanbul). In or around these settlements or along the road system stand numerous remains of fortifications, buildings, viaducts or aqueducts, roads, and bridges. Two of the most famous roads were the Via Militaris from Singidunum (Belgrade) to Konstantinopolis and the Via Egnatia from Dyrrachium to Thessolonika. Only the first of these roads survives as the route of a main railroad and road, while

the second – one of the great routes of antiquity – has only a few relics from the past.

Perhaps the most outstanding series of Roman relics found at a single site in the Balkans exists at Salona (Solin), the capital of the Roman province of Dalmatia and a springboard for Roman penetration into this area. The remains include those of a basilica, amphitheater, forum, water supply system, and baths. Here as well as anywhere, the Roman relics illustrate not only the political grandeur of Roman rulers, but also the extent of social change they introduced – Christianity, culture, technology, and trade.

No doubt the Roman personality who most affected the Balkan landscape was the Emperor Diocletian. In AD 285 he split the empire into western and eastern components along a line from Sirmium, above present-day Belgrade, upstream along the Sava River, and then south to the Adriatic Sea near Kotor. This division influenced the subsequent history of the area, for to the west of this line the Latin alphabet and Roman Catholic religion have persisted, while to the east the Cyrillic alphabet and the Orthodox religion have prevailed. This important cultural schism can be seen in the landscape through variations in churches, settlement types, and levels of economic development. These are mentioned in later sections.

What is generally considered not only the finest single Roman relic in the Balkans, but also the largest and most perfect example of Roman palatial architecture extant also made Diocletian famous. In the fourth century, after abdicating the throne, he retired to a large palace that had been built at Palatium (Split) during his reign. Today, the palace, in reality an extensive walled fortress 500 ft (152 m) in length on each side, with square towers on the corners and with four major gates, dominates the central core of this Yugoslav port. Later construction replaced many of the original Roman structures inside the fortress, but the Peristyle, Mausoleum, Vestibule, and Temple remain. The four hundred or so small houses from later periods today crowd within the walls and represent a cross-section of unrivaled architectural history in Dalmatia.

3. The strategic fortress

As mentioned earlier, some fortresses served as political centers, but more often they performed administrative or military functions. Some were isolated while others were part of a spatial system of strong points; in most cases, they were occupied successively by different military forces and symbolize the insecurity of a multi-

national environment in Eastern Europe for two thousand years. In the Balkans, especially good examples of fortresses established by the Byzantine forces still abound. One, the ruin of Caričin Grad dating from the sixth century and occupying a site at the confluence of two rivers in southern Serbia southwest of the city of Leskovac, includes walls, acropolis, mausoleum, episcopal palace, and church. The theocracy of the Byzantine empire is reflected in the association of secular and religious buildings on the same site. The mausoleum is even in the shape of a Greek cross.

One of the best-known Balkan fortresses is Kalemegdan in Belgrade. Situated on a high point at the intersection of the Danube and Sava Rivers, its location was ideal to control movement through the Balkans. Consisting mostly of Austrian inputs, the fortress at various times was occupied by Celtic, Roman, Byzantine, Slavic, Turkish, Austrian, and Hungarian forces, truly reflecting the multinational environment of the past.

The old mining town of Novo Brdo represents an isolated relic in southern Serbia dating from the twelfth and thirteenth centuries when this center was the Balkan's leading producer of gold and silver; the early miners were Saxons from Germany. Associated with the Serbian Empire, the town evolved next to a large fortress and apparently flourished, for merchants from as far as Ragusa resided here. The town declined under Turkish rule, and today the crumbling ruins of the fortress and a few foundations are all that remain from an important past.

Still another fortress of the Serbian medieval empire is located at Smederevo on the Danube River east of Belgrade. This fortress, placed near the strategic Morava River route running southward from the Danube, served as one of the most powerful Serbian strongholds. In the fifteenth century Prince Djurdje Branković built it in the shape of an irregular triangle featuring nineteen towers, five gates, and a surrounding moat. At later dates the Turks, Austrians, and Serbs occupied this citadel.

Hundreds of other fortresses throughout Eastern Europe emphasize the role they played in an insecure multinational environment. The most concentrated belt of these castles is in northern Yugoslavia where conflict between east and west raged for hundreds of years. The belt actually corresponds to the historic and strategic frontier between Croatia-Dalmatia and Bosnia. Except for short periods, Croatia and Dalmatia have remained Roman Catholic from the time of the division of the Roman Empire, while Bosnia has been

Orthodox and, later, under the influence of the Turks, Moslem. The Holy Roman Empire, Italian states like Venice, and finally the Austrian Empire maintained this frontier against Byzantium and the Turks.

The importance of this frontier led to the formation in 1575 of the famous *Militärgrenze* (Military Frontier), a chain of fortified cities and villages together with blockhouses and watchtowers which the Austrians constructed in defense against the Turks. The frontier extended from the Adriatic sea to the Carpathian Mountains and was settled by *graničari*, or frontiersmen, generally Serbs, who received grants of land in this depopulated landscape in return for military service. Many of these Serbian settlers established villages in eastern Croatia and Slovenia, thus forming a wedge of the Orthodox Church in Catholic areas and complicating future Serb-Croat problems. Beyond the overall density of fortresses in this zone, little remains in the landscape other than the presence of Orthodox churches of Serbian residents (in Catholic areas) and a few relics in some cities to mark this historic frontier. In Karlovac, for example, the Austrian star-shaped fortress, surrounded by a moat, is preserved as are certain other garrison buildings dating from this period. Farther east, the fortress of Peterwardein (Petrovaradin), which caps a hill overlooking the Danube across from the city of Novi Sad, was also a part of the Military Frontier (see Photo 5.5). In the Carpathian Mountains flanking Transylvania on the south, no systematic military frontier existed as it did in the west, but various fortresses guarded the passes for the Hungarians against the Byzantines and later the Turks, e.g. Bran.

4. *The Turkish legacy*

Relics of the Turkish period – with the mosque probably the most typical – are distributed throughout the Balkans. These settlement relics are tied to roads and to town facilities along these routes. Some similarities exist to the Roman road network, particularly the Belgrade-Niš-Sofia-Istanbul road and the old Via Egnatia from Durrës to Thessaloniki; by Turkish times, however, Ragusa (Dubrovnik) had become an important Italian city-state, and caravans from this city traveled up the Neretva valley to Mostar and Sarajevo before turning south toward Skopje and the road to the east; another main route led to Poland. The Turks apparently maintained this road system well, for wagons carrying flour and barley could travel from Belgrade to Constantinople in a month. To facilitate travel, the

Photo 5.5 As a relic of the Austrian Military Frontier, the fortress of Peterwardein (Petrovaradin) on the Danube River opposite the city of Novi Sad, Yugoslavia, reflects the multinational environment.

imperial forces constructed many bridges in typical arched design and a variety of overnight accommodations for travelers (see Photo 5.6). Inalcik (1973: 148) says that in Bosnia-Hercegovina alone the state constructed 232 inns, 18 *caravanserais*, 32 hostels, 10 *bedestans* or covered markets, and 42 bridges. One of these relics, the bridge at Višegrad, formed the focal point of the novel by Nobel-prize winner Ivo Andrić – *The Bridge on the Drina*. Andrić eloquently describes the multinational environment and especially the impact of the Turkish Empire on the Balkans.

As the most imposing of the overnight accommodations, the *caravanserai* or *han* comprised a large fortified building with rooms on one or two levels around a courtyard used for wagons, horses, and storage of goods. In 1974 I visited a *caravanserai* near the town of Vranje in Dalmatia. Built in 1644 and listed in the *Blue Guide* for the Adriatic Coast (1969: 112) as one of the best examples of its type in Yugoslavia, this structure, unfortunately, was being used as a farm-

Photo 5.6 One of the best examples in the Balkans of the arched Turkish bridge spans the Neretva River at Mostar, Yugoslavia. Note the minarets of the mosques and the rugged Dalmatian mountains in the background.

house when I saw it. Although in poor repair, this huge, impressive building still gave a glimpse into the former importance of such way-stations in a precarious environment that apparently existed along the Turkish roads. A *caravanserai* in better condition exists in Novi Pazar. The Hanul lui Manuc in Bucharest also reveals the former atmosphere of such an inn; built in the early nineteenth century, it has been restored for use as a hotel and restaurant.

Sarajevo typifies a city that developed under Turkish influence to become the great center of Bosnia. Its relics of mosques, markets, and housing with overhanging second stories make it the most western expression of Turkish influence in the Balkans. Today, Bosnia retains a largely Moslem religious affiliation and thus its designation as a religious republic in the federation of Yugoslavia.

The legacy of the Turks emerges in other ways in today's Balkan landscape, e.g. in attire such as skull caps, pantaloons worn by female

Moslems, and shoes with turned-up toes (*opanci*); with the presence of gypsies, who apparently came as camp followers of the Ottomans; in the growing of tobacco, paprika, and the attar-yielding rose – a flower which flourished in the upper Tundzha River valley of Bulgaria; and lastly, as Vucinich (1963: 92–4) points out, in the coffee hause (*kafana*), which continues as one of the most conspicuous gifts. After the Turkish conquest, the Koranic edict against wine prohibited the medieval practice of serving wine with meal. Thereafter, the coffee house became a favorite social center for Moslems who gathered to exchange gossip, tell stories, and discuss the political and religious issues of the day. Any visitor to the Balkans will recall an experience in a coffee house, a stronghold of male chauvinism, where a clean tablecloth may be a rarity.

Economically, the relics left by the Turks in the Balkans tell largely a negative story of social change. Although the road network, *caravanserai*, and town markets indicate commerce, much of the indigenous population lived in isolation in the mountains where advantages for preserving cultural traditions were offset by limited contact and retarded economic development. Even the relative autonomy enjoyed by the Christians was countered by the superior status of Moslems, both Turks and Slavs, that prevailed in this theocratic empire where Christians were socially ostracized and economically repressed. In addition, the Orthodox Church was controlled by Greeks who also were important in commerce and Turkish administration. Vucinich (1963: 82) speaks for many historians when he states that Ottoman rule primarily led to the social lag of the Balkan peoples. In this respect, the Balkans contrasted with the northern part of Eastern Europe where even in a feudal environment progress was greater.

Of the various regions in the Balkans with a Turkish legacy in the landscape, the Kosovo perhaps shows the greatest effect. Here many cultures intermingled, a situation which reflects a multinational environment. The Kosovo consists of an area of upland plains surrounded by mountains in the heart of the Balkans. These plains have long served as primary nodal points of settlement because excellent routeways of the Ibar and Drin Rivers bisect them, geographical characteristics mentioned in connection with the medieval Serbian Empire. Strangely enough, this empire was the only Balkan power ever to use the Kosovo as an important core area for unification of the peninsula. At other times, the frontier nature of this region has served to make it a zone of conflict between Catholics of

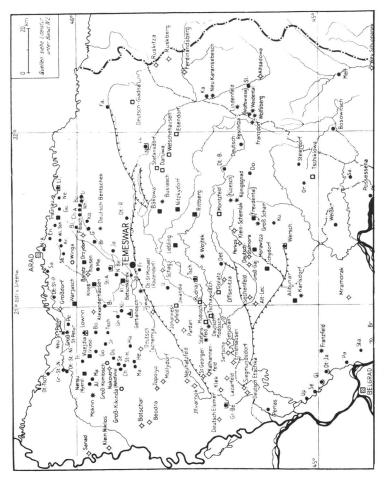

Fig. 5.4 The Banat region north of Belgrade, Yugoslavia: the Austrian planned settlements in the latter part of the eighteenth century. (Source: Petersen 1933: 230.)

Schimscha (1939) and Kallbrunner (1943) provide details on the entire colonization process in the Banat and emphasize that this process was a reflection of the absolutist government system. The strategic location of the Banat prompted the government to handle it as a province of the empire rather than as a Hungarian county. In fact, the entire colonization policy – political, military, religious, and economic – was established in Vienna and carried out from the administrative center of Temeswar or Temeschwar (Hungarian, Temesvár; today, Timişoara in Romania). Official policy perceived the Germans as more reliable settlers than the Hungarians for filling the gaps between the major fortress cities of Arad, Szegedin (Szeged), and Temeswar (Temesvár). Colonial settlement was concentrated in the grazing area of the Prädien northwest of Temeswar and called for a change from extensive raising of livestock to a more intensive cultivation of grain crops. The initial objective of this colonization – 20 000 families and 80 000 people – was not realized because only one-half of this number – 11 000 and 42 000 – reached the Banat.

A personal visit to the area in the 1970s revealed a remarkable persistence of this settlement pattern with its amazing uniformity of village layout (see Fig. 5.5). A map of Sándorháza (today Şandra) shows the checkerboard plan of these villages – indeed, they are called *Schachbrettdörfer*. This uniformity resulted from precise Austrian regulations which produced an imposing image of state intervention on the landscape. Various features that characterize this alikeness include: wide streets (main ones of 100 ft [30 m] and secondary of 40 ft [12 m]), an important consideration for preventing the spread of fire; lots for a church – often in the square at the intersection of the two main streets – a parish house, a school, and an inn; wells on each street; same type of house (*Streckhof* mentioned in Ch. 4, see Fig. 4.9); narrow, deep lots featuring a street frontage of 75 ft (23 m) and a depth of 450–500 ft (137–152 m); and all structures, residential and agricultural, lined on one side of this lot and thus separated by the open *Hof* (court) one from the other, another measure designed to prevent fire from spreading. These pronounced features of the *Schachbrettdorf* and *Streckhof* produce an overall impression on the Banat landscape of early settlement planning in one part of the Empire.

Although the density of population may be higher today and the individual lots smaller, one reverts to two hundred years ago while walking down the dirt streets, side-stepping geese, and conversing in German with the residents. The gables of the houses still show

165

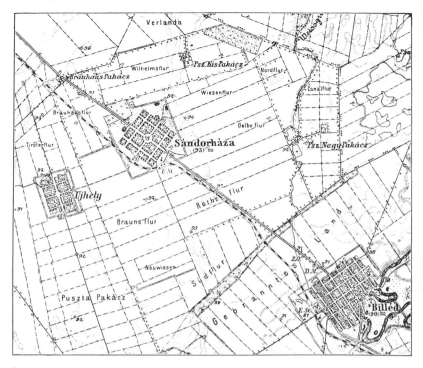

Fig. 5.5 An example of the checkerboard pattern of villages in the Banat. (Source: Petersen 1933: 238.)

the names of the German builder (see Photo 5.7). Sándorháza (now Şandra), although founded later as a private colony in 1833, resembles the other villages, but I include it here because maps of 1833 and 1933 are available to illustrate the changes that have taken place (see Fig. 5.6). This village, originally known as Alexanderhausen, is used in the Westermann *Atlas zur Weltgeschichte* (1956: 121) as a typical example of planned Habsburg settlement in Eastern Europe.

Another village nearby, Lenauheim (originally Csatád), is named after the poet, Nikolaus Lenau, who was born there. His poems reflect his Austrian parentage, his later experiences in both Hungary and Germany, and especially his feelings emphasizing the solitude of the Hungarian plain (Schmidt 1971: 86). His statue in the village seems to symbolize a dimension of the Germanic contribution to the development of the Banat's historical landscape. Beyond this, the total Austrian colonization scheme demonstrated the state role as *Landschaftgestalter* (molder of landscapes) and director of social

166

Photo 5.7   The *Streckhof* houses of Alexanderhausen (later Sándorháza and today Şandra, Romania) still are occupied by German descendants and bear the name of the German builder.

change; this gave state intervention, discussed in the early section of this chapter as a multinational ideology, an undisputed imprint on the landscape.

b. The tanya. In complete contrast to the planned villages of the Banat and yet originating in a similar multinational frontier situation is the landscape of dispersed farms (*tanya*) located on the Hungarian plain (Alföld). These farms lie between large towns which in the past were also rural in nature but now have become considerably modernized. The *tanya* consists of farmstead, stable, barn, and other outbuildings, which, before the socialist era, were set in the middle of the fields to be worked. Prosperous-looking *tanyas* still alternate with those in poor condition. A primary problem always has been the isolation of these dwellings from public services including especially health and education. The sweep well near most of the farms stands

167

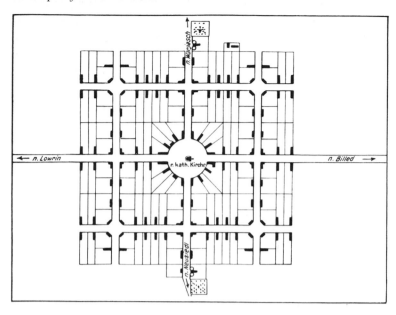

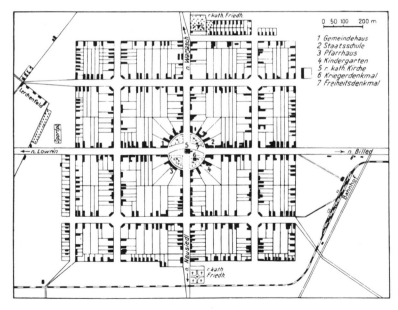

Fig. 5.6 Sándorháza (Şandra) in 1833 (top) and 1933 (bottom). Note the increased density of settlement. In the 1970s, the village was much the same as in the lower map. (Source: Petersen 1933: 239.)

alone as the most visible landmark across a plain that is flat for as far as the eye can see. The Hungarian poet John Arany, quoted in the *Geographical Magazine* (October 1938: 371), said of the sweep well: 'One might mistake it for a great mosquito, sucking the blood of our old earth.' But it is the dispersed pattern of individual farms that is so unique in Eastern Europe. Visitors today are bound to be curious as to the origin of these landscape relics. They may also wonder how the communist party is handling the problem of bringing collective life to the *tanya*. Historically, the *tanya* illustrates the changing role played by settlement in an evolving society – from empire to national state to socialist state.

To understand the origin of *tanya* settlement one must go back to the Turkish period of occupation when the inhabitants of the smaller villages (communes) fled for protection to the larger market centers of their areas. These larger villages grew so much from the influx of refugees that they assumed the size of towns. As such, they received favorable status from the Turkish rulers, including title to the communal land of the vacated villages. The administrative area of these towns thereby became immense, e.g. Debrecen, which had a population of 30 000 in the eighteenth century, covered an area of almost 386 sq. miles (1000 sq. km), an area equal to the five boroughs of New York City today.

During the long period of Turkish occupation, the quality of the Alföld environment deteriorated until much of the land was suitable only for pasture. Cultivated land, therefore, was restricted, and a pastoral economy dominated the enlarged communal land of the towns. A system prevailed in which the animals (horses, cattle, sheep, and swine) found their own summer grazing and in winter were brought to quarters near the towns. Hungary became a source area of livestock, especially cattle, for markets of central Europe to which the animals were driven by foot. This pastoral economy prevailed long after the Turkish occupation ended.

How did the actual *tanya* evolve in response to the vacuum created as the Turks were pushed out of the Alföld? The towns, where most of the population lived, originally prohibited permanent settlement in the countryside so as to keep residents involved in municipal responsibilities. As a consequence, out on the rural grazing areas, shelters of herders from earlier times often formed the nuclei of temporary dwellings and stables used for the livestock economy. Eventually, wheat was raised on this land when reclamation of the Tisza River increased the cultivated area by six million acres and ex-

tension of the railroad provided for shipment of grain to central Europe.

Gradually, however, several factors caused this temporary settlement to become more permanent. In the first place, the cultivation of land spread farther and farther from the town and the 'divided' settlement pattern became less practicable in terms of the work necessary. Second, increasing population strained the housing in the towns. Third, as the extended family ties became looser, *tanya* lands were given to children, who often lacked the economic means to maintain both residences; these new *tanyas*, often located beyond the administrative limits of the town, became the personal property of the settler. Finally, wheat growing, which required only temporary residence, gave way to more intensive livestock farming where a permanent settlement with stables for animals was necessary (Enyedi 1976: 237).

In the years from 1900 to 1945, population increase forced more town and village residents out onto *tanya* land. Thus, by the Second World War, isolated settlements of varying condition had spread over the Hungarian plain. Den Hollander (1960–61: 161) remarks that the territory of Kecskemét had 12 *tanyas* in 1830 and 8225 in 1925. Lettrich (1969: 155) adds that in the first half of the twentieth century, nearly one million people on the Hungarian plain lived in *tanyas*. In this way, a process of voluntary dispersed settlement served to transform the face of the Alföld, filling in a vacant frontier after the departure of the Turks. Today, the relics of these farms, now being altered under communism (see Ch. 7), illustrate not only particular characteristics of a past multinational environment but also forces of social change (see Photo 5.8).

6. Italian settlement in Dalmatia

Anyone who has visited the cities of the Dalmatian coast like Zadar, Trogir, Split, and Dubrovnik (Ragusa) cannot fail to be impressed by the Italian legacy of settlement – Roman, Venetian, and modern Italian. Dominian (1917: 85) relates that Dalmatia's history, its most notable monuments, and its whole culture are products of either Roman or Venetian influence; the cities especially reflect this impact. Yet the Italian legacy has been modified by a Slavic image: architecture in large cities represents a blend of Venetian and Slavic cultures, while some cities and most villages are entirely Slavic. Geographically, therefore, Dalmatia is a borderland between cultures. Here both Venetian and Slav become Catholic, a legacy of the long Latin

Photo 5.8 The dwelling, corn crib, outbuilding and well are typical of a dispersed *tanya* on the Hungarian plain.

influence. Nevertheless, 100 miles (161 km) inland over the mountains one finds the most significant cleavage of the Balkans – that between Catholic and Orthodox/Moslem. This line, which dates from the division of the Roman Empire, had a great impact on the entire Balkans but especially on Dalmatia.

Renowned for its physical appearance, especially the mountain chain towering over the coast and creating several fjord-like bays, Dalmatia has little room for agriculture and city support. This region, dominated by karst topography, is described in Chapter 2. Some of the features that develop in this type of terrain include sink-holes and underground drainage – caused by water from precipitation dissolving the limestone – and large tectonic basins called *polja*, which have sizable flat areas for cultivation. Elsewhere endless stone terraces, built by hand labor over hundreds of years, support olive trees, vineyards, and small plots of corn. Cisterns must be built and utilized to catch the water that is otherwise lost underground: The ecology of Dalmatia is a delicate one, especially in recent years as tourism has increased.

This topography set the stage for the conflict of cultures that took place in the Dalmatian borderland. Towns were established along the Adriatic coast as border fortresses, situated topographically for defense and at the same time located close to routes inland. The permanent settlements thereby became important not only in utilizing the Adriatic Sea, but also in establishing commercial relationships with the inner Balkans. From the beginning, then, the Dalmatian coast served as a center of multinational power politics, and at various times Greek, Roman, Byzantine, Croatian, Serbian, Bosnian, Hungarian, Venetian, French, and Austrian powers controlled sections of the coast. As in other parts of Eastern Europe, a multinational 'environment' existed. As one power replaced another, the cities became places of refuge, particularly for Latin and Slavic groups caught in the middle. This function from early times formed an ancient city network, and municipal charters testify to early independence before cities were forced to accept the protection of a more powerful state. Even after these cities became dependent, their local municipal tradition allowed for some degrees of autonomy or at least a negotiated basis for allegiance (Violich 1972: 163).

At the present time, the landscape of these cities primarily bears the imprint of Venetian control from 1420 to 1797. Venice and Ragusa (Dubrovnik), the latter an independent city-state on the Adriatic coast, controlled most of Dalmatia. Both cities established extensive trade networks throughout the Balkans and with Constantinople, exchanging mostly raw materials like wheat, metals, beeswax, silk, honey, and hides for manufactured Italian goods, mainly textiles and salt. The 'Lion of Saint Mark', a bas-relief in marble or stone that looks down from many public buildings or gates, symbolized Venetian hegemony over the area. However, it is in architecture that attention focuses on the general influence of Venice or Italy, with the Loggia (open gallery) in most cities exemplifying the impact along with the pointed arches in Venetian Gothic, the carved balconies, and the two-light and three-light windows. Perhaps the most complete and striking expression of Italian influence is Ragusa (Dubrovnik), a remarkably preserved fortress city (see Photo 5.9). However, the Slavic heritage – the imprint of Croatians who also lived in this city and others – blended with the Italian image. Sebenico (Šibenik), for example, has this Slavic aspect. As a Croatian art historian informed me, the Renaissance style, although originating in Italy, became an international style, a trait certainly evident in the cities of the Adriatic coast. However, more than this,

Photo 5.9 The city of Dubrovnik (formerly Ragusa) on the Dalmatian coast of Yugoslavia rivaled Venice as a Mediterranean power.

these cities illustrate aspects of social change – art, architecture, and literature – that provided a strong contrast with the interior of the Balkans where Turkish rule prevailed.

In the nineteenth century, one would expect the differences between a progressive Italian coast and a backward Turkish interior to break down, for the Austrians controlled both the coastal region and eventually Bosnia and Hercegovina. However, as mentioned earlier in this chapter, Austrian regional politics required that any economic improvement, which might aid the nationalistic aspirations

173

of the Slavs, be restricted. This policy was particularly important in curtailing new road or railroad links between coast and interior, which would aid Slav unity. Up to the 1960s, only one railroad, a narrow-gauge line completed by the Austrians along the Neretva River valley in the 1890s, crossed the Dalmatian Mountains to the coast. For strategic reasons, the Austrians built in southern Dalmatia a famous road of twenty-six serpentines over Lovćen, the Black Mountain (Montenegro). Both of these early aspects of development are still used. The Habsburgs also wanted to restrict ports along the coast from competing with Trieste and Fiume, ports for Vienna and Budapest, respectively; the Italian appearance of these two cities, therefore, changed as central European elements were introduced. Today, Trieste looks Austrian and Italian as the two cultures intermingled in creating the cityscape.

Religious relics

Scattered across Eastern Europe, the thousands of relics associated with religious activity – churches, monasteries, shrines, and cemeteries – bespeak the role of religion in a multinational environment. Although this role varied from place to place, church and state were closely interwoven in this environment. In Austria, the Roman Catholic Church loyally supported the Habsburgs, and in Poland this church has been related closely to the Polish state for a thousand years, as symbolized by the defense of the Jasna Góra monastery against Swedish armies in 1655. In Hungary the Matthias Church in the castle area of Budapest was the coronation site for many Hungarian kings. Early imperial rulers of the Balkans – Byzantine, Bulgarian, and Serbian – possessed both temporal and religious sovereignty. Later the Ottoman rulers brought a state religion with them to the Balkans, and the relics of mosques in what had been Catholic or Orthodox territory attest to this change. At the same time, the Ottoman influence (according to Vucinich 1963: 95), compelled the Orthodox Church in the Balkans to dedicate itself to preserving religious and cultural traditions, a role it filled in places like the Rila or Bačkovo Monasteries in Bulgaria. It can be said, therefore, that the landscape relics of religion in Eastern Europe illustrate (1) degrees of interrelationship between church and state that existed in multinational environments and, indirectly, (2) both negative and positive effects of social change.

The primary religious spatial systems from which relics survive

in the landscape today represent the hierarchies of the Roman Catholic and Orthodox Churches. The division of the Roman Empire into two parts led eventually to two systems of religious spatial organization. The dividing line ran from north to south through the Balkans so that Romania and the South Slavs except for Slovenia and Croatia became part of Byzantium and, therefore, Orthodox. The rest of Eastern Europe remained Catholic and tied to Rome. Catholicism and Orthodoxy had important ensuing effects on the landscape, the most important one being architecture. In addition, the work of Cyril and Methodius, Slav missionaries of the ninth century who were responsible for developing the Cyrillic alphabet, had profound effects on the lives of all residents and travelers in the Balkans. Today, persons from countries which use the Latin alphabet have a problem reading most words displayed in the landscape – street signs, store names, transportation information – in Bulgaria and sections of Yugoslavia.

The Catholic Church has persisted as the most important religious influence in Poland, Czechoslovakia, Hungary, Slovenia, and Croatia. This Church, called the most formidable religious institution in the history of the world, possesses an intense hierarchy of spatial organization from Rome down through the ecclesiastical provinces, dioceses, and parishes. In the fifteenth century, archbishoprics existed at Magdeburg, Gniezno, Prague, Gran (Esztergom), and Kalocsa; three of these have continued to the present as the sites of important churches in the territories of Poland, Bohemia, and Hungary. In Poland, Gniezno, northeast of Poznań, was both a political center and the first archbishopric (founded in the year 1000) of the state. It was here, according to legend, that Lech, the early sovereign, found the nest of a white eagle and made it the emblem of the Slav tribe which he headed. Although the cathedral has been rebuilt, the marvellous twelfth-century bronze door remains. In Prague, Saint Vitus Cathedral, where Bohemian kings were crowned and buried, dominates the Hradčany castle complex just as it does the skyline of the city. Gran (today Esztergom), a medieval center of the Hungarian state, was also an archbishopric. The early basilica is gone and in its place a nineteenth-century cathedral – built in classical style with a portico supported by Corinthian columns – stands out as a landmark over the landscape of the Danube River north of Budapest. Only the Bakócz Chapel remains from the sixteenth-century basilica.

In Dalmatia, archbishoprics existed at Zara (Zadar), Spalato

(Split), and Ragusa (Dubrovnik) as primary nodal points in Catholic spatial organization along the Adriatic coast. Zadar has the largest and finest Romanesque church in Dalmatia, while the one at Split represents a conversion of the old mausoleum of the Emperor Diocletian. In Dubrovnik, a Baroque cathedral replaced the original Romanesque basilica that was destroyed in the earthquake of 1667. Much of the church architecture along the Adriatic coast illustrates a mixture of Italian and Croatian influence, a point mentioned before in connection with administrative relics.

The Orthodox churches and monasteries of the Balkans, including Romania, contrast with those in the Catholic sections of Eastern Europe. These Orthodox relics in the landscape were established under the influence of Byzantium, which, according to Sherrard (1966: 170), 'set the seal of its civilization on the whole Balkan world'. This seal from the early period is less evident, although the great sixth-century basilica at Poreč is a prime relic of Byzantium in the peninsula. The seal is revealed best in the square layout and dome profile seen in later Byzantine churches and monasteries. In the square plan, derived from the Greek cross of four equal arms, the central space below the dome is used for the Mass, while the altar itself is screened off by an iconostasis. The dome is perhaps the most notable and impressive Byzantine contribution to architecture. The plan and dome make Orthodox churches unmistakable in the Balkans, and together they reflect the imprint of a temporal/religious ruler on multinational landscape. The icon (images of Christ, the Virgin Mary, and saints in fresco or mosaic form) is also a distinguishing part of Orthodox churches or monasteries; in most cases it serves as an interior decoration, but in some cases it appears on the outer walls. What seems to distinguish this Byzantine art of the Balkans is the exclusive preoccupation with ecclesiastical subjects, a contrast to the variety of Western Europe.

Although the Byzantine style predominates in the Balkans, most of the outstanding churches bear the imprint of modifications by separate cultures which gained a degree of clerical autonomy. Both the Bulgarian and Serbian churches obtained patriarchal status and thereby implanted their own cultural imprints, still evident today, on religious buildings. For example, some have a polychrome design in which bands of white stone alternate with brick. Especially notable are the monasteries of southern Serbia, all built in the thirteenth to fifteenth centuries. The Serbian rulers, like those of Byzantium, controlled the Church and thus reflected a close link with the state.

They also strongly involved themselves in choosing the monastery sites (e.g. Dečani just below the Albanian Alps) since the monks had the responsibility not only for disseminating the Orthodox faith into the mountain areas, but also for exploiting the resources of these uplands (Wilkinson 1955: 183). The rulers, in addition, desired remote sites because these monasteries were to be their mausoleums. Studenica, for one, is quite isolated, as I discovered during a long ride on a poor road at night. The long nave of this great monastery – a deviation from the square plan – illustrates the penetration of Latin influence (Cichy 1964: 147). On the other hand, Gračanica, also built by the Nemanja dynasty, is pure Byzantine with equal arms of the Greek cross.

Two patriarchal centers for the Serbian Orthodox Church are Žiča and Peć, both also bearing the imprint of imperial rulers. The church at Žiča, built by Stephen the First Crowned, is painted red so that it resembles the famous monastery at Mount Athos in Greece. Although built in a multinational era, its link to the later nationalistic period is mentioned by Rebecca West in *Black Lamb and Grey Falcon* (I, 1944: 557) when she describes how Milan Obrenović, ruler of Serbia in the nineteenth century, had himself anointed there in the manner of all the Nemanja dynasty in the Middle Ages. Because Žiča was located in the Ibar River valley, and thus exposed to enemy attack, Peć, a more isolated place, became the patriarchal center of Serbia under Stephen Dušan; it remained, with few interruptions, the residence of Serbian archbishops and patriarchs until 1766. The entire cluster of monasteries, found within a rather small area of southern Serbia, marks the ancient homeland of the Serbian culture.

In northeastern Romania, a group of Orthodox monasteries, built in the fourteenth to the sixteenth centuries by the princes of Moldavia, stands out as a unique series of monastic structures reflecting the impact of a particular culture. These religious buildings and the construction of extensive fortifications for their defense against Turkish forces attest once again to the close ties of state and church in multinational environments. Clustered within the eastern Carpathian Mountains and centered on the town of Suceava, these monasteries – named Putna, Sucevița, Humor, Voroneț, and Moldovita – are distinct not only because they represent the beginnings of a characteristically Moldavian type of architecture – Byzantine, Romanesque, and Gothic features grafted onto native styles – but especially because they have unusual frescoes painted on their exteriors. This type of illustration arose in the sixteenth century to

portray Bible stories to illiterate peasants. The paintings cover the walls of churches and monasteries like the sequences of a film. The impression one receives in this hilly area of northern Moldavia when looking down into the basin where Suceviţa lies, surrounded by walls and with the monastery itself entirely covered by frescoes, is vivid and lasting (see Photo 5.10).

Both the southern and northern parts of Eastern Europe witnessed religious changes that later affected the existing spatial systems of Catholicism and Orthodoxy. In the south, the Turks introduced the Moslem religion which left numerous mosques and minarets scattered over southeastern Europe. This landscape extends even to Hungary where today well-preserved mosques exist in Pécs. According to some authorities, the form of the mosque was copied by the Turks from Saint Sophia, the great Byzantine church in Constantinople. In the north, the Protestant Reformation started in what is now East Germany. The city of Wittenberg and Wartburg castle near Eisenach were both associated with Martin Luther. In Prague's Old Town Square, where Russian tanks sat in the summer of 1968, the Tyn Church and a memorial commemorate the Hussite religious reform movement of the fifteenth and sixteenth centuries, including the Thirty Years' War. Farther south in Bohemia the Hussites founded the town of Tábor, which served as a regional center for the Protestant revolutionary forces. Today, a number of relics testify to this important period in Czech history; narrow streets, designed to facilitate the defense of the town; a stone table for communion; a monument to the Hussite leader Jan Žižk; and the baptismal pond of Jordan. Debrecen, Hungary, a stronghold of Calvinism and a nineteenth-century seat of revolutionary government, contains still another Protestant relic in Eastern Europe: the Great Reform Church that stands in the main square was the site of the anti-Habsburg proclamation issued in 1849.

Two special religious relics confined to small areas in Eastern Europe are the large tombstones of the Bogomils in the south and the structures of the Uniate Church in the north. The Bogomils were a religious sect which rejected both Catholicism and Orthodoxy after the twelfth century and then disappeared under the influence of Islam. Their existence is marked by huge tombstones, engraved with a variety of life scenes including hunting and dancing, found in Hercegovina, Yugoslavia, near the city of Mostar; one of the best sites is the village of Radimlje. The Uniate, or Greek Catholic Church, was established by the Pope during the reign of the Polish king Sigis-

Photo 5.10   Suceviţa, one of a group of Orthodox monasteries in the northern part of the Romanian province of Moldavia, occupies an impressive site in a valley on the edge of the Carpathian Mountains.

mund (1587–1632) to attract the peasants away from the Orthodox Church in the eastern borderlands. A considerable following developed in eastern Galicia and adjoining regions. Spiritual allegiance is to Rome, but the liturgy is Orthodox. Actually, considerable conflict eventually developed between this Church and the Catholic Church, largely because the Uniate Church became a focus for Ukrainian and Romanian nationalism in the nineteenth century. In the 1970s I visited a Greek Catholic Church in Prešov, a town in eastern Slovakia, and was startled by the dualism it presents: a picture of the Pope at the entrance and an Orthodox iconostasis inside. Incidentally, worshippers completely filled the church.

The Jewish synagogues and cemeteries found in only a few places in Eastern Europe form the final examples of religious relics. Perhaps the best known is the cemetery in Prague, which includes a museum on Jewish traditions and customs. With its gravestones crammed side by side to mark the multilevel of burials in strata-fashion in the ground below, the cemetery illustrates in death the inferior position in life of Jews in Eastern Europe mentioned earlier in this chapter

Photo 5.11 The density of gravestones in the Jewish cemetery of Prague, Czechoslovakia, provides a clue to the social position of this group in Eastern European society.

(see Photo 5.11). Often excluded from the larger towns, the Jews settled in the smaller ones, generally confined to high-density ghettos that reflected social pressures and their own desire to be together. Hostility toward this group was latent, but eventually, of course, it manifested itself in the Nazi program for racial purification, which during the German Third Reich essentially eliminated the Jews as an ethnic group in Eastern Europe. The concentration camp at Auschwitz (Oświęcim, Poland), 'preserved' as a 'museum' of this Holocaust, is a grim and unforgettable experience for a visitor and a reminder of man's inhumanity to fellow man. In the towns, remains of the ghettos have disappeared; only an occasional monument still exists to indicate this peculiar aspect of the pre-Second World War urban landscape of Poland and certain other countries.

The foregoing relics illustrate indirectly the influence of religion on geography and on social change in Eastern Europe as several systems of religious spatial organization overlapped – Catholic, Orthodox, Moslem, and Protestant. The relics of these systems indicate:

180

a hierarchy of state control, as under the Turks; a place, generally a monastery, where a Balkan culture survived several hundred years of Ottoman occupation; frontier zones where religious influences were mixed, as in Yugoslavia between Catholic and Orthodox; aspects of cultural individuality, as in the case of Romanian monasteries; and, finally, religious or ethnic conflicts like the Reformation and the repression of the Jews. Religion, therefore, represents a very significant force in the multinational environment of Eastern Europe.

Industrial relics

Information on the geographical pattern of industry in Eastern Europe at different times during the long multinational period is difficult to compile. Turnock (1978 4: 44) says that the location of industry before the First World War can be explained in an imperial context which is related to an ideology of state intervention. An early part of this chapter contains an analysis of this ideology. In the nineteenth century, when the Industrial Revolution reached Eastern Europe, only the major empires, particularly Prussia-Germany and Austria–Hungary, had the authority and resources to influence industry. From the beginning, the location of factories was related closely to railroads, a relationship that was often related to state ownership. However, private enterprise also played an important role, although with degrees of state support.

Eastern Europe was ill-equipped in the nineteenth century to receive the seeds of industrialization that were spreading across the continent: instead of commercial capitalism, there was recent serfdom; instead of urban life, there was mostly a rural population; and instead of a constitutional bourgeoise-democratic government, there was autocracy. Such an environment helps to explain the limitation of extensive industrialization to the eastern margins of Prussia-Germany and Austria.

A map of industry in Eastern Europe in 1914 illustrates that considerable imbalance existed (see Fig. 5.7); indeed, the map supports the A–B–C transition of economic landscapes across Europe – a concept mentioned first in Chapter 4. An overwhelming proportion of this industry occurred in the German and Austro–Hungarian Empires, more specifically in central Germany, Silesia, and Bohemia–Moravia. Hamilton (1970a: 301) reports that before 1940 75 per cent of East European industry operated in a triangular area between Halle, Łódź, and Budapest. Within the

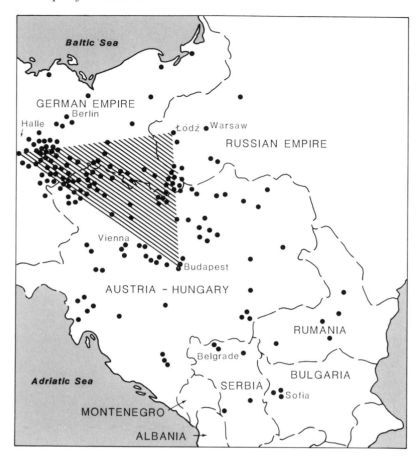

Fig. 5.7 The pattern of industry in Eastern Europe before the outbreak of the First World War. Note the concentrations in the north and west, especially within the 'triangle' marked by Halle, Łódź, and Budapest. (Adapted from a map by Mellor 1975.)

Austro–Hungarian Empire, Bohemia, Moravia, and Slovakia were important, for Mellor (1975: 187) informs us that although these areas constituted only one-fifth of the Habsburg territory, they contained three-quarters of the imperial industrial capacity. The following sections of this chapter examine the basis for the various concentrations in Eastern Europe and some outstanding industrial relics that resulted.

Turnock (1978: 52) feels that two types of industrial processes which were taking place before 1918 might account for the difference

in pattern between north and south in Eastern Europe. First, a tradition of craftsmanship existed in the north and led to the conversion of small cottage industries to factories producing for the local market. Second, state agencies and private banking firms invested in resources and railroads, especially those most accessible to the empires of Prussia-Germany and Austria, namely, in Silesia, Bohemia, and northern Moravia. In these areas industry often preceded railroad development, which eventually became quite dense. However, the situation differed in the southern parts of Eastern Europe. As previously explained, a number of factors led to backwardness of economic development and to concentration of industry in a few places like capital cities or along railroads. The state often assumed either an active role as builder of industrial establishments and railroads or a more indirect one by stimulating investment for factory development. Some railroads were built early to export grain from Hungary but others were constructed later to develop regions. An example of the latter was the Austrian state railroad to Trieste.

The geographer can use the landscape as a key for analyzing these early industrial concentrations by isolating locational factors of raw materials and transport together with tradition and governmental influence. Several types of industrial landscapes have evolved as a part of multinational environments – those of medieval origin, those based on coal development in the nineteenth century, and those isolated nodes around ports and large cities.

1. *Multinational industrial landscapes of medieval origin*
In Chapter 3, we observe the medieval origin of mining and craft industry established in Eastern Europe by German colonists attracted by the mineral resources of the Harz and Ore Mountains. This tradition continued in the modern period. Early silver mining gave way later to lead, copper, and zinc, which led to metal industries in the towns located in the valleys of these mountains. Smelting was based on water power and charcoal. The mining practices, as described by Georg Agricola in the sixteenth century, were taken from mining camps in the Ore Mountains like Altenberg and Schneeberg. Freiberg was the site of the earliest mining school from which technology diffused across Eastern Europe. Today, in East Germany, much of this mining has ceased except for lead and zinc near Freiberg; both of these ores are smelted nearby. Textiles were also produced by hand in these mining towns. With the decline of

183

mining after the Thirty Years' War, many miners and metal workers turned to skilled industries; today, optics (Jena), printing of maps (Gotha), watches (Glashütte), and porcelain (Meissen) represent the work of skilled artisans in the area.

In Bohemia, a similar landscape exists in both the Ore and Sudetes Mountains, where older industries like ceramics (Karlovy Vary), textile mills (Liberec), and glass (Jablonec, formerly known as Gablonz) are located. Wanklyn (1954: 262) reports that Maria Theresa and her son Joseph II encouraged the porcelain and glass industries at Karlovy Vary (in German, Karlsbad) – still another indication of what could be called a multinational environment.

2. Multinational 'Black Country' landscapes

The 'Black Country' landscapes, so named because of grime and pollution associated with coal mining and ferrous and nonferrous metallurgy, account for the largest industrial concentrations in Eastern Europe. The most extensive of these are Upper Silesia, northern Moravia, Kladno in Bohemia, Miskolc in Hungary, Reschitza (Reşiţa) in Romania, and Jesenica (Jesenice) in Slovenia. In all of these areas, the state role either in ownership or in support of industrial facilities was important. Upper Silesia, now entirely in Poland, is the largest industrial region in Eastern Europe, a conurbation of a dozen large cities and many small ones that covers an area of 150 square miles (389 sq. km) and includes a population of over three million. At the other end of the scale stands Jesenice, an iron and steel complex that is crammed into the Drava River valley of northwest Yugoslavia. These 'Black Country' landscapes, whose origins go back to the eighteenth and nineteenth centuries, are based on bituminous coal and/or iron ore.

The map shows the various stages in the development of the 'Black Country' landscape of Upper Silesia (see Fig. 5.8). Although some of the early smelting was carried out by certain Prussian noble families (explained in Ch. 4), the most extensive expansion occurred under Prussia-Germany as a part of the nineteenth-century imperial support. A frontier location on the eastern margin of the Prussian state helps to explain its peculiar geographical pattern.

In the eighteenth century, Prussia handled Upper Silesia almost like a colony: decisions made in Berlin allocated Silesian resources for Prussia and not for Silesia. Early development depended on the mineral resources of iron, lead, and zinc in the rocks between Tarnowitz (Tarnowskie Góry) and Beuthen (Bytom); for example,

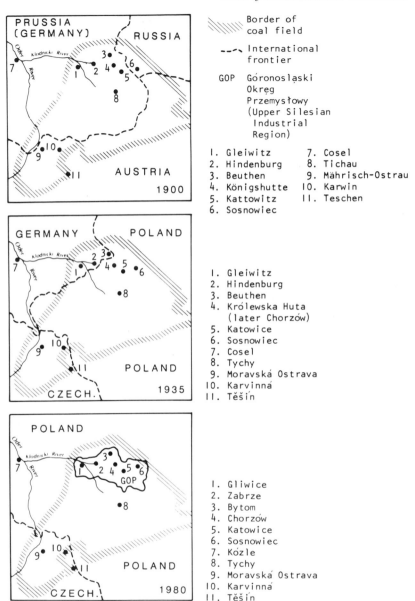

Fig. 5.8   Three stages in the spatial organization of Upper Silesia. The history of this large industrial region has been marked by division between empires and states. Only after 1945 was the major portion of the area organized as one unit in Poland.

Frederick the Great utilized the iron to increase Prussia's supplies of armaments, most particularly at Malapane (Ozimek). Later, coal was used to provide fuel for the water pumps in the lead mines and, still later, for smelting iron and zinc. Finally, under the industrial policy of von Reden, who was the Prussian administrator in charge of mining in Silesia, coal mining and factories were developed using new industrial innovations introduced from western Europe.

The frontier location also manifested itself in the rapid transition from a feudal agricultural structure with some metallurgical development to an imperial industrial 'colony'. Since no intermediate commercial period existed, mines and factories were superimposed on a landscape of villages (Hartshorne 1934: 437), which helps to explain the lack of 'urban' character in this district, a feeling that still can be sensed just by wandering through it. A peripheral location to the Prussian state also hindered a balanced industrial development, primarily because of the distance to markets. As a result, heavy industry – especially ferrous and nonferrous metallurgy – became predominant. The development of raw materials here offset the exposed position on the margin of the Empire. This lack of balance established then remains today.

An old canal relic in the landscape provides an interesting clue to the early frontier nature of Silesia and especially to the role of this province in a multinational environment. Transportation of Silesian industrial products to the core of the Prussian state at Berlin was provided originally by using the Oder River and its tributary, the Klodnitz, which penetrated into the coal area as far as Hindenburg (now Zabrze) (see Fig. 5.8). To facilitate the transport of coal and industrial products to the west, the Klodnitz River was canalized in the early part of the nineteenth century from Hindenburg to the Oder River at Cosel (Koźle). However, this canal proved too narrow and eventually, after 1850, the railroad became more important (Pounds 1958: 37, 62, 71, 168–9). This Klodnitz Canal survives in a slightly altered form (Gliwicki Canal) as a result of use in the 1930s under the Nazis. It functions as an artery for tourist excursions and as a symbol of early imperial attempts to develop the resources of a frontier area.

Visible boundaries of early political fragmentation make up a second characteristic of the Upper Silesian district (see Fig. 5.8). Three empires – Prussia, Russia, and Austria – met in the eastern corner of the district, the so-called *Kaiserdreiecke* (Emperors's three

corners). These international lines divided political control and prevented complete unity of development within the coal-field area. Even today one can see faint evidence in the landscape of the differences that existed in 1918, particularly between the Prussian portion, which exhibited considerable urban activities, and the Russian area, where despite recent progress under communist influence the lack of consistent state support in the nineteenth century is evident, especially in urban underdevelopment. However, a few industrial relics show traces of investment made for a short time by the government of Congress Poland in this eastern part of upper Silesia; since this aspect of the landscape can be considered national in nature, it is treated in the next chapter.

The Upper Silesian district displays a third characteristic that dates from the imperial period, i.e. an unattractive, formless appearance. The map shows the six primary cities that coalesced rapidly in the nineteenth century (see Fig. 5.8). When industrialization began in Upper Silesia, these cities were really only villages and, therefore, the rapid development of mines and factories appropriated most of the land, leaving very little for continuous urban expansion. The intermixing of housing, mines, and factories created an unplanned agglomeration which has persisted. Only Gleiwitz (Gliwice) and Beuthen (Bytom) had market places and churches to provide a historic core, and these two cities, together with modernized Kattowitz (Katowice), still appear the most urban in the district. Within this large agglomeration, one can even see manor houses of a few old estates, illustrating the overlap of multinational and feudal eras. In addition, deteriorating, ugly, pre-1918 apartment blocks still contain occupants; waste heaps, quarries, and gravel pits usurp land between the built-up areas, preventing expansion; and stagnant water collects after rainstorms in depressions caused by subsidence from underground mining. Although many of these landscape features are being removed by socialist planning, enough remain to show the influence of the multinational period.

The Upper Silesia 'Black Country' landscape extends into Czechoslovakia to the south, where in the nineteenth century it formed a principal heavy industrial base for the Austrian Empire (see Photo 5.12). Many of the same characteristics of rapid, formless development took place as they had in the Upper Silesia region. Indeed, Moravská Ostrava, the central city in the region, has one of the most distinctive industrial landscapes I have ever seen. I vividly recall the

intermixture of residences and businesses with factories and mines; after an overnight stay in a local hotel, my car was covered with a layer of sinter from a nearby blast furnace.

A second major 'Black Country' landscape in Eastern Europe is the remarkable concentration of chemical factories centered on Halle in what is now East Germany. Early development, encouraged by the imperial Prussian-German governments in the late nineteenth century, consisted mostly of privately owned factories. Although the famous deposits of potassium salts at Stassfurt provided the basis for fertilizer production in the last quarter of that century, Turnock (1978: 161–2) reports that the decision by a western German company, Chemischefabrik Griesheim, to apply the electrolysis of brine at Bitterfeld in 1895 using regional salt and lignite deposits was unquestionably the chief force in making central Germany the center of the German electro-chemical industry. The product of this process, caustic potash, was used in making indigo for textile dyes, but within a few years the company concentrated its entire chlorinated hydro-carbon section at Bitterfeld to preparing bleaching

Photo 5.12   An aerial view shows Moravská Ostrava in Czechoslovakia. This city, located in the coal mining area of Moravia, was a primary base for heavy industry in the Austro-Hungarian Empire.

powder. Supplementing this development was the establishment in 1896 of the Agfa firm at nearby Wolfen, using their own lignite mine to produce cotton dyes and photographic materials. The expansion of the chemical industry in the Halle district, both before and after the First World War was partly the result of its distance from sensitive frontiers. Lignite was taken largely from shaft mines, and the extensive open pit developments only came after the First and Second World Wars. Today in this middle Elbe region one can see relics of early settlement from this German imperial period, e.g. those along the Geisel River to the west of Merseberg and Leuna.

3. Isolated industrial centers

As the map of East European industry illustrates, many of the isolated centers outside the Halle–Łódz–Budapest triangle were mining centers, especially in the Balkans. All of this scattered industry was initiated within a multinational framework or within states formed in the nineteenth century as Turkish power declined. Associated with some of the coal mining areas were iron and steel centers like Reşiţa and Jesenice, mentioned under the 'Black Country' landscapes, which also have visible relics from the late multinational period. Southern Poland (then Galicia in Austria) shows relics of early petroleum production, as does Romania near Ploieşti. In Serbia, remains from mining can be seen, operations that began in the early part of the twentieth century. In some of the larger cities like Berlin, Posen (Poznań), Prague, and Sofia, the seeds of engineering production emerged, although few relics remain. One that does is the Č-K-D, an engineering factory in Prague which, according to Carter (1975), illustrates social change around the turn of the century in terms of its new products and its role in establishing large-scale rural-urban migration.

Relics of a multinational landscape system: Austria-Hungary

The foregoing landscape relics did not exist in isolation, but were parts of multinational systems of spatial organization. However, since only fragments of these systems still exist, analyzing them by relics was easier than by complete systems – Greek, Roman, etc. Nevertheless, I feel that some effort should be made to show how these relics fit together to form a landscape system in one empire. This approach, using the Austro-Hungarian system as a model, can serve as a useful, pragmatic conclusion to the chapter. The variety

and number of relics remaining from this Empire give a feeling for the imperial influence in a multinational setting, even though this realm ceased to exist after 1918. This imperial system also serves to illustrate the behavior and attitudes of the rulers mentioned earlier in this chapter. This ideology included such motivations as territorial aggrandizement, unification of the state with policies promoting loyalty and assimilation of multinational subjects, state economic intervention, and regional politics.

The relics that survive today to mark the Austro-Hungarian imperial system of spatial organization extend over a wide area in *seven* countries – Austria, Czechoslovakia, Hungary, Poland, Romania, Russia, and Yugoslavia. This empire represents an attempt to weld a political-economic whole which was centered on the Hungarian plain. Above all, it represents the impress of central authority on the landscape – what Hassinger (1932) called *Der Staat als Landschaftgestalter*, or the state as a molder of landscapes. In this case, the state was Austria (later Austria-Hungary), which for several hundred years tried to make a multinational empire function. The main physical links in the nineteenth century were rail systems centered on Vienna and Budapest, a pattern shown as it finally emerged around 1900 (see Fig. 5.9). Lines focused on the two major cities like the spokes of a wheel, but connections between the spokes were lacking. This radial pattern of rail transport explains the present location of relics that otherwise would be impossible to understand if analyzed in the context of the individual states that appeared after 1918. The map shows that the rail systems were designed to serve the two major components of the Empire, Austria and Hungary. This pattern is particularly evident in the irrational tie of Galicia and Bukovina, including the important town of Lemberg (L'vov in the Soviet Union), to Vienna, demonstrating several ideological bases of imperial rulers: territorial aggrandizement, strategic location north of the Carpathian Mountains, control of heterogeneous ethnic groups like the Poles and Ukrainians, and regional politics.

The map also discloses the concentration of industrial relics in the Austrian portions of the Empire, particularly Bohemia-Moravia – an illustration of the regional-politics theme presented earlier as an imperial ideology. Berend and Ránki (1974a: 114), for example, show that in the middle of the nineteenth century, Austrian industrial production came mainly from Bohemia-Moravia (34%), Lombardy-Venice (27%), lower Austria (16%), and Galicia (7.5%) and that the share of the other provinces including Hungary amounted to only

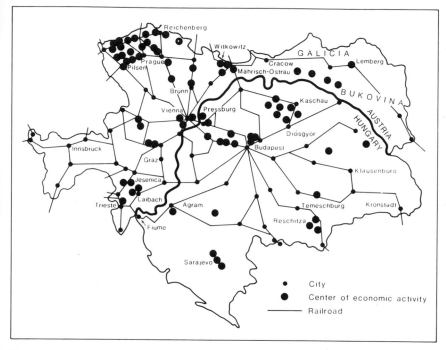

Fig. 5.9 Elements of economic spatial organization within the Austro-Hungarian Empire in the nineteenth century. Note the association of economic activity with radial patterns of transportation from Vienna and Budapest. Today, these relics are located in several different countries.

15.5 per cent. Thus, regional politics were responsible for regional imbalance.

Many present-day relics in the landscape of Eastern Europe originally exhibited spatial ties to this radial system of railroads, and to varying degrees were located or supported by the Austrian or Hungarian governments. These relics, in part, have already been mentioned separately, but now are linked together in an imperial system for brief discussion in five categories: administrative, economic, colonization, cultural, and defense.

Administrative

Cities that served as administrative centers and garrison points for the empire became the primary nodal points in the rail system. As mentioned before, Vienna was the hub of the imperial system and

each city in the monarchy, even Cracow and Prague, owed much of its appearance and culture to Habsburg rule. I am amazed that the similarity of these imperial cities has been preserved through relics even though the cities now are located in different countries, e.g. Pressburg (Bratislava) and Kaschau (Košice) in Czechoslovakia, Temeswar (Timişoara) in Romania, and Agram (Zagreb) in Yugoslavia, all of which served as administrative centers in the Empire. One notable characteristic was pervasive: the use of yellow or ochre wash as a historic color for public buildings; Macartney (1968: 116) remarks that God may bless Maria Theresa for her addiction to the shade of yellow which bears her name. This practice represents a good example of the political grandeur attitude already mentioned – the Habsburg ruler shaping a landscape in all parts of the Empire; indeed, today one can almost delimit its former reaches on the basis of Maria Theresa yellow.

Economic

The location of many relics of early economic activity within the Austro-Hungarian imperial area are explained again on the basis of state support and linkage by the radial rail network. Once more, the multinational ideology of direct or indirect state intervention must be acknowledged. The dots on the map show some major early relics of imperial economic activity that still exist, but are now part of national state networks of spatial organization (see Fig. 5.9). These include the major industrial regions of Bohemia and Moravia, especially the iron and steelworks at Witkowitz (Vítkovice) and the armament works at Pilsen (Plzeň), both mentioned previously (see Photo 5.12). Early state ironworks were established at different times by the Austrian State Railway Company and by the Hungarian government. The state, with the help of Rothschild financing, built the *Südbahn* Railroad, which not only connected with the major port at Trieste but also provided a link with the ironworks at Jesenica (Jesenice). Hamilton (1964: 54–5) writes that this ironworks had advantages of a location close to local labor skilled in iron working, halfway between Styrian markets and Trieste shipyards, and in proximity to Austrian imperial objectives in the Balkans. Establishing the railway to Trieste, including ties to Fiume (now Rijeka in Yugoslavia) and other places, again provides a good example of the application of multinational ideologies such as territorial aggrandizement,

unification of a multinational state, state intervention in industry, and regional politics. The last point is well illustrated by the dual ports of Trieste and Fiume (Rijeka), which served Vienna and Budapest, respectively.

The influence of Germany on cities in the northern part of the Austrian Empire is also unmistakable. An example is the city of Reichenberg (now Liberec), a textile center in the Sudetes Mountains of northern Bohemia. A current visitor to this city, by ignoring the recent socialist changes, notices its German rather than Austrian appearance. This is not surprising, for Reichenberg like much of the Ore and Sudetes Mountain area has always been exposed to Germanic influence. The city even became the capital of the Sudeten-German region after the occupation by the Nazis in 1938. Today, this German cultural influence lingers, perhaps best reflected in the massive city hall built in German Renaissance style in 1888–93. Other industrial centers of this region like Aussig (Ústí-nad-Labem) and Eger (Cheb) also retain a German aspect.

Colonization

The Austrian role in state colonization in the Banat area of what is now Yugoslavia has been discussed. Villages similar to those of the Banat exist as relics in the Bačka area to the west between the Danube and Tisza Rivers. These relics again illustrate the multinational ideology of establishing by state edict a stable settlement pattern in a vacuum left by the retreating Turks, thereby offsetting Hungarian interest in the area.

Cultural

The state role in forming the landscape of an imperial system can be demonstrated further by an unusual type of relic – the healthspa of Austria. The Habsburgs supported all of these resorts, which as a result bear their imprint in terms of architecture. The best known, of course, are Karlsbad (Karlovy Vary) and Franzenbad (Františkovy Lázně), both located in the Ore Mountains of Czechoslovakia north of Prague. Two others are Abbazia (Opatija), on the Adriatic coast west of Rijeka in Yugoslavia, and Herkulesbad (Băile Herculane), in the Banat Mountains of southwestern Romania. These fashionable spas, centered around mineral springs, attracted many people of wealth and position including the Habsburg emperors; today, these

are health resorts run by the socialist governments of their respective states. Yet, a visitor sees their similarity in design as they illustrate through an Austrian image the impact of the Habsburg spatial system into the far corners of the Empire. A walk on the heights above Herkulesbad, tucked away in the narrow Cerna River valley, can easily project a visitor back into the nineteenth century. The most imposing buildings, including the Casino, are in Austrian Baroque style and date from the last half of the nineteenth century. In Opatija, the Kvarner Hotel (formerly the Humler and Quarnero) also retains its Austrian appearance.

Defense

Security, always an important component of Habsburg multinational ideology, is best illustrated by a few relics of strongholds built by the Austrians as a *Militärgrenze* against the Turks. As mentioned earlier, the most significant fortresses are at Karlstadt (Karlovac) and Peterwardein (Petrovaradin), both in what is now northern Yugoslavia.

The imperial landscape system of Austria–Hungary illustrates the A–B–C concept (see Fig. 4.7). Both the map of East European industry in 1914 and the map of the Austrian imperial system portray the sharp transition from Bohemia (A) through a belt connecting Moravia, western Hungary, and Slovenia (B) to the largely agricultural portion of the Empire in the southeast (C) (see Figures 5.7 and 5.9). This transition is still apparent to a traveler and is supported by a map of industry in the *Atlas der Donauländer* (sheet 221, 1971). However, regional changes that began in the interwar period and continued under socialism are obvious in Slovakia, Transylvania, and Bosnia. This economic backwardness of the southeastern parts of the Empire could be attributed to regional politics, already discussed, which favored Austria, at least until 1867; Turnock (1978: 52), however, points out that this backwardness actually might be attributed to a long-range historical process, which resulted from attitudes among the landowning class and political elite of Hungary, who were unfavorable to industrialization. Ethnic fragmentation of the empire also hindered its development as a unit. When the Empire was dismembered after the First World War, the new states that emerged reflected the one-sided structure of the past – a situation that intensified their economic problems.

Summary

This chapter completes the analysis of the third layer in the palimpsest of culture that makes up the landscape of Eastern Europe. For over two thousand years the political environment of this region has been primarily multinational. Although not all political units have been empires, the predominant decision-makers have been imperial rulers, often based in capital cities outside the area. These empires, especially the absolute ones of Prussia–Germany, Austria, and Russia, were held together by a variety of forces: loyalty to the emperor, agreements between emperor and nobility, a class structure that cut across nationalities, and methods of forced cultural association, e.g. Prussianization or Russification. Imperial ideologies as seen in territorial expansion, state intervention, and regional politics are reflected in the landscape today. One sees multinational relics that include Greek colony, Roman road, Prussian capital, Turkish fortress and *caravanserai*, Austrian colony, Hungarian *tanya*, Venetian city, Orthodox monastery, porcelain factory, and spa. All of these were associated in some way with multinational systems of spatial organization. Although most relics represent the dominant forces of imperial authority, some – like those connected with the Reformation – represent opposition. These relics, though scattered across several states of Eastern Europe, collectively tell a story of multinational behavior that affected social change in the region. This environment was eventually altered by the process of nationalism, which brought about not only a new system of political organization of space, but also new patterns of economic and social organization in the landscape.

6
Landscapes of nationalism

In the preceding three chapters, we have seen how German medieval colonization, feudalism, and multinationalism intertwined as processes in explaining social change and landscape patterns in Eastern Europe. A fourth process – nationalism – supplemented the others in forming the landscape. Its origin lies far back in history and yet it embodied a modern political ideology.

In Eastern Europe, nationalism appeared in the nineteenth century, representing early national movements such as economic planning in Congress Poland or the National Revival movement in Bulgaria; for respective examples, consider the textile center of Łódź and the Balkan Mountain town of Tryavna. However, the greatest number of national landscape relics date from the interwar period when the old multinational map of Eastern Europe disintegrated and new states emerged with capital cities and realigned patterns of regional economic development. A capital city like Belgrade grew rapidly and reflected its new role of political center; at the same time, the Yugoslav industrial center of Zenica was subsidized in Bosnia, away from vulnerable borders with other states. A variety of landscape relics exists, therefore, to show that new forms of spatial organization were replacing those of the multinational era. The remainder of the chapter examines the nature of nationalism and how its ideology affected social change and the landscape in Eastern Europe.

The nature of nationalism

In the preceding chapter, the distinction was made between multinational and national states. In doing so, it was pointed out that

nationality refers to a group of people speaking the same language and observing the same customs. When loyalty to this group becomes paramount, especially in the formation of a nation-state in which this nationality is dominant, we called it nationalism. We observed that, for a variety of reasons, loyalty to such groups in Europe tended to lag behind patriotism or loyalty to a territory or rulers, features more common to the multinational state. Only in the modern era did the ideology of nationalism begin to affect political organization and in turn affect social change and the landscape.

Nationalism does not always lead to the creation of a nation-state. Yet the nation-state remains the goal of most national movements, and after the sixteenth century in Europe the conditions that had kept nationalities fragmented began to change. As Hayes (1926: 30–60) shows, literature, politics, economics, and religion began to be nationalized, and the basis of national ideologies emerged. In the first place, vernacular literatures developed with writers stressing what was common to a particular national area. Second, the rise of cities and a middle class served to break up the rigid class structure and to provide a base for the demands of self-government. Third, a series of nation-states appeared in Western Europe that, although encompassing 'foreigners', retained a core that was national in terms of language, traditions, and patriotism. Fourth, within these states, policies of mercantilism were established that put the emphasis on the economic growth and self-sufficiency of the nation-state; domestic production was encouraged and foreign importation discouraged. Finally, international Catholicism was weakened by the Protestant Reformation, thus somewhat dissolving the bonds that held diverse nationalities together and giving religious sanction to different groups.

By the seventeenth century in western Europe, therefore, the states of Sweden, Denmark, France, Spain, Portugal, and England could be called nation-states. The governments of these states often were absolute in nature with the rulers exercising a centralized form of government over a large territory dominated by one nationality. Kohn (1942 66, 100) feels that the absolute state, a form discussed in the previous chapter, served as a pacemaker for nationalism, because it provided a cohesive political framework for the dissemination of new liberal-spiritual ideas of the French Revolution. In Kohn's words, nationalism was unthinkable before the emergence of the modern state in the period from the sixteenth to the eighteenth centuries. This state provided the container for nationalism as the

nation within it exhibited new powers of cohesion and a group consciousness based on a common tradition of territory, language, and ethnic descent. This cohesion was helped by the Commercial and Industrial Revolutions which served to break down class structures and to create a middle class that integrated the masses on a scale not theretofore possible. In addition, technology associated with improved transportation reduced the former isolation of rural areas.

Above all, however, a new doctrine of popular sovereignty and national self-determination derived from the French Revolution held the nation-state together. The former 'subjects' of the absolute state now became the 'citizens', participating in the actual government of a nation-state; a new form of corporate will emerged among the citizens of a state. These changes manifested themselves in France: political democracy replaced monarchial aristocracy, class privileges broke down, local and provincial distinctions declined, and most French-speaking peoples joined in the national state and became infused with a national spirit. State policies, like elementary education in the French language and military conscription, focused on national patriotism and furthered this spirit. Even journalism emerged as a force in appealing to nationalist feeling. From the French model, therefore, arose an ideology of nationalism based on popular sovereignty that diffused throughout Europe and the world. This ideology was to affect social change and the landscape in both Western and Eastern Europe.

The ideology of nationalism in Eastern Europe

Conditions for the evolution of the nation-state and feelings of nationalism in Western Europe differed from those in the eastern part of the continent. Although ideas of national self-determination and liberal democracy spread into the latter area in the nineteenth century, the political and socioeconomic conditions prevented nationalism from easily being translated into nation-states. The three primary factors in this delay in nation-state development in Eastern Europe included the multinational environment, the internal antagonisms among the subject nationalities, and the socioeconomic conditions in the region.

The lack of a nation-state frame into which nationalism could be disseminated as it had in Western Europe constituted the first factor inhibiting the transformation of nationalistic forces into nation-states in Eastern Europe. Instead, four large empires dominated the

multinational environment from external capitals at Berlin, Saint Petersburg (later Leningrad), Vienna, and Constantinople (later Istanbul). These empires were able to erect barriers not only to liberal ideas from the West, but also to economic developments connected with the Commercial Revolution. Eventually, in the nineteenth century, the subject nationalities began to express ideas of national self-determination that culminated in the successful revolutions of 1848. After this period, policies aimed at the imposition of an imperial ideology repressed such ideas; for example, attempts were made to Prussianize or Russianize the Poles and to Magyarize the Slovaks, Romanians, and Croats.

An imperial environment also permeated the Balkans where expansionist policies of Austria against the declining 'sick man' of Europe – Turkey – ran into the opposition of both the national groups and the Russians, who for political reasons were promoting a Pan-Slav doctrine. In contrast to the northern portion of Eastern Europe, however, the imperial structure of Turkey tended to isolate the national groups. Vucinich (1963: 85–9), for example, notes that two social aspects of spatial organization furthered this isolation: (1) the older, medieval state structure dominated by fragmented kinship domains, e.g. tribe, clan, and extended family; and (2) a linkage between these widely separated groups consisting of an ecclesiastical *millet* system under which Orthodox Christians were grouped spatially into units that did not correspond to a unified territory, a homogeneous ethnic group, or a people possessing the same legal status. Although kinship and *millet* systems did serve to insulate and thus preserve certain national traditions of the past, the degree of isolation and parochialism also helped to retard economic, social, and political development. Thus, liberal and technological ideas from the West penetrated slowly. The first Serbian Revolution of 1804–12, for example, was hardly more than a peasant rebellion. Actually, Serbs and Bulgarians, who were exposed to Western ideas either by living abroad or in the Austrian-occupied areas, were in great part responsible for the rise of their nation-states. The state-making process, therefore, evolved slowly in the Balkans.

A second factor impeding the appearance of nation-states in Eastern Europe was the presence of internal antagonisms that existed among the subject-nationalities themselves. This characteristic leads Seton-Watson (1975) to refer to this region as the 'sick heart' of Europe. The Austro-Hungarian Empire particularly suffered from such internal fragmentation. In the Austrian parts of the Empire,

199

subjects were expected to devote their first loyalty to the Emperor. In the Hungarian areas, loyalty had to be focused on the Hungarian 'nation', an ideology enforced by a Magyarization policy that limited use of national customs among the subject-nationalities. These two forms of imperial loyalty, of course, conflicted with the rising national loyalties. However, among the separate cultural groups an intolerance based on various antagonisms toward minorities, clergy, nobles, peasants, and political leaders rendered a nationalistic ideology ineffective. In Bohemia, for example, the nationalism of the Czechs was a reaction against the militant nationalism of the German minority, which had supporters for a large Pan-Germanic movement. In Hungary, the poet Petöfi had espoused liberal reforms in 1848, but his words could not fit into the nationalist policy of Kossuth, the Hungarian revolutionary, who wanted independence for the Hungarians but not for the Slovaks, Romanians, and Croats (Seton-Watson 1946: 39); this policy was one of strict Magyarization. In Serbia, antagonisms existed because of the differences between the Austrophile Obrenović dynasty and the Russian-leaning Karadjordjević dynasty. In Croatia, a part of Hungary, the nationalist group representing the aristocracy, church, and intellectuals was opposed by the peasant movement. Other factors in the internal differences within East European national groups centered on the conservatism of the Roman Catholic Church, expressions of anti-Semitism, and the rise of worker-rights movements.

Finally, a third factor that played a role in delaying nation-state evolution in Eastern Europe was the class system and backward state of economic development. The previous chapters reveal that a feudal environment dominated by the nobility persisted for a long time in many parts of Eastern Europe. In contrast to Western Europe, where nationalism found its impetus in the bourgeoisie of urban areas, no such stimulus existed in the east. This lag in development, while delaying nationalism and social change, also stimulated it. Berend and Ránki (1974a: 9–10), for example, explain that this backwardness, especially in comparison to Western Europe, was a main factor in promoting nationalism in the area. They say that the national aspirations operating hand-in-hand with the demand for transformation of the socioeconomic structure constituted the chief driving force behind the irregular reforms and halting economic progress of the nineteenth century.

Kohn is explicit in differentiating between the process of nationalism in Western and Eastern Europe. He feels (1945: 457) that

the primary factor was timing: 'While the new nationalism in Western Europe corresponded to changing social, economic, and political realities, it spread to Central and Eastern Europe long before a corresponding social and economic transformation.'

The national groups of this area, therefore, developed what Kohn (1942: 65) calls *cultural* nationalism – a *Volkgeist* with manifestations of nationalism in literature, folklore, the mother tongue, and history. To justify their existence as future nation-states, East European nationalities had to look backwards into their history – back to the glorious days of Jagellonian Poland, Saint Stephen's Hungary, Simeon's Bulgaria, and Dušan's Serbia. This process was facilitated by the efforts of linguists like Karadžić and Kazinczy, who made available histories and poetry to ethnic groups, thereby permitting a national identity (Sugar 1969: 42). Unfortunately, this cultural nationalism actually became a form of imperialism because these groups believed that all people within the historic boundaries should be included in the nation, even if they were of a different nationality. Such a solution, of course, would leave large minority groups existing in nation-states, thereby preventing the cohesion so necessary to effective development. Furthermore, it was assumed in states like Poland and Hungary that the nobility should continue to dominate the power structure. The legitimacy and unity of these new nation-states was confirmed by constitutionalism – what Sugar (1969: 23) calls the strongest single influence shaping nationalism in Eastern Europe. These constitutions represented older contracts between ruler and the estates that could justify the reestablishment of states in the same territories and with the same social orders. Thus, one concludes that nationalism in Eastern Europe stemmed from historic rights while in Western Europe it rested on human rights.

Religion also was a factor in East European nationalism through its function as a force for both unity and disunity. For example, the dissolution of the medieval Bulgarian and Serbian states increased the importance of the Orthodox Church as an institution with which these cultures could identify during a long Turkish occupation. The same was true of the Catholic Church in Poland through the period of the partitions. On the other hand, the Reformation was a source of disunity. One of the the primary ideological aspects of the anti-Habsburg forces in Hungary was a desire for freedom of religion, and thus it is not surprising that many of the Hungarian insurrectionists were Protestants (Várkonyi, 54 [quoted in Sugar 1969: 33]); the Great Reform Church in Debrecen in eastern Hungary was the

site of the Declaration of Independence in 1849. In the Balkans, the cleavage between Slovenian-Croatian Catholics and the Orthodox peoples in the rest of the peninsula was also a source of fragmentation.

Although nationalism in Eastern Europe possessed certain common characteristics that differentiated it from that in Western Europe, variations from state to state did exist (Sugar 1969: 46–54). Czech nationalism exhibited bourgeoisie characteristics because the close geographical association with German-speaking areas allowed sharing in the intellectual and economic progress of the West. A strong and active bourgeoisie had developed and was ready to assume leadership by the time nationalism began to be a force in politics; on the other hand, the aristocracy, because of its foreign origin, could not capitalize on its power. Serbia and Bulgaria lacked a large noble class in the nineteenth century, giving their nationalism more of a popular character based on peasant support. The most aristocratic nationalism occurred in Poland and Hungary, although Polish lords found it much easier to gain the allegiance of Polish masses than did the Hungarian nobility, who had to contend with peoples of different nationalities. Romania exhibited more of a government-supported nationalism after the union of Wallachia and Moldavia in 1859.

Sugar (1969: 43), I feel, cogently sums up the East European type of nationalism when he calls it *intolerant* (my emphasis). In an environment in which nation-states did not exist and in which conflicts flourished in terms of class, religion, and culture, only an ideology of nationalism based on inequality – with all individual and class demands subordinated to the national interest – could weld nations together in the face of the numerous external and internal difficulties. In this context, the subject nationalities of Hungary were not equal to the Hungarians. In Western Europe, on the other hand, equality was more apparent within states because multinationalism was less evident. To the east, an inegalitarian nationalism, which not only allowed certain inequities to persist but also inhibited political and economic development, helps to explain why social change moved so slowly in this area before and after independence. A class system that kept the peasants on the land, thereby preventing development of a middle class, weakened the chances of social change as did the feelings of antagonism that existed between nationalities within the new states – feelings which led to such regional domination as Czechs over Slovaks and Serbs over Croats.

This section provides the background for understanding the

ideology and late rise of nationalism in Eastern Europe. In essence, the nineteenth century illustrates the transition from multinationalism and feudalism to nationalism as a process of landscape change. Although multinational aspects of the landscape prevailed, the different cultural groups became more aware of the architectural heritage of their past as reflected in certain monasteries like those of Bulgaria, Serbia, and Moldavia. As nation-states emerged, new focal points of nationalism, such as capital cities, developed. The process began in Congress Poland, a national entity whose limited autonomy from Russia lasted until the 1830 uprising. During the years 1815 to 1830, the government of Congress Poland initiated a program of national development that is still evident in the landscape. Other nation-states emerged in the Balkans during the nineteenth century – Serbia in 1804 and 1829, Moldavia-Wallachia in 1858, and Bulgaria in 1878 and 1885.

Economic progress and social change

Actually, political independence was achieved in the Balkans ahead of areas to the north because of the weakness of Turkey. Thus, the changes in the landscape that took place as a result of political status stood out because of the backwardness of much of this area. Vambery (1906: 343–4), for example, describes the changes in Sofia, Bulgaria, after independence:

> Five-and-twenty years ago, Sofia was full of crooked and dusty streets, such as we still see in Adrianople, Yanina, Monastir, etc., without any features to commend itself either for beauty or convenience, and with the exception of several places of worship, barracks, and prisons, there was nothing to denote any degree of culture. Since Sofia has been under Bulgarian government, one would scarcely recognize the place on account of the many improvements and changes which have been made. It now possesses straight wide streets, public squares, theaters, museums, zoological and botanical gardens, electric light, tramways, telephone, etc. And not only Sofia, but also Varna, Philippopolis [Plovdiv], and other towns, have been Europeanized. Romania, Serbia, and Greece, as well as Bulgaria, have been illumined by the light of civilization since they have become independent states.

This account characterizes how nationalism was responsible for landscape and social change in Eastern Europe.

By the outbreak of the First World War, Eastern Europe was showing signs of progress in both those areas that remained within

empires and those that had become independent. Berend and Ránki (1974a: 132–3) feel that in terms of general transformation of the whole economy, Eastern Europe was experiencing aspects of an industrial and commercial revolution: agriculture showed signs of capitalistic reorganization with an emphasis on grain exports; a banking and credit system was established; transportation networks expanded; foreign money – most notably in Romanian oil and Serbian nonferrous minerals – was invested in the Balkans and, although exploitive in nature, began to bring currency into the economies. Factory industry appeared in most nation areas and was responsible for some expansion of a middle class and of urbanization.

Stavrianos (1963: 190–6) points out specific aspects of social change in the Balkans that accompanied this economic progress. He relates, for example, that Serbian, Bulgarian, and Greek merchants (1) brought back to their native towns and villages examples of Europe's Enlightenment, particularly lavish gifts of books, equipment, and money; (2) frequently financed the education of young countrymen to foreign universities; and (3) supported the publication of books and newspapers in their native languages in addition to the translation of political works of writers like Voltaire and Rousseau. Accordingly, Stavrianos feels that political, economic, and scientific forces from the West were felt in the Balkan peninsula. A new age of secular and national ideas and aspirations was emerging. Even the manner of everyday living changed: tea and coffee became less of a luxury, lamps replaced candles, purchased clothing and household equipment appeared more important than homemade ones, and iron and steel plows became common.

However, in contrast to Western Europe, this industrial revolution was still a limited one, incapable of stimulating overall modernization. Most of the eastern nation-states were still agrarian and classified 'C' in terms of development: the food branch, for instance, continued to be the leading industry; in Western Europe, on the other hand, most countries had shed their earlier agrarian nature and were becoming thoroughly industrialized, able to generate their own capital for investment and possessing sizable internal markets for manufactured products. As cited in Chapter 5, three countries – Great Britain, Germany, and France – produced 72 per cent of Europe's industrial output in 1914 while the entire Austro-Hungarian Empire produced only 6 per cent! Within Eastern Europe, the gradient of social change ran from west to east. For example, Stavrianos (1963: 211) reports that regional illiteracy in the Balkans

immediately after the First World War showed higher rates from west to east: 8.8 per cent in Slovenia, 32.2 per cent in Croatia, 65.4 per cent in Serbia, and 83.8 per cent in Macedonia.

In the next two sections, I examine Poland and Bulgaria as examples of nationalism in nineteenth-century Eastern Europe with certain consequent effects on the landscape. Then in the following sections, I look at the interwar period when the political organization of national space became predominant and caused even more alterations in the landscape.

Nationalism and the landscape in the nineteenth century: Poland

Early seeds of nationalism and some effects on the landscape

Ideas of nationalism appeared quite early in Poland after the partitions of the eighteenth century, when French influence penetrated the area as a result of the Napoleonic Wars. The old Polish nation, dominated by the nobility and excluding both Polish and non-Polish masses, had been united on the basis of shared privilege rather than on a common bond of language. Their nationalism consisted of 'a sense of territorial patriotism, a loyalty to the commonwealth that safeguarded its golden liberty' (Brock 1969: 311). After the partitions, the concept of 'nation' was broadened under the influence of reformers like Kołłątaj and Staszic to include all social classes speaking a similar language. This change came in part because the state on which territorial loyalty was based had ceased to exist, and language seemed the logical basis on which to build a new one. This trend was influenced by the spread of German ideas of romanticism with emphasis on *Volk* culture as preserved by the peasants. A linguistic and cultural nationalism slowly took shape alongside the older, more limited concept of nation.

Although many Poles accepted denationalized roles within the territories of the three partition powers, others continued to work for the resurrection of the Polish state. Some felt their best hope rested with France and, therefore, Polish legions were formed to fight with Napoleon, trusting that military action could influence geopolitics. Others cast their lot with Russia, particularly after 1801 when the liberal czar, Alexander I, ascended the throne. In contrast to the liberal ideas of the French Revolution, the Russian orientation was influenced by the Slavophilic idea of resistance to a decadent and

materialistic West. The first solution to the French-Russian impact on the Polish nation represented a compromise – the establishment of the Duchy of Warsaw in 1806, ruled by the neutral king of Saxony. Although not really independent, this state nevertheless was Polish and of great historical importance to the nation as a whole. In Wandycz's (1974: 63) words, 'Its existence contradicted the verdict of the partitions; its army not only revolutionized the Polish military tradition but also served to educate the masses in a patriotic and liberal sense.' In a way, the Polish problem in the early years of the nineteenth century served as the first example of a small nation struggling to find its place on a continent dominated by big powers. This problem only magnified after 1918.

The period of the Duchy of Warsaw saw certain changes in political, economic, and social conditions that were representative of changes in Europe as a whole at this time. Although compulsory peasant labor reduced the impact of the abolition of serfdom, other aspects of modernization could be seen. The Napoleonic civil code, which protected property and contracts, and the commercial code created favorable conditions for economic development. Deprived of their land monopoly, the gentry were drawn into the processes of change along with an expanding middle class. Consequently, the Duchy of Warsaw as the creation of Napoleon was identified with France and the national struggle for independence.

The sequel to the Duchy of Warsaw was Congress Poland, a territory created in 1815 by the Congress of Vienna after the defeat of Napoleon (see Fig. 6.1). Again, this state represented a paradox in that the Great Powers both reaffirmed the partitions, yet recognized the existence of the Polish nation. Congress Poland actually was placed under Russian control but retained degrees of autonomy. However, many Poles lived outside this state within the empires of Russia, Prussia, and Austria. Economic progress in these parts of partitioned Poland – discussed in the previous chapter – was uneven and would complicate the reorganization of the state after 1918. On the other hand, economic development in Congress Poland was substantial, representing in the minds of Poles a very crucial first stage in national development. Politically, this territory reflected the transition of romantic nationalism from a largely literary movement to a political movement centered on the nation as an ideal and based on liberty.

Congress Poland covered the territory centered on the middle Vistula River including Warsaw and Lublin but excluding the free

Fig. 6.1   Congress Poland in the middle of the nineteenth century. Note the 'national' industrial developments around Łódź, in the Holy Cross Mountains, and in a part of Upper Silesia.

city of Cracow (see Fig. 6.1). It also included a prong extending to the northeast centered on the city of Augustów, where today a canal serves as a relic of Polish attempts to gain a water outlet around Prussian territory to the Baltic (see Photo 6.1). Although the Constitutional Charter for Congress Poland provided for a certain amount of political independence and civil liberties, effective power remained with Russia and the Polish propertied classes. The eastern link was crucial, especially in the attempt at industrialization, for Russia with an underdeveloped industry opened up new market possibilities for Polish factories. The government began to organize industrial de-

207

Photo 6.1 Boaters fill a lock on the canal at Augustów in northeast Poland. The canal, a relic of the early nineteenth century, fulfilled the need of leaders of the Congress state to gain a water outlet around Prussian territory to the Baltic sea. (Source: *Poland*: p. 131.)

velopment projects and to formulate town construction plans. The state in this period exerted an effect on the landscape of Congress Poland that is still visible. Today Poles are quick to point to the period of 1815–30 as important in terms of national economic progress, especially because it was carried out despite the lack of true independence.

Under the leadership of Staszic and later Drucki-Lubecki, state industrial planning centered around saline springs on the Vistula, iron smelting in the Holy Cross Mountains, metal works in the Dąbrowa area of Upper Silesia, and textiles in the Łódź region (see Fig. 6.1). At Ciechocinek, south of Toruń on the Vistula, the salt-graduation towers – large wooden structures – still stand and are in use as a part of this spa complex. Only a few relics of mines and smelters, which originally were based on water power and charcoal, exist today in the Holy Cross Mountains. On the other hand, the Dąbrowa region, originally oriented to the east as a part of Congress Poland and later Russian Poland, is fully integrated into the Upper Silesian industrial region. The state Bank of Poland established a major relic, the Huta Bankowa (now called the Huta Dzierzyńskiego) as a coke-using iron works based on Dąbrowa coal (Pounds 1958: 124).

Present relics and street layouts from Warsaw's days as the capital of Congress Poland also illustrate the planned effects of this period. One of the largest schemes involved the redevelopment of Bankowy Square, now known as Dzierzyński Square (Gutkind, VII 1972: 101). On the western side of this square, monumental buildings for the Revenue and Treasury Commission, the Ministry of the Treasury, and the Bank of Poland and Stock Exchange replaced former private palaces. The joint planned effect of these Neo-Classic buildings is still evident today, although the buildings are used for different purposes.

Cracow, of course, is the most Polish of cities and as an entity symbolizes national feeling, although the city had served as a Polish capital before the modern period of nationalism. Thus I discussed the great landscape relic of Wawel castle in the previous chapter on the multinational period. However, one important national relic that arose here in 1820 during the Congress period was the mound commemorating Tadeusz Kościuszko, from which one can view the entire Cracow area. Kościuszko's heart reposes in a chapel next to the mound but his actual grave is in Wawel cathedral.

Relics of early Polish nationalism in the landscape of Łódź

The landscape of Łódź and its surrounding area bears the most lasting impress of the national planning in Congress Poland. The development of the city as a textile center (the 'Polish Manchester') illustrates not only the impact of rapid industrialization on a landscape, but also the difference between state planning in the early period and *laissez faire* development in the latter part of the nineteenth century. Today

the overall plan of the city represents the former, while the association of large factories, tenements, and palaces reflects the latter. Łódź itself was a village in 1815 when the state selected it as a site for textile mills because the location offered several advantages for planned, artificially stimulated development: much of the land not only was state owned, but also had waterpower sites and was close to Prussia, a source of skilled textile workers. The undeveloped Russian markets to the east also beckoned, especially since the tariffs between the Polish Kingdom and the Empire were either nonexistent or small. Finally, the Polish army also constituted an important market for cloth.

Analyzing the plan of Łódź in some detail is important because it strongly reflects the original national planning of the Congress period. The map shows the chronological development of the city (see Fig. 6.2). South of the original village, a new town of regular layout was constructed in 1823 around an octagonal square, where the Neo-Classic town hall of 1827 still symbolizes the changed character of Łódź. In this new town, craftsmen produced handmade woolen cloth and also raised food from plots laid out systematically to the east. Several miles to the south an axis of settlement transverse to Piotrkowska Street developed along the Jasień River, where grain mills based on water power were converted to linen production, which required bleaching, dyeing, and printing; sales from this production took place in the market at the south end of Piotrkowska Street. The state plan then called for connection in the 1820s of the north and south cores by planned settlement along Piotrkowska Street. Over five hundred plots of land were laid out – smaller ones for weavers along the street and larger ones for growing and spinning flax a block away. Later, cotton production either supplemented or replaced that of linen. In the 1830s, coal began to replace water power in the mills. Until the 1860s, therefore, Łódź expanded in an orderly fashion under state control of planning and ownership of factories.

Capitalist development replaced state planning within Łódź after 1860 when large, privately owned factories were established at random throughout the city. One factor aiding new enterprises was the cheap labor provided after 1864 by the emancipation of the serfs within the Russian Empire. The coming of the railroad in the 1860s facilitated the conveying of coal, raw materials, and finished products. However, a more significant factor was the expansion by one industrialist, Karl Scheibler, who cornered the supply of American cotton in the Civil War period, giving him the means to buy out

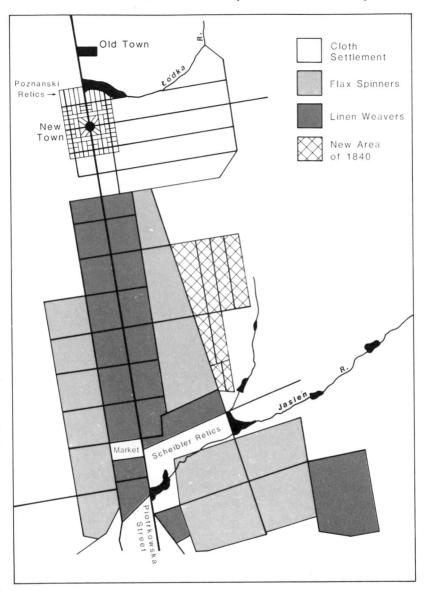

Fig. 6.2 Łódź in the middle of the nineteenth century. Note the importance of Piotrkowska Street as a connection between the new town in the north and mills along the Jasień River in the south.

other Łódź establishments and to increase his holdings to one-sixth of the city's total. Several other textile entrepreneurs – some of them German or Jewish – appeared, each constructing a complex of factories and tenements. As their fortunes increased, these men built large palaces that symbolized wealth and power based on the exploitation of labor. Władisław Reymont (1899) vividly describes this new industrial environment in his famous novel entitled *Ziemia obiecana* (Promised Land). This city exhibited a population growth typical of industrial cities in Europe during the nineteenth century: from 20 000 inhabitants in 1850 to over a half million in the next sixty years, when the impact of the Industrial Revolution was maximized (Straszewicz 1959: 74–7). With the exception of Leeds, England, this growth probably surpassed that of any city in Europe.

Today, the landscape of Łódź exhibits many relics from this period, even though the entire textile industry is now under state ownership and operation. Perhaps the most evident relics are the large complexes of Scheibler in the south and Poznanski in the north. The large agglomeration of buildings built by Poznanski remains much as it was in the 1890s – a large factory and tenements of red brick adjacent to the palace; the latter, in Baroque style, is now used as museum (see Photo 6.2).

A variety of other relics from this period exists throughout Łódź – indeed, the city is a virtual outdoor museum of early industrialization in Poland. Can one call this a landscape of nationalism? Probably so, in terms of the early state role. Ostrowski (1966: 38–40) feels that Łódź is an example of rational state planning of an industrial center unique in the history of European town development.

Nationalism and the landscape in the nineteenth century: Bulgaria

The rise of nationalism and some effects on the landscape

Poland, located in the northern part of Eastern Europe, provides one early example of the impact of nationalism's process on the landscape in the nineteenth century. Bulgaria, with its southern location in the Balkans, provides another. Today, a variety of relics that represent the so-called Bulgarian 'national revival' can be seen in various parts of the country (see Fig. 6.3). Many of the best remains are located in settlements of the Balkan Mountains, where the Turkish occupation forces were less numerous; however, some historic cities of

the lowlands like Plovdiv were also important centers of the revival. Finally, Sofia, as the new capital of the Bulgarian state in 1878, reflected the rising national spirit. The following section examines the process of nationalism in Bulgaria and relates it to the relics that are still evident.

The Bulgarian nation struggled to keep its cultural heritage alive during the Turkish occupation of over five hundred years. This situation differed somewhat from Poland's, where the partitions were much shorter and Congress Poland served as a symbol, albeit weak, of national unity. In providing many details on the rise of Bulgarian national consciousness, Pundeff (1969: 93–165) points out that nationalistic activity developed despite the oppressive rule of the Turks. The role of monasteries, whose charters and established privileges were honored by the sultans, demonstrates this effort; furthermore, the fortified and inaccessible nature of most monasteries helped them as sanctuaries for the preservation of Bulgarian culture. In the seventeenth century, some 120 Orthodox monasteries served a popu-

Photo 6.2   The Poznanski textile mill of Łódź, Poland was built in the nineteenth century and is now owned and operated by the state.

Fig. 6.3 Bulgaria after independence in the latter part of the nineteenth century. Note the original state of 1878, which was supplemented by Eastern Rumelia in 1885. In addition, Bulgaria had traditional ties in Macedonia.

lation of one and a half million. Their libraries included not only religious texts and the charters from kings and local magnates, but also copies of medieval documents that kept alive the early heritage of Bulgarian empires. The monasteries organized schools that utilized the native language in preparing young men for the Church and for lay pursuits such as clerks for merchants, thereby helping to develop a lay intelligentsia. In short, the monasteries as exemplified by the large Rila complex south of Sofia are symbols not only of early Byzantine imperialism (mentioned in the previous chapter) but Bulgarian nationalism as well.

The accomplishments of the medieval Bulgarian state provided an important legacy for later nationalistic trends. In the Middle Ages, the Bulgarians successfully resisted Byzantine domination in acquiring a cultural identity that, while not yet classed as nationalistic, represented a significant historic force in later years. The role of the Cyrillic alphabet was crucial in resistance to the Greek alphabet

of Byzantium as it provided a distinctive national alphabet, which not only facilitated a religious and secular literature, but also aided in the establishment of a national church whose independence was recognized by Constantinople in 927. As a base of the international language of Slavic civilization, Old Bulgarian carried cultural traits throughout the Balkans and to Russia. This provided the Bulgarian intelligentsia with a consciousness of the role of their culture in the world which found expression not only in the idea of Trnovo as a religious center rivaling Rome and Constantinople – even before this idea was expressed by the Russians for Moscow – but also in the idea of Bulgaria as the seedbed of Slavic civilization (Pundeff 1969: 98). In addition, a rich folk tradition from the medieval period of greatness served as a source of common history, identity, and hope for freedom among Bulgarians of later periods.

Nationalistic tendencies during the eighteenth century developed in Greek and Serbian areas, activities not easily visible to Bulgarians isolated in the southeastern Balkans. Nevertheless, to certain Bulgarian clergy like Father Paisii, who traveled throughout the Balkans, fell the role of writing about these ideas as they encountered them in centers of national cultural life, e.g. Mount Athos in Greece and Sremski Karlovci in Serbia. Father Paisii's *History of the Bulgarian People* (1762) placed this culture in the context of the Slav peoples and in history in general. His work, a patriotic history, inculcated pride in the national past and resistance to the strong Hellenization of Bulgarian culture. Other scholars began to collect materials on national identity and to publish them in grammars, dictionaries, and folklore and historical studies. Demands for patriotic education increased, and in 1835 the first secular school opened in Gabrovo (see Fig. 6.3).

National liberation in Bulgaria involved throwing off Greek economic and religious domination before any attempt at political resistance against Turkey (Pundeff 1969: 116). Greeks in Bulgaria controlled both commercial life and the Orthodox Church. The few Bulgarians who attained wealth and status in the towns tended for convenience to become Hellenized and to merge into the Greek bourgeoisie. After the 1830s, anti-Greek feeling intensified. The economic interests of the rising Bulgarian middle class clashed with those of Greeks in the towns. Nationalist propaganda alleged that the Greek merchants and clergy were bent on denationalizing the Bulgarians to keep them subjugated. Finally, the increasing pressure of European powers on the Turks encouraged the Bulgarians to seek a national-

ized church. This agitation for Bulgarian rather than Greek bishops and priests within the Orthodox Church of the nation finally culminated in 1870 by Turkish recognition of a Bulgarian exarchate (see Fig. 6.3). This large territory, extending from the Black Sea to the Aegean coast and as far west as Ohrid and Niš, was vital to the political issues of the Balkans, because it formed the basis of what the Bulgarians hoped would be a new national state that would reflect, in its geographical extent, the medieval state (Pundeff 1969: 115). Unfortunately, Greece and Serbia also claimed part of the western area, known as Macedonia. The city of Ohrid, today in Yugoslavia, long served as a landscape symbol to both Bulgarians and Serbs because of their medieval associations with this city.

Successful religious nationalism in creating a Bulgarian church was connected to political nationalism against the Turks (see Fig. 6.3). In this regard, Bulgaria was constrained by power politics in the Balkans, but the details are not essential here. Suffice it to say that revolutionary activity supported the rising nationalist sentiment; this culminated in the uprising of 1876, which was so ruthlessly suppressed by the Turks that moral indignation arose throughout Western Europe. When Turkish authorities rejected proposed reforms, Russia intervened and decisively defeated the Moslem power – a victory marked today near the site by the golden domes of a Russian memorial church which can be seen when approaching the Balkan Mountains at Šipka (see Photo 6.3). From this victory emerged an enlarged Bulgarian state; political liberation had supplemented religious liberation. However, the Russian orientation of this state with a Mediterranean coastline alarmed England and Austria; the resultant Congress of Berlin in 1878 reduced independent Bulgaria to a principality located north of the Balkan Mountains and returned the Maritsa valley (Eastern Rumelia) and Macedonia to Turkey. A disappointed Bulgaria continued to press for unification of all territories with Bulgarian population. This nationalist thrust was reflected geographically in the transfer of the capital from Trnovo to Sofia, a site which was better situated to control routes both north and south of the Balkan Mountains. In 1885, Eastern Rumelia was united with the principality, and Bulgaria with minor exceptions assumed the geographical form it retains today.

In the twenty-five years before the Balkan Wars of 1912–13, the country made tremendous national progress. However, an aggressive foreign policy of territorial expansion within the Balkan area led to successive defeats in 1913, 1918, and even later in 1944. Each of these

Photo 6.3 The nineteenth-century memorial church at Šipka, Bulgaria, stands near the site of the Russian military victory over the Turks. This victory paved the way for Bulgarian independence and symbolizes traditional friendship between Bulgaria and Russia. (Source: Cash 1949: p. 134).

defeats resulted from nationalistic policies attempting to gain what was perceived as Bulgarian territory from the illustrious medieval past – Macedonia, an Aegean coastline, and southern Dobruja.

217

Relics of early nationalism

The national movement in Bulgaria, which began in the last part of the eighteenth century and continued to gather force in the nineteenth, appeared in the landscape in a different way than in Poland. In the latter country, industrialization was much more important than it was in Bulgaria where an expanding bourgeoisie class – artisans, merchants, and even small industrialists – affected social change and the landscape. Indeed, Stavrianos (1963: 194) feels that the history of the Bulgarian national revival reflects the history of the craft guilds. The rise of a middle class was especially strong in certain historic cities like Trnovo and Plovdiv, which served as centers of national ideas; in addition, smaller towns on the slopes of the Balkan Mountains – Tryavna, Gabrovo, Koprivstica, and Karlovo (now Levskigrad) – also were affected because they were less exposed to Turkish influence (see Fig. 6.3). The two major landscape symbols of this national urban renaissance in architecture were the clock tower and the private house.

The clock tower in cities like Tryavna, Berkovitsa, and Shumen (now Kolarovgrad) reflect both the changing economic life and the attempt to create a new Bulgarian style in architecture. Toward the end of the eighteenth century, craftsmen's guilds with the permission of Turkish authorities assumed control of economic life, particularly the production and sale of goods. Various crafts began to concentrate in different streets, and gradually a town commercial district emerged. In enforcing the fixed working hours of the guilds, each artisan or merchant had to know the time; this necessity gave rise to the clock tower, a distinctive landmark that has survived in many Bulgarian towns. The clock tower of Tryavna, built in 1813, is a model of many of these structures (see Photo 6.4). It includes a lower section of rough stone that tapers upward before joining a square portion, faced with wood and housing the clock mechanism. The superstructure terminates in a pointed roof. Bichev (1961: 58) feels that this tower, so visible throughout the town above the low houses, symbolized not only the economic progress but also the inevitable end to alien rule. I concur.

The private residence, constructed in a style that is unique in Europe, forms the second symbol of the Bulgarian national revival. The style is called 'Bulgarian Baroque' because of characteristics reminiscent of Viennese architecture. Yet the style has an individuality of its own which, when it appeared in the middle of the nine-

Photo 6.4 In the Balkan mountains of Bulgaria, clock towers like this one in Tryavna represent economic progress in the nineteenth century and the end of Turkish rule.

teenth century, could not be traced back to the earlier traditions of Bulgarian architecture. By using symmetric layout instead of the asymmetric plan of the earlier folkstyle house, this new residence reflected class differentiation, prosperity, and a penchant for showiness on the part of the nascent bourgeoisie. The most impressive feature is the curved pediment, also found on public buildings and churches in the country. Relics of these residences, now preserved as national monuments, are most frequent in the cities of Trnovo and Plovdiv as well as in towns in the Balkan Mountains. Good examples are the Georgiadi residence in Plovdiv and the Kableshkov house in Koprivstica (see Photo 6.5); the clock tower of Botevgrad and the Holy Trinity Church in Svishtov also have curved pediments. Although this feature is perhaps a unique aspect of national style, other features like projecting upper floors, wide eaves, wooden shutters, and decorated façades are also typical.

While clock towers and residences seem to be the most widespread relics in Bulgaria reflecting the national revival, Bichev (1961: 73, 78) mentions that other buildings also display this turning point in cultural life (see Fig. 6.3): (1) the large inn in Trnovo, built in 1858, not only illustrates in its arcades (which resemble those of the Rila Monastery) an architectural theme of Bulgarian history, but also reflects the changing role of Bulgaria in the Ottoman Empire; and (2) the Aprilov high school in Gabrovo, a monumental public building completed in 1873, serves as a symbol of early public education in an era of nationalism. Both buildings are prominent in the landscape today.

The effects of nationalism on the landscape of Bulgaria actually are twofold. During the national revival period, which lasted some hundred years from the latter part of the eighteenth century until the liberation of 1878, the changes described earlier illustrated connections with the Bulgarian past. However, after liberation a new period of capitalism developed which, although it reflected elements of national style, typified urban development taking place around the world. Tashev (Gutkind, VIII 1972: 58) confirms this break with the past and points to its effect on urban development when he says that 'after the liberation, the development of towns was detached from the progressive traditions of the National Revival Period'. At this time, a group of town planners and engineers began to draw up plans for the modernization of major towns. The primary element in these plans was a new, rectangular layout superimposed on the narrow, irregular pattern that had dominated through the Turkish occupation. Today the gridiron patterns of Sofia, Plovdiv, Stara Zagora, and Varna testify to this radical shift in morphological orientation, although older radial streets did not entirely disappear. In addition, new public buildings were constructed as symbols of national life.

As noted earlier in a quote by Vambery, the transformation of Sofia was very noticeable. The rectangular layout, focusing on several broad squares and preserving five radial streets, grew out of the plan drawn up by Amadier in 1881 (Gutkind, VIII 1972: 68). This transformation of Sofia between liberation and 1914 can be recognized today by the mixture of irregular and regular layouts and by

Photo 6.5 In Bulgaria, the national revival period of the nineteenth century is illustrated in architecture, especially residences with curved pediments like the House of Kojumdžioglu in Plovdiv. This building now serves as the Ethnographic Museum.

the large number of public buildings erected as a part of this early national period: the National Assembly, Alexander Nevski Memorial Church, the University (central part), Law Courts, Ministry of War, National Bank, National Theater, Ministry of Foreign Affairs, Bulgaria Hotel, Concert Hall, and Ministry of Interior; in addition, residential buildings, both villas and apartment houses, were constructed. Jelavich (1977: 281) points out that much of this construction used European cities like Paris or Vienna as models, employing foreign architects and making little attempt to build on national foundations. This trend, which represents a break with the 'national revival', influenced both the landscape, making it much more cosmopolitan, and social change.

In conclusion, the process of nationalism affected the present urban landscape of Bulgaria in two ways during the two hundred years before the First World War: (1) a period of national revival was represented by certain symbols like the clock tower and the Baroque residence; (2) supplementing this revival was the modernization of cities in a capitalistic sense following European models.

Nationalism in the interwar period and the landscape

Ideologies behind the new states after the First World War

The two examples of Poland and Bulgaria illustrate how the process of nationalism began to affect the landscape of Eastern Europe during the nineteenth century. Today, the Poles still speak proudly of the progress made by the Congress state, while the Bulgarians are no less bashful about their National Revival Movement. However, these exemplify merely two nationalist movements which were found throughout the area and which affected both social change and the landscape. Some movements, like those of the Poles, Serbs, Romanians, and Bulgarians, reflected degrees of political independence before 1914. Others, like those of the Czechs, Slovaks, and certain south Slav groups, had to wait until the interwar period, when a tier of new states shattered the old multinational framework of Eastern Europe (see Fig. 6.4).

The peace conferences following the First World War produced a new framework of political organization in Eastern Europe that did not necessarily meet the aspirations of the national states. Furthermore, the pattern was not ideal for the establishment of viable economies from a spatial point of view. Understanding the ideologies of

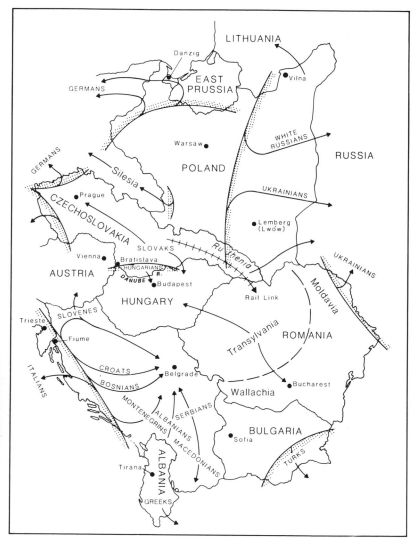

Fig. 6.4 Eastern Europe: the forces exerted by ethnic groups that hindered the cohesion of national states after 1918.

the decision-makers who delineated these states is important, therefore, because they illustrate limitations which had to be overcome in organizing space and transforming landscapes. In addition, we have to consider the ideologies of external powers, especially Germany. Finally, the ideologies of the national states themselves

223

also affected the pattern of states that emerged, as we will find in Poland.

Little doubt existed that some new spatial framework would be created after the First World War to reflect the rising national hopes of these groups. In this sense, a basic ideologic factor behind the decision to change the map of Eastern Europe was idealistic: an experiment to see if small powers could exist in their own right. Woodrow Wilson's Fourteen Points certainly reflected an idealist motive based on the principle of national self-determination; but beyond this motive arose the more practical one of power politics: emasculating the strong empires that had controlled Eastern Europe for so long. France, for example, saw the establishment of Poland, Czechoslovakia, and Yugoslavia as weakening both Central Powers – Germany and Austria; furthermore, alliances with these new states might exert a check on future German expansion. In addition, since Western Europe feared the rise of a large communist political unit in Russia, the establishment of a tier of states was viewed as an effective barrier to Soviet ideological expansion.

Although the peace treaties of the First World War partially met the nationalist aims of culture groups in Eastern Europe, there still remained a legacy of ethnic fragmentation and economic weakness that would prove fatal twenty years later. Kosiński (1969: 393) estimates that over one-third of the total population of Eastern Europe in 1930 (34 million out of 94 million) consisted of minorities. This figure is astonishing and tells realistically why Eastern Europe was labeled the 'Shatter Belt'. The map shows some of the geographical effects of these minorities (see Fig. 6.4). In struggling to reconcile new political boundaries with the mosaic of ethnic groups and with a former imperial pattern of economic development, the victorious powers created states that were far from viable. Promises made to certain powers, e.g. Italy, during the First World War also caused deviations. In creating a new map, therefore, the treaty makers had to utilize certain approaches to political spatial organization – corridor to the sea, divided plebiscite zone, and free territories – that made Eastern Europe an outstanding laboratory for the study of political geography. Finally, economic development was hindered not only by a world-wide depression but also by attitudes of the leaders and peasants: the former feared a large worker group that would attract communist activity whereas the latter viewed urban and factory development with suspicion. Each state established after 1918, therefore, reflected to varying degrees a spatial pattern that deviated in

reality from what was desirable in a rational geographic sense.

Although these newly created states in Eastern Europe reflected the basic process of nationalism, the external powers continued to play a strong role in the area, both in establishing the states and in their development during the interwar period. This persistent external influence is an important spatial characteristic of the Shatter Belt. The primary power, of course, was Germany which not only dominated the area economically, but also raised the specter of a *Mitteleuropa* commanded by the Third Reich. The concept of *Mitteleuropa*, primarily a geographical term until the First World War, began to change during that war. With the loss of its overseas colonies, Germany was more dependent upon the resources of central Europe. In 1915 Friedrich Naumann published his famous book, *Mitteleuropa*, which advocated a new federation of states in central Europe under German leadership. Although he did not intend his plan as an argument for German imperialism in the area, many construed it as such. The non-German nationalities of the region rejected his idea, but many Germans seized upon it in a geopolitical sense. In the next twenty years, German geographers writing in the *Zeitschrift für Geopolitik* increasingly referred to *Mitteleuropa* as a *Kulturraum* – a region extending from the Saar to the Ukraine which had been influenced by German culture since the Middle Ages. The concept of *Mitteleuropa*, according to Meyer (1946: 190–1) became 'a weapon for aggression and domination . . . With the Munich settlement, the decisive step was taken toward a continental racial imperialism'. *Mitteleuropa* was no longer a term for a vague area in Central Europe or even a concept of bourgeoisie German nationalism, but the basis for an ideology of expansion.

In looking at these new states, therefore, we find geographical patterns and landscapes that reflect ideologies of the peacemakers, those of the adjacent powers, and those of national states themselves. Now let us examine some examples of the effects of such ideologies on individual states.

1. Poland

Although many East European states had aspirations of recreating a political entity that reflected its early glories, only Poland managed to form a state that in certain ways resembled the past – the Polish-Lithuanian commonwealth of 1772. After the First World War, Polish forces, capitalizing on weaknesses of Soviet revolutionary armies and fortified by military aid from the Allies, managed to

occupy large areas of western Russia and Lithuania (see Fig. 6.4). Minority groups of over five million people were included in the eastern portions of the new state – Lithuanians, White Russians, and Ukrainians. Haskins (1920: 164) relates that after the First World War most Poles perceived their country not as an ethnographic Poland, but as the whole expanse of Jagellonian Poland of the eighteenth century. They envisioned the eastern area as dominated by Polish culture, an area from which many national leaders had originated, e.g. Kościuszko, Mickiewicz, and Pilsudski. The chief cities of this area, Wilno and Lwów, were considered Polish cities although their populations were multinational. In a sense, the reconstruction of a new state in the 1920s on the basis of the historic boundaries of 1772 was viewed as a release from the historic injustices that the nation had suffered after the partitions. The Allies, swayed by Woodrow Wilson, let this Polish imperialistic view prevail after the First World War. Evidence indicates that, although Wilson was unsympathetic to Polish expansion, his earlier liberal views favoring the establishment of a Polish state and his indebtedness to the Polish-American vote in the US election of 1916 influenced his acceptance of boundaries that diverged widely from a rational organization of political space.

As one of Wilson's Fourteen Points, the creation of an outlet to the sea for Poland represented a basic ideological point that was to affect its landscape. As mentioned earlier in this book, German colonization along the Baltic coast areas had resulted in creation of a Polish-German borderland. A rather continuous band of German settlement in Pomerania and Masuria was intersected by a belt of mixed Polish-German population along the lower Vistula River. This mixed zone seemed to be the logical place for a corridor to the sea as it would not only minimize the German-Polish conflict but also would keep the Vistula River, the core area of the Polish nation, within one state. Although this selection caused hard feelings in Berlin, because it separated East Prussia from the German state, it did facilitate interaction between Poland and Danzig, a port city mainly of German population.

Still another ideological problem that affected the landscape of Poland was presented by Upper Silesia, the largest industrial concentration in all of Eastern Europe. The development of this region within a multinational framework is discussed in Chapter 5. After the First World War, the industrial significance of Upper Silesia made it a critical issue in the peace settlement. The split in the area between

German and Polish populations complicated the spatial solution. The Council of the League of Nations finally divided Upper Silesia into two parts largely on the basis of the voting pattern in a plebiscite (see Fig. 5.8). The greater part of the region was given to Poland, but large numbers of Germans and Poles were left in each other's territory. The new boundary greatly disrupted the spatial organization of what should have been one economic unit. Pounds (1959: 413) shows that 11 of 22 major industrial firms had their properties divided, e.g. zinc mine from smelter. The entire region was pulled in two different directions as Berlin and Warsaw tried to integrate their own sectors with national economies. Today, some traces (e.g. German concrete blockhouses) of this old interwar frontier running through the area are still visible in the landscape, although the region now operates as one unit within communist Poland.

2. Czechoslovakia

Geography was a vital factor in Czech nationalism, because this Slavic group, as the western vanguard of the Slavs, was exposed to the expansion of German-speaking peoples. Similarly, the Slovaks were thrust by geography into a strong dependence on the Hungarians. This historical difference in geographical orientation between Czechs and Slovaks was a barrier when the new state of Czechoslovakia was artificially created after the First World War (see Fig. 6.4). However, the two ethnic groups were similar in language and, in addition, the Slovaks resented earlier attempts at Magyarization. The Allies wanted to link Czechoslovakia and its ally Romania against Hungary by adding the territory of Ruthenia, inhabited by Ukrainians. The ideology of the peace-makers, then, was in part anti-Hungarian. But creating this new state across the middle of Europe was not easy. No railroads connected Bohemia-Moravia with Slovakia, and Prague – located off-center to the west – did not serve the country well as a capital. Furthermore, the Allied Powers in giving the state access to the Danube River east of Bratislava included large numbers of Hungarians, thereby providing for a future minority problem. The result was a precarious state at odds geographically with the previous imperial patterns of spatial organization. Not only did the lack of east–west railroad links cause difficulties, but also the presence of minorities – Germans, Hungarians, and Ukrainians – caused instability: in the late 1930s, the Sudeten Germans provided Hitler with the main excuse for the conquest of Czechoslovakia.

3. Yugoslavia

In the Balkans, the perception of the peace-makers was that one state incorporating the south Slavic groups would be more viable than a series of small states. As a result, Yugoslavia contains several south Slav groups, the most important being the Serbs, Croats, and Slovenes (see Fig. 6.4). The link between these groups was mainly cultural but, as in the case of Czechoslovakia, they were oriented in different directions. The Catholic Slovenes and Croats had been a part of the Austrian Empire and were more advanced economically than the Orthodox Serbs, who had been under Turkish influence for a long period. Nevertheless, the Serbs, as the major ethnic group numerically and the only one with some nineteenth-century experience as a nation-state, became dominant in the new state and exercised a strong central control from the capital at Belgrade. Actually, some degree of regional autonomy probably would have been wise, because considerable ethnic friction between eastern and western parts of the country resulted in terrorism characteristic of Balkan politics.

Strong animosity developed between Yugoslavia and Italy, again reflecting the impact of an external power on a weak Shatter Belt state (see Fig. 6.4). In 1915, the Allied Powers promised Italy major sections of the Dalmatian Coast, including ports, in return for entering the war against the Central Powers. The tradition of Italian settlement along this coast provided some basis for these promises. Since the entire hinterland of Dalmatia is Slavic, however, giving major ports and other parts of the coast to Italy represented deviation from rational geography for political purposes. Thus, when Trieste and Fiume (now Rijeka), were awarded to Italy, even though their hinterlands were now Yugoslav, the effect of drawing an international boundary between a port and its hinterland became clear. Moodie (1945: 220) in 1934 observed the results in terms of trade: 'The railway tracks of Fiume were literally grass-grown, there were only a few tramp steamers at the berths and the equipment of the quays gave every impression of disuse and neglect'. In short, Italy achieved military security in the northern Adriatic region at the cost of trade and the economic destruction of Trieste and Fiume. The designation of one or both of these ports as a 'free territory' would have made more sense geographically; in fact, Fiume was so designated after the First World War before Italian pressure forced a change.

4. Hungary

Dismembered and reduced to a small rump state, Hungary became the most bitter of the Central Powers after the First World War (see Fig. 6.4). For hundreds of years, the Hungarian nation had controlled the Pannonian basin and its mountainous rimland area. This historic pattern of geographical interdependence had much logic behind it, especially in terms of managing the rivers that originated in the highlands before reaching the basin. Nevertheless, this interdependence did not offset the Allies' ideological determination to free the three major subject nationalities of pre-1914 Hungary – Slovaks, Romanians, and Croatians – from Hungarian rule, even though this action left over 2.5 million Hungarians outside their own state. The Peace Treaty was based on national self-determination, and the nationalities were incorporated, in so far as possible, into new nation-states. Hungary itself was reduced to a country of 8 million people in which the Magyars constituted a real majority – 7.2 million. The loss of the rimland area created an imbalance, and Hungary became an agricultural state without the minerals, water power, and forest resources of the past.

These examples explain some of the ideologies behind the spatial patterns of four of the states established in Eastern Europe after the First World War – Poland, Czechoslovakia, Yugoslavia, and Hungary. In turn, these patterns were to affect the transformation of the landscape. Far from national in terms of spatial organization, these states included a variety of divisive forces such as minorities, languages, and religions; thus, they actually retained many multinational characteristics. They also faced considerable readjustment of their economies – especially transport – from an imperial framework to a national one. The four mentioned had the greatest adjustments, but certainly Romania and Albania faced similar problems (see Fig. 6.4). Romania, created in the nineteenth century by the unification of the principalities of Moldavia and Wallachia, was enlarged after 1918 by the addition of Transylvania, an area rich in resources but with physical and historical orientations toward Hungary, factors which made national cohesion difficult in the interwar years. Albania was created as a new state on the western flank of the Balkan peninsula. Although fairly homogeneous in terms of culture, its economic backwardness and isolation made national progress difficult and in the 1930s strong Italian influence developed. Finally, Bulgaria alone of all the states in Eastern Europe retained its prewar form.

Problems of economic development between the wars

The extensive changes in political spatial organization of Eastern Europe after the First World War necessitated a long period of economic and social adjustment. The primary problem involved the establishment of new, viable states from a previous imperial pattern of economic spatial organization. In the case of Poland, for example, three imperial segments had to be welded together. Unfortunately, the period of readjustment was short – only two decades separated the two world wars – and included not only reconstruction, which slowed down economic progress after 1918, but also a world-wide depression, which struck in 1929. Hence, the amount of economic progress made by 1939 was relatively small, especially in comparison with the dynamic changes that had taken place just before the First World War.

A first major weakness of the new states was the disruption of the old imperial patterns of regional specialization. Before the First World War in Austria-Hungary, Bohemian industrial products had moved to Hungary in exchange for food products. Similar regional specialization existed in the other empires, although to a lesser degree. The new boundaries, however, cut off these patterns of exchange which had made the empires viable. The new states found themselves with one-sided economies that were dependent on trade with external powers. Although Czechoslovakia could export industrial products, most of the other countries had peasant populations and could only export agricultural products and certain minerals in exchange for needed manufactured items; they also lacked capital for their own modernization.

A second weakness of the new states resulted from their peasant characteristics (summarized in Ch. 4). Except in Czechoslovakia, the peasant population (either tilling small plots or laboring on large estates) ranged from 50 per cent to 80 per cent of the total population. Modernization of agriculture remained vital, yet land reforms actually retarded economic progress. Carried through in all the countries except Poland and Hungary, these reforms indirectly reflected nationalism in the sense that they provided land to peasants for the first time, enabling them to share in the collective progress of the nation-state. The land reforms, therefore, represented strong examples of social change initiated by nationalism. Unfortunately, such wide distribution of land in fragmented parcels only slowed up the possibilities of altering the one-sided peasant economies. Unlike

Western Europe, industry, which could reduce rural overpopulation by attracting peasants, lagged. Some 50 per cent of the peasant work force could be characterized as underemployed (Berend and Ránki 1974a: 296). Furthermore, the lack of urban markets restricted the sale of farm products which would provide domestic capital to agriculture and in turn would enable modernization to occur. Thus, the cleavage between the two parts of Europe remained. Although some East European countries exported grain and livestock products, this activity actually resulted from the weaknesses of agriculture, since it represented one of the few methods of accumulating capital – the surpluses being the taxes and rents from both peasant strips and large inefficient estates.

A third weakness or barrier to economic development after the First World War was the attitude of the ruling elites toward the possible consequences of industrialization. Denitch (1978: 15–17) points out that the leaders of Eastern Europe, including even those of church and small towns, were wary of increasing the numbers of working-class people, thereby enabling the socialist and communist parties to challenge the existing social order.

In the face of an environment of new political boundaries hindering trade within Eastern Europe and of populations dominated by a conservative elite and peasant proprietors, the new states at first initiated mercantilistic policies of autarky or self-sufficiency. Tariffs were used to protect economies from outside competition. For example, the Danubian states raised tariffs to protect their own infant industries against manufacturing imports from Austria and Czechoslovakia. Finally, laws restricting the importation of foreign capital also reflected nationalistic policies. In the long run, however, these policies of economic independence failed. The lack of resources and the backwardness of the economies restricted self-sufficiency, exports of goods, and accumulation of domestic capital. As a result, the countries had to seek foreign help.

Foreign capital, therefore, began to penetrate this economic vacuum in Eastern Europe and according to Berend and Ránki (1974a: 237) had a 50 to 70 per cent of the total in financing the economies during the interwar period. These investments sought primarily to exploit raw materials, particularly bauxite in Hungary (by the British), oil in Romania (British, French, and Americans), timber in Yugoslavia (Italians), metals in Yugoslavia (British and French) and electricity in Hungary (Americans). Although presently obscured by aspects of socialist modernization, the landscape still contains relics

of this foreign financial involvement. However, this capital was not successful in generating growth in the various countries, because only a small amount was used for productive investments, e.g. for the infrastructure or transportation. Furthermore, the interest payments on use of such capital was beyond the capacities of these countries except Czechoslovakia, which had a more industrialized structure.

Of the foreign countries exploiting Eastern Europe for its raw materials, Germany was by far the most important (Berend and Ránki 1974a: Ch. 11). In the late 1930s, Nazi economic planners established a *Grossraumwirtschaft* (Extended Economic Area) in central and eastern Europe as a base for German territorial expansion. A series of bilateral treaties, which enabled the Nazis to gain needed raw materials in exchange for manufactured goods, linked this area to the German economy. The economic weakness of these states gave them little choice in becoming dependent on this external power. In a strategic sense, the *Grossraumwirtschaft* made sense to the Germans, because in a war situation supplies could not be cut off. The similarity between this region and that of Friedrich Naumann's *Mitteleuropa*, described earlier, has been made by some sources (Meyer 1946: 179). German investment in Eastern Europe continued during the Second World War and is manifested in the landscape today, an example being the alumina-aluminum plant at Ajka, Hungary (Turnock 1978: 149).

Although linked to foreign countries in a dependent situation and unable to generate much capital of their own, the East European states did make some progress in industrialization, which, like the foreign capital just discussed, left persistent traces in the landscape. While separating the relics established independently by the states and those supported by foreign capital is often difficult, the latter usually involved raw material development for export. The autarkic nature of policies for growth resulted in considerable state ownership of industry. In Poland, Berend and Ránki (1974a: 261) report that by 1939 the government ran a hundred industrial enterprises including all the armament factories, 80 per cent of the chemical industry, 40 per cent of the iron industry, and 50 per cent of other metal industries; the most apparent state intervention in Poland involved the initiation of a Central Industrial Region at the confluence of the Vistula and San Rivers. The governments of other countries such as Yugoslavia, where Bosnia became a new focus of iron and steel, also participated in economic development and ownership. In general, however, light industry ran ahead of heavy branches while the machine industry –

an important base for modernization – remained largely undeveloped.

Regional imbalance continued as the predominant geographical characteristic. The map of industry in Eastern Europe in 1914 utilized in the previous chapter can also be applied to 1939, because the concentration of economic activity in Saxony, Bohemia-Moravia, Upper Silesia, and Budapest still existed (see Fig. 5.7). The interwar developments, while altering the landscape, did not really force a change in the overall pattern. Large shifts of industrial capacity were rare, although the Polish Central Industrial District and the Yugoslav Zenica region do represent state attempts to create more viable units with less strategic exposure near the frontiers. The Romanians also initiated some expansion in Transylvania with the use of natural gas, but again this was not enough to change the basic concentration in the north and west of Eastern Europe. Thus, the strong cleavage in industrial development persisted between west and east in Europe. A table of *per capita* industrial production and national income in European countries for 1938 supports these differences.

Country	Industrial production per capita (in dollars, 1938)	National income per capita (in dollars, 1938)
Great Britain	140	378
Germany	132	337
France	76	236
Belgium	96	275 (with Lux.)
Sweden	122	367
Austria	59	179
Czechoslovakia	57	176
Hungary	26	112
Poland	21	104
Romania/Bulgaria	12(R)	68(B)

Sources: I. Svennilson, *Growth and Stagnation in the European Economy*, Geneva, 1954: 306, and *Economic Survey of Europe*, 1948: 235.

The cleavage between west and east in Europe is apparent while the gradient from north to south in Eastern Europe proper is significant.

At a different scale of generalization, however, it should be noted that regional imbalance existed within the new states created after 1918. In many cases, these regional differences corresponded to the broad one described for Eastern Europe as a whole. For example, western Poland was ahead of eastern Poland in economic development, and the same was true of Bohemia as compared to Slovakia.

Hamilton (1970a: 302, 304) shows that in 1939 Slovakian contribution to total industrial output in Czechoslovakia was only 8 per cent and that 78 per cent of Yugoslav industry in 1938 was located north of the Danube–Sava Rivers line.

Evidence in Fig. 4.7 and in the table on industry and national income demonstrates that in the interwar period the greater part of Eastern Europe was classified 'C' zone (Van Valkenburg and Huntington, 1935: 7); that only what is now East Germany and the areas of Silesia, Pomerania, and Bohemia were 'A' zone; and that a thin band of 'B' zone ran through central Poland, Moravia, western Hungary, and Slovenia. In other words, when the socialist regimes came to power after the Second World War, they faced a rather backward area of peasant economies with limited industry.

The discussion of the political environment in Eastern Europe after the First World War and of the economic changes that took place serves as a background to actual changes in the landscape itself. Much of this economic development was constrained to some degree by the new political framework. Yet the nationalistic ideology was reflected in these landscape changes as the new states tried to overcome these limitations and to create independent, viable entities. In the sections which follow, I cite examples of relics in the landscape that survive from this period.

Selected relics of interwar spatial organization

1. Capital cities

The establishment of capital cities represented one of the most obvious effects of new independent states on the landscape of Eastern Europe. These cities served as centers of spatial organization for the new states and reflected new national institutions in their public buildings. Of the seven capitals, only Tirana, Albania, was completely new. Warsaw had been a capital before the partitions and served this role in Congress Poland after 1815. Budapest had been a capital within a dual empire, while Bucharest and Sofia were centers of states created in the nineteenth century. Belgrade had been the center of the new Serbian state after 1830 and was retained as the capital of the Yugoslav territory created after the First World War. Finally, Prague had served as the capital of a kingdom within both German and Austrian Empires and on one occasion became an imperial capital.

The population growth of these cities as shown in the table illustrates the impact of full independence after 1918. These increases are remarkable considering that only a 20–30-year-span was involved and included many problems of reconstruction and economic dislocation.

Warsaw	820 180 (1919)	1 265 700 (1938, est.)
Prague	616 631 (1910)	922 284 (1947)
Budapest	880 371 (1910)	1 115 877 (1939)
Bucharest	345 628 (1917)	648 162 (1939)
Belgrade	158 378 (1911)	388 246 (1948)
Sofia	102 812 (1910)	434 888 (1947, est.)
Tirana	12 000 (1918, est,)	61 000 (1942)

As might be expected, the greatest relative increases occurred in the Balkan capitals where the lengthy Turkish occupation had allowed for little urban development up to that time. If one goes back to the actual dates of independence, the urban growth is even more impressive; for example, Sofia grew from a small town of 18 000 in 1878 to a city of over 400 000 by 1945, and Belgrade, although the capital of a semi-independent Serbia in the nineteenth century, doubled in size between 1910 and 1945 as the capital not only of the Serbs but of other south Slav groups as well. Bucharest also benefited as the capital of an enlarged country rather than of the two principalities of Wallachia and Moldavia. In the northern countries, the absolute increases were also great, as Budapest, for example, absorbed large numbers of Magyars, who returned from provincial cities that became parts of new states.

The landscape of capital cities in particular is composed of a variety of elements. I have pointed out in earlier chapters that one can recognize contributions made to a city like Prague by different segments of society, i.e. by German colonists in the old town, by feudal lords in the palaces of the Malá Strana, and by imperial leaders in the Hradčany castle. Yet a fourth urban element just as apparent and often more ubiquitous than the others is the national one. Although all these elements of the pre-1945 urban landscape of capital cities in Eastern Europe may be overshadowed by the more recent socialist changes, the 'national' landscape nevertheless remains an important component. The Balkans most notably reflect this element, for the successful independence movements against the

235

Turks in the nineteenth and early twentieth centuries represented the first real urban population growth and modernization. The transformation of Sofia is a good example of such modernization, reflecting the social change that was taking place in this newly formed state. The 'national' landscape includes not only relics that symbolize new independence like a parliament building or a national theater, but also office buildings and residential or industrial areas. Although the events of the Second World War, resulted in damage or destruction of certain 'national' relics, many have been restored in their original form.

Table 6.1 classifies some of the more important 'national' elements in the landscape of six East European capitals; two capitals are excluded: Tirana, because recent data are restricted although one report states that royal buildings of King Zog still remain (Biber 1980: 543); and Berlin, because it essentially evolved as an imperial capital. Although strict comparison between the relics is difficult, the table itself is revealing. Two types of 'national' form appear – pre-nationalism and post-independence. The first includes the older relics, like a palace which originated before nationalism became an important process in Eastern Europe, but which represent to the people a symbol of medieval power by a nation. This type is found in the northern states of Poland, Bohemia, and Hungary, where royal castles and even cathedrals, while reflecting multinational spatial organization, also illustrate images of national culture from the past. A second type of 'national' form in the capital city – the one designed after independence – includes all the functions that a nation feels must be represented as a collective expression of national culture: 'national' assemblies, theaters, concert halls, operas, museums, art galleries, libraries, and monuments. Many of these buildings are characterized by a heavy Neo-Classic style of architecture and do not necessarily reflect the particular culture of the country. These forms represent degrees of social change that occurred in these countries as a result of nationalism. I have included some of them in the table as examples.

Using Belgrade as the national capital of Yugoslavia is difficult because the city actually evolved in the nineteenth century as a Serbian capital; even after 1918, when it became the capital of the south Slav state, the other nations, especially the Croats, did not view it as such. Certainly, the royal palace and cathedral are Serbian, while the parliament building, national theater, museum, and university all had their origins in the Serbian state of the nineteenth century;

Photo 6.6 The Yugoslav monument to the unknown soldier, located on the Avala hill south of Belgrade, was one of the first created to show the unity of the south Slav groups making up this multinational state.

only the Avala monument to the unknown soldier seems truly national in a Yugoslav sense. In this memorial, located on a hill south of Belgrade, an attempt is made to symbolize in statuary the different ethnic groups making up the state (see Photo 6.6).

Sofia, the Bulgarian capital, is of interest because certain relics of the national period still illustrate the close ties of this country to Russia. The latter power played a strong role in the liberation of the nation from the Turks in the 1870s, and the Bulgarian people have not forgotten it. This Russian–Bulgarian link was first symbolized in the monuments at Šipka in the Balkan Mountains, where a crucial battle took place in 1877. At the base of the mountains stands the Memorial Church with its golden domes (see Photo 6.3), while on Mount Stoletov a memorial commemorates the Russian soldiers who were killed. Later, as Sofia became a national capital, the Bulgarians perpetuated this Russian connection by several forms that remain today: (1) the large equestrian statues of Alexander II (the liberator),

Table 6.1 Relics of nationalism in capital cities

	Poland	Czechoslovakia	Hungary	Romania	Bulgaria	Yugoslavia (Serbian)
Palace	Royal (1300s)	Royal (10th century on)	Royal (15th century)	Royal (1930–1937)	Royal (1878–1900)	Royal (White) (1929)
Cathedral	St John's (1300s)	St Vitus (13th century on)	Coronation (13th century)	Church of Patriarchate (1654–1658)	Alexander Nevski (1904–1912)	Orthodox (1837–1845)
Square and Old Town	Old Town Square (Rynek Starego Miasta)	Old Town Square (Staroměstké náměstí)	Medieval market place (Dísz tér)	Union Square (Piaţa Unirii)	National Assembly Square	Terazije Square
Boulevard	Krakowskie Przedmieście-Nowy Swiat	Wenceslas Square (Václavské náměstí)	Andrássy Ave. (later Népköztársaság)	Calea Victoriei	Ruski	Kralja Alexandra (later Bulevar Revolucije)
Parliament	Sejm (1851–1853) (1925–1928)	National Assembly (1930–1934)	Parliament (1885–1902)	National Assembly (1907)	National Assembly (1884–1928)	Parliament (1907–1918)
Theater	Grand (1825–1833)	National (1880s)	National (1875)	Athenaeum (1886–1888) (old National Theat. destroyed)	National (1923–1929)	National (1868–1870) (1920s)
Museum	National (1862) (1926–1938)	National (1885–1890)	National (1837–1847)	Folk Art (1905)	Natural History (1889)	National (1902–1903)

Park	Łazienki (1764–1780)	Stromovka (15th century)	City Park (Városliget) (1797)	Liberty Park (1904–1916)	Freedom (1900–1940)	Kalemegdan Fortress (1723–1736) (park–1868)
Govt. Office	School of Planning and Statistics (1925–1926)	Municipal Transp. Enterprise (1927)	Nat'l. Bank (1905)	Post Office (1900)	Nat'l. Bank (1939)	Nat'l. Bank (1889)
University	Warsaw (1818)	Carolinum (1348)	Eötvös Lorand (1898–1900)	Bucharest (1856–1869)	Sofia (1934–1944)	Belgrade (1863)
Hotel	Bristol (1899–1901)	Alcron	Duna	Athénée Palace	Bulgaria	—
Monument	Sigismund (1644) (later changes)	National Memorial on Žižkov Height (1929–1932)	Millenary Mem. (1896–1929)	Arch of Triumph (1935–1936)	Liberators' Monument (1907)	Avala (1934)

in Liberator's Square in front of the National Assembly; (2) the Alexander Nevski Cathedral, named after the patron saint of Russia and dedicated to the liberating czar (see Photo 6.7); and (3) the Russian monument erected in 1882 on the spot where the Ottoman troops in Sofia retreated. In no other East European country does one find so many pre-1945 monuments to Russia in the landscape. In contrast to these other countries, therefore, the Bulgarian landscape reflects a nationalism that is intermixed with a strain of Russian paternalism.

On the other hand, the Polish brand of nationalism has anti-Russian overtones. Despite the proximity of these two states, almost no pre-1945 symbols of any cultural link to the Soviet Union appear in the Polish scene; even the postwar landscape includes fewer monuments and slogans to Russian–Polish friendship than in East Germany or Czechoslovakia. In Warsaw, the Palace of Culture, a 'Stalinesque' skyscraper erected as a gift to the Poles by the Russians, is considered an architectural and cultural intrusion, while the relic of the citadel, built in the nineteenth century to repress the Poles, is a grim reminder of past differences between the two states. Perhaps the most nationalistic symbol of Warsaw is the Old Town (Rynek Starego Miasta), whose reconstruction after almost total destruction in the Second World War was a decision backed by the masses, including the Communist Party.

In all of the capital cities of Eastern Europe, many residential areas date from the national period and represent an attempt to develop inexpensive but adequate housing for an expanding middle class. Such housing estates were socially and architecturally progressive. One of the best examples is the Żoliborz WSM Housing Estate, built in the northern part of Warsaw during the interwar period. The *Atlas of Warsaw's Architecture* (1978: 232) reports that this estate is one of the most significant achievements of functional residential architecture constructed in this particular period. Certainly its simplicity and elegance are still recognizable today; I personally enjoy the crescent of apartments on Suzina Street (see Photo 6.8).

Finally, one recognizes in capital cities, and other large cities of Eastern Europe, hotels that date from the interwar period, e.g. the

Photo 6.7 Central Sofia contains national monuments of Bulgaria: on the right, the National Assembly and, in the background, the national cathedral of Alexander Nevski.

Photo 6.8 This building on Suzina Street in the Żoliborz district of Warsaw, Poland, exemplifies the new residential architecture built between the wars.

Bristol in Warsaw and the Athénée Palace in Bucharest. Even Tirana has the Dajti. Under socialism, new hotels have risen, but, surprisingly, the old ones still remain popular with nationals and foreign travelers who have long memories.

2. A fragmented country: the case of Poland

The major problem of Poland after the First World War concerned welding together three partition areas – German, Russian, and Austrian – that had been oriented toward different capital cities. In all of these areas, minority groups existed to hinder unification. In addition, Poland faced certain other problems: the loss of the Russian market to the east, as the Soviets embarked on a planned economy; the contraction of older industries like coal and metal working that had developed within imperial frameworks; and a small domestic market. Despite these factors, the country made remarkable economic progress between the wars in terms of industrialization.

The most significant aspect of the new pattern of spatial organization, and one that had great effects on the landscape, was development of a new north–south axis from Upper Silesia to the Baltic Sea via the Polish corridor (see Fig. 6.4). This axis was a direct result of the corridor to the sea created by the Allied treaty powers. Because of uncertainties regarding the use of the free city of Danzig, the Poles undertook the construction of a rival port, called Gdynia, at the site of a small village on the coast to the north; the city increased in population from 1300 in 1921 to 120 000 in 1939 and eventually became a complete port in every sense, ranking among the top Baltic ports and sharing Poland's trade with Danzig. After the completion of the north–south railroad connection with Upper Silesia, Gdynia became an important coal export outlet. This city is perhaps the most significant national element created in the interwar economic landscape of Poland and, according to Zweig (1944: 95), was regarded by the people as a symbol of their drive to the sea and economic independence. It is important to note that two spatial characteristics of the new Poland created by the treaty powers after the First World War were involved in the new axis. The corridor to the sea made it possible, but the weakness of a divided Upper Silesia helped make it necessary.

Supplementing the port of Gdynia as a symbol of Polish nationalism was the program of national planning which focused on the central part of the country. The key element was the creation of

an entirely new Central Industrial District (CID) in a triangle at the confluence of the Vistula and San Rivers. Although the Second World War interrupted construction, the results of remarkable progress between 1936 and 1939 are still visible in the landscape. To the Polish nation in the 1930s, the project represented significant national progress in addition to social change. The location of the District was not accidental, but had been planned carefully. In the first place, according to Taylor (1952: 83), Poland felt that more regional balance was needed, since much of its industry was located west of the Vistula – in Silesia, Częstochowa, Łódź, and Warsaw. Second, the CID was located away from the more vulnerable cities of Upper Silesia on the German frontier. Third, as a frontier region between Russia and Austria, the area had been neglected in terms of development but had a large surplus of agricultural labor; the plan, therefore, presented opportunities not only to raise the economic level of the district but also to utilize the labor. Other advantages included a central location accessible to deposits of coal, oil, and natural gas plus raw materials like copper, phosphorus, and low-grade iron; the nearby Vistula River represented an alternative means of transport. Included among the individual projects completed under this plan and which remain visible today are the large reservoir at Roznów on the Dunajec River, state armament factories at Kraśnik, and the state steel works at Stalowa Wola. The Central Industrial District represents a successful example of large-scale economic planning until that development was terminated by the Second World War.

Other relics remain from Polish economic progress made during the interwar period, e.g. the famous nitrate fertilizer plant at Chorzów. Although founded by the Germans during the First World War, the plant in reality developed after 1918 under the management of Professor Mościcki, who became president of the Republic in 1926 (Taylor 1952: 87–8). This plant provided a link between industry and agriculture and led to an expansion of the chemical industry in national Poland.

Another type of relic, the Polish national park system, dates from the period of development between the wars. Other countries of Eastern Europe have such systems, but Poland's is particularly noteworthy, because it originated with Białowieza forest from which a national park developed in 1921 (Szafer 1938). For centuries, this large forest had been the hereditary property of the Polish crown and included hunting quarters for the reigning king; in the nineteenth

Photo 6.9   Created in 1921, Białowieza was an early national park of Poland. Located next to the present Russian border, the park contains virgin forest and a herd of European bison.

century, the forest became a part of Russia but was returned to Poland after the First World War. In addition to its primeval character, the park is noted for its herd of European bison – the only one of its kind on the continent (see Photo 6.9). Although nearly exterminated in both wars, the herd is increasing in numbers. Because of the post-1945 boundary alignment, part of Białowieza forest now lies in the Soviet Union. In the solitude of this centuries-old forest, one senses the past, especially the hunting activities that were such an important function of the imperial period.

3. A town divided by a national frontier

One of the most noteworthy geographical disputes arising from the peace treaties of the First World War concerned the territory of Teschen, which had been a part of the Austrian Empire. The area held great industrial importance for the Hapsburgs because of the presence of coking coal and the existence of one of the largest iron and steel complexes in the empire at Trzynietz (Třinec). Since the area was inhabited by both Czech and Polish populations, the Allied Powers held a plebiscite to decide its future status. The result gave the western part containing the greater part of the coal and industry to Czechoslovakia (Bowman 1928: 415–16). The new frontiers split the major city of Teschen along the small river flowing through it, thereby creating two cities which after 1920 faced each other across the frontier: Český Těšín, a Czech town, to the west; and Cieszyn, a Polish town, to the east. The latter contains the primary core of the old municipality.

4. A national center of heavy industry

A few miles north of Sarajevo, the capital of the central Yugoslav province of Bosnia, a large integrated iron and steel plant dominates the landscape near the city of Zenica. This complex exemplifies the role of a state in developing an industrial site for strategic reasons. The Yugoslav metallurgical concerns inherited from the Austro–Hungarian Empire after 1918 were situated in a vulnerable location on the northwestern margins of the new state and at a considerable distance from sources of iron at Ljubija and Vareš (in Bosnia); they were also poorly placed for distributing their products throughout the country. However, according to Hamilton (1964: 55–7), not until the late 1930s, when Nazi Germany posed a threat, did the Yugoslav government decide to move the focus of the iron and steel industry from the more exposed northwest to the central part of the country at Zenica. This location close to the sources of iron and coal maximized the strategic, raw material, and distribution factors. After 1937, the state-controlled Jugoslovenski Čelik a.d. firm with headquarters in Sarajevo was formed. The small, existing steel mills were modernized and enlarged, surprisingly through the aid of the Krupp Steel Company of Essen, Germany, with the aim of fulfilling most of Yugoslavia's requirements for raw steel. This complex, although now the primary center of iron and steel under the communist government, remains in the landscape as a symbol of early national planning.

5. Resources under foreign control

Driving south along the upper Ibar River in the mountains of southern Serbia, an enormous metallurgical complex near the town of Zvečan suddenly looms into view (see Photo 6.10). This complex dates from the 1930s, when an Anglo–American company opened a lead and zinc mine at nearby Trepča and constructed a concentrating plant and smelter at Zvečan on a main north–south rail line of Yugoslavia. The crushed ore was (and still is) sent from mine to smelter by aerial cable. Until the Zvečan smelter was opened in 1939, the lead and zinc concentrates were exported via Salonika to Belgium. After the Second World War, the complex was nationalized by the Yugoslav government. Nevertheless, it serves as a symbol of international ownership and development of certain natural resources in Eastern Europe that took place between the wars. Allcock (1977: 553–7) feels that this complex illustrates the satellite nature of Yugoslav economic development under which ores left the country and, as a consequence, domestic industry failed to evolve. Also in Yugoslavia, the French development of the Bor copper mines is another example of this type of dependency upon Western Europe: oil production in Romania and Hungary illustrates foreign (American) control of resources in these two countries.

6. Impacted environments

In the heart of Romanian Transylvania along the Tirnava Mare River, a traveler cannot avoid one of the most polluted industrial sites in Eastern Europe. Located just west of the well-preserved old Saxon town of Mediasch (Mediaş), the city of Copşa Mică developed in the interwar period as a chemical center based on newly opened methane gas deposits. The earliest products were carbon-black and ammonia, used for producing tires and fertilizer, respectively. Since that time, chemical production has expanded and diversified, but the control of air pollution has not kept pace. Copşa Mică symbolizes not only early chemical industrial expansion after the First World War, but also the seeds of environmental problems based on a new source of energy – natural gas. Evidently the persistence of this pollution illustrates that the socialist desire for production, like that of the capitalist, frequently overrides the environmental concern.

The effects of humans on the physical environment are equally impressive today in East Germany where open-pit mining of lignite coal has transformed the landscape of the Halle and Cottbus areas. As mentioned in Chapter 4, central Germany in the late nineteenth

Photo 6.10   The large lead smelter at Zvečan near Trepča in southern Serbia, Yugoslavia, originated from early foreign ownership and exploitation of national resources.

century was an important early center of the chemical industry based on both lignite and salt (rock and potassium). Most of the lignite was mined from shafts, but in the interwar period great open pits were developed west of the Elbe River in a large area around Leipzig. Today, many relics of these pits exist as exemplified by the landscape near Leuna (see Fig. 6.5). Leuna itself represents one of the largest chemical complexes in the world. Exploitation of brown coal in the west Elbe field continued after the Second World War but the greatest expansion has taken place east of the Elbe in the Cottbus district. Between the wars, lignite was used in the production of chemicals including sulphuric acid, alkalis, nitrogen compounds like ammonia, and coal tar products including dyestuffs and photographic materials. (The concentration of factories in this district naturally made it a chief target of Allied bombers during the Second World War.) In addition, much of the lignite also was (and is) used for the production of elec-

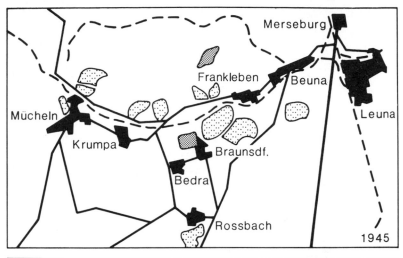

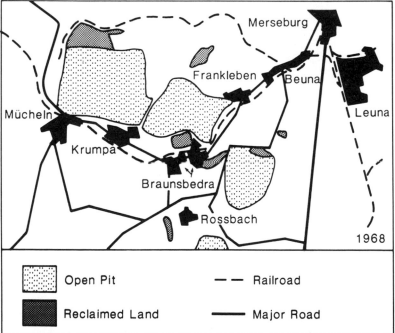

Fig. 6.5 The major areas in 1945 (top) and 1968 (bottom) of German brown coal mining west of Leipzig. Major changes include the expansion of open pits and attempts at reclamation. (Source: *Atlas der Erdkunde*, VEB Hermann Haack, Leipzig, 1978, p. 11).

tric power, which has contributed to the air pollution of the Halle district.

7. An international industrial center

In Moravia, the town of Zlin, now called Gottwaldov to reflect the name of a postwar communist leader, has been expanded and altered considerably under the communist government. It is best known as the interwar center of the famous Bat'a international shoe empire. As one of the most successful entrepreneurs in Czechoslovakia before the Second World War, Tomáš Bat'a built up a modern industrial complex utilizing assembly line techniques and employing 65 000 employees, some of whom were located in foreign branch plants. Gradually the name Bat'a became a symbol throughout the world not only for shoes but also for a new approach of combining the responsibility of the craftsmen, inherent in many Czechs, with the speed and cheapness of production on a vast scale (Wanklyn 1954: 284). Even today relics of the system persist, e.g. in Gottwaldov as well as in Yugoslavia, where the old Bat'a factory at Borovo in Croatia is now the center of the state-controlled shoe industry and where the name 'Borovo' serves as the state symbol of footwear.

8. Past national events

Certain places in Eastern Europe stand as symbols of past history and glory to individual cultures in the area. In many cases, the historical events associated with these places occurred before the relatively recent period of nation-state consciousness. Later, with the consolidation of nation-states after the First World War, the places (often battlefields) became national shrines, e.g. Kosovo, the 'field of blackbirds', a plain along the Ibar River, where the Serbians were defeated by the Turks in 1389. The battle marked the beginning of Ottoman tyranny in Serbia and remains as an important date in the history of this culture. However, no actual relic from this battle remains in the landscape, a contrast with Poland's most famous national place – the monastery of Jasna Góra at Częstochawa, where the Swedish invaders were repulsed in 1655. Historically, the Polish victory is steeped in the legend of the Black Madonna, a portrait which tradition says was painted by Saint Luke the Evangelist and which is kept at the monastery. The abbot supposedly held the portrait of the Black Madonna aloft before the advancing Swedes, who turned and ran. Ever since, the monastery has been the scene of annual pilgrimages

by Catholics, and the Black Madonna has become a symbol of Polish nationalism. Lech Walesa, leader of the Solidarity movement, in 1981 wore a representation of it as a badge.

9. Statues of national leaders

The role of nationalism in Eastern Europe today conflicts with the international ideology of Marxism–Leninism, which discourages separate roads to communism; the national feelings of East European cultures, however, are difficult to repress and are reflected, for example, in the persistence of statues of former cultural leaders from both the national and imperial periods. Seemingly, the earlier the national figures the more exposure they have today. Statues of famous medieval figures are common, e.g. Saint Stephen of Hungary. Petöfi Square in Budapest, which includes a statue of this famous poet who was connected with the revolutionary events of the mid-nineteenth century, was an important site in the 1956 Hungarian revolution against the communist regime. In general, national leaders of the interwar period receive little exposure in the form of statues, e.g. Tomáš Masaryk, first president of the Republic of Czechoslovakia after the First World War. In 1959, I saw a statue of him in the village of Hodvodonica south of Liberec; I wonder if it is still there.

10. Peasant strips and villages

Peasant land holdings as relics in the landscape of Eastern Europe are the product of several processes – German colonization, feudalism, imperialism, and nationalism. However, the evaluation of most writers is that these holdings reflect the long feudal era in which the lords dominated the peasants' lives. The early peasant uprisings, which occurred from time to time, represented protests against obligations to the lords and were not national movements. I deal with the peasant strip as a landscape relic, therefore, in Chapter 4. However, in the modern era, the effects of nationalism and national states did have an effect on peasant status and on the landscape; therefore, it is important to illustrate how the peasant period overlapped the feudal and national eras.

Serfdom actually disappeared in Western Europe by the sixteenth century, but certain obligations of peasant-tenant to lord remained. What is more, the peasant had no political rights and occupied the lowest rung on the social ladder. Not until 1789 in France did the

first complete emancipation sweep away all the restrictions and obligations of the peasant class. These changes reflect the liberal ideas that were being diffused throughout Europe at that time. Although such reforms were successful in Western Europe, they were blocked by the absolute states of Eastern Europe, where reform in the nineteenth century was limited to emancipation. Most freed peasants gained no land and, of necessity, continued to work on the estates as laborers. Mitrany (1951: 109–10) feels that the land reforms after the First World War reflected the growing importance of the state in economic and social affairs, a trend that could be called nationalistic. Political peasant parties, led after the First World War by people like Švehla, Witos, Stambulisky, and Radić, grew in importance and helped to promote these reforms. Overall, such reforms, which took place in every country but Poland and Hungary, represented important social change for the peasant class in Eastern Europe: it meant that widespread capitalism was introduced into the countryside through peasant land ownership, enlarged markets, and improved methods. Such change was important socially even if it did not necessarily mean a great improvement in agricultural production. As pointed out in Chapter 4, these reforms were laid out on the feudal lines of the three-field strip system which, because of its fragmentation, prevented capital inputs and increased efficiency. In addition, the lack of industrial development in the cities prevented rural–urban migration and reduction of large rural surpluses of population.

Thus, by the outbreak of war in 1939, peasant strips existed as the usual land tenure system in five of the countries of Eastern Europe (see Photo 3.1). In the other countries – Poland, Hungary, and the area that is now East Germany – large estates prevailed. However, after 1945, the new Marxist regimes in an attempt to curry favor with the large peasant class distributed land to all peasants in the eight countries. For a short period in the late 1940s, then, the small, narrow strips dominated the entire East European landscape. However, when the communist state governments started collectivization, the landscape began to change into large fields, a process discussed in the next chapter. Only Poland and Yugoslavia successfully resisted collectivization, and today strips in these two countries survive as landscape relics of a field system introduced by German colonists in the Middle Ages, perpetuated under feudalism, and finally liberalized in the nationalist era.

251

Supplementing the strip field is the peasant village. As Blum (1960: 22) so vividly points out, the village has a timeless quality, and its face seems to change very little. In isolated parts of Eastern Europe, this impression may be valid, for peasant folk traditions remain in periodic festivals, but in more accessible places the village is changing under the influences of communist modernization, especially through the daily commuting of peasant-workers to the cities and towns. This phenomenon is discussed in the next chapter.

11. Other changes in the landscape

The previous sections serve to illustrate the diversity of changes in the East European landscape that resulted from the establishment of new national states. Many others could be listed. For example, those states with access to the sea had to readjust their economic patterns of spatial organization to accommodate port cities that had been less important during the imperial period. In Yugoslavia, no real port existed because Fiume (now Rijeka), the old imperial port for Hungary, had been given to Italy as part of the peace settlement, and its suburb, Sušak, which became Yugoslav, was too exposed strategically to be developed. A decision was made, therefore, to develop the port of Split, located farther south on the Adriatic coast. With the help of a new railroad line to Zagreb and subsidized rates for merchandise on the state railways, Split grew until by 1938 it handled more goods than Sušak (Geographical Handbook, *Yugoslavia*, Vol. III 1945: 330). Other national ports like Varna in Bulgaria, Constanţa in Romania, and even Durrës in Albania assumed different roles and became changed cities as parts of national states.

Not overlooked is the effect on the East European landscape of the Nazi period of the Second World War, when German occupation was complete, a reflection once again of multinationalism as a process. Destruction marked the overall impress of German presence, especially during the retreat before the Red Army. Scars throughout the region attest to the ruthless policies of the Nazis, e.g. concentration camps like Auschwitz in southern Poland and the Czechoslovakian town of Lidice – completely wiped out in a reprisal. Then there is the relic of a bunker at Rastenburg in East Prussia (now Kętrzyn in Poland), where an attempt was made in 1944 to assassinate Adolph Hitler.

Summary

This chapter includes a discussion of nationalism, a fourth historical process involved in forming the palimpsest of landscapes in Eastern Europe before the modern socialist era. The process of nationalism followed but also overlapped with earlier processes of German colonization, feudalism, and multinationalism. Nationalism essentially represents a recent process in Eastern Europe whereby seven new nation-states evolved from a multinational framework of four empires. However, the creation and progress of these national states were hindered not only by the antagonism existing among the subject nationalities that were seeking independence but also by the feudalistic conditions that persisted in most parts of the area. Unlike Western Europe, where nations corresponded fairly well to states when nationalism prevailed, the East European nations had no such ready-made political framework. New states had to be created out of an imperial framework and most states were forced to include sizable ethnic minorities. In some cases, an ideology existed of using a multinational model of the past, e.g. Poland. The ideology of nationalism in Eastern Europe, therefore, often had intolerant and inegalitarian overtones. Finally, the nationalism of this area was much affected by the attitudes of the Great Powers who, in creating new states after the First World War, deviated from rational geographic solutions to satisfy political aims.

The creation of nation-states, begun in the nineteenth century and continued after the First World War, affected the landscape accordingly. Examples of Poland and Bulgaria are used to illustrate the nineteenth-century period – national planning in Congress Poland and the national revival in Bulgaria. Relics in the landscape in the textile city of Łódź, Poland, and Plovdiv or Tryavna in Bulgaria illustrate these national movements. In the interwar period, all the new states had difficulty developing national patterns of spatial organization from previous imperial frameworks. Many of the important existing landscape relics from this period represent attempts to create viable political and economic entities, especially during a period of reconstruction followed by a world-wide depression. Capital cities certainly reflect the most persistent national changes. However, other relics like new ports (Gdynia and Split), foreign investment (Trepča), divided towns (Teschen), strategic centers of heavy industry (Zenica), an international industrial town (Zlín), peasant land reforms, and statues of national leaders also illus-

trate not only the process but also the aspects of social change. Although these relics tell a story of considerable economic progress by 1939, Eastern Europe still remained generally backward in comparison to the western half of the continent. After 1945, socialism became the dominant force in the area. The effects of this new process on spatial organization and the landscape are discussed in the next chapter.

7

Landscapes of socialism

The previous chapters have focused on four historical processes affecting spatial organization – German medieval colonization, feudalism, multinationalism, and nationalism – which in influencing social change in Eastern Europe have left their marks on the landscape. A main hypothesis has been that certain relics of the 'environment' created by these processes persist in the landscape and can be analyzed geographically. These four aspects of the historical landscape, interwoven with each other, collectively form what Wagner (1972: 102) has called a palimpsest of recorded culture on the ground.

The latest process affecting spatial organization must be analyzed to complete the historical evolution of the East European landscape. Since 1945, the area has been dominated by a different political system and ideology, that of communism, or at this stage, socialism. This form of political, economic, and social organization was diffused into the area from the Soviet Union after the Second World War and was superimposed on national states as well as on a portion of prewar Germany. Thus, the persistent pattern of external influence from outside the region, a characteristic of the Shatter Belt throughout its history, has continued. However, the fragmentation of Eastern Europe between national states has intruded, for many of them – most notably Yugoslavia, Romania, and Albania – follow different roads to socialism. Nevertheless, a certain break with the past is apparent. Despite intermittent opposition to communism in certain countries since the Second World War, the area in general has exhibited a degree of stability that seems strangely at odds with the past. During this time, remarkable progress in the modernization of the economies has occurred. Indeed, a theme of this chapter is that

255

stability and modernization since 1945 represent perhaps the most apparent contrasts with the past. Everywhere in the East European landscape one sees evidence of economic and social change. An important question involves ascertaining the connection between this modernization and the socialist ideology that accompanies it.

The purpose of this chapter, then, is to examine the changes that socialism has made in the landscape of Eastern Europe and some of the factors that explain these changes. In contrast to past chapters where I deal only with relics from past periods, I now confront a current landscape that is in a process of transformation by socialist governments. Before analyzing these changes, however, I must first examine the 'socialist landscape' in general, the political changes in spatial organization that took place after the Second World War, and the nature of socialism including the roles of planning and ideology.

A socialist landscape?

Anyone visiting Eastern Europe today is generally impressed with the changes that have occurred since 1945. In the countryside, the large fields with machinery represent the communists' attempt to develop a rational, mechanized agriculture. Although the peasant village of the past remains ubiquitous, it has been transformed and currently exhibits not only an increased diversity of services, but also contacts with nearby cities through the commuting of peasant families who work in factories. The cities, too, have vastly changed to include factories, neighborhood residential areas of apartment blocks, and different collective institutions. A number of entirely new towns have appeared. Altogether, one is tempted to call this new landscape 'socialist' or at least 'socialized'.

These changes pose questions for the geographer, especially a student of the landscape: is the spatial organization introduced by the communists in these countries different from that found in capitalist societies? If so, what role does the socialist ideology play? Can we call this landscape socialist? Such questions are difficult to answer. Hamilton (1971a) and French and Hamilton (1979: 3) provide some support to the view that socialism does have certain specific effects on the landscape. They not only isolate certain principles of industrial location that they feel are important in guiding Marxist decision-making, but also support (with certain qualifications) the idea of a special form for the socialist city. Kansky (1976) in his study of urbanism in Czechoslovakia also feels that the Communist Party has

played a unique role in manipulating population and settlement patterns, especially through central control of housing policies. On the other hand, Turnock (1978: 10–11), who has compiled a thorough study of industrialization in Eastern Europe, takes the view that the economic geography of this area is unlikely to have any intrinsically 'socialist' content and that western geographers have substituted an ideological explanation for locational trends which, given modern technology, are a natural outcome of economic, political, and strategic forces.

My own position in this controversy has changed somewhat. My original concept of a possible existence of a 'socialist landscape' was criticized as being incapable of empirical proof. A modified version given at an international conference on East European geography in Austin, Texas (Rugg: 1971), created a discussion that produced both pro and con support. At present, I still see elements of the socialist ideology in the landscape, but these are intermingled with other ideologies discussed earlier in this book. However, I feel that the point is missed by stressing an element of uniqueness which can probably never be isolated. Certainly, it is not suggested that recent modernization in Eastern Europe (or the Soviet Union) could not have occurred in another type of political system. In fact, progress might very well have been greater. But the real point, I feel, is that a Marxist environment exists and scholars must deal with it. My aim in this chapter is to discern the spatial effects of the communist approach to modernization in Eastern Europe. I do not try to show that this approach is unique or different but merely that it is there and helps to explain the landscape patterns. Obviously, the central control and planning, which exist to varying degrees in the region, provide a strong input that is less apparent in the West, even in the welfare economies of Western Europe.

Changes in political spatial organization after the Second World War

Soviet influence over Eastern Europe after the Second World War caused significant changes in political spatial organization. With the support of the Red Army, communist regimes established governments in seven of the prewar national states and a portion of Germany. The Soviet Union accordingly controlled an area from the Elbe River to the Pacific Ocean. H. J. Mackinder's warning in 1904 of the danger to the world balance of power from a strong state or

group of states controlling the Heartland of Eurasia finally seemed to have materialized. The Iron Curtain, a forbidding landscape of walls, electrified fences, mined strips, and armed observation towers unique in world history, descended over Europe, separating West from East.

An entirely new political environment developed in Eastern Europe as a result of Soviet influence. This environment is reflected in three different political changes that formed a geographic background for socialist change of the landscape: ethnic homogeneity, the partition of Germany, and a new administrative framework. Each is discussed briefly.

The eight states of Eastern Europe and their some 135 million people today are much more ethnically homogeneous than they were before 1939. Although the fragmentation of some states among major culture groups continues, the old Shatter Belt characteristic of minorities has been considerably reduced as a result of two changes: removal of the German minority and annexation of territory by the Soviet Union. An estimated 13 million Germans moved out of Eastern Europe, either voluntarily during the war or involuntarily under the Potsdam agreements. Even though many of these Germans were *Volksdeutsche* (ethnic Germans), who had lived in the area peacefully for hundreds of years, their removal as an ethnic minority group was deemed necessary despite the human costs. Today only a half million Germans remain in the entire area of Eastern Europe, with half of them in Romania, especially in the old towns of medieval colonization in Transylvania (Siebenbürgen). The Soviet annexation of territory – eastern Poland, Ruthenia (from Czechoslovakia), and northern Bukovina and Bessarabia (from Romania) – created a second basis for greater ethnic homogeneity. The Yalta agreement of 1944 provided for these annexations at the conclusion of the war, and even though a high percentage of the population in the affected areas spoke languages related to Russian, not all necessarily desired incorporation within the Soviet Union.

Thus, with the elimination of Germans and Russian-related groups together with the Nazi extermination of some 4 million Jews, the ethnic map of Eastern Europe after 1945 was not as fragmented as in pre-Second World War days. Kosiński (1969: 393, 397) shows that, although minorities still exist in the area, the number as of 1960 had been reduced from 34 million to 7 million; in terms of the total population of Eastern Europe, this amounts to a decline from 36 per cent to 7 per cent.

A second important political change in Eastern Europe after the Second World War involved the partition of Germany. This alteration of the map was part of a Soviet plan of communist expansion which the Allied powers did not perceive until too late. Although provisions had been made for the 'temporary' occupation of a defeated Germany, the Allies relied on future withdrawal of all forces and the establishment of a democratic state. Instead, the Soviet Union presented the Allies with a *fait accompli* – the creation of a belt of communist states including a Russian occupation zone in Germany. The goal of the Russians lay not only in dividing Germany so as to reduce its future influence, but also in establishing a viable communist state of Poland. Since the Soviet Union had acquired the eastern part of prewar Poland with large numbers of Belorussians and Ukrainians, Poland under the Yalta agreement was to be compensated in the west by territory in Brandenburg, Pomerania, and Silesia vacated by the expelled Germans. Poland, therefore, was moved westward after the Second World War, becoming ethnically homogeneous and gaining a sizable Baltic coastline (see Fig. 1.1).

The Soviet plan to partition Germany and eventually to transform the occupation zone into a communist state was resisted for years by the Allied powers, who still hoped for reunification of the country. This Allied position was supported by their occupation rights in West Berlin, which existed as an enclave behind the Iron Curtain in the Soviet Zone. As long as West Berlin remained tied to the West, the Soviet Union found it difficult to establish a separate communist state; therefore, the Russians tested the Allied commitment to the city in 1948 by a blockade, which finally was broken by the famous Berlin air lift. East German refugees continued to find a route to the west through Berlin, but this was closed in 1961 when the 'Wall' became an 'Iron Curtain' through the middle of the city. Eventually, both West and East Germany became independent states – oriented to different ideologies. One nation has formally become two states, while West Berlin remains as a relic of the Cold War, an enclave within East Germany. The landscape of Berlin today reflects a divided city with the western portion limited in terms of contact not only with East Germany and East Berlin, but also with West Germany.

The communist framework of administration formed the third political change in Eastern Europe that provided a new geographic background for landscape change. This framework reflected the need to facilitate economic planning as well as attempts to reduce regional

traditions from the past. In East Germany, for example, the old *Länder* (states) were abolished in favor of fourteen new *Bezirke* (districts). However, the presence of major ethnic groups in two countries led to federal constitutions that reflect certain degrees of autonomy: for Serbs, Croats, Slovenians, Bosnians, Macedonians, Montenegrins, Hungarians, and Albanians in Yugoslavia; and for Czechs and Slovaks in Czechoslovakia. This move diffused the Serb and Czech traditional dominance of the past, but it by no means solved the problem of animosity. In addition, Romania created an autonomous region for some 1.7 million Hungarians, but traditional enmities finally forced the authorities to gerrymander this group among several districts.

These political changes have given the individual countries of Eastern Europe fewer minorities than ever before in history, and certain administrative changes have been made to handle existing cultural differences where they do occur. A new communist state of East Germany has been created which might reduce the potential impact of a united Germany but which has left a divisive legacy that is hard to erase. Finally, and perhaps most important of all, an Iron Curtain divides Europe into two parts, which are at odds with the increasing tendency toward international interaction and cooperation.

The nature of socialism

Background

An understanding of the landscape under socialism necessitates a brief analysis on the nature of this social system. We begin with communism – a word derived from the Latin *communia*, common or belonging to all – a collective theme that stands in contrast to the emphasis placed on the individual in capitalistic societies. A principal, long-range goal of communism is a collective society that provides equality and economic security for all. Communist doctrine rests on the theories of Karl Marx as interpreted and modified by Lenin. A strong stimulus to Marx's early ideas resulted from the exploitation of workers by factory owners during the Industrial Revolution in nineteenth-century Britain. He hypothesized that the key to history is the relationship between different classes of people in *producing goods*, i.e. history passes through certain inevitable stages of class struggle for the means of production with each stage leading to a higher level of economic and social development. Thus, feudalism

had been succeeded by capitalism, which in turn would eventually be succeeded by the highest state – communism.

Under capitalism, the production of goods is controlled by the bourgeoisie who, according to socialists, use their ownership of the means of production to exploit the people, especially the proletariat, who do not receive full value for their labor. An inevitable class struggle, therefore, would take place between bourgeoisie and workers, because the former would not willingly relinquish its power. Capitalism would eventually be destroyed and the proletariat would set up a classless communist society in which the ownership of the means of production would be reserved for public bodies. In such a society, goods would be made available on the basis of need. However, as most scholars agree, this stage has not been reached, and goods are still distributed on the basis of work. Thus, the countries of Eastern Europe like the Soviet Union are called socialist republics, and the focus in this chapter is on this social system. These socialist countries are ruled by communists, however.

What is the nature of socialism as practiced in the Soviet Union and Eastern Europe? Heilbroner (1970: Ch. 5) provides an illuminating comparison of capitalism and socialism that helps us to understand the effects of the latter system on the landscape. Although capitalist and socialist societies may vary, he feels that two basic characteristics differentiate them: all capitalist societies have the structural elements of *private property* and a relatively free market backed by a *business* ideology or value system; on the other hand, the structural counterpart to the market system in socialist societies is the *planning* mechanism which allocates resources and fixes prices. This planning, in turn, is supported by an ideology that focuses on the reshaping of society along *egalitarian* lines – equality of classes, income, housing, health, goods and services, and even regional development. Both of these characteristics – planning and an ideological commitment to an egalitarian society – are crucial to our analysis of landscape changes under socialism, necessitating a further probe.

According to the communists, the operation of a free market creates and perpetuates inequalities; hence, a primary goal of socialism, backed by a planned economy, is to remove them. Obviously, this goal of controlling the production and distribution of goods in a world of scarcity is difficult to achieve while at the same time striving for equality. As a consequence, the socialist societies of Eastern Europe and the Soviet Union have exhibited strong

differences between what socialism should accomplish in theory and what the system does in reality. All socialist regimes have been forced to compromise to different degrees on their goals of equity in order to reward performance, whether it be a collective group like a factory or an individual like a party leader, engineer, or ballet dancer. Furthermore, Connor (1979: 306), who has written a book dealing with equality in socialist societies, points out that equity means not necessarily equality in a strict sense but a fair distribution of benefits to citizens.

Role of ideology

This contradiction between what socialism should do in theory and what it does in practice is related to the role of ideology, a subject that has stimulated much controversy among scholars. In Chapter 1, ideology was defined as the complex of values, beliefs, and sentiments that bind together members of a society and so differentiate them from other societies. However, in socialist societies, the ideology is much more prominent than in other societies because of a strong commitment to social change, even to public intervention to accomplish its goals of equity. Bornstein (1966: 74) and Kolakowski (1982: 45) both feel that the ideology is used systematically to justify and legitimize the communist power system. In this sense, the regimes can use the ideology to rationalize the differences between socialist theory and practice, i.e. the discrepancies between what the party has said it will do and what it does. An acceptance of the ideology by the masses is more crucial than widespread belief in it. Ideology thus authenticates the regime to the people and shows them that the Party is omnipresent, which is especially helpful when the masses are called on to sacrifice material goods like consumer wares or immaterial wants like travel to the West.

Socialist ideology lays much of its claim to legitimacy on being able to modernize society more rapidly and effectively than capitalism. This theme of socialism was particularly important in Eastern Europe immediately after the Second World War, when growth policies of heavy industry were instituted. The communist regimes wanted to show immediate success as a contrast with the failure of the interwar administrations. They also knew that to modernize they must institute radical changes to reduce rural peasant overpopulation and then utilize this labor as the basis for industrialization. Finally, the regimes wanted urban working populations as a base for communist party support.

The equity which occupies a prominent place in the socialist ideology has a spatial context that interests geographers, who have addressed the subject for both the Soviet Union (Pallot and Shaw: 1981) and Eastern Europe (Fuchs and Demko: 1979). According to socialist ideology, geographical differences within a country should be eliminated, including those between town and country, regions, settlements, and even within cities. The removal of these regional inequities obviously affects the landscape. However, geographical equity has a peculiar meaning in socialist societies. The East German geographers, Lüdemann and Heinzmann (1978: 121–4) report, for example, that the planning goal is

> not an even distribution of all branches of industry over an entire country, i.e., a regional balance in the degree of industrialization. . . . Rather, it involves the formation of regional centers in all parts of the country and the concentration of industries in those locations where economic conditions are best for them. . . . Despite differing economic structures in individual districts of the German Democratic Republic, the evenness of the regional distribution of productive forces becomes apparent by virtue of the fact that in all regions full employment is guaranteed, that there are no basic regional differences in wage levels, and that in all parts of the country every citizen has the opportunity to make use of a wide range of work places.

Such an interpretation of equity seems to place a premium on *access* to the benefits of a socialist society.

Certainly the environments in which socialism evolved exhibited strong inequities. In Russia and Eastern Europe, regional variations in equity were extreme, for in most areas – excepting East Germany and Czechoslovakia – the agricultural sector dominated with large proportions of the population living as peasants producing mostly for themselves. Areas of industrial production using modern technology were few in number. The Marxists believed that this environment of inequality would eventually be transformed into a Marxist environment where spatial inequalities would disappear through a process utilizing modern methods of production in both industry and agriculture.

Role of planning

After examining some of the characteristics of socialist ideology, we turn briefly to national planning, especially in its application to Eastern Europe, as a basis for changes in the landscape.

Neither Marx nor Lenin really considered planning in any detail

263

before the Russian Revolution. Only when the need arose for some means to replace the market mechanism in economic decisions did planning evolve as a major feature of socialism. In fact, E. H. Carr (1947: 20), in an oft-quoted statement, remarks that 'the economic impact of the Soviet Union on the rest of the world may be summed up in the single word "planning" '. Owing to the difficulties encountered in modernizing a backward Russian society, Lenin and the other party leaders realized that a planned economy was necessary. Gradually, under Stalin the traditional centrally planned 'command economy' evolved. Marer (1979: 282–3) gives the following seven characteristics of this economy:

- All significant means of production are nationalized or collectivized, with the agricultural sector being a partial or near-full exception in several countries.
- Economic decision making is hierarchical so that inter-enterprise relationships are vertical, i.e., determined through the respective administrative hierarchies, rather than horizontally, through the market.
- Planning is pervasive and is mainly in physical units rather than in value terms; it involves the administrative rationing of inputs and outputs.
- Managerial and worker incentives stress fulfillment and overfulfillment of quantitative production targets.
- Prices are set administratively, tend to remain unchanged for long periods, and, as a rule, do not fully reflect costs and demand-supply pressures.
- Consumers can choose among the goods already produced, but their choice will have little influence on what will be produced.
- Foreign trade is a monopoly of the state; its principal function is to secure goods that cannot be produced domestically at all, or only in inadequate quantities.

In the early 1980s, the landscape of Eastern Europe reflected more than thirty years of socialist planing, but the nature of the planning had varied over this period. Its relationship to socialist ideology also had changed. Specialists have distinguished at least three periods of planning, each contributing somewhat different inputs to landscape evolution (see Pounds 1969: 167–75; Mellor 1975: Ch. 8; Turnock 1978: Ch. 5; Enyedi 1976: Ch. 4). Although various terms have been used for these periods, they are often referred to in regard to their focus – autarky or self-sufficiency, regional specialization and trade, and economic reform coupled with expanded trade with the West.

Outlining the characteristics of the three periods is important because planning and its effects on the landscape differed in each of them.

1. Autarky

A primary goal of planning in Eastern Europe until the 1960s was autarky or attempts at self-sufficiency. From the beginning, the influence of the Soviet Union was paramount as it made attempts to reconstruct its war-ravaged economy. The East European countries, referred to as Satellites, were stripped bare of resources and equipment, either by direct confiscation or through reparations. A tense political environment reflected the Cold War situation between East and West, exacerbated by the Berlin blockade and airlift of 1948. Such an atmosphere enabled the Soviet Union to isolate the socialist Bloc from the West and to justify a policy of self-sufficiency when programs of heavy industry were instituted. This policy of autarky also suited the Russians because they were able to prevent the East European countries from joining the newly formed Common Market of Western Europe. Even cooperation within Eastern Europe was discouraged, forcing those countries to depend on the Soviet Union for needed raw materials. Thus, Bloc autarky did not necessarily mean autarky for each country.

The command economy model used in the Soviet Union dominated the planning connected with autarkic policies. Five-year national plans were established and implemented from the top down. Heavy industry as a base for the modernization of relatively backward areas received the main priority. Ideologically, this base was to be established in all parts of a country because it was felt that backward regions hinder overall progress. The plans, therefore, emphasized considerable dispersion of industry into new areas so as to utilize surplus labor or unexploited resources. Needless to say, this type of dispersion was not always efficient in terms of return on capital invested. Furthermore, agriculture bore a large part of the cost of these expensive programs, for collectivization was carried out in part to create capital through selling state products in the cities at a profit. Autarkic policies also deprived the masses of consumer goods and saved on foreign exchange by reducing imports. Nevertheless, the continuous Cold War situation, which included a hot war (Korea), provided sufficient justification for autarky by emphasizing the need for maximum sacrifices in a conflict with the 'imperialist West'.

Difficulties connected with autarkic policies became evident even

before Stalin's death in 1953. Attempts to develop heavy industry often led to unfruitful investments and overdiversification of economies on the basis of scarce resources. Also, the domestic markets were too small to sustain manufacturers on a scale large enough to realize economic savings. Perhaps the primary weakness, however, was that under an autarkic system countries found difficulty in specializing in those products for which they had comparative advantages, as in the case of the more developed economies of East Germany and Czechoslovakia. In all countries, domestic products were often more expensive than foreign imports, either from other Bloc countries or the West. Furthermore, the poor quality of Bloc exports made it difficult to generate hard currency. The Soviet Union realized that further progress toward modernization required buying technology in the world market, something not easily accomplished under autarkic policies. Finally, increasing pressure for change came from neglected sectors – agriculture, consumer goods, and housing. Actually, by the late 1950s, the autarkic policies had been responsible for establishing an improved base for industry and, therefore, an ideological shift in planning could be more easily justified.

Albania reflects a socialist state that in the late 1970s rejected cooperation and adopted a policy of autarky long after other socialist states had abandoned it. Here is an economy that, insofar as possible, exists independently of the rest of the world. This country severed its ties and support from the Soviet Union in 1961 and from China in 1978 because, among other things, Albanian leaders believed that these two countries by dealing with the West were betraying communism. The present policy of self-reliance and isolation is apparent in the landscape. A banner in the city of Shkodër reads: 'Let us fulfill all our obligations and smash the blockade' (Biber 1980: 530). The country is a throwback to the Stalinist era, and, indeed, a statue of the late dictator flanks a major boulevard in Tirana, the capital. Other aspects of this country, communism's most dogmatic, are visible: brigades, composed of ordinary citizens who must work a month each year, are mobilized to support an autarkic policy and are seen everywhere, working in the fields, on railroads, etc.; closed churches testify to the complete repression of religion as the country becomes officially atheistic (Shkodër Cathedral is reportedly a basketball arena!); the Elbasan iron and steel project, and also the oil refineries at Cërrik, Qytet Stalin (formerly Kucovë) and – most recently – Ballsh, reflect heavy industry and the drive for self-sufficiency emphasizing national resources, especially oil; and finally,

the ubiquitous civil defense bunkers guard against a perceived external threat.

2. Regional specialization and trade

Except in Albania, autarky ended in 1957 when Khrushchev announced that it was not possible or profitable to do everything at once and, instead, the division of labor between countries should be encouraged. A second era of planning began which emphasized greater economic efficiency based on regional specialization and trade, especially within the East European Common Market – Council for Mutual Economic Assistance (CMEA) or Comecon. This organization had actually been formed in 1949 as a visible counterforce to the West European Common Market (ECM), but had not been used because it did not fit the autarky framework. Up to the late 1950s, therefore, Comecon had only provided for barter agreements between countries and a few joint arrangements such as an electricity grid or use of railroad cars. By the 1970s, new forms of integration included joint ownership (e.g. cotton yarns by East Germany and Poland) and specialized coordination of economic activities (e.g. chemical fibers by all members) (Marer and Montias 1981: 151–2). Actually, Comecon is quite different from the West European Common Market: enlargement of markets through reduced tariffs, quotas, etc., so important in the West, remains less important than attempts at coordination of national planning. Private firms dominate international activity in the West, whereas the government controls it in the East. Furthermore, members of Comecon have become dependent upon the Soviet Union, because this country dominates the organization. This latter characteristic is reflected in the Friendship Pipeline, which brings Soviet oil to the deficient areas of East Germany, Poland, Czechoslovakia, and Hungary.

As priorities for specialization were worked out, not all of the countries were pleased, especially Romania, which had been allocated a role of supplying raw materials – grain and oil – to Comecon countries. A very nationalistic country with considerable resources and a desire to industrialize and sell finished industrial products on the world market, Romania found the decision hard to accept and embarked on a long attempt to take an independent road to communism. Since political deviation did not accompany this economic independence, the regime did not encounter the opposition of

other Comecon countries that had faced Czechoslovakia in 1968. Romania's economic stand is demonstrated in its own iron and steel plant at Galaţi (none had been built during the autarkic period) and by the decision to build – with Yugoslavia, an even more independent communist state – a hydroelectric project on the Danube River.

A greater emphasis on balance and efficiency keynoted planning in the period of regional specialization and trade. Investments in other sectors than industry – agriculture, consumer goods, and housing – increased in a relative sense, thereby raising living standards and diversifying the employment structure. Spatially, the ideologic thrust of regional balance in each country was still applied, but efficiency in terms of savings through external economies and economies of scale certainly was of equal importance. The old areas of development thereby received much investment, although not always in the core: for example, the peripheries of Budapest and Upper Silesia received the bulk of new industry. Even in Yugoslavia, where backward areas like Macedonia and Montenegro had received special subsidies under autarky, the more developed areas of the north like Croatia and Slovenia now could convince many planners that it was cheaper to invest there.

3. Economic reform and increased contacts with the West

By the late 1960s, it was obvious that even further changes were necessary in planning, not only in structure but also in increased contacts with the West. Considerable pressure was exerted among Comecon members for more decentralized managements, the introduction of profitability in a quasi-capitalistic sense, and the importation of Western technology, especially computers. However, planners realized that contacts with the West would be useful for more than technology. The East European countries like those of Western Europe are small in terms of resources and markets and therefore depend on trade, e.g. in Hungary, trade accounts for 40 per cent of the national product. Limiting much of this trade to Comecon would restrict the possibilities of overcoming weaknesses such as feed for livestock and Western help in producing material goods like automobiles.

A liberal model for economic reform has existed in Yugoslavia since 1948, when this country split with the Soviet Union over the degree of central control necessary in a planned economy. Yugoslavia's ethnic fragmentation, which is reflected in a federal structure,

was a major factor in a policy of decentralized economic development. Planning in this Balkan country relies on (1) decentralization by transfering decision-making to an enterprise itself and (2) the free market to accomplish the allocation of resources. Autonomy has been given to individual enterprises in pricing and production policies and in the distribution of income between wages and investment.

Of the other countries, Hungary has gone the furthest in reform. Enyedi (1976: 116) summarizes the characteristics of the New Economic Mechanism (NEM). The aim is to realize the central objectives as laid down in the national economic plan by means of economic regulators – taxes, credit, state subsidies, and partially fixed prices – instead of plan directives. Producers are given a direct interest in efficient and economical production, enabling them to make decisions on their own through analysis of their economic situations. Central decisions are only made with regard to investments in large installations, e.g. oil refineries.

Economic reforms on a lesser scale have taken place in the other East European countries. However, in none of the countries, including Yugoslavia and Hungary, has the regime relinquished any political power. All economic decisions must be made within the constraints of a highly circumscribed political framework.

Although the economic reforms have emphasized changes in decision-making and use of market factors, planning in Eastern Europe has also included increased attention to economic efficiency. Less is heard about pure equity and more about spatial links within a settlement system. Today, fewer new factories are located in isolated areas unless they can make a significant contribution to national growth. However, plants can be located in transportation corridors between major centers, thereby remaining accessible to commuters, who, at the same time, are close to education, health facilities, and other services. Attempts are being made to economize by greater agricultural integration through larger specialized farms and even industrial factories on the farms to process the raw materials, i.e. the so-called agro-industrial enterprises.

Present contacts with the West appear throughout Eastern Europe. For instance, Austria and Hungary exchange electrical energy, and foreign corporations like Fiat and International Harvester have sold licenses to produce cars and farm machinery, respectively. To pay for Western technology, these countries sometimes export products, e.g. Polish food, to the detriment of their own populace, which must

go without. Many of these countries have borrowed heavily from Western banks and now have accumulated sizable debts. All in all, the road to modernization has not been easy.

Economic progress and social change

A valid assessment of the achievements of the planned economies in East European countries is hindered because data are not easily obtained or even comparable with Western classifications. Ideally, these countries should be compared with those of Western Europe, but perhaps the fairest comparisons are with the past. How much progress have the socialist regimes made? An assessment is important to provide a framework for the later sections of this chapter, which deal with an analysis of geographic changes within the region. Based on limited data, I conclude that the planned economies have made remarkable progress over the interwar situation, but these advances have not enabled the socialist countries to catch up with Western countries. I concur with Brzeski's evaluation (1969: 9) that Eastern Europe, while no longer a 'C' area, still ranks as a 'B' on the scale mentioned earlier in this book.

Certainly one of the most significant indicators of modernization in any country is the employment structure. Data provided by the World Bank (1982: 147) show how East European countries have changed in this regard:

	Industry (%)		Agriculture (%)		Services (%)	
	1960	1980	1960	1980	1960	1980
Eastern Europe						
Bulgaria	25	39	57	37	18	24
Czechoslovakia	46	48	26	11	28	41
East Germany	48	50	18	10	34	40
Hungary	35	53	38	15	27	32
Poland	29	39	48	31	23	30
Romania	15	36	65	29	20	35
Yugoslavia	18	35	63	29	19	36
Soviet Union	29	45	42	14	29	41
United Kingdom	48	42	4	2	48	56
West Germany	48	46	14	4	38	50
United States	36	32	7	2	57	66

Before the Second World War, peasants constituted 50–80 per cent of national populations everywhere except Czechoslovakia and East Germany. Today this imbalance has been reversed with industry dominating except in Albania, for which data are unavailable but where agricultural workers are probably the largest category. The East European countries, consequently, are now producing more food but with far fewer workers – an important aspect of modernization. Nevertheless, communist agriculture exhibits definite weaknesses as we shall see later in the chapter. The services – those activities employing white-collar workers – which in advanced countries like the United States and West Germany now dominate the work force, also show increases in Eastern Europe. The northern countries in the Bloc still have more industrial employment than those of the Balkans, but the latter exhibit sizable increases over 1960. The Soviet employment structure appears to be somewhere between the two groups.

Visitors to Eastern Europe realize the emphasis on industrialization when they see factories and apartment buildings as ubiquitous features of urban and even some rural landscapes. Quantitative figures, however, are unavailable to capture the total impact of this modernization, but Volgyes (1980: 112) provides a significant fact: from the time of collectivization to the mid-1970s, 9 million people or 12 per cent of the total population of Eastern Europe moved from rural to urban locations. Hamilton (1979a: 215) adds that industrial workers, between 1960 and 1975 alone, increased by 5.7 million. He also mentions that at least 75 per cent of the investment since the Second World War has been in the productive sector (industry, construction, and transport), a contrast to the interwar period when it was 65–70 per cent in the nonproductive sector (trade, housing, and services).

As we shall see, this progress in industrialization has not been even in its spatial distribution and, furthermore, has run ahead of urbanization. Owing to a deliberate policy of saving on housing and other urban infrastructure by encouraging rural residence and commuting, the rural population of approximately 45 per cent exceeds the agricultural employment of 25 per cent (Kosiński 1974: 143; Lazarcik 1981: 592). In other words, the benefits of socialism are not necessarily equal for the many workers who commute, i.e. peasant-workers.

Despite the economic progress made by East European countries, the rest of the world has also moved ahead, a fact which places this modernization in perspective. Table 7.1 shows data which permit

Table 7.1 Selected comparative economic data

	GNP* (per capita US $)	Electricity† (billion kw. hours)	Steel† (million m. tons)	Cement† (million m. tons)	Auto Registrations† (per 1000)	Energy Consump.† (barrels per cap.)	Teleph.† (per 1000)	Persons‡ per doctor
	(1979)	(1981)	(1981)	(1981)	(1981)	(1981)	(1981)	(1976–78)
Eastern Europe								
Bulgaria	3,630	37	2.5	5.4	56	28	120	504
Czechoslovakia	5,190	73	15.2	10.6	149	35	201	458
East Germany	6,310	101	7.4	12.2	152	40	183	549
Hungary	3,780	24	3.6.	4.6	85	20	111	478
Poland	3,770	115	15.7	14.2	67	26	91	623
Romania	2,100	70	13.0	13.9	11	22	59	828
Yugoslavia	2,370	60	4.0	9.8	108	13	85	897
Soviet Union	4,040	1,325	149.0	127.0	31	31	84	390
United Kingdom	7,390	278	15.6	12.8	276	27	477	770
West Germany	12,200	369	41.6	31.6	377	33	434	543
Italy	5,730	183	24.6	43.0	310	19	318	—
United States	10,610	2,448	108.8	66.1	537	59	791	621

Sources: * 1981 World Bank Atlas, 1982: 6.
† Handbook of Economic Statistics, CIA, 1982: 26–7.
‡ F. E. Ian Hamilton, The Planned Economies, 1979b: 12.

comparisons between capitalist and socialist countries. The respective levels of developments are shown by GNP *per capita* for which the East European countries correspond in general to the Soviet Union but, in general, lag behind the United States and selected West European countries. Within Eastern Europe, the level of development for the Balkan countries is lower, although the migration of Yugoslav 'guest workers' to and then from Western Europe explains the larger number of automobiles in this state. Differences in communications as shown in telephones and in electricity are to be expected. However, the communists have given priority to heavy industry and, therefore, production of steel and cement compares favorably with West European countries except for West Germany. Furthermore, in their commitment to social services, the East European countries show up well in health (e.g. doctors) and education. Finally, because certain items like food, transportation, and housing are subsidized in socialist countries, individual income actually is worth more.

Closely related to economic progress, of course, is social change. What has been the nature of this change in Eastern Europe under socialism? Connor (1977: 17–21) feels that, above all, the regimes as a social consequence of rapid industrialization created new possibilities for occupational mobility within the population. A sharp break with the past occurred as the old Eastern Europe, dominated by localized economic development and immobile peasant populations, has been transformed. The thirty-five years of communism has been characterized by mass movements of population from old to new habitats of work and life. Opportunities, which never existed before, now exist for changing one's status. Perhaps the major social change has been from peasant to worker: the peasantry, which constituted a majority of the population in all countries but East Germany and Czechoslovakia, yielded nearly half its offspring, on the average, to form the new working class. Changes from peasant to white-collar worker or from blue-collar to white-collar were smaller but also significant.

The credit due to socialism for this social change is, of course, subject to controversy. Connor (1977: 22–3) says that the socioeconomic expansion and not the revolutionary introduction of a socialist order is responsible for the increased mobility. He feels that a capitalist system could have had the same effect, but the record of this system in Eastern Europe is modest at best, for only limited social change occurred between the wars; however, the time was short and

conditions including a depression were not conducive to social change. Yet, in looking at Greece in the postwar period, when that country received vast Western economic aid, the discrepancies between wealth and poverty are shocking (Seton-Watson 1975: 59). Thus, I find the argument that progress in a socialist country would probably have been greater under a capitalistic system not only incapable of proof but also pointless. We have to look at what has been done under socialism. In this connection, Rostow's (1971: 162–4) statements are interesting: he feels that communism's contribution to a society rests in the ability of a centralized state to supply the preconditions for economic 'take-off' into a drive for technological maturity. Such an ability to mobilize the forces of modernization is one factor attracting Third World countries to communism.

If we concede that communism has certain advantages in transforming a society, especially one dominated by peasants, what about the chances for maintaining this momentum after the initial provision of occupational mobility? Here the evidence shows the existence of what Connor (1977: 25–32) calls deferred costs of this initial success. All three social strata in Eastern Europe – while-collar, blue-collar, and peasants – now find upward mobility curtailed and no longer can they contrast their success in material rewards with that of earlier milieu. Economic growth has slowed except perhaps in certain Balkan countries, like Romania, where a rich resource base occurs and urban opportunities for occupational change still exist. For thirty-five years, the people of Eastern Europe accepted political repression because economic conditions were improving, but now, as social change is curtailed, they are beginning to question whether the repression is worth it.

If social change as measured by occupational mobility has slowed, what about class equality? The landscape certainly may 'appear' more equal as the differences between residential districts subside from those of the interwar period. Most authorities agree, however, that a new hierarchy exists under socialism largely to reward specific skills – scientific, managerial, cultural, etc. – creating an elite class, whose members receive certain benefits such as a dacha in the country or access to special shops. Evidently constraints on class equality break down in any society.

Having provided background on the roles of socialist ideology and planning in East European countries together with an assessment of economic progress and social change, we now turn to the effects of

socialist policies on modernization of rural, industrial, and urban landscapes.

The modernization of the rural landscape under socialism

The importance of a state-run agriculture

Socialist ideology emphasizes creation of a new environment in which differences between town and country are removed, primarily through the application of large-scale methods of production to agriculture and the modernization of rural areas. The creation of such an environment was especially difficult because the Communist Revolution took place in Russia, where some 80 per cent of the populace consisted of peasants and where no real middle class of workers existed. This formulated change placed a severe strain on the ideology, because Marx had not envisioned a situation in which a capitalistic worker class was lacking.

To handle this paradox meant modifying the revolution to accommodate the large proportion of peasants, who obviously had to be integrated into the new socialist society. Lenin first gained their allegiance by granting them land, i.e. a so-called peasant revolution (Mitrany 1951: 77). Then, in the 1920s, a form of capitalism – the New Economic Plan – was employed to restore productivity, but agriculture remained backward with underemployed peasants on the land retarding progress. Furthermore, the peasants withheld crops and remained alienated from the cities. Perhaps the major factor, however, was agriculture's failure to make capital available for building-up industry. Finally, with the threat of a world war bringing things to head (Schlesinger 1947: 14–15), Stalin instituted forced collectivization of the land. By 1936, after the loss of millions of lives, collectivization in the Soviet Union was 90 per cent complete.

Why do socialist regimes place such an emphasis on collectivization, especially when it is resisted so strongly by the peasant? The primary reasons are the furthering of both ideological and planning goals – differences between town and country are reduced and a large-scale agricultural system is more efficient. But couldn't private agriculture achieve these results? Why must there be a *state-run* agriculture at the expense of alienating such a large group of people like the peasants of Russia and later those of Eastern Europe? Specialists

275

have isolated several advantages – even *essentials* – that justify the extreme measures of collectivization and lead to radical transformation of the landscape.

1. *Intensive and efficient use of manpower and resources*

As shown in Chapter 3, peasant populations represent a vast reservoir of underemployed labor, especially if labor-intensive methods are required. For example, the inefficient strip system not only prevents the use of machinery and the grazing of animals but also requires extra travel time. The Marxist emphasis on large-scale methods, like that of many capitalist farms, utilizes capital inputs in the form of machinery and fertilizer to increase per-person and per-acre yields. Moreover, this system decides on the crops to be grown and the method of marketing them, theoretically making for more systematic planning.

2. *Food and labor surpluses*

Large-scale socialized operations in agriculture, designed as capital intensive to increase output per person, attempt not only to release peasant labor to the cities for industry but also to provide surpluses for export, raw materials for industry, and food for factory workers in cities. The exports are meant to be exchanged for industrial equipment and military goods.

3. *Capital savings*

The possibility of capital savings forms one of the most important advantages of a collectivized system. Tomasevich (1958: 50) explains that the compulsory quotas delivered by the farms to the state actually are a heavy land tax paid in kind. By paying low prices for the quotas, the regime insures savings by selling to the urban market at higher prices and thus providing an accumulation of capital. Furthermore, since these urban prices are still relatively low, general wage levels are depressed, accounting for further savings.

4. *Control of peasants*

Along with the economic reasons for collectivization goes the political-ideological one of peasant control. Mosely (1958: 49) emphasizes that the peasants, because of their numbers and their parochialism in terms of attachment to land and local culture, are feared by the communist leadership. Collectivization allowed the Party to penetrate the countryside and by indoctrination and other

techniques to eradicate peasant mentality, transforming the people into agricultural workers for the state. Decision-making in the village became a communist function. Mosely (1958: 58) adds that Soviet leadership from the beginning felt 'the future socialist society could not be built so long as one part of the society, numerically the larger part, operated on the basis of private interest, private decisions, and private marketing. . . . It was absolutely necessary, according to the communist program, to transform the village and the agricultural sector in the image of the urban and proletarian sector.'

The economic and political advantages of collectivization are difficult to separate because they actually are interwoven. The peasant had to be eliminated as a political threat and to be exploited for economic purposes. Industry and agriculture had to be *joint* carriers of the revolution, thereby confirming the social objectives of the ideology and carrying out modernization in both town and country. This integration of political, economic, and social factors in collectivization is supported by Stalin's statement in 1929 to the Conference of Marxist Agricultural Scientists: 'The great importance of collective farms lies in the fact that they are the basis for introducing machinery and tractors, for transforming the peasant, for transforming his psychology in the spirit of proletarian socialism' (quoted in Sennow n.d.: 99)

Collectivization in Eastern Europe

Communist regimes of Eastern Europe, established with the support of the Soviet Union after the Second World War, encountered the same problem of transforming large peasant societies as that existing in Russia in 1917. Here again, a high degree of underemployment prevailed. Dumont (1957: 495) reports that in 1948 in the eastern Slovakian village of Mijslava the average peasant had work for only 165 days a year and sought employment for 200. This indicates the vast untapped potential of labor. But how was this reality of small-scale peasant farming in Eastern Europe to be changed to fit into the large-scale plans of Marxism? Again, temporary compromises had to be made by the regimes so as to neutralize the peasants; in addition, left-wing political organizations, including peasant parties, joined with the Communist Party in popular fronts. Land reforms were instituted, thereby gaining the support of the peasants, especially the poorer ones who held no land. This process, in essence, completed the land reform programs of the interwar years, especially

in Poland and Hungary, which had retained large estates until the Second World War (see Fig. 4.8).

Under these reforms of the late 1940s, land was allocated in strip form, following the historic pattern and landscape relic described earlier: the formation of the three-field system of the German colonists (Ch. 3); the transformation under feudalism as the estates were enlarged at the expense of peasant land (Ch. 4); the appearance again of the strip as a product of national land reforms in the separate countries in the interwar period (Ch. 6); and, finally, the further appearance of this landscape feature as the result of communist land reforms in the years after 1945. Except in Poland and Yugoslavia, these strips eventually disappeared under programs of collectivization, but immediately after the Second World War they were perhaps more prevalent in the total East European landscape than at any time in history.

After 1948, when the communist regimes felt themselves firmly in control, collectivization programs began. Evidence indicates that the US Marshall Plan for the economic recovery of Western Europe indirectly hastened the process: it forced the communists to tighten control so as to preserve Soviet domination over the East Bloc countries and to reduce the possibilities of any economic ties with Western Europe. At first the regimes encouraged voluntary entry into 'cooperatives' – the word collective was purposely avoided. Gradually, pressure increased, especially against the *kulaks* or large land-owning peasants, who were most resistant. Rákosi, the Hungarian communist, stated that 'Stalin reminded us that the class struggle in rural areas is carried on with the poor peasants acting in support of the working class, with the medium peasant as a class ally, and the *kulak* as a class enemy' (Dumont 1957: 486). Because machinery was extremely limited, machine-tractor stations serviced a number of collective farms from a central location. The collectivization process took longer than it had in Russia, the delays possibly resulting from the crises in Yugoslavia (1948), Hungary (1956), and Poland (1956).

By the late 1960s, collectivization was essentially complete in six of the countries. In the other two – Yugoslavia and Poland – the process was resisted and private farms remain, although the government is represented through state farms. Tomasevich (1958: 48) explains that in Yugoslavia a combination of factors caused collectivization to be abandoned in 1951–52: stubborn opposition of the peasants; effects of droughts on production; consideration for the vital economic and political relations with the United States after the

Cominform attack on Tito; introduction of the 'new economic system'; and the overriding need to increase agricultural production. Piekalkiewicz (1979: 89–92, 99) points out that factors in the failure to socialize the Polish landscape are many and complex. One important factor involved the need to employ a large growing population, a situation different from other countries with smaller population increases. Thus, in Eastern Europe most countries but not all followed the ideology of collectivization.

In all of the countries, however, the peasants along with their traditional life in the village were affected as never before: the communists organized them, forced them to attend meetings and rallies, and increased their contacts with the outside world. Village parochialism became a thing of the past. Aspects of modernization such as electricity, new housing, and commuting to the cities became evident in the landscape. Although much of this intrusion by the Party into the village was for purposes of economic production and political control, in Romania's case it served a nationalistic purpose in the 1960s when peasant folk traditions were emphasized to gain support in the attempt to be independent of the Soviet Union.

Socialist agriculture is based on two types of large-scale units – the collective and the state farm. The collective operates like a cooperative – indeed, it is often called a producer's cooperative – in that net profits, after the state's quota is subtracted, are distributed among the members, partly in cash, partly in kind, on the basis of work measured by a so-called 'labor day'. Different types of cooperatives exist. The most socialized type involves the farmer relinquishing all private control over his land, livestock, and equipment; however, members of all types receive about an acre or so on which they may cultivate for themselves and keep livestock. Supplementing the collective is the state farm – the true socialist form – owned by the state and financed by the national budget. Employees receive wages in the same way as industrial workers, and the net profits revert to the state. State farms usually are in areas where population densities are low and where specialization in one type of crop or livestock is feasible; they also serve as models for management, experimental functions in terms of technology, and supply sources for high-quality seeds and selected breeding stock. Today, collectives still exceed state farms in total numbers and area, but the goal is for the latter to become the prevailing form, a situation now evolving in the Soviet Union.

In the alteration of presocialist tenure into a socialist agricultural

system, the collective generally came first because it was easier to establish in areas where high, rural population densities prevailed. The primary problem was a lack of machinery, a situation handled by machine-tractor stations (MTSs), which not only supplied machinery to several collectives but also served as another arm of the Party in controlling production. Today, the collectives have their own machinery and, except in Albania, the MTSs serve as repair stations.

The main recent change in socialist agriculture – one reflected in the landscape – is integration both between farms and between farms and factories. Bulgaria has been the leader in this movement, but other countries are following suit. The first stage in Bulgaria was the creation of agro-industrial complexes (APKs) in 1970, a move which represented horizontal integration of smaller socialist farms into larger ones that would permit greater specialization and economies of scale in use of capital, e.g. fattening complexes for 200 000 pigs. In the 1970s, vertical integration supplemented horizontal integration as several APKs were transformed into industrio-agricultural enterprises (PAKs) designed to superimpose industry and marketing institutions on top of the agricultural ones. A good example is sugar beets with factories located right on the farms, representing the ultimate in socialist 'industrialization of the countryside'. Again, the motive is greater efficiency in the use of capital, following the lead of vertical integration in industry.

I viewed horizontal integration in Dedelow, East Germany, where enormous silos tower over the landscape and reflect the production of feed for livestock on a large scale. The former mixed feeding of dairy cows, beef cattle, and pigs in each district is now more specialized with only one type of animal (e.g. dairy cow) being fed.

The major residues of capitalism found in the six East European countries where the socialist sector predominates are household plots of the collectives, which provide vegetables, fruits, grapes, and meat – products which require considerable individual care. The regimes realize the importance of these plots and even encourage them, although generally classify them within the socialist sector to avoid invidious comparisons. O'Relley (1977: 357–8) points out that Hungary, for example, in 1975 had approximately 800 000 household plots and 120 000 small private gardens, orchards, or vineyards. These holdings accounted for 13.6 per cent of the total cultivated area and were responsible for 35 per cent of the vegetables, 46 per cent of the

fruit, 42 per cent of the wine, and over 50 per cent of the pork production.

The collectivization programs in Eastern Europe were responsible for one of the most significant processes of landscape and social change in the history of the area. Percentages of population in agriculture in various countries fell drastically as peasants moved into industry, either by migrating to cities or by commuting. This change was particularly apparent in six of the countries where agricultural populations in 1950 had been 50 per cent or more (assumed for Albania). Thus, two of the primary problems of Eastern Europe in the interwar period – rural overpopulation and underemployment – were drastically reduced (Brzeski 1969: 5).

Despite the reduction of numbers in agriculture since 1950, absolute production has increased. In other words, the goal of the Party to produce more food with fewer people has been successful. Lazarcik (1974: 335: 1977: 294; 1981: part 2, 594) shows that total agricultural output increased from a prewar index of 100 to 179.4 in 1973; similarly, an index of 100 in 1965 rose to 149.3 in 1979.

By 1979, therefore, fewer people in Eastern Europe were working in agriculture yet were producing more. However, this increase in production represented an ever-decreasing share of the Gross National Product as industrialization progressed even faster. As late as 1965, agriculture was still the most important sector in several East European countries, but by 1979 the highest share of agriculture in GNP (excluding Albania) was 24.5 per cent in Romania and the average for all of Eastern Europe was 16.9 percent (Lazarcik 1981: part 2, 591–2).

How can the overall performance of East European agriculture under communism be evaluated? Most experts agree that the attempt to transform a traditional system of estates and peasant plots into a mechanized, large-scale operation has had only mixed success. In six of the countries, the creation of large fields for machinery has helped the Party to make progress toward the goals of releasing labor and food surpluses to the cities while at the same time creating capital and assuming complete control of the countryside. There has been some decentralization of management and, most important, better incentives in the form of higher prices. These incentives have led to greater flexibility in decision making. A greater diversity of production has resulted as industrial crops, fruit, vegetables, and livestock feed have been expanded. Some progress has been made in

producing more fertilizer and machinery, thus increasing yields per acre and per person.

Agricultural modernization among the countries of Eastern Europe has shown uneven progress. Lazarcik (1981: part 2, 588) points out that in the 1970s these countries became divided into two groups – centralized and decentralized. East Germany, Czechoslovakia, and Bulgaria remain consistently in the first group; on the other hand, Poland and Yugoslavia, where private farms predominate, have been decentralized with the decisions made by individual farmers. Recently Hungary and Romania, owing to recent policies promoting decentralized management and incentives, have joined Poland and Yugoslavia in this group. In most comparative aspects of agriculture, excluding mainly outputs per worker, the performance of the decentralized countries has been better than that of the centralized ones. This performance, accomplished despite less nonagricultural inputs, tends to indicate that management and incentives are more important factors than tenure since the decentralized countries have both state and private forms of ownership in operation.

International comparisons of agriculture are difficult. Although Eastern Europe is more self-sufficient in agriculture than Western Europe, this does not imply a weakness on the part of the latter, but merely a preference for using industrial production to pay for food imports. Western Europe actually is more mechanized and has greater yield per livestock unit than Eastern Europe, but the latter compares favorably in terms of fertilizer production (Lazarcik 1981: part 2, 625).

The landscape can provide clues to weaknesses in East European agriculture: idle machinery rusting in the open, signifying the unavailability of spare parts; peasant workers, often women, using hand methods in rural labor; draft animals supplementing the work of tractors, particularly in Poland, where 2 million horses are used on the small fields; many unbelievably poor roads, especially in the spring when melting snow creates impassable morasses; small field strips in Poland and Yugoslavia, perpetuating barriers to the use of machinery and, therefore, modernization. Perhaps the most conspicuous and damning evidence of the current state of communist agriculture appears in the cities: long queues of people waiting to buy food, especially meat. Urbanizing populations traditionally demand more meat in their diets, but the regimes have been unable to provide the feed to produce it, causing East European countries to become in-

creasingly dependent upon regular imports of feedstuffs. In Poland, where private agriculture exists, large quantities of meat, notably hams, have been exported to help pay debts accumulated under programs of industrial modernization. Meat shortages have been a primary factor in the rise of the Solidarity movement.

The presence of an agricultural labor force that averages over forty years of age and is often female is an especially significant weakness and requires brief comment. These peasants have been left behind by the young, able-bodied people, who have been attracted to the city by higher wages, by shorter, regular working hours, by pensions and paid vacations, and by urban services. These factors combine to create a new class of 'peasant-workers,' who commute daily to towns. The traditional peasants feel that a change of occupation at their age would be difficult and, therefore, choose to remain in agriculture. What will happen when this older generation of workers passes on? This is a question the regimes are now debating.

A final weakness of East European agriculture is the limited degree of regional specialization in crops and livestock needed for intra-bloc trade within Comecon. Considerable potential exists for greater specialization, but up until 1980 autarkic policies in agriculture have restricted it (Jaehne 1980: 231–2). This policy seemingly results from short supplies – itself a reflection of weaknesses mentioned previously – and from the realization that a stable food supply must be based on a balanced domestic foundation of production. One of the few evidences in the landscape of agricultural specialization is the fleet of *Bulgaria* refrigerator trucks carrying fruit and vegetables to Western Europe.

Changes in the rural landscape

Socialist ideology emphasizes the modernization of rural areas with the goal of removing differences between town and country that exist under capitalism. The landscape reflects these changes, especially through the collectivization process. In portions of East Germany, Poland, and Hungary, vast prewar estates with large fields were rather easily converted into collective or state farms. On the other hand, where small strip holdings prevailed and high population densities existed, the collective farm became dominant as a first stage in communization of agriculture. However, the relationship between the old settlement pattern and the new farms is important. In Eastern Europe the commune or township centered on a village is the his-

torical form of local political organization. This village generally becomes a site for socialist farm buildings, a residence, and economic-cultural activities for farm workers. As socialist farms were organized, the area of the commune sometimes comprised parts of several collectives and state farms, e.g. the village area of Csepreg in western Hungary included portions of two collectives, one state farm, and a state forest. Other times, a single collective or state farm incorporated several villages. Whatever the case, the total effect of collectivization on the rural landscape is impressive. Several aspects of change in the rural landscape are discussed in this section as part of a typology: (1) fields, crops, and irrigation; (2) farm buildings; (3) villages; and (4) settlements.[1]

1. Fields, crops, and irrigation

Large fields now distinguish six of the East European countries from Yugoslavia and Poland, which retain the small strips. However, large fields are seen in the state farms of these two countries: in the Danubian plain of Yugoslavia and in the western and northern areas of Poland (formerly German territory). In East Germany, most socialist farms were formerly Junker estates. Field changes in one of these at Stresow, south of Greifswald (see Fig. 4.8) complement the changes portrayed earlier during the feudal period. In 1946, this Stresow estate has broken up and parcels were distributed to peasants as part of a land reform program; these small fields were then enlarged in the 1950s as part of collectivization.

Until the 1970s, the socialist farms ranged in size between 2500 and 12 000 acres (see Photo 7.1). Under new integration programs, however, sizes have dramatically increased. In Bulgaria, the industrio-agricultural enterprises (PAKs) average over 120 000 acres (Wiedeman 1980: 119). The enormous fields of these Bulgarian complexes – indeed they are called 'massives' – cross former collective and state farm boundaries.

Within this structure of larger fields (except in Poland and Yugoslavia), increased diversification of crops is apparent. Enyedi (1967) mentions that in all eight countries of Eastern Europe considerable emphasis was placed on raising more industrial crops in line with the Marxist goal of modernizing society. As a result, one sees extensive fields of sugar beets, sunflowers, tobacco, hemp, and flax in portions of the area. In addition, fields of seed grasses for fodder such as clover and alfalfa reflect an emphasis on livestock. Intensity of land use is also evident in greater production of fruit, vegetables, and grapes for

Photo 7.1 Machinery and large fields, as here on the Wallachian plain in Romania, demonstrate collectivization and the advantages of large-scale farming, which replaced the uneconomical strips. Horse and wagon are not completely eliminated.

wine, although a good proportion of these crops are derived from the private plots of collective farms.

The agricultural systems of Eastern Europe have become more intensive through irrigation programs. Perhaps the most important project in terms of landscape change was the construction of a large canal in eastern Hungary through an area east of the Tisza River that had been characterized by droughts. The project – called the Eastern Main Canal – was developed in the 1950s under the first Five-Year Plan and connects the Tisza and Berettyó Rivers, crossing the dry Hortobágy and Hajdúság regions (see Photo 7.2). Over 200 000 acres were brought under irrigation with water dispersed from the canal to fields via irrigation ditches. The large reservoir backed up by the postwar dam at Tiszalök on the Tisza River supplies water to the canal. In Hungary as a whole, irrigation under socialism has expanded from only 35 000 acres in 1939 to 1 million acres in the early 1970s (Mellor 1975: 291).

Albania also exhibits notable landscape changes connected with irrigation. Although accurate data cannot be procured, Mellor (1975: 326) reports that reclamation schemes begun in the interwar period in the coastal plain with American and Italian assistance have been expanded under the socialist regime. This project represents an attempt to restore fertility to an area damaged by harmful practices. Although the plain was once a granary for Rome, the overcutting of trees in the mountains for fuel and for shipbuilding led to erosion and blocking of streams debouching onto the plain. With the natural drainage obstructed, the plain became marshy and endemic with malaria. Today, drainage has erased much of the marsh, and the cultivated area of Albania has increased by two-thirds, 40 per cent of which is irrigated.

2. Farm buildings

To take advantage of external economies, socialist regimes found it most convenient to construct new collective and state farm buildings on the edge of villages. In East Germany and Poland, old feudal

Photo 7.2　A socialist change in the landscape of the Hungarian plain is an extensive irrigation network.

Photo 7.3 Large barns for cows and pigs create ubiquitous aspects of collective farms of Eastern Europe, as seen here in northern Bulgaria.

estates whose buildings could be transformed were utilized. A majority of the new structures relate to livestock (see Photo 7.3). In peasant agriculture between the wars, livestock rearing was extensive in nature because feed was not plentiful. The upheaval and destruction of the Second World War did not help the situation. When collectivization programs began, individual members were allowed to keep a few animals, but most livestock was grouped together in an attempt to improve the quantity and quality of production through large-scale methods. Since structures for large herds or flocks did not exist, new ones had to be constructed.

In an early geographic study dealing with the farm elements of collective and state farms, Horbaly (1951: 85) mentions the emphasis in Czechoslovakia in 1949–50 on the construction of feeding barns for pigs; propagation of this quick-maturing animal would help alleviate the meat shortage. At the 'Gigant Smiřice' state farm in eastern Bohemia, ten large pig-fattening structures – 500 ft (152 m) long by 44 ft (13 m) wide, each accommodating 1000 swine – were constructed. Other building types mentioned by Horbaly include cow and poultry barns, calving sheds, storehouses, a slaughter house

and meat processing plant, and dehydrating plants for potatoes and hay. Dumont (1957: 506) adds information on Czechoslovakia: 'Cooperative stock-rearing had led to the construction of enormous collective cow houses, which were subsidized on condition that local materials were employed and used economically, and that the members themselves should supply practically all the labor.'

With this emphasis on farm buildings for livestock, animal husbandry is obviously more important than in the past. Although peasant characteristics of tenure and method still hinder livestock raising and the climate in parts of the Balkans is not ideal for fodder crops, the production and consumption of meat has increased in the years since the Second World War (Terhaar and Vankai 1981: 563).

One structure enduring from the past is the old manor house that still stands, either in a village or isolated in the countryside. This relic, particularly evident in East Germany, Poland, and Hungary where the estates lasted until the Second World War, is discussed in Chapter 4; included is a map of Leezen, East Germany, showing the changes in settlement that occurred under socialism (see Fig. 4.3). Although many of the old estate buildings remain, a number of new residences and other facilities have been built. Even the road pattern has been altered slightly. I should repeat that under Marxist ideology each building must serve a functional purpose. These manor houses, therefore, often contain administrative headquarters for a collective farm – a common use in East Germany – or fill other uses as well, e.g. that of a museum or health institute.

3. Villages

Socialist plans for altering villages often start with the construction of a collective or state farm on the edge and then include changes in other parts of the settlement. In East Germany, one of the principles of village planning concerns the development of separate but adjacent areas of residence (*Wohnbereich*) and economic activity (*Wirtschaftsbereich*). The theoretical pattern of the socialist village as shown in the graph (see Fig. 7.1) is taken from Ogrissek (1961: 101). Although theoretical, Schröder (1964: 303) explains that the plan is actually implemented throughout the northern plain of East Germany. Placing residential and economic areas together follows the ideological principles of reducing differences between town and countryside as the *Wirtschaftsbereich* becomes a 'factory in the village', a place where all economic processes related to the collective or state farm are concentrated. The adjacent *Wohnbereich* is usually a village that

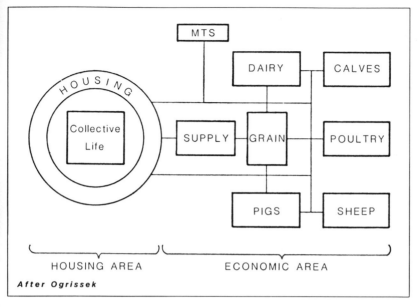

Fig. 7.1 The theoretical structure of a socialist village in East Germany. The collective or state farm is attached to the village as its 'economic area'. MTS refers to Machine Tractor Station, which was important in the early days of collectivization. (Source: Ogrissek 1961.)

in many cases has been altered by the addition of apartment buildings and single-family houses for agricultural and even industrial workers. The village also performs certain functions – political, economic, and social – that taken together determine its position in the socialist hierarchy of settlement.

The hierarchy outlined for East Germany, however, is ideal, and each village may differ according to local circumstances. A concrete example is Marxwalde, formerly called Quilitz, a village about 20 miles (32 kms) northwest of Frankfurt/Oder. While visiting this village, I verified that the map by Ogrissek (1961: 109) accurately portrays a socialist model (see Fig. 7.2). As a German *Angerdorf*, Marxwalde has been adapted to conform remarkably well to the theoretical plan for development of a village with 'residential' and 'economic' areas. The former noble's house with park has been turned into an administrative center. Grouped around the wide portion of the village common are administrative buildings, a school, shops, a church, and a cultural house. An electronics plant

289

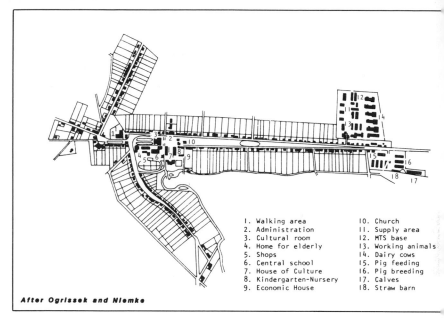

1. Walking area
2. Administration
3. Cultural room
4. Home for elderly
5. Shops
6. Central school
7. House of Culture
8. Kindergarten-Nursery
9. Economic House
10. Church
11. Supply area
12. MTS base
13. Working animals
14. Dairy cows
15. Pig feeding
16. Pig breeding
17. Calves
18. Straw barn

After Ogrissek and Niemke

Fig. 7.2 The village of Marxwalde in East Germany. The author in a 1980 visit noted the similarity of this village to the model of Fig. 7.1 and to the models of Ogrissek (1961) and Niemke (1956).

accompanied by apartment buildings for workers demonstrates Marxist 'industrialization' (see Photo 7.4). At one end of the village is the 'economic area' of the collective farm whose dominant buildings are elaborate stables for cows and pigs, with others for oxen, the breeding of pigs, and storage of machinery for the farm; the stables for calves are located near the meadowland; because of the possibility of disease, sheep and poultry installations lie farther out. This emphasis on livestock was pointed out in the preceding section in regard to the postwar construction of barns for feeding purposes.

The modernization of housing constitutes a striking change in the village landscape of Eastern Europe. In all the countries except Albania, which I have not visited, villages exhibit a mixture of old and new; houses that look little different from what they did in the nineteenth century, possibly with a few repairs or extensions, represent the old; the impact of industrialization in fostering houses or apartment buildings represents the new. Those villages located close to cities or towns with factories contain large numbers of peasant-workers whose residences are quite evident. In Kaszów, a

Photo 7.4 This apartment building in the village of Marxwalde northeast of Berlin houses workers for an electronics plant (Dynamo).

village west of Cracow, Poland, I saw villas representing the investment of these workers who benefit from both agricultural and industrial incomes (see Photo 7.5).

Perhaps the most distinct 'socialist' structure in the village, however, is the House of Culture or, in smaller settlements, the club or reading room. These centers comprise outlets for the communist cultural programs and, therefore, act as foci of Party influence in the rural areas where isolation and traditional resistance of the peasant to regime propaganda exist. The official goal is for the culture center to replace the local church and tavern as a focus of rural life. In varying degrees, these facilities are part of the landscape of all countries of Eastern Europe, having been copied from the Soviet Union. I have viewed many centers in Romania, including new ones under construction, and was told that they are typical – along with the school and police station – of the 'village-scape' (see Photo 7.6); a Romanian atlas (*Atlas Geografic*, 1965: 101) indicates their wide regional distribution and increase in numbers since the Second World War.

4. Settlement patterns

Supplementing changes in the individual villages under socialism are

the overall changes in the settlement patterns. In Eastern Europe, villages dominate this pattern, except in Hungary where the *tanya* plays a role and in Poland where many dispersed farms were established during the land reforms after the Second World War. Within the village network, planning interest has centered on the functional role each should play in a socialist settlement hierarchy. Before the Second World War, high rural overpopulation and village isolation meant that any hierarchy of functions was vague. School, church, and tax collector might have been present, but other central-place activities such as police and consumer goods were quite localized. With the advent of communism and the attempt to reduce differences between town and country, the outline of a hierarchy of central places becomes more evident. Uren (1969: 136–42) points out that in Hungary socialist planning for rural areas includes designating villages suitable for development with state help at one of three levels in the hierarchy, based on the population threshold necessary to support different functions: (1) 900–1500 – service for two collectives to include a four-room school, basic shopping, and administration; (2) 2400–3000 – service for three to five collectives to include an eight-room school, kindergarten, house of culture, physician, pharmacy, fire department, police, sports field, water and sewage, and small shops; (3) 5000 and over – service for six collectives to include technical institutions, district administration, courts, department stores, and market places. Public transportation varies with the size of the village.

Industry has also invaded the rural landscape. Tatai (1976: 77–83) indicates that between 1959 and 1973 industrial workers living in Hungarian villages increased by 130 000. Examples of such villages are: Visonta, coal; Borsodnádasd, sheet iron; Balatonfüzfö, nitrogen; Szigatszentimiklós, aircraft; Tolna, silk; Martfü, shoes; and Szerencs, chocolate.

A special problem of settlement change under socialism concerns the role of the *tanyas* (dispersed settlements) of Hungary (see Ch. 5), because they are not easily incorporated within a collective farm

Photo 7.5 The largest residences in farm villages of Eastern Europe generally are built by peasant-workers who commute to factories in the city. This residence is in the village of Kaszów near Cracow, Poland.

Photo 7.6 The House of Culture, found in the villages of Eastern Europe, serves as a source of Party control and influence.

293

system. The basic problem is their isolation from services, especially utilities, health, and education (see Photo 5.8). In many cases, only the dwelling remains now as *tanya* land was added to collective farms (see Fig. 7.3). N. Volgyes (1980: 182–3) indicates that the Alföld landscape in the late 1970s actually included four types of *tanya* residents: labor-intensive producers of fruit and vegetables for market; farmers who lived there and worked on collective farms but produced livestock products of their own for sale; commuters to industrial jobs in the cities and who used the *tanya* for subsistence purposes; and urban dwellers who kept a *tanya* for weekend recreation and gardening. The *tanya* persists because it reduces urban housing investment and because these farms collectively make an important contribution to Hungarian agriculture. In doing so, however, this settlement form hinders the socialist ideological goal of removing differences between town and country.

The character of the giant town-villages of the Hungarian plain has also changed under socialism. Kecskemet, a large town of about 60 000 inhabitants in south-central Hungary, exemplifies this transformation. Today this center is beginning to resemble a city: the outer zone of rural residences with haystacks is less evident and the inner core displays both a greater variety of commercial facilities and an industrial zone of factories and blocks of apartment buildings. The city attracts many commuters to its plants.

The peasant-worker

What have been the effects of collectivization on peasant society in Eastern Europe? Considerable evidence shows that the peasant groups so graphically portrayed by Doreen Warriner (1939) in the interwar period have been radically changed. In sponsoring programs in industrialization and urbanization, the communist party offered the first real outlets to large peasant populations that Warriner had depicted as underemployed in the 1930s. The isolation of the village was broken down and with it the parochial attitudes that were based on the security provided by land, family, and village. In the Balkans, the old extended family (*Zadruga*) had vanished. Most pronounced of all is the magnetism of an urban way-of-life on the younger peasants, a pull that fits in with the Marxist goal of reducing differences between urban and rural areas. The Party hopes to create a socialist countryside in which collective institutions will dominate and agroindustrial complexes can exist.

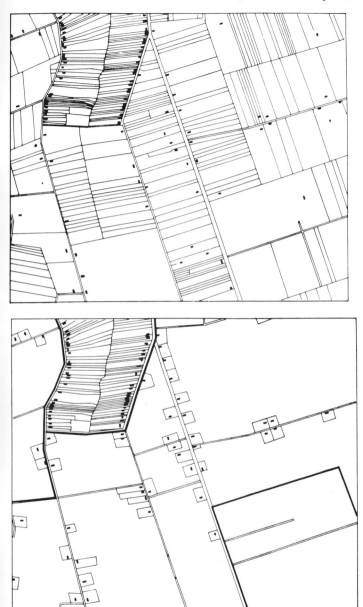

Fig. 7.3 Changes in *tanya* settlement under socialism. The top map shows the small holdings and dwellings of the *tanya* on the outskirts of Szarvas, Hungary, in 1945. By 1965 (bottom map) most of the land had been added to collective farms, and the *tanyas* remained only as dwellings. (Source: Petri 1971: pp. 175–6.)

However, the attempt to industrialize rapidly, using labor released by collectivization and agricultural modernization programs, creates problems in Eastern Europe. The most prominent one, ironically, is this very rapid influx of new workers into cities from rural areas. As mentioned earlier, this rural–urban migration contributed to an increase in urban population from 36 per cent in 1950 to over 50 per cent thirty years later. Yet, 50 per cent does not reflect the true degree of urbanization, for actually only about 25 per cent of the labor force in Eastern Europe is employed in agriculture. Several million industrial workers continue to live in villages and commute to cities because housing is unavailable, i.e. industrialization has run ahead of urbanization. Members of this rural nonagricultural labor force, known as peasant-workers, comprised the following percentages of the total nonagricultural labor force in 1973: Czechoslovakia, 40; East Germany, 33; Hungary, 30; Yugoslavia, 30; Bulgaria, 25; and Poland, 20 (Hoffman 1980: 33).

The communist party looks on this phenomenon of peasant-worker with mixed feelings. On the one hand, such a group tends to perpetuate some of the rural–urban differences and thus delay the creation of a 'collective' society focused on urban areas; on the other hand, it permits savings on housing investment by using the village as a base for commuting. Dienes (1973: 363) remarks, for example, that such restrictions on urban expansion in Hungary meant that in the early 1970s one-third of the total nonagricultural labor force lived in villages and hamlets, most of them commuting to the cities. Barta (1976: 106–7) supplements this by reporting that these villages had lower ratios of services including running water, sewers, gas, and health care.

The creation of a class of peasant-workers, therefore, is a spatial characteristic of postwar Eastern Europe. These persons live in the village and may even farm part-time while commuting to a job in the city. Eventually, they might move to the city but periodically return to the village, thereby maintaining their physical and cultural ties for some time. The village, consequently, feels the impact of the peasant-worker – economically through expanded income and goods and socially through aging of the agricultural work force. At the same time, the city or town also reflects the influence of the peasant-worker. This mutual urbanization and ruralization reduces the differences between town and country without doing away with them; a specific and temporary hybridization of urban and rural society is

involved, the nature of which is not yet wholly clear (Mihailović 1972: 83).

In Yugoslavia, the peasant-worker makes up a very high proportion of the farm population. For example, in 1969, 43.8 per cent of all agricultural households involved peasant-workers (Crkvenčić 1977: 7) One-half of these people had assumed this status after 1963, so it is a relatively new phenomenon. Furthermore, it is widespread. By 1969, peasant-workers composed sizable percentages of the total nonagricultural work force in all the republics, ranging from 26 per cent in Slovenia to 58 per cent in Bosnia-Hercegovina. However, ethnic differences in Yugoslavia affect migration since movements across certain republic lines are reduced, i.e. from the 'eastern' ones to the 'western' ones of Croatia and Slovenia (Hawrylyshyn 1977: 381). The underdeveloped republics, e.g. Bosnia-Hercegovina, have high percentages because the peasant-workers tend to dominate the industrialization process as it develops.

Peasant-workers in Yugoslavia tend to commute to the nearest urban center (80% traveled less than 12 miles [20 km]) and to work in blue-collar jobs, especially construction, where seasonal employment is important. It is the peasants from the smallest holdings that become part-time workers as they are motivated by the wages, pensions, and health benefits in the city, while their agricultural property is too small and fragmented for any real security in the rural environment. Finally, many of the *Gastarbeiter* (guest workers) who migrate to northern Europe, especially West Germany, from Yugoslavia seeking jobs are peasant-workers who, when they return, may use their savings either to improve their original holding or to build a house in the town as they abandon part-time farm status. Crkvenčić points out that the migrants might choose fringe locations in cities – as in the case of Rudeš in Zagreb – where they can grow vegetables and raise poultry and pigs, helping to retain a part-rural landscape.

The village of Orašac in Serbia illustrates the peasant-worker in Eastern Europe. Although some may argue that this village is not typical because of the historical influence of the Party, the rather complete documentation of changes offers advantages. This documentation was compiled by Joel Halpern (1956; 1972), an anthropologist who lived in the village for an extended period and who revisited it on several occasions. In addition, I made a personal trip to the village.

The village shows considerable change under socialism. In many ways, a paradox exists in that the village is a mixture of old and new. For example, characteristics of small, fragmented land holdings, importance of grain over animal production, use of hand methods, and small capital investment persist. However, the impact of the state comes through the cooperative which provides machinery, seed, and fertilizer at low costs. Since almost half of the 450 families in Orašac work in a factory or other job in towns like nearby Arandjelovac, supplementary income is available for things like fertilizer, which has helped to double the yields of crops. At the same time, the absence of young men has led to the decline of the *Zadruga* or extended family organization, which was so important in Orašac in the past. The relationship between man and wife seems to have increased at the expense of the old father–son tie that dominated the *Zadruga*. The village is left with a higher proportion of older persons, especially women, who must do a greater share of the agricultural work. Visible urbanization of the village results from the influence of the state, which paved the road to the town, instituted bus service, and brought electricity for the first time. Other state influences include an elementary school and television. However, the most apparent change – the modernization of housing – is a product of both the state and individual effort.

The impact of the village on the town is also evident, most particularly through the values of the peasants who have migrated there or who commute daily. Almost three-fourths of the 10 000 inhabitants of Arandjelovac have moved there from villages like Orašac, pulled by the possibilities of jobs, education, and higher living standards. However, these peasants prefer their own houses over apartment buildings – because the latter include 'strangers' – so with the cooperation of friends, they build a house over a long period, using evenings and weekends as in the village. Having a garden, chickens, and even a pig furthers the similarity with the village. Electricity may be accepted but not the feeling of necessity to tie into the water and sewer networks, if they exist. Thus, the 'peasantization' of the town can be real. At the same time, however, family ties with the village become difficult to maintain.

The overlap between village and town is consequently more complete in Yugoslavia than in the past when a clear separation existed between urban and rural; indeed, the two were often antagonistic in their relationships. In the past, Arandjelovac was a market town for the surrounding area, but now it is a factory town with branches of

national enterprises replacing the former shops and with cars replacing carts. Still, it has peasant overtones. On the other hand, Orašac clearly no longer is a village. The peasant-workers partake of both worlds through their commuting or returning on weekends, yet they are part of neither. They can never really return to the village tradition, yet they do not possess an urban mentality. This mixed legacy is one dilemma of at least the first generation, a group which may make up one-third of the total Yugoslav urban work force.

The modernization of the industrial landscape under socialism

Widespread industrialization of the East European landscape, most of it in urban but some also in rural areas, reflects the high priority placed on this process of modernization. In the following sections, I emphasize the factors explaining the location of this industry and the degree to which the ideological goal of greater regional equity has been realized. Both location and equity are related to the three periods of planning that took place after 1945: autarky to 1957; regional specialization and trade through the 1960s; and, finally, economic reforms in planning coupled with trade with the West in the 1970s.

Major regional disparities in industrialization within Eastern Europe relate to historical differences in development, e.g. the backwardness of eastern Poland as a result of Russian repression during the partition period, Slovakia's treatment under Hungary in contrast to Bohemia's position under Austria, and the isolation of Serbia and Macedonia compared to the more Westernized Slovenia, Croatia, and Dalmatia. On the other hand, north–south differences in East Germany and Poland relate to the presence or absence of raw materials. As Mihailović (1972: 8) points out, polarization of economic development is inevitable in a backward economy because the volume of industry is insufficient to cover the whole country. A fundamental goal of socialist ideology has been the elimination of these backward areas that were assumed to exist in territories with capitalistic backgrounds.

The factors that explain the socialist location of industry in Eastern Europe after 1945 vary. Hamilton (1971a) relates them to certain Marxist planning principles: proximity to raw materials or markets; attainment of regional autarky or regional specialization; dispersion throughout an area for ideological reasons; placement in backward

regions occupied by an ethnic minority; elimination of differences between town and country; strategic location for defense purposes; and specialization within the East European Common Market (Comecon). Examples of all of these principles can be found, but their application does not follow any consistent pattern in time. Frequently, more than one is involved in explaining changes in spatial organization.

Selected types of industrial landscape that have evolved under a framework of socialist planning in Eastern Europe are the focus here.

Heavy industry: steel

In the 1950s, a policy of autarky with an emphasis on heavy industry dominated both centralized planning within the Soviet Bloc and the more decentralized planning of Yugoslavia. As an initial base for this policy, each country built a large integrated iron and steel plant, which represents a striking element of the landscape from this period. The locations of these plants did not seem to follow the traditional economic factors of raw materials, transport costs, labor, and market. Although the plants were more or less located in backward areas and thus furthered dispersion, the sites seemed to be related as much to military-strategic factors as to ideological ones. Four of them – Eisenhüttenstadt (formerly Stalinstadt) in East Germany, Nowa Huta in Poland, Košice in Czechoslovakia (see Photo 7.7), and Galaţi in Romania – were built in the eastern parts of their respective countries, close to the Soviet Union (see Fig. 7.4). Indeed, the dependence on the Soviet Union for raw materials (especially iron ore) was perhaps a primary factor in the eastern location, although the sites might vary. Dunaújváros (formerly Sztalinváros) in Hungary on the Danube below Budapest and Kremcikovi near Sofia in Bulgaria are located farther west in their respective countries, but dependence on the Soviet Union remains basic. Galaţi, which was built in the 1960s – considerably later than the others – represented Romania's delayed attempt at autarky after this policy was abandoned in the other countries in favor of specialization within CMEA. Eisenhüttenstadt, Nowa Huta, and Dunaújváros are new towns.

This dependence on the Soviet Union is not true of steel plants in Albania and Yugoslavia. Mellor (1975: 325) reports that the small steel works at Elbasan in Albania was originally dependent on Soviet aid and later on the Chinese, but its present base seems to be autarkic. The plants at Skopje (in Macedonia) and Nikšić (in Montenegro)

are examples of Yugoslavia's early attempts to develop bastions of socialism in the underdeveloped republics. Nikšić, located in an isolated karst region, also represented a strategic location away from Soviet threats after the 1948 Cominform break. Both Skopje and Nikšić had problems – Skopje from the use of low-grade ores and coking coal, and Nikšić from a location 150 miles from sources of raw materials; the latter, as a consequence, had early losses of 3 million dollars annually, a fact that seems to support ideological and strategic factors in location over economic ones. Furthermore, neither served as an ideal growth pole, because the plants were capital intensive rather than labor intensive.

The wide dispersion of these plants in Eastern Europe originally created an impression that the Party was serious about its ideology, especially the spread of industry into underdeveloped areas. To the people of the respective countries, these plants are physically impressive, as they are meant to be. The site of Galați on a bluff overlooking the Danube is very imposing. What one should keep in mind, however, is that a variety of factors in industrial location are interrelated here: the eastern parts of four countries besides being close to the Soviet Union and farther from western military forces were also underdeveloped. Here ideology and strategy happened to

Photo 7.7   A view of the large iron and steel plant constructed in the 1960s near Košice in eastern Czechoslovakia. Iron ore comes from the Soviet Union.

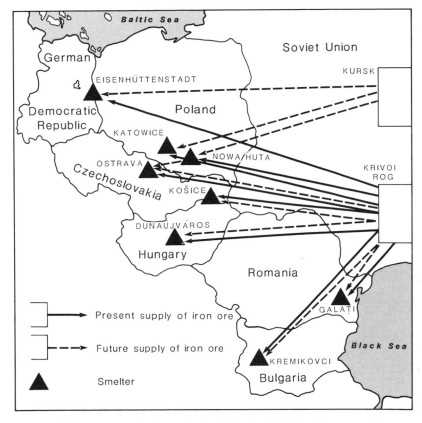

Fig. 7.4 Links between the iron and steel industry of Eastern Europe and the sources of iron ore supplies in the Soviet Union. The smelters represent the new integrated plants built after the Second World War. (Source: Harke and Dischereit 1979: p. 50.)

combine as factors, as did pride and autarky. One Pole summed it up: 'The first real iron and steel plant constructed by Polish hands and one that will make us more self-sufficient in heavy industry.' Finally, even the political factor looms important in Poland where citizens frequently tell visitors that Nowa Huta was located near Cracow to proletarianize a bourgeoisie city; even the location of a second integrated plant at Częchochowa is cited by Hamilton (1971b: 83) as industrialization of this pilgrimage center of the Polish Catholic Church.

Heavy industry: energy and minerals

Policies of autarky and heavy industry in the 1950s also supported new industrial regions based on unexploited energy and minerals. A good example of this concept is the postwar development of the Bezirk of Cottbus as a coal and energy base for East Germany. This district produces over one-half of both the brown coal and electric energy for the country (Kohl *et al.* 1976: 140). The massive transformation of the landscape here impressed me tremendously: large machines stripped away the overburden and laid bare the coal to be used in new electric plants; at the same time, conservation was being practiced with old pits converted to lakes for recreation, e.g. Senftenberg. Two new towns – Hoyerswerda and Lauchhammer – have developed as centers of brown coal use for energy purposes. Hoyerswerda is a residential site for workers at the Schwarze Pumpe complex, which became famous in the 1950s for production of coke from brown coal for metallurgical production; this coke, apparently unsatisfactory in quality for that purpose, is now used for producing gas for industry and heating.

Poland also illustrates regional changes in industrialization based on exploiting new raw materials for national growth purposes but not necessarily as part of autarkic policies. Wilczewski *et al.* (1978: 85–8) explain how five new industrial regions based on raw materials have emerged since 1950 and tend to bring more balance to the industrial map of Poland (see Fig. 7.5). These regions demonstrate the difference between equality in an absolute sense and that defined under socialism in which strict equality is not a goal. For example, these locations previously provided little or no industry whereas now they not only provide greater access to jobs and services for the people in these areas than before, but also transform the presocialist landscape. However, collectively in the mid-1970s, they only accounted for 5.5 per cent of gross industrial capital and 3.8 per cent of industrial employment in Poland. This reflects new thinking in Marxist industrial-location policy in which national growth interest becomes a major factor in initiating new regional development. The five regions illustrate the diversity of raw material sources that are being exploited: brown coal at Konin, copper at Legnica-Głogów, sulphur at Tarnobrzeg, natural gas at Puławy, and oil at Płock. The last is unusual because the oil comes by pipeline from the Soviet Union. All these regions seem to represent minor growth sectors in Polish industrial development. Some plants based on these raw

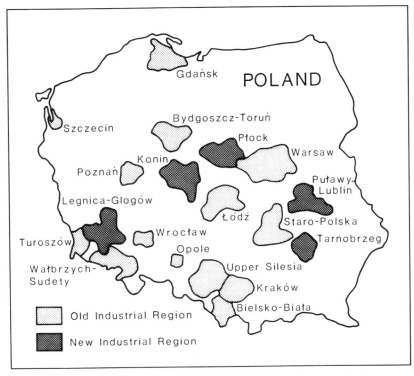

Fig. 7.5   Industrial regions of Poland. The five new regions have provided more regional balance to modernization. (Source: Wilczewski 1978: p. 82.)

materials include aluminum smelting and fabricating in the Konin region, copper processing at Glogów, nitrogen fertilizer at Puławy, and petro-chemicals at Płock. These cities are of medium size and reflect socialist policy to deconcentrate industry where possible.

Ethnic regions

Hamilton (1971a: 189–90) finds that early locational dispersion of industry in Eastern Europe was affected by political attempts to equalize the economic base of ethnic or minority areas, although other factors of local raw materials, the ideology of developing backward areas, and military strategy were important, too. The two outstanding examples of the ethnic factor affecting industrial location are Czechoslovakia and Yugoslavia, the only two states in Eastern Europe which have federal systems of government that represent

304

attempts to handle multinational situations.

In Czechoslovakia, the Slovak area historically has been much less developed economically than the Bohemian-Moravian portion, but postwar industrialization raised its contribution of total state output from 8 per cent in 1939 to 24 per cent in 1967 (Hamilton 1971a: 183). Although the need for ethnic balance was a crucial motive in this significant progress toward equity, the developed state of the Czech economy and the surplus Slovak labor were contributing features. In addition to the ethnic factor, strategy played a role in Slovak industrialization because this area is located on important routes — east–west to the Soviet Union and north–south to Poland and Hungary. Slovak industrialization, consequently, is widely dispersed in the landscape. One outstanding example besides the Košice steel plant is the series of hydroelectric plants along the Váh River.

Socialist attempts to develop backward ethnic regions played a part in Yugoslavia's construction of the Belgrade to Bar railroad. The separation of the Adriatic coast from the interior by the Dinaric Mountain barrier has long been a handicap to the integration and development of the country. Since existing railroad lines traversed Slovenia, Croatia, and Bosnia, the socialist regime planned to construct the newest line from Serbia through the southern republic of Montenegro. This line, begun in the 1950s but frequently interrupted by high costs, was finally completed in the late 1970s and seems to reflect persistent planning goals for developing the resources of backward areas. In its long route through mountainous terrain, across numerous bridges, and through extensive cuts and tunnels, this railroad not only alters the landscape but also symbolizes the integration of a country.

The Belgrade-to-Bar railway is but one manifestation of continuing Yugoslav efforts to channel funds into the developing republics of the south. Although the Slovenes and Croats object to subsidizing Bosnia, Macedonia, Montenegro, and Kosovo, the federal government's allocation in 1978 was some 700 million dollars. Pressure for government support is especially strong in Bosnia, where the Moslems have achieved a special identity with some even agitating for Pan Islamism.

National and international tourism

A specialized type of resource that has led to dispersion of a service industry comes from scenery and tourism, with the most outstanding

examples being the resorts built along coastlines of East European countries. All of these facilities provide recreation for the proletarian masses, but the ones along the Black Sea and Adriatic coasts cater to Western hard currencies as well. The rising demand for this service explains why expansion of facilities has been continuous since 1950 and is not confined to a particular time period. Places like Mamaia ('not Miami', as an advertisement in the *New York Times* stated some years back) in Romania, the Golden Sands in Bulgaria, and Makarska in Yugoslavia have international reputations, although they do not measure up to the quality of the Riviera. Along the Baltic coast, the short summer season restricts use to regional people, but accommodations are booked solid by worker groups on state vacations.

Poulsen (1977, Ch. 11), in providing details on the expansion of tourism along the Adriatic coastline of Yugoslavia, reports that the stimulus for state promotion of the tourist industry came from Yugoslavia's 1948 break with the Cominform and the ensuing need to earn hard currency for essential imports. As a result, the state increased investments in hotels and restaurants from 0.7 per cent of total national budget in 1960 to 7.4 per cent in 1970. Financial assistance from the World Bank and the US government helped to build a modern road along the coast, giving rise by 1972 to accommodations for over 600 000 persons. The increase in tourism in the 1970s was phenomenal – 4 million foreigners, especially tourists from West Germany, spent time here each year. Yugoslavia became one of the world's most important tourist countries, ranking with Switzerland and ahead of Greece. The $1.3 billion spent annually in the 1970s represented 22 per cent of Yugoslavia's foreign currency. In addition to international visitors, one-sixth of the domestic population spends time on this coast.

My interest lies in the impact of tourism on the Dalmatian landscape, a 600-mile stretch of coastline, which before the Second World War was a backward area except for a few cities, but which now has been thoroughly transformed in several ways:

1. New facilities for tourists

A new all-weather road of 640 miles now runs between the Italian and Albanian borders, linking a series of hotel complexes both in major cities and smaller localities (see Photo 7.8). This coast can safely be called the Yugoslav Riviera, although the atmosphere differs in that foreigners are not permitted to own land, thus reducing the international set. Many Yugoslavs, especially the workers returned

Photo 7.8 The resort of Makarska, located on the Dalmatian coast of Yugoslavia south of Split, exemplifies the post-Second World War attempt to attract Western hard currency.

from jobs in Western Europe – West Germany in particular – have invested in guest houses, pensiones, restaurants, and automobile facilities.

2. New settlements for workers

In the early 1970s, the tourist industry of Dalmatia employed 175 000 persons, as each year some 8000 workers migrated to the coast to fill the jobs in service and construction. Others commuted daily or weekly. To house these migrants, a new series of settlements arose, some of which represent squatter residences in the suburbs of towns. Others include the transfer of whole villages from the slopes of the mountains to the narrow coastal plain; thus, Donja ('lower') Brela replaced Gornja ('upper') Brela.

3. Abandonment of farm land

The migration of workers from both the adjacent mountain areas and islands of Dalmatia has resulted in considerable loss of agricultural land – either abandoned completely or inadequately cared for in terms of labor. An example is the fertile Ravni Kotari region south of Zadar, where mile after mile of olive groves are no longer tended or harvested, even though Yugoslavia suffers from a shortage of olive oil and must import it from other Mediterranean areas.

4. New agricultural areas

At the same time, new areas of agricultural specialization have emerged to supply the tourist industry with food. Examples include the delta of the Neretva River, with fields of vegetables, citrus orchards, and grapes near the resort town of Primošten.

5. Second homes

Still another aspect of this transformed landscape is the presence of second homes (*Vikendici* – weekenders) built by Yugoslav residents from the interior. Poulsen estimates that 15 000–20 000 such houses exist.

6. Effects on the environment

The changes incurred by the Dalmatian environment are a classic example of technological impact and population pressure. In the days before tourism, the environment of the barren limestone mountains and narrow coastal plain displayed a fragile ecological balance in terms of people's use of the land. The ancient stone terraces which perch precariously on the slopes with plots of corn, vineyards, and olive trees reflect this balance. Once the tourist boom struck, however, this delicate balance was upset and the natural environment has suffered tremendous damage, some of it irreparable. Furthermore, air pollution from plants producing cement, aluminum, carbide, and refined petroleum products, e.g. the aluminum factory in Šibenik, harms both ancient buildings and human health. Water pollution is also a problem as is damage to buildings and roads from vibration caused by increased vehicular traffic. The ancient town of Trogir, an impressive historical relic, demonstrates the collision of modern technology with historical preservation by its location in the flight pattern of the new Split airport.

The rapid modernization process along the coastline has produced

great contrasts in social change, e.g. the average income in the Zagora mountain area behind the coastal city of Šibenik is only 22 per cent of the average income of Croatia, the republic in which Dalmatia is located; the proportions of coastal population by occupation have changed – 80 per cent to 30 per cent in agriculture, 10 per cent to 30 per cent in industry, and 10 per cent to 40 per cent in tertiary services; and, finally, six out of ten coastal inhabitants now engage in some phase of the tourist industry.

Traditional centers of industry

The previous examples of socialist industrial development illustrate spatial patterns of dispersion and, therefore, provide support for the socialist goal of greater regional equality. However, regional concentration of industry in traditional centers of Eastern Europe has remained important through all periods of autarky, regional specialization, and economic reform. In an absolute sense, the increase in industrial employment has been greater in the traditional regions than in the newer ones, although the latter, starting from a lower base, have had high relative increases. A map of Polish industrial growth from 1946 to 1975 supports this hypothesis (see Fig. 7.6). In the 1960s and 1970s, decision-makers increasingly favored the older regions because of external economies, i.e. the savings generated by being near large cities and their markets, labor supply, transportation, and so on. Thus, the efficiency–equity trade-off seemed to be tipping in favor of efficiency owing to increased costs of industrial dispersion into new areas and the advantages of using existing centers. Much of the growth in these older regions, however, has been peripheral, representing a spatial pattern of decentralization.

The main area of industrial concentration has been in a triangle between Halle, Łódź, and Budapest, where three-fourths of East Europe's industry was located before the Second World War (see Fig. 5.7). Although dispersion reduced this to 50 per cent in the early 1970s, the concentration remains impressive (Hamilton 1971a: 176, 179). Actually, the triangle constitutes a series of historic manufacturing subregions including Upper Silesia (Poland), Saxony and Anhalt (East Germany), portions of Bohemia-Moravia (Czechoslovakia), and Budapest. In addition, presocialist areas of heavy industry based on raw materials have expanded in northeast Hungary, southwest Romania, and central Yugoslavia as well as in the capital cities

309

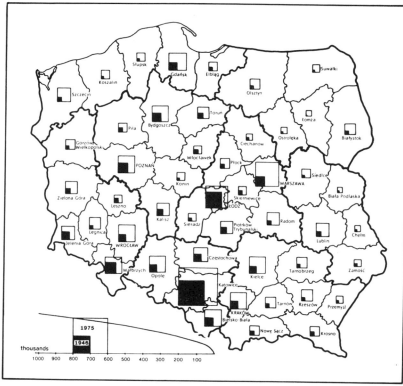

Fig. 7.6 Poland: industrial growth between 1946 and 1975. Although the absolute increases have been highest in the areas that were most important in 1946, relative increases have been very large in the lesser developed regions. (Source: Misztal and Kaczorowski 1980: p. 204).

and certain regional centers like Poznań (Posen), Györ, Brno (Brünn), Braşov, and Zagreb.

The outstanding example of the traditional industrial region where raw materials serve as a locational factor is Upper Silesia (see Fig. 5.8). This region is discussed in earlier chapters in terms of its primary geographical characteristic of political fragmentation – first between three empires and later between Germany and Poland during the interwar period. After the Second World War, however, the entire region came under Poland, a spatial factor that has facilitated its development. As the largest industrial-urban agglomeration in Eastern Europe, Upper Silesia in 1980 included some 3 million persons, with about one-third of the labor force employed in

310

manufacturing. The area retains its 'mono-industrial' structure with coal mining, ferrous and nonferrous metallurgy, and engineering still dominating the regional economy. However, Wilczewski *et al.* (1978: 92–6) point out that significant structural changes have taken place by which mining and metallurgy have declined in relative proportion of employment from 72 per cent to 58 per cent. On the other hand, machinery and chemicals have increased from 15 per cent to 25 per cent.

The landscape of Upper Silesia reflects this mixture of old and new, which are correlated spatially with inner and outer regions as designed officially by planning authorities (see Fig. 5.8). Of the two zones, the inner shows less evidence of change except for the rebuilding of certain factories and residences and the expansion of service facilities in cities, especially Katowice. The most apparent problems are air pollution and subsidence from coal mining. The outer zone, however, reflects more changes. During a recent trip through the area, I observed new mines and factories plus a series of dormitory settlements (e.g. Nowe Tychy) for workers who commute into the region. Most of the new coal mines are located near Rybnik to the west of the conurbation. The landscape's most impressive new factory, with its long, covered beltway for transferring iron ore from Soviet railroad cars, is the large integrated steel works east of Katowice at Dąbrowa Górnicza. This project, which reflects the personal politics of the former Polish Communist leader Gierek, who is of Silesian origin, is one of the largest ever undertaken in Poland and, as such, severely strained the economy.

Spatially, this expansion of a traditional industrial region into new locations near, but outside, the core area of Upper Silesia represents what Hamilton (1971a: 183) calls 'dispersed localization' or what others might term 'decentralization.' Another example of decentralization of industry around a traditional region relates to brown coal mining near Halle in East Germany, already mentioned in the chapters on multinationalism and nationalism in connection with the early development of the chemical industry. Exploitation of brown coal has been even more intensive during the socialist period, as shown in an East German map of open-pit mining changes between 1945 and 1968 (see Fig. 6.5). The equipment used, perhaps the largest in the world, removes the overburden, extracts the coal, and returns the overburden, all in one operation (see Fig. 7.7).

Within the Budapest agglomeration, changes in industrialization also occurred through decentralization of factories to the suburban

Fig. 7.7 Example of open-pit mining of brown coal in East Germany. Such advanced technology includes reclamation for future use. (Source: Barthel 1962: Annex No. 10.)

zone. By the 1970s, Compton (1979: 468–77) reports that the landscape of Budapest had evolved into three distinct zones. The first is the central city, a highly administrative, commercial, and residential zone; the residential section is composed of a mixture of older villas, apartment houses from presocialist times, and some socialist housing blocks. The second zone – suburbs – exhibits uneven development: large, industrial settlements like Újpest, Kispest, and Csepel, with factories and residential blocks standing in contrast to rural-like centers such as Cinkota and Pestimre with their single-family houses along unpaved roads. This zone contains most of Budapest's industry. The third zone is the outer ring of 44 villages and small towns lying within 10 miles (16 km) of the city boundary. This ring of settlements has the fastest growing population in Hungary, virtually all a result of net in-migration to accommodate workers who commute to factories in Budapest and, in part, live there because the city itself lacks housing (see Fig. 7.8).

International cooperation

The emphasis in the two preceding sections has been on national efforts to achieve a more effective distribution of industry under socialism. However, international policy as developed within Comecon has also affected the spatial organization of manufacturing and the landscape, especially after the autarkic period ending in 1957. Under the leadership of the Soviet Union, this so-called Common Market of Eastern Europe – including all East Europe countries (Albania was participating then but is not now) except Yugoslavia (an observer) – has established a number of facilities that are linked together.

Some of the industrial landscapes mentioned previously are closely related to policies of Comecon, most noteworthy being the large steel plants. But it is in the field of energy that the effects of Comecon are the most evident (Hoffman 1976; Bornstein 1981).

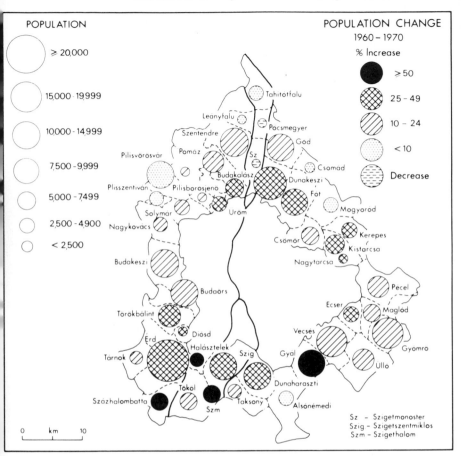

Fig. 7.8 Budapest. The outer zone of the metropolitan area has a rapidly increasing population of migrants, who live in villages and towns while commuting to jobs in the city. (Source: Compton 1979: 476.)

Eastern Europe still depends more on solid fuels than does Western Europe. In the 1970s, consumption of primary sources of energy in Eastern Europe was distributed 66 per cent in solid fuels, 19 per cent in oil, and 15 per cent in natural gas; comparable figures for Western Europe were 24 per cent, 57 per cent, and 15 per cent. The bloc itself supplied most of these solid fuels, which represented not only greater production of coal in traditional regions like Upper Silesia but also brown coal in newer areas like Cottbus (East Germany) and Konin (Poland). However, the consumption of oil and gas quadrupled

313

between 1960 and 1974, and, except for Romania, these countries have very little of their own. According to a Radio Free Europe Report (Hudson 1980: 14–15), 80 per cent of the oil required in Eastern Europe in 1980 was to come from the Soviet Union although non-Soviet imports were increasing. The Russians supply this oil to northern countries of Eastern Europe via pipelines from Volga-Urals and Siberian sources. The map shows the effects of the 'Friendship' oil pipeline (see Fig. 7.9): the creation of new bases for industrial dispersion at the refineries of Leuna and Schwedt (East Germany), Płock (Poland), Záluží and Bratislava (Czechoslovakia) and Leninváros (formerly Tiszapalkonja) and Százhalombatta (Hungary). Three of these cities – Schwedt, Płock, and Leninváros – are new towns. In Romania, the new refineries, for the most part, are based on domestic oil. Petrochemical plants have appeared at most of these new refinery sites, which, in general, are located in under-industrialized regions and are very apparent in the landscape (e.g. Schwedt).

The supplying of oil and gas to Eastern Europe, however, is a double-edged sword for the Russians: positive in view of making Comecon dependent on them for these vital resources, but negative in view of depleting their own reserves. Obviously, this procedure must be strategic for the Soviets because they are willing not only to sacrifice a precious resource, but also to sell it to the Bloc at a lower price than they could sell it to the West. In return for this oil, the Soviet Union in the future can probably demand higher prices, closer integration of economies, and political loyalty.

A network of electricity supplements those of iron-steel and oil-gas in the landscape of Eastern Europe. On a trip in eastern Hungary, a friend pointed to an east–west line of high-voltage transmission towers and said that it extends to the Soviet Union. This line, part of the Mir (Peace) electric grid that connects the seven major countries of Comecon, seems to support Lenin's emphasis on electricity as a key to industrialization: 'Communism is Soviet power plus electrification of the whole country' (Kuusinen 1963: 647). As a result, many prewar areas without electricity now have it and the international grid permits better adjustments to peak loading times in many areas.

With a 50-mile (80 km)-long lake that has submerged a series of rugged gorges and with a dam that has obliterated a barrier of rapids in the river at the Iron Gate near the Romanian city of Turnu Severin,

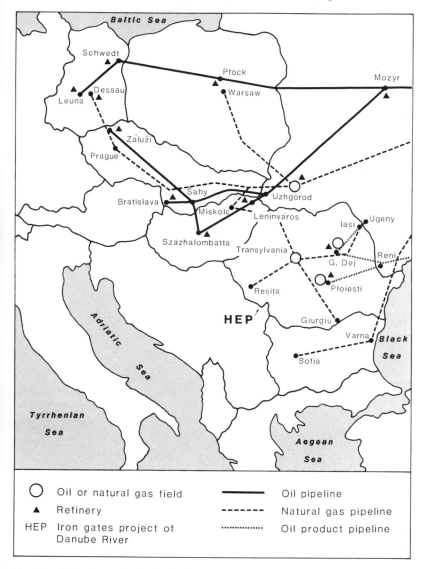

Fig. 7.9 Oil and gas distribution in Eastern Europe: the spatial effects of modernization. The emphasis is on connections with the Soviet Union; developments in Yugoslavia and Albania are not shown. The joint hydroelectric power project (HEP) on the Danube River between Romania and Yugoslavia is indicated. (Source: adapted from *International Petroleum Encyclopedia* 1982: p. 213.)

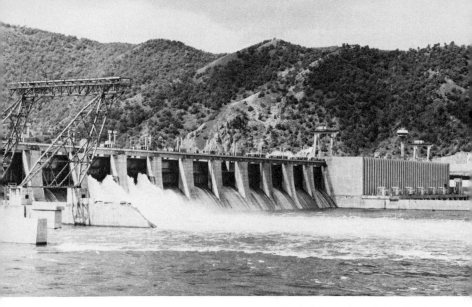

Photo 7.9 Romania and Yugoslavia cooperated in building a large hydroelectric power plant on the Danube. The dam created a large lake in former gorges above the Iron Gate.

the hydroelectric complex built on the Danube River between Romania and Yugoslavia stands out as a convincing illustration of landscape transformation in Eastern Europe (see Photo 7.9). In addition to its large-scale physical attributes, the plant – the largest of its kind in Eastern Europe – invites ideological reflections of Romanian nationalism and its early dissent with prescribed roles for countries within Comecon. Cooperation between the two countries, however, falls mostly into the production of electricity, for integration of regional planning on both sides of the Danube is negligible. A surprising gap in East European cooperation involves the Danube itself, largely because the river often flows along vulnerable borders.

Impacts of industry on the environment

Socialist countries have both advantages and disadvantages in handling environmental problems (Dienes 1974). In controlling the economy, they can effect a mix of output that minimizes environmental disruption. Also, their lag behind the West in consumer-goods production reduces the output of disposable products and

316

private cars, both of which are responsible for many of the water and air pollution problems. Furthermore, surplus, cheap labor supplies the work force for the collection of waste and the cleaning of streets and public places – a notable aspect of urban landscapes.

Reality, however, does not seem to agree with theory, for the socialists, ignore the environment much the same way that many capitalists do. Aspects of a degraded environment, including air and water pollution, catch the attention of anyone who has traveled in Eastern Europe. In Chapter 5, I mention that Copşa Mică in Romanian Transylvania has one of the worst environments from air pollution that I have seen. This chemical center, based on natural gas as a raw material, developed in the interwar period but has expanded considerably under socialism. Similar degrees of air pollution are seen and felt in Upper Silesia, especially in the core city of Katowice, which, according to a Polish scientist, may have the worst pollution problem in the world (Timberlake 1982: 56). This contamination extends even to the historic city of Cracow some 50 miles (80 km) to the east. I personally viewed how this city has received the ecological impact of new metallurgical developments from Upper Silesia to the west and Nowa Huta to the east. I was told that statistical data on this pollution are classified and that planners are extremely worried about the problem, because industrial dust exceeds the acceptable national limit by nine times.

Another aspect, this one a peculiar but still visible force, of the environmental landscape is subsidence of surface soil from coal mining in the Upper Silesian coal field. Removing layers or seams of coal close to the surface causes slumping which leaves surface depressions that fill either temporarily or permanently with water. This modification of the terrain restricts not only urban development but also the extension of coal mining under cities or settlements. To combat subsidence, socialist planners now pump sand underground to fill worked-out coal seams. Today, the large sand bunkers established near mines and the 300 miles (483 km) of rail lines to supply these bunkers become modern aspects of the landscape. The same is true of small lakes formed in areas of subsidence.

What are the factors explaining this apparent failure of socialism in Eastern Europe to handle environmental problems, given the advantages of a planned economy? A primary factor, according to Hamilton (1970b: 95–6), comes from the perceptions of socialist decision-makers, who regard the environment in terms of potential

productivity rather than potential habitability. In the early stages of autarkic development under socialism, these states were more concerned with opening up unutilized resources in all parts of the country regardless of costs. In this way, regional equity of production can conflict with regional equity of environment. The socialists were possibilists, believing – as did Stalin in his early plans to build shelter belts across vast areas – that people can tame their environment. Such perceptions tended to ignore the risks of environmental disruption in the interests of providing development in regions that exhibited potential, i.e. the economic costs of opening up backward areas were put ahead of the social costs of environmental harm. More recently, when external economies have favored concentration of production in large cities, efficiency has been favored over equity, and the regimes have hesitated to set rigorous environmental standards and enforce them. Furthermore, in socialist countries, where prices are subsidized and kept low, environmental costs are not passed on to the consumers.

The modernization of the urban landscape under socialism

We have now analyzed two aspects of the socialist landscape as it evolved in Eastern Europe after the Second World War. The first of these – the rural – was associated especially with collectivization of agriculture and the transformation of fields and small settlements, attempting with mixed success to reach an ideological goal of greater equity between town and country. The second aspect of landscape change – industrialization – was associated with an ideological goal of regional equity, again with only partial realization. We now turn to a third aspect of landscape evolution – the modernization of the urban areas, which is broken down into two logical sections, interurban and intraurban. At the macro scale, we are dealing with the changes in the overall network of settlements and the degree of balance which the socialist regimes have set as an ideological goal. Such balance refers to reduced concentration of population in large cities and a more rational distribution of goods and services through a hierarchy of settlement. At the micro scale, we are examining the variations within cities, especially the ideological goal of balance in the provision of services.

Separating the socialist landscape changes into rural, industrial,

and urban components, it must be stressed, is artificial, because the processes of modernization are interrelated. Planning priorities within the three components have varied, and industry frequently has run ahead of both agriculture and urban development. These differences justify a separation, which seems to me to be an important characteristic of this socialist landscape.

Interurban landscapes

Most industrial landscapes are associated with cities, making urban areas implicit in these patterns. However, we will now be more explicit and focus directly on the urban centers. Interurban networks comprise a hierarchy of settlements designed to provide goods and services for the 135 million people in the region. Here again, the socialists make the claim that they can provide a better overall balance of services like jobs, housing, health, education, and consumer goods than can capitalistic societies. In providing such services, the socialist regimes must implement policies designed to correct imbalances in population and settlement, such as the agrarian north of East Germany with its inadequate services or the primate city of Budapest with its large proportion of Hungarian population and industry. As we shall see, these imbalances placed considerable pressure on the goal of equity.

The relationship of interurban networks to landscape needs clarification. As mentioned in Chapter 1, landscape is most easily associated with individual forms, and the notion of an entire settlement system as a landscape is more abstract. Nevertheless, the concept is important in discussing spatial organization in socialist societies, which place considerable emphasis on national settlement plans and the ideology of equity. In this section, we look at landscape elements as part of a system. Following a brief discussion of urbanization levels in Eastern Europe, we examine settlement policies of dispersion, underurbanization, and national integration in their effects on the landscape.

Today, a visitor to Eastern Europe sees a landscape that is definitely more urbanized than in the past. The table (p. 320) shows the changes that have occurred since the 1930s in percentages of urban population in each country (Kosiński 1974: table 1; and *United Nations Demographic Yearbook* 1980).

319

	Pre-Second World War	*Recent*
Albania	15.4 (1938)	33.8 (1971)
Bulgaria	21.4 (1934)	62.1 (1980)
Czechoslovakia	38.9 (1930)	66.7 (1974)
East Germany	72.2 (1939)	76.2 (1980)
Hungary	33.2 (1930)	53.1 (1979)
Poland	37.3 (1939)	57.7 (1978)
Romania	21.4 (1930)	48.6 (1978)
Yugoslavia	13.2 (1931)	38.6 (1971)

These figures show that socialist programs of industrialization have definitely affected urbanization. Six of the countries are close to or above 50 per cent urban with only Yugoslavia and Albania lagging behind. The method of urban classification, which varies in each country, affects the data, but nevertheless the large changes are obvious.

The progress in urbanization is not evenly distributed, and the existing differences show up in the urban landscape. In general, urbanization decreases from west to east and from north to south, the highest being in East Germany and the lowest in Albania and Yugoslavia. Regionally, Bohemia is more urbanized than Slovakia, and Slovenia more than Serbia, Montenegro, or Macedonia. Yet urban differentials between north and south have contracted: towns in the Balkans had only 22.9 per cent of all East European urban dwellers in 1950 but 34 per cent in 1975. High growth rates in many ports and regional centers also indicate progress in urbanization, e.g. the eight major ports of Eastern Europe – Rostock, Szczecin, Gdańsk, Gdynia, Constanţa, Varna, Burgas, Rijeka, and Split – all doubled in population in the socialist period as did some thirty regional centers.

Kosiński (1974) points out that both rural to urban migration and high birth rates were responsible for rapid urbanization after the Second World War. Until the 1960s, the programs of collectivization (except in Poland and Yugoslavia) released large numbers of agricultural workers for jobs in cities. These rural transplants initially kept the fertility rate high, but gradually over the years it declined, in some cases to the extent that the regimes provided incentives to produce larger families. A major factor in the reduced birth rates was the socialist environment itself – lack of housing, increased numbers

of women in the labor force, and the general availability of abortions and contraceptives. More often than not, having large families in socialist cities was not convenient. East Germany presented a different situation: the loss of several million refugees in the 1945–61 period left a stagnant population and even caused the decline of some urban centers.

1. Early policies of settlement dispersion under autarky

In the 1950s, under a policy of autarky, the planners encouraged the dispersion of industry, thereby affecting patterns of urbanization. In doing this, they followed the ideological goal of reducing regional differences, including those between town and country. Such a policy would avoid excessive population concentration in large cities, which they believed was associated in capitalist cities with congestion, pollution, and inequities of living conditions. They discovered, however, that this policy was not easy to implement, particularly because dispersal led to increased costs, especially the establishment of new infrastructure, e.g. transportation. In reality, therefore, economic and social goals often contradicted each other. Nevertheless, throughout the 1950s and into the 1960s, planning emphasized greater settlement equity. The landscape of medium-sized towns, such as Płock in Poland and Veszprém in Hungary, both of which had been service centers, underwent a transformation by industry (Hamilton 1979a: 222). At the same time, attempts were made to reduce regional concentrations of population in large cities like Budapest or to increase the urban characteristics of backward areas like Slovakia (Kansky 1976: 166–70). Finally, new roads as connecting links to settlements were deemed vital, one being the new *Autostrada* across Yugoslavia from Italy to Greece.

Sixty or so newly built towns attest to an early policy of urban dispersion in Eastern Europe. Although new-town policy has not been as important as in the Soviet Union, where vast areas were without settlements, the effects on the landscape, especially in undeveloped areas, are very visible. However, the new-town policy seems to have been a product of the autarkic period, and in recent years additional new towns have not been initiated. The total population in new towns involves some 2.25 million people or 3 per cent of all urban dwellers in Eastern Europe (Hamilton 1979a: 183). The most important new towns are:

Eisenhüttenstadt	GDR	Komló	Hungary
Halle-Neustadt	GDR	Leninváros (formerly	Hungary
Hoyerswerda	GDR	Tiszapalkonja)	
Lauchhammer	GDR	Oroszlány	Hungary
Schwedt	GDR	Dr Petru Groza	Romania
Nowa Huta	Poland	Gheorghe Gheorghiu-	
Nowe Tychy	Poland	Dej	Romania
Płock	Poland	Victoria	Romania
Wodzisław Śląski	Poland	Bregovo	Bulgaria
Havirov	Czechoslovakia	Dimitrovgrad	Bulgaria
Ziar nad Hronom	Czechoslovakia	Novi Beograd	Yugoslavia
Dunaújváros	Hungary	Novi Zagreb	Yugoslavia
Kazincbarcika	Hungary	Titograd	Yugoslavia
		Velenje	Yugoslavia
		Qytet Stalin (formerly	Albania
		Kucovë)	

The early history of these new towns varies. Several represent settlements built out of the countryside, where perhaps only a village or small town existed before, e.g. Wodzisław Śląski, Titograd, and Schwedt; a few such as Halle-Neustadt, Nowa Huta, and Nowe Tychy are satellite towns near large cities. New portions of Belgrade and Zagreb represent attempts to relocate government functions away from crowded cores. Dunaújváros is a large, self-contained town and according to Enyedi (1976: 240) has the functions of a central city for a rather large area.

Practically all of these towns have industrial functions and serve as showpieces for socialism. Three of them – Eisenhüttenstadt, Nowa Huta, and Dunaújváros – emerged to serve new iron and steel plants built during the Stalin period; indeed, all were named after Stalin, but their names were changed in the late 1950s. On a visit to Gheorghe Gheorghiu-Dej, a new town in eastern Romania named after the postwar Communist leader, I was told that the town grew out of a decision to utilize the petroleum, coal, and salt resources of the area for construction of industrial products (see Photo 7.10). Now the complex includes an array of petrochemical factories and the town has reached a population of over 50 000.

Nowa Huta, the industrial satellite town for Cracow, is home to a great integrated iron and steel plant – built after the Second World War – which now has a capacity of 10 million tons of steel. It uses coking coal from Poland and Czechoslovakia and iron ore from the Soviet Union. The town, built for the plant workers, numbers over 200 000 people and is organized along socialist principles

Photo 7.10   The new town of Gheorghe Gheorghiu-Dej was established in the 1960s in eastern Romania as a focal point for industrial development using the resources of an undeveloped region.

with shopping and collective installations located to serve the residents of multistoried apartment houses. Hamilton (1979a: 204) points out that original plans did not provide for later expansion of the steel plant, a development which eventually forced the town to encroach on the green belt between this city and Cracow, creating congestion and increased air pollution. One aspect of Nowa Huta reflects Polish nationalism: a modern church constructed in the 1970s in the heart of the town exists, according to one Pole, as a symbol of the persistence of the Catholic Church in a communist society, especially in a socialist workers' town.

Another example of a new town is Schwedt, located on the Oder River in the German Democratic Republic. The primary raison d'être for this settlement is a pipeline, which brings oil from the Soviet Union for the refinery and large petrochemical complex nearby. The pipeline was purposely planned to traverse the less industrialized northern sectors of Poland and East Germany so as to serve as a

growth point. While visiting this town, I became impressed with the internal planning that went into its inception. The town of 50 000 is made up of three components – the original new town and two recent additions – connected by major arteries. Each has certain service facilities to include daily needs plus schools and recreation, with the more periodic requirements being handled in the core of the settlement by the Cultural House (with theater), library, and hospital. The primary focal point is the Platz der Befreiung (Square of Liberation), which is surrounded by a department store, a hotel, and service facilities to include restaurant, clothing, hair salon, etc. The amount of green space is noteworthy. A surprisingly large number of cars are seen on the streets and in the parking places provided outside the apartment houses, even though the average waiting period for purchase is ten years.

All the new towns of Eastern Europe show certain weaknesses in terms of economic and demographic balance. For example, Boros (1970: 55–64) has shown that Dunaújváros, the new steel center on the Danube River south of Budapest, has 61 per cent of its employment in industry, whereas the average for all Hungarian towns (including Budapest) is 38 per cent; this imbalance causes services to lag behind demand. Boros also notes that the age structure in Dunaújváros is heavily unbalanced by young people, mostly migrants from surrounding agricultural counties. The age distribution, in turn, leads to a larger-than-average increase of population per thousand – 8.2 in the new town versus 3.0 for Hungary as a whole in 1965.

2. A policy of under-urbanization

Despite the progress noted for urbanization in Eastern Europe, the process tends to lag behind industrialization, a spatial phenomenon just the opposite of the Third World. In the programs of socialist modernization, industrialization has always had the highest priority and, therefore, planners have encouraged a policy of commuting to save investment in urban infrastructure – an approach that leads to under-urbanization (Konrád and Szelényi 1974).

Throughout the area, mass transportation by bus carries workers into cities and towns from residences in villages, a phenomenon touched on in the section on collectivization, which dealt with the peasant worker. Now it is necessary to examine it from an urban viewpoint. Data on this commuting, unfortunately, are not easily compiled, but Fuchs and Demko (1977) have assembled some infor-

mation on the process as it evolved in the northern, more industrialized countries of East Germany, Poland, Czechoslovakia, and Hungary. They find, for example, that the number of commuters runs into the millions and range from 20 per cent of the working force in Poland to nearly 50 per cent in Czechoslovakia. In Hungary alone, the number doubled between 1960 and 1973 – from 613 000 to 1 300 000. Most of this commuting is daily, but some involves going to the city for a week or more and living in a dormitory or hostel near the place of employment. Buses provide the primary means of movement, although trains and sometimes even automobiles are used for long distances. As mentioned, the commuters are typically young, male, and manual or low-skilled workers. Commuting times vary: in the German Democratic Republic, the intense commuting zone is 40 minutes, but in Hungary, where such daily movement is especially noticeable, 35 per cent of all commuters have journeys of over one hour.

A map by Carter (1973: 25) shows not only the wide extent of commuting around Sofia, the capital of Bulgaria, but also the relative importance of travel by bus or train (see Fig. 7.10). The commuting density is particularly high in the areas to the north, since topography is more restrictive in the south. Bus service dominates up to 16 miles (25 km), and the axial train route to Vratsa is important. Although many of the villages around Sofia serve as dormitories for peasant-workers, society in these villages has remained remarkably stable despite the great social change that has taken place. For example, Sanders (1977: 125–133) compared data from the 1970s with that from the 1930s for Dragalevtsy, a village south of Sofia that he had studied before the Second World War. He found that a high proportion of the families still represent three generations. However, the older members, who in the 1930s exercised authority, now work on the collective farm to qualify the family for a private plot and also to care for the children while the other members of the family commute to jobs in Sofia.

The most significant aspect of this commuting process reflects the close interrelationship between policies of industrialization and urbanization. In all East European countries, the Communist party instituted programs of forced industrialization, causing intense permanent migration to these centers of production. However, migration outpaced the provision of housing and other urban services, because the latter, as unproductive activities, were assigned lower investment priorities. In other words, industrialization ran

325

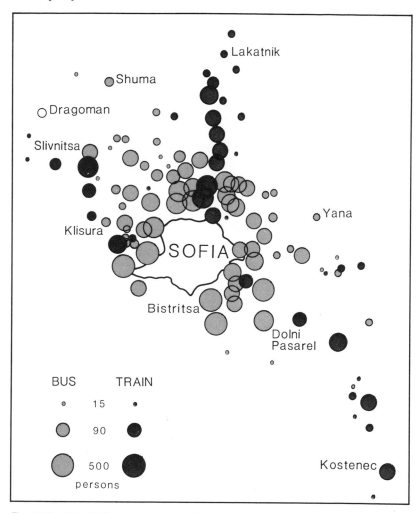

Fig. 7.10   Sofia, Bulgaria: the commuting area in the 1970s. Public transportation is used because private cars are not numerous. (Source: Carter, 1973, Fig. 7.)

ahead of urbanization, thus accounting for the higher number of rural residents in comparison with the number of people actually employed in agriculture. This gap, one of the most significant in the spatial organization of Eastern Europe today, explains the continued importance of a peasant landscape in the area, but it is misleading because, as explained before, many rural residents are commuters. Another way of putting it is that industry is much more concentrated

in cities and towns than are industrial workers. Thus, the surplus labor remains in the villages, and commuting becomes a substitute for urban housing. Some of this commuting is involuntary because many workers would like to move. On the other hand, some is voluntary, because workers perceive the advantages of improved village housing and food production from private plots.

The spatial disparity between jobs and labor supply, i.e. industrialization and urbanization, forced the socialist regimes into a policy of compromising between two alternatives: dispersing industry to smaller cities close to the labor supply or providing the housing and services in cities for increased permanent migration. Both options would have slowed industrial growth, the first by ignoring agglomeration economies and the second by diverting capital. Therefore, a middle road was chosen to solve the problem of industrial labor needs, i.e. a short-term goal which encouraged commuting thereby saving on the urban costs of housing, infrastructure, and services. Negative factors of commuting – long journeys, strain on public transport, impact on villages through daily loss of young people, and environmental problems – had to be accepted. In summary, rural-urban differences in *per capita* incomes, living conditions, and available services are perpetuated (Fuchs 1980: 83).

3. Later settlement policies emphasizing national integration

In the 1970s, the regimes increasingly located industry and population in large centers, a policy which was more economical than dispersion; because this policy collided with the ideology of equality, they sought a compromise in which concentrations of population could be retained within a framework of greater equity. The planners began to change their definitions of urbanization in a socialist society, moving away from narrow definitions, which saw urbanization as the growth of many cities with increasing concentration in some of them, to an interpretation of urbanization as a complex process linked with productive forces and with forms of social communication (Musil 1980: 5–6). Cities were viewed less as adjuncts of production – mines, power plants and factories – and more as centers of socialist modernization and opportunity. Fuchs (1980: 85) summarizes the change by saying that the former concern with preventing excessive concentrations in large metropolitan areas is increasingly construed in the more positive terms of developing a balanced or unified hierarchical system of urban settlements. The original goal of a greater equalization of industry throughout a

327

country is modified to regional equity in terms of economic opportunity and access to public services. This approach appears to seek a balance between economic efficiency and social equity. Good examples of this approach to national settlement are found in Hungary, Poland, and East Germany, but other countries are now examining urbanization strategies within a systems context.

Hungary exemplifies a case of an early national settlement policy, because it had a remarkably distorted settlement pattern in the period after the Second World War. In 1949, for example, Budapest with 1.6 million people commanded the role of a primate city with one-fifth of the total population and over 40 per cent of the industrial employees. The rest of the country was poorly served by urban centers, i.e. second-order cities averaged only 100 000 population and rural market towns prevailed at the lower level. Through a variety of planning measures, the proportion of the nation's industry in Budapest has been reduced to 32 per cent by programs of decentralization while regional towns like Miskolc, Debrecen, Szeged, Pécs, and Györ have doubled in population through enlargement of industry and services. Finally, even the most backward region – the Great Plain – exhibited startling change as its share in the number of industrial workers increased from 16 per cent to 21 per cent between 1965 and 1974. All these changes, however, should be evaluated with caution, because disparities still exist.

In Poland, a settlement plan for the year 2000 exists and takes a middle route between economic (efficiency) and social (equity) criteria (Chełstowski 1974). Certain large metropolitan areas will be allowed to grow, although middle-sized ones in the northern and central parts of the country will be favored, and growth will also take place in corridors connecting these selected cities. Thus, interaction between a large proportion of the population will be maximized, thereby facilitating accessibility to services. This goal is a compromise between concentration of production and accessibility to services. Because of its emphasis on the growth of multiple centers, the plan has been called 'moderate polycentric concentration'. Under this arrangement, the acceleration of economic growth and urbanization in less-developed areas does not rest inevitably on the location of industrial plants there (Wilczewski *et al.* 1978: 88). The areas between corridors are reserved for agriculture, forest, and recreation. Much of this planning took place just before the Solidarity union evolved in the early 1980s. One wonders what effects this movement will have on such a national settlement policy.

Lüdemann and Heinzmann (1978: 123–6) illustrate how related concepts of rational development of all regions and equal access to settlements are being applied to the German Democratic Republic. The basic regional difference before the Second World War was between the agrarian northern districts and the more heavily industrialized southern ones. Thirty years of planning have not made the north and south 'equal', but the north has been transformed by the addition of industry and the modernization of agriculture. The table (p. 330) shows how industry now dominates the employment pattern of these northern districts, a reversal of 1939. However, this does not mean that industry in these districts in absolute terms compares with that in the three southern districts; it simply means that industry is now a part of the environment in the north to a much greater extent than it was in 1939 and that the growth rate of both industry and urban centers over 10 000 population has been much higher in the north than in the south.

Data provided by Lüdemann and Heinzmann also show that the northern and southern districts are now fairly equal in the availability of special consumer goods (e.g. televisions, refrigerators, and washing machines) and education. They maintain that the rational, development of all areas combined with improved accessibility to urban nodes has permitted the majority of the population to benefit from socialism. These East German geographers may be biased, however, for an American geographer found inequalities in retail sales, housing, and services that resulted from a policy of reducing costs through concentration of population (Berentsen 1980: 298). Consequently, an objective evaluation of the degree to which East European countries have balanced social equity with economic efficiency must be withheld.

Irrespective of differences between regions, East German authorities like those in other socialist countries are planning for the spatial distribution of goods and services in all regions within the context of a central-place hierarchy. When I visited the Neubrandenburg district in the northern part of the country, I saw the results of this policy. The map shows the existing hierarchy, which is confirmed in the field by observation (see Fig. 7.11); smaller villages have lost population; regional centers like Prenzlau and Neustrelitz have more industry and services than in the prewar period; and the town of Neubrandenburg has doubled its population and has completely evolved from a small prewar market town into a large industrial center. The town's factories and worker apartment buildings lie just off

329

District	Employment: 1939		Employment: 1975		Index of industrial gross production 1975 (1965 = 100)	Urbanization increase in towns over 10 000 (1955–75)
	Industry	Agriculture	Industry	Agriculture		
North L						
Rostock	45.4	54.6	69.3	30.7	184	+10.5
Schwerin	32.5	67.5	59.7	40.3	213	+7.1
Neubrandenburg	33.4	66.6	51.2	48.8	232	+11.2
South						
Halle	69.4	30.6	83.7	16.3	180	+4.9
Leipzig	80.4	19.6	85.1	14.9	173	+1.5
Karl-Marx-Stadt	86.0	14.0	91.2	8.8	180	+2.3

Source: Lüdemann and Heinzmann 1978: pp. 123–4, 126.

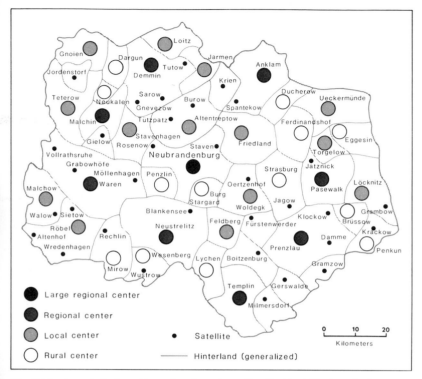

Fig. 7.11 A central-place hierarchy of services: the *Bezirk* of Neubrandenburg, East Germany. Socialist planners have emphasized this approach. (Source: Kohl *et al.* 1979: p. 177.)

the widened boulevard that follows the circular course of the old city walls, and the central core has been entirely rebuilt to include a pedestrian mall.

Intraurban landscapes

The preceding sections deals with changes in the interurban landscape under socialism and their effects as seen in a macro system. Now, attention turns to the intraurban landscape, where the scale is micro and where individual forms reflect the influence of the socialist commitment to equity in terms of living environment. In contrast to capitalist practice, socialist ideology speaks of unique roles for the city core, retail enterprises, public space, and housing districts. Each of these roles is considered here, especially in terms of the degree to

331

which the ideology has been translated into practice. Is the individual socialist city really different from a capitalist one and, if so, how?

The political environment of East European cities contrasts strongly with that of American cities. The United States has no national urban policy to compare with those of Eastern Europe, and each American city, while it has benefitted from certain aspects of federal help, is fairly independent in promoting economic growth and a healthy environment. As Hamilton (1979a: 201–2) shows, cities of Eastern Europe, like those of the Soviet Union, are dependent on the central government in four ways: (1) the legal status of a city may change in line with centralized decisions regarding alterations in administrative frameworks, e.g. the number of provinces may be reduced, something that never happens to American states and counties; (2) central decisions regarding allocation of resources and location of enterprises affect the growth patterns of cities; (3) central ministries establish a variety of norms which strongly influence the design, appearance, and quality of urban areas, e.g living area per person; and (4) central governments generally determine the degree of authority that city authorities have over their own administrative area.

Thus, the political environment of socialist cities reflects close interdependence between national and local authorities. One would assume that such a relationship would be advantageous in terms of planning and in many cases it is. However, in Poland, for example, a lack of coordination exists between the economic plans of national authorities and the physical-spatial planning of the local authorities. One problem is that the procurement of satisfactory sites for factories or housing often does not correspond to the changing economic allocations, thereby causing the landscape to reflect either congestion, when the site is not large enough, or wasted land, where it is too large. Such disparities are recognizable in socialist cities such as the new Polish town of Nowa Huta, where the expansion of the steel plant has forced urban development toward Cracow, thus encroaching on the green belt between satellite and mother city.

Like the political environment in which socialist cities are developed, the economic one differs from that of capitalist cities. In the latter, site rent and transport costs are primary variables influencing the allocation of land uses in the city. The two are reciprocal in their effects, because good access, i.e. low transport costs to a site, causes a demand for that site, thereby leading to higher land values. Capitalist cities trade off the two, e.g. the department store profits from

an accessible site which it can develop intensively in order to pay the site rent, while the single-family resident in the suburbs pays the higher commuting costs in order to purchase cheaper land. Thus, the land-value surface consists of a series of peaks, which represent multiple nodes of high access and value surrounded by a lower undulating surface of values.

The socialist city is quite different, for the effects of site and transport costs are much less applicable: the state nationalizes or appropriates, if necessary, land which it needs and keeps transportation costs low by subsidizing public transit systems in the absence of alternatives, especially the automobile. These measures produce a more uniform land-value surface than found in the capitalist city, making location a much different process. Moreover, sites can be allocated by the state to enterprises, institutions, and housing. Workers find that travel to work and to shop is cheap, although often time consuming.

In the absence of constraints on land and transport, at least in the capitalist sense, socialist planners are still restricted by urban development costs – those related mostly to buildings and the infrastructure, i.e. roads, sewers, gas, water, and electricity. Because the regimes have had to economize on urban costs in giving industry a higher priority, resources for urban construction are scarce, a factor encouraging long-distance commuting. Urban development, when it takes place, has to be compact, especially the infrastructure. These economies help to explain the star-shaped pattern of socialist cities with high-density residential areas extending outward along the axes or corridors followed by public transport and by utilities, an axial pattern such as found in Warsaw. All together, the landscape reflects certain aspects of collective savings that are less apparent in capitalist cities.

Although public land dominates the socialist city, the outskirts frequently contain significant amounts of private land. A map of Warsaw (Hamilton 1979a: 211) shows the high percentages of private land in the gaps between the state lands along the axes of new development. These gaps include landscapes of older housing – single-story or villa-type residences of wood, stone, or brick with stucco. Furthermore, the Polish government, in an attempt to preserve the better agricultural land near cities, has placed higher prices on it than on the poorer land. This action has influenced a pattern of sharp contrast between urban and rural land on the outskirts of Polish cities that is less evident around sprawling American cities. Farther out,

clusters of 'second' or 'weekend' homes create a new phenomenon found not only in Poland but also in other East European countries.

Detailed employment data are not available for East European cities. Hamilton (1979a: 215), however, provides some information that permits limited comparisons with capitalist cities: (1) high industrial employment, which in 1960 amounted to almost 50 per cent of the total – about double the average for the United States – is reflected in the landscape through the number of factories; (2) employment in retail trade involved only 5 per cent, about one-fourth that found in the USA but normal in socialist landscapes, where consumer goods are not emphasized; (3) employment in welfare services – health, education, and social security – ranked high and are visible in collective institutions such as schools, hospitals, parks, and day-care centers; this emphasis is in keeping with the socialist ideology that holds public services to be free – necessary rights for the full cultural development of every person.

The political and economic environments of the socialist city have been described as background to the more detailed landscape changes that are taking place. These changes are analyzed under four headings: central-city core as a political-cultural center; subordinate role of retail trade; importance of public space over private space; and the explosion of standardized housing projects. Each of these internal aspects of the socialist city reflects the eras of planning that have taken place.

1. Central-city core as a political-cultural center

In preceding chapters, I indicate the contribution of major landscape processes to the evolution of the city in Eastern Europe. In the medieval period, German colonists contributed the institution of town law and associated landscape elements of a regular plan, a city hall, and a market place. During the later and persistent feudal period, the lord was responsible first for castle and city walls and later for residential palaces. The multinational ruler in his *Residenzstadt* added the royal palace and a variety of other public buildings that reflected his power. Finally, during the recent era of nationalism, not only new capital cities expressing the individual cultures of the region but also commercial outlets, factories, and apartment blocks represent the input of a small but growing middle class.

It is this heterogeneous city composed of landscape relics from a thousand years of history that the socialist regimes have tried to change into an urban area reflecting a socialist ideology. One model

for this transformation was Moscow, which Frolic (1975: 309) indicates was to serve as a blueprint for socialist countries. A primary aspect of this model is the development of the central portion of the city into a political-cultural center rather than a commercial one. This contrast surprises Western visitors, for they find little evidence of a Central Business District (CBD) with large commercial and office buildings and numerous automobiles. The difference in structure lies partly in ideology and partly in the limited availability of consumer goods. The Soviet regime devoted much of its investment to heavy industry as a basis for modernization, leaving little place for a free market economy with an emphasis on retailing. Furthermore, the regime hoped to use the central city core as a political focus of socialism – a place where the influence of the Party was continuously present. Accordingly, this part of the city was developed on a grand scale to impress the populace with the power and grandeur of socialism.

The diffusion of the Moscow urban model into Eastern Europe after 1945 varied, depending on the amount of war destruction and on the degree of Soviet influence: in East Berlin and Warsaw with severe damage, the transformation from presocialist cities is impressive, especially in East Berlin where Soviet influence on state policies has been more evident; in Cracow and Prague with little damage, the impact of socialism is less apparent; in Budapest, where some destruction occurred, the presocialist townscape is nevertheless quite evident. The Balkan cities experienced less severe war destruction, but Soviet influence in Bulgaria – a tradition explained in Chapter 6 – exceeded that in Romania or Yugoslavia. Sofia radically transformed its central core in the image of Moscow – even with a mausoleum to a national leader – while Belgrade and Bucharest retained presocialist faces. Despite this varied imprint of war destruction and Soviet influence, a socialist image emerges in most cities in certain showpieces: East Berlin and Sofia have squares and massive buildings patterned on Moscow; Warsaw and Bucharest have skyscrapers resembling those in Moscow – indeed, they were 'gifts' from the Soviet Union to the Poles and Romanians; Belgrade and Zagreb have constructed new socialist civic centers on the outskirts of the cities; finally, Tirana, Albania, still has a massive statue of Stalin on a central boulevard.

a. East Berlin This city perhaps more than any other in Eastern Europe displays the influence of Marxist ideology on the design of

335

the central core. After the Second World War, Berlin as a part of the Soviet occupation zone of Germany was divided among the Four Powers. Although the Russians attempted to dislodge all Allied occupation rights there, these efforts failed, and the city remained divided – the Allies in the western part and the Soviets in the eastern. This separation was completed in 1961 with the erection of the Berlin Wall. East Berlin became the capital of the German Democratic Republic and West Berlin an exclave of the Federal Republic of Germany. In visits to this city over the years, I found that Berlin offers a unique opportunity to make a comparison between the impacts of two different ideological systems – socialist and capitalist – on the urban landscape. These striking effects are especially notice-able because much of Berlin had to be rebuilt after the Second World War.

In dividing Berlin after the war, the central district (Mitte) of the German city was left in East Berlin, thereby offering an opportunity to perceive how Marxist planners handle the problems of historical relics in urban design. This combination of old and new forms creates a primary aspect of the landscape today. Although the impression is subjective, I have the feeling that here we are seeing urban forms that reflect two imperial systems – Prussian-German and socialist – existing side by side, each symbolizing the power of a centralized regime. In Chapter 5, I discuss the ideology behind imperial Berlin, and recalling this gives one the feeling that many of these ideas are being re-created by socialist planners.

Heineberg (1979) analyzes the systematic transformation of the former Berlin-Mitte of the prewar period into a new political-cultural center of the German Democratic Republic. This process was facili-tated not only by the destruction of the Second World War, but also by the exodus of capitalistic firms to West Germany. Furthermore, preserving the old imperial street pattern and certain historic build-ings was influenced by the high costs of a complete reconstruction of the infrastructure and by the feeling that the new socialist city should retain elements of the past to preserve German national culture. The basis for planning in the central core – indeed, the basis for much of the postwar planning of cities in the German Democratic Republic – was a series of principles expressed by planners as early as 1950 (Werner 1976: 132–4), modified, and then applied through master plans: political-cultural functions were to dominate the core of East Berlin (1) by making the center an international point of contact with hotels, embassies, and tourist and trade functions; (2)

by constructing administrative buildings for state and city; (3) by establishing organizations connected with culture, research, and education; (4) by setting up shops of a specialized nature; (5) by building large residential blocks nearby; and (6) by creating a meeting place not only for the population of East Berlin but for the whole country (the GDR) as well.

The core of East Berlin today reflects the application of these socialist planning principles. This district with its large public square for demonstrations and broad boulevards (*Magistralen*) lined with prestigious buildings – 'architectural dominants' designed to impress the socialist image upon the whole townscape – resembles its counterpart in Moscow but differs in layout. Instead of adopting the concentric format, the older axial layout has been preserved. Heineberg (1979: 308) in using ideas of Näther, the chief architect of Berlin in the early 1970s, portrays in map form the theoretical-ideological conception for the socialist master plan (see Fig. 7.12). The plan stresses an east–west axis composed of three elements – the old, renowned avenue of Unter den Linden; a new political and cultural center between Karl-Liebknecht-Strasse and Rathausstrasse; and a residential-shopping boulevard called Karl-Marx-Allee (formerly Stalin-Allee).

Unter den Linden still retains the old imperial image, especially along its eastern portion with many reconstructed buildings of the imperial era – library, university, theaters, and museums – described in Chapter 5. The west end, however, features a postwar administrative zone with lesser ministries and the prestigious headquarters of two mass organizations – the Free German Trades Union and the Free German Youth – plus the embassies of three socialist countries, including the Soviet Union's massive structure. Crossing Unter den Linden is the sub-axis of Friedrichstrasse, a historic commercial street, whose function is supplemented now by cultural attractions such as theaters; in addition, two international hotels have been built. A station of the pre-Second World War *Stadtbahn* or elevated train affords excellent access to the area.

The political-cultural center between Karl-Liebknecht-Strasse and Rathausstrasse – a showpiece for socialist planning and the second element of the axis plan – contains the two great squares: Marx-Engels-Platz on the west end is laid out on the site of the former imperial palace and is flanked by three massive buildings in modern style – the Ministry of Foreign Affairs, the Council of State, and the Palace of the Republic; Alexanderplatz on the east end is a historic square that has been enlarged as a meeting place for the city with new

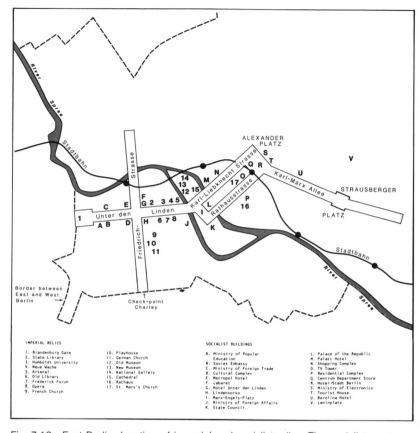

Fig. 7.12 East Berlin: location of imperial and socialist relics. The socialist master plan is based on the east–west axis of Karl-Marx-Allee, Karl-Liebknecht Strasse, and Unter den Linden. Along this axis, relics of the Hohenzollern imperial period are intermixed with new socialist structures.

focal points of the International Berlin Hotel, the Centrum or department store, and a large international travel center (see Photo 7.11). A series of other public, cultural, commercial, and residential structures flank Karl-Liebknecht-Strasse and adjacent Rathausstrasse. The chief 'architectural dominant' is the television tower, but nearby remain three symbols of historic Berlin – the *Rathaus* (city hall), the Marienkirche (Mary Church), and the Alexanderplatz station of the *Stadtbahn.*

    The third element of the axis is Karl-Marx-Allee, lined by blocks of apartment buildings in ornate Stalin-baroque architecture; the

Photo 7.11 Alexanderplatz has been transformed into a socialist center of culture for East Berlin. Shown here is the international hotel Stadt Berlin with shops and restaurants on the lower level. Note the ever-present political slogans.

ground floors typically contain stores and tourist offices. During the Stalin period, this rebuilt street was the solitary expression of postwar recovery and planning in a socialist city that was slow to recover – in vivid contrast to West Berlin. Like a movie set, the buildings along this street stood as a façade for the empty, debris-cleared lots behind it. Since 1965, however, other buildings have been built to fill the gaps.

Along the central axis with its political-cultural functions are compact residential areas of high-rise apartment buildings, the largest of which are located to the south of Unter den Linden along Leipzig-gerstrasse. This section of old Berlin has probably witnessed a greater change from the pre-1945 pattern than any other district. Leipzig-erstrasse, formerly a leading shopping street in Greater Berlin, today has only local neighborhood services available in ground-floor enter-prises of the apartment buildings.

A walk along the total length of this axis from the Brandenburg Gate to Strausberger Platz enables one to capture something of the spirit of urbanism in a socialist country. The German imperial image of the past blends rather naturally with the international image of

socialism. In fact, the intermixture of both periods of design portrays a Marxist-Leninist version of compatibility between past and present. The German heritage of the past can be preserved without compromising either modernization or the representation of a socialist image. The massive Hohenzollern and socialist buildings established up and down a wide boulevard reflect the power of the state – at least this is the feeling I have. On this long walk, an observer also sees the changes in socialist architecture and planning, from the heavy Stalin-baroque of the 1950s along Karl-Marx-Allee to the more modern style of buildings like the Palace of the Republic or the apartment buildings of Leipzigerstrasse. Another impression indicates that function might not follow form under socialism. In some cases, the imperial function of the past has not changed, e.g. the theater, opera, university, and museum; but, in other cases, a new function has been superimposed, e.g. the conversion of the former Reichsbank to the headquarters of the Sozialistische Einheitspartei (SED) – the Communist party of East Germany – or the Zeughaus (Arsenal) to a museum for German history emphasizing socialism.

A final impression in the landscape of central East Berlin comes from the lower density of buildings and enterprises, giving a spread-out aspect that may be related to the attempts at grandeur in a socialist capital. Of course, government control of this land permits these low densities. Many functions, however, are spatially concentrated; for example, Heineberg (1979: 314–15) reveals that the entire insurance system of the GDR is localized on three sites in the eastern city center. Legal and medical services are also concentrated, as are tourist facilities, which I can verify from personal experience with the Haus des Reisens (Travel House) on Alexanderplatz.

b. Other examples of transformed central-city cores Although East Berlin exhibits extensive change of its central core in line with Marxist ideology, Sofia, Warsaw, and Katowice also deserve mention.

In making a comparison of Sofia and Prague, Carter (1979: 427) emphasizes the great influence of Stalinist ˍrchitecture on the former. The central portion of Sofia underwent radical transformation so as to focus on political and cultural activities. As in the case of East Berlin, the most notable aspect of the plan is a wide boulevard which links two squares. On the west end is Lenin Square, bordered by the ponderous Stalinist buildings of the Balkan Hotel, Communist party building (with its red star on top), and central department store. From this ensemble of socialism, the wide Boulevard Ruski runs to

the southeast past the Square of 9 September, a counterpart to Red Square in Moscow even to a mausoleum, in this case, Georgi Dimitrov's, the Bulgarian communist who died in 1949. The axis which dominates the core of Sofia is not entirely socialist in character – nationalist sentiment has allowed the preservation of historic buildings, the three major ones being the former palace, the Alexander Nevski Cathedral, and the National Assembly. Whereas the palace is now an art museum and the Cathedral is infrequently used in this communist country, the Assembly serves its original purpose.

On the other hand, Prague resembles Cracow, Budapest, and Bucharest in not overly reflecting socialist ideology in planning and architecture. The main reason for this stems from minimal rebuilding after the war, whose destruction largely by-passed both the medieval core and the later imperial-national elements described in earlier chapters. The historic squares – Staré Město (old town) and Václavské (Wencelas) remain the foci of activity. Function fails to follow form in the examples of government offices that are frequently located either in former palaces of the nobility or in the Hradčany castle complex which, like the Kremlin, serves political as well as tourist uses.

Two cities of Poland – Warsaw and Katowice – also show the effects of socialist planning, although less of the Stalinist influence. Warsaw's center core is a curious mixture of old and new (*Atlas of Warsaw's Architecture* 1978). On the east is the old, established axis of Krakowski Przedmieście–Nowy Świat–Ujazdowskie that retains its presocialist image of palaces and shops. At the north end is the Rynek Starego Miasta (old town square), whose reconstruction from the rubble of the Second World War duplicates the original appearance. This brick-by-brick restoration was endorsed by everyone, communist and noncommunist alike, and reflects Polish nationalism. To the west and parallel to this axis runs another axis – Marszałkowska Boulevard – which has been impressively transformed. The principal landmark, of course, is the Palace of Culture, a high tower in pretentious Stalinesque style that evokes no admiration from the Poles, not only because it is unattractive but also because it is a gift from the Soviet Union. Directly across from this skyscraper is the 'Ściana Wschodnia' (east side), a complex of department stores, restaurants, theaters, offices, and residences built in the 1960s. This complex boasts a pedestrian mall, perhaps its most attractive feature, which is located away from but parallel to Marszałkowska Boulevard. MDM, a large housing district built in the

early 1950s to form a background for Constitution Square, extends from the south end of this boulevard. Along Marszałkowska and its intersecting boulevards – Świetokrzyska and Jerozolimskie – socialist planning has reduced the number of enterprises compared to that along Krakowskie Przadmieście and Nowy Swiat to resemble in part the wider individual frontages seen in East Berlin on Karl-Marx-Allee. The modern central railway station is very accessible to the immediate south of the Palace of Culture.

The socialist alteration of the urban landscape appears in a second Polish city – Katowice. As explained earlier, this city was one of six major settlements forming part of the Upper Silesian conurbation based on coal and heavy industry (see Fig. 5.8). After the First World War, Katowice became the center of the Polish portion of the district, a role which continued after the Second World War under the communist regime. With over 300 000 inhabitants, the city is now the largest of the Upper Silesian centers, but the nature and extent of the industrial conurbation make it difficult to distinguish administrative boundaries between Katowice and the other cities. The socialist regime has made an effort to redesign the central core of this city to reflect its place in a socialist society. The primary contrast is between the old core of narrow streets centered on the railway station and the new axis that extends northward along Ulice Armii Czerwonej (Red Army Street), an impressive, wide boulevard designed as a series of functional nodes separated by green spaces. A positive assessment of this new axis with its office buildings, hotels, restaurants, shops, a sport stadium, a large residential complex of apartments (with underground parking for cars), a cinema, and a supermarket can be deceptive: even though the use of space is appealing, the visitor senses the attempt to impress the population with the accomplishments of socialism – in other words, with a show place; moreover, this axis of development, unlike those mentioned in East Berlin and Warsaw, suffers from being a major traffic artery for both the city and other parts of Poland. Vehicular congestion is severe – doubtlessly unforeseen in the 1950s when few Poles owned automobiles.

The transformed socialist city centers in East Berlin, Sofia, Warsaw, and Katowice represent the most apparent examples for the big cities. Many examples exist for small cities, like Bacău in eastern Romania, which exhibit completely new centers – perhaps the first ones they have ever had. A second type of socialist city center – the new one constructed on the edge of the city to accommodate future growth – provides another subject of interest and comment. The two

best examples of this type are Belgrade and Zagreb in Yugoslavia. Novi Beograd (New Belgrade) located across the Sava River from the main city includes not only a commercial area and apartment blocks, but also a series of large public buildings focused on one for the Federal Executive Council, the ruling body for the country. Again, one has the feeling that New Belgrade was built to show the population what socialism can create.

Since the Second World War, Zagreb has tripled in population – from 250 000 to 750 000. The old city was built on the contact line between hills and plain, with a primary square centered in Gornji Grad (upper town) and one in Donji Grad (lower town). Steep streets and a funicular connect the two sections of the city. Early post-Second World War growth extended east and west along this contact line, but planners had long felt that the main thrust of growth should be southward to the Sava River. The primary natural focus for Novi (New) Zagreb became the river, which lies a mile (some two kilometers) south of the Donji Grad. After measures were completed to protect the area from floods, the plan for the new town called for a series of belts containing varied types of land use parallel to the river and connected to the old town. The northern axis – the Ulice Proletarskih Brigada (Worker's Brigade Street) – has become a new political-cultural focus similar to that described in other socialist cities. Again, low density of buildings and the aspect of grandeur are the impressions gained. The primary public buildings include the Zagreb city hall, concert hall; worker's university; hotels; offices of leading Croatian banking, trading, and industrial organizations; and a shopping center. Farther south on both sides of the river are residential areas with local services, medical and hospital facilities, a hall of culture, recreation areas, and the new grounds of the Zagreb Trade Fair. All in all, Novi Zagreb resembles a new town except that it is not; instead, it represents a socialist attempt to compromise between the old and new in an era of rapid modernization.

2. Subordinate role of retail trade

The dominance of political-cultural functions in the central cores of socialist cities contrasts strongly with the landscapes of Western cities. Another and related unmistakable observation concerns the subordinate role of retail trade, an impression largely subjective and hence difficult to substantiate with data. Land use maps are not available for cities in the Bloc, and the Western geographer is restricted from mapping; however, one statistic helps: in the United States,

average urban employment in retail trade is about 19 per cent, but Hamilton (1979a: 215) informs us that in 1960 this category was less than 5 per cent in Eastern Europe. In addition, the proximity of West Berlin to East Berlin permits some objective comparisons, which support the subordinate role played by retail trade. In the GDR, principles set forth by the Ministry of Trade and Supplies in 1965 regulate the spatial patterns of retail trade. Heineberg (1979: 315–16) refers to three principles that affect the retail landscape:

a. Spatial concentration in large complexes Under this principle, a diversified range of goods is sold in large enterprises. A primary example is East Berlin's new Centrum or department store that faces on Alexanderplatz. This store with 16 750 sq. yards (14 000 sq. m) of floor space resembles an American counterpart, except that being unique in the central core of the city it is more crowded; in fact, the after-4 pm throngs of workers make it almost impossible to move, as I found out personally. Only one large department store for the central core of a city of over one million illustrates a subordinate role of retail trade in a system where decisions are not based on demand. A second example of the spatial concentration principle is the group of specialist shops located near the East Berlin TV tower. These shops are large factory sales outlets, e.g. the optics shop of Carl Zeiss Jena has a frontage of 98 yards (90 m).

b. Concentric construction and the locational pattern of sales outlets Heineberg (1979: 317) shows data from 1971–73 for East Berlin that illustrate how this principle affects the spatial pattern of retail trade. First, the five commercial areas of the central core included only seventy-five enterprises. Second, of this number, the most numerous groups were education-arts, textiles-clothing, and food, whereas outlets selling furniture, vehicles, and jewelry were few. Third, a surprising number of stores such as the 'Exquisit' shops along Unter den Linden sold goods that are luxuries or in infrequent demand, e.g. Meissen china or expensive clothing; since few East Germans can afford extravagances, the purpose of these stores raises the question of the propaganda intent to show the achievements of socialism. Fourth, only a prescribed range of stores existed in each commercial area, e.g. textiles-clothes, books, and art in Unter den Linden; this restricted range of products is based on the third principle of retail distribution – that of territorial concentration. Fifth, stores filling daily needs

were not represented in the core but were decentralized to the various residential complexes.

These principles invite a comparison between socialist and capitalist landscapes of retailing not only between East and West Berlin but also within East Berlin itself. A primary aspect of this comparison is in density of enterprises, which shows up amazingly well. Heineberg (1979: 320–2) and Schöller (1974: 428) provide a map (see Fig. 7.13).

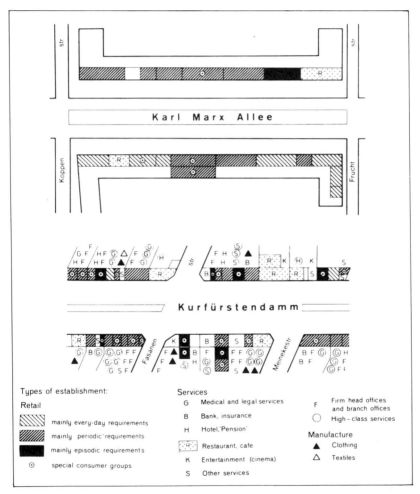

Fig. 7.13   East and West Berlin: a representative comparison of services along blocks on two main streets. (Source: Schöller 1974: p. 428.)

that illustrates the contrast between Karl-Marx-Allee in East Berlin, where only seventeen enterprises are located in the block shown; and Kurfürstendamm, the opulent shopping street of West Berlin, which has forty-two in an equivalent distance. Some of the East Berlin enterprises are, in reality, specialized department stores with specific clientele, e.g. 'The Children's House'. The small-shop characteristics of Western Europe do not occupy an integral part of planned portions of socialist cities, because the regimes choose to control the supply and distribution of consumer goods through state enterprises. In addition, the large outlets serve as an image of socialist urban progress, which actually masks deficiencies in retailing.

In contrast to Karl-Marx-Allee, the persistence of the capitalistic approach to competition in retail sales within East Berlin can be seen along a portion of Schönhauser Allee in the northern part of the central core. Frontages of the smaller retail units here average 10 yards (9 m) in an area where 40 per cent of the shops were privately owned in the mid-1970s. This street reflects large portions of East Berlin that have not yet been converted to a socialist urban pattern. The primary attraction of these shops lies in the variety of services they provide – restaurants, jewelry, etc – that are not available along the socialist-style street.

The data provided for retail trade in East Berlin are not easily available for other socialist cities. In general, a similar pattern of fewer enterprises and restricted goods and services applies to the planned sections of cities, but in unplanned areas a variety of shops still exists (see Photo 7.12). Nevertheless, certain aspects of the landscape prevail everywhere, especially the uniform, characterless store fronts that denote state ownership and/or control. Queues for certain scarce consumer goods at some stores do not go unnoticed but become part of the daily scene.

3. The importance of public space over private space

Visitors to communist countries are impressed not only by the alteration of the central core and the subordinate role of retail trade, but also by the emphasis on public space over private space. This emphasis, of course, fits in well with the ideological focus on collective aspects of society rather than on individual ones. Hence, Western visitors are likely to be surprised by the significant role of public facilities – parks, extensive transportation systems, museums, exhibition halls, educational and health institutions, squares and wide boulevards, concert halls, recreation of all kinds, and kiosks selling

Photo 7.12   A state book store and crowded shopping street in the old core of Katowice, Poland.

a variety of daily needs. Visitors discover the ever-improving quality of international hotels, which in many cases – like the Metropole of East Berlin – charge Western prices. Unchanged, though, is the display of symbols that explain or glorify the ideology – statues, red banners, flags, slogans, and posted party newspapers. Finally, overall cleanliness; absence of clutter like billboards, signs, and above-ground utility lines; plus safety from criminal activity make an impression. Not so conspicuous is the limitation of private space. For example, single-occupancy houses are the exception; apartments are small, located in large complexes, and often without many conveniences the Westerner has come to expect. Indeed, the generalized residential environment in America with the single-family home and its green areas typifying the emphasis on private space is often the reverse of the Marxist one. After some study, it appears as though the socialist environment not only reflects the collective ideology, but also tries to compensate the urban resident for the lack of consumer goods and mobility provided by the automobile.

Anthony (1979) applies this concept of public versus private space in socialist societies to Moscow, but it can be used for most large socialist cities in Eastern Europe. She mentions five characteristics

347

– choice, size, design, physical condition, and symbolic function. All of these are visible in socialist cities to some degree, especially in the central cores of urban areas as already discussed.

a. Choice Ample choice in the variety and number of facilities is an obvious feature of public space in large cities of Eastern Europe. Perhaps the most apparent example is the park of 'rest and culture'. In public transportation, riders select schedules and routes from comprehensive networks using mostly streetcars and buses, which feature cheap fares as the result of subsidization. Extremely crowded conditions prevail, however. Public entertainment presents a wide variety of inexpensive concerts, operas, movies, circuses, and sport events.

The choice of private space, on the other hand, lags far behind that of capitalistic societies, especially the United States. In Eastern Europe a person might wait years for an apartment, although once it is obtained, the rent is incredibly low. Private housing or cooperatives allows more choice than in the Soviet Union, but again this alternative is limited, with the possible exception of weekend homes outside some cities like Prague (Carter 1974: 544). The resident of a socialist country might never be able to buy an automobile, a form of private space that remains a dream for the greater percentage of the population. The greatest divergence toward possibilities of private space occurs in Yugoslavia, especially through the migration of temporary workers (*Gastarbeiter*) to Western Europe. These people often use their earnings to bring back a car and/or to build a private residence after returning to Yugoslavia

b. Size Large size characterizes public space in Marxist countries, often because land is controlled by the state and can be developed on an extensive scale. The tremendous size of squares, boulevards, and public buildings has been discussed in connection with the planning of central cores in East Berlin, Warsaw, and other East European cities. Although no square in the world can compare in size with Tiananmen in Beijing, China, the expanse of Red Square in Moscow has made it a socialist model for others in Eastern Europe. Boulevards in cities of these countries tend to be broad and extensive, which especially calls to mind the wide pedestrian mall of Prager Strasse in Dresden with its elaborate fountains, a theater in the center, and four large international hotels, stores, restaurants, and blocks of apartment buildings on the sides (see Photo 7.13). Then there is the

Photo 7.13   Prager Strasse in Dresden is an example of socialist urban design. Here several international hotels, a theater, stores and restaurants flank a new pedestrian mall with fountains.

towering Palace of Culture in central Warsaw with the new buildings across from it on Marszałkowska Street. Large dimensions even carry over to monuments as exemplified by the National Memorial on Žižkov Hill in Prague, which includes a mausoleum and an equestrian statue 10 yards (9 m) tall; or the Soviet War Memorial in the Russian cemetery of East Berlin, which features a gigantic bronze statue of a Red Army soldier.

Smallness, on the other hand, describes private space in apartments, generally less than 14 sq. yards (12 sq. m) per capita as allowed by planners – a figure considerably less than in the United States or Western Europe. In fact, the cramped quarters and doubling-up of families promote the widespread use of public space – in some cases just to pass the time by windowshopping.

c. Design   Socialist design is difficult to characterize except to say that it differs from that in the West. I agree with Yurick Blumenfeld (1968: 60–1), who believes that the Stalinesque skyscrapers of Warsaw, Bucharest, and Sofia – modeled on those of Moscow with 'wedding-cake' form, 'frosted' with pediments and pseudo-rococo

ornamentation – have a distinctive period flavor (see Photo 7.14). Since the Stalin era, however, the influence of Marxist ideology upon architectural design has weakened. Hutchings (1968) feels that factors of cost efficiency and foreign influence were instrumental in reducing in Soviet cities the early architectural themes like 'proletarian triumph', and this conclusion seems applicable to Eastern Europe. Nevertheless, the new styles, while closer to the West in some respects, also tend to reflect in their uniformity a Party-directed mass culture, devoid of real originality and based above all on a master plan, all of which create 'dreary, monotonous blocks of brick or concrete [which] seem to be bereft of spiritual feeling or human content' (Blumenfeld 1968: 60). The variety made possible in Western cities by contrasting store fronts with attractive and colorful window displays, the use of different architectural designs and materials (e.g. glass and aluminum), bright street lighting, and the presence of advertising and neon lights vanishes in socialist cities. In addition, one finds examples of barren, sterile landscape around many apartment buildings (private space); overcrowded transportation; and inadequate services. As mentioned before, severe air and water pollution exist in many places. Perhaps a lack of warmth, character, or personality best symbolizes the socialist city and its public space.

The uniformity of socialist cities fits the collective goal, but whether it is based on ideology or efficiency is hard to say. Ciborowski (1975: 4), a leading Polish architect, presents the dilemma of socialist urban planning when he asks how both egalitarianism and variety can be implemented at the same time in the landscape.

I wish to point out that the socialist architecture does not completely ignore nationalist feeling. Even the Stalinesque Palace of Culture in Warsaw incorporates decorative designs copied from the medieval Cloth Hall in Cracow. In Dresden, the new Palace of Culture combines a mural depicting the development of the German working class with bronze doors portraying episodes from the city's history.

d. Condition The physical condition of public space in East European cities commands much more attention than that of private space, though this impression is a mixed one. Certainly the cleanliness of streets and public places stands in contrast to many Western counterparts. Public employees sweep these places at frequent intervals – labor seems abundant and cheap – and litter is much less apparent

Photo 7.14   The Scinteia Publishing House building in Bucharest, Romania, is a gift, like the Palace of Culture in Warsaw, Poland, from the Soviet Union. The 1950's Stalinesque architecture emphasized monumentality and exterior decoration. Note the statue of Lenin.

than in the United States. However, most public buildings except the most outstanding historical structures show neglect and, indeed, look as if they have not been touched for decades; old residential districts suffer from even greater shabbiness. In fact, one strong impression I have after many years of visiting Eastern Europe is the dearth of refurbishing and renovating – as if everything stopped after the buildings were made usable. What a shame that a great legacy of history is ignored. Although movements exist for historic preservation in all countries, their priorities are not high. In Poland, three cities stand out as having made great progress in restoration – Cracow, Gdańsk, and Toruń. But as Abrams and Francaviglia (1975: 262) point out, the constraints are great, especially because of the cost in making old buildings and districts fit modern needs.

Maintenance of private space is not adequate, either. East European friends speak of difficulties in getting apartment utilities repaired

and the impossibility of finding automobile parts, if they are lucky enough to have a vehicle. In general, restaurants operate under trying conditions, mostly because the relatively few such establishments are overused, e.g. tablecloths and restrooms are apt to be dirty, especially at the end of the day. Hotel supplies for guests may be wanting, particularly in the nontourist hotels where towels, soap, and toilet paper are often missing.

e. Symbolic function Anthony's fifth characteristic of public space in Soviet cities – a symbolic function for each – can be applied to East European cities as well. Large, visible squares for the assembly of people fulfill this function as do the massive proportions of structures designed to impress – symbols touched on in previous pages. The most penetrating and lasting impression, however, comes from never being very far from some symbol of the Party – the aforementioned Party flags, banners and slogans, red stars, posted newspapers, statues of Red Army soildiers and, finally, real-life policemen and soldiers. Even street names reflect socialism. In short, symbolic function in socialist countries is omnipresent (see Photo 7.15).

4. Explosion of standardized housing projects
Standardized housing projects introduced into the cities of Eastern Europe after the Second World War have changed the landscape as much as any other force – a virtual explosion. The panorama from any high point in a large socialist city confirms the preponderance of large blocks of apartment houses rising four to twelve stories (see Photo 7.16). The scale of these structures reflects the socialist ideology that calls for housing equity. In addition, these projects represent an emphasis on modernization and industrialization of society. As we have seen, the percentage of industry in the economies of these countries – especially those of the Balkans – has increased and with it the percentages of urban residents, represented by millions of former peasants who have migrated to the cities to set in motion degrees of social change never before experienced in this region. Hamilton (1979a: 236) reveals that new residential neighborhoods house at least half (35 to 40 million) of East Europe's urban population. In Poland alone the period of 1950 to 1975 witnessed the construction of 4 million apartment units and 7500 schools. Whatever one may say about the quality of this housing, the mere scale of the process is overwhelming. The outstanding characteristic from the landscape point of view is the similarity of these buildings regardless

Photo 7.15   A poster in rural Bulgaria stresses the 'eternal' friendship of the Soviet and Bulgarian Communist Parties. Although symbols of the communist party are most apparent in cities, they are also evident in the countryside.

of country, a trait which extends to the Soviet Union. Actually, one must look to that country for the early development of planning principles for housing, which were later introduced into the East European countries.

Socialist ideology centers on urban life, where environments can reflect social objectives not only of providing equal opportunity for all members of society but also of reducing feelings of separateness between different social groups. Jensen (1976: 38) states that residential areas in the Soviet Union, therefore, should be relatively heterogeneous in terms of occupation, income levels, and other social features, but relatively homogeneous in their physical organization so as not to attract or repel different segments of society. Urban physical planning has been considered a means of bringing about this social change. To accomplish these goals, Soviet planners have focused on a policy of constructing a hierarchy of relatively self-contained residential areas composed of apartment buildings, and this strategy, with variations, also has been followed in Eastern Europe.

Photo 7.16 Large neighborhoods of apartment houses dominate the skyline of socialist cities in Eastern Europe, as does this residential area along Leipziger Strasse in East Berlin.

Apartment houses, of course, are an efficient way of housing large numbers of people, especially since utilities and other periodic/daily services can be shared. Furthermore, Fisher (1962: 252) points out two advantages in standardizing housing: savings are realized by using one set of blueprints and the landscape reflects the classless society.

The spatial organization of housing in socialist cities is based on a hierarchy of residential units designed to provide urban services to the population, utilizing the central core only for the most specialized requirements. French and Hamilton (1979: 11) emphasize that the basic unit of housing construction in all socialist countries is the micro-region or district, a neighborhood which generally includes 6000–12 000 inhabitants, each of whom is theoretically allotted 11–14 sq. yards (9–12 sq. m) of floor space. An ideal model of such a district provides apartment buildings with daily services including certain commercial enterprises, a school, public eating facilities, recreational space, and a day-care center for children of working familes.

Several micro-districts are grouped together to form the next level of the hierarchy which includes higher-order or periodic services: shops, movie theater, library, public health establishments, and specialized recreation. At both levels, norms prescribe the kinds and extent of services for each group of 1000 residents. The principle of self-containment is important because if services and even jobs (i.e. factories) are located in proximity, the amount of travel and congestion – assumed by socialist planners to be typical of capitalistic cities – is reduced.

The micro-district concept actually resembles other groupings of residential units in various parts of the world. What sets it apart or gives it a socialist image is the central determination of design standards having nation-wide application, its special role in developing a unified system of urban services, and the large number of districts that have been constructed.

After this brief summary of the theory and ideology behind Soviet and East European residential planning, we ask to what extent reality coincides with theory. There is little doubt that the physical living environment has been improved for millions of urban residents. However, as pointed out, the emphasis has been on production with factories having priority over housing and urban infrastructure. As a result, housing construction lags behind demand, constricted living space requires the doubling-up of families, and millions of workers must commute from villages on the outskirts of cities. This demonstrates that equity goals of housing and urban life have been reached for only a portion of the population. Some favored groups like party members, technocrats, athletes, and performers of the arts obtain better city housing and even country residences. Aside from the housing gap, the most notable deviation from theory is the lag of consumer goods and services behind demand – long queues form part of the ordinary shopping landscape. Even the goal of reducing intraurban commuting to jobs by locating factories close to residential areas has not been feasible, and considerable cross-town traffic still occurs.

Attainment of social goals also remains elusive. Strumilin's (1961) ideas for future communal living – shared dormitory, eating, and recreation facilities – have been unacceptable to date in both the Soviet Union and Eastern Europe; attempts to promote neighborhood-centered life also appear to be out of touch with reality. Jensen (1976: 40) suggests that the micro-district in the Soviet Union, while improving housing conditions and dispersing urban services, has not

355

necessarily promoted a feeling of local community within the city. Soviet specialists evidently find that their attempts at organizing life around planned neighborhoods conflict with urban life characterized by frequent trips throughout the city. These defects of the micro-district – lag of services and lack of neighborhood focus – are applicable to Eastern Europe. Hamilton and Bennett (1979: 266) suggest that the crowded housing and search for consumer goods lead to an increased attraction for the central city, even though this part of the urban center is not designed for daily use. Like capitalists, socialists seemingly utilize the whole city, seeking contacts in diverse places. Hence, physical planning does not seem to influence social interaction.

A visitor to a socialist country, while noticing a uniformity in housing landscapes between countries, is also aware of differences between time periods. Richter (1974) identifies four phases of planning in the German Democratic Republic, and these correspond in general to those found in other countries: (1) conservative formalism from 1945 to 1956; (2) socialist realism from 1956 to 1962; (3) mass production utilizing prefabrication from 1962 to the present; and (4) private ownership of dwellings from 1971 to the present. The first two, for example, can be seen in proximity in the central part of Dresden, where the socialist conversion after the war created 8 large housing blocks out of 26 smaller blocks from the prewar pattern (see Fig. 7.14). To the east of the Altmarkt (Old Market), stand a series of massive apartment buildings with a variety of ornamentation, each structure built in a closed form around a courtyard. This project illustrates conservative formalism – phase 1 – that existed when the socialist countries of Eastern Europe imitated the Soviet Union during the Stalin era. To the west of the Altmarkt is a completely different style of housing block – the closed–court form has been replaced by free-standing apartment buildings aligned in rows; these structures exhibit a plainer style of architecture. This project representing socialist realism – phase 2 – resulted from Khrushchev's action at the 1956 party congress in Moscow. The Soviet leader, when he asked for acceptance of Western styles and rejection of the expensive and unnecessary ornamentation of the *Zuckerbäckerstil* (confectionary or 'wedding cake' style), was responsible for a complete turnaround in socialist planning and architecture.

This second phase in most socialist countries was short, for in the 1960s the emphasis shifted to mass-production of housing by means of prefabricated methods – phase 3. The approach represents an at-

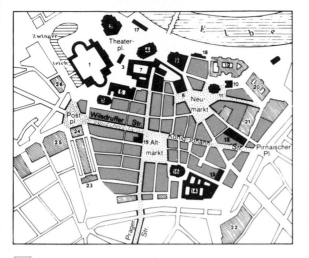

1 Zwinger
2 Semper-Oper
3 Wache
4 Kath. Hofkirche
5 Sophienkirche
6 Palais am Taschenberg
7 Schloß
8 Johanneum
9 Standehaus
10 Koselsches Palais
11 Frauenkirche
12 Landhaus
13 Gewandhaus
14 Neues Rathaus
15 Altes Rathaus
16 Kreuzkirche
17 Ital. Dörfchen
18 Brühler Terrasse
19 Kunstakademie
20 Albertinum
21 Polizeipräsidium
22 Kreuz-Gymnasium
23 Markthalle
24 Fernsprechamt
25 Hauptpost
26 Schauspielhaus

▨▨▨ Important streets and squares

PUBLIC BUILDINGS
■ of historical value
▨ other

OTHER DISTRICTS
▥ developed in the style of
conservative formalism

▨ developed in the style of
socialist reality

☐ unchanged

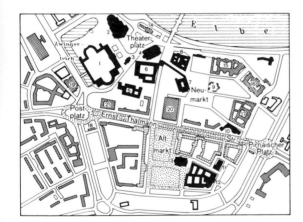

1 Zwinger
2 Semper-Oper
3 Wache
4 Kath. Hofkirche
5 Palais am
Taschenberg
6 Schloß
7 Johanneum
8 Ständehaus
9 Frauenkirche
10 Landhaus
11 Gewandhaus
12 Neues Rathaus
13 Kreuzkirche
14 Ital. Dörfchen
15 Kunstakademie
16 Albertinum
17 Polizeipräsidium
18 Post
19 Schauspielhaus
20 Haus der sozialistischen
Kultur
21 Großgaststätte
"Am Zwinger"

▨▨▨ Important streets and squares

PUBLIC BUILDINGS
■ of historical value
▨ other

OTHER DISTRICTS
▨ old core
☐ old suburbs

Fig. 7.14   The transformation of a portion of Dresden, East Germany, after the Second World War. The top map shows the pre-1939 pattern, and the bottom map illustrates the different phases of socialist design of apartment complexes. (Source: Richter 1974: p. 185.)

tempt to reach two important goals of a socialist ideology: living space for every worker and the image of a collective way of life. Phase-3 style features high, narrow buildings in large clusters – in East Germany called *Wohnscheiben* or housing 'walls' of concrete – which are a rational means of accommodating large numbers of people in a short time and yet representing the ultimate in standardization – a true 'classless' image. These 'high walls' of housing appear throughout Eastern Europe and signify modernization accompanied by considerable uniformity and monotony. In East Germany, this approach only became important in the 1970s owing to shortages of materials and labor, the latter especially associated with the movement to the West of workers before 1961 and the Berlin Wall. Housing plans in the GDR call for construction of 3 million apartments between 1976 and 1990 using the new mass methods of construction.

A good example of this third phase of socialist housing construction is Halle-Neustadt in East Germany. This settlement – a satellite town to Halle modeled on Kryukovo outside Moscow – was designed to handle overspill from Halle and to accommodate workers who commute to chemical works, especially at Leuna. Four microdistricts exist, each with services for daily needs, e.g. food, drugs, household items, and elementary school. Between the five districts is a regional center for periodic services such as health, library, sports and recreation, post office, fire station, and gasoline pumps. Areas exist for town expansion and for urban utilities. However, despite the apparent advantages of this new socialist residential environment, problems exist. Certain services like entertainment (movies, etc.) are missing and distances to jobs are lengthy. In addition, residents complain of the 'unhealthy' prefabricated concrete slab buildings, which, unlike brick or stone, cannot 'breathe' (Hamilton 1979a: 240).

The third phase of housing construction in Eastern Europe overlaps with the fourth – private housing. In East Germany, this last phase began in 1971, when the Eighth Party Congress recognized the need to supplement state construction of housing with other means. In this option, which is available to certain workers with financial means, especially those with more than three children, the state provides assistance in construction through credit and equipment. In other socialist countries of Eastern Europe, various options provide for private or cooperative dwellings.

What about the quality of life in these new socialist neighborhoods? Hamilton (1979a: 241, 244) provides a revealing summary of a questionnaire survey taken in the new socialist subtown of Novi

Beograd across the Sava River from Belgrade. Residents apparently were satisfied with this location in terms of access to work, public services, and connections to Belgrade. However, considerable dissatisfaction was expressed with living conditions in the neighborhood projects, opinions that agree with those expressed in other socialist countries. The major complaints were: small size of apartments – the living room for 61 per cent of the respondents served as a bedroom, and the balcony had to be used for drying clothes; insufficient daily services, especially repair, cultural, and recreation for children; noise associated with the large numbers of people in high blocks of buildings over ten stories; and inaccessibility – difficulties getting from ground level to upper stories, perhaps because of elevator problems. In general, lack of privacy was a common complaint of adults, one that I heard frequently throughout Eastern Europe. Apparently a collective life style is not always compatible with human nature.

Parking space for cars was not needed in early residential planning in socialist countries, but with private automobiles becoming more numerous, a problem has arisen. In some cities in Yugoslavia, where returning migrant workers from Western Europe park their cars in neighborhoods without parking space, this practice often leads to traffic congestion in areas where children play.

Although these four phases of socialist housing construction can be distinguished in the large cities of Eastern Europe, they are intermixed in location, extending from central core to the city edge and giving the overall landscape an aspect of large apartment houses. Dawson (1971) in a study of Warsaw feels that socialist transformation of the city has led to increasing uniformity of population and housing density over that during the prewar period. The factors involve the reduction of densities in the center through the development of wide boulevards and public space and the increase of densities on the periphery with the planned construction of apartment buildings. Hence, the outward decreasing density gradient of population and housing, which in North American cities is related to the predominance of single-family houses, is less characteristic of the Polish capital. Dawson does find, however, that the internal distribution of this housing tends to be axial, because placement occurs reasonably close to public transport along the major arteries leading out from the city center.

In examining other East European cities, I find that Dawson's ideas of a uniform density gradient and axial development to be applicable, although the presence of presocialist relic features can raise

densities in the core. One can conclude that the suburbs of East European cities are quite distinct from those in the United States: housing in East European suburbs resembles housing in the rest of the city, because all are worker settlements created by rural to urban migration; in the United States, however, suburbs are stratified as a result of migration from a declining, central city to single-family houses on the periphery.

Summary

This chapter deals with socialism, the final historical process affecting the landscape of Eastern Europe. Instead of using relics as a basis for creating geographic environments of the past, we examine a current landscape system. Supported by the Soviet Union, the states of Eastern Europe, including the eastern portion of Germany, established communist governments after the Second World War. Although their overriding goal was the modernization of their economies through programs of industrialization, these countries are unique because of their commitment to social change, spelled out in Marxist-Leninist ideology which includes reference to geographical goals of greater equity – between town and country, regions, cities, and urban neighborhoods. These industrial programs have been carried out through a series of national plans which have been helped by the public ownership of the means for production and controlled allocation of resources.

After almost forty years of socialism, the landscape reflects the imprint of this planning. Collectivization programs, which have been implemented in six of the countries, created large fields and significant alterations in village structure; in the other two countries, private farming in small strips remains predominant. The pattern of industrial location under socialism eludes easy analysis, because a variety of explanatory factors are present including autarky, military strategy, ethnic minorities, unexploited raw materials, existing centers, and cooperation through the East European Common Market. All of these factors were responsible for widespread changes in the landscape so that the total influence of socialism has been impressive. Examples include large, integrated steel plants in all countries, the improvement of backward areas like Slovakia, the decentralization of older industrial regions like Upper Silesia, and an oil pipeline from the Soviet Union to four countries. Changes in urbanization have also been impressive, although this feature has

lagged behind industrialization, with the commuting of peasant-workers from villages acting to hold down even greater progress. Finally, the internal landscape of cities has changed as the planners have stressed political rather than commercial cores, public space over private, and rapid expansion of prefabricated apartment projects instead of single dwellings.

Have the socialist regimes reached their goals of social change and equity? This is difficult to say. In the 1950s, a period emphasizing a policy of autarky, a noticeable upward mobility of major portions of the population occurred as peasants migrated to jobs in the cities and blue-collar laborers became white-collar workers. The ideology of regional equity received considerable attention and many new factories and even new towns arose in backward areas. In the 1960s and 1970s, however, this rapid growth abated as the regimes encountered difficulties. A shift in policy from self-sufficiency to regional cooperation and specialization within a Common Market took place, reforms of the economic planning systems occurred, contacts with the West increased, the commitment to spatial equity weakened, and goals of economic efficiency became evident. Despite accommodations to the ideology of Marxism-Leninism, the economies and landscapes of the East European countries have been transformed beyond recognition. Let us now review in a final chapter the making of the East European cultural landscape and consider some assessments for the future.

Note

1. Case studies of collective and state farms with detailed maps are not easily obtained. Some of the best are shown in a publication on agricultural land use (Kostrowicki, 1965: 5). Others are by Uren (1969), Knübel (1968), and Kwiatkowska (1976).

361

8
The East European landscape

Eastern Europe! A nebulous area between Western Europe and Russia that spawned two world wars and a 'Cold War' between communism and the West. The zone sealed off by an Iron Curtain. Average Americans hold vague concepts of this region, even though some of their ancestors or those of many of their fellow citizens might have originated there. Because of its importance as a center of world geopolitics, Eastern Europe became a model – called the Shatter Belt – devised by geographers to exemplify a band of small countries subjected by external powers to domination, raising the question of whether these small countries could exist in their own right or would remain catspaws in world politics. The most recent of these external powers – the Soviet Union – has exerted varying degrees of influence over this region since the Second World War.

The processes

My interest in Eastern Europe was stimulated by the many landscape relics representing the marks of earlier social orders responsible for spatial organization in the area. I became fascinated by the possibility of using these as clues to the geographical environments of the past. Classifying these relics led me to four processes of historical development in Eastern Europe – German colonization, feudalism, multinationalism, and nationalism – which preceded the present process of socialism.

German colonization
Today, a series of relics, which extend across the East European landscape from the Baltic to Transylvania, tell a story of German medi-

362

eval colonization. These forms – towns, mines, field systems, villages, and monasteries – help us to re-create the environment of progress which the German colonists diffused to the east. Such social change included a market economy, town law, and a technology of agriculture and mining that completly transformed the landscape. Eastern Europe began to resemble the western part of the continent.

Feudalism and serfdom
The next layer of the landscape tells a different story, one of stagnation and repression. These remains – castles, palaces, manor houses, planned towns, and barracks for farm laborers – project an environment of feudal serfdom that stifled the innovations developed by the German colonists. At the very time in Western Europe when commercial activities were leading to a flourishing town life and to the development of a middle class, the eastern area was becoming increasingly agrarian and backward. This cleavage between the two parts of Europe developed as the nobility in the east began to expand their land for the growing of grain and other products for export. Peasants, who formerly had certain rights, became serfs tied to the land. The lords as masters of the countryside restricted social change in their domains for six hundred years.

Multinationalism
Still another series of landscape relics help us to re-create the political environment of multinationalism, which dominated the history of Eastern Europe for so long. Today, reminders of these states – empires, kingdoms, or principalities – are scattered across the boundaries of several modern states, illustrating the changes in political systems of spatial organization. The multinational nature of these units led to cohesive forces of loyalty to ruler or territory rather than to nationality. Rulers made special arrangements to insure the loyalty of the nobility. The Austrian Empire exemplifies the remnants of administrative centers, military fortresses, colonial settlements, spas, factories, and railroads – all established to serve the interests of a strong ruler, often absolute in nature and making decisions from a capital external to the region. Religious relics also remain to represent a force generally supportive of this ruler but sometimes in opposition.

Nationalism
A final series of landscape features re-create the political environment

of nationalism, which in the nineteenth century replaced multi-nationalism as an ideology in Eastern Europe. Relics of nationalism generally are confined within the boundaries of new states, whose base was loyalty to nationalities. In its regional planning of 1815–30, Congress Poland reflected in places like Warsaw, Łódź, and Silesia attempts to keep the national spirit of the Poles alive during the early period of partition. Farther south, in the Balkans, the national revival of Bulgaria in the nineteenth century illustrates nationalism through certain relics in places like Tryavna and Plovdiv; other remains in Sofia show its progress as a new capital after the country became independent of Turkey. After the First World War, other new states developed national environments through such forms as capital cities, ports, industrial areas, monuments, and national parks.

Socialism

Superimposed on the palimpsest of four environments from the past in Eastern Europe is the present environment of socialism trans-planted from the Soviet Union after the Second World War but modified since then by national communist governments. These regimes have instituted planned programs of modernization based on the ideology of Marxism-Leninism, which includes a commitment to equity in providing a quality environment – jobs, housing, goods, and services. An important aspect of this equity is the spatial one – between town and country, between regions, and between cities. Evidence of landscape transformation under socialism abounds in all respects: collective farms, industrial districts throughout the countries, new towns, and modernized settlements of different sizes.

Can we call a landscape that exhibits such pervasive change a 'socialist landscape'? As mentioned previously, this question is controversial. Some feel that the degree of central planning together with an ideology that retains a commitment to social change constitutes arguments for such a landscape. French and Hamilton (1979: Ch. 1), in asking if the socialist city is fundamentally different from a capitalist one, argue that it is but with qualifications that are based on the presence of varying national backgrounds. They feel the term 'socialized city' is more appropriate and perhaps 'socialized landscape' would be, too. Certainly, after years of studying this question in the field, I conclude that the landscape has a new element under socialism that cannot be subsumed by merely calling it 'modernization'. The socialized landscape was best typified in the 1950s under programs of autarky, when equity goals remained uppermost in the minds of

planners. In the 1970s, cost-effectiveness enjoyed at least equal time with equity and the landscape reflects this. Does this mean that ideology is now a 'hollow ritual' as Vucinich (1981: 25) states? I do not believe so, at least in certain countries like East Germany and Bulgaria. I also remain impressed by the overall modernization that has occurred, although, of course, disparities remain between regions.

The palimpsest of landscapes

When considered together, the landscapes of Eastern Europe tell several stories: external influence, lack of social change, and incompatibility between traditional and modern social orders.

By examining in total the relics from the past, one can make an important first conclusion: many of them had their origin from outside the region, a confirmation of the persistent external influence from powerful states on the margins. A few examples suffice:

Greece: ruins of colony at Apollonia, Albania
Rome: palace of Diocletian at Split, Yugoslavia
Byzantium: Orthodox monastery at Rila, Bulgaria
Germany: mining town at Kremnica, Czechoslovakia
Austria: spa at Băile Herculane, Romania
Italy: architecture of Dubrovnik, Yugoslavia
Turkey: mosque at Sarajevo, Yugoslavia

In a deeper sense, these forms are visible evidence of penetration by the cultures of these external powers as manifested in trade, politics, religion, and technology. Even the basic ideology of nationalism came from the outside.

Despite this contact with external powers, however, the landscape also tells a second story of restricted social change dating from the fourteenth century and continuing to the present. In contrast to Western Europe, gaps appear in the landscape chronology – an underrepresentation of relics of the Commercial, Agricultural, and Industrial Revolutions. One factor explaining this negative aspect of social change has been the isolation of the area from innovations from other parts of the world. Even today, the Iron Curtain acts as an effective barrier to continental interaction. The barriers placed by communist regimes on political freedom and the refusal of some to recognize national feelings present in these states also affect social change.

365

How do we reconcile this paradox: external influence and yet isolation from innovations necessary for social change? One answer is that, except for the German colonists, the external influences were largely exploitive. The external powers, mostly empires, utilized Eastern Europe as a base for expansion, and the cultures within the area had little opportunity for independent development. Even the lords restricted social change in repressing the peasants and limiting innovations in agriculture, commerce, and industry. No real middle class existed and nationalism arrived late. Thus, external control by a multinational state was often characterized by a feudal environment.

A third story seen in the total landscape of Eastern Europe is the degree of incompatibility between the traditional forms and those of socialism. An attempt to create compatibility between past and present is seen in East Berlin where Hohenzollern and socialist forms portray an image of state power. In most cases, however, modernization is not compatible with the past. The landscape lacks character: there is uniformity or monotony to the socialist forms and there is drabness to the older forms. The pace of modernization in transforming or preserving older landscape forms has been slow, a contrast very evident in comparing changes in West and East Berlin in the years since 1945.

The future landscape

In the 1980s, Eastern Europe continues to modernize, but one now hears less about Marxist goals of equity, for there appear to be limits to the extent to which an industrial space economy can be manipulated to achieve social objectives. Greater efficiency in spatial organization seems to be the major motive as seen in attempts at agro-industrial integration and specialization – larger fields, specialized operations, and even factories in the countryside. Investments in backward areas may take place if they serve the national interest, although existing centers are often more economical. Efficiency is also a factor in reforms that allow some decentralization of decision making and increased Western contacts as reflected in Fiat autos produced under license.

Yet, seeing certain things in the landscape – an aging, often female work force in agriculture; peasant-worker commuters, who bear the costs of underurbanization; a deteriorating environment; and a shortage of consumer goods and housing that contradict the promises

of socialism – raises questions for the future. How will the regimes handle the problem of stimulating young people to remain in agriculture? How can urbanization catch up with industrialization? Will socialists continue to injure the environment because they perceive it in terms of potential productivity? What measures will be taken to fill the demands of citizens for consumer goods? A basic question remains: can the socialist states, which established the preconditions for economic 'take-off', show progress in the drive to maturity? This lack of progress in second-stage modernization together with the problem of sustaining upward occupational mobility makes one doubt the possibilities of convergence of socialist and capitalist societies.

New forces might possibly be leading to a different political alignment in Europe. In the early 1980s, the crisis in Poland showed that the Communist party there has not learned how to cope with social change and might face continued resistance as a consequence. On the other hand, the debts owed to the West by East European countries could force these countries into greater dependency on the Soviet Union, even though the latter has its own problem of scarce resources. At the same time, the basing of nuclear missiles in Western Europe has caused rifts in the Atlantic Alliance. Perhaps, this is the time for the 'Yalta Order' of the Second World War to dissolve and for a neutral Europe – West and East – to emerge. If so, the Iron Curtain, which disrupts the logical unity of a continent, could disappear.

Today, other Shatter Belts exist in the world. Most of them involve Third World countries that are experimenting with variants of socialism and capitalism as approaches to modernization. The location of many – Southeast Asia, the Middle East, Africa, and Central America – makes them centers of world geopolitics. In these areas, the lesson of the Shatter Belt of Eastern Europe remains paramount: can small states find their places in today's world without being catspaws in world politics? One hopes so.

References

Abel, W. (1962) *Geschichte der deutschen Landwirtschaft*, Eugen Ulmer, Stuttgart.

Abrams, Irwin and Richard Francaviglia (1975) Urban planning in Poland today, *Journal of the American Institute of Planners*, 41, 258–69.

Allcock, John B. (1977) Aspects of the development of capitalism in Yugoslavia: the role of the state in the formation of a 'Satellite' economy, pp. 535–80 in Francis W. Carter (ed.) *An Historical Geography of the Balkans*, Academic Press, London.

Andrić, Ivo (1959) *The Bridge on the Drina*, George Allen & Unwin, London.

Anthony, Kathryn H. (1979) Public and private space in Soviet cities, *Landscape*, 23, 20–5.

Arany, John (1938) quoted in Countess of Listowel, The indigestible Magyar, *Geographical Magazine*, 11, 361–76.

Atlas der Donauländer (1965–) Austrian Ost- und Südosteuropainstitut, Vienna.

Atlas Geografic-Republica Socialistă România (1965) Editura Didactică şi Pedagogică, Bucharest.

Atlas Istoric (1971) Editura Didactică şi Pedagogică, Bucharest.

Atlas of Warsaw's Architecture (1978) Arkady Publishers, Warsaw.

Aubin, H. (1934) Die deutschen Stadtrechtslandschaften des Ostens, *Veröffentlichen der Schlesische Gesellschaft für Erdkunde*, Heft 21, 27–52.

Aubin, Hermann (1928) Wirtschaftsgeschichtliche Bemerkungen zur Ostdeutschen Kolonisation, *Aus Sozial- und Wirtschaftsgeschichte*, Gedächtnisschrift für Georg von Below, Stuttgart.

Aubin, Hermann (1966) The lands east of the Elbe and the German colonization eastwards, pp. 449–86 in M. M. Postan (ed.) *Cambridge Economic History of Europe*, Vol. I, Cambridge University Press.

Barraclough, Geoffrey (1970) Towards a new concept of European history, pp. 7–14 in F. Graus *et al.*, *Eastern and Western Europe in the Middle Ages*,

Harcourt Brace Jovanovich, New York.

Barta, Gy. (1976) Changes in the living conditions of the rural population, pp. 89–110 in Gy. Enyedi (ed.) *Rural Transformation in Hungary*, Akadémiai Kiadó, Budapest.

Barthel, Hellmuth (1962) *Braunkohlenbergbau und Landschaftdynamik*, VEB Hermann Haack, Ergänzungsheft No. 270 of *Petermanns Geographischen Mitteilungen*, Annex No. 10, Gotha.

Benthien, Bruno (1963) Karten zur Entwicklungsgeschichte des vollgenossenschaftlichen Dorfes Stresow (Kreis Greifswald), *Geographische Berichte*, 8, 1–9.

Berend, Iván T. and György Ránki (1974a) *Economic Development in East-Central Europe in the 19th and 20th Centuries*, Columbia University Press, New York.

Berend, I. T. and G. Ránki (1974b) *Hungary: A Century of Economic Development*, Barnes and Noble, New York.

Berentsen, William H. (1980) Spatial pattern of retail sales per capita in the German Democratic Republic and East Berlin, *Die Erde*, 111, 293–300.

Biber, Mehmet (1980) Albania: alone against the World, *National Geographic Magazine*, 158, 530–57.

Bichev, Milko (1961) *Architecture in Bulgaria*, Foreign Languages Press, Sofia.

Biegajło, Władysłav (1965) Borysówska, Grodzisko, and Hruskie villages in the northeastern undeveloped corner of Poland, pp. 29–60 in J. Kostrowicki (ed.) Land Utilization in East-Central Europe: Case Studies, *Geographia Polonica*, No. 5, Warsaw.

Bjorklund, Elaine (1964) Ideology and culture exemplified in southwestern Michigan, *Annals of the Association of American Geographers*, 54, 227–41.

Blue Guide (1969) *Yugoslavia: The Adriatic Coast*, Ernest Benn Ltd., London.

Blum, Jerome (1948) *Noble Landowners and Agriculture in Austria, 1815–1848*, Johns Hopkins Press, University Studies in Historical and Political Science, Series 65, No. 2, Baltimore, Md.

Blum, Jerome (1957) The rise of serfdom in Eastern Europe, *The American Historical Review*, 62, 807–36.

Blum, Jerome (1960) *The European Peasantry from the Fifteenth to the Nineteenth Century*, Service Center for Teachers of History, Washington, D.C.

Blumenfeld, Yurick (1968) *Seesaw: Cultural Life in Eastern Europe*, Harcourt, Brace and World, New York.

Bornstein, Morris (1966) Ideology and the Soviet economy, *Soviet Studies*, 18, 74–80.

Bornstein, Morris (1981) Soviet–East European economic relations, pp. 105–24 in Morris Bornstein *et al.*, (eds) *East-West Relations and the Future of Eastern Europe*, George Allen & Unwin, London.

Boros, F. (1970) Geographical aspects of Dunaújváros, pp. 55–64 in Béla Sárfalvi (ed.) *Recent Population Movements in the East European Countries*, Akadémiai Kiadó, Budapest.

References

Bosl, Karl (1970) Political relations between East and West, pp. 43–82 in F. Graus *et al.*, *Eastern and Western Europe in the Middle Ages*, Harcourt Brace Jovanovich, New York.

Boswell, A. Bruce (1953) Poland, pp. 154–71 in A. Goodwin (ed.) *The European Nobility in the Eighteenth Century*, Adam and Charles Black, London.

Bowman, Isaiah (1928) *The New World: Problems in Political Geography*, George C. Harrap, London, Chs 13–18, 20.

Brock, Peter (1969) Polish nationalism, pp. 310–72 in Peter F. Sugar and Ivo J. Lederer (eds) *Nationalism in Eastern Europe*, University of Washington Press, Seattle.

Brzeski, Andrzej (1969) Two decades of East European industrialization in retrospect, *East European Quarterly* 3, 1–14.

Carr, Edward Hallett (1947) *The Soviet Impact on the Western World*, Macmillan, New York.

Carsten, F. L. (1954) *The Origins of Prussia*, Clarendon Press, Oxford.

Carter, F. W. (1973) Postwar structural and functional changes within the Sofia conurbation, *Occasional Papers*, University College, Department of Geography, No. 21, London.

Carter, F. W. (1974) Concentrated Prague, *Geographical Magazine*, 46, 537–44.

Carter, F. W. (1975) Č-K-D Employees, Prague, 1871–1920: some aspects of their geographical distribution, *Journal of Historical Geography*, 1, 69–97.

Carter, F. W. (1979) Prague and Sofia: an analysis of their changing internal city structure, pp. 425–59 in R. A. French and F. E. Ian Hamilton (eds) *The Socialist City*, John Wiley, New York.

Cash, J. Allen (1949) Contrasts in Bulgaria, *Geographical Magazine*, 22, 132–41.

Chełstowski, Stanisław (1974) A regional plan for the future, *Polish Perspectives*, 17, 5–13.

Christian Science Monitor (1978) Dresden as art capital, 9 June, p. 27.

Ciborowski, Adolph (1975) We must develop, *Poland: Illustrated Magazine*, 3–4, 19.

Cichy, Bodo (1964) *The Great Ages of Architecture*, G. P. Putnam's Sons, New York.

Cohen, Benjamin J. (1973) *The Question of Imperialism*, Basic Books, New York.

Compton, Paul A. (1979) Planning and spatial change in Budapest, pp. 461–91 in R. A. French and F. E Ian Hamilton (eds) *The Socialist City*, John Wiley, New York.

Connor, Walter D. (1977) Social change and stability in Eastern Europe, *Problems of Communism*, 26, 16–32.

Connor, Walter D (1979) *Socialism, Politics, and Equality*, Columbia University Press, New York.

Crankshaw, Edward (1963) *The Fall of the House of Habsburg*, Popular Library, New York.

Crkvenčić, Ivan (1977) Part-time farming and some aspects of the attitudinal and behavioral change in the rural sphere of Yugoslavia, unpublished manuscript.

Curry, Leslie (1964) Landscape as system, *Geographical Review*, 54, 121–4.

Curry, Leslie (1967) Chance and the landscape, pp. 40–55 in *Northern Geographical Essays in Honour of G. Daysh*, Oriel Press, Newcastle, England.

Dawson, A. H. (1971) Warsaw: an example of city structure in free market and planned socialist environments, *Tijdschrift voor Economische en Sociale Geografie*, 62, 104–113.

Delaisi, Francis (1929) *Les deux Europas*, Payot, Paris, Ch. 1.

Demek, Jaromír and Miroslav Střída (1971) *Geography of Czechoslavokia*, Academia, Prague.

Den Hollander, A. N. J. (1960–61) The great Hungarian plain: a European frontier area, *Comparative Studies in Society and History*, 3, 74–88, 155–69.

Denitch, Bogdan (1978) *Society and Social Change in Eastern Europe*, American Society for Advancement of Slavic Studies.

Dickinson, Robert E. (1942) The development and distribution of the medieval German town, *Geography*, 27, 9–21, 47–53.

Dienes, Leslie (1973) The Budapest agglomeration and Hungarian industry: a spatial dilemma, *Geographical Review*, 63, 356–77.

Dienes, Leslie (1974) Environmental disruption and its mechanism in Eastern Europe, *Professional Geographer*, 26, 375–81.

Dollinger, Philippe (1970) *The German Hansa*, Stanford University Press.

Dominian, Leon (1917) *The Frontiers of Language and Nationality in Europe*, American Geographical Society, New York.

Dumont, René (1957) *Types of Rural Economy*, Methuen, London.

Dunman, Jack (1975) *Agriculture: Capitalist and Socialist*, Lawrence and Wishart, London.

Durand, E. Dana (1922) Agriculture in Eastern Europe, *Quarterly Journal of Economics*, 36, 169–96.

Dziewoński, K. (1943) The plan of Cracow: its origin, design and evolution, *Town Planning Review*, 19, 29–37.

East, Gordon (1961) The concept and political status of the shatter zone, pp. 1–27 in Norman J. G. Pounds (ed.) *Geographical Essays on Eastern Europe*, Indiana University Publications, Russian and East European Series, Vol. 24, Bloomington, Ind.

Enyedi, György (1967) The changing face of agriculture in Eastern Europe, *Geographical Review*, 57, 358–72.

Enyedi, György (1976) *Hungary: An Economic Geography*, Westview Press, Boulder, Colo.

Ferguson, William S. (1941) *Greek Imperialism*, Biblo and Tannen, New York.

References

Fisher, Jack C. (1962) Planning the city of socialist man, *Journal of the American Institute of Planners*, 28, 251–65.

French, R. A. and F. E. Ian Hamilton (eds) (1979) *The Socialist City: Spatial Structure and Urban Policy*, John Wiley, New York.

Frenzel, Reiner (1970) *Palaces of Europe*, Hart Publishing Co., New York.

Frolic, B. Michael (1975) Moscow: the socialist alternative, pp. 295–339 in H. W. Eldredge (ed.) *The World Capitals*, Anchor Press, Garden City, N.Y.

Fuchs, Roland J. (1980) Urban change in Eastern Europe: the limits to planning, *Urban Geography*, 1, 81–94.

Fuchs, Roland J. and George J. Demko (1977) Commuting and urbanization in the socialist countries of Europe, *Bulletin-Association for Comparative Economic Studies*, 19, 21–38.

Fuchs, Roland J. and George J. Demko (1979) Geographic inequality under socialism, *Annals of the Association of American Geographers*, 69, 304–18.

Geographical Handbooks (1944–45) *Yugoslavia*, Vols I–III, Naval Intelligence Division, London.

Gerhard, Dietrich (1959) The frontier in comparative view, *Comparative Studies in Society and History*, 1, 205–29.

Goodwin, A. (1953) Prussia, pp. 83–101 in A. Goodwin (ed.) *The European Nobility in the Eighteenth Century*, Adam and Charles Black, London.

Gross, N. T. (1973) The Industrial Revolution in the Habsburg Monarchy, 1750–1914, in Carlo M. Cipolla (ed.) *Fontana Economic History of Europe* Vol. IV, Collins, London.

Gutkind, E. A. (1964) *International History of City Development*, Vol. I, *Central Europe*, Free Press, Glencoe, Ill.

Gutkind, E. A. (1972) *International History of City Development*, Vol. VII, *Poland, Czechoslovakia, and Hungary*, Free Press, Glencoe, Ill.

Gutkind, E. A. (1972) *International History of City Development*, Vol. VIII, *Bulgaria, Romania, and the USSR*, Free Press, Glencoe, Ill.

Hajdu, J. (1978) The German city today, *Geography*, 63, 23–30.

Halecki, O. (1952) Imperialism in Slavic and East European history, *American Slavic and East European Review*, 11, 1–26.

Hall, Arthur R. (1955) Mackinder and the course of events, *Annals of the Association of American Geographers*, 45, 109–26.

Halpern, Joel M. (1956) *A Serbian Village*, Columbia University Press, New York.

Halpern, Joel M. and Barbara Kerewsky Halpern (1972) *A Serbian Village in Historical Perspective*, Holt, Rinehart and Winston, New York.

Hamilton, F. E. Ian (1964) Location factors in the Yugoslav iron and steel industry, *Economic Geography*, 40, 46–64.

Hamilton, F. E. Ian (1968) *Yugoslavia: Patterns of Economic Activity*, Praeger, New York.

Hamilton, F. E. Ian (1970a) Changes in the industrial geography of East

Europe since 1940, *Tijdschrift voor Economische en Sociale Geografie*, 61, 300–5.

Hamilton, F. E. Ian (1970b) Aspects of spatial behavior in planned economies, *Papers of the Regional Science Association*, 25, 83–105.

Hamilton, F. E. Ian (1971a) The location of industry in East-Central and Southeastern Europe, Ch. 5 in George W. Hoffman (ed.) *Eastern Europe: Essays on Geographical Problems*, Methuen, London.

Hamilton, F. E. Ian (1971b) Decision-making and industrial location in Eastern Europe, *Transactions of the Institute of British Geographers*, 52, 77–94.

Hamilton, F. E. Ian (1979a) Urbanization in socialist Eastern Europe: the macro-environment of internal city structure, and spatial structure in East European cities, pp. 167–261 in R. A. French and F. E. Ian Hamilton (eds) *The Socialist City*, John Wiley, New York.

Hamilton, F. E. Ian (1979b) *The Planned Economies*, Macmillan, London.

Hamilton, F. E. Ian and Alan D. Bennett (1979) Social processes and residential structure, pp. 263–304 in R. A. French and F. E. Ian Hamilton (eds) *The Socialist City*, John Wiley, New York.

Hamlin, Talbot (1953) *Architecture through the Ages*, G. P. Putnam's Sons, New York.

Handbook of Economic Statistics (1982) Central Intelligence Agency, Washington, D.C.

Harke, M. and M. Dischereit (1979) *Geographische Aspekte der Socialistischen ökonomischen Integration*, VEB Hermann Haack, Gotha.

Hartshorne, Richard (1934) The Upper Silesian industrial district, *Geographical Review*, 24, 423–38.

Haskins, Charles Homer and Robert Howard Lord (1920) *Some Problems of the Peace Conference*, Harvard University Press, Cambridge.

Hassinger, H. (1932) Der Staat als Landschaftgestalter, *Zeitschrift für Geopolitik*, 9, 2, 117–22 and 3, 182–87.

Hawrylyshyn, Oli (1977) Ethnicity as a barrier to migration in Yugoslavia: the evidence from interregional flows and immigration to Belgrade, pp. 379–99 in Alan A. Brown and Egon Neuberger (eds) *Internal Migration: A Comparative Perspective*, Academic Press, New York.

Hayes, Carlton J. H (1926) *Essays on Nationalism*, Russell and Russell, New York.

Heilbroner, Robert L. (1970) *Between Capitalism and Socialism*, Random House, New York.

Heineberg, Heinz (1979) Service centers in East and West Berlin, pp. 305–34 in R. A. French and F. E. Ian Hamilton (eds) *The Socialist City*, John Wiley, New York.

Henderson, W. O (1958) *The State and the Industrial Revolution in Prussia, 1740–1870*, University Press, Liverpool.

Henderson, W. O. (1969) *The Industrialization of Europe, 1780–1914*, Harcourt,

References

Brace and World, New York.

Hitze, Otto (1914) Die Hohenzollern und die Adel, *Historische Zeitschrift*, 112, 494–524.

Hoffman, George W. (ed.) (1971) *Eastern Europe: Essays in Geographical Problems*, Methuen, London.

Hoffman, George W. (1976) Energy politics in Eastern Europe: structural changes in production and consumption, and resource dependence, *Proceedings: International Ex-Students Conference on Energy*, Center for Energy Studies, University of Texas, Austin, Texas, 137–51.

Hoffman, George W. (1980) Rural transformation in Eastern Europe since World War II, pp. 21–41 in Ivan Volgyes *et al.*, (eds) *The Process of Rural Transformation*, Pergamon Press, New York.

Horbaly, W. (1951) *Agricultural Conditions in Czechoslovakia*, 1950, University of Chicago, Department of Geography, Research Paper No. 18, Chicago, 55–94.

Hoskins, W. G. (1957) *The Making of the English Landscape*, Hodder and Stoughton, London.

Hoskins, W. G. (1973) *English Landscapes*, British Broadcasting Corp., London.

Hudson, Cam (1980) *Eastern Europe and the Energy Crisis: An Overview*, Radio Free Europe Research, RAD Background Report, 136, East Europe, pp. 1–17.

Hutchings, Raymond (1968) The weakening of ideological influence upon Soviet design, *Slavic Review*, 27, 71–84.

Illyés, Gyula (1971) *People of the Puszta*, English translation from Hungarian original of 1936, Chatto and Windus, London.

Inalcik, Halil (1973) *The Ottoman Empire*, Praeger, New York.

International Petroleum Encyclopedia (1982) Penn Well Publishing Co., Tulsa, Oklahoma.

Jackson, John B. (1980) *The Necessity for Ruins*, University of Massachusetts Press, Amherst.

Jaehne, Günter (1980) Problems of agricultural integration within the CMEA, pp. 221–35 in Ronald A. Francisco *et al.* (eds) *Agricultural Policies in the USSR and Eastern Europe*, Westview Press, Boulder, Colorado.

Jelavich, Charles and Barbara (1977) *The Establishment of Balkan National States, 1804–1920*, University of Washington Press, Seattle.

Jensen, Robert G. (1976) Urban environments in the United States and the Soviet Union, pp. 31–42 in Brian J. L. Berry (ed.) *Urbanization and Counterurbanization*, Sage, Beverly Hills, California.

Kallbrunner, Josef (1943) Die Planung der deutschen Siedlung im Banat unter Mercy und Maria Theresia, Sonderabdruck aus *Deutsches Archiv für Landes- und Volksforschung*, 7, 453–8.

Kansky, Karel Joseph (1976) *Urbanism under Socialism: The Case of Czechoslovakia*, Praeger, New York.

Kiełczewska-Zaleska, M. (1965) On the types of rural settlement networks

and on the plans of their transformation, *Przeglad Geograficzny*, 37, 457–80.

Knapp, Vincent J. (1976) *Europe in the Era of Social Transformation, 1700–Present*, Prentice-Hall, Englewood Cliffs, New Jersey.

Kniffen, Fred B. (1936) Louisiana house types, *Annals of the Association of American Geographers*, 26, 179–93.

Knight, David B. (1971) Impress of authority and ideology on landscape: a review of some unanswered questions, *Tijdschrift voor Economische en Sociale Geografie*, 62, 383–7.

Knox, Brian (1971) *The Architecture of Poland*, Barrie and Jenkins, London.

Knübel, Hans (1968) Die LPG Dolen Tschiflik, *Geographische Rundschau*, 20, 22–5.

Kohl, H. *et al.* (1976) *Ökonomische Geographie der Deutschen Demokratische Republik*, VEB Hermann Haack, Gotha.

Kohl, H. *et al.* (1979) *Geographie der DDR*, VEB Hermann Haack, Gotha.

Kohn, Hans (1942) *World Order in Historical Perspective*, Harvard University Press, Cambridge.

Kohn, Hans (1945) *The Idea of Nationalism: A Study in Its Origins and Background*, Macmillan, New York.

Kolakowski, Leszek (1982) Ideology in Eastern Europe, pp. 43–53 in Milorad Drachkovitch, *East Central Europe*, Hoover Institution Press.

Kolarz, Walter (1946) *Myths and Realities in Eastern Europe*, Lindsay Drummond, London.

Konrád, György and Ivan Szelenyi (1974) Social conflicts of underurbanization, pp. 206–26 in Alan A. Brown *et al.* (eds) *Urban and Social Economics in Market and Planned Economies*, Vol. I, Praeger, New York.

Kosiński, Leszek A. (1969) Changes in the ethnic structure in East-Central Europe, *Geographical Review*, 59, 388–402.

Kosiński, Leszek A. (1974) Urbanization in East-Central Europe after World War II, *East Europe Quarterly*, 8, 129–53.

Kostrowicki, J. (ed.) (1965) Land utilization in East-Central Europe: case studies, *Geographia Polonica*, No. 5, Warsaw.

Kötzschke, R. (1912) *Quellen zur Geschichte der ostdeutschen Kolonisation im 12. bis 14. Jahrhundert*, B. G. Teubner, Leipzig.

Kozenn Atlas-Österreichisches Mittelschulatlas (1961) 86th ed., Verlag Ed. Hölzel, Vienna.

Krebs, N. (1930) *Landeskunde von Deutschland*, Vol. II, Der Nordosten, B. G. Teubner, Leipzig.

Kuhn, W. (1955) *Die deutsche Ostsiedlung in der Neuzeit*, Vols I–II plus map volume, Böhlau Verlag, Cologne.

Kuhn, Walter (1937) Die deutschen Siedlungsräume im Südosten, in *Deutsches Archiv für Landes- und Volksforschung*, I, 808–27.

Kuusinen, O. V. *et al.* (1963) *Fundamentals of Marxism-Leninism*, Foreign Languages Publishing House, Moscow.

Kwiatkowska, Eugenia (1976) New forms of rural settlement in the

Voivodship of Toruń in the thirty years of People's Poland, *Przegląd Geograficzny*, 48, 637–48 (in Polish).

Lazarcik, Gregor (1974) Agricultural output and productivity in Eastern Europe and some comparisons with the USSR and USA, pp. 328–93 in Joint Economic Committee, U. S. Congress, *Reorientation and Commercial Relations of the Economies of Eastern Europe*, GPO, Washington, D.C.

Lazarcik, Gregor (1977) Comparative growth and levels of agricultural output and productivity in Eastern Europe, pp. 289–332 in Joint Economic Committee, U.S. Congress, *East European Economies, Post-Helsinki*, GPO, Washington, D.C.

Lazarcik, Gregor (1981) Comparative growth, structure and levels of agricultural output, inputs and productivity in Eastern Europe, 1965–1979, pp. 587–634 in Joint Economic Committee, U.S. Congress, *East European Economic Assessment*, Part II, GPO, Washington, D.C.

Leopold, Luna B. (1969) Landscape aesthetics, *Natural History*, 78, 37–44.

Lettrich, E. (1969) The Hungarian tanya system: history and present-day problems, pp. 151–68 in Béla Sárfalvi *Research Problems in Hungarian Applied Geography*, Akadémiai Kiadó, Budapest.

Lichtenberger, Elisabeth (1970) The nature of European urbanism, *Geoforum*, 4, 45–62.

Lowenthal, David and Hugh C. Prince (1965) English Landscape Tastes, *Geographical Review*, 55, 186–222.

Lüdemann, Heinz and Joachim Heinzmann (1978) On the settlement system of the German Democratic Republic: development trends and strategies, pp. 121–43 in Niles Hansen (ed.) *Human Settlement Systems*, Ballinger, Cambridge, Massachusetts.

Lynch, Kevin (1960) *The Image of the City*, MIT Press, Cambridge, Massachusetts.

Macartney, C. A. (1968) *The Habsburg Monarchy, 1790–1918*, Weidenfeld and Nicolson, London.

Macartney, C. A. (1953) Hungary, pp. 118–35 in A. Goodwin (ed.) *The European Nobility in the Eighteenth Century*, Adam and Charles Black, London.

Mackinder, H. J. (1904) The geographical pivot of history, *Geographical Journal*, 23, 421–44.

Marer, Paul (1979) East European economies: achievements, problems, prospects, pp. 244–89 in Teresa Rakowska-Harmstone and Andrew György, *Communism in Eastern Europe*, Indiana University Press, Bloomington.

Marer, Paul and John Michael Montias (1981) CMEA integration: theory and practice, pp. 148–95 in Joint Economic Committee, U.S. Congress, *East European Economic Assessment*, Part II, GPO, Washington, D.C.

Mayhew, Alan (1973) *Rural Settlement and Farming in Germany*, Batsford, London.

Mellor, Roy (1975) *Eastern Europe: A Geography of the Comecon Countries*,

Columbia University Press, New York.

Města Hrady a Zámky (1970) Odeon, Prague (photos and endcover map).

Meyer, Henry Cord (1946) Mitteleuropa in German political geography, *Annals of the Association of American Geographers*, 36, 178–94.

Mihailović, Kosta (1972) *Regional Development: Experiences and Prospects in Eastern Europe*, Mouton, Paris.

Mikesell, Marvin W. (1968) Landscape, pp. 575–80 in David L. Sills (ed.) *International Encyclopedia of the Social Sciences*, Vol. 8, Crowell, Collier, and Macmillan, New York.

Misztal, Stanisław and Wojciech Kaczorowski (1980) Spatial problems of Poland's postwar industrialization, 1945–1975, *Geographia Polonica*, 43, 199–212.

Mitrany, David (1951) *Marx Against the Peasant*, George Weidenfeld and Nicolson, London.

Moodie, A. E. (1945) *The Italo-Yugoslav Boundary*, George Philip and Son, London.

Mosely, Philip E. (1958) Collectivization of agriculture in Soviet strategy, pp. 49–66 in Irwin T. Sanders (ed.) *Collectivization of Agriculture in Eastern Europe*, University of Kentucky Press, Lexington, Kentucky.

Muncy, Lysbeth Walker (1944) *The Junker in the Prussian Administration under William II, 1888–1914*, Brown University, Providence, Rhode Island.

Musil, Jiří (1980) *Urbanization in Socialist Countries*, M. E. Sharpe, White Plains, New York.

Naumann, Friedrich (1915) *Mitteleuropa*, Verlag Georg Reimer, Berlin.

Niemke, W. (1956) *Dorfplanung am Beispiel Marxwalde*, Berlin.

Obenaus, H. (1975) Zur Umgestaltung des Gutssiedlungsbildes in Mecklenburgischen Raum durch die demokratische Bodenreform, pp. 159–84 in Hans Richter *Entwicklung der Siedlungsstrucktur im Norden der DDR*, VEB Hermann Haack, Gotha.

Ogrissek, R. (1961) *Dorf und Flur in der Deutschen Demokratischen Republik*, VEB Verlag Enzyklopädie, Leipzig.

O'Relley, Z. Edward (1977) Hungarian agricultural performance and policy during the NEM, pp. 356–78 in Joint Economic Committee, U.S. Congress, *East European Economies, Post-Helsinki*, GPO, Washington, D.C.

Ostrowski, Wacław (1966) History of urban development and planning, pp. 9–55 in Jack C. Fisher and Wojciech Morawski (eds) *City and Regional Planning in Poland*, Cornell University Press, Ithaca.

Pallot, Judith and Denis Shaw (1981) *Planning in the Soviet Union*, University of Georgia Press, Athens.

Parker, W. H. (1960) Europe: how far? *Geographical Journal*, 126, 278–97.

Petersen, Carl et al. (1933) *Handwörterbuch des Grenz- und Auslands-deutschtums*, Ferdinand Hirt, Breslau, Vol. I, pp. 207–86. Maps on pp. 230, 238–9.

Petöfi, Sándor (1951) A Magyar nemes (The Hungarian nobleman), 1845, p. 340 in *Collected Works*, Vol. I, Akadémiai Kiadó, Budapest.

Petri, E. (1969) The collectivization of agriculture and the 'tanya' system, pp. 169–81 in Béla Sárfalvi *Research Problems in Hungarian Applied Geography*, Akadémiai Kiadó, Budapest.

Piekalkiewicz, Jaroslaw A. (1979) Kulakization of Polish agriculture, pp. 86–107 in Ronald A. Francisco *et al.* (eds) *The Political Economy of Collectivized Agricultural*, Pergamon Press, New York.

Poland (1977) Sport i Turystyka, Warsaw.

Postan, M. M. (1970) Economic relations between Eastern and Western Europe, pp. 125–74 in F. Graus *et al., Eastern and Western Europe in the Middle Ages*, Harcourt Brace Jovanovich, New York.

Poulsen, Thomas M. (1977) Migration on the Adriatic coast: some processes associated with the development of tourism, pp. 197–215 in Huey Louis Konstanick (ed.) *Population and Migration Trends in Eastern Europe*, Westview Press, Boulder, Colorado.

Pounds, Norman J. G. (1958) *The Upper Silesian Industrial Region*, Indiana University Publications, Slavic and East European Series, Vol. XI, Bloomington, Indiana.

Pounds, Norman J. G. (1959) Planning in the Upper Silesian industrial region, *Journal of Central European Affairs*, 18, 409–22.

Pounds, Norman J. G. (1969) *East Europe*, Aldine, Chicago.

Pounds, Norman J. G. (1971) The urbanization of East-Central and Southeast Europe: an historical perspective, Ch. 2 in George Hoffman (ed.) *Eastern Europe: Essays in Geographical Problems*, Methuen, London.

Pounds, Norman J. G. (1973) *An Historical Geography of Europe, 450 B.C.–1330 A.D.*, Cambridge University Press.

Praga Bohemiae Metropolis (1954) Prague. Map showing historical monuments of the city.

Price, Edward T. (1968) The central courthouse square in the American county seat, *Geographical Review*, 58, 29–60.

Pundeff, Marin V. (1969) Bulgarian nationalism, pp. 93–165 in Peter F. Sugar and Ivo J. Lederer (eds) *Nationalism in Eastern Europe*, University of Washington Press, Seattle.

Reymont, Władysław (1927) *The Promised Lands*, Vols I–II, Knopf, New York. English translation from Polish original of 1899.

Richter, Dieter (1974) Die sozialistische Grossstadt: 25 Jahre Städtebau in der DDR, *Geographische Rundschau*, 26, 183–91.

Rogers, Everett M. and F. Floyd Shoemaker (1971) *Communication of Innovations*, Free Press, New York.

Rostow, W. W. (1971) *The Stages of Economic Growth*, Cambridge University Press.

Rugg, Dean S. (1971) Aspects of change in the landscape of East-Central and Southeast Europe, Ch. 3 in George W. Hoffman (ed.) *Eastern Europe: Essays in Geographical Problems*, Methuen, London.

Rugg, Dean S. (1978) *The Geography of Eastern Europe*, American Association for the Advancement of Slavic Studies.

Sanda, J. and M. Weatherall (1951) Czech village architecture, *Architectural Review*, 109, 255–61.

Sanders, Irwin T. (1958) The peasantries of Eastern Europe, pp. 24–48 in Irwin T. Sanders (ed.) *Collectivization & Agriculture in Eastern Europe*, University of Kentucky Press, Lexington, Kentucky.

Sanders, Irwin T. (1977) Dragalevtsy household members then (1935) and now, pp. 125–33 in Huey Louis Kostanick (ed.) *Population and Migration Trends in Eastern Europe*, Westview Press, Boulder, Colorado.

Schenk, H. G. (1953) Austria, pp. 102–17 in A. Goodwin (ed.) *The European Nobility in the Eighteenth Century*, Adam and Charles Black, London.

Schimscha, Ernst (1939) *Technik und Methoden der Theresianischen Besiedlung des Banats*, Rudolph Rohrer, Baden, Austria.

Schlesinger, Rudolf (1947) *The Spirit of Post-War Russia*, London.

Schlüter, Otto (1906) *Die Ziele der Geographie des Menschen*, Antrittsrede, Munich.

Schmidt, Hugo (1971) *Nicholaus Lenau*, Twayne Publishers, New York

Schöller, Peter (1974) Paradigma Berlin, *Geographische Rundschau*, 26, 425–34.

Schröder, Karl Heinz (1964) Der Wandel der Agrarlandschaft im ostelbischen Tiefland seit 1945, *Geographische Zeitschrift*, 52, 289–316.

Schröder, Karl Heinz and Gabriele Schwarz (1969) *Die Ländlichen Siedlungsformen in Mitteleuropa*, Bundesanstalt für Landeskunde und Raumordnung, Forschungen zur deutschen Landeskunde, Band 175, Bad Godesberg, West Germany.

Sennow, A. (n.d.) *Zur Frage des Gegensatzes zwischen Stadt und Land.*

Seton-Watson, Hugh (1946) *Eastern Europe between the Wars, 1918–1941*, Cambridge University Press.

Seton-Watson, Hug (1975) *The Sick Heart of Modern Europe*, University of Washington Press, Seattle.

Sherrard, Philip (1966) *Byzantium*, Time, Inc., New York.

Školní Atlas Československých Dějin (1959) Kartografie, Prague.

Škrivanić, G. (1977) Roman roads and settlements in the Balkans, pp. 115–45 in Francis W. Carter (ed.) *An Historical Geography of the Balkans*, Academic Press, London.

Smith, C. T. (1978) *An Historical Geography of Western Europe before 1800*, Praeger, New York.

Spaziergang durch die Geschichter Berlins (1978) Information, Berlin.

Stavrianos, L. S. (1963) The influence of the West on the Balkans, pp. 185–226 in Charles and Barbara Jelavich, *The Balkans in Transition*, University of California Press, Berkeley.

Straszewicz, Ludwig (1959) The Łódź industrial district as a subject of investigation of economic geography, *Przegląd Geograficzny*, 31 (supplement), 69–91.

Strumilin, S. (1961) Family and community in the society of the future, *Soviet Review*, 2, 3–29.

References

Sugar, Peter F. (1963) *Industrialization of Bosnia-Hercegovina* (1878-1918), University of Washington Press, Seattle.

Sugar, Peter F. (1969) Nationalism, pp. 3-54 in Peter F. Sugar and Ivo J. Lederer (eds) *Nationalism in Eastern Europe*, University of Washington Press, Seattle.

Svennilson, I. (1954) *Growth and Stagnation in the European Economy*, Geneva.

Szafer, W. (1938) The national parks of Poland, *Geographical Magazine*, 10, 129-40.

Szulc, Halina (1972) The development of the agricultural landscape of Poland, *Geographia Polonica*, 22, 85-103.

Tashev, P. (1972) Urbanization in Bulgaria, in E. A. Gutkind (ed.) *International History of City Development*, Vol. VIII, Free Press, Glencoe, Illinois.

Tatai, Z. (1976) The growth of rural industry, pp. 71-88 in Gy. Enyedi (ed.) *Rural Transformation in Hungary*, Akadémiai Kiadó, Budapest.

Taylor, J. (1952) *The Economic Development of Poland, 1919-1950*, Cornell University Press, Ithaca.

Terhaar, Allen A. and Thomas A. Vankai (1981) The East European feed-livestock economy, 1966-85: performance and prospects, pp. 561-86 in Joint Economic Committee, U.S. Congress, *East European Economic Assessment*, Part II, GPO, Washington, D.C.

Thompson, James Westfall (1915) East German colonization in the Middle Ages, *Annual Report of the American Historical Association for 1915*, Washington.

Thompson, James Westfall (1928) *Economic and Social History of the Middle Ages, 300-1300*, Century, New York.

Tihany, Leslie C. (1976) *A History of Middle Europe*, Rutgers University Press, New Brunswick, New Jersey.

Timberlake, Lloyd (1982) Poland's pollution crisis, *World Press Review*, 29, 56.

Time-Life (1965) *Eastern Europe: Czechoslovakia, Germany, Poland*, Time Incorporated, New York.

Tomasevich, Jozo (1958) Agriculture in Eastern Europe, *Annals of the American Academy of Political and Social Science*, 317, 44-52.

Tourist Guide Book of Albania (1969) Nam Frashëri Publishing House, Tirana.

Turner, Frederick Jackson (1893) The significance of the frontier in American history, *Proceedings of the State Historical Society of Wisconsin*, Madison.

Turnock, David (1978) *Eastern Europe*, Westview Press, Boulder, Colorado.

United Nations (1949) *Economy Survey of Europe: 1948*, Economic Commission for Europe, Geneva.

United Nations (1980) *Demographic Yearbook*.

Unstead, J. F. (1923) The belt of political change in Europe, *Scottish Geographical Magazine*, 23, 183-92.

Uren, Philip Ernest (1969) *The Impact of Socialism on the Rural Landscape of Hungary*, University of Ottawa, PhD dissertation, Ottawa, Canada.

Vambery, Arminius (1906) *Western Culture in Eastern Lands*, J. Murray, London.

Van Valkenburg, Samuel and Ellsworth Huntington (1935) *Europe*, John Wiley, New York. 1.

Violich, Francis (1972) An urban development policy for Dalmatia, *Town Planning Review*, 43, 151–65, 243–53.

Volgyes, Ivan (1980) Economic aspects of rural transformation in Eastern Europe, pp. 89–127 in Ivan Volgyes *et al* (eds) *The Process of Rural Transformation*, Pergamon Press, New York.

Volgyes, Nancy (1980) The Hungarian tanyas: persistence of an anachronistic settlement and production form, pp. 175–90 in Ivan Volgyes *et al.* (eds) *The Process of Rural Transformation*, Pergamon Press, New York.

Vucinich, Wayne S. (1963) Some aspects of the Ottoman legacy, pp. 81–114 in Charles and Barbara Jelavich, *The Balkans in Transition*, University of California Press, Berkeley.

Vucinich, Wayne S. (1981) Major trends in Eastern Europe, pp. 1–28 in Stephen Fisher-Galati *Eastern Europe in the 1980s*, Westview Press, Boulder, Colorado.

Wagner, Philip L. (1972) *Environments and Peoples*, Prentice-Hall, Englewood Cliffs, New Jersey.

Wandycz, Piotr (1974) *The Lands of Partitioned Poland, 1795–1918*, University of Washington Press, Seattle.

Wanklyn, H. G. (1941) *The Eastern Marchlands of Europe*, George Philip and Son, London.

Wanklyn, Harriet (1954) *Czechoslovakia*, George Philip and Son, London.

Wanklyn, H. G. (1944) The artisan element in the Slav countries, *Geographical Journal*, 103, 101–19.

Warriner, Doreen (1939) *Economics of Peasant Farming*, Oxford University Press, Oxford.

Watson, J. Wreford (1959) Relict geography in an urban community: Halifax, Nova Scotia, pp. 110–43 in R. Miller and J. Wreford Watson (eds) *Geographical Essays in Honour of Alan Ogilvie*, Thomas Nelson and Sons, London.

Werner, Frank (1976) *Stadtplanung Berlin: Theorie and Realität*, Part I: 1900–1960, Verlag Kiepert K. G., Berlin.

West, Rebecca (1944) *Black Lamb and Grey Falcon*, Vols I–II, Macmillan, London.

Westermanns Atlas zur Weltgeschichte (1956) Georg Westermann Verlag, Braunschweig.

Whittlesey, Derwent (1935) The impress of central authority upon the landscape, *Annals of the Association of American Geographers*, 25, 85–97.

Whittlesey, Derwent (1944) *The Earth and the State*, Henry Holt, New York.

Wiedemann, Paul (1980) The origins and development of agro-industrial development in Bulgaria, pp. 97–135 in Ronald A. Francisco *et al.* (eds)

Agricultural Policies in the USSR and Eastern Europe, Westview Press, Boulder, Colorado.

Wilczewski, Ryszard, *et al.* (1978) Spatial industrial changes in Poland since 1945, pp. 80–98 in F. E. Ian Hamilton (ed.) *Industrial Change*, Longman, London.

Wilkinson, H. R. (1955) Jugoslav Kosmet: the evolution of a frontier province and its landscape, *Transactions of the Institute of British Geographers*, 21, 171–93.

Willis, F. Roy (1973) *Western Civilization: An Urban Perspective*, D. C. Heath, Lexington, Massachusetts, Vol. II.

World Bank (1982) *World Development Report, 1982*, Oxford University Press, Oxford.

Yates, P. Lamartine and D. Warriner (1943) *Food and Farming in Post-War Europe*, Oxford University Press, Oxford.

Zweig, Ferdynand (1944) *Poland between Two Wars*, Secker and Warburg, London.

Index

383

Index

DATE DUE

	DE 20 '93		
MAY 11 1999			
GAYLORD			PRINTED IN U.S.A.

CPSIA information can be obtained
at www.ICGtesting.com
Printed in the USA
JSHW021335261119
2649JS00001B/4

Back, Steven M. Tipton; *Front, left to right,* Richard Madsen, Ann Swidler, Robert N. Bellah, William M. Sullivan. Photo by Jane Scherr.

Recipient of the National Humanities Medal, **Robert N. Bellah** is Elliott Professor of Sociology Emeritus, University of California, Berkeley, and the author of several books, including *The Robert Bellah Reader.* **Richard Madsen** is Professor of Sociology, University of California, San Diego; his most recent book is *Democracy's Dharma* (UC Press). **William M. Sullivan** is Senior Scholar at the Carnegie Foundation for the Advancement of Teaching and the author of *Work and Integrity, Second Edition.* **Ann Swidler** is Professor of Sociology, University of California, Berkeley; her most recent book is *Talk of Love.* **Steven M. Tipton** is Professor of Sociology and Religion at Emory University and the Candler School of Theology, and the author of *Public Pulpits.* The authors also collaborated on the writing of *The Good Society* and co-edited *Meaning and Modernity* (UC Press).